Also by David Hoffmeister

Going Deeper
Only One Mind
Healing in Mind
My Meaning in Scripture
Purpose is the Only Choice
Awakening through A Course in Miracles
Movie Watcher's Guide to Enlightenment

David's writings are available in print, e-book and audio formats. Select materials have been translated into Chinese, Dutch, Finnish, French, Norwegian, Portuguese, Spanish, and Swedish.

Online Materials

www.acim.cc
www.acim.biz
www.acim.me
www.awakening-mind.org
www.livingmiraclescenter.org

UNWIND
YOUR MIND
BACK TO GOD

Unwind Your Mind
Back to God
Experiencing *A Course in Miracles*
by David Hoffmeister
ISBN: 978-0-9913839-1-7

First Printed Edition 2014

Living Miracles Publications
P.O. Box 789, Kamas, UT 84036 USA
publishing@livingmiraclescenter.org
+1 435.200.4076

Living Miracles

This book was joyfully produced by the Living Miracles Community –
a non-profit ministry run by inspired modern-day mystics devoted to awakening.

UNWIND
YOUR MIND
BACK TO GOD

Experiencing *A Course in Miracles*
David Hoffmeister

About David Hoffmeister

David Hoffmeister has touched the lives of thousands with his consistently peaceful state of mind, radiant joy and dedication to Truth. He is a modern-day mystic who has been invited to over 30 countries and 49 states to share the message of Love, Oneness and Freedom. His journey involved the study of many pathways culminating in a deeply committed practical application of *A Course in Miracles*. His immersion was so total that when he put the book down, to his surprise, the Voice of the Course continued speaking to and through him.

David was always known for questioning everything rather than accepting conventional answers, thus he was delighted to find in the Course support and encouragement for his careful examination of every idea, belief, concept and assumption in his mind. Jesus became David's internal teacher, answering his every question, guiding him to hand over the day-to-day management of all relationships, circumstances and events in his life. David stepped back and "let Him lead the way," W-155 withdrawing all investment in the ego and the world. Students began to appear, engaging with David in deep dialogues and sparkling correspondences like the ones that grace these pages.

In 1996 David was guided to a small house in Cincinnati, Ohio, called the Peace House, where he welcomed those desiring to step back from the world to go deeply into the mind to discover the Christ within. Living Miracles communities have since sprung up in Utah, Hawaii, Canada, Spain, Mexico and Australia. Under David's living demonstration of taking the Course all the way, those devoted to awakening have come together to join in living the steps laid out in the Course for unwinding the mind out of the world, back to God. They join David in extending his non-compromising teachings through a vast internet ministry, audio/video media forums, written publications, inspirational gatherings using music and movies for awakening, live stream web events, and an annual "Strawberry Fields Music Festival and Enlightenment Retreat."

David has also shared his insight on many spiritual talk shows and radio programs. The multiple forums through which David freely shares his heart allows those with a deep call to connect from wherever they find themselves. The material in this book has been collected from his email messages, website postings, and interviews as well as transcripts of in-depth dialogues from the earliest days of David's work with those who came from around the world to join with him.

For those who hope that enlightenment in this lifetime is possible, David is pure inspiration. His gentle demeanor and articulate non-compromising expression touches all who listen. His interest in practical application means the Answers are for everyone. You will recognize the questions asked of him, as there is only one mind and it is yours! You will recognize the Answers for the same reason. As you enter this book you are accepting an invitation from deep within your own heart. You are joining with mighty companions devoted to awakening. Awakening requires the dismantling of all that we made as a cover over the Light that "I Am." As David did, we must invite the Holy Spirit to unwind our mind from all ideas, concepts and beliefs—everything we think we think and think we know—until all that is left is the Love that we are. David Hoffmeister's life is a living demonstration of the Awakened Mind.

Message from the Holy Spirit

I will work with your beliefs, guiding you step by step as you unwind your mind from the many false concepts you believe keep you safe and make you happy. Only the release from these false beliefs will bring you True Happiness and lasting Peace.

Editors' Notes

❖ David often gives voice to thoughts within the mind. These thoughts are presented in italics rather than within quotation marks.

❖ The words "the Course," and the acronym ACIM, are used interchangeably throughout this book to refer to *A Course in Miracles.*

UNWIND YOUR MIND
BACK TO GOD
Experiencing *A Course in Miracles*

Bibliography

A Course in Miracles
Second edition, 1996

Foundation for Inner Peace
P.O. Box 598
Mill Valley, CA 94942
www.acim.org

Course quotes are referenced using the following system:
T: Text
W: Workbook for Students
M: Manual for Teachers

Example:
"All real pleasure comes from doing God's Will." (T-1.VII.1.4)
T-1.VII.1.4= Text, Chapter 1, Section VII, paragraph 1, sentence 4

BOOK ONE
LAYING THE FOUNDATION

CONTENTS

Chapter One

Chapter Two

Chapter Three

Chapter Four

Chapter Five

Chapter Six

Chapter One

A Message from the Holy Spirit on Form and Content

When your mind is riveted on the holy purpose of healing God's Son, then you know what the world is for. This is content. To focus solely on content (the Holy Spirit) is to give the world a unified purpose. It is only by seeing past the ego's separate purposes – form-based purposes – that true happiness and joy can be found.

The world of form, of specifics, was made as an attack on God, as a hiding place for the mind that was terrified of the believed repercussions of separating from God. The mind is addicted to form because form is a defense against truth. The mind that believes it separated from God is terrified of the truth – it has become totally dependent on form for its survival because it believes that its source of life is within the world of form.

To perceive specifics and treat them as whole units in and of themselves is to close the mind to healing. The mind that is focused on form is asleep. It has forgotten wholeness, communion, Oneness; it has forgotten God. The way back to this remembrance is through the healing of distorted perception. A unified purpose is given, and is to be transferred and applied to every aspect of the mind, to every experience, in order to return the mind to a focus on content. Content sees two categories: love and a call for love. Every moment is an opportunity to join in the holy instant, where there is no past, no bodies, and no world.

To focus on form is idol worship. To decide upon form goals and outcomes is to lose the understanding of purpose.

The mind is always choosing. A decision is made in every moment and the focus is either on form or on content. The ego uses form – the body, the world and all forms of communication – for pride, pleasure and attack. Form is used to build a self-concept, the self-concept is used in competition with what is perceived to be other self-concepts; defense and attack become major distractions. Every war, from the grand scale of a world war and genocide, to a battle of wills over who will wash the dishes this evening, stems from a focus on form. Only when a brother is seen as a body can upset and attack be experienced. Only when the world of form is seen as causative can defense even be considered.

To focus on form is to judge. Form is the past; form is an illusion of the past. The mind that reacts to anything of this world, including interactions with brothers, is reacting to the past, to associations that are held in mind. Success and failure in this world are always judged upon form outcomes: *Did the couple stay together? Did the job get finished? Were you hired or fired? Shall we celebrate or commiserate?*

Content sees all things as the same. Content sees all brothers as one. Content sees every moment as an opportunity to forgive, to release the past, to offer a reminder of innocence, and to remember that all things—past, present, and yet to come—are gently planned by One who knows the best outcome for all concerned. When all things are seen to be working together for good, the mind can rest. When the mind is at rest, love returns to awareness.

It takes great willingness and trust to begin to turn away from the deeply ingrained and completely upside-down belief system of the ego. Every belief is to be loosened from the mind and seen as having an unreal cause. God is Cause. God is the Source of life.

Moment by moment I will work with your beliefs, taking you step by step as you unwind your mind from the many false concepts that you believe keep you safe and make you happy. Only the release from these false beliefs can bring you true happiness and lasting peace.

Many Forms, One Correction

David: As a spring board for deepening our understanding of form and content, we begin with the section called *The Equality of Miracles*. The first sentence is a common idea that you are probably familiar with in working with the Course:

> The only judgment involved is the Holy Spirit's one division into two categories; one of love, and the other the call for love. T-14.X.7

The Holy Spirit sorts all the varied messages that the mind seems to receive from the outside world into two categories. One is the extension of love and the other is a call for love. The first is when you feel the warm resonance of receiving love. Whenever someone is in fear or believing in the lack of love, that is just a call for love. When love is being extended, you feel loving. When there is a call for love, answer it with love.

The ego has a third category and that is attack. If you do not perceive love or a call for love—you perceive attack; either you think you have attacked someone or you think someone else is attacking you. The defenses come up because of this misperception. The key is that all you have to do is be tuned in with the Holy Spirit. He only has two categories—love or a call for love. In either case you will extend; you will answer with love. As this paragraph goes on, we think: *it is so simple; why can I not perceive everything as either just love or a call for love? Why do I perceive attack?*

> You cannot safely make this division, for you are much too confused either to recognize love, or to believe that everything else is nothing but a call for love. You are too bound to form, and not to content. What you consider content is not content at all. It is merely form, and nothing else. For you do not respond to what a brother really offers you, but only to the particular perception of his offering by which the ego judges it. T-14.X.7

Here is the idea of form and content. In the one sense when you read something like this you think: *Well, I can see that that is my problem. I am confused; I am too bound to form.* For me the next question was always, "OK, teach me more about this distinction between the form and content so I can really start to tune into content." Another way of coming at this is Workbook lesson 161. This helps put form and content into some kind of a context:

> Complete abstraction is the natural condition of the mind. But part of it is now unnatural. It does not look on everything as one. It sees instead but fragments of the whole, for only thus could it invent the partial world you see. The purpose of all seeing is to show you what you wish to see. All hearing but brings to your mind the sounds it wants to hear. Thus were specifics made. W-161.2

In this sense specifics are analogous to the form; form is always specific. Every object that we could name in the cosmos is specific. It seems like "book" is specifically different than "leg," or "finger" is specifically different than "nose," and so on. The whole world of specifics is the dream world, but then he turns around and says:

> And now it is specifics we must use in practicing. We give them to the Holy Spirit, that He may employ them for a purpose which is different from the one we gave to them. Yet He can

use but what we made, to teach us from a different point of view, so we can see a different use in everything. W-161.3

And here is a glimpse of the end, in the next paragraph:

> One brother is all brothers. Every mind contains all minds, for every mind is one. Such is the truth. Yet do these thoughts make clear the meaning of creation? Do these words bring perfect clarity with them to you? What can they seem to be but empty sounds; pretty, perhaps, correct in sentiment, yet fundamentally not understood nor understandable. The mind that taught itself to think specifically can no longer grasp abstraction in the sense that it is all-encompassing. We need to see a little, that we learn a lot. W-161.4

These passages bring the problem into focus. I am thinking specifically now, I am thinking compartmentally, but my mind in its natural condition is abstract.

That tells me that in order to come to peace, a transformation of my consciousness, a transformation of the very way that I think is necessary. That gives me a context; at least I am not in the dark about what this is about. In the past I have thought: *if I could just find the right relationship, attain some worldly recognition, or fame, or a goal, and that would bring me happiness.* It is great to come to the point of realizing that I have to change my thinking. It is not about just thinking happy thoughts or positive thoughts. I have to learn how to return thinking to the Holy Spirit so that my perception becomes unified.

This next paragraph was very helpful for me. I remember studying all kinds of theories in psychology, philosophy and spirituality. Theories can be fascinating, yet you can get caught in the fascination of studying theories about the mind. The ego loves that. The Course tells us to go for the *experience*. You deserve peace of mind! Do not get side tracked.

> The ego is incapable of understanding content, and is totally unconcerned with it. To the ego, if the form is acceptable the content must be. Otherwise it will attack the form. If you believe you understand something of the "dynamics" of the ego, let me assure you that you understand nothing of it. For of yourself you could not understand it. The study of the ego is not the study of the mind. In fact, the ego enjoys studying

itself, and thoroughly approves the undertakings of students who would "analyze" it, thus approving its importance. Yet they but study form with meaningless content. For their teacher is senseless, though careful to conceal this fact behind impressive sounding words, but which lack any consistent sense when they are put together. T-14.X.8

You can see that if the ego enjoys studying itself; that is another trap to watch out for. There can be many words. I heard our friend saying, "I do not want to get caught in words." The ego would just as soon have people go around spouting the Course verbatim, while still hanging onto a self-concept of separation. There is that feeling of *too many words*, of trying to hide behind a mask of words and intellectualization. We must go into the silence for the experience. Still your mind! That is where the experience is.

Now that we have a little introduction on form and content we can zoom in further with the section titled *Many Forms; One Correction*, in the second section of Chapter 26. The Workbook lessons that go along with this section are lessons 79 and 80. "Let me recognize the problem so it can be solved." Lesson 79 explains that as long as you keep defining your problems in terms of form – in terms of specifics – you will never come to peace of mind because that is not where your problems are. You have a perceptual problem that has to be solved. This section boils it down to one correction.

> It is not difficult to understand the reasons why you do not ask the Holy Spirit to solve all problems for you. He has not greater difficulty in resolving some than others. Every problem is the same to Him, because each one is solved in just the same respect and through the same approach. The aspects that need solving do not change, whatever form the problem seems to take. A problem can appear in many forms, and it will do so while the problem lasts. It serves no purpose to attempt to solve it in a special form. It will recur and then recur again and yet again, until it has been answered for all time and will not rise again in any form. And only then are you released from it. T-26.II.1

There is great cause for rejoicing that there is only one problem! There seem to be layers and layers of obscurity and complexity. Dealing with problems, whether they are relational, financial, health-related … it is like trying to plug little, tiny holes in a dam. Each day seems to bring with it another wave. You may feel like you can get a handle on it; you have been handling them every day for years and years, but do you not want the waves of problems to stop? Wouldn't it be restful if you did not have to deal with waves—if you could just be in a place of stillness?

Yes! Yes! I want them all to be solved in one swoop, in one instant!

> The Holy Spirit offers you release from every problem that you think you have. They are the same to Him because each one, regardless of the form it seems to take, is a demand that someone suffer loss and make a sacrifice that you might gain. And when the situation is worked out so no one loses is the problem gone, because it was an error in perception that now has been corrected. One mistake is not more difficult for Him to bring to truth than is another. For there is but one mistake; the whole idea that loss is possible, and could result in gain for anyone. If this were true, then God would be unfair; sin would be possible, attack be justified and vengeance fair. T-26.II.2

Take a look at that one sentence: "For there is but one mistake; the whole idea that loss is possible, and could result in gain for anyone." If there is only one mistake we want to get clear about that one mistake. That is where the release comes in. What are some of the thoughts that come to mind? What are some of the losses that seem tangible and real in this world?

If a bank repossesses your house, it feels like someone gains a house and someone loses a house. Or if there are five candidates up for an award, somebody gains the recognition, respect, and perhaps even money. And then you have the category of the losers. Say several companies bid for a big project; one company ends up winning the bid and the others lose it. Even in arguments between persons it can seem to be a battle of wits, of bringing forth more evidence to support your position. It can go on and on, as if it is a battle that can determine who is right. The one who seems to end up proving a point (*I told you so*) seems to be the right one and the other one seems to be the one who is wrong. Often it is based on two people desiring different outcomes. Whichever way the outcome occurs it can seem as if the one who gets their way is the happy one.

The whole world, as it is set up, is based on loss and gain. And this is based on bodies. Bodies seem to lose and gain. The whole free enterprise system is based

12

on competition, on loss and gain. The whole world as it is constructed is based on that and that is why I have to loosen my mind from bodily identification and get back to this condition or state called *mind*. That is the only condition where there is no loss and gain.

We have been touching on many overtly physical things. Now let us move to the mental realm. You have heard of voodoo dolls, where pins are stuck in a doll in order to bring bad things to another person. It seems as if someone is being harmed, this time in more of a psychic way. Or you have heard of people saying that someone has damaged or played with their mind, someone like Charlie Manson, Jim Jones or David Koresh. Some of these figures come to mind, as if they have brainwashed others. Just think about the belief that has to be beneath that. Obviously there is a belief that minds can be controlled and that minds can be harmed, whether it is through voodoo or brainwashing. There is the idea that some minds are vulnerable and others are dominant. It seems that vulnerable minds can be attacked.

It seems as if the leader or the guru gains control. Stronger bodies seem to dominate weaker bodies; bigger corporations seem to wipe out little businesses, in the physical sense. In the mind sense, as long as loss and gain are believed to be possible, peace of mind is not. The Sonship is cleaved into two camps: the victims and the victimizers. We are working our way to the miracle which sees loss and gain as impossible. A key idea is the belief in private minds. Private minds seem to be dominant or submissive.

> This one mistake, in any form, has one correction. There is no loss; to think there is, is a mistake." T-26.II.3

Just think of the idea of loss. Would loss come from God? If everything is an idea, which we have started to get at, loss is an ego idea. It is one of the cornerstones of the fear-based thought system.

> There is no loss; to think there is, is a mistake. You have no problems, though you think you have. And yet you could not think so if you saw them vanish one by one, without regard to size, complexity, or place and time, or any attribute which you perceive that makes each one seem different from the rest. Think not the limits you impose on what you see can limit God in any way. T-26.II.3

Fairness is a great topic to go into because in this world justice is often equated with fairness. But then the question is: What is fair? Some say that fairness is equality—equal pay for equal work. That sounds pretty good, but then you read the parable in the Bible about the land owner who goes out in the morning and hires some people to work his land. He says he will pay them a denary for a day's labor. Then he goes out at about two o'clock and hires some more workers and says, "I will pay you a denary." Around four o'clock and again at six o'clock he again hires more workers, saying, "I will pay you what is fair." At the end of the day he pays every worker one denary. Of course the workers who came earlier in the day are not very happy.

Friend: Hot under the collar.

David: Hot under the collar! *You mean those who have been working for a few hours get the same pay?* I remember when I first went over that parable with a friend she said, "That is not fair! You should give those earlier workers more money—they deserve it!" Jesus is using this as a teaching. He is saying that this is what the Kingdom of Heaven is like. You get the same thing no matter how long you work at it.

When there is upset the usual phrase is, "It is not fair!" But no matter how you try to attain equality in the world—you can try to pass your laws, with equal opportunity, etc.—but you would never reach it. At some point you sense that the idea of equality in form does not work. It is not that some are greater and some are worse; the whole Sonship is equal. *But there cannot be equality in form.* As long as you are looking for equality in form you will never find it, but you can find it in the miracle; the miracle is the Holy Spirit's perception and He sees everyone as the same. In the miracle, voodoo is impossible. Cults are impossible. One mind dominating another is impossible. The Holy Spirit sees them all as a ridiculous idea.

The Holy Spirit trains us to see that there is no guilt. The one who seems to be the mass murderer in the world's eyes is relieved big time! The world says: *Fry him,* or, *Lock him up for life.* And then there is the other one over here who seems to be leading the ideal life, a philanthropist, giving away lots of money. In the world's eyes there is no comparison between these two.

Friend: They are not equal.

David: They are not equal in any way, shape, or form. But Jesus is saying: *Your perception is messed up.* That helps me to recognize that I cannot evaluate; I cannot weigh the scales of justice. I do not have to be angry at some and have pity for others. I just need to see the world differently. I need to see how mistaken I have been about *EVERYTHING.* This is very different than spiritualities that define what is good or sacred, or that dictate what needs to be done to get to Heaven. There are quotes in the Bible about the wicked being gathered up and burned. People take that literally.

To understand the wheat and tares parables is to see the wheat as right-minded thoughts and the tares as wrong-minded thoughts. Yet in the end they all are gathered up and the one is seen to be illusion and dissolves. You are left with the fruit. The fruit is the part that is edible; you are left with the good part. To me, those parables are all about teaching that what you are thinking is what needs to be sorted out.

Friend: So there is good even in that one bad person? Is that what you are saying? It is going to be sorted out? It is still going to be the One mind?

David: This pulls it away even from persons. Remember, it just pulls it back to: *Oh, it is my lesson, it is my mind, and right now there is a mixture between the wheat and the tares. It seems like the ego thinking has grown in there and that my mind is infested. It still has the wheat, it still has the Holy Spirit's thought system, but it is mixed.* The Holy Spirit guides you through the sorting. Then you start to see that right-mindedness is content or purpose. I do not have to pay attention to all the forms that my brother seems to make. I just need to get in touch with right-mindedness, or right thinking.

It often comes back to the body. It hurts when you are judging others. And when you are judging this body it hurts just as much; the shame, blame and guilt get dumped on this body. *Holy Spirit, I do not know who I am. I want you to help me sort that out in my mind so I can come to the experience of who I really am*—which is mind or Spirit, not body.

The miracle of justice can correct all errors. T-26.II.4

Two Voices

Hi David,

I feel sometimes as if two persons are living in me at the same time—one that I feel as "I," who is very quiet and simply exists with no thoughts; the "I" who becomes "joy." And the other one who pushes me and tries to take me off of my path. I have everything under control, but sometimes I feel like a butterfly flying against the wind; I want to say, "Stop bothering me now!" In these moments I understand what people mean when they talk of the "devil" being a person. It really seems as if somebody is talking to me from inside. Can you please tell me if this is a normal step on the spiritual path?

Beloved One,

What you speak of is common on the spiritual journey, for often the ego seems to literally be a voice which is heard in one's mind. The ego always speaks first and can seem pushy because it always has an agenda or a form outcome for what it "thinks" it wants. It does not know what it wants nor does it really "think," for the ego has no unified goal and no power of real thought. The ego is just an unreal stream of pretend thoughts and it is a Joy to pay the stream no heed.

It is important to be firm in commitment or attentiveness to the Guidance of the Spirit within and to the Still State of Being beyond all words that is the real "I" you experience at times. This is what you are doing when you say or think: *Stop bothering me now!*

A version that I seemed to use was "Get thee behind me, Satan." (Luke 4:8) The form matters not, for in a moment of temptation it is the willingness to be Still, or to hear only God's Voice, that matters. And God's Voice is our Voice in Christ.

Thanks be to God for leading the Way. All Glory to the One.

Love, David

God is a Pure Idea, as is Christ

Hi David,

I live in Australia. I continue to read from your awakening-mind site with great interest; it is so helpful and much appreciated. I notice that you do not seem to judge the ego, or at least the ego takes a back seat in your writings.

Other sites emphasize it all differently. In a recent post, this point was made: If you believe that you know what Love is, and that you can of yourself forgive, or you have something that others do not have and you can give it to them (like love), you are believing that you are God. As long as you think that the world is real and that the body is alive, you believe that you are God.

When I first read the Course, God completely disappeared. I found myself thinking that there is no God. So shall we see God as completely made up? The Course does say that even God is an idea. The ancient Gnostics used to be of the opinion that when one has transcended, one sees that you are THAT. To my way of thinking, THAT is our very essence. We become God. Love is what you are. According to the above post, is one just being arrogant to think this way? Like a no-win situation?

Beloved One,

Forgiveness clears the way for remembrance of God, so that is always the focus. Until the mind releases the error of ego, the fear of a make-believe "god" is buried deep in the unconscious mind. In this respect it takes forgiveness, or release of the entire ego belief system, before the Memory of God's Love can return fully into awareness.

God is a Pure Idea as is Christ. When the mind is emptied of false concepts and beliefs, the Pure Idea remains – Eternal and Perfect.

"I am as God created me" W-110 is another way of saying: *Love is what you are.*

I am grateful that the website has been helpful for you. Thanks for writing and I hope to see you soon.

Love always, David

How did the Mind Make the Ego?

David: We are reading from *The Ego and False Autonomy* section where Jesus says in the first paragraph:

> It is reasonable to ask how the mind could ever have made the ego. In fact, it is the best question you could ask. There is, however, no point in giving an answer in terms of the past because the past does not matter; history would not exist if the

same errors were not being repeated in the present. Abstract thought applies to knowledge because knowledge is completely impersonal; examples are irrelevant to its understanding. Perception, however, is always specific and therefore quite concrete. T-4.II.1

There is no sense of going on a witch hunt and looking back into the past, or in asking how the guilt and the ego could have come about. Jesus tells us not to go looking in the past for the answer. You need to have a present experience. As long as you are feeling upset in any way, then by your experience you can tell that the same mistake is being repeated.

Friend: But that does not answer the question of how the mind could have made the ego?

David: Here we go. In the fourth paragraph of the introduction to the *Clarification of Terms* section, Jesus addresses this question directly, saying that there is no answer to it. There is only an *experience*. Seek the experience rather than allowing questions like this to delay you. In other words, to get bent on the question of how the impossible could have happened can put one into a metaphysical, theological tailspin. Beneath the question there is an underlying assumption. The underlying assumption is that the impossible could happen and has happened.

Why would you ask how it happened unless you already believed that it did? Answering the question makes the error real. It is the same as wanting a good, solid definition of the ego. Rather than defining the ego, we talk about the miracle, about the right mind and about the correction. The state of the miracle is what the ego is *not*. It is about choosing the right mind – choosing the miracle. It is not about analyzing the ego.

The mind ran from the light in an instant of terror. The ego belief is that God is going to get you because you have really pulled off the separation from God. The mind was terrified and moved into the darkness away from the light. For an instant there was a belief in the ego. That is all it is, the unholy instant. Here is the unholy instant where that tiny belief was believed in, and here comes the Holy Spirit simultaneously, as the answer to that, right there in the mind. God placed the answer to the insanity right where the insanity was. He did not put the answer out in the world because that is not where the puff [insanity] is; the puff is in the mind. He placed the answer right where the problem was. But the mind is so terrified of that light that it kind of moved out towards the form and got engaged in bodies and survival and judgment.

> God is my life. I have no life but His. I was mistaken when I thought I lived apart from God, a separate entity that moved in isolation, unattached, and housed within a body. Now I know my life is God's, I have no other home, and I do not exist apart from Him. He has no Thoughts that are not part of me, and I have none but those which are of Him. W-223.1

How Do You Turn Your Ego Off?

Hi David,

My problem, since I was as young as two to three years old, has been fear and always thinking the worst. I wish I could just turn off my ego fear but it has always been my downfall. I know I have to look within, read more and meditate more. How do you turn your ego off? Is it just constantly being aware and rejecting it at all times? I worry so much it drives me crazy.

Beloved One,

Thanks for your question and for writing what is on your heart. One does not turn the ego off; one unplugs it by withdrawing faith in it. First you begin by paying attention to thoughts and feelings and perceptions. The chatter and emotional roller coaster ride and distorted, unstable perceptions attest to an insane ego belief system that dictates these swings. The ego must be exposed and brought to Light before the swings will give way to a consistent, stabilized perception. Until faith is withdrawn from the ego, the mind will seem to swing between darkness and Light. You made the ego by believing in it and can dispel it by withdrawing all belief from it. Without the power the mind seems to give it, the ego will seem to cease to be. Right Now Christ is Present. The ego was an illusion of past/future, but the Light has come and in this Light the error has vanished.

Be willing to move inward and question all assumptions. Fear is an assumption and thus dissolves in the Presence of Light. Protect no belief from the healing Light of the Holy Spirit and you will see that there is nothing to cling to. Yield and merge with the Will of God, for it is our Will as well. Miracles come from trust in God; as trust increases, fear disappears. Your willingness will seem to open into readiness, and readiness will seem to open into mastery. All Glory to God and thanks to the Holy Spirit for Guiding past the illusion of fear to the forgiven world and on to the Memory of God.

Who Wrote the Course?

Friend: You keep saying, "He says…" Is the Text supposed to be Christ's words?

David: The entire Course seems to be written in first person singular and uses the second person; in other words he says "I," and "you," and makes references to his involvement in the crucifixion, the resurrection, the apostles, etc., as it happened to him. The supposition is that Jesus is speaking. I had already studied many different paths and spiritualities when I first picked it up in California. I had no idea who wrote it, I knew nothing about it. I just picked it up and started reading the ideas. It was some time before I even happened to get to some of those passages that were speaking in first person about the crucifixion and the resurrection. All I knew was that the resonance inside me and everything I was feeling and everything I was reading – everything – was guiding me towards wholeness. That was really strong – very, very strong. And then when I got to those parts, it was kind of like: *Oh, who wrote this book?* Of course I already had a sense of it.

Jesus as the author is symbolic. There is a Whole Mind that is Awake; this Course is coming from that Whole Mind. He says that he was just the first to awaken (implying that there have been others). It is not person-specific and it is not specifically a Christian path just because it uses Christian terminology. I just see it as ideas – as a metaphorical ladder that is coming from a whole mind.

In this world – which represents the belief in an authority problem – authors are thought to be people. Add to this the illusory concept of channeling, and then authors are thought to be distinct entities which come through persons. Such is the case with "Jesus" and "Helen." Verily, verily, none of this has anything to do with Authoring as God Authors, for to Author is to create in Spirit. The concept of a "personal author" is a contradiction in terms that has no meaning whatsoever. Zero. Zilch. Nada. This realization is the escape from fear and opens the way for the remembrance of Love.

ACIM is form, a collection of words, and form has no author. The infinite is Authored by God. The finite is unreal and has NO author. The Thought beyond the veil of illusion (a veil that includes the book called *A Course in Miracles*) is Christ – a Whole, Pure, Perfect, Abstract Idea in the Mind of God. The closest approximation to what this world calls "author" is the Holy Spirit or the Voice for God. The Holy Spirit is synonymous with the Voice for Christ. Forgiveness, itself an illusion, was "made" (not created) as a counter-dream to the world of judgment. Yet even the "forms" the Holy Spirit seems to take – words, angels, visionary dreams, the forgiven world – are all illusion and will dissolve when the belief in time is no longer cherished. Time, space, and form have no Divine Author! God is the Author of Reality, and there is no Author but God! Reality is Eternity. God is not the "author" of time, space, and form. "God knows not form." T-30.III.4 God Authors Christ in Spirit and only in Spirit. The Eternal creates Eternally. The Infinite creates Infinitely. Reality is Spirit. To Awaken Now, simply follow the instruction in the ACIM workbook: "Forget this world, forget this course, and come with wholly empty hands unto your God." W-189.7

Identity is an Experience, not a concept. God (Abstract Spirit) Authors Reality. Reality (Abstract Spirit) is All there Is, having no opposite. There is no Author but God. Belief in opposites has no reality whatsoever. To Author is to create in Spirit. Authorship is Spirit, is All Meaning. Form is belief and thus has *nothing* to do with Authorship.

ACIM is a symbol of undoing belief, nothing more and nothing less. ACIM is a book, not Reality. God is the Author of Reality, and form is authorless. Words are but symbols of symbols, twice removed from Reality. Reality is an Experience and cannot be described, explained, or defined. Reality simply Is – far beyond illusory beliefs and concepts and words.

The ego time belief (illusion) seemed to invent a time-space cosmos (also illusion), yet neither ego nor its cosmos have reality. The belief in ego and cosmos seem to deny Reality in awareness, yet Reality is beyond belief entirely and can only be Known. Like all images, ACIM is part of the realm of belief and is illusion.

The ego asks who the author of ACIM is, yet Christ has no question – being certain of Identity in God. Can an illusion have an author if God Authors Reality and God is the only Author? ACIM seems to be a collection of words, yet the words point beyond the words. The Meaning of Life is the Experience these words point to: God is the Author of Reality and I am as God created Me.

Words can seem to represent the Holy Spirit. The Holy Spirit is Abstract in Reality. Yet Holy Spirit seems to take the form of a voice for God with regard to the time belief, so that the time belief may be undone. The Voice for God is the Voice for Christ; for as Creator and Creation are One, Abstract Spirit, the Voice which temporarily represents Reality is One as well. The simple message of the Holy Spirit is this: God is Spirit. Christ is Spirit. God Authors Christ Eternally. Spirit is All there Is, having no opposite. There is no Author but God.

Forgive all symbols and accept our Self Now, for God creates Spirit as Spirit. Divine Mind is singular. Christ is One Being in the Mind of God. Forgive all symbols, even Jesus, for the man was but an illusion. History has no meaning. God is Now. Christ is Now. All Meaning is Now. I Am Now. The holy instant is all there is to behold. Be Still and Know, for the past is gone and the future was but false imagination. How obvious and simple is the Experiential Answer of our Identity in God.

Therefore lay aside foolish questions and distractions and enter into the Silence of Being. Certainty is an Experience beyond words and questions. The "I Am" Presence is real. Issues of the world are not real. Desire Reality wholly and Experience All God created Holy. There are no holy books or words or people or places or things, yet the Spirit of the "I Am" is forever Holy. There is nothing else to behold.

Apply the Ideas

David: The truth is within us; let's come together with the intention of becoming very clear in our discernment between the ego and the Holy Spirit. This requires looking closely at the mind and how it works. As we allow the Spirit to come among us, questions are asked, answers come, and experiences are shared. We want to take practical examples from our lives and apply the ideas to them. If we do not *use* the Course, it is just a book filled with high ideas of metaphysics and theory. All spiritual teachings are meant to be *applied*. We need to live the teachings. If there are parts of our lives that are not congruent with them then it is helpful for all of us to be aware of those things so the mind can shift and be a demonstration of the truth. As upsets come up in daily life they can be traced back through the metaphysics, which are meant to be practical and useful. We must always come back to the awareness that it is our own perception that needs to be healed! Our minds make the decision to heal or not; there is never anything happening in the world of form that causes a change in mind.

There really is only one question that the mind keeps asking over and over on a very deep level: *Who am I?* The ego asked the first question ever. There was no question in Heaven, there was just Oneness. There have been an awful lot of questions raised since this first question of: *Who am I?* It was the ego that asked it. Christ did not ask this question. There is complete certainty in Heaven. Every other question has come from that first question, including all the questions about the world, about the sub-atomic levels, about science, about philosophy. All the other questions are just stacks and stacks and layers upon layers of questions on top of that first one. In the deceived state the mind is still asking that basic question: *Who am I?* [laughter]

The ego has many answers: you are a man or a woman, you are a son or a father or a brother, you are a sister, a husband, or a wife. You are a construction worker, an engineer, a mathematician, a tennis teacher. The ego gives us lots of answers and it is constantly in there saying you are a combination – you are this, this, this, and this. Underneath it all, the mind just is not sure because it is still asking that central question: *Who am I?* Identity seems to keep shifting and changing. I was a son, now I am a father or now I am a grandfather. Or, I was a banker, now I am into this or that. It is very unstable and constantly shifting. We want to keep working it back down deeper and deeper into the mind, to get at that central question of *Who am I?*, and to find where the *experience* of the answer is.

Every question asked within this world is a double question. We cannot really come to an understanding of the answer if we cannot even ask the right question, if we are asking questions that are nonsense questions; questions that ask and answer in themselves. They are circular questions that do not go anywhere:

> All questions asked within this world are but a way of looking, not a question asked. A question asked in hate cannot be answered, because it is an answer in itself. A double question asks and answers, both attesting the same thing in different form. The world asks but one question. It is this: "Of these illusions which of them *is* true. Which ones establish peace and offer joy? And which can bring escape from all the pain of which this world is made." Whatever form the question takes, its purpose is the same. It asks but to establish sin is real, and answers in the form of preference. "Which sin do you prefer? That is the one that you should choose. The others are not true." T-27.IV.4

When we pull this back to our daily lives we see that the dominant theme of each day comes from the seeming situations that make up the menu of the world, and they are all illusions. We spend a lot of time and frustration debating the seeming options: *Do I want to go here to eat dinner or there? Do I want to call this person or not? Do I want to date this person or not? Do I want to buy this kind of car or not? Do I want to invest in this mutual market fund or do I want to invest in CDs?* There is a lot of strain and energy put into which illusion is true. Which ones are the best? Underneath that is the mind's belief in a hierarchy of illusions. It does not see that these are just projected images. It has the images ranked: *These are my top illusions. I spend a lot of effort and energy pursuing them. Then there is the middle level which I am indifferent about. Let people pursue those illusions if they want, I do not really care about them. And then there are the negative ones, the illusions I spend my energy avoiding. I do not want to be around this person. I do not care if they are illusion or not, I don't like them. Or, I do not like this kind of weather. If I move to Hawaii I can get away from this weather. Hawaii has better weather.*

You can see that there is a hierarchy there. Most questions that are asked both ask and answer. That is where the preferences come in. Each person has this hierarchy. Everybody has their version of the good life, which can be different, because everybody has an unconscious sense of the good life. You have to really take a look at these questions that you are asking. "What can the body get that you would want the most of all? It is your servant and also your friend. But tell it what you want, and it will serve you lovingly and well." T-27.IV.4 Jesus is speaking sarcastically here because this is how the ego thinks: "And this is not a question, for it tells you what you want and where to go for it. It leaves no room to question its beliefs, except that what it states takes question's form." T-27.IV.4

In this world it has been forgotten that we are Spirit, that we are Mind. In the deceived state the ego says: *God made you a body. Very well. You already know that you have a limit here so you better make the best of it. You better go for all the gusto you have got. You know you are stuck and you are limited. You have already separated from the Kingdom and thrown away your spiritual inheritance; you might as well just go for the gusto: Eat, drink, and be merry for you shall die.* [laughter]

Friend: I have certainly done my share of that.

David: And the ego does not tell us, with all its aiming for the gusto, that the world is the last place we could ever find peace and happiness. The world was made as a smoke screen so we would not go back in our minds, in meditation, and sink down inside to be with the Holy Spirit, where our true happiness and salvation resides. You know that the old Bible says, "The Kingdom of God is within you." (Luke 17:21) The ego says: *No, it is without.* It is that co-dependent relationship; go for the relationship, go for the possessions, go for the fame, go for the glory, go for something out there. We have had a lot of examples of people who have followed it all the way out. I think of extreme examples like Marilyn Monroe. She had all the money, all the fame, all the sex appeal; she was married to Joe DiMaggio and Arthur Miller–all these variations of the ego's premise of, "Seek and do not find." T-12.V.7 The Course gives us the framework to see this. It is very different than the biblical, "Seek and ye shall find." (Luke 11:9) The world keeps putting the carrot out front–fame, fortune, money, good looks; we keep looking for these satisfactions in form and we keep asking these pseudo questions. And Jesus says, "A pseudo-question has no answer. It dictates the answer even as it asks. Thus is all questioning within the world a form of propaganda for itself." T-27.IV.5

Later he says:

> An honest question is a learning tool that asks for something that you do not know. It does not set conditions for response, but merely asks what the response should be. But no one in a conflict state is free to ask this question, for he does not *want* an honest answer where the conflict ends. T-27.IV.5

This is about the very instant that this powerful, powerful mind seemed to buy into this tiny, mad, ridiculous belief in separation. Giving such a powerful mind as that of the holy Son of God, to the ridiculous thought that he could separate from his Creator was literally the Big Bang in the mind. That is where all the guilt arose. The answer to this was not given *after;* it was given simultaneously. The instant the belief seemed to be bought into, the Holy Spirit was given as an answer for it. The good news is that your only problem has been solved. It is already solved. That is good to know because it can seem at times like it is still open to question whether this is solved or not, because of the feelings that are experienced. The number one question for the ego mind is: *How could this happen in the first place?* History would not exist if you did not keep making the same mistake in the present. The present moment is your point of power; that is where you make decisions and that is where you can choose salvation.

We conceptualize ourselves as having been on the spiritual journey for a number of years and we are moving back towards awareness of God, towards wholeness and completion. We think of salvation as in the future; someday, if we really keep at it, salvation will come. Why would God place salvation in the future? Wouldn't the time that you have to suffer through between the present and the future make God cruel, kind of like the idea that Jesus died for our sins? What kind of father would have his son shed his innocent blood? God did not place salvation in the future. He put it in the present. All of salvation is offered to you this very instant. There is a lot of relief with that, but the ego can jump right in there and go: *Oh, I should be able to get this now, please help me get this, I want it now.* [laughter] Basically Jesus has 1,200 pages that say you are terrified of the Holy Spirit; you are terrified of accepting that answer right now. That is why linear time was born. The past and the future are the mind's attempts to evade and avoid the present. On a conscious level that can seem like: *Well, that is kind of funny because I feel like God is my friend and the Holy Spirit is like my partner and now Jesus is telling me that I am terrified of the Holy Spirit!* This makes sense when you see that during the blip, when the tiny mad idea seemed to happen, the mind believed that it actually had usurped Heaven, that it had usurped God's place in Heaven. And the ego counseled: *Run! You have done it now, run away from that light because if you ever come back that light is going to get you, because you have really done it, you have pulled it off, you have separated from your father and your father is angry!*

This whole world has been an attempt to run from the light into the darkness, into the fragmentation, into the duality. No one wants to ask an honest question because he is afraid to hear the answer. What we are learning is that the Holy Spirit *is* the answer. Into this darkened mind that believes that it separated from God, God placed a spark of light that is the Holy Spirit. That light will grow and grow until it literally illuminates the whole mind. But the mind is very afraid of it.

The ego is a belief in the mind that projects out the world. Now would God have placed the answer where the problem is not? Would God have placed the answer in the world if the problem is in your mind? No, God placed the answer right where the problem was. The answer is in our mind; the Holy Spirit and the problem are in the mind. The belief in separation is in the mind. This world is a smoke screen, a giant distractive device that keeps you from going down into the mind and questioning all the assumptions and beliefs. In the analogy of the World Trade Center, both the Holy Spirit and the ego are in the basement. All the floors of the World Trade Center are layers of beliefs. The mind is so terrified of the light that it has stacked on all of these layers of dark floors so it can forget about the light. The deceived mind has literally tried to dissociate and just forget about the light. The mind has dissociated also because light and darkness do not go together; they are kind of like oil and water. When one is present, the other is absent. And the mind could not stand the intolerable condition of holding two thought systems that are not reconcilable – the ego thought system and the Holy Spirit's thought system. The ego's answer is to forget about one. Dissociation is to forget about the light. There seems to be a little bit of relief, but really it is just buried and the mind is still in pain because it is not in its natural state.

In Heaven the mind is a state of oneness, completion and wholeness. When the split is in the mind, it is very uncomfortable and intolerable. Therefore the mind projects it out into the world. All of a sudden the smoke screen became a "real world" of duality. Instead of the duality being these two thought systems in the mind, now it is seen in the world. For example, male/female, hot/cold, fast/slow, tall/short; we could go on all night. The whole world seems to be just extremes of duality. Now the mind seems to get some kind of relief, because it believes it is a little teeny figure on the screen. It has forgotten that it is this vast, vast powerful mind. Now it is this little teeny person. And in a sense, it is a little whole person, even though it does not feel very whole sometimes. In a sense, that is the trick. You can see that this is an identity that has been made up, that it is not our true identity. Our true identity is Christ. But this little, bitty identity has got all this stuff made up in the dream world: *I was born in such and such a place and these were my parents. I grew up and I have this life history and these were my main life events. My fourth grade teacher embarrassed me, and I had my first kiss when I was thirteen.* This is a substitute because the true identity is magnitude – it is vast, powerful spirit. In this world, when we identify with the teeny, little person that we think we are, it feels very tiny and very limited.

Not only that, but it seems like there is this gigantic world around this teeny, little person, where people seem to be competing against it all the time – competing for jobs, competing for love, competing for resources. There are hurricanes and tornados; there are things it has to constantly defend against and watch out for, when really it is just a dream.

The problem is that it is identified with this little, teeny speck of flesh instead of the vast light which is its reality. As you go through life you seem to be confronted with all of these issues and problems out on the screen – financial problems, relationship problems, health problems. But really you just have one problem and it is down in the basement. And you have one solution to your one problem, thank Heaven; it is down in the basement of your mind. We start from where we perceive the problem, up here on the top of the World Trade Center which is on the screen of the world in this analogy. *I have a problem with this person, they bug me; this is what bugs me about them.* You start from describing the problem as you perceive it and then you start tracing it back into concepts and beliefs that are in the mind; the floors of the World Trade Center that really are the cause of the problem. All of those dark floors sprung from the ego, they are all just false beliefs.

That is an overview of the metaphysics of the Course. We do not start our discussion with the idea that *God is love*, or *I am the Christ*, because most people do not have that in their experience. We start at the level of perception; most people perceive themselves as being impinged upon by the world and are struggling to keep their head above water emotionally and financially. When the mind is identified with this little speck on the screen, it seems as if the world has caused *it*. The mind that believes it is a body believes that its origin is on the screen as well; it thinks that its earthly parents are its origin. The mind that believes it is a body holds grievances: *I did not ask for this; I do not want a life like this; I do not like these things happening to me all the time; I want it to be different than it is.* The cause of everything is believed to be something on the screen – the economics, the IRS, genetics, the husband, the wife, the heart condition, childhood trauma – some event out here on the screen is the cause of my life being in shambles. But it is not the memories that are the cause of trauma. It is the interpretation in this very instant; the interpretation that we are giving it in the present is causing the trauma to our minds. And where is this interpretation coming from? The mind is calling the memories forth from the vaults of the past and trying to keep them.

It is all over in the holy instant. We are guiltless and innocent *right now*, but the mind is afraid of that. It keeps calling the past into the present and keeping things complicated because it is too terrified of the holy instant; it is too terrified of the Holy Spirit. This insight is a very helpful lens through which to look at our life and all the problems we think we have on the screen. If you try to change the behavior but do not really start opening up and going within, you are not really making a change at all. You will probably have other symptoms that will spring up. You are just shifting the form. Ultimately it is really time which is at the root of all problems. There are a lot of psychotherapies starting to get into beliefs, but the Course points to the awakened mind that has literally transcended the ego entirely. That is what makes it such a clear and powerful tool. That is also why there is such enormous resistance to working with it. The ego is *very* resistant to it because it is a very sharp tool for cutting away and dissolving the deceptions.

And the belief in time and space is at the bottom of it, at the very bottom floor of the World Trade Center. But when people wake up in the morning for their 6:30 a.m. meetings their mind is usually not at a place where it is questioning linear time or questioning space. Usually it is already off on its plan of action and pursuits. There have been a number of therapies that talk about living in the present moment but they have not gone quite so deeply into *how* to live in the present and *how to undo the belief in time and space.*

You cannot just talk about this stuff and read about it; you have to live it. My life has been a process of going down and raising this stuff up, and coming to the point where I have examined concepts and literally stepped out of them. Then I could say: *I am not this, I am not that.* You keep going. It is about starting to move towards a point of stepping out, just trusting that things will be provided and letting the Spirit come through. If you have issues or things going on in your life, we want to come together, let the Spirit come amongst us, and get some clarity on those things. We have a metaphorical framework to work with. We have a basic agreement on some of the metaphysics and now we want to really put it into application.

Friend: How do we get into the present? How do we actually apply this so that we are not planning for the future and worrying about the past?

David: Remember we said that there was a God-substitute made, or a substitute-self, made in place of the Christ. That is what the self-concept is. The self-concept is the purpose of the learning of the world. Everyone comes here without a self and makes one as he goes along. We learn things, whether we think we learn them from our parents or we learn them at school; we learn how to judge: *these are the good things in life, these are the things that will make you secure and safe, these are the bad things in life, these are the things you need to avoid.* That is all part of the ego system. The judgment that we learn in this world is which things to pursue and which things to avoid. This is part of the defense system against trusting in the holy instant – against trusting that the Spirit can do it. In this world mature judgment means learning the ways of the world very well, but true wisdom is the relinquishment of judgment. That can be unsettling. Having come here and learned how to be a "good judge" of right and wrong you start to see that your whole system of discernment is still part of the ego system.

Any kind of evaluation in a positive or a negative way literally denies that everything is equally illusory. It is like you have constructed a maze from all

29

your judgments. You have a maze of complexity going here. And the Holy Spirit is your guide now; he is going to guide you out of the maze. The Holy Spirit is evaluative. In other words the Holy Spirit does judge but he is capable of judging truly because he can see the past, the present, and the future. Think of when you are trying to judge in the maze. Do you have cognition of the past and the future? Do you know the results of every decision that you make and how it will affect everyone else? It is not that you *should not* judge, but to see that you *cannot!* You are not capable of accurately judging. That is why you need the Holy Spirit. In that sense the Holy Spirit is judgmental. In a maze you can only go left or right. At every point we have all these seeming decisions to make and the Holy Spirit is in there guiding us. *Go left, go right.* He knows the way out of the maze.

Friend: And how about when someone who is evil is affecting you? I am serious! I went into business with this 24-year-old man who has the ability to make hundreds of thousands of dollars per year. He is, in my eyes, evil; he has power. I believe that he has power in his voice—he could walk into a room and just [clicking fingers] steal you blind and you would not even know it. I got into business with this guy with all these big expectations and came to find out this guy is the biggest crook I have ever met in my life. What is going on right now is that he wants to sue me. I feel in my heart I did nothing wrong, he is the one that wronged me. It is crazy. [laughter]

David: What I am hearing is that you are feeling the tension; you are feeling the fears, frustrations, and anger. You have no idea of the extent of the self-hatred that is in your own mind. We have to unveil the extent of that self-hatred. What happens with this intolerable split in the mind—with this intolerable hatred—is that it gets projected. That is the way that the ego deals with it. It wants to project it. That is this whole idea of evil out in the world, what is sometimes called a devil or a force. It seems to be very active, very powerful, and very destructive. The devil is the ego—a belief in your own mind. Someone asked Gandhi about the devil once and he said, "The only devils in this world are those running around in our own hearts, and that is where all our battles should be fought." It sure can seem in this projection like there are evil forces around us, but that thinking is false. The Course is a book that can systematically walk you through the correction.

Our brothers are mirrors for us on an unconscious level. Relationships can be used to flush up the unconscious beliefs. People will often say: *Wait a minute now, I can see mirroring to a certain degree but I have witnesses and examples that will only go so far.* They will say for example: *I know a person who is very sloppy and lazy and I am not sloppy and lazy. I do not care what the Course says.* [laughter] It is not about the behavioral level. The mirroring goes back to our beliefs. In other words, if we judge somebody as being sloppy or lazy, there is a box that we have—a sloppiness box or a laziness box—and we have a certain group of behaviors that we put together in there and we read it on to the screen. You have to go back into your mind and look at these boxes that you have constructed. And we have *lots* of boxes. That is what the ego system is. There are judgments, categories and boxes. In business there are a lot of boxes because the ego is so tied into appearances. Ultimately we need to let go of relying so much on our physical senses and to start to trust this intuitive voice; we are fooled and deceived by what our eyes see and what the ears hear. It is fun to be on a path that is guiding us to think: *Oh thank you, now I am going to let go of some of my judgments and start listening and opening to my intuition.* That is literally our safety, our joy, and our happiness. It is great that you can just be. It seems like it is all coming right up there, you are not stuffing it. You are definitely not stuffing it; it is like a volcano. [group laughter]

Friend: Right now I have a person in my life that is going through reactions. I listened to him and thought: *Why can't you see what is really going on?* I tried to explain to him what is really going on, even though I know you cannot do that. And then I stopped seeing him through love, stopped seeing that he is the Son of God just like I am the Son of God. I love that term because it keeps us all the same, except I forgot. I know I was acting out of fear—I wanted to change him and I could not. I wondered why he could not see what he was doing. He was seeing all this as bad, and I was trying to say: *Hey man, you are missing the point. We do not judge because what we see is not real.* It did not work.

David: In the past you have suppressed and denied the ego system. The ego has not been raised to awareness, but once you start to raise it to awareness and the stuff starts getting flushed up, there is a strong tendency to want to project. Even though the ego is now being unveiled, you are seeing that the mind is still very strongly invested in it and that is where the guilt comes in. The transcendence will eventually come where we are able to detach in our mind from those false thoughts, from the attack thoughts; we will be able to just calmly see the false as false. But that is one of the stages that we go through. Once it starts to get flushed up there is a real tendency to project—to be what Jesus calls the unhealed healer. You want to go around and give healing without having healed yourselves and it is just to watch as we do this, and go through it.

Last night the self-concept of being a parent came up. A gentleman said: "I have a son and he has a duty to clean the bathroom and he does not. I suggest, I remind, but it is just filthy. I start to get angry just describing this whole dynamic." The parent is another role with a lot of unconscious beliefs, about *good mom* and *good dad; good moms and good dads do it this way*. We have these unconscious beliefs that are down there. The basic situation with parents and children is that there is often a big struggle over control. This is not just with parents and kids; it can be in all kinds of relationships. The world teaches that you have to tame and train this ego to at least adapt and become somewhat normal in order to function. It teaches that there are things that you have to do in life. You can always tell when you are sliding into ego; it is that control feeling and the tone of voice–when the demanding and the commanding starts coming out. The Holy Spirit never commands and never demands; he reminds and suggests.

Friend: He does not teach high school!

David: Right away the intent will come in relation to certain situations or certain children: *Wait a minute. I have reminded and suggested to a certain point, then I have to really bear down here!* But really it is always our own lesson. Children are great mirrors. Whenever we start feeling we are off the beacon, whenever we start feeling controlling or angry, we can pull back to a level of Spirit or a mind level of: *What is the deal, we are equals here. Did you forget?* There are just these roles now. *Wait a minute this is the role: I am the dad, you are the son and you are the daughter.* As soon as the mind clicks into *I am the role*, then control comes in. There are not any roles in Heaven.

Friend: But is that not a fact? I mean, it is an illusion, but it is also a fact, right?

David: It is an *interpretation*. The only fact is that of Christ or Oneness. But within the dream world these identities, these self-concepts that we make up, include a lot of roles.

Friend: We also have perceptions about what the roles mean. As a parent, the role issue sometimes is hard to let go of when you have to say: *You need to do this; you need to do that…*

David: Yes, the real problem is the authority problem. The authority problem is with God. It comes down to the question: *Can I create myself or was I created?* What happens is when you get into *I can create myself*–that is where the self-concept comes in. Not only *can I create myself,* but *I have!* I chose to be a parent, or to go into education, or to take a business job, etc. You can see that all these lessons that come up are really ways to start to loosen our identification with these roles. And we see that all of the expectations that we place on our brothers, that seem to be violated by their behaviors, are really just expectations. We are reading meaning into a situation from our own goal.

Being identified as a male or as *A Course in Miracles* teacher I perceive somebody as trying to weaken my position; here it goes again. I have another concept or construct that I have to let go of. As long as there is defensiveness or fear, or anything that is uncomfortable within us, we are still clinging to some kind of role or some kind of a concept that we believe is more valuable than the truth.

Friend: When it comes to kids I feel that I have to put on a different hat because they have certain rules and regulations they need to follow in order to get where they need to be, or where I think they need to get to.

David: It is really about judgment. "You are afraid … because you believe that without the ego, all would be chaos. Yet I assure you that without the ego, all would be love." T-15.V.1 See that when the mind had these dark beliefs in it and there was all this seeming horror and chaos—when it seemed to buy into the belief in separation—all this judgment was a way to try to bring some control and order into the chaos.

> Yet the very fact that you can do this, and bring any order into chaos shows you that you are not an ego, and that more than an ego must be in you. For the ego *is* chaos, and if it were all of you, no order at all would be possible. Yet though the order you impose upon your mind limits the ego, it also limits you. To order is to judge, and to arrange by judgment. Therefore it is not your function, but the Holy Spirit's. T-14.X.5

It takes a lot of trust to let go. You are talking about these ideas and beliefs—about letting go of these constraints and restrictions and judgments about your children. The underlying belief is that if you let go of that, all hell is going to break loose. You are afraid they will grow up and be a reflection on you; *what wild children you have!* You see how it goes? The ego will just run with that. It does take a lot of trust to generalize this to your family situation.

It is by watching your emotions and reactions that you can tell whether you are listening to the Holy Spirit. "Let your yea be yea; and your nay, nay." (James 5:12) But be really clear that if there is still egocentricity and codependency involved, if we associate following the Holy Spirit with saying *yes* to everything and everyone, you can see how you could just totally give away your sense of integrity. The Spirit is in there. If we just stay with our emotions and keep surrendering, the Spirit will tell us when to say *yes*, when to say *no*, and when to set some sort of guideline that could be helpful.

We can set guidelines but must watch for that insistence, the demanding and commanding and getting upset when others do not seem to follow it. The whole lesson for us is to always be extending the light and extending the peace. It really does get at our own beliefs and expectations and roles. That is always the lesson: *What do I value in my mind? What am I holding onto that is more important than seeing the Christ in this person or child?*

Friend: I can think of certain conflicts that I have had with my children, and the thought that came to me was that if I get into a conflict there is obviously something I am not willing to see. But I lose patience and say: *I am not ready; I am not willing to go that far. Let me just do this, let me get into the conflict of it.* When I can just pause I get the answer, so to speak. Maybe it is just about taking that extra moment to wait in order to see it. So in a situation, maybe a classroom situation, it is not necessarily to let it go, it is about asking what I need to see. And like you said, is this something that I can say *yea* to or is this something I can say *nay* to.

David: And be at peace with either way.

Friend: Right. I think teachers have a really hard time because society puts so many role expectations on teachers and what they are supposed to get out of each student in order to go from grade to grade. So you cannot just have that free will kind of attitude that you can in other jobs or other situations.

David: That is one of those sneaky ego ploys—that certain situations or certain people have it more difficult or easier. And really what that does is fly in the face of the first principle of miracles which is that "There is no order of difficulty in miracles." M-22.1

That is the hardest one! If you can get the first principle you do not even need the other forty-nine. But the ego's strategy towards all kinds of conflicts is basically to always say: *if only something were different in the world*. It is always trying to change something on the screen to bring about the peace. The mind is resistant to seeing that it just takes a change of perception in the moment. That is the one thing that the mind in the deceived state is so resistant to. In the end, that is what the Atonement is – to start to see there is nothing outside of me that can give me peace or take away my peace. To do that though, you literally have to transcend the roles.

One guy asked one of these channeled entities, "How can I be enlightened and still be in the corporate world?" And the answer came back: "You cannot!" The deeper we go and the more we transcend the concepts, the more we will be used in ways that we cannot even fathom or foresee. But the ego wants to take all the seeming concepts and situations and project them out into the future. I see this as a path of being present in the moment – whatever the situation is that you seem to be in – and using those opportunities without getting too concerned about the next steps or trying to figure out: *How is this ever going to work? Am I ever going to be a teacher and be enlightened?* Or: *Am I going to have kids?*

It really takes that internal guidance of being shown. *Ok, where do I go from here God? Holy Spirit, what is the next step?* That first step – that *all learning situations are helpful* – is a very big step. But sometimes people will take it too literally. It does not matter if you are on a factory line, if you are hang-gliding, what country you are in, it does not matter – you do not want to get too anchored to the situation and use it as a justification.

For example, a woman I know had problems in her job for years. She would say things like, "I am going to get it; I have to be able to get it while at this job. I know it is not the job that is the problem; I know it is in my heart, so I am going to stay with the job year after year because I know I should be able to get it here."

But that is not how it works either. There are times when it is time for a shift, whether in a relationship or in a job situation or whatever, where the Holy Spirit will give that internal guidance that it is time to move on.

That is the really fine line between not getting so identified with the particular situation or role and then turning that around and using that as a justification. The ego will do that as well, but just try to be in touch with the intuitive voice that recognizes if it is time to move on. That happens with relationships too; the big question is: *How do I know whether I should stick it out with this partner, or if it is time for me to move on?* It really comes back to the intention. *Am I trying to run from something, or am I really being guided on to something else?* That is really helpful.

Friend: Sometimes even our language is a good place to start examining. Like the word *should*, for example, and all of those qualifiers.

David: I know that idea comes out in a lot of literature and yet I have gone through the Course and I have seen Jesus use the word *should*. You cannot make blanket statements about words because it is truly about the intention that is behind the words. It comes down to: *What is my intention?* It does not work to try to identify specific words as ego words. I will give you a good example. There is a line from the Bible that is explained in the Course: "Vengeance is mine, saith the Lord." T-3.I.3 You could jump in right away and say *that is an ego statement.* In the Course, Jesus amazingly takes, "Vengeance is mine, saith the Lord" and turns it around and gives it a different interpretation. He says it is like the Holy Spirit saying: *My little child, vengeance is Mine. That idea does not belong in your Holy Mind, give it to me.*

Wow, what a turnaround; thank you! We can do the same thing for song lyrics. You hear a song and you think that it is such a "special relationship" song, *I can't live if living is without you,* or something like that. You think: *That is an ego statement if I ever heard one!* Then the little voice in my mind goes: *Turn it to God; I can't live if living is without YOU.* What a relief! It is a good example of form versus content. There are ways of reinterpreting things such that we do not have to get into saying something is an ego form or a Holy Spirit form.

Friend: Can you talk more about roles and responsibility?

David: The mind is so conditioned to forms and roles and the concrete; that is all it knows. That is where the mind is. That is where the mind watching comes in. The mind watching starts to pull you away from form and move more to a sense of mind. In the *Song of Prayer* Jesus talks about asking for specifics. He says that in the beginning that is the only way the mind can pray. Prayer is a desire of your heart; if you believe in specifics you are going to ask for things. *Please help me pay the rent; please help me get a better job; please....* It is all about asking for form. Ultimately you keep moving inward and start to ask what the Will of God is for you. You start to ask that question in all aspects of your life. You can see how that is a fundamental shift from asking for specifics.

Now it is not to say that there is anything wrong with those earlier things because they are all stepping stones. I have heard a lot about abundance and manifesting—using the power of your mind to bring certain results, whether it is houses, cars, better jobs, or parking spaces. This is a big stepping stone for the mind. If the mind believes that it is this powerless little victim, helpless in the face of the world, then it can be a great witness when you do have that goal that seems to be achieved—the car, the house, the money, and so on. It can be a step to say: *Gee, I am not this puny little powerless thing. My mind is powerful.* It can be a good affirmation of that, and the only thing that the Course says is: *Ok now, right. You have a powerful mind. Instead of trying to run with the ego and get as many possessions and collect as much stuff as you can—to build up your self-concept—why not use your powerful mind for a goal as high as peace of mind, or eternal peace?* Even those things, everything that we do along the way are steps towards asking what the Will of God is in everything. There is a real gentleness and ease that comes when I think of it that way, instead of the panic of: *Am I doing the right thing? Should I change relationships? What should I ... do, do, do, what do you want me to do?*

Friend: My friend was talking earlier about living in the now and the first thing that came to my mind was when my son comes up to me and says "I want to do this with you," and immediately [clicks finger] I am right in the now. The perfect way that I get into the now is being reminded of those things in my life that need to be attended to right in the here and now.

David: To me that question about living in the now runs really deep. It is basically assumed that there is a world and that there are causes in the world and there are consequences. If you do not water a plant during a hot sunny summer; the plant dries up and dies. Cause: sun, heat; consequence: dead plant. Have sex without birth control—cause/consequence. If you do not pay the rent you will be evicted; cause and consequence. The whole world is based on causes and consequences. But the world is just an effect. It is a bunch of images that are dancing shadows on a screen. That is a phenomenal idea because it totally overturns the way we do everything. All of our thinking and planning, and the way we go about things used to be based on fear of consequences. Fear of consequences is all very much tied in with the ego's use of time. The ego says: *You have been guilty in the past. Look at the closet full of things that you said you were going to do that you have never done, or that you did that you should not have done.* It is the guilt that is saying: *You will have to pay for that; you will pay for it in the future.* That is where fear comes in. That is where the ego's use of time is very fearful: *You have been guilty in the past and you are going to pay in the future.* Fear of consequences can be a simple thing like: *I have to keep my head above water because the world is going to get me in the future.* Or it can be the fear of God. A lot of people project the fear of God out onto a final judgment day; they will pay for their "sins" on a final day of judgment. But when I really started to look at my life I asked, "What would it be like to live with the complete relinquishment of fear of consequences?" If you could do anything that you wanted to and you could really just tune into Spirit, what would you do?

Friend: How do we turn our life into wanting to gain pleasure and just enjoy life rather than basing it on avoiding pain?

David: The basic thing with pleasure/pain, or looking for enjoyment, is that we have still identified it as being in the world and so we are still seeking. The Course is teaching us that the world is past. I mean if you have just done the first ten workbook lessons you have probably come to number seven: "I see only the past." It can be a startling lesson.

Friend: Yes. All of the thoughts in my mind are based on everything that I have already seen. And that is what I base my future on, which is an illusion. My life is a series of organized drifting with unexpected opportunities along the way, but there are beautiful and wonderful miracles at times as well.

David: And you can see where this linear-ness is. The ego needs linear time to keep it going. The holy instant – or coming to live in the now – releases the worry about the future and the guilt and regret about the past. In holy encounters we literally see our brothers without the past. The past is made up of judgments and reactions. Do I have a good relationship with this person or a bad one? You mentioned your issue with your friend – all those are like memories and the ego's saying: *Yes, that is who that guy is, all those bad memories, and that is why you should be afraid of him whenever he comes close.* But it is really about starting to live in the moment and trust – and it does take a lot of trust because all of our seeking to avoid those fearful consequences in the future is based on past learning. The intuition is a lot different than: *This is the way it worked in the past and I know this will work and da, da, da.* The intuition says: *Let go of all of that and just trust to be guided in the present moment.*

Let your judgment thoughts come up and look at them all, both positive and negative, and realize that both extremes are part of the judgment. A lot of times it is like you want to just let go of all negative judgments; you want to put positive judgments or positive thoughts in place of them. But your positive judgments will hurt you as much as your negative judgments. The Course differentiates from other spiritual paths where they just bring the positive in and try to get the negative out. It's the positive expectations that we have – the hierarchy of illusions – that we get so defensive about. If we are really identified with our looks in a body sense, or with a car or a house or whatever, then when something seems to threaten that, we just flip out!

Friend: What I hear you saying is that for there to be a positive you have to have a negative?

David: Opposites again.

Friend: And to look at them both equally, not make judgments on either of them. Is that right?

David: Yes. Like the Zen way of watching the trains of thought go by; some of the trains will be positive judgments and some of the trains will be negative judgments. The Course is saying that spiritually we are very small children and that we cannot tell the difference between pain and pleasure. In this world it seems obvious. It seems like we can tell the difference between pain and pleasure. You pursue one, you avoid the other. But the ego never lets it into awareness that the pursuit of both pain and pleasure reinforces the body as being real. Reinforcing the body as being real keeps the guilt and the belief system denied and keeps us from waking up to our spiritual reality.

Ultimately it is not a path of relinquishment or sacrifice. When we start to get miracle minded – when we let the Spirit come through us and we connect and join – we start to experience such an intrinsic joy that is not based on getting something external to satisfy or gratify us. A momentum starts to grow and we feel like we are fulfilling our function. It is like: *Oh, this is what I came here for, oh yeah, now I am remembering.* Then the joy and the peace start, and the other stuff, the addictions and the whatever, just fall away because the momentum just takes over. This makes a lot of sense to me because I know I have struggled with a lot of things regarding pain, pleasure, gratification, repression, and indulgence. In this world it is like: *Oh, go for the indulgence. Oh I should not be doing that. I am going over the boundary lines here. Pull it back. Oh, I am repressing. I really would like to be doing that, I am thinking about that all the time.* The miracle just brings our mind into clear focus.

The miracle is the option. There is indulgence, there is repression, and then there is the miracle. The indulgence and repression do not go anywhere; they stay horizontal, but the miracle goes up. We go back up to the Source.

Approaching the Atonement – Discouraged by Time

Hi David,

Jesus says in *The Meaning of the Last Judgment* section, "Just as the separation occurred over millions of years, the Last Judgment will extend over a similarly long period, and perhaps an even longer one." T-2.VIII.2 With Last Judgment he means that man finally judges himself as forgiven and sees himself as God does. Does this mean the healing of the whole Sonship will take many millions of years?

When I look at my own journey, I see how rigidly I hold my perceptions in place and how seeing differently can seem to take enormous persuasion. Those times that I had a glimmering that my seeing was wrong, and what the truth really was, seemed like they were a change the size of a grain of sand. I think I am going to need millions of years to see completely differently to shift my perceptions so wholly! This really freaks me out because I really thought: *Wow! Cool! I really have the solution finally so all I have to do is read the Course and hey, presto, my life will change and everything will be wonderful.* Now I am seeing how much it took just to see that tiny bit differently and I am disappointed that I will not have enough time to get it in this life time! I do believe in reincarnation, but who wants to go through more death experiences? I have become very disheartened by this. Can you help?

Beloved One,

Thanks for sharing what is on your heart. Do not be disheartened by the thought of time, for the world you perceive was over long ago. This world is the past. It was just a symbol and represents only the meaning that was given it. It seemed to last but an instant and was forgiven immediately by the Holy Spirit. Process is a time concept; miracles are simply a gentle use of time to collapse time while you still believe in it. In this sense, time is under the control of the miracle worker. Christ arranges time and space for the miracle worker as the miracle worker seems to perform miracles, and Atonement is the first and last miracle, the Alpha and Omega, and all the miracles which seemed to come in between.

Atonement means Correction; it is the awareness that the separation never happened. This cannot be difficult to accept, for no illusion can stand in the Light of Truth. Do not be discouraged by the "process" of Awakening. All thoughts of process are transitory metaphors that simply disappear in the twinkling of an eye. Truth is true and has no exceptions. There was never a time when illusions could replace truth and time cannot replace Eternity. Spirit and time cannot be reconciled, for Spirit is true and time does not exist. Awakening is nothing more than *this* realization.

Life is neither of the body nor in a body. Life is an Eternal State of Mind. There is no death, for nothing real can die. Forgiveness shows the falsity of illusion and thus makes way for the remembrance of God and Christ. Christ is not born and does not die, remaining Eternal as God created Christ in Spirit. If you seem to be discouraged by judging "progress," remember the teaching of Christ: "Judge not, lest ye be judged." (Matthew 7:1) Time is self-judgment. The Holy Spirit's only use of time is to teach that there is no time.

These words witness to this simple fact; for Christ is fact, and time and Christ cannot co-exist. It only takes one instant for Atonement, yet this instant is without an opposite and thus is completely Certain. Miracles will seem to build your trust, yet Atonement is a moment of complete trust that yields to Absolute Certainty. You cannot fail to accept what is inevitable and God's Plan for Salvation IS inevitable. Innocence is our Birthright, and nothing can change what God created Perfect and Eternal.

I use many symbols and metaphors. These are transitory illusions that point beyond themselves. "What Is" is literally beyond symbols and metaphors. Complete forgiveness rendered time past and gone. I rejoice in the holy instant and ask but that Christ be glorified by recognizing the Self God created forever Pure and Innocent. In this recognition is God Glorified.

All Glory to God forever and ever! Amen.

Form/Content Question about Approaching Salvation

Hi David,

I read something you wrote that I would like some help on: "It matters not what road you have taken, be it the Bible, *A Course in Miracles*...." As you know, I started ACIM about a year ago (after a number of years "doing" Eastern spiritual stuff like Transcendental Meditation). ACIM re-sparked an interest in Christianity. In September I did the "Alpha course" – a non-denominational introduction into Christianity. I also attended the particular church that held this course (an evangelical/Pentecostal church). It appealed to me because, unlike some of the more traditional churches I had been exposed to when young (where, in my opinion, there was much "man-made" ritual and a distinct lack of God or the Holy Spirit), this was more like a Gospel church.

I agree with your statement and it has been my philosophy, but my question is this: The particular Christian church mentioned above points to a single passage in the Bible (in John's Gospel) where Jesus says no one can come to God except through him. They then continue: *Therefore anyone who puts their faith in lay-lines or Zen or Buddha or Allah etc., is misguided, since only through Christ Jesus comes salvation.* Can these two seemingly different stances be reconciled?

Beloved One,

The Universal Spirit is the Way, the Truth, and the Life. The Spirit is One, and the Christ Spirit or Holy Spirit, or One Spirit. "No man comes unto the Father, but by me," (John 14:6) is the Universal Call to remember Eternal Oneness.

The "paths" and the "forms" of the world seem to be many and different, but the Call remains the Same. There can be no "truth" or "absolute" in form, for form was made by the ego to deny and cover over the Abstract Oneness of Spirit.

The statement you refer to from John's Gospel is true in Content, for Christ is Spirit and is Identity in God. The ego does not understand Content, for all the ego recognizes is form. Christ and the Kingdom of Heaven are the same in Spirit, and thus the Universal Spirit is the Way to remember God.

Jesus is a symbol that has been used to point to the Christ – the Universal Spirit which is beyond form entirely. Jesus, as a form or symbol, is an illusion, as all forms are illusion. The ego wants to make an idol of Jesus or anyone or anything to maintain the belief in illusion. The Holy Spirit's use of symbols is to lead beyond symbols, as the Holy Spirit's use of time is to lead beyond time. Time and Eternity cannot *be* reconciled for one is illusion and One is Truth. The Truth is true, and only the Truth is true.

So in answer to your question, two stances about form can never be reconciled, for the dualistic perspective which sees two is the error – is the ego. The unified or single Perspective of the Holy Spirit is the Content, which is beyond the possibility of contradiction or duality or multiplicity. What is the Same cannot be different, and What is One cannot have separate parts. Oneness is natural. Oneness simply Is.

Love and blessings forever and ever, Holy One.

Q&A Session

Friend: What was/is paradise?

David: Pure Spirit/Eternity/Light/Love/Infinity.

Friend: What is "heaven on earth?"
David: Seeing the world without judgment.

Friend: Do you believe it is possible?

David: It is a stepping stone or metaphor in Awakening to Spirit.

Friend: What is healing of the world?

David: Accepting that the mind is whole not fragmented.

Friend: How can you socially help, so a soul that is experiencing a dream of dying from hunger in Africa can experience Truth?

David: Release the belief in separate souls/private minds/private thoughts and the world is healed. There is no problem apart from the mind.

Friend: How do you classify out of body experiences and the forms on higher vibrational planes like Christ plane or etheric planes?

David: Out-of-body experiences are perceptual metaphors for a mind which believes it is "in" a body. Christ is Reality and therefore not a belief, level, plane, or concept. When the sleeping mind is emptied of all concepts and beliefs, Divine Mind is recognized as Reality. Such is the Christ. Spirit never enters into form. When the illusion of ego is raised to the Light it dissolves. Such is Awakening.

Friend: You said that there is no Mind/Spirit in matter. Is Spirit/Mind present in you?

David: Spirit is ever present. The word David is a symbol or representation, not Reality. Spirit, Being Abstract and limitless, is beyond personality. The "I AM" is Spirit.

Friend: Was/Is Spirit/Mind present in Jesus?

David: The word Jesus is also a symbol or representation. Jesus the Christ is a phrase indicating the apparent representation or demonstration of Reality. Yet Reality is One, beyond any/all symbols.

Friend: What about Neo's mastery over illusion (stopping bullets) in the movie *The Matrix*? Or in the movie *Dark City*, isn't that the Holy Spirit's work in mainstream media?

David: These are excellent symbols of Mind over matter and the power of forgiveness, to have dominion over the world of images. Yet the Holy Spirit does not work in the world, but in the mind that believes the world is real. The point of healing is the release of the illusory lens of fragmentation.

Interpreting the Holy Spirit as using symbols is accurate, yet it must be remembered that the Holy Spirit uses time to teach there is no time, and symbols to teach a unified Perspective in which symbols are no longer necessary. Thus forgiveness is more accurately the *unlearning* of everything one knows about the world than learning in the sense of accumulating skills and abilities in the world.

Friend: Can you feel Oneness with me and with all that is true in this illusion? If yes, what is the rush to the formless world?

David: Unified or healed perception is feeling the Oneness and Love that comes from the experience of non-judgment. Non-judgment is a Perspective where you are joined with the Holy Spirit—and realize you are not in the illusion. The dreamer of a dream, aware that the world is only a dream, is not identified as being a figure or participant *in* the dream. The fear was generated by the belief that one is in a dream, a body. The peace comes with the dreamer of the dream Perspective, joined with the Holy Spirit.

Friend: Do you vote and for whom?

David: No. Peace is seeing that there literally are no sides to take and no change possible in the world. This is what changing your mind about your mind means. Change the lens and not the script, for right-mindedness is a real alternative with which to view the dream. It is impossible to change a script that is past, that is already written. Seeing this is peace. Seeing this is the Correction. It is about accepting the Holy Spirit's Correction instead of attempting a personal correction, which of course is no correction at all.

Chapter Two

Is the Function of the Holy Spirit to Translate Reality into Form?

Hi David,

Is the special function of the Holy Spirit to translate reality into form?

No, Beloved One,

This is a very basic error. The Holy Spirit's function is *not* about "translating reality into form" – quite the opposite. The Holy Spirit reinterprets the dream, as error is brought to truth and darkness is brought to light, not vice versa. Understanding this is fundamental to Awakening. It is impossible to bring truth to illusion or reality to fantasy. That is a fundamental teaching of ACIM.

> You who have spent your life in bringing truth to illusion, reality to fantasy, have walked the way of dreams. For you have gone from waking to sleeping, and on and on to a yet deeper sleep. Each dream has led to other dreams, and every fantasy that seemed to bring a light into the darkness but made the darkness deeper. Your goal was darkness, in which no ray of light could enter. And you sought a blackness so complete that you could hide from truth forever, in complete insanity. What you forgot was simply that God cannot destroy Himself. The light is *in* you. Darkness can cover it, but cannot put it out. T-18.III.1

> The Holy Spirit does not see the body as you do, because He knows the only reality of anything is the service it renders God on behalf of the function He gives it. T-8.VII.3.6

> The Bible says, "The Word (or thought) was made flesh." Strictly speaking this is impossible, since it seems to involve the translation of one order of reality into another. Different orders of reality merely appear to exist, just as different orders of miracles do. Thought cannot be made into flesh except by belief, since thought is not physical. T-8.VII.7

45

All figures in the dream are idols, made to save you from the dream. Yet they are part of what they have been made to save you *from*. Thus does an idol keep the dream alive and terrible, for who could wish for one unless he were in terror and despair? T-29.IX.3

In gentle laughter does the Holy Spirit perceive the cause, and looks not to effects. How else could He correct your error, who have overlooked the cause entirely? He bids you bring each terrible effect to Him that you may look together on its foolish cause and laugh with Him a while. *You* judge effects, but *He* has judged their cause. And by His judgment are effects removed. T-27.VIII.9

Bringing illusion to truth, or the ego to God, is the Holy Spirit's only function. T-14.IX.1.4

The Holy Spirit reaches from the Christ in you to all your dreams, and bids them come to Him, to be translated into truth. He will exchange them for the final dream which God appointed as the end of dreams. W-pII.6.4

The major difficulty that you find in genuine forgiveness on your part is that you still believe you must forgive the truth, and not illusions. W-134.3

This metaphysical teaching is essential to experiencing forgiveness as it is, and not merely intellectualizing according to the ego's plan. It is the ego that counsels that Holy Spirit goes about translating reality into forms. Forgiveness is a retranslation of perception (Atonement) that is the gateway to Reality, which is Abstract and Eternal. Reality, or Knowledge, is far beyond perception and cannot be translated or shrunk down to form or perception.

Without this understanding, there is no experience of forgiveness, and it remains an ego concept which serves to make the error real in awareness, or reinforce that illusions are true. Error must be brought to truth, not vice versa. Reality cannot be translated or brought into form.

Can Enlightenment be Received by "Hands-On" Transference?

Hi David,

I had a very interesting chat with my friend today about diksha (hands-on transference). I feel to ask you to give me your views on diksha and this whole expanding movement. I have deep trust in you and value your clarity. Is this phenomenon serious in your eyes and do you think it can cause an actual permanent change and lead to permanent enlightenment?

Beloved One,

Thanks for writing. There are many concepts that are stepping stones toward Enlightenment, yet all of them must evaporate before the mind is emptied of false belief. There is no body or action or time-space event that can save the mind or set it free, for there is nothing apart from mind. Your desire and willingness will call forth witnesses to Awakening, and there is nothing in form that can speed up Awakening—for form but witnesses to the desire within. People and actions are symbols, and mastery of mind can be reflected with symbols, yet there is no shortcut or substitute for the requirement of emptying the mind of every thought and belief.

A Course in Miracles is a very direct path when the desire for Awakening is strong, and all books and teachers and events can but reflect the desire of the heart. Enlightenment is never a matter of time, of study, or proximity/transference with a guru, or a special energy transmission, for these are but effects of belief. All beliefs must be exposed and released to make way for complete forgiveness, which is an experience that transcends specifics in its wholeness.

There is no causation in form, and this includes the concept of diksha. The mind must be emptied of all specific concepts, even those about energy, in order to be still and at rest forever.

Form versus Content

Hi David,

It was a rainy, foggy morning and not a particularly up day. The Workbook lesson for me today said that the peace of God is shining in me now. As seems to be shared by many, it has been difficult for me to reconcile the Course teachings with everyday life in the world, especially when what I have projected may not always be extraordinary, but much of which is often so compelling.

Business worries and problems took center stage for most of the day, and at this time of the month – hey, this is relevant – I am hormonally challenged. (I mention all that I do here to paint a portrait of my day as an example of the conflict I am experiencing.) In the late afternoon, the sun seemingly miraculously came out, and I took off on my bicycle towards the path by the river. The air was so clean and almost crisp and a dry wind was blowing lightly. It was not quite sunset and as the first formal day of fall, that moment colored the sky in perfect synch with the date's designation. It was suddenly so gorgeous outside.

Okay, so what is the point? It is a question, really. Given the above scenario, you will understand if I sound a bit testy or sarcastic. I do not mean to. But if we are to believe that all of these circumstances in the world of form do not really exist, then are all the values we have associated with the pleasant and the unpleasant invalid wastes of time and energy? I lose sight of the alternative to thinking this way. Is it as pointless to allow one's self to be occasionally seduced by pleasure and beauty as it is to collapse into fear? Are they both traps? Or are these lovely experiences a glimpse of the even more splendid stuff on the other side?

I hope I am making myself clear. I think I am feeling guilty about helping myself feel better by seeking out the goodness in the world of form, when I am learning that it is neither substantive nor meaningful. Are we to believe that the feelings we get from watching the sunset and such are merely distractions? I used to think they were gifts from God, sometimes even signs that all is well. Do I have to abandon that notion since it is not true? Or could it be in some way that would not compromise the Truth?

Many thanks for your website, your wise counsel and gifts, and for giving me a forum in which to vent today. Please attempt to enlighten me when you can.

Beloved One,

Thanks for sharing and venting what is on your heart. You are dearly loved and fully appreciated. Your questions get to the subtleties of the mind training required for Awakening, because in dreaming things are not as they seem to be.

Everything that appears in this world of dreams is given its meaning by the mind of the dreamer. The dreamer is asleep and dreaming of forms aplenty, unaware of the Abstract Light of Mind Awake. The sleeping dreamer believes in both love and fear, dissociates these feelings, projects the split onto the dream, and perceives a world of opposites as reality.

Thus beautiful and ugly, good and bad, sunny and rainy, clear and foggy, unpleasant and pleasant, etc. seem to be real descriptions of real sights and sounds and smells and conditions in the dream. There are even spiritual paths that tell students to accentuate the positive and eliminate the negative, as if it is possible to tell them apart.

The one right use of judgment in Awakening is discernment. How does one feel? Is one happy, peaceful, joyful? Are one's perceptions stable and consistent?

The experience one has is a barometer of the stability of one's perception. In order to be consistently peaceful, mind training is required. This involves the relinquishment of judgment, releasing the belief that one is actually capable of judging anything at all. Each step inward is more and more humbling, until the mind reaches a point at which it can honestly say, "I do not know what anything is for." W-25 This is the point at which the mind can experience the meaning of forgiveness.

Be gentle with yourself on this inward journey. Accept the symbols that come to you with gladness and appreciation. Let the Holy Spirit use the symbols to remind you of the Inner Beauty that is far beyond appearances. Let the colors and the sights and smells and sounds wash through your mind as reminders of the Vastness and Glory of Being! Discover the Beauty of the Holy Spirit's Purpose.

Without judgment are all things equally acceptable. Without judgment one can see the Big Picture, the Tapestry of the Cosmos. Without judgment there is nothing "outside" the mind and everything is therefore included. Without judgment, nothing can be rejected and there is only harmony. Without judgment conflict and competition are no more. And without judgment, One is happy, simply Being, and in this Being is everyone and everything included.

The alternative to judgment is acceptance. There is another way of looking upon the world, and this new, fresh Perspective is worth the mind training that seems to precede It. As self-concepts are laid by, so are the expectations and the stress.

Behold the world anew and see a forgiven world without agendas and controls and rules. As one is light-hearted one perceives a light-hearted world. Notice the synchronicities and the melody and the orchestration of the big picture, and observe it all with Supreme Detachment. There is a Joyful Passion in beholding all things with Detachment.

Who One is, the Christ, is truly Gorgeous. The opening to this State of Being is worthy of the attentiveness to mind training and the opening to the Holy Spirit's Purpose. True Beauty dawns as Content of Mind, and as this transformation occurs all the forms light up and are seen as the same. It takes faith to keep attentiveness to mind training and to be open to miracles. The miracles stabilize and clear one's perception and are truly worth the effort and practice. I am joined with you in miracles and know that every bit of willingness to allow the miracle into awareness is something to rejoice about! As you proceed, the ego's emphasis on form will be eclipsed and transcended by your alignment with the Holy Spirit's Content.

Preliminary Questions on Memory, Creations and Consciousness

David: The lesson in the Course about holding on to your function of forgiveness basically says it entails two phases: recognizing that forgiveness is your only function, and giving up all the other functions that you think you have. The self-concept comes in when there are agendas; when things have to go a certain way with certain outcomes. So what is my priority? Am I going to really hold forgiveness as my only function or am I going to let these other agendas come in and take forgiveness off the front and hold those up instead? It has to be either or.

Friend: There is an old Indian saying that says, "I use memory. I do not let memory use me." That really helps me out a lot in my interpretation.

David: I always associated memory with the past, until I read in the Text about using memory to remember the present. That is a revolutionary idea. It says that memory is an ability you made. You are used to associating it with the past but you can actually use it to remember the present! That is where you would have the memory instead of just letting the memory automatically have you. It is an experiential thing. When you let go of the outcomes and just follow the guidance, there is a joyful stepping aside from a lot of these concepts.

Time and space are deeply rooted beliefs. Once you start to see these as constructs then all of a sudden there is a real ease that comes. You start to take to heart the saying that you cannot help but be in the right place at the right time. That is a great one to hold out front when you are traveling a lot. It takes the struggle out of it. It takes out all the *Oh, gosh, did we make a right turn? What did you do with the map?* That whole thing that comes from feeling like you are not in the right place at the right time, or you are too early or you are too late. It is a practical kind of an experience. There is a shift of mind, like being above things. It is almost like you are on a carpet ride and the only way you stay on the carpet, of course, is to stay divested of the outcomes. If you really hold on to your intention and just want to stay at peace and have holy encounters without knowing how it is going to look, it makes it a lot of fun. The struggle in my life always came from trying to control the outcomes, people, or situations.

Friend: Can you talk about creations, our creations?

David: Creation is totally at the level of Heaven. You do not know your creations in the sleeping state, but the Father extended Himself – Created the Son in his likeness and image, and then the Son extended himself and these are the things that are called creations. It is entirely at the level of spirit. In other words spirit begat spirit, begat spirit. It is all a continuous line. In the sleeping state where perception is distorted you have no remembrance, no recognition of your creations. It is one of those things that you can really only go so far in talking about. We know they are eternal, we know they are changeless. They are perfect; they are infinite – like the Father and the Christ.

Friend: Ken Wapnick talks about how in Heaven God has no consciousness. I felt upset when I heard that. I always thought in terms of the mind being conscious, and then I thought *there will be nothing!* There was an immediate sense of fear but I heard this small voice say: *You know, when you think of what makes you happy, it is always thoughts of Love.* There was an overwhelming feeling that those thoughts would be more magnified than anything I could even think of and I was suddenly at peace with it. But, I could feel how quickly I shifted out of that, into that ego thinking of: *Oh my God, I have picked up a book that says God has no consciousness. I won't have a conscious mind to think.* It was a real learning experience. I sense that the thoughts that make me most joyous are those thoughts that I cannot even express. I do not know how else to say it. They are just....

David: Beyond the words.

Friend: Yeah.

David: I think it does help to be precise about the words. Like what if we asked, "What does consciousness mean to everybody in this room?" The Course describes consciousness as "the receiving mechanism." Of course messages can be received from the ego, or messages can be received from the Holy Spirit. Consciousness is literally the mind that, in this deluded state, is receiving messages from two diametrically opposite voices. Consciousness can be trained to approach the real world; at the highest level, consciousness is aware of the real world. Transpersonal psychology talks about training the mind, about using meditation and mind training to the point of being able to overlook and not hop on the trains anymore – which means you have reached the real world.

Now that is still a metaphor because there are no levels, in the ultimate sense. We talk about a structure of the split mind but there is not a split mind. It is like a ladder is lowered down into the mind that believes it is split. The ego level is where the teaching is needed, as if there is an "individual mind." The ultimate metaphysics are that there is only one mind. We talk sometimes about collective egos, and the split mind, and this other person's lesson was this, and my lesson was that. Basically the idea of an "individual mind" is useful because if you believe in bodies, you also believe that there is a separate individual mind that goes with each body, rather than believing and experiencing the truth of there being only one mind. The split mind sees a subject/object split and perceives itself as fragmented but there is only one mind and by golly, it is mine! It is always my lesson regardless of how much the ego wants to throw it out there onto somebody else.

Consciousness as used in ACIM

Hi David,

I never expected to actually write a question or comment but here goes. You said, "Consciousness (split mind) seemed to come into existence with the belief in separation from God, from Oneness." Do you mean ego-consciousness, the ordinary self-awareness that appears to exist in a body and has a name and so forth? I ask because I use the term consciousness to mean that which creates and animates the illusory form; that which is an Aspect of God and never leaves His

Mind – a part of the Mind of God. My understanding is that this Consciousness, being an Aspect of God, is eternal and plays and plays and plays, extending Love first in one direction, then in another, including making up and pretending to experience an illusion of separation, complete, with amnesia about Reality.

You continued somewhat later with: "God knows not form. God creates the eternal, and Christ is an eternal Idea in the Mind of God. Christ creates the eternal as well. Creation is eternal extension."

I am reminded that ACIM tells us God is within us. We can only hear the Voice for God (Holy Spirit) by going within. We are part of God, as in "My Father and I are One." Certainly I did not take this to mean within the body (like the throne of God is somewhere near the liver), but I did take it to mean within our mind or consciousness (not brain), which is part of Mind. That part of Mind knows form, doesn't it? It is aware of itself as currently playing in the illusion of duality, isn't it? Otherwise a part of the Mind of God would be unaware – which is impossible.

Greetings Infinite One,

Thanks for taking the time to write. I use the term consciousness as it is used in *A Course in Miracles*. ACIM states:

> Revelation unites you directly with God. Miracles unite you directly with your brother. Neither emanates from consciousness, but both are experienced there. Consciousness is the state that induces action, though it does not inspire it. T-1.II.1

> Consciousness, the level of perception, was the first split introduced into the mind after the separation, making the mind a perceiver rather than a creator. Consciousness is correctly identified as the domain of the ego. The ego is a wrong-minded attempt to perceive yourself as you wish to be, rather than as you are. Yet you can know yourself only as you are, because that is all you can be sure of. Everything else is open to question. T-3.IV.2

> Very quietly now, with your eyes closed, try to let go of all the content that generally occupies your consciousness. Think of your mind as a vast circle, surrounded by a layer of heavy,

dark clouds. You can see only the clouds because you seem to be standing outside the circle and quite apart from it. From where you stand, you can see no reason to believe there is a brilliant light hidden by the clouds. The clouds seem to be the only reality. They seem to be all there is to see. Therefore, you do not attempt to go through them and past them, which is the only way in which you would be really convinced of their lack of substance. W-69.4

In the *Clarification of Terms* section the idea of individual consciousness is described as immaterial because it is synonymous with the separation. Studying the separation does not lead to knowledge. Consciousness is described as the mechanism that receives messages from both the Holy Spirit and ego, in other words, the split mind.

Consciousness is the focus of the mind training lessons in the Workbook; it can be trained to reach the forgiven world that Jesus calls the real world. This is the *dreamer of the dream* Perspective that I speak of frequently which is a state of consistent peace and non-judgment. Revelation and miracles emanate from the Light beyond consciousness. God and Christ, Being Pure Eternal Abstract Light and Oneness, have nothing to do with consciousness (which is "split" into illusory levels). In this sense there is no "God Consciousness" for Oneness and split mind are not reconcilable. God and Christ are True and consciousness is make-believe or false. God and Christ are Spirit and consciousness is the belief that there is "something else" in "addition to" Spirit. Awakening could be described as the "release" of the make-believe "something else."

Creation is the Light beyond consciousness. Consciousness, being the domain of the ego, does not have creative ability. God creates the Eternal and the ego or error "makes" the finite, temporal, illusion of time-space. It is consciousness which seems to unlearn the ego (or split) and thus learn of forgiveness (perceived wholeness), yet the quotation above saying "it cannot reach knowledge" reflects the realization that consciousness is an illusion which must disappear before remembering the Knowledge of Heaven or Pure Oneness.

You wrote: "I use the term consciousness to mean that which creates and animates the illusory form; that which is an Aspect of God and never leaves His Mind—a part of the Mind of God. My understanding is that this Consciousness, being an Aspect of God, is eternal and plays and plays and plays, extending Love first in one direction, then in another, including making up and pretending to experience an illusion of separation complete with amnesia about Reality."

Christ never leaves the Mind of God, yet consciousness is the belief that Christ has left the Mind of God. Creation extends Eternally and as ACIM states: "God knows not form." T-30.III.4 Christ is an Eternal Idea in the Mind of God. It is the ego domain of consciousness which seems to be making up and pretending to experience an illusion of separation complete with amnesia about Reality. God does not forgive, for God has never condemned, yet forgiveness (release – letting go) applies to consciousness and thus to releasing the obstacles (what was ego-made) so that the mind can remember God, Christ, and Eternal Creation.

One of the key metaphysical ideas for understanding the importance and necessity of forgiveness of illusion and the release and detachment from the judgment of the world is stated in ACIM as follows:

> The world was made as an attack on God. It symbolizes fear. And what is fear except love's absence? Thus the world was meant to be a place where God could enter not, and where His Son could be apart from Him. Here was perception born, for knowledge could not cause such insane thoughts. W-pII.3.2

God Is. Christ is Awake in the Mind of God. The mind which sleeps and dreams of images appears to play with idols, toys of its own "making," yet the Holy Spirit uses what was made to go far beyond what was made. The Holy Spirit Made a waking Dream cleansed of judgment. The Holy Spirit knows the distinction between the real and the unreal, and the judgment of the false AS false is the only meaningful judgment to be made. This Atonement is the gateway to freedom beyond all dreaming – to remembrance of Self as Christ in the Mind of God. God and Christ are Abstract Eternal Love, and the seeming world of parts and specifics is the veil which HAS BEEN forgiven.

"The Kingdom of Heaven is within." T-4.III.1 I will use the metaphor mentioned in the ACIM Workbook. If Divine Mind were a vast Circle of Light and if this Circle was seemingly surrounded by dark clouds of false belief and perception, consciousness would be the illusory experience of being "outside" of the Circle. In sinking beneath the clouds of illusion, the experience is One of Pure Light. In Truth Light cannot be surrounded or circumscribed, for Light is literally the Allness of God and Christ which Know Perfect Oneness.

I rejoice in the forgiveness of illusion, for a Child of God cannot be limited in awareness except by illusory belief. And happily this need not be. I love You forever and ever!

What is the World?

The world is false perception. It is born of error and it has not left its source. W-pII.3.2

David: The world came about from the ridiculous belief that you could separate from your Creator. This conveys that ideas leave not their source. It seems as if the world has been projected out of our mind. It seems like there is really an objective world out there where there are plane crashes and hurricanes and people sick and dying, and there are continents and cultures and histories; and all of it seems concrete. It has been there long before mankind even came. Carl Sagan would say: *Billions and billions of years... This planet has been around long before there was human life or even evolution. These rocks and these geological formations have been around long before man.* Jesus is saying: *No, no, no, the world is a projection from your mind and it has not left its source.* In other words the world is still in your mind. The world is nothing more than a bunch of ideas in your mind. But the ego would say: *Get out of here. No way! The world has left its source and not only that, you have left your source.* The Course says we were Created as an Idea in the Mind of God. The ego says: *You left! You were created as an Idea in the Mind of God but you usurped God. You turned your back on God. You are out of the Kingdom now. You have left your Source.*

As I have had shifts of self-concepts and as I started to step out of these beliefs, it has been more of an experiential sense that *the world is in my mind.* There is a big perceptual problem going on. The world is in your mind and all the perceptual things that seem to happen on the screen are just witnesses. You look first within your mind and you have all these dark crazy beliefs that your Father did not create, then you feel weak and frail and tiny and guilty. Then you will call forth witnesses in the world that will represent: *I am weak, I am tiny, I am frail, I am little.*

Friend: We have forgotten what the Kingdom is, we have forgotten what Love is, and so to let go of all these things that we have made is very frightening. What do you have left? Just not knowing what is on the other side.

David: The ego says if you let go all this familiar stuff in the world and even these beliefs that are the underpinnings of the world then the ego says you will go into the void. That is the ego's version of going back to the light. But the Holy Spirit is saying you will be everything. You will be exactly as you were Created. You will be abstract Light with no needs, no cares, and no worries; nothing but eternal peace so deep that you do not even have a glimmer of how deep it is. So you can see how there are two different versions of going within.

Friend: Oh, yes. They are total opposites.

David: The ego's belief is that all your security rests on meeting your survival needs and then it goes on beyond that with: *Well, why not have joy in life and comfort; more comfort for the body; more pleasure for the body,* etc. In a sense that is worshipping death because letting go of the mind's identification with the world and the body is where the freedom and joy come in. You can see how this is a big turnaround. We have been seeking our happiness and salvation out on the screen in the specifics and that keeps covering over our deep sense of loss which really comes from the belief that we have separated from our Father in Heaven.

Friend: So it is really that we are totally outside of ourselves. And not really going within to find the joy, the happiness, the love and the peace. It is not in anything outside of us and we are using everything outside of us to find the joy, the happiness, the love and the peace. [laughter]

David: And we are discovering: *Hey, this is not working!* [more laughter]

The World the Ego Made

Friend: Did the ego make everything on this planet? What about angels or chakras or things that people consider good, higher or spiritual? And are we really here because of our wrong-minded thoughts or is this a place that God wants us to be for soul growth and learning?

David: The first part of that question really comes down to looking at consciousness or perception. You might say that consciousness is the domain of the ego as shared in ACIM. So all of perception: time, space, the cosmos, all specifics are a projection of the ego. So yes, the ego did make the cosmos of time and space. The ego made all the images and symbols. We could say that in the sense that you think of angels as cherubs or as beautiful beings with big wings, these are images and they are part of the specifics of the cosmos. Again those are made by the ego. We could talk about the seven chakras. Seven is more than one. It is a multiple number and the specific seven chakras that are often associated with the spine and different positions on the body are again part of the ego's system.

The Holy Spirit is simply a purpose in the mind, this light, this remembrance in there that uses all the specifics. It certainly uses symbols like chakras and angels in a very helpful, loving way to bring comfort and blessing so that when the mind is frightened it has a symbol of a helper. And certainly angels are a good example of that.

The wrong-minded perception that we are here is part of the ego's perception of the world. You might say that God or Christ is part of abstract Heaven. The realm of Heaven does not really know of the realm of perception because, as the Course teaches, "Nothing real can be threatened, nothing unreal exists." T-in.2 The Eternal is what Heaven is, it is what God is; it is what Christ is. The ephemeral, the phenomenal, the time-space cosmos is ever-changing and temporary and by definition is unreal. So you might say that it is a wrong-minded perception to try to bring God into the world and say that God put us here for a reason or that we are here to learn lessons that God set up to test us, or anything like that, because God is just pure Oneness and Love and Abstraction.

It is wrong-mindedness to believe that you are here. Jesus says in the Course that you may wonder how you can experience perfect peace while you are still in a body. He suggests to ask yourself who is it that is in a body? So when you get questions like that you see that Jesus is hinting that truly you are at home in Heaven right now, eternally; you are just dreaming of exile. That is what perception is all about.

On Pleasure and Pain

David: The deeper I have gone, the more my life has simplified. But it has not been a simplification based on the ascetic paths; the old way was sacrifice, like in some of the old mystical paths where people would literally do harm to their bodies, to sacrifice.

Some of you have probably heard about Gnosticism. The Gnostics were a group that came right after, or around the time of, Jesus. A lot of the Gnostics got Jesus' teaching: "My Kingdom is not of this world," (John 18:36), and "The Kingdom of God is within you." (Luke 17:21) The Gnostics really got the fact that the world was not real, that Jesus was speaking of a Spiritual Kingdom, that it was not an earthly kingdom that the Apostles and the Jews were looking for. But the ego's belief in sacrifice is so deeply rooted in the mind and the Gnostics kind of fell into the ego traps of making the error real; they thought: *If the world is not real, then the world must be bad. The body is part of the world so the body must be bad therefore I will starve the body, or I will go out into the desert and I will do things to harm my body, to prove to myself and to God that the world is not real.* Unfortunately the ego loves that. That is like playing into its hands, because whenever you judge something as negative or bad in the world you make it real. Remember when we talked about projecting duality and judging things as good and bad? Once you judge something as negative in the world you reinforce it in your mind as being real.

Then there was another sect of the Gnostics. They kind of said: *The world is not real, so we can indulge in all the vices and pleasures of the world.* They taught that if you did not get them done in one lifetime you would reincarnate and come back and you could just keep indulging in the vices of the world until you were free of them.

But that does not work either, because vices and both pleasure and pain make the body real. If any of you have ever tried to do the lessons "I can see peace instead of this," or "There is nothing to fear," when you have a splitting headache – they just do not go together. Pain is like a witness that says, "I am hurting here, I am guilty," or "I am fearful," or "I am frail." And pleasure does the same thing, because pleasure focuses the mind on the body. It identifies the mind with the body and the sensations of the world. The Hindus and all the great mystics of the world are onto this thing of pleasure and pain. They are like two sides of the same coin. The ego does not tell us that. The ego says to maximize pleasure and minimize pain. *Avoid pain,* isn't that pretty common wisdom in the world? The mind in a deceived state actually believes it can tell the difference. Do pain and pleasure seem the same to you? In a deceived state they seem to be very, very different, but they are just two sides of the same coin.

There are passages such as, "It is impossible to seek for pleasure through the body and not find pain." T-19.IV.B.12 There are physical things that seem to be attractive, like a little band-aid over the terrible loneliness and emptiness that is felt inside. It is like: *This is a quick little fix, I can have that hot fudge sundae that I love. It brings me a lot of pleasure and takes my mind off the loneliness and despair that I feel*—for about ten minutes—and then in another couple of hours: *What is next? What am I looking for?* It is the attraction to guilt, whether it is alcohol or marijuana, sexual addictions, or food.... You can use movies, wanting to just sit in your house all day and watch movies; *I do not want to face the world. I want to just be distracted.*

The Course is so great because it unveils the ego and all of its schemes, showing us just how crazy and insane its thought system is.

> Under fear's orders the body will pursue guilt, serving its master whose attraction to guilt maintains the whole illusion of its existence. This, then, is the attraction of pain. Ruled by this perception the body becomes the servant of pain, seeking it dutifully and obeying the idea that pain is pleasure. It is this idea that underlies all of the ego's heavy investment in the body. And it is this insane relationship that it keeps hidden, and yet feeds upon. To you it teaches that the body's pleasure is happiness. Yet to itself it whispers, "It is death." T-19.IV.B.13

What is Underneath my "Physical Addiction"?

Hi David,

What does the Course say regarding addictions? I am addicted to cigarettes and it has been impossible for me to quit. That sounds negative, but I have tried everything, from positive thinking to support groups, and everything else. Part of me blames my lack of self-control or will-power. Is that really it? I just feel like there is something more going on here. I feel like my battle with cigarettes represents my battle with my ego mind. I was wondering if you have any insights regarding addictions. Thank you so much for all that you have given us. You truly are a blessing.

Beloved One,

Clearing the way to inner peace means exposing and releasing the belief in addiction. What seems to be a physical addiction, such as smoking, is always only a symptom of the mental addiction to judgment. And the release of judgment is the release of the ego. Judgment always involves concepts and comparisons, and this entire cosmos is built upon the premise of judgment. The Being which God created One is beyond judgment, for what is there to compare in Pure Oneness that is Changelessly Eternal? All specific judgments are an attempt to evaluate the Self, yet the Self God created is far beyond the possibility of evaluation.

Wholeness is eternally complete. The belief in lack, therefore, is a belief in addiction.

What seem to be physical addictions are covers or distractions from looking within and moving through the fear to the Love inside. While many are aware that addictions feel like misery, the fear of looking within may seem more frightening to a sleeping mind than the thought of keeping the addiction. Yet when the mind is willing and ready, feelings long repressed are allowed into consciousness, to be moved through and released. This is the opening to healing, and healing is synonymous with the release of judgment.

As the Heart opens the Love inside is revealed. While once it was believed that the Heart needed protection, suddenly it is seen that the Heart revels in extension. And with this opening the Love pours forth and flows without condition or limit, and the remembrance of True Love – ever extending Love – is restored in awareness. Love is never absent – the only choice is whether to be aware of It or not.

Free Will is free forever and One with God. Choice and judgment arose with the belief that it was possible to separate. A premise of any "choice" is duality, and the Atonement or Correction of error sees the impossibility of duality. What is One now is One forever and can never be split apart. As the mind looks inward, it is Guided past the fear and guilt it once sought to hide and protect, and Guided on through to the Light.

I am joined with you in experiencing the Light of Love within. When the journey inwards seems intense and frightening, remember... this too shall pass. The release of error is worth the determination. And the bliss of Being, free of addictive judgments and thoughts, is unspeakably Glorious. Here's to the looking inward. Here's to the Letting Go!

The Original Belief in Separation

Hi David,

I read the text of ACIM in about a year. The reading coincided in time with the seasons, as Jesus mentioned them, which delightfully surprised me, as my picking up of the book was not planned. I proceeded with the lessons and arrived at the first review with the objects in the world sometimes looking as if they had only a front side and around them and from behind glimmered light. This encouraged me.

During a meditation somewhere in the review I felt as if falling. Not falling down, but forward. I knew what was happening and at that point the ego freaked out and fear welled up that I had not experienced since childhood. At that point I fell away from the Course for a while until now, as I am beginning the lessons again.

Here is my question that has been haunting me. God being perfect means His Creations are perfect. How then could His Creations begin to create imperfectly to cause the separation? I know the separation was healed in an instant and what I am experiencing now is only a memory of it. But how could the separation have happened at all?

Blessings and love from a holy rolling stone trying to find his way back home.

Beloved One,

The spiritual journey is the pathway inward, the undoing of every scrap of belief that stems from this core belief. You have had glimpses of the "light behind the veil" and this is very encouraging.

The ego is terrified of the surrender and when the mind is identified with it, you experience its feelings. The ego is terrified of the Light. The ego is the belief in separation; the spiritual journey is its undoing.

I am glad you are turning back to the Course; we are deeply joined in our holy shared purpose of awakening to truth. It is a pathway through the darkness to the light, so the fear will come up, along with all kinds of other uncomfortable emotions (that are all really just fear), but when you have a firm context, knowing that you are going for a healing, for a mind-overhaul, then there is no need to run away from it.

The mind, in the full awareness of the Atonement, knows that the separation never happened. The full awareness of the Atonement is that the separation never happened.

I always hear the same questions, "How did the impossible occur?" "To whom did the impossible occur?" I call them the top questions. How did this happen in the first place? How could perfection, how could God, ever make a mistake? Or how could Christ, who is a perfect Being, ever make a mistake?

And basically, it is a statement. When you ask the questions, "How did the impossible occur?" or "How did this happen in the first place?" there is an assumption underneath the questions. And what is that assumption? That it happened! Of course the ego likes that assumption. Then it can ask all kind of questions including how this happened.

It is like you are on a wild goose chase to find the right theology, the right teacher, the right technique, the right mantra. Oh my gosh, the guilt of trying to solve that question. But the very assumption is something we have to learn to release.

There will be no theology that will come along to get you out of this. There is not going to be a concept. There will be an experience that will come that will end your doubting. In the Course that experience is the Atonement. The Atonement is full awareness that the separation never happened. In this respect, *A Course in Miracles* is a launching pad. You are on a launching pad where you are ready to take off in a rocket and get up in orbit where you have no sense of gravity. You are happy and free. *A Course in Miracles* is a book that is just designed to help you get up into orbit, into Being-ness, into your perfection.

Chapter Three

A New Interpretation: Part 1
Metaphors of the Course and the Bible

Friend: David, you said we could talk about and clarify the ego; what the ego is, or what we think it is and what it really is instead. It seems like everybody has the same twenty four hours, the same day. You have a good day. Someone else has a bad day. You have a great day. The Course is saying that our perception is an illusion and that is why everybody can have these different good days and bad days. Now we, as a majority of folks out here, might not believe that we have the separation, ok? But I believe God is fully aware that we are under this illusion. I am having a real difficult time with my own personal illusion but I have to deal with everybody else's illusion at the same time. I do not know how to get any real congruency with this thing, or how to work this in toward a common basis so to speak, or a common perception of reality.

David: The reason we seem to have a problem is because our perception is so twisted and distorted. It is like we are looking through a lens. If you are looking through a very dark lens you are unable to see clearly. It is like it says in Corinthians, "For now we see through a glass, darkly." (Corinthians 13:12) The Course is saying that the only way we will ever have consistent peace is when we have a healed perception.

Let's go back to one of your earlier statements that God knows about this. In fact God, being infinite Spirit and Love, only looks on Itself. In other words Love—something that is infinite and eternal—does not look on something that is finite and temporary. Now the Course is saying: *my child sleeps and I must awaken it.* It is like the analogy that you are a parent and your child has been tossing and turning, as if he is in a nightmare. As a parent you do not know what the content of that nightmare is, all you know is that your son seems to be tossing and turning. Metaphorically God, the Father, gave the answer—the Holy Spirit—to His Son to solve the problem. The Holy Spirit is aware of our illusions, being God's answer or Messenger, but He does not believe that they are real. He is very clear that they are just illusions because He is anchored in Heaven and knows the true essence and the true reality of the Son.

The Holy Spirit has a dual function. You can look at it as if He had one foot in Heaven, so to speak, and one foot in the illusion, to help the Son awaken.

The Holy Spirit is in the mind, working with the mind on giving up the false beliefs and ideas. The only way that perception can be healed is by giving up the false beliefs.

Another idea about the ego is that it is nothing more than a puff of madness. The way it is described in the Course is that the whole ego system is a very logical thought system. It seems so sneaky because one premise falls on another. If you have studied logic, you know a thought system is only as good as the first premise. If you have a false premise, then the whole thing is false. That is what makes the ego so sneaky. The basic underlying premise of its thought system is that it is possible that you have separated from your Creator, which is a false premise. All the other beliefs are stacked on top of this premise.

One very deeply rooted belief is the belief in time. If you can imagine this stack of beliefs like an inverted pyramid with the ego down at the bottom, at the apex, the belief in time comes right near the ego.

Heaven is eternal. There is no time or increment of time. God Is. Heaven Is. It is the state the Course calls Knowledge or Eternal Oneness. Time is a belief. For example, a lot of times we talk about spiritual paths as if – *I am on the path to God and maybe in several lifetimes or several more hundred lifetimes I am going to make it back.* But God is not holding up a carrot or saying *okay, just a few more millennia,* because God is not involved in time. The idea that there could be time apart from Heaven is our invention.

So time is a very deeply rooted belief. You were saying that we seem to all have twenty four hours a day – but the Course breaks it down a little further than just our day. It basically says that you believe in linear time, in which there is a past, a present and a future. The ego believes in linear time; its version of time is: *you are guilty in the past, look at your life! Look at all the things that you messed up with, the things you did that you should not have done, the things you should have done that you did not do.* The ego says the present is determined by your past; that is a common belief in this world, that your past determines your present. It says, the past extends into the present and then your future is just an extension of that too. You are guilty in the past, so you are guilty in the present and you are going to be guilty in the future! That is very depressing. To really get into the ego's use of time is depressing.

The Holy Spirit says, "The past is gone." T-28.I.1 Remember when we spoke earlier about how the answer was given immediately to that first belief that *seemed* to be believed in? When God answered your world of separation, fragmentation, sickness and death, it was answered immediately and was over. All the pain and the suffering and the sickness is over!

We were discussing this concept of destiny tonight at dinner. The mind believed it separated from God and the plan of correction, of Atonement, was established simultaneously because God's plan is apart from time. God did not say, "Ok, the first hundred billion years you will do this and the second hundred billion you will do that!" God gave immediate answer. The correction was given simultaneously. However, for the mind that believes it is in time it seems to take a lot of years; there seems to be a time lag. The Holy Spirit's use of time says: *You are completely healed and free and atoned for in the present, and the past is gone; at any instant, at any single instant, if you completely let go of the ego belief system in your mind, you will remember God.* This is good news for a mind wondering how long it is going to take to give up all judgments, false ideas and beliefs. The good news is it has already happened but you just do not believe it; you think that it is still unfolding.

Friend: So it is a matter of accepting what has already occurred?

David: Yes. The mind is terrified of accepting what has already occurred. The ego feels threatened every time you have the experience of sinking down into your mind in meditation. The mind is very afraid of the stillness and the inner light. The ego is telling the mind that if you go back to this light it is going to get you; *you are going to be hurled into oblivion because God is angry with you.* Because the mind believes in the ego and listens to that voice, it is afraid of going within. That is the reason why it is easy to get distracted by addictions and things in the world that seem to cover over the pain but never really get to the core belief underneath.

Friend: We appear to have good and evil, up and down–this dualism. Are you saying that there is only good, that this illusion or this evil that we are seeing, is something that we project, not something that we are creating, and that it has no outside metaphysical force about it?

David: That was a question I always had about this devil idea. The devil can seem very active, powerful and destructive in your life when you give power to this belief. But the good news is, when you withdraw your mind's power from this belief, when you start to squeeze out the ego's belief system and point it out for what it really is you can say: *No way, this has brought me nothing but pain and misery. I do not want this anymore.* You withdraw your mind's power from it. It is like the wicked witch of the West, in the Wizard of Oz, when they throw water on her and she simply melts away. The ego is not overcome by fighting against it or by defeating it, but it is overcome by pulling the plug on it. And you cannot pull the plug on it until you know what it is.

Friend: What about Jesus' life?

David: Jesus literally transcended the ego and in that sense is a wayshower. It is a little different in the Course than the traditional approaches that tend to deify him. In the Course Jesus tells us to think of him as an elder brother and says, "There is nothing about me that you cannot attain. I have nothing that does not come from God. The difference between us now is that I have nothing else. This leaves me in a state which is only potential in you." T-1.II.3 If you are going to have a model or a wayshower to transcend the ego it is helpful to have someone who has overcome the world. Be of good cheer!

Friend: "I am the way the truth and the life and no man comes to the Father but through me." (John 14:6)

David: Yes. You can think of Jesus as someone who has transcended the ego and literally *is* the Voice for God that is speaking through him.

Friend: It was as if he was saying, *I the Holy Spirit*, because that was who was speaking through the person of Jesus. The *I*—the Holy Spirit—is the way the truth and the life. And the Holy Spirit is the truth that is within each of us, whether we have ever heard of the person Jesus Christ or not!

David: Or the Holy Spirit!

Friend: Or the Holy Spirit, right, the truth is still there, whether you are in China or India or you are an aborigine. I had an argument with my cousin about this. We got into a real philosophical and religious conversation. I said, "Dick, all these people in Africa that have never heard of Jesus, they are all going to hell? They are all damned? You have kind of damned a whole lot of these folks out here." And he said, "Well, they never heard of Jesus." And then I said, "I do not think God operates that way, Dick."

The scriptures have said that he has revealed those things of the Earth. And if you have that expectation to find it, then by chance you might. But if you never seek it or you never expect it, then you will never know it when you walk by it.

David: That is the basis of what Jesus is saying here about perception too; what you are looking for within – what you are really sincerely, devotedly looking for within – you will see without, in the world. "What you seek you will find." T-12.VII.6

Friend: The Bible says, "Ask and it shall be given you; seek, and ye shall find; knock and it shall be opened unto you." (Matthew 7:7)

David: The Course uses educational and psychological terms more so than in the Bible, to get at the same initial thing. Also, in the Course Jesus reinterprets certain statements from the Bible that the ego has used for its purposes. The ego loves to quote scripture. There are a lot of things that have been taken out of context from the Bible and used in the name of fear, damnation and hell. Jesus is saying those are just misinterpretations. Some of the thoughts that he has worked with are amazing to me! For example, "Vengeance is mine sayeth the Lord." T-3.I.3 When I read that I thought: *Ooooh!* Jesus reinterprets it. He says it is as if the Holy Spirit is saying to you: *My child give me that idea of vengeance, it does not belong in your Holy Mind. Vengeance is mine, give it to me. I can handle it.* Wow, what a better interpretation of one that I had looked at as a very negative and condemning statement! And about Judas, he says, "I could not have said, 'Betrayest thou the Son of man with a kiss?' unless I believed in betrayal." T-6.I.15

When you read the traditional Christian stories it seems like there are twelve apostles and then there is the bad guy, there is the *Judas* who turned on his master. Jesus is saying that the crucifixion was just an extreme demonstration of how when the Father's and the Son's will are lined up, you cannot kill the Son of God; the mind is all powerful and the body is literally worthless. Jesus reinterprets the crucifixion in the Course: "The only message in the crucifixion was: teach only love." T-6.III.2 That is a pretty radical interpretation when the ego perceives the crucifixion as: *One of God's beloved sons had to suffer and die, to be the lamb of God, literally, to take all the sins, of all the world on himself. An innocent Son had to do it!* If you really trace that thinking back, you would still get back to: *What kind of God is it that would have his innocent beloved Son go through a suffering trial and turmoil, in order to get to Atonement or Salvation?* From Jesus' perspective, he did not perceive that he was being attacked. Through the ego lens it looks like attack when somebody is kicking you and spitting upon you and screaming, "Kill him!" However Jesus says that he did not share that perception; He saw it as a call for love. "Father forgive them for they know not what they do." T-2.V.A.16

Jesus calls us to similarly change our way of seeing. We can have such a trained mind that we go beyond the perception of being attacked and learn instead to see everything as either love, or a call for love. It takes a highly trained perception!

A friend was talking tonight about the soul, about being "soul to soul." This is what the Course is saying. When you realize that your brother is just calling out for love – instead of perceiving him as attacking you – then you will respond with love. That makes a lot of sense. It is not that you perceive attack and then somehow forgive out of the kindness of your heart or because you are more advanced spiritually. That is not forgiveness.

A New Interpretation: Part 2
Touching on Form and Content

Friend: What do you do if people attack you, your beliefs, your name, or your status?

David: It is a process of starting to dis-identify from the beliefs that you thought identified you. In other words, everyone who comes to the world has learned ideas of what it means to be a person, or a man and a woman. A lot of the arguments between the sexes get to statements like, men are like this, women are like that.... What the Course is saying is that you do not know who your brother is; you have a lot of judgments about him that are based on what you believe you are. The deeper you go the more you start identifying yourself as a spiritual being. You get away from even identifying yourself with the world. For example, you no longer defend when someone starts to bad-mouth something you used to be attached to. What I have learned is that when defenses start to come up it is because of my mind's identification with or attachment to whatever is being challenged, whether it is a particular city, team, hero....

Friend: An insecurity.

David: Yes it is a sign of insecurity; it is definitely not aligning with the Holy Spirit or Jesus in my mind. As we start to dis-identify with our attachment to figures in form we do become more defenseless – because we start to identify with the spirit or the soul in each and every one. Insecurity happens when the mind is not so sure of what it is; it has two different voices running. The mind will attempt to use all kinds of defense mechanisms to get around this insecurity or to cover it over, things like denial and repression, or projection. The ego is quite ingenious in coming up with tricks that will minimize insecurity and fear without letting it go. It knows that if you were to ever let go of all the fear and insecurity *it* would be out of business; it would not have a life any more. Defenses are the sneaky mechanism designed to reduce the fear, but not to eliminate it.

It is a good practice just talking about these things. I enjoy it when people question and share their views and perceptions. Once I invited a gentleman who was a philosopher to our meeting. We were having lunch and I heard all these groans up and down the table, like: *you do not want him at your meeting because then we are all going to be in trouble.* This philosopher was someone who had a lot of questions and wanted to really get clear on all this stuff. I said, "This is great!" That is what we want, is it not? Why would we want to leave somebody out who is ready to ask questions? In fact, it turned out to be a tremendous four hours of really plunging into things.

If someone has a belief or an opinion and you notice a reaction or a defensiveness coming up, it has to be your own perception that is producing the uncomfortable feeling. Jesus was able to come and speak the Word because he had transcended the ego system. There was nothing threatening to him, not the Pharisees or any of the different groups that would come to claim blasphemy; *how dare you forgive people's sins? No one but the Father can do that.* Jesus was able to remain above the battlefield because of his certainty of who he was. The Course is saying that if you remove all falsity and false beliefs – then you will have that certainty too. There will be nothing in the world that can take away your peace. There is a lot of comfort in that. It helps you to let go of planning and trying to fix people, circumstances or outcomes. It helps you to be more accepting and trusting, knowing that things are working out. "All things work together for good." T-4.V.1

Friend: …and there is not just one right way of getting to that understanding, right?

David: In form there are many expressions of the universal curriculum but in terms of *content*– no matter what the spiritual path is – it is about transcending the ego. In content or a mind sense they are all the same. But there can be a lot of distortion in discerning between form and content. Content is purpose. Whenever we are speaking of content – we are speaking of purpose: *What is this for?*

As far as schools and pathways go, the Course is one among many. It does not answer questions like: *Should I do this or should I do that? Should I watch the TV show tonight or should I read my Course.* The Course asks: what is your *purpose* for watching the TV show? Is it to have a distraction – something to take your mind off things in order to forget your sorrows and problems? What is your purpose for reading the Course? You know a lot of times people can read the Course and just move their eyes over the words and go: *ah this does not work,* and heave the book. But what the Course does is ask: What is your purpose? That is the crucial thing – not the form.

Many spiritualities fall into a pattern of rituals (form), instead of content. If I do so many particular prayers or Hail Mary's, or so many rites or rituals – if I do enough, or accumulate enough – that will get me back. But the Course is saying: *it is the thinking that is the problem.* Your behavior comes automatically from your thinking so the only place that you can have significant substantial change is by changing the way you think. There are only two thought systems in your mind; the ego's and the Holy Spirit's. Basically the Course is here to help you discern between the two.

The simplest way to identify the two is to see that for every cause there is an effect. And there is only one Cause, with a capital C! That is the Creator; that is the Cause and you are the Effect; you were created by your Creator. You were also created in His likeness and image in the sense that: He is eternal – you are eternal. He is changeless – you are changeless. He is magnitude – you are magnitude. There is only one seeming difference between the Father and the Son: the Father (Cause) created the Son and the Son (Effect) did not create the Father. There are some new age systems that literally say that "I" am God, but this path differentiates. Jesus said in the Bible "the Father and I are one," but he always talked about the *Father and I.* And he would always point back to the Father: Why callest thou me good? There is none good but one, that is, God. (Mark 10:18) He would always point to the Father.

The ego picked up on this seeming difference and said: *What! Why should you settle for number two? Why just be the created, why not be the kingpin, why not be number one all by yourself where you literally can make up a world where you are the kingpin?* That is what this world is, where Cause and Effect are split off, the thought that the Son could somehow be separate from the Father. Cause and Effect are turned around backwards such that it seems that the things that are happening on the screen of the world cause our emotional states. You know how when we were little kids we would stomp off with: *you make me angry* or, *you hurt my feelings.* But that is backwards; *I* hurt my feelings.

Friend: By my thinking.

David: By my thinking.

Friend: And by my perception.

David: If you are identified with the ego that is what hurts because that is denying your Christhood. If somebody seems to steal from you or harm you the world would say you are just an innocent victim; you have nothing at all to do with that, you just happened to be in the wrong place at the wrong time. But the Course says that "I am responsible for what I see. I choose the feelings I experience, and I decide upon the goal I would achieve." T-21.II.2 In other words I can choose to see peace and healing in every situation or I can choose to see separation, defensiveness, etc. A lot of new age systems will say you are responsible for things in form, but as we were talking at dinner tonight, what happens when you take a mind level principle like: *I am responsible for my state of mind,* and you take a worldly perception from the level of form, cancer for example; you put these two together, you get: *I am responsible for my cancer.* Ah ha. The guilt comes in – from taking something on the level of form and then taking a metaphysical principle of mind (I am responsible for my state of mind), and cross-pollinating or bringing those two together.

Friend: That is the level confusion.

David: Yes, that is level confusion. The question comes up straight away: Who in their right mind would choose sickness? And I always say that of course nobody in their right mind would choose sickness. You would have to be operating in the ego or the wrong mind to call forth such a witness in the world. And sickness is a very strong witness. The mind has to believe that it is guilty to call forth a witness such as sickness. The good news is that once we learn to choose and be in our right mind consistently then we are free of the guilt and therefore we do not call forth the witnesses to reinforce that guilt. That is really the only escape from all pain and misery and suffering. It is like you said: join with Jesus. If you are with Jesus and the Holy Spirit you can discern between the purposes of the ego and the Holy Spirit; you understand that one is a fear based thought system and one is a thought system of love. The ego is backwards; it believes that things out there in the world are taking away your peace of mind. But this is the flipside: the ego also tells us that things in the world can bring us peace of mind. *I know a particular island that I can picture and just be there. Or: There is a particular thought that is always peaceful to think, but when my attention comes back to my job, I lose it.* That is backward thinking because as long as we think that there are things in the world that can give us peace or take away our peace then we are literally co-dependent. Do not listen to that ego because it is telling you that there are things that you can get in this world that are going to bring you happiness and peace; and it is a scam, it is a big scam. Go within. That is where meditation comes in; go within your mind, sink down beneath these clouds of darkness of the ego, meditate and go down beneath them to the Kingdom of Heaven. "The Kingdom of Heaven is within." T-4.III.1 And if you have trouble meditating, then relationships can really speed things up because they will bring up all the unconscious beliefs in your mind.

You are dreaming a dream of fragmentation. God did not make this dream; it is a projection from your mind. The first thing to do is to turn around cause and effect. You believe you are the victim of this world that you have made up. As long as you continue to believe that you are a victim with no power, you are stuck. You need to turn cause and effect around and give cause over to the Holy Spirit. The Holy Spirit knows that there is no real cause in this world because the ego is not real. God did not create the ego. So what we have to do is to expose the ego; every time you are tempted to blame anything, your spouse, your job, the IRS, you can choose a miracle. The miracle helps you to remember Cause and Effect. The miracle also reminds you that nothing has the power to take your peace away and the thing that seemed to cause distress must not be real. The more we transfer this and practice it in our daily lives the better we get at realizing that there is nothing in this world that can take our peace away.

We are afraid to do this all the time, but as we practice little by little and the more we start to generalize it the more we become convinced that there is nothing in this world that can take away our peace. Then instead of being this little, bitty dream figure, this little body that is subject to all these forces in the world, we start to see ourselves as the dreamer of the dream. Just like when you are sleeping at night—you go to bed and seem to have all these things that happen. When you wake up you go: *phew, I am glad that was just a dream.* There will come a time when you hear only the Holy Spirit—the Voice for God. You will go: *phew, that was just a dream,* and you will wake up to the Kingdom of Heaven. It makes a lot of sense to actually apply these ideas instead of just reading and talking about them, since you actually get happy and your life gets joyful. You can actually sense real shifts take place in your life. The proof is in the pudding; the more peaceful you start feeling, the more you know you are moving on. Of course there is no compromise between everything and nothing. As long as you have even a scrap of fear in your mind then the ego still has a toe in the door. Jesus is our wayshower, because when he completely one hundred percent transcended the ego he became a model for us. He is not tempted any more by the ego, he knows it is false.

Friend: When you meditate who do you communicate with, how do you communicate or what do you see? I do not know how to meditate, how do you meditate?

David: I see meditation as really just trying to be very receptive. There is a lot of chatter when you first start out because the ego does not like your intention to go within. It knows that if you get real still you are going to start hearing the voice of the Holy Spirit, Jesus, or something else that you feel to call it, and the ego "I" is very threatened by that. So there is this shrieking yakety, yak, yak that goes on: *oh I got to take care of this; I have to remember to go to the bank and remember to pick up the kids.* The mind just wants to race in and get distracted.

Use the methods in the Workbook. There are guided meditations. He starts out very gradually. In the early lessons he does not put in any structure because he knows that it takes willingness just to be able to put your mind to this Course, much less to expect miracles and wonders right off the bat. Little by little structure is introduced because the mind is untrained and needs a certain amount of structure. But then in the later lessons there is less and less structure so that the mind does not get into rituals. The ego would try to get in there in any way it can to make a ritual out of it. So it is all in the book. He will say something like: try to settle down, sit quietly, and try to watch your thoughts as dispassionately as possible; see them come and go. If it helps, think of them as a parade going by. He gives you all kinds of analogies and metaphors because he knows that you are new to meditation and he knows that you need some guidance. He literally gives you Zen-like mind training exercises to help you be dispassionate; to watch your thoughts go by. What makes it so great is that he knows that is what is going to happen, he is prepared. It's like a master psychologist designed these 365 lessons. They are really well suited to an untrained mind.

Thoughts are like trains, you have heard about trains of thoughts. You are sitting there and you are detached, watching your thoughts go by and before you know it you are on the train. One train leads to the next, then you wait a minute and you hop off the train, then you hop back on invariably, then you hop off, then you hop on. In the beginning stages of meditation you are going to hop on some of those trains and some of them are going to be thoughts like:

I will never get this and *I am not making any progress, I do not know how to do this.* They are just ego thoughts, like ego trains. A technique from Christian Science—for discerning whether thoughts are ego or Holy Spirit thoughts—is to put "sayeth the Lord" at the tail end of the thought. If it sounds ludicrous, like *I cannot believe that person did that,* sayeth the Lord … well, can you imagine Jesus complaining about somebody? You feel it is ridiculous and so you can let that one go! There are techniques like that you can use to start to sort what is in your mind.

Friend: There is one point where he says your thoughts do not mean anything and he also says to recognize them for what they are.

David: In the Workbook the lessons rotate back and forth between what you think you see in the world and what you are thinking in your mind. To an untrained mind what is out there in the world seems a lot different than what is in the mind. Say you are at a party and you really start judging somebody. You have the thought: *boy I am glad they do not know what I am thinking about,* or something like that, because the mind believes it is private. It does not believe minds are connected, and that is why Jesus starts to talk about the perceptual world in lesson 1, "Nothing I see means anything." Then the second lesson continues with "I have given everything I see all the meaning that it has for me." A great example of different perception and how everybody reads meaning into what they see is when a group of people go to a movie and afterwards talk about the movie. You get five or ten different views and interpretations. The second lesson brings it back to: I have given everything I see all the meaning it has for me. It is not that the events are giving the meaning or telling me how things are happening, it is the thoughts. In lesson 4 he literally says "these thoughts do not mean anything."

A New Interpretation: Part 3
Form, Content and Responsibility for Sight

David: The Course says you may be surprised at how different the goals that this Course is advocating are from the goals that you hold in your mind. This is a Course that is turning us around and having us go within to try to hold a constant purpose in mind—to stabilize our perception. And what often happens when people start working with the Course is a sense that the Course will ask me to give up something that is valuable, something that I like and I enjoy. This is the belief in sacrifice. Sacrifice is a very, very deeply rooted idea in the mind.

In a metaphysical sense the mind has turned away from the light and identified with the self-concept in all its forms. It is basically afraid of the light. When going toward the light it now believes it has to give up things of real value, things that it is very familiar with, things that it is very attracted to, the status quo. There are certain things about the status quo that the mind likes and it is seen as: *Oh, oh I do not want to rock the boat; I do not want to change the status quo.*

The mind defends against the Holy Spirit by its ordering of all the thoughts. Even though these thoughts are images it is in the ordering of them where the judgment comes in. One of the common ways to judge is to condemn your brother. It is in the ordering of images and the hierarchy of illusions that judgment takes on a finer point and you start getting into subtleties of preference. Those subtleties are so important to see because from those orderings, those self-concepts, goals come forth and that is where expectations come in, even if it is something as simple as driving along and seeing an open parking space. You are trying to get there and someone comes along and gets in there and you feel a little sense of frustration that someone beat you to the parking space. There was an expectation; *that is mine; I pictured myself in that parking space,* or whatever. It is very subtle.

Friend: It occurred to me that the problem is interpretation. Something happens and we interpret it. It became clear to me that it is an expectation that somehow *it is my parking space and someone intentionally took it away from me and I feel victimized.*

David: Yes, why would it be offensive unless we could trace it back to something that was offending me; there is that "me" again. Another question is: Who *is* the "me"?

Friend: I would be more concerned about the dynamics around the reverse of that: I see a parking space and I am oblivious to the fact that another person is aiming for that space and I get the space and there is this driver behind me who is red in the face and just about to explode! Now do I feel any responsibility because I was insensitive to his sense of ownership?

David: Yes, once we break it down and look at the parts it can get away real quick. We have to get back to the idea of purpose. Under the Holy Spirit's teaching there are not any losers, everyone gains, in fact the whole Sonship gains from every decision we make with the Holy Spirit. Underneath what you are saying is: can anybody else be a cause of my upset or is there responsibility involved, for other people's feelings, in any way or to any degree? That is a very core issue – taking complete responsibility for your own state of mind. The sole responsibility of the teacher of God is to accept the Atonement for himself, or as I like to say, "It is always my lesson." If I am really at peace, if I really am in a defenseless place I will automatically perceive this as a call for love and the response then is completely involuntary, whether it be a smile or a kind word, or something else. We are not responsible for choosing our behavior; we are responsible for lining up with the Holy Spirit. As soon as we do that, whatever comes through will be most helpful for the whole Sonship. It is crucial to see the guilt that comes from the belief that I can upset someone else, or that someone else can upset me. It is key to see that believing that the screen is causative, thinking that actual harm can be done from something on the screen or that something did not go the way I wanted, brings me back down to helplessness and powerlessness.

Friend: I hear you saying that it is not about being clever enough to respond in the right way, which is the way psychology would approach it. It is simply to be clear in your own center and then trust the automatic response; because of your own clarity you can trust your response. I still have to own the fact that I am not always in what I would call perfect peace, it is sort of relative peace and there is always something in my cage that can rattle under some circumstances. But I recognize that it is my cage that is rattling and I am responsible for that part of it.

I guess the question I am asking is that I certainly felt relatively at peace, but it did not have the appearance of a peaceful situation and that is why I am raising the question. If one were truly at peace with the situations that surround us, can one be truly at peace and have a bomb drop?

David: What we are getting to is that it is not *situational*; peace is not tied into appearances in any way. Jesus is a good example of accepting the Atonement and choosing to see the world differently. And yet what seems to be happening on the screen seems to go on – including even an angry mob of thousands in one accord yelling "crucify him," – which you may not consider peaceful. He did not share their perception. He did not perceive it as an attack because he was holding onto the torch of peace regardless of what was happening on the screen. That is a good, extreme example of *it is just my choice*. I have to be very clear though, and when we get back to that responsibility we get back to clarity.

The Holy Spirit has only two orders of thought. He perceives everything as love or a call for love. The Course says you are too bound to form to perceive consistently like the Holy Spirit. You are too bound to form and not to content when you have definitions of who people are and what certain behaviors mean. Whenever we start to interpret behaviors we get away from: *what is my purpose, what am I to be holding on to?* That is where the reaction comes in.

Friend: It seems I am more concerned with form than content.

David: From a deeper perspective the mind denied all these attack thoughts and tried to push them out of awareness. Then another way the ego counsels is that the way to get rid of attack thoughts is to project them out onto the screen. If you consider what we would call a frightening situation, the form has become a concrete form of fear. There is something in my mind that I cannot accept and look at and take responsibility for. It really is just a thought that I have or I made up and I do not want to look at that so I keep it buried in the unconscious and then I project it out, and therefore I see something objectionable in someone else or some other situation or thing. That is the deeper dynamic that is going on beneath what we are talking about.

Friend: Then I guess I go back to the earlier part of the question which was: did I attract this to myself? I can accept that all things are lessons that he would have us learn, but I have been dealing with asking what the lesson is. There is this sense that nothing comes into our lives that we have not asked for at some level. Did Jesus ask to be crucified? I think I hear you say on one level no and on another level yes?

David: It was the power of a teaching demonstration. There is a line in the Course that says that everything I seem to ask for I receive as I have asked. Let's look at the metaphysical idea of responsibility. We are only responsible for accepting the Atonement. The only thing we are responsible for is choosing to be in our right mind, for choosing the Holy Spirit. When the idea of responsibility is taken into the level of form then you get into guilt. Take ideas like the law of attraction and then cancer. Now you can see we are going to confuse the levels and you can see immediately how the guilt comes in. I attracted this cancer to me. Whack, whack, whack! I am doing the Course wrong, I should be better; I should be able to heal myself. This is a misunderstanding of the statement, *I am responsible.* Here is the truth: *I am responsible for choosing the right mind,* but once I raise the body thoughts up – the cancer – to the level of mind, I have hooked the idea of self-responsibility in with that form which I am judging, that terrible awful thing; then guilt automatically results. This is bringing the mind to see that the only way that correction can take place is by changing the thoughts. There is no amount of changing behavior that will help, no matter how many versions of *if only* you can come up with; if only I had done this differently, if only I had a mammogram, or eaten a lot of beta carotene. But we say, wait a minute, I am not going to look at the behavior level. I have a choice and I want to perceive this situation differently, I want to link with a different thought system in my mind, a thought level that can give me a different way of perceiving this. I want to choose right-mindedness; I want to choose the way out.

Friend: A thought occurred to me when I was taking a Science of Mind course last year; it addressed the importance of clarifying exactly what you are treating for. I heard that if I am trying to train in patience, for example, then I am probably going to get a lot of things coming into my life that are going to teach me patience. If I can get on past that, to the acceptance level – to accept that patience is my divine right and patience is mine now – then I may get through or past some of these lessons. And my thought was that I was not sure I was thinking enough that I need more patience. True enough I get opportunities around patience and that would be a step short of acceptance of the fact that patience is indeed mine.

David: We can talk about the law of karma. This one basic law has taken many different words and forms; *giving and receiving are the same,* or *as ye sow so shall ye reap.* If the mind gets exactly what it wants always – as ye sow so shall ye reap – then the question is, does the deceived mind know what it wants? The definition of a deceived or split mind is a mind that has two thought systems; it has the ego and the Holy Spirit's thought systems. Does it know what it wants? I want the Holy Spirit, I want the ego, I want the Holy Spirit; no I want the ego. If the mind is confused, if it is split, it does not know what it wants. But it gets exactly what it wants – so it gets confusion! You see? You see how this works? That is why it is so important to learn to choose the Holy Spirit's thought system.

Blessed are the pure of heart for they shall see God. If there is not a pure intention, if one does not have a mind with pure thought – the thoughts that only come from God – then one is going to keep calling forth witnesses in the world that will attest to confusion and conflict. That is why it is so important to get really clear about these two thought systems and to let the ego's go. Otherwise you are just going to continually call forth witnesses of littleness and frailty and that you are able to be harmed by the slightest thing going wrong. That is the ego's thought system and as long as one holds onto that thought system that is what is going to happen.

Friend: So another way to look at having a confused thought would be to say that I am experiencing confusion when I want to experience peace and so this is an invitation to peace, I want to choose peace. It is a reminder of that?

David: We went into detail last night about backward thoughts and forward thoughts. Backward thoughts we defined as cause and effect being split off and turned around; there is something on the screen – there is something in the world that has the power to give peace, or to take away peace. You see how both extremes get back to that codependency. If there is something in the world that can give me peace then I am dependent on it and I am going to try to pursue it. If there is a certain person, a certain place, a certain career, if there is a certain physical way of looking; whatever it is you believe can bring you happiness and peace you will be codependent on. Conversely, if there are crime areas, if there are areas with bad weather, areas where the economy is terrible that are identified as things that can take away your peace then you are codependent there too, because you are going to have to find the areas that do not have crime, or better economies, or ones with better weather. You can see how you can be on an endless chase to try to pacify the ego in order to try to get peace of mind. If you really pull it away from there being anything external that can give you peace then it comes back to: *what is it in my mind that can give me peace and happiness?* Your function and your happiness are one. As long as I am holding onto my function happiness will be in my awareness.

Friend: Then the reverse would be true; there is nothing that can take my peace away and so that comment you made about: *did I call it to me* or *did I create it*, well yes – by my interpretation of it, by how I chose to look at it, I certainly did.

David: It is the interpretation that upsets us. The question of whether you called it to yourself implies that the mind still perceives itself in a linear world with linear events that happen to it. The script is written, it has played out. We have talked about the feeling of resistance to the script being written, that you may think it sounds like predetermination or destiny. *Yuck, where is my choice, where is my free will?* The script is written but you do have a choice; you have the choice of *how* you look upon the script. Which lens are you going to look through, which guide are you going to listen to? That brings us back to Content or Purpose. The ego has the purpose of death, it wants to call forth witnesses to prove that sickness and pain and death and destruction are who you are; that you are teeny, and you are little. The Holy Spirit has given the purpose of healing to the world. It is a completely different purpose – but it takes a lot of practice and mind training to hold that completely different purpose of healing in mind.

The mind that is deceived believes that this world is real. It believes that it is a real person and that there are real events that are happening to it. *I really lost my job; I really do not have enough money to pay the rent.* That is how it feels. It really does not see it as a dream. When we go to bed at night and dream, do we react to the dreams? There is running and sometimes fear and lots of emotions that seem to go on in those dreams. Why? Because the mind thinks it is in the dream. If you really let go of judgment you will start to see more and more that you are the dreamer of the dream, you are the cause of the dream. If I am in the dream it does not seem like I am the cause of the dream and I am not in control of it, but if I step back and realize that I am the dreamer of the dream, then I can accept another purpose for it. OK, I am going to change the purpose – out with the ego and in with the Holy Spirit! The Course calls that the happy dream. There is nothing on the screen that has changed, there are still the same things going on, what the world describes as wars and so on but my purpose for the world has changed.

Friend: Is that the same script? I mean we are not changing the script?

David: Right.

Friend: It is just a way of looking at things; everything else is the same?

David: Yes. That seems to be a very high concept, because wait a minute, it seems like I am a person, I can choose to raise my arm or lower it, that is changing the script and it is that sort of thing that makes it difficult to pull back, because the mind believes that bodies are autonomous and behavior is autonomous. I can decide to go from Seattle to Coney Island to Cincinnati or not. No, the script is written. The script is just playing itself out and behavior is not autonomous. What you do comes from what you think. You have a choice in what you think – and that is the only choice you have. The behavior follows automatically from the thought system you choose to think with.

Friend: This is my pet topic! You said that I can make a choice to interpret what happens and that if I am choosing to listen to the Holy Spirit, I can choose to act in the direction with the Holy Spirit. But I am still choosing, right? Or if I want to be right I can choose to act with the ego and perhaps thumb my nose at this guy, I can be right and I can be obnoxious and I am still making a choice? I would love to walk out of here clear about these things.

David: "You may believe that you are responsible for what you do but not for what you think. The truth is that you are responsible for what you think for only at that level is real choice possible." T-2.VI.2 It sure seems convincing in this world that we are individual, unique little persons that have free choice. And not only that, there are other individual unique persons on the planet that can also choose and when they make a choice, does it reflect my choice? No. But the mind has denied that this is like an optical illusion, that this is a screen that it has projected out there. This is all about the subject/object split. There are all these objects, like a jigsaw puzzle with hundreds of little pieces. I pick one out and say: *this is me*. Out of the whole puzzle I pick one little piece. Now there is a *me* apart from all the other pieces. There is fragmentation because now I have this piece as me and this other piece I am going to move over here because I do not like that one. These are the ones I like; I will surround myself with these. You can see there is still a sense of otherness, there is *me* and there are *the others*. That is what the optical illusion of this world is; it is that split that you believe is there between you and your brother. That is what the fragments are—bodies. I am a person which includes a body and this is another person and once I perceive that split there then it seems that I am constantly battling against all these other fragments and I need my space, I need autonomy, I do not want to become too codependent; that whole tug of war comes into play.

Friend: If I recognize my oneness with the Sonship then that is where I get confused. That is when I feel like I should back my car out and give them my place because he or she is more upset than I am about having it or not having it. Then I get irritated and that is crazy. I know that that is still dealing with form and I know that I am responsible for the peace within myself, but there is a piece missing....

Friend: That is choice in behavior. Choosing the thought would determine the behavior. I can choose thoughts which are peaceful and my behavior can stem from that. That is what I want. I either line up with the Holy Spirit or with the ego. Choosing between illusions is not a real choice.

A New Interpretation: Part 4
Talking About the Script and Linear Time

David: We are talking about coming to this purpose. This purpose is so denied. I use the analogy of a skyscraper, where the purpose is the light in the basement. That is the Holy Spirit's purpose. It is so buried and covered over; that is why it takes a lot of practice to let go of our investments. As long as we have expectations they cover over that purpose.

Friend: But I am still wanting to back it up again, because I am still making the choice for peace, both of these are peaceful, I am still making the choice.

Friend: I hear what you are saying. Is there a sense that if you were really at peace you would feel that what would occur is that when you pulled into a parking place there wouldn't be anybody upset about it?

David: Our friend has a point, a key point. This is what the Workbook is trying to teach the mind—that cause and effect are not separate. In other words, there are no hypotheticals. The ego does not like that. When we get into all of our examples, including the example of the parking spaces, we are out into the hypothetical *what if*.

Friend: It is the ego saying *what if*.

David: If we took it that way, we would have to have a formula, or we would have to have a giant book or something—a huge catalogue—four trillion, eight hundred and ninety-nine million situations. You can see the variables are endless. It really gets back to the sense of simplicity—that prayer:

> I do not have to worry about what to say or what to do,
> because He Who sent me will direct me. T-2.V

Now that is a principle; in the moment, we will be guided. Ask yourself, "How am I feeling right now?" It is always helpful to monitor your own reactions and your own emotions right in the moment. *How are you feeling right now?*

Friend: If I will be guided, am I guided according to how the script is written?

David: I will give you another line. The Course says:

> You do not need guidance except at the mind level. T-2.VI.3

That is where you need it. In other words, bodies do not get guidance. Minds get guidance. If you are really open and willing, you will be guided.

Friend: When you say that the script is written do you mean that the script is written on the mind level?

David: In the perceptual/form everything has already happened. "Written" is past tense. Jesus comes at it from the same angle when he says in Workbook lessons 5, 6 and 7: "I am never upset for the reason I think," "I am upset because I see something that is not there," and "I see only the past." "I see only the past," is literally restating that the script is written. What the mind perceives when it perceives bodies and cars and stars and airplanes and rugs is all the past. And the reason why it gets very upset about the past is because it believes that the past is not over.

Friend: So "the script is written" means that we see only the past?

David: Yes.

Friend: That is what that means?

David: That is it!

Friend: I got it! [laughter]

David: And when is truth available? It is always available now! Whenever you are upset about what is the past, you obviously do not believe that the past has gone. Otherwise, why would you be upset? Really, the Course is just the path to help us see that the past is gone. Let's take it another step further, because we have only gotten to lesson 7. Lesson 7 explains the first seven lessons. And lesson 8 is: "My mind is preoccupied with past thoughts." Now we are getting to the thought level. The only reason I am seeing all these shadows of things in form is because in my mind I have these dark thoughts that are like a projector. The light shines and here are the dark thoughts—the projector, and here are all the forms on the screen. Do you know what happens if you let go of the dark thoughts? Light! You have just pure light because there are not any obstructions to it. That is the escape. The escape is lesson 23: "I can escape from the world I see by giving up attack thoughts." He works all the way up to the first 22 to bring it to that. So really, it gets to be simple! All I have to do now is to get in touch with those attack thoughts and not be afraid of them. I have to be able to raise them to awareness and look at them and see them for what they are, a bunch of backward thoughts, and then let them go. That is what salvation is! It is that simple!

Friend: I was watching a TV series on the brain and on memory. The neurosurgeon made an interesting point that without memory we have no sense of self, which I think is delicious because that is what we are really trying to do, to shed this sense of self that comes from the ego. Without it we just *are*. They said it is memory that makes us look back.

David: Yes! The word memory is usually associated with the past. There is a section in the Course called *The Present Memory* in which Jesus says that memory is an ability that you made after the separation, but he says you can use it to remember the present. This is a reinterpretation because of the mind's associations: memory/past and past/memory.

Reading that section gives you a new way! The present moment is revelatory; it is pure light. It is not perceptual. It does not have anything to do with images or form. The mind is really terrified of remembering the present. That is why it keeps trying to hang onto the past.

Friend: When you can come to a point where you can see or remember the present, do you still see the script, do you still see the past?

David: The present is the holy instant, and in those revelatory points, you do not even perceive. Jesus calls them the Great Rays, with a capital G and a capital R. He describes it another way in the *I Need Do Nothing* section. It says, "At no single instant does the body exist at all. It is always remembered or anticipated." T-18.VII.3 In other words, when you think: *How will so-and-so react?*—you are using thoughts that are projected out in the future. And when you think about what seemed to happen in the past, like how someone reacted to you, etc., you see how it is always the past or the future. But the present is pure light; it is literally an experience of revelation or the holy instant. It is not even perceptual in that sense.

Friend: I do not understand memories. Here it is present when it just said it is past. So what is the memory for?

David: The Holy Spirit—the light—is buried and there are dark layers, past memories, stacked because the mind is afraid of the light. The light is the present. Our gateway to eternity is the light of the Holy Spirit. That is a memory that is buried very, very deeply in the mind. The whole world, the whole self-concept that the mind constructed, was made to forget that light. That is the reason why the mind has to completely cease judging before it can remember the light.

The metaphor of peeling an onion kind of gives us the idea of a process, but all of the layers of the onion are the same. The ego is like a tree trunk. Here are the branches of the tree. The ego and the branches are identical, and until you see that the branches and the trunk are identical, you can go through a lot of twigs thinking thoughts like: *It seems like I have a belief in time and space and concept of size, concept of bodies, etc.* Those are like all the limbs and the branches and the twigs. But the instant that the mind can see that the image-maker (the trunk) and the images are identical, then it is dispelled.

It is the self-concept that makes it seem like you are attached to a body, or a car or a person, or a job. Those are all the branches and the limbs. But the mind does not want to look at what it is that made up all the branches and limbs. *Who is this "I" that is so attached to this body and so attached to different people and everything?* Ultimately you have to get back to the image maker. You can count those images forever (four hundred and ninety-nine billion). It just seems like there are all of these images, but ultimately we have to get back to the image maker. And when the mind can see that the image maker and the images are the same, what is it that can see that? It has to be a very clear mind, a mind that is not deceived in any way, a mind that has now stepped back from the image maker.

Friend: Can a partially clear mind see this?

David: It would not be "partially" at the instant it sees. You either see or you do not see.

Friend: It seems like I, for a moment, can have a clear mind and see something. I keep trying to unravel this stuff with the ego, and it makes me feel crazy, but when I can remember that: *Oh, there is a Holy Spirit, and Holy Spirit I want you to see this part of what is going on right now*, then all of a sudden I can feel the peace come in, but I do not feel that I can always maintain that clarity.

David: There is a section in the Course called *The Immediacy of Salvation* T-26. VIII. If you really follow Jesus' thinking in that section, it makes a lot of sense. He asks why God would put your salvation in the future. When you stop a minute and think about it, that is what the deceived mind believes in this world; *OK, now I am reading this Course, and if I do this enough, and if I really practice this enough, then eventually* (in the future) *I will achieve salvation* (or the totally clear mind). Why would God place salvation in the future? Wouldn't that be cruel? If God gave you salvation would He not have put it in the present instead of in the future? Would it not be cruel for God to hold out a carrot and say: "Ha ha, you will get it in another millennium"?

Friend: Oh, we make that future. It is obvious that salvation must be present. The problem is accepting it. That is the only problem I have.

David: Time is a projection of the ego; it is made up. But it is not always helpful to say it is just an illusion in the sense that you could use it as a kind of denial while you still believe you are in it. The Course gives us a stepping stone towards realizing that time is but an illusion. It does the same thing that it does with everything, with the body, and relationships and everything else. It says: OK, you made time. The Holy Spirit can use time too! He can use everything you made. You made a world. He can use it to lead you out of it! You made bodies. He can use them! How do the Holy Spirit and the ego each use time? The ego wants to promote a linear view of time. The Holy Spirit is teaching us that there is one time–Now! And the ego says: *No, there is the past, and here is the present, and there is the future.*

It is helpful to really look at what else the ego says about time, which is basically that you are guilty in the past. You are a body. *Look at all the things in your life that you did not do and should have done, and look at all the things that you have done and should not have done. Look at all the things back there that you feel guilty about.* Basically the ego says: *You have got it, you are guilty in the past; there is no doubt about that.* Now, it says: *And the present is just a gateway to the future. You have been guilty in the past, you cannot do anything about it in the present, and you are going to be guilty in the future*–Hell! Hell awaits you in the future! A fearful world awaits you in the future. The ego's linear idea of time basically says that you will pay in the future for the sins that you have committed in the past.

It is helpful to see the role that pleasure and pain play in this. Both pleasure and pain reinforce that the body is real. This is the sneaky trap about pleasure; the ego asks: *Didn't you like that? Think back to that experience in the past* (whatever it was that you associate your mind with that was pleasurable–it can be anything). *Think of a really pleasurable event. Now, don't you want to repeat that event in the future?* That is how the ego makes linear time continue. *You had pleasure in the past, and if you do such and such and such and such, you can repeat that in the future.* That is how linear time continues; the mind still believes that there is something valuable in the past that it wants to repeat and strive for in the future. That keeps linear time going. We have talked about how pain and pleasure are just two sides of one coin: "It is impossible to seek for pleasure through the body and not find pain." T-19.IV

The ego does not want that idea to be brought into awareness. You may even feel some resistance starting to come up in yourself right now; it is because that is an idea that is very important to maintaining linear time and it is very important to the ego that the mind does not make the connection. It is one of those things that the deeper you go, the more you start to see. Have any of you read in the Course the term, "attraction to guilt"? T-19.IV On the surface that seems ludicrous! *Attraction to guilt? Why would I want to be attracted to guilt? Guilt is what I want to give up!* And yet, why did Jesus use so many pages to talk about it? Because when the mind is in the deceived state, it is actually attracted to guilt. It wants to use it to perpetuate itself. In this world, it is pursuing pleasure and avoiding pain. That is what it means to have pretty good judgment, to know the things that are good and pursue those, and avoid the things that are painful. And what the Course is basically saying is: *My child, your mind is very twisted. You have a lot of darkness in it, and you cannot even tell the difference between the two.* There is this thing called joy that has nothing to do with anything physical, it is completely intrinsic; it kind of wells up from within. Your joy comes from fulfilling your function and when you are listening to the Holy Spirit, and you are being truly helpful, you will feel a joy that is so intense and indescribable. Doing the Father's Will is indescribable happiness. Those other things which seemed to bring you happiness, those little bits of pleasure, those little bits of fleeting things that you grasp for in the world, they will fade from your awareness because that joy will expand. Now, *that* I can go for! If you just take the first part of the equation about pleasure and pain, it is like: *Hey,* what is *in it for me?* When you say, *Joy is in it for me,* that is what we are moving toward. That is the positive experience.

Also, if you think you really know what pleasure is, and you are really sure that you have experienced it, and you have something in mind that you want to repeat to get that back, there is *deprivation* involved in the interval between now and the time you can get it. Maybe you would like a drink, and maybe there is a certain kind of drink or beer or soda that you are thinking about as you are going down the street to the pub…

Friend: …your mouth opens wide.

David: Yes, just by thinking about it. There is a sense of lack until: *Ahhh.* Like in that old Fresca commercial: *Fill your senses and then blow it away.* You can see that there is a sense of deprivation or lack involved until that sensation will be satiated by some external thing.

Friend: I think the most common one we can talk about is sex, using the body for the seeking of the pleasure. Or even eating candy, it is not that different. I love red hot candy. Sometimes I bite my lip. All I can feel is pain. It is an ego gimmick; if I am feeling pain, I cannot be at peace. I used to wonder why I banged my finger, or something. What has that got to do with me feeling separated from God? It has a lot to do with it. This is part of the ego's smoke screen for me. If I can hone in on peace when I get up in the morning – that is my function during the day. If I pick up a piece of hot candy and eat it, I have lost my function. It is ridiculous, but I do not hone in on peace while my mouth is munching. I have to get away from the body.

Friend: That is what I find; it does not matter if it is pleasure or pain or sex or security; it is all seeking, you know, it is *project and pursue*; I am just chasing my own carrot.

David: "Seek not outside yourself." T-29.VII.1 You have every right to happiness; that is your inheritance, but you cannot look for it on the screen. It is within you, it is the Holy Spirit's Purpose. And about pleasure and pain, let's face it; in this world, pain and pleasure seem to be very different. Experientially, they seem to be very different. So what makes them single or unified? They are two things that share the same purpose; that is what makes them the same. How do pain and pleasure share a purpose? They both reinforce the body as being real. It is the same thing whether you are in ecstasy eating something you love or you have a throbbing headache. Is God in your awareness with one extreme or the other?

How to View Time-Space and "The Script"

Hi David,

I would very much like to know what you think about this. The Course says that we are at the end looking back. I have been thinking about this a lot. It seems that if you follow this to its obvious conclusion, then we would have no way to change anything we are experiencing in the dream. It would simply appear to continue to happen because it has already happened. We will only choose to view it through the ego or through Holy Spirit. The more we choose the Holy Spirit (true perception) the more we wake up.

My friend thinks that since all possible scripts have been written and happened simultaneously, then each time we make a choice, we experience life differently.

We are not writing a new script, but simply experiencing the already written script that applies to our most recent decision. In that way, we do affect how our script plays out. (The Course does mention "all dimensions of time.")

There is a reason I care about this answer; it is not just idle curiosity. I was always afraid to fly and though I do it, I would take a tranquilizer or have a drink to calm my nerves. Once I realized that everything has already happened and I am just viewing it, I started concentrating on seeing it through the Holy Spirit. I found that I am no longer afraid to fly. In fact, I find this view very comforting. The alternative view would be a little different, but fine, too. I am just saying that I really have a reason for wanting to know. I try not to get too much in my head and to concentrate mostly on the experience, but some things, if I have some sort of understanding, are helpful to me.

What do you think about this?

Beloved One,

Thanks for your thoughtful question and wonderful witness to the healing Power of the Holy Spirit. The Present is before time was. To mind asleep this Blazing Light has been completely pushed out of awareness with the dream of time and space. Your question is very practical, for it asks for the Helpful View of time from the Holy Spirit's Perspective.

In Reality there is no time-space; practically speaking time-space lasted but a seeming *instant* and was simultaneously Corrected (Healed) by the Holy Spirit. Only via the ego does this unreal instant seem to be repeated over and over and over again, making a ghost or illusion of linear time-space, which has been called the script. The phrase *the script is written* emphasizes that the dream of the world was over long ago. Time, practically speaking, is over and gone and in Reality never happened. Experiencing time as simultaneous is the decision to see that cause and effect are together, not separate, and that there is no world apart from mind, or apart from what you think. In simultaneity there is no duality, no past and future, no inner and outer, and no subject and object.

You wrote about the dream: "It would simply appear to continue to happen because it has already happened, and we will only choose to view it through the ego or through Holy Spirit. The more we choose the Holy Spirit (true perception) the more we wake up."

This is an accurate description of the seeming "process," although it must eventually be realized that the decision is without exception and therefore beyond the belief in degree (that is, "more" or "less"). Salvation is no compromise of any kind; this applies to the release of the error of linear time-space. Atonement entails the realization that linear time-space cannot be changed because linear time-space is an illusion, and illusion, being false, cannot change. Your experience seems to change from the ego's ever-changing uncertainty to the Holy Spirit's tranquil and certain and stable Perspective. Peaceful Perspective is a choice, a decision, an acceptance and this happy dream of non-judgment is the goal to which ACIM points.

In Happiness simply review what has already gone by, and make no attempt to change or fix or rearrange the images of the script. Seek not to change the dream. Seek rather to change your mind about the dream. This is the meaning of the phrase: "I need do nothing." T-18.VII Remember these happy passages from ACIM:

> Therefore, seek not to change the world, but choose to change your mind about the world. T-21.in.1

> Time is a trick, a sleight of hand, a vast illusion in which figures come and go as if by magic. Yet there is a plan behind appearances that does not change. The script is written. When experience will come to end your doubting has been set. For we but see the journey from the point at which it ended, looking back on it, imagining we make it once again; reviewing mentally what has gone by. W-158

> Let me recognize my problems have been solved. I seem to have problems only because I am misusing time. I believe that the problem comes first, and time must elapse before it can be worked out. I do not see the problem and the answer as simultaneous in their occurrence. That is because I do not yet realize that God has placed the answer together with the problem, so that they cannot be separated by time. The Holy Spirit will teach me this, if I will let Him. And I will understand it is impossible that I could have a problem which has not been solved already. W-90.3

> The unforgiven is a voice that calls from out a past forevermore gone by. And everything that points to it as real is but a wish

that what is gone could be made real again and seen as here and now, in place of what is *really* now and here. Is this a hindrance to the truth the past is gone, and cannot be returned to you? And do you want that fearful instant kept, when Heaven seemed to disappear and God was feared and made a symbol of your hate? T-26.V.8

Forget the time of terror that has been so long ago corrected and undone. Can sin withstand the Will of God? Can it be up to you to see the past and put it in the present? You can *not* go back. And everything that points the way in the direction of the past but sets you on a mission whose accomplishment can only be unreal. Such is the justice your All-Loving Father has ensured must come to you. And from your own unfairness to yourself has He protected you. You cannot lose your way because there is no way but His, and nowhere can you go except to Him. T-26.V.9

Would God allow His Son to lose his way along a road long since a memory of time gone by? This course will teach you only what is now. A dreadful instant in a distant past, now perfectly corrected, is of no concern nor value. Let the dead and gone be peacefully forgotten. Resurrection has come to take its place. And now you are a part of resurrection, not of death. No past illusions have the power to keep you in a place of death, a vault God's Son entered an instant, to be instantly restored unto his Father's perfect Love. And how can he be kept in chains long since removed and gone forever from his mind? T-26.V.10

From the *Rules for Decision* section:

We said you can begin a happy day with the determination not to make decisions by yourself. This seems to be a real decision in itself. And yet, you *cannot* make decisions by yourself. The only question really is with what you choose to make them. That is really all. The first rule, then, is not coercion, but a simple statement of a simple fact. You will not make decisions by yourself whatever you decide. For they are made with idols or with God. And you ask help of anti-Christ or Christ, and which you choose will join with you and tell you what to do. T-30.I.14

Your day is not at random. It is set by what you choose to live it with, and how the friend whose counsel you have sought perceives your happiness. You always ask advice before you can decide on anything. Let this be understood, and you can see there cannot be coercion here, nor grounds for opposition that you may be free. There is no freedom from what must occur. And if you think there is, you must be wrong. T-30.I.15

The second rule as well is but a fact. For you and your adviser must agree on what you want before it can occur. It is but this agreement that permits all things to happen. Nothing can be caused without some form of union, be it with a dream of judgment or the Voice for God. Decisions cause results *because* they are not made in isolation. They are made by you and your adviser, for yourself and for the world as well. The day you want you offer to the world, for it will be what you have asked for, and will reinforce the rule of your adviser in the world. Whose kingdom is the world for you today? What kind of day will you decide to have? T-30.I.16

Chapter Four

The Serenity Prayer – No Control Over the World

David: Let us go to the very core of the matter so we can be clear that this need not be a long journey. I want to go right for the core, so there is clarity.

A Course of Miracles is a 1,200 page book. The wisdom at its core is contained in the *Serenity Prayer*.

> God grant me the serenity to accept the things I cannot change, the courage to change the things I can, and the wisdom to know the difference.

In a nugget, the Course is about receiving the wisdom to tell the difference between the first two statements – the things I can change and the things I cannot. To accept the things we cannot change and change the things we can – we need the wisdom to know the difference. That is where discernment and discrimination come in.

We want to go deeply into it, to see those first two statements for what they are. Once you see the first two steps for what they really are, all striving ends; it is not a linear journey anymore.

> You still cannot will against Him and that is why you have no control over the world you made. T-12.III.9

Take a close look at that statement for a moment. Observe what comes up around it. What are your feelings about that? What does it mean to you to have no control over the world you made?

Friend: My first reaction is: *Oh, no! This is bad news if I have no control over the world I made.* Then as I look at that statement, there is more of a feeling of relief; if I do not have control over the world I made then I do not have to keep trying to control it. There is relief in the thought that there is no point in trying to control what is not controllable. I can just take my hands off it because it is pointless to keep them in there when it is of no avail. It is a waste of time, a game. Why would I want to put my mind and attention there?

David: Can you see how all-encompassing that statement is? You have *no control over the world you made.* Earlier we had a discussion about someone whom you felt was talking too much. That is a circumstance that fits under the umbrella: "You have no control." Can you see how that fits in here, as well as all conceivable problems relating to specifics, or wishing things could be different than they are?

Friend: Yes. That is coming to mind ... all those examples of wishing things were different than they are, and the idea that if they were different then things would be so much better.

David: We spent a whole session one time talking about the restlessness you were feeling. We traced it very carefully back to the belief that you had a choice in the world in form. Can you see how that is encompassed here? The whole concept of having to choose between things, circumstances, events and objects – all of the strain and struggle and even the restlessness of wondering what to do next, or feeling like you should be doing something different – can you see how it all gets blanketed under *you have no control over the world you made?*

Friend: Yes, that seems clear but I do have this thought that the control lies with my mind, that keeping my mind focused on my intention will give me control over the world. There is still a thought that the world might change or people might change as a reflection of the change in my mind. That would be the control I would have. The control would come through my mind and be reflected out into the world.

David: People say things like: "As I get clearer, the evolution of the world will improve and it will become a more peaceful place." That is a subtle example of still believing I have control over the world in some way. It is about getting to the point of the Serenity Prayer, where you can see the things that you can change.

Friend: That would be my mind only.

David: The Course says: "For you do have control over your mind." T-12.III.9 That states it pretty clearly. While you have no control over the world you made, you do have control over your mind. That is where the control is. That sentence says *nothing* about the world. Nothing!

Friend: But the world is in my mind. So how is it different?

David: When we speak of having "no control over the world you made," T-12.III.9 we are speaking of the projected world or "the script." You could even call it the wrong mind – thoughts and the world that was projected from them. There is no control over that. But there is control over the purpose that I give the world. We are making a clear distinction between form and content. The idea that you do have control over your mind brings the two purposes in the mind into focus – the ego's purpose and the Holy Spirit's purpose. That is where you have the control, because that is the decision. In fact, purpose is the only decision you have. It is still a metaphor because in Heaven there is no decision at all. Yet you cannot reach that state of being until you can see the choice where it is, until you see where you have the control.

What I can change is my mind; I can decide between these two purposes. The line: "accept the things I cannot change," refers to the script or the projected world. As the Course puts it, "…seek not to change the world, but choose to change your mind about the world." T-21.in.1 That fits right in with: Seek not to change the world. Why? Because you have no control over the world that you made! It is pointless and fruitless to try to change something where no change is possible.

Friend: So the idea that the world is a reflection of the mind does not in any way imply that there is control over the script? Only the way I look upon it will reflect the purpose I bring to it? If I bring the ego purpose to what I see, then that is what will be reflected back to me from the script. And from that same script, the Holy Spirit's purpose will be reflected back to me, if that is what is in my mind.

David: Yes. In that sense the world is symbolic; it is representative of the purpose I am holding onto. The only thing that I have control over is the choice of the purpose that I give to the world. The "real world" is seeing and embracing the Holy Spirit's purpose as the only alternative. That is the world given a completely different meaning than the ego's purpose for the world, which is to just reinforce the separation and the guilt. But even the real world has no real purpose in the sense that once it is reached, it is seen as purposeless. If it had a real purpose it would have a reality, but the real world is an illusion as well. We do not want to jump the gun too quickly here. We just want to follow this inward with the *Serenity Prayer*, to see the only thing you *can* control.

Friend: For me it is important to remember that the reflection that comes back to me does not have any objective existence. It all depends on how I am looking at it. There is not anything about it apart from how I am looking at it. I am thinking about what someone said to me recently, "If I start looking at things differently, will things in form change?" But it is not about anything changing in form. It is only about my perception, or the interpretation I am assigning to that form.

Friend: Yes. It is not a change in form. It is really a change in how I am seeing the script. The script is written! A change in my mind does not change anything about the script. It only changes my perception of the script.

David: We began with a simple thing: "You have no control over the world you made." Now you are bringing in the element of "the script is written." That would seem to go with "you have no control over the world you made." If it is written, if it is past tense, it is over and done. How do you change a painting that is finished? How do you change something if it is already over and done? This brings in the sense of time. The metaphysical reason why you have no control over the world is because it is all past. Lesson 7: "I see only the past." My mind is preoccupied with past thoughts. Those past thoughts are showing me a past world and therefore if I think I can change the screen, so to speak, or change the script, then what do I believe? I believe I can change the past!

Friend: Or I believe it is not really past, that it is the present instead of the past.

David: Yes. When looking through the body's eyes we are seeing through the deceived mind. The deceived mind sees only the past. As this is illuminated to us, we come to see that any attempt to change things in the world is an attempt to change the past. That is the whole basis for special relationships. The mind believes it has been deprived. It keeps seeking outside of itself because it keeps trying to tinker with the screen. Another body, another relationship, another car, another house, another climate, more money, more idols in whatever form they are. But underneath it all is the thought: *I have been deprived in the past and I believe that I can tinker with the screen or change the content of consciousness and rearrange it in some way that I can find a way to get what I was deprived of.* But it will not work. It cannot work, trying to make up for something in the very place where the deprivation was believed to happen. The only place of completion is in my mind. The Holy Spirit is the answer to what I seem to be feeling as a lack. Suddenly all the sections on special relationships start to click in with these basic underlying metaphysics.

Friend: Is it to recognize that there is no deprivation in the world? The only void or vacancy or lack of fulfillment is in the mind that believes that there is a lack.

David: And whether you call it scarcity principle, or lack, or deprivation, it is the ego's purpose. There are only two purposes in the mind. Therefore the only way to see a solution to the problem is by changing the purpose in the mind. It has nothing to do with the world.

Another quote that dovetails with this is, "Only a constant purpose can endow events with stable meaning." T-30.VII.3 Of course! It is the ego's purpose that makes everything seem dis-united and like separate events. The constant purpose is the thread that ties all the events together. The script is really a continuous thing, rather than discreet events. *I did this next and this happened, then I went there.* That is the way it is talked about when the mind believes in sequential time and events. But once we get a sense that there is a purpose that ties them all together, that is when the fusion between all the events takes place.

Friend: I am glad we are looking at purpose and couching it in the context of the script having been written, because when we remember that the script is written, it takes everything out of the "doing" altogether. The script is written. There is nothing for me to *do* in relation to the script.

David: Yes. Minds do not do. Minds do not act. Purpose is not in the realm of actions.

Friend: So anytime I think I am *doing,* I am not looking at it from my purpose?

Friend: There is that whole choice thing: *Do I do this or do I do that? What is it I am supposed to do right now?* Then I have totally forgotten that it is already done, that the script is already written. *What is it that I am supposed to do?* That is the wrong question.

David: I would like to clarify this a bit more, because we are talking about rungs again. In the Workbook, he says to ask the Holy Spirit very specifically, "What would You have me do? Where would You have me go?" W-71.9 Someone could read that and think: *What if I am guided to do something, to call someone? That seems to be a "doing." What if I am guided to move someplace, or this or that?*

Friend: I think when the guidance is there and it is clear, that question does not come up. It is so obvious.

David: Yes, but we want to go deeper to the point that I am talking about. Accepting the Atonement is accepting a purpose in the mind, and that is an abstract purpose. It is coming to the point of seeing the impossibility of doing. It is reminiscent of the *I Need Do Nothing* section, when he talks about sinking into your mind. The unholy instant is the time of bodies, but in no single instant does the body exist at all. Those are the kind of statements that point to what we are talking about; minds do not *do.* There must be level confusion if I perceive myself doing anything; sitting in a posture for eight hours, going out and traveling the country, speaking, or anything we have talked about as the metaphors that are part of the Holy Spirit's plan. We want to move to the place of sinking into the mind beneath all the concepts – moving towards accepting the Atonement. That is the purpose. From our discussion here, that should be coming clear. Salvation is a thought in the mind. It has nothing at all to do with the world. This is why we talk about moving into mysticism. It should be another step to begin to see that there is no other place to go but into mysticism, in the sense that the solution is in the mind. What enfolds our discussion is the experience of being drawn into the silence to hear that voice, and to accept that purpose.

Friend: This really resonates with me. I am trying to see how what you are talking about is consistent with some of the other things that we have talked about doing. Sometimes when we talk about those other things, there is something that does not feel quite right. Like when we talk about the "doings" – of going here and there and doing this and that. Somehow I have to see that those things are still stepping stones. But I think at times: *Why are we putting so much energy and attention into things that are just stepping stones? Why do we not just go for the ultimate step, the final step, instead of taking these stepping-stone steps?*

David: It is good that you bring that up because as I said, the whole point is to come to that clarity. As we go into this ultimate stuff, it should feel inviting to go into the silence. Everything that we talk about – like doing gatherings and so on – it is all peripheral. That is all for a mind that has resistance to the ultimate. Maybe I could put it in the context of sinking down into the mind. Completely letting go into the silence; opening the mind up to the revelatory experience is the ultimate. The question I hear coming in is: "Where does the perceptual stuff, of going places and doing things, fit with that?" The best description is in the early part of the Course where Jesus talks about miracles and revelation. He says that when the mind is too afraid of revelation, too afraid of the light, miracles are necessary to prepare the mind. Miracles reduce fear; they seem to collapse time. In a sense this discussion is a miracle. Actions, like those you do when you are in your purpose, are like time-collapsers; they are all preparations for the mind.

Friend: Yes, I have experienced that. Because of the miracles, the trust has deepened. And the attraction of turning to the light or towards the revelatory experience has increased, as the trust deepens. It all is simultaneous. It happens together. This answers my question why it seems to be necessary to do all that stuff. It is really not necessary but it is helpful in alleviating the fear.

David: Another way of couching the same thing we are talking about is the description of miracles as the *means*, and revelation as the *end*. To reach the end, you have to want the means. Everything we do—when we talk about starting with specifics and working it back to *what is my perception of this in my mind*—is always working back to the miracle. You have to desire and want the means if you are going to reach the end. The end is terrifying to the deceived mind. It is not that the deceived mind has so much difficulty with the miracles but it is terrified of the end. It does not want the means. It would rather focus on the specifics and the body and use that as its means for its Atonement with a small "a," which is really death. The ego has a purpose for the world and the means of achieving it are to focus on the specifics and use them to get what it wants. Underneath all that is the intent to reinforce the separation, perpetuate the sleep and protect itself. The turnaround is: *miracles are the means to reach revelation*. They reduce the fear. They collapse time and eliminate guilt. Revelation is offered. It is a *given* from God, but there is the matter of being aware of it, and opening to receive what has already been given. If the mind is too afraid, it is not going to be open. The characteristics of teachers of God start off with trust, and the last characteristic of a teacher of God is open-mindedness. That makes sense because what is left when the advanced teacher of God has laid aside all fear and ego is the receptivity to receive what has always been there but has been denied.

As long as there is even a subtle identification with the body, there is still personification. It is not even necessary for the mind to believe that it *is* a body, but as long as it believes it is *in* a body or working through a body—that is still a personification. There is still a subject/object split. There is still some personhood. With that there is fear of revelation; revelation seems to be a threat to that construction of the world. As long as there is a belief in personhood, there is ordering of thoughts. A person is seen as being different than a pencil, different than a tree, or a car or a rug. There is still a sense that the mind is working in and through a body. The body then seems to be pretty significant, more significant than the pencil. There still seems to be an ordering of thoughts. The body does not seem to be just another image on the screen, it seems to be important. In the *Manual for Teachers*, in a section called, *How is Healing Accomplished*, Jesus says:

> There is no form of sickness that would not be cured at once. What is the single requisite for this shift in perception? It is simply this; the recognition that sickness is of the mind, and has nothing to do with the body. What does this recognition "cost"? It costs the whole world you see, for the world will never again appear to rule the mind. For with this recognition

is responsibility placed where it belongs; not with the world, but on him who looks on the world and sees it as it is not. He looks on what he chooses to see. No more and no less. The world does nothing to him. He only thought it did. M-5.II.3

You have to see that the mind is the decision maker. It is a common perception in the world to believe in persons—to believe that I am a person and that there are separate persons with separate private minds, and that each of these persons has their own decision-making mechanism. It cannot be so. That is the belief that different figures can make decisions in the dream. That is not the case at all. It is the mind. The right mind is one decision and the wrong mind is another decision. Heaven and hell are decisions. Seeing the two purposes in the mind as decisions, versus persons-making-decisions, lifts it back from the screen. To accept the Atonement you must see that the mind is the only creative level. It is the only place where decisions can be made.

At the very end of this section it says that to accept this, the insignificance of the body must be an acceptable idea. This goes full circle with what we are talking about, seeing that the body is no different than a pencil. In the end we see that there are not any separate objects. There is nothing in the world that exists in and of itself. It is all a tapestry. One illusion is all illusions. Illusions are one; the ego, the tree trunk and all the different branches are the same.

Friend: To even speak of something as *in and of itself* is to imply that there is something apart from the mind. Otherwise there would be no *in and of itself*-ness.

David: Workbook lessons 183 and 184 really get to that. "I call upon God's Name and on my own." W-183 The fourth paragraph reads:

> Repeat the Name of God and little names have lost their meaning. No temptation but becomes a nameless and unwanted thing before God's Name. Repeat His Name and see how easily you will forget the names of all the gods you valued. They have lost the name of god you gave them. They become anonymous and valueless to you, although before you let the Name of God replace their little names, you stood before them worshipfully, naming them as gods. Repeat the Name of God and call upon your Self, Whose Name is His. Repeat His Name, and all the tiny, nameless things on earth slip into right perspective. Those who call upon the Name of

God can not mistake the nameless for the Name, nor sin for grace, nor bodies for the holy Son of God. W-183

The lesson closes with this paragraph:

All little things are silent. Little sounds are soundless now. The little things of earth have disappeared. The universe consists of nothing but the Son of God who calls upon his Father. And his Father's Voice gives answer in his Father's holy name. In this eternal, still relationship, in which communication far transcends all words, and yet it is seen in depth and height, whatever words could possibly convey, is peace eternal. In our Father's Name, we would experience this peace today. And in His Name, it shall be given us. W-183

It is this sense we are talking about–this silence. Anything that could seem to be done or anything within the perceptual realm is just to come to this point. It is not about traveling the country and saving the world or evangelizing the Course. It is not about reaching people, or corresponding with people or helping anyone else get clear; there is not anyone else. It is about having a burning desire to just have the Name of God in my mind. Period. This sets the table for accepting the Atonement. You cannot accept the Atonement until you can discern the *wisdom to know the difference*; until you can discern between the things you cannot change and the things that you can change. That is the discernment between form and content.

Friend: That is the end of level confusion, of thinking there is cause in the world.

David: Yes, in all the different ways that we are saying it, that is the end of level confusion. It all says the same thing, from different angles. It is so simple.

It is good to get the metaphors clear. A common one that I have used in the counseling, talks and presentations that I have done is the metaphor of the right mind and the wrong mind–and the seeming vacillation between the two. It seems as if the mind can choose either/or; as if there is a decision maker. Clarity is coming to see that the right mind is a decision and the wrong mind is a decision, and they are mutually exclusive.

Friend: If they are mutually exclusive, it cannot be a sometimes kind of thing that allows for vacillation. If one is real, then the other is not. There is nothing else to go toward except what is real.

David: Step off the rung; it is the top of the ladder.

Friend: We are back to the idea that truth is all there is.

David: God's will is all there is. That is the advanced form of practice, so to speak. First you look at all the seeming obstructions and see that all the obstructions are one. Then you embrace all that there is. The truth is truth and only the truth is true. There is nothing causative in the world; there is nothing that can be controlled or changed in the world – absolutely nothing. You have to have examined and explored deeply to see that. That makes way for, "The truth is true and nothing else is true." W-152.3 But you cannot just jump to that without doing a thorough examination, without first coming to the realization that there is nothing you would hold back from the light, no remnants of personhood....

Friend: Without that examination, could the statement, "The truth is true and nothing else is true," be anything but an idea? Could it ever be an experience except from the examination of all the beliefs that stand in the way?

David: That is right. Hence, this is a Course working from the bottom up, not from the top down. You must bring illusions to the truth. You cannot bring the truth to illusions. It can seem on the surface like there is a shortcut to bring truth into illusions. But you can see that it does not work. It produces the illusion of enlightenment, not the *experience*.

Ask yourself if there are any images in your mind that seem to be causative or images you think you can still control. That would be a denial of "the truth is true." To start from the bottom up is to hold onto the intention to let go to the Holy Spirit and have him orchestrate. Start off with where the mind assumes it is, and what it assumes to be true, and then peel the layers away, or dissolve the question. That is truly bringing the illusions to truth. This brings the mind to a point of stillness where all the questions would be dissolved, an absoluteness where the questions have dissolved into the experience, into the silence.

What about Prayer and God's Will?

Friend: I'd like to talk about prayer. The intention of prayer has always been to make the "out here" be what we think it should be, or "better." So what is the Will of God? I do not understand how the Will of God is my will. It's all stirred up for me. It does not fit together.

David: You have some good questions. The Bible says: "Seek and ye shall find; knock and the door shall be opened unto you." (Mathew 7:7) The law of karma basically states: "As you sow, so shall you reap." No matter how you take it, it all points to the fundamental belief that giving and receiving are the same.

There is a part in the *Song of Prayer* where he refers to a ladder. When you are really bound into the world of form, you cannot help but pray for the world of form. This is the lower rung of the ladder. *Help me; help my child; help my Aunt Martha on her trip to India; help to end world hunger and poverty.* If you believe in the reality of the world around you, you cannot help but pray like that.

It is not wrong to pray in that way, but there are higher realms of prayer. *Help me see this differently* is a prayer the Course offers in many different ways, because it brings it all back to being a perceptual problem. *My perception is distorted; I need another way to look at this. I need to see peace instead of this.*

Prayer is your desire. If your desire is single and whole, your prayer, of course, is always answered. If your prayer is for God and nothing but God, then the state that you receive is a state of joy and peace. You may have it tainted with desire for other things. For example, Marianne Williamson puts it something like this, "Do I want peace or do I want him to call?" It is a good example because sometimes *getting a call from him* seems more important than peace of mind.

At those levels of desire, you can start to see how important it is to get in touch with unconscious beliefs, how important it is to start to get in touch with what the ego's beliefs are and what its purpose is and say: *Hey I do not want those. I am not going to keep plugging this appliance in. I am not going to keep following this ego – because I want peace.* Who wants pain and misery and not happiness? That kind of addresses the topic of prayer. It certainly gets away from the prayers for specifics.

A lot of prayers, even among Unity and other New Age thinking, are tied in with abundance – praying and using the mind to visualize the kind of life you want. This prayer for specifics is not the highest form, but it is more like the middle rung. If you visualize and then experience something, you hold it in mind and it seems to come, that is a powerful experience. It points to how powerful the Mind is. It is a definite experience that flies in the face of: *I am a weak little helpless nobody and I am at the whim of and the victim of everything in the world.* But what the *Song of Prayer* does and the Course in general is to say: *Okay now you are beginning to learn that your mind has power and you actually can seem to manifest things.* It seems that way. The script is written and you are still just watching the past but it seems as if the things you want are coming to you.

Once you can see that your mind is powerful, how about Peace of Mind, Enlightenment, and Salvation as your only goal? Take that powerful mind you are beginning to realize you have and give it to the Holy Spirit. Start putting peace as your only goal. Peace is an abstract kind of purpose that may be hard to get a grasp on. How am I at peace when I am with my brother or my sister? Peace and judgment do not go together. Peace and its interpretation definitely give a lot of experience, but those are the higher rungs. Instead of praying for specifics, like *please give me this, please give me that, please end world hunger, please have it be a hot sunny day when we are having our family picnic*, hold this goal of abstract peace in mind! And allow and accept, then you do not have as much of an investment in the form. The peace comes because you are not invested in the form.

You start to feel so content as you ascend up that ladder that nothing is seen as a sacrifice. Those things that seemed so important, that seemed like a really big deal…. The joy starts to be so intense; the well starts to bubble up inside so much that you wonder how you could have thought those things could bring you happiness and peace. But at the time you could not see that.

Aside from prayer you also mentioned *Will*. God's Will for his Son (for us) is perfect happiness. I have heard people say "Well it must be God's will that people starve…," but God's Will is for perfect happiness. God's Will is not known in this world. This world is made to cover over and make up an alien will (the ego), apart from God's Will – and that is where pain and fear and misery come in. Free Will is when the mind has accepted the Atonement and is healed. Then the will is free because the Father and the Son's Will are One and the Son knows this. The Son knows his Will is not apart from his Father's. Jesus knew this as a Fact.

Touching on Manifesting and Prayer

David: The Holy Spirit does not really work in this world. He is in the higher mind. He is this abstract light that shines and reminds us that we are whole and complete. Then we have these dark beliefs that we hang on to and the way the shadows come out on the screen can be interpreted like, *the Holy Spirit brought my car back* or *the Holy Spirit got me a parking space* or the Holy Spirit got me to win the lottery, etc. That is still attributing something in form, as if the Holy Spirit is moving things around. What is actually happening is that He is working with us in our mind; as we let go of our concepts and beliefs our mind opens up to His light. It is the interpretation of what we see that seems to witness that we are being taken care of. This is a very subtle point, but if you go back to the belief that the Holy Spirit works in the world – you start asking metaphysical "why" questions, such as *why did He help me?* But, the script is written. Look through the right lens and you will be at peace.

For some people the whole idea of manifesting is a big step. If you perceive yourself as a powerless, helpless little victim, a little peon, and you start to use affirmations and things start to seem to happen – that can be a witness to the idea that your mind is powerful. And that is a big step from *I am a powerless victim.* The Course just takes it a step further. It gives you the way to give that powerful mind over to the goal of peace of mind, as opposed to accumulating this and that. Like I said earlier, manifesting can be a stepping stone.

Friend: So we have to know that our mind is powerful.

David: I think a good example is in the *Song of Prayer*, the little twenty-page pamphlet that Jesus dictated. It deals with the topic that we are just touching upon now. When the mind is in a deceived state, it believes in specifics: specific persons, specific everything in this world. It has forgotten the abstract reality of light and Spirit. In a deceived state it cannot help but pray for specifics, whether it be for desires for things to work out, or perhaps just wanting someone to not make so much noise, or having goals and ambitions for specific things like a good job. The mind prays without ceasing and when it believes in specifics it cannot help but ask for specifics. But ultimately, as described in here, we really go inward; our purpose becomes very single and unified – just wanting God above all else. Our prayer becomes unified such that we literally want God above all else and ask always: *What is your will for me, Father?* This is the question we move towards.

Helen Schucman was a good example. She was quite fearful of Jesus. She would ask him for green panty hose, you know, "Where do I get green panty hose?" She is the scribe of the Course and has this highly trained ability to tune in and listen to Jesus speak to her, and she wants to know where to get green panty hose or a Borgana coat, as a specific preference. What does he do? He tells her where to go. He knows how important the Course coming into the world is, so to speak; he is trying to save time and he knows it would be a delay if she just goes about in her analytical ways of shopping all over New York City for the green panty hose or for a coat. Time is precious so he joins with her where she thinks she is and he helps her. I think that is a good lesson for all of us in the sense that when we pray there is a gradual letting go of desires for specifics and things of the world. It may seem to take the form of getting our prayers answered in that way for a while. But slowly we get clear in our mind and begin asking in any situation: *What do I want?*

One Universal Goal

David: I was always taught that it is good to be goal-oriented. By the time I finally got to the Course I was thinking: *Being goal-oriented – that is a bunch of baloney.* All those goals were specific and they were all based on the self-concept. That is where all form goals spring from. It can be thought of as an aquarium with the little pump at the bottom that blows the bubbles and pumps the air into it. The bubbles that seem to come up and float up to the top and pop on the surface are like all the specific goals. Make more money, get this, get that, develop these skills, do this and do that. That is the *pop, pop, pop;* those are all the bubbles. The important thing is to question the little thing generating the bubbles! I finally came to the point in my life where I thought: *I am going to finally get down there to the generator and question the mechanism the bubbles seem to be coming from.*

Friend: So all specifics come from a self-concept?

David: Yes. Lessons 24 and 25 in the Course address this very directly. Does that mean we should not have any goals? No, no, the Course is not advocating that; the Course is advocating you should have *one* goal, and only one goal. And that goal is abstract, it is universal and it does not have a specific reference. What does that mean? It is not quantifiable; it is not measurable. It is a goal of purpose. It is not a specific goal. It is not a goal with x amount of dollars, or a better job, or better physical health, or a warmer climate, or a better looking mate, or all the specifics goals that keep popping up here on the surface. This universal goal has to be learned very carefully because the mind can only think in terms of specifics. That is what it prays for all the time. Its prayer is its desire. It is always praying for specific outcomes. Even when you have the thought, *Gee, I am hungry*, something specific comes to mind that would seem to satisfy that hunger. When you seem to have to go to the restroom it pops into the mind where the restroom is. And you seem to go and urinate and it seems to satisfy that momentary, temporary need. Those are all answers to prayers. Going to the bathroom is an answer to prayer. Having a Dorito chip is an answer to prayer. Having sexual intercourse with someone is an answer to prayer. Going for a walk on a sunny day is an answer to prayer. Everything on the screen is an answer to prayer. It is just bringing witness to what the mind wants and also what the mind believes will answer that want or satisfy that want. This is what makes up the surface.

The key is to see that all these splintered desires are part of the self-concept bubbling away down there. It is what is sending all these bubbles up. The only way out is to have a single unified goal, to bring it to the point that my desire is single; I want only God and nothing else! If you think of the center of the mind as being like an altar, it is like saying: *I want to remove everything on the altar except God.* God cannot be on a defiled altar. He cannot be on something that is made unclean. You cannot put pure Source on a dirty altar, on a split altar.

All the Spirit will do is wait. The Spirit will not come in and try to take over the mind again. The mind has to willingly empty its altar. The Holy Spirit is not going to try to wrestle this world away from the mind. Even if the beliefs are unreal, the Holy Spirit respects or honors them in a sense, because the Son of God or the mind that fell asleep made them. And He has to honor that mind because of what it truly is.

Friend: So he honors the source of the mind?

David: Yes. He honors the source of it; He honors the true power of that mind. He is a gentle reminder for that mind to voluntarily bring those beliefs to the light or to at least question them. There is no coercion involved; there is no forcing.

The ego belief system in your mind may tell you: *If you follow this all the way out, if you really follow what he is saying, you could end up in dire straits because you are withdrawing all your seeming support in the world, what was before regarded as your support system; you are cutting your support system.* That is the ego's interpretation of following Jesus; you are cutting your support system. All that learning we talk about; we talk about resumes, learning, and all the different things that seem to be such symbols of support you have worked so hard to build. Build it, polish it, build it, polish it, build it … as if that is your support. When you really start to follow this you say: *Wait a minute, this direction is completely the opposite. This is a 180-degree turn around.* This is where the trust comes in—where you thought something was asked of you or you thought you were asked to sacrifice something. At one point in the *Manual for Teachers*, Jesus says, "The teacher of God finds a happy lightheartedness instead." M-4.I.A.6

> The world can teach no images of you unless you want to learn them. There will come a time when images have all gone by, and you will see you know not what you are. It is to this unsealed and open mind that truth returns, unhindered and unbound. Where concepts of the self have been laid by is truth revealed exactly as it is. When every concept has been raised to doubt and question, and been recognized as made on no assumptions that would stand the light, then is the truth left free to enter in its sanctuary, clean and free of guilt. There is no statement that the world is more afraid to hear than this: I do not know the thing I am, and therefore do not know what I am doing, where I am, or how to look upon the world or on myself. Yet in this learning is salvation born. And What you are will tell you of Itself. T-31.V.17

Joining the Messengers of Peace is like a witness or a symbol of giving your mind permission to let go of everything it believes–knowing that it is going to be safe, though it may seem disorienting at times…. Like, *what am I doing? Where am I?* We are metaphorically holding hands and saying, *Yeah that is the way it is going to seem at times.* We keep gently reminding each other: *Good, good, you are not nuts; you do not need to be locked up in an insane asylum. This is a good sign!* The deeper you go, it seems like you, at times, are non-functional. You cannot function in the world; good! It is another good sign.

A Discussion about Needs

David: In this discussion I would like to get into some of the metaphysics of the Course and how the mind works without being too abstract and theoretical. The deceived mind believes so much in the specifics of this world that we have to start with the specifics and work our way back from the bottom up. We begin with the way we perceive things initially, our presenting problem or situation, and then we will work it back to the mind. We will trace it to the beliefs and what is going on in the mind because that is really where our release is. We want to hold the intention to get very clear about the ego–to be able to see the ego for what it is and to remain above the battlefield. First you get to notice where your attachments are. There is much to be grateful for with this, because you cannot begin to let go of something until you can see it. Whenever questions come up in your mind, if you have a question for me, just feel free to express it. There are not any good questions or bad questions. Is there anybody who has any questions now?

Friend: About money... [laughter] I have been trying to get straight in my mind about applying the Course and then having things manifest a certain way. Explain it to me.

David: That whole question of manifesting.

Friend: Well, I just keep reading how you can make these corrections and then you suffer no consequences, that part, and somehow it links up into being at peace and....

David: It is true that the Course just comes straight out and says that it has one goal and that is peace of mind or the peace of God. Often people wonder what the Course says about abundance, or manifesting, etc. Basically, the first thing that needs to be worked on with the Course is the realization that everyone that comes to this world in some sense perceives themselves as very tiny, weak and frail. You can deal with that in certain ways. Some people try to overcompensate with money or possessions, or with particular relationships. But your worth is established by God; nothing you think or say or do is needed to establish your worth. Yet the mind believes it is a very small person in a body and it has to constantly strive and struggle to keep its head above water, whether it is financially or health-wise, or in any number of ways.

There are a lot of metaphysical systems that talk about the idea of manifesting; if you really focus on visualizing or holding a certain thing in mind it will come to you. I would see that as a stepping stone. The highest aim of prayer is for the Atonement, for peace of mind. A stepping stone along the way may be that you discover that you do seem to be able to manifest certain things, helping you to see that your mind is powerful. But once experience shows you how powerful your mind is—then you have to ask what you really want the goal to be? Why not have the Atonement, or peace of mind, be your goal?

Now, about money: there can be a fear of not having enough. For me, it was about letting go of my worldly pursuits, letting go of trying to achieve and also to not judge outcomes. It requires trust to follow this in, and see that everything is working out. The Holy Spirit is the safety net, but sometimes it feels like we are walking on a tight rope. We hear the Holy Spirit is in there but it is usually not until we seem to teeter or fall off and land on the net that we realize it has always been there for us. It comes down to *what is it for?* Content is purpose in our mind, content is the question of purpose; *what is it for?* That is a very alien question to the ego. The ego is bent on form outcomes, on setting specific external goals and then striving to achieve them. When you do, you feel like: *Gee, I still am not happy. What is next?* The game of *I will be happy when ...* goes on and on.

That peace is a decision is a powerful idea. In a way that is where the Course veers away from many of these psychotherapies and practices of going into your past to get in touch with unconscious memories and scenes that are believed to be the cause of the problem. There is nothing in your past that is causing the problem. This is radical considering so many psychotherapies say you must delve into your past. Your peace of mind, as well as guilt, fear, and anger, is based on a present decision, a decision you are making this very instant. Instead of going on a witch hunt into your past the focus is on a present decision. Now if we follow that in a little further—a decision is a conclusion based on everything that you believe. So my peace of mind or my state of mind is dependent on a present decision and the decision is a conclusion based on everything that I believe.

It is important to get in touch with the unconscious beliefs in our mind. Without raising them to the light to look right at them and see what they are, assumptions will just continue to lurk under the surface. Then it is more like being a robot. Getting up in the morning, brushing your teeth, getting ready for work; you go through the motions. How many of us get up in the morning, sit up in bed and ask: *What is the nature of reality? I do not even want to brush my teeth until I get a handle on this.* [laughter] It is like you click into gear and then maybe during your lunch hour or sometime at work you will have some of those questions come in. Sometimes they come in the form of: *What am I doing here? What is the purpose of any of this?* Often these questions will get brushed aside by all the things you think you have to do; it is like all the "practical things" get in the way of starting to investigate these questions. The ego would have us keep those questions out of mind because the more we start to go into the mind the more we begin to question the beliefs that this world is built upon.

When we talk about the idea of decision we also get into the whole idea of choice. When I was growing up I always had a sense of destiny but I really did not like the idea of pre-determination. The idea of destiny and pre-determination seemed to eliminate my choice. In psychology I studied behaviorism, which claims that everything is predetermined by your environment—stimulus-response; you just keep reacting to your environment. I did not like that idea much because it means I am just a victim or I am just completely determined by my circumstances. I liked the idea of choice but then I would hear about psychics and people who would literally read the future or read the past; it was like they were reading from a script or something. How could these psychics be predicting things that would happen? How could they read the future and see a destiny? How do you put the two together? How do you put free will or choice together with destiny?

The Course brought it all together for me. The script is written. During the holy instant all the scripts and all the perceptions were spun out—in one instant—and the Holy Spirit was given as a simultaneous answer. All the happenings took place in one, specific instant. Where does choice come in then? Your only choice is about how you are going to look at what is on the screen. You always have the choice of whether you are going to look through the ego's lens or the Holy Spirit's lens. Within the dream framework that is the only choice we have. That is not the way it seems because it seems as if we are persons in this vast world and it does not seem, at the beginning, like we are dreaming a dream; it seems like we are figures in the dream that we go through every day. And it seems like we have choices, as persons. In other words we can choose what to wear in the morning, what to eat, where to go, and those kinds of things. In this world that is what choice stands for. The ego counsels for example that the more money you have the more choice, the more freedom you have, right? *A Course in Miracles* says the only choice you have in every instant is how you look upon what is happening. That is where the freedom lies. The freedom does not lie in choosing between the illusions so to speak—choosing between a blue shirt and a green shirt. Do not arrest your mind in choosing between illusions. You can have a big dilemma, do I want to read the Course tonight or do I want to watch this TV show. Basically what it comes down to is the real question of: *What purpose will I bring to reading the Course? What purpose will I bring to watching the TV show? What is this for? What is the purpose?* The only way you can wake up to the eternal reality of your true identity as Christ, the Son of God, is to see the choice where it is; you have to see the problem where it is.

In the deceived state problems seem to be on the screen—in the world. The problem is not having the rent money or being cut off on the highway, or having a hang nail, or cancer, or a mother-in-law who won't speak to you. If you perceive the problem to be on the screen or in the world you are stuck because there is no solution to the external problems. We seem to come up with solutions; we seem to come up with enough rent, etc. For example polio seemed to be a big problem and then we seemed to come up with a polio vaccination;

Ah, a solution! It is more like having a dam break and just pushing a bunch of little things in there to plug the hole. The reason why it is important to see the decision, the choice, and the problem where it is, is because it can never be solved out there in the world. The ego counsels: address the issue of scarcity by getting a job that pays lots of money—as if that will take care of your problem with scarcity. That is the obvious way of dealing with the problem. But scarcity is a belief in your mind! And the only way you will ever completely heal it is by bringing the belief in scarcity to the Holy Spirit. Then the belief will be gone and you will not have the problem anymore.

Friend: That is what I want to know about! I want to know about the belief in scarcity being gone. Then I will not have the problem because I will have money! [laughter]

David: No. The perception will change.

Friend: I am just slow, I am sorry.

David: It is good! We can use the issue of money because the issue with money or the issue with anything else is basically the same thing.

Friend: I know it is not out there, but I cannot figure out how to fix it in here. I mean I need a house to live in, I think I know that, don't I?

David: In one of the very, very earliest sections in the Course—*The Illusion of Needs*—Jesus says that the idea of the order of needs arose because there was a fundamental error being made. The fundamental error is the belief in lack, the belief I am lacking or not complete or whole.

> ...having made this fundamental error, you had already fragmented yourself into levels with different needs. As you integrate you become one, and your needs become one accordingly. Unified needs lead to unified action because this produces a lack of conflict. The idea of orders of need, which follows from the original error that one can be separated from God, requires correction at its own level before the error of perceiving levels at all can be corrected. T-1.VI.2-3

Let's bring it back to the practical. When we think about the world, when we think of ourselves as persons in the world, it seems that we have needs on different levels. We can talk about the mental level; we can talk about the emotional level. Is anyone familiar with Maslow's hierarchy of needs where he talks about the basic levels of needs—food, clothing, warmth, sex, etc.? He also talked about self-actualization needs, of reaching your full potential. To be more specific, what if we went around the room and talked about things that we are really interested in and believe in? Some people might talk about environmental issues; others may talk about eradicating AIDS. Other people may have interpersonal problems on their minds, problems with their husband or daughter, or it may be financial needs, chronic conditions, sickness or disease. There are so many different topics. It seems like saving the dolphins, cancer, and the interpersonal relationship with your mother are really different things. This is the illusion of levels of needs. Workbook lessons 79 and 80 teach, "Let me recognize the problem so it can be solved," and then "Let me recognize my problems have been solved." If you read point-blank, "Let me recognize that my problems have been solved" it is like: *Wait a minute, I do not feel that way.* It seems like every day you have to deal with problems, interpersonal problems, survival, and so on and so forth. But you only have one problem and there is one solution to that problem. Isn't that nice to think it is so simple? If there is such a thing as truth, it will be simple—one problem and one solution. If I perceive the problem to be in the world, it cannot be solved because the Holy Spirit is the one answer to that one problem and the Holy Spirit is in the mind. God did not place the answer where the problem was not. He did not place the answer out on the screen. He did not place the answer in the world; he placed the answer in the mind of the sleeping Son. And that is where the Holy Spirit is.

The Course constantly reminds you to bring illusions to the truth. Bring your false beliefs to the light, to the Holy Spirit in your mind. The false ideas and false beliefs that are in the mind are all backwards. They all have the basic error that there is something on the screen that is causative, and your mind is the effect. For example, you mentioned preferring an 80-degree day over a 60-degree day; the mind has beliefs in preferences of temperature. Some like it hot and some like it cold. It seems like there is something on the screen—the sun—that makes you feel hot. If you do not put enough food in this body then that is what makes you hungry. You do not see that the hunger has something to do with the belief in your mind that you have separated from God. You believe you are hungry because you do not have enough food. It is kind of like when you were a kid and got into fights with your little sister or with a neighborhood child. You would run to mom and tell her that so and so made you mad or hurt your feelings. Or maybe your boss told you off today which just made you fume and lose your peace of mind. The world and the ego teach that there is always something on the screen that is the cause of your upset, and not only that, there is always something on the screen that is the cause of your happiness, like that giant hot fudge sundae; I am happy tonight because I get to eat my hot fudge sundae. Or, I got the woman I was chasing all my life; she finally fell in love with me so now I am happy and we go into the sunset. No matter what it is: I have the right job, I got the right promotion, I have the right car, and I am living in the right area. No, no, our peace of mind and our upset has nothing at all to do with what is happening on the screen, but it has everything to do with our *interpretation* of what is happening on the screen.

You are always reading into things all the meaning that you are feeling. All the feelings you have watching a movie, for example, are coming from within you. You never react to what happens directly—you always react to your interpretation of what is happening. What you need to work with is correcting your interpretations and perceptions. How many of us have tried to correct things in a behavioral sense? I am too fat; I will go on a diet. I do not have enough money; I will go get a better job. I have a certain kind of illness so I will go to a specialist that does an operation or that gives me a particular kind of medicine. Or behavior modification: I want to be a good Christian like Jesus and be kind so I am going to try to be a kind person. Meanwhile inside there is anger or rage, but we are trying to put on a nice mask because we think we want to do the kind thing. Forget about your behavior. Behavior will follow automatically from your thoughts and perceptions. Do not try to fix things out there with your behavior but follow me inward with this. Look at perception and raise up the false beliefs. Then you will have a transformation of your mind. Behavior will follow automatically. Doesn't that make sense? Intuitively you can see where this is going.

Friend: I can see how it makes sense but I think what is confusing sometimes is when we are taught that what is in our world is a reflection of what is in the mind. I think: *Okay well let's go to the source here and if this is changed— if I become one with God—then this will automatically follow.* It is unrealistic to think that we will suddenly become millionaires. But if you come to the consciousness and really realize you are not lacking or you are not sick, would there not be some kind of change in the outward world to reflect the change in the mind?

David: The error is that the deceived mind really believes that there is an objective world out there, a world that is apart from me and you, but all perception is completely subjective. Every time any "fragment" looks through the ego's lens, he sees the world in a distorted way.

Friend: So the shift is to see there never was a lack in the first place and we never really were sick in the first place?

David: There is the clarity of seeing this choice where it is, of seeing that it was just a misperception.

Friend: I notice sometimes that if I am faced with a big bear in the middle of the road of this dream I am in, what has been helpful is to recognize that my goal for the day is the peace of God—just for today. Sometimes that is all I can do.

David: That simplifies things; it really brings it home. The important thing is to stay with the peace and to be open to the Holy Spirit's guidance. The Holy Spirit does not work in the world. He is in the mind. That may be very scary, but the Holy Spirit will reach you wherever you believe you are. If you believe you are a mother and you believe you have three kids and you only have five dollars left, then, when you really set aside the chatter and focus on peace as the goal, you may receive specific guidance on steps to take. In this case it is not really helpful to just sit there and think about how God is abstract and does not know about this world. Focus on the peace and then be open to who to call or what to do next. That makes it very practical. And do not look for outcomes, even in the slightest way. Judging or gauging how well you are doing by the outcome is a trap.

Many people fall into this trap with sickness. We talk about sickness being a decision, and that our state of mind is completely our own responsibility; there is nothing outside of us and there is no blaming God and no blaming the medical model or blaming the doctors. People will take that idea and put that together with a diagnosis of cancer, or the flu, and start to think: *I should be able to do better than this.* This is still identity confusion. To say that I am responsible and then to put that with *Oh, I have cancer* is to try to combine two different levels. Remember, we are responsible for the way we look at things; when you bring it down to *and I have cancer;* there is an "I" confusion there. If you look at the idea that sickness is a projection of guilt onto the body. *Oh my gosh, what am I doing to myself?* That is level confusion. Is Christ projecting sickness on himself? With "my body" there is a very strong identification in the mind with "this is me." The Course is gently guiding us away from this body identification to a point of seeing that we are mind. We can get clear on what the ego is and pull our mind from it. In other words, take the juice away from it, take the power away, then we will choose peace at that point. But as long as we think the ego offers us something and we still buy into that, our minds are not willing to choose the peace; we want to make exceptions. We want to say that there is order of difficulties in miracles. This one right here is more difficult than that one. We want to hold onto exceptions.

> Every thought you have makes up some segment of the world you see. It is with your thoughts then that we must work if your perception of the world is to be changed. If the cause of the world you see is attack thoughts you must learn that it is these thoughts which you do not want. W-23.1

Attack thoughts would be analogous to the backward thoughts we were talking about; the ego-based thought that the cause is outside my mind.

> There is no point in lamenting the world. There is no point in trying to change the world. It is incapable of change because it is merely an effect. W-23.2

Those are some very strong statements. It is like the analogy of the movie screen. You have a projector and some film with dark images moving through it. When the light shines through the dark images, shadows dance on the screen. Have you ever gone to one of those movies where there is a glitch in the film? When we try to change things in the world, or look to the world for things to change, it is like going up and banging on the screen instead of going back to the manager in the projection room. We can see that it would be silly to do that. Literally, it is like the film that is going through the projector. Once you are able to overlook those dark thoughts, the world lights up, so to speak. The Course even talks about light episodes and gives some metaphors for that. When we let go of attack thoughts our perception will literally light up. Now that does not tell you anything about what is going on out there. In other words when Jesus accepted the Atonement it did not seem that the world exactly changed a whole lot; the Jews continued to fight the Roman Empire. The world seemed to still be kind of a mess, but Jesus is saying that is just twisted perception. When you see war and conflict and fighting, it is the ego's lens that you are looking through; that is what is twisted. It is not about anything out there in and of itself.

Friend: I think that no matter what, the world is going to be screwed up. Like with a film, if you do not like a certain scene you can fast forward through it but then after a while another scene you do not like will come up. If it is not one thing, it is another. You can even make this world a pleasant place to live in to a certain extent but in the final analysis you are going to have to look at all those problems and say: *who cares.* That is the way Jesus did it. He said, "In this world you need not have tribulation because I have overcome the world. That is why you should be of good cheer." T-4.I.13 You have to rise above it and not even see the problems as problems.

David: Yes, it is a real healing to be able to rise above them like that.

Friend: That is what I meant that it is not so much to heal the world but to heal yourself. And once you heal yourself the problems in the world do not matter anymore because you will not even see them.

David: That is what got me going initially. I talked earlier about not being able to reconcile what I was seeing with these eyes, with God. I had a feeling that God was all knowing and all loving and all powerful. That all seemed to resonate, but then I have these eyes and ears, like watching the nightly news. When you say *I do not care* – that is the good news; the world as you perceive it through the distorted lens, is not reconcilable with God. There is no use trying to fit them together. Philosophy and science have tried; all kinds of efforts have been made to reconcile how this happened. God did not create sickness; God did not create war; God did not create these things! But when you are looking through a twisted lens, you see it outside yourself. Healing is about seeing that the split is in your own mind. Then you can see that the correction is also in your mind.

I like to use the analogy of overhead projectors. There is this beautiful pure, white light on the screen and then all the overlays are brought in. You can imagine drawing a body on it. Now there is an overlay with the body; now we have form. Then the ego names this body as male or female and puts some skin color on it: some black, some white. Then we can put age in there. And there we have all the problems – ageism, sexism, racism…. It seems as if those are big problems in the world; you hear about them on the news. But the Course basically says that ageism is in your mind, sexism is in your mind, racism is in your mind. The ego belief system is in your mind! The problem of inequality is not in the world. It is in the split mind.

You can see that it is really an unlearning or a subtraction process. It is not like you need to attend x number of seminars or read x number of books and then someday in the future – if you are lucky – you will finally arrive. It is really more of a subtraction thing. [laughter] You are *it* right now. But these other things are laid on. That is why it is so valuable to look together at all the constructs in our minds that we believe we are. They are just beliefs.

There are many mind training exercises and guided meditations in the Course that are designed to help you sink down beneath the thoughts and beliefs. It is important to realize that this is a course in transforming your mind; it is not a course in just memorizing text and talking about it. Sinking down beneath the thoughts is very, very important. The rest of the book helps you start to become aware of the backward thoughts and some of the concepts and ideas that you have, but really it comes down to a constant job of what I call mind watching.

Controlling the Body, Controlling the Past

Hi David,

A while ago you wrote: "Weight control, like any attempt to 'control' the script or the body, is an attempt to control the past." Can you help with that line? I would like more explanation as to how it is an attempt to control the past. How is controlling the body like controlling the past?

Beloved One,

In the workbook the Course makes the statement: "The script is written." In the beginning of the workbook Jesus explains that the reason the first six lessons are true is because of lesson 7: "I see only the past." The script of the world – everything perceived with the five senses – is the past.

Everything in the script was over long ago; the mind is just reviewing it as if it is still happening. To attempt to control the weight of the body is one example of trying to change the past or control the script. It is *only* possible to control the direction of thinking in the mind. That is, right-minded thinking is a choice that can be made with increasing consistency, yet the script is beyond the possibility of change or control.

The script is like the film in the projector. It just *seems* to play out, when actually all the images are past. The optical delusion of the world seems to offer the ability to control "things," but it is impossible to control something that is already finished and done! The body is part of the past.

> Time is a trick, a sleight of hand, a vast illusion in which figures come and go as if by magic. Yet there is a plan behind appearances that does not change. The script is written.

119

When experience will come to end your doubting has been set. For we but see the journey from the point at which it ended, looking back on it, imagining we make it once again; reviewing mentally what has gone by. W-158.4

The mind can change its mind about itself. One has no control over the world. The body and the world are the same; they are past.

The world you perceive is a world of separation. Perhaps you are willing to accept even death to deny your Father. Yet He would not have it so, and so it is not so. You still cannot will against Him, and that is why *you have no control over the world you made.* It is not a world of will because it is governed by the desire to be unlike God, and this desire is not will. The world you made is therefore totally chaotic, governed by arbitrary and senseless "laws," and without meaning of any kind. For it is made out of what you do not want, projected from your mind because you are afraid of it. Yet this world is only in the mind of its maker, along with his real salvation. Do not believe it is outside of yourself, for only by recognizing where it is will you gain control over it. For *you do have control over your mind, since the mind is the mechanism of decision.* T-12.III.9

Seek Not to Change the World

The world is a mirror of the thoughts you think you think and the identity you think you are – as long as perception lasts. The world will never change. The eyes and the ears of the body will still seem to offer separate images and sounds; they will continue to report differences. For this reason they were made; until perception disappears entirely they will continue to do what they were made in hate to do. Yet the healed mind realizes none of them are true; thus it IS possible to see the world from a Higher Perspective and experience the peace of the forgiven world.

This is the goal of *A Course in Miracles.* You still perceive the world, but from this right-minded Perspective there is no longer any attempt to judge between that which is all the same. Images are the same, they are not different. The Holy Spirit's Perspective is indeed different from the ego's personal slant and this discernment – or mind training – is the goal of all effort to reach inner peace and tranquility.

The world is like a mask that was made to hide the truth. The mask seems to shift and change, but do not be fooled by appearances. The world will never change. Come within in peace and accept this simple statement. Lay aside all attempts to judge any person or aspect of the world you perceive. Lay aside the desire to fix or improve or change that which was made as a distractive device to keep you blind and preoccupied. Rest now, for you are entitled to happy dreams from a New Perspective that surely awaits your recognition in awareness.

Do not try to complicate what is simple and obvious with attempts to intellectually "understand" the book as a collection of concepts. Forgiveness is not the study of the ego. The Course aims at an experience of the Present Moment. All so-called knowing and understandings must be released to the Holy Spirit. Accept that you know nothing and thus open the mind to an experience of the New Perspective. Each miracle gives a glimpse of the New Perspective. Remember that not one thought the world believes is true. Relax in the awareness that the ego has no contribution to make to the truth! Not one opinion or specific judgment has any validity or value. From this clean and open-minded Perspective is the world shown to you Anew, and it is obvious that the world will never change. Change your mind about your mind by accepting the Mind's changeless State of Innocence and Perfection. Make way for the Vision of Christ. It is the only sight there is to See. The Light of Understanding is Visible to the Spiritual Eye. Do not attempt to "see" with the body or to understand images. There will come a time when all images have gone by and the mind will rest in Eternity. There is no need to delay what is simple and natural.

"Nothing real can be threatened. Nothing unreal exists." T-in.2 The metaphysics of these statements are clear and straightforward. Apply the Workbook lessons and refrain from making any exceptions. Many teachers focus on the principles and words and give little attention to practical application and transfer of training. If you would forgive you must experience that there is no such thing as partial forgiveness. Only complete forgiveness or Atonement brings lasting peace. "Judge not" is not an injunction to stop judging. Rather it is an invitation to the awareness that judgment is forever impossible. You need not make amends for past judgments, for by understanding that judgments are unknown to God, to Love, you realize that only Love is real and judgment is impossible. How Innocent is the Being God creates in Wholeness and Spirit. To know the Christ as Thy Self is inevitable.

The symbols and the gifts and the tools of Awakening are noticed everywhere once you have opened your heart to them. They are free and Freely Given. They come with blessings and with no cost or sacrifice. They come easily to a willing heart and open mind. Be not afraid of Love. Love comes as a Friend and the Holy Spirit is Friendly and Gentle.

I come in Peace.

I come in Joy.

I come in Love.

I come in Happiness.

The Light has come. Seek not to change the world. Change your mind about the world. The world will never change.

What I Can Control versus what I Cannot Control

Hi David,

I listened to your tape *No Control over the World*. It raised lots of confusion in my mind. When I was young, I thought I had control over everything in my life (work, who my friends were, what I did for pleasure and time off, what I did for hobbies, etc.). I thought I had no control over sickness, violence from others, war, accidents, etc. Now that I am getting older I need to wear glasses and find I cannot see with them or without them, my memory is failing, my ability to learn new technologies is getting more difficult, etc. I find that I have less and less control over the loss of function, and that I am heading to where my mother is – in a wheelchair in a home. I seem to be at a loss to control the human decline. If I understand the message of *No Control over the World*, I might as well accept the fact that the body is aging and function is leaving. The mind would be at least relieved of the worry. It too is not as sharp as it was. I cannot remember people's names and often words I know simply do not come, or come in the wrong language.

In spite of the detailed questions and resulting confusion, I did get a clear visualization after listening to No Control over the World, which is that my life is like a person on a carpet (the carpet you spoke of that rolls up when time is done). So for every decision I make on the carpet, the carpet unrolls according to my decisions. If I decide to turn right, it also turns right and unrolls before me, and if I look down the carpet I see my imagined future. If I look back over the carpet, I see my past story. If I turn left, the carpet precedes me. When the mind dis-engages, no longer seeing itself as part of the person on the carpet, it appears that the whole carpet (past and present) is really a dream; it is not in the reality of the mind that was identified with the person before. Thus you say it "is past" because it is outside of timelessness. The visualization also explains to me why there is no randomness in reality – because all is Mind, and mind is both love and knowledge at the same time, so once one is identified with the Big Mind, then they could never see randomness which implies action without intelligence....

Anyway, I am sure that your words of wisdom will shed clarity on these issues, so this is lesson 1 of "How to recognize what I can control versus what I cannot control?"

Beloved One,

Thanks for writing and sharing your questions and ponderings. Awakening is simply the clear awareness that State of Mind (Peace, Happiness, Freedom, Joy) is true Self Responsibility and the belief that seemed to make the cosmos (ego) has had no effect on Reality (Truth of Spirit).

To live in the Present is to be free of the illusory limits of time-space. You can control the direction of your thinking and can therefore align with the Holy Spirit in the Present Moment. Practicing with willingness the ability to choose the Holy Spirit will yield the experience of Being, which is far beyond the illusory concept of choice.

It is true that nothing is random. The script of the cosmos played out in one seeming "unholy instant" and was corrected or neutralized by the Holy Spirit. Flow with the Love of the Holy Spirit and it becomes apparent that all seeming decisions in form are already made. This is the experience of the happy dream of non-judgment. Prayer, mind watching, and forgiveness lead to the experience that all form is false appearance and past, and what is past cannot be changed – only recognized as over and gone. Time and space are one illusion; peace of mind comes the instant the illusion is forgiven or released.

Life is our Spirit, which is Eternal. The body only seems to decline and age to the ego, which *is* the belief in time. Be comforted to know that Holy Spirit will arrange time and space for the miracles you will be sharing. Our joining shows that time has had no effect on our Identity in God. Nothing can change Eternal Love. What seems to fade was never Love, for Love is Everlasting.

Continue to open to the miracles the Holy Spirit offers. Listen to the gatherings offered online, pray for the Holy Spirit's Loving Interpretation, and everything will be revealed. Awakening is a Moment of readiness and willingness and actually has nothing to do with time at all. Give your mind permission to rest and soar in the Divinity within. Miracles offer an effortless way of flowing in the moment; you will recognize them by the Ease through which they come. Release all attempts to control persons, places, and events, and watch with the Holy Spirit. Keep watch and there is only an experience of light-heartedness. Nothing else really matters.

Releasing the "Control" Addiction

Turning something over to the Holy Spirit is a leap of faith that lets go of attempting to control outcomes. The core of alcoholism, anorexia, bulimia, smoking and a host of things the world calls addictions is control. The little willingness the Holy Spirit asks is the key to letting go of the attempt to manage the body and the world, which is the insane attempt to maintain a self-concept image that God did not create. An idea to contemplate from the Course is this:

Seek not to change the world, but choose to change your mind about the world. T-21.in.1

The requirement is to change your thinking, not to focus on behavior and form. Behavior flows from thought, and transformation of the mind is synonymous with changing thought patterns from ego-based to Spirit-based.

Control and judgment are the addiction; the focus is always on releasing them since God creates only Mind Awake and these abilities are unnatural, being illusions. The development of trust in the Holy Spirit goes hand in hand with the release of judgment/control. And it becomes more and more apparent that trust would settle every problem now.

Chapter Five

Clarifying the Meaning of Free Will

Free Will is another name for God's Will, for it is eternally free, happy, peaceful, and joyful. This State of Mind is Perfection or Reality or Truth. The Will is free in perfect Oneness and Union; this freedom is a characteristic of Spirit or Eternal Creation, which is the abstract Light of unconditional love sometimes reported in "near death experiences." This Light is total understanding and Love, or Oneness. God creates only Light and Oneness. Duality is the illusion of the ego.

Choice did not seem to arise until the "fall from Grace" that reflects the belief that separation from God is possible. This belief in separation produces what appears to be a dualistic dream-world of extremes and opposites: the time-space cosmos. These seeming "choices between specifics" which are the common "choices of the world" are a distraction from understanding that the choice of purpose in one's mind is the only meaningful choice remaining to the dreamer of the dream-world.

No one can serve two masters; the ego's voice and the inner voice of the Spirit are as different in purpose as night and day. Learn to discern between these two voices. Lay aside the ego. Align completely with the Voice for God. This is the goal of life, for God's Will for us is perfect happiness. The Voice for God leads to awakening from the dream-world of fear to the Reality of Eternal Love and Oneness.

What does it require to remember God? Nothing in Reality. You do not need to do anything to Be What You Are. If the illusion of time still seems real, what is your only need? You know the answer; the forgetting of this world of fragmentation, the forgiveness of illusions, the releasing of the past. Do not put your faith in the ego and its laws of economics, medicine, nutrition, physics, friendship, and its doctrines, rituals, and creeds that tell you that you must "struggle" to survive.

Let go of the belief that you are confined to a body. Let go of the belief that you have a past or a future. Watch your cares and concerns disappear from awareness. Behold the blazing light of your True Identity in God, changeless and timeless. The truth is now, the present moment, free of all illusory restrictions and limitations.

In Awakening to God you will first have a happy dream, cleansed of judgments and grievances. Joy and laughter will replace sadness and sorrow. The mind becomes completely "saved" from the belief in error. What was error but a mistake to be corrected by the Holy Spirit, the Answer within. Now is the time of release, for happy dreams lead to Awakening to Love and Light, Peace Eternal. Welcome Home Holy Child of the Living God!

A Prayer to Be in Touch with the Comforter

Hi David,

My heart is so weary and seeks solace. I have perused your website for some time and have found comfort in your materials. I have yet to be aware of the Comforter Himself. Sometimes I think and hope that I feel Him. I have demonstrated to myself that HE is there with me even in the presence of many others. It still remains true for me that I just, so often, do not know what to do or what to say. I guess I just do not yet know how to trust.

I am often very scared, especially of late. Thoughts of persecution and attack haunt my mind, most of them seeming to take the form of opposition towards my person. It does seem to me that the world does not want what I, in my highest hopes, want with all my heart, but am too afraid to grasp. Oh! Why do I still resist?

I am touched by the Course. I am touched by the story of Jesus in *The Urantia Book*. I am touched by Augustine's Confessions. And I am also touched by Christian Science as taught by Mary Baker Eddy herself and her earliest followers. It seems that, in some way, they all point towards the same glorious truth. In some ways, there seem to be discrepancies, but I can accept that this must be due to my ignorance, and that if I could just fasten on the glory of God, that the ambiguity would disappear. And then, I often wonder if I just want to be in conflict and lament the whole thing.

Now, I am a student at a University. I am often afraid because I do not know what my future will be. Everything that I believe and would profess is directly antagonistic to the common opinion and beliefs held. I would so welcome the atmosphere of questioning these things, but no one really wants this. I have one friend that is open to me and what I say, but I do not see any support elsewhere. There is no degree or major offered by the

University that I believe I would be happy in. I am interested in about any discipline you can name, but do not really believe that I could pick just one. I do not think I would be happy being a priest for I fear the hypocrisy in the churches, and in those that have stepped away from the truer idea and would attack it in the name of almighty God. These are the many things that fill me with dread.

I do not know you, but from what I can understand, you seem to be at peace and filled with hope for the future. If this is so, I would do anything you said. And if I do not mean what I say, then I should be checked for my insincerity. You studied the Course passionately for two years! My God – the courage! I do not wish to throw cheap flattery at you, but I really mean this. I have had the thought of doing this myself but do not see how, in terms of worldly circumstances, I could do it. And I am not even sure if I am ready for that. I may be too naive in this whole affair. I have felt what I think is peace. The feeling is very strong and powerful and quiet. It seems that physical changes happen as well. Sometimes, I do see little sparkles of a brilliant white light. Also, I have had interesting dreams. Sometimes the most perfect moment seems to happen where I am so sure I love someone. A simple smile, kind eyes, and a pure heart go such a long way, even unto Infinity! But, oh, these moments are so few! My tired heart... God, I am so weary and beaten on the path of thorns.

I read Mary Baker Eddy's book and am touched by everything she says but afraid at the same time. I believe that she really healed physically, and while this is certainly not the lesson in itself, the physical part seems to be glossed over in the emphasis of mind only in connection with those who discuss the Course. And while I know that this must be the ultimate, I would hope that God so loves us that He comforts us even here in our false belief so that we may be led out of it. And that was the place I thought physical healing had in the grand scheme of things. I think that all of my conflicts involve my belief in the body and that I am a body. I do not see how to reach God without being relieved of these material difficulties. I feel like I am denying what seems to be so obvious; like I am trying to fix on the spiritual idea and hold it even though the physical senses show just the opposite and pronounce me a liar.

I know that some of this may be vague, but I think I have written about all I can for now. I know that you answer the letters addressed to you as you are Guided, and considering how busy you may be, when you have time. I appreciate this and eagerly await your answer with a spark of hope.

Beloved One,

Thanks for writing and unburdening your heart. You are receiving your Calling as many are right now. The glimpses of truth have shown you that our Being is not of this world. And you are on the right track when you realize that you must trust in the Holy Spirit to release the laments of the past and fears about the future. To you there seem to be many things that fill you with dread, but I assure you that only the ego dreads and its one dread is present joining. This joining is the Purpose that dissolves the fear forever.

You have called forth beautiful texts and videos and music and witnesses to remind you that you have a Purpose you must embrace. The situations and circumstances around you will all seem to shift as you embrace your new Purpose. Time is in the hands of the miracle worker, and Christ will arrange time and space to suit your function. You are being Called out of the thinking of the world because you are the Light of the world. When you give your mind's loyalty to the Holy Spirit you withdraw your faith in the ego. It is impossible to serve two masters that have no meeting point. Love and fear can never be reconciled since one is true and the other false. Now is the time to be gentle with yourself and nurture along each nod of willingness that you give to the Holy Spirit.

I can relate to your feelings and beliefs about a future in the educational system, for I was once tempted to believe and feel the same things. You wrote: "There is no degree or major offered by the University that I believe I would be happy in. I am interested in about any discipline you can name, but do not really believe that I could pick just one." This describes my perception during most of the 10 years of University study I completed. The skills and abilities you have seemed to develop in college can and will be used by the Holy Spirit in the Plan of Awakening. Skills and abilities are neutral. It is the purpose to which they are put that either frees the mind (Holy Spirit) or imprisons it (ego).

You wrote: "I am often very scared, especially of late. Thoughts of persecution and attack haunt my mind, most of them seeming to take the form of opposition towards my person. It does seem to me that the world does not want what I, in my highest hopes, want with all my heart, but am too afraid to grasp." Deep down everyone wants what you want in your highest hopes, for everyone must inevitably know our Creator and remember our Eternal Oneness. Attack thoughts are the only things that stand in the way of recognizing the Truth of Spirit. It would be wise to give your mind to a mind training discipline such as the workbook lessons in ACIM, for that will clear the way in your function as a miracle worker.

Workbook lesson 23 is: "I can escape from the world I see by giving up attack thoughts." The belief that you can attack and/or be attacked is central to the ego's thought system and its attempt to maintain fear, guilt, and pain. You must realize that attack thoughts never serve to bring peace of mind. If the Peace of God is your goal, attack thoughts must be relinquished. As your trust in the Holy Spirit increases you will see that you have no need of attack thoughts. The willingness to Awaken must start and end with your heart.

You wrote: "I would so welcome the atmosphere of questioning these things, but no one really wants this. I have one friend that is open to me and what I say, but I do not see any support elsewhere." This is exactly how I seemed to feel years ago, yet I was determined to persist in questioning everything I believed in because deep inside I knew there had to be another way of living. I kept the faith during all this questioning even though doubt thoughts would come and go then come again and again. I came to the awareness that Waking Up from the dream of sickness, pain, and death to the Eternal Joy of Heaven was the only Purpose worthy of my effort and energy. Once I came to this admission it was easy to study the Course for 8 hours a day, for I saw in this devotion my whole way out of the dream of the world.

You are zooming in to a very, very direct relationship with the Holy Spirit. Never forget this. You wrote: "I have demonstrated to myself that HE is there with me even in the presence of many others." Yes!!! The Holy Spirit is always Guiding you; the Holy Spirit's Voice is as loud as your willingness to listen. Brothers and sisters everywhere are hearing and Answering the Call to Awaken, the Call to Salvation, the Call to enlightenment. I have traveled many places in the past 14 years and I can attest to these witnesses for the desire to Awaken. I will be traveling to Chicago and New York City this month and meeting with many more witnesses to Awakening. They are everywhere. Your willingness will show them to you just as my devotion has brought them into my awareness. They are all sweeties in my mind!

All healing is in and of the mind. It is helpful to be reminded that you were looking through a darkened glass at the world when you perceived sickness or any form of error. The message of the Atonement is that the past is over and gone and, in fact, never happened. Symptom removal is but a reflection of a shift in perception. When the mind is wholly aligned with the Holy Spirit's Perspective there is no perception of separate persons, places, things, events, or situations. Linear, situational thinking was the problem that the Holy Spirit has already Corrected. The only task for a sleeping mind is to accept this Correction; that is your goal now. Time and Eternity cannot co-exist.

You are ready to open to your Heavenly function. Christ does not ask for a spiritual resume, yet your willingness will carry you farther along than you can imagine. It cannot be difficult to do all that Christ has appointed for you, for it is Christ Who will do it through you until the realization dawns that You are the One. If you knew Who walks beside you along the way, fear would be impossible. I am always with you and you can always Call on the "I Am" Presence to join you in whatever circumstance you seem to be facing.

My heart goes out to You Beloved One, for You are my Self. Our joining carries the power of All of Heaven! Trust in That and watch the fears of the ego melt away and disappear forever.

The Ladder of Prayer – Crossing the Barrier to Peace

Hi David,

I wrote you last year when I was out of work and concerned for my family. My wife and I had to trust that Holy Spirit would provide. Someone who reads these messages was led to offer assistance, and I found employment shortly thereafter.

I would appreciate your prayers and guidance. Also for my wife, who desperately needs an operation that we cannot afford and my three beautiful children who have been through their own challenges.

Thank you my brother. I am not afraid. Peace and Love

Beloved One,

Thanks for pouring your heart out and being open and willing for Guidance about prayer. You and your family are in my thoughts and prayers. Now for some Guidance about prayer: Prayer is desire. A heart which knows no desire has cleared the Altar of mind and desires that there be no idols before God.

Desirelessness is Completion. God created Christ Whole and Complete. Desirelessness means that there is nothing to add or wish or want beyond the Perfection that God Gives Eternally. Single or unified desire is Creation; this is the meaning of "Let Thine Eye be Single."

Christ has Given *The Song of Prayer* as direct Guidance about the topic of prayer. I invite you to read it, that you may ask the Holy Spirit within for further clarification and illumination.

As the Altar of mind is made clean, freed from the desire for the impossible, the Memory of God will return to awareness. Release the past, for it is gone. No longer seek to repeat what is already over and gone. Prayer for specifics asks that the past be repeated in some form the mind believes is desirable. Desirelessness is of the Present Moment, this holy instant.

Be Content with What is forever Real and True. God Gives only Love.

Prayer: Clearing the Altar of the Heart

In this past world, the linear world of time-space, prayers were often believed to be petitions, requests, or questions. Lord grant me ... Lord, I ask that ... Please Lord, I beckon You to ... Lord I have a favor to ask ... It is as if there was a Power (up there, out there, or apart) that was looking down and watching over the world – a Power Who had the ability to, at times, grant wishes and favors to human beings. It also appeared to be the case that prayers were not always answered. This view could not have avoided seeing God as fickle or inconsistent or, very strangely, a Being that was capable of playing favorites. These are the concepts and perceptions of prayer that arise from an allegiance to the ego, the impossible belief in scarcity and lack. They were but witnesses to false belief and thus were never accurate or true. Yet there is another way to see prayer.

True prayer is a way back to the recognition of the Kingdom of Heaven. True prayer is an opening and clearing of the heart – a return to the purity or singularity of desire. For prayer IS desire and, as such, prayer is continuous. Prayer never starts or stops and it is never strong or weak, sincere or insincere. One is never absent from prayer or the power of prayer. Like faith, prayer can seem to be misplaced, yet even this illusion cannot but testify to the power of the mind from which the illusion was made. Just look at the time-space cosmos. A belief in separation can seem to make a "Big Bang" out of literally nothing. As the saying goes, *be careful what you pray for, because prayers ARE answered.*

Prayer is actually the meditation of the heart. As visualization is the imagination that seems to arise from belief, belief is the illusory ego wisp that draws from and is powered by prayer. Heaven Itself is beyond belief, for God can be but Known.

Prayer is the energy of God. In Heaven, Prayer is the Song of Gratitude that echoes forever as the Eternal Oneness of Creation. In time-space, prayer is the energy which infuses all appearances and powers belief. Prayer is Itself in the Divine Silence within, in which the Beloved of God rests in peace. The Heart which is One has no division, for there is nothing unlike Itself.

True prayer accepts "what is." "What Is" remains forever changeless as a Gift of God. Creation is Eternal; God's Will is Perfect Happiness, Now and Forever. Wholeness is complete and total. There is nothing to be wanted in the Wholeness of God. There is nothing to "get" in the Reality of Allness. The "I Am" Presence is very literally the Kingdom of Heaven – from which nothing can be absent.

The belief in linear time IS the belief in lack. The belief in linear time is the belief in "Seek and do NOT find," T-12.IV.1 or as the song says, "Looking for Love (in all the wrong places)." Eternity and time cannot co-exist. One is real and one is not. One is Eternal Innocence, and one is the illusion of guilt. How could innocence be found in guilt, or love be found in fear? And how could Spirit be found in a string of images, sequenced and arranged in a line? Divine Love, Christ, is the Inheritance and cannot be found in specifics of time-space. The holy instant Calls. The experience of Now is the Answer.

Pray truly Holy Child of God: Holy Creator of Me, what is Your Will for Me? And Hear: Beloved Child, Thy Will is Mine, One forever. You are created as Perfect Happiness in Eternity, and remain so forever. We shall not be content with the littleness of time-space. We shall not ask for what can never content our Holy Mind. Blessed are the pure in Heart, for... You Know the Rest!

Foolish beliefs have fallen from the inner altar of prayer Now, swept away by the Wind of Eternity. The Light is free to radiate completely without obstruction. A heart made free of the pursuit of idols is a Heart which loves the Lord Thy God with all Its Being. My Heart abides forever with God. Amen.

Opening to the Experience Beyond Manifesting

Hi David,

What is your guidance on the magic of manifesting? Since becoming aware of the dream and myself as the dreamer, I seem to be experiencing a period of lack after over 40 years of never seeming to go without a relatively comfortable lifestyle in this world.

I have heard you talk about manifesting as "magic" and that it is merely a way of showing people they are not victims, and that the mind is truly powerful. Yet, as you and the Course say, this world is not real! Any manifestation is simply more dreaming and I do not want to prolong the dream (in my wrong mind that is, for as we know it was over as quickly as it began!) for one second longer than absolutely necessary.

Do you see it as a necessary step in one's spiritual development to learn the skills of manifesting? Or can I somehow learn how to let go of any attachment to money (and the seeming security it seems to provide) and surrender into the abundance of what I really am without experiencing the concept of manifesting. And, if this second step is possible, how does that look and feel in this world?

I want to help my brothers wake up, I want to fulfill my one function and purpose in this world and it is bringing up fear and feelings of limit and control. What can I do to ease this transition and release this fear with grace?

Beloved One,

The best indicator of connection to God is how one feels; this indicator is the best because it is not dependent on any particular "form outcome." A mind that looks to "form outcomes" is deceived and will not experience a lasting Peace. State of mind (how one feels) IS the outcome of which thought system one is aligned with (God or ego). Such is the case with "manifesting" money, skills, resources, etc. Money, for example, is nothing. If a mind believes in ego (belief in lack/reciprocity), money is endowed with false value. The belief in lack/reciprocity is the belief in substitution, for the ego is the chosen "substitute" for Source, for God.

The reason money seems valuable is because it seems to be highly exchangeable for many "things" that meet illusory needs, whether they seem emotional, physical, or spiritual. Like medicine, money is like the magic spell of the world that seems to make illusory problems disappear for a while. Yet until the ego has been released entirely, the mind perceives needs and external means (false sources) to meet the perceived needs.

It all comes down to this: one must accept One Self as Changeless Divine Mind. The only step to this is realizing that the world cannot change, for it is an unreal effect of an unreal cause. The world CANNOT change. Asking for things to be different than they are is an impossible request.

Money, like all effects (images of the ego) is never a source. The meaningful request is a request to see the world differently (as an unreal effect of an unreal cause) and to thus accept the Fact that there is only One Source. God is the ONLY Source. The only question/problem/confusion is one of identity and has absolutely nothing to do with money. Trust would settle every problem now, for to trust is to be God dependent. The reversal of thought necessary to realize God dependence is a full three hundred and sixty degree turn around, so to speak, and this means the realization that there are no cause/effect relationships in this world that are true.

If all the images (including money) are effects, there is no cause or source to be found in this world. God is True Source and Christ the True Effect. Therefore the secret to true prayer is to forget the things you think you think and think you need by withdrawing faith in the temporal and transitory. What is eternal is valuable, as what is of time is valueless by definition. With regard to this world, Purpose is the only "value" that can be given faith if you would be God dependent.

Giving and receiving are one. One always receives EXACTLY what one asks for. The problem or confusion one may seem to experience in perception comes about from the belief in "manifesting," which IS the belief in "time." Eternity does not manifest, Being One forever. Manifesting is the belief that the Eternal can take form, that Infinity can become finite, that Spirit can enter matter. Awakening is the experience of forgiving the illusion of "manifesting," for What Identity Is is Spirit. Christ comes not into form, but Calls you "out of the world" to recognize your Self as Eternal Spirit.

Is there a willingness to release the idea of manifesting forever and experience Peace of Mind? This is the same as asking "Are you willing to accept your Self as God created You instead of trying to make yourself?" The belief in manifesting can be released for it is not true. Spirit can and inevitably must be accepted, for It is true. The belief in linear time is a defense against the holy instant, for time is but a denial of Eternity.

Beloved Child of God, you have been released of the grievance of time and there is no delay in what Your thoughts create instantly and forever. The belief in time and manifesting is an unwillingness to accept the Instant Answer Now, and one can only receive what one is willing to hear and see.

When one asks for a sign, or an outcome or for accountability or money donated – one asks amiss, for one is asking out of lack. When one has voluntarily released the beliefs in manifesting and time, one can then honestly ask: "God, what is Your Will for me?" Prayer is always answered according to what the mind is willing to receive. And in the deepest prayer of the heart you shall realize what is meant by the statement "My thoughts create eternally."

There is a difference between create and make, and a difference between extension and projection. Love creates; the ego makes. Love extends; the ego projects. In Love, being and having are the same. To the ego, possession and having are the same. In a world of lack, what you get is what you have. How utterly impossible is manifesting/getting and how absolutely true is Creation/Giving.

Reciprocity is a question of identity. Trust is the way out of the false belief in a worldly identity. It takes trust to change your mind so completely that you forget the concepts of time and manifesting forever. And happily it requires only willingness and not time. If you drop the "thought process" entirely you make way for the Vision of Christ. If this be your desire, the world of unreal effects will be shown to be causeless, and you will laugh at the thoughts that money or any image could be a real "source" or that the Holy Child of God "needs" anything. One's real thoughts create eternally, yet no thoughts of the past or future are real thoughts. The Stillness of Now is the Answer.

The Holy Spirit will direct your thoughts and actions very specifically if you allow Him. Give all concepts of money and manifesting and time to Him to use for His Purpose, and they shall be removed from your Holy mind. For You are Wholly Mind, and nothing of the world can ever BE understood. Who You are IS the Meaning.

Now everything is very, very simple. I make no demands, have never charged a fee for anything I share, do not command or confront, live in complete Divine Providence for everything without exception, go only when and where I am invited as Guided, make no attempt to convince anyone or change anyone's mind and am completely affiliated with Spirit. I live in the Present Moment and let the Spirit Give all that I experience.

I call this God dependence. It works. It also requires lots of mind training to listen to only One Voice, the Voice for God. The benefits are immediate and wonderful. I am with you all the Way beloved One.

The Ladder of Prayer – More on Manifesting

Hi David,

Since I began my journey back up the ladder, there are obviously things I do not understand. Hoping you can clarify something for me. To manifest something that you want, two things must be true: 1) It must be what you really, really want. 2) It needs to be in accordance with God's Will because God wants for us what we really want. Right?

Sometimes though, I feel like I am really asking for what I want, but I still do not get it. Does this mean that I am not in touch with what I really want or is it really what I want and I just do not have the necessary faith to make it happen? I am unclear about this.

Beloved One,

God's Will is for perfect happiness, though this is Abstract and only forgiveness reflects God's Will in this world. This prayer is for the Big Picture. The Holy Spirit gives nothing that would delay the Awakening. Our Will is universal and cannot be content with form of any kind, yet while one believes in lack one's perceived needs are met by following the Holy Spirit and many whims, as such, are granted if they will not foster delay.

When you pray for our shared Purpose to be experienced, this is helpful. Purpose is not specific. Prayers for specifics are requests that the past be repeated in some desired form, and the goal is to see that the past is gone. Specific prayers seem to be "manifesting" and yet symbols can only represent the desires of the heart. The secret of true prayer is to forget the things one thinks one needs; this is our gift to the Holy Spirit. Then everything that is helpful appears in awareness effortlessly. This is how prayer is meant to work in the truest sense, until prayer returns to its formless state (a song of gratitude).

Trust Would Settle Every Problem Now

In the simplicity of Divine Providence everything is taken care of through Inner Listening and following Guidance. Whatever is offered in Christ's service is received as well in Christ's service. The healed mind makes no demands and therefore is under no demands. The healed mind is at peace and content with

What Is, and therefore has no need to confront anyone or anything. The peaceful state of mind is incapable of being challenged, for there is no threat to peace and the present moment has nothing to be vulnerable about. Time drifts by the Perspective of the forgiven world, and no stress or strain is possible in the present moment. Everything that is helpful in God's Plan is freely Given and freely Received. In trusting the Holy Spirit all perceived "needs" are easily met; no effort is required once the Holy Spirit's Purpose is accepted without exception.

The examples of Divine Providence which come to mind are Jesus, Buddha, Mother Teresa, Peace Pilgrim, and Saint Francis, to name a handful. They gave fully of the Spirit and allowed the Spirit to lead and direct the way and provide whatever was needed for their vocation on earth. They offered a state of mind freely. They lived simply and had very few material needs and wants. And reciprocity, for those who trust, is a thing of the past. They did not charge fees for the words they spoke. They had transcended the concept of reciprocity – of giving to get – for in Giving as God Gives there is nothing apart from the Giving. The Giving of Love is extending. Extending Love has no cost, no price, no rent, no wage, no cares, and no concerns. What is Provided comes freely without any strings attached.

In this world Divine Providence seems rare to impossible to the untrained mind, for reciprocity is learned and trust is unknown until it is developed. It is relatively easy for the ego to learn and accumulate skills, to learn how to do mundane meaningless tasks and participate in the economic dance of reciprocity. What takes initial effort is the willingness to open to God dependence – to listen and follow the Holy Spirit and let go of the pride and Self-sacrifice ideas such as "earning in return for work" and personally "making a living," for the mask of personhood is in need of undoing before the Light of Christ can shine through unrestricted.

Christ has no "job," Being Eternal Love. Christ pays no "dues," Being Whole and Complete. To know Thy Self as Christ it is only necessary to forgive or release the illusion of a self, of a world, of an identity that God did not create. As one advances in mind training one experiences that the Purpose of forgiveness entails the means and the end of happiness. St Augustine said, "Love and do what you will." Christ Calls to the sleeping mind: "Forgive and Be as You are." Identity as Christ is a creation of God and can only be remembered. Forgiveness simply removes the obstacles to the awareness of Love's Presence. Trying to "run the show" is tiring only because the ego is the one "trying." In Purpose, everything is given effortlessly. The Divine Ease is always the indicator as to the Divine Advisor the mind is following in the moment.

Relax. There is no need to keep trying so hard. Let go. It is easy to trust the Holy Spirit and difficult to try to "make a living" on "your own." If you find the world to be a struggle or a series of unending challenges and confrontations and problems, resign now as your own teacher. Let the Advisor Who Knows the Way guide and direct. Say and mean, "I will step back and let Him lead the way," and watch the dance with Happiness and Peace and Joy!

Divine Love has met and will always meet every human need as long as the perception of lack persists. And in Heaven there is nothing lacking. Relax in trust and watch the illusory "problems" dissolve away in Love. Darkness cannot even seem to exist in the Presence of Light. The world is upside-down and backwards; in forgiveness it is apparent that nothing of the world means anything. Pride is nothing. Personal achievement is nothing. Not one speck of the learning of the world offers the slightest bit of lasting Happiness. Seen from the forgiven world Perspective it is apparent that there is no world apart from thought, and conflict is forever gone from awareness.

I join You, Beloved One, in the Great Awakening to Life Everlasting. The Christ can never die or change or grow, Being forever One. It is easier to be One than to attempt to struggle against Oneness. The recognition comes with a sigh of Happiness and deep Peace.

All Glory to God for creating Christ as One with All Creation.

Speak on Forgiveness

Friend: Can you talk about forgiveness? Whatever you feel inspired to share on that topic would be wonderful.

David: Yes. It is a topic that is the central teaching of *A Course in Miracles*. To forgive is to release the ego. The world's view of forgiveness is to forgive what happened. The Course teaches that you forgive your brother for what he did not do. This is quite a radical dive into the true experience of forgiveness. In the Workbook of *A Course in Miracles* Jesus says, "The major difficulty that you find in genuine forgiveness on your part is that you still believe you must forgive the truth, and not illusions." W-134.3

At first when you read it you wonder what he is talking about. He is saying that the thoughts, the beliefs, and the perceptions that you seem to see and hear and feel and touch every day are part of this hallucination that in truth has not occurred. The biggest frustration that people feel with forgiveness is that they say or feel things like: *So and so was cussing and shouting; they did steal the money; they did murder the person.... Now what are we supposed to do? Bless them as if they are white as lilies and pure as snow when they did it?* In some cases there is "proof:" *I've got the evidence on video tape. What do you mean they did not do it? It is recorded, preserved for posterity.* But in Truth it did not occur. It is only this belief in linear time that seems to string together these persons, places, things and events. That makes it seem as if you have a real movie going on when actually it is just a bunch of shadows dancing on the screen that has no reality whatsoever.

The first step in forgiveness is to be attentive to your feelings. Your feelings are inroads to your thoughts and your thoughts are inroads to the beliefs. It is important to be attentive to all of these because in the end you have to empty your mind of everything you think you think and think you know as well as all of these beliefs that are underneath the thoughts.

> Simply do this: Be still, and lay aside all thoughts of what you are and what God is; all concepts you have learned about the world; all images you hold about yourself. Empty your mind of everything it thinks is either true or false, or good or bad, of every thought it judges worthy, and all the ideas of which it is ashamed. Hold onto nothing. Do not bring with you one thought the past has taught, nor one belief you ever learned before from anything. Forget this world, forget this course, and come with wholly empty hands unto your God. W-189.7

That passage ends with coming to God with open arms. It is an invitation into Divine Silence in which you rest in the present moment and let go of the past/ future collage of images; just sink into the Light within your mind.

Forgiveness as Jesus really intended it is the releasing of illusions. It is important to distinguish true forgiveness from a sense of false forgiveness which says: *This really happened, now how am I going to deal with it?* Once you have established the reality of error, the reality of images, you are stuck trying to figure out how you are going to dispel "reality." This is an impossible thing. Learn to recognize that this world is an impossible situation. Without judging it or trying to analyze, fix or figure it out—rest deep within and watch it. See it for what it is; you can see the false as false and then let it go. That is a summary of forgiveness.

What it means to Decide for the Light

Friend: Is forgiveness about focusing on the Light, or is it a process of looking at the negative and see it for what it is – nothing?

David: When you join with the Light, the whole purpose is to look at the false and look past it. To forgive or overlook, that is really where the two come together, in a sense they are one and the same. Jesus says things like: *Take my hand, dear little child, we will go down and look at this dark stuff.* These are metaphors for joining with the Light. It is not about just looking at the negative intellectually.

Friend: What would you look at the negative with? You look with the Light. How would you be able to look at it if it was not with the Light? One decision seems to be to just turn to the Light and one decision seems to be turning to the Light with my individual intellect.

David: Let's come back to the metaphysics in this way. We are making a decision to decide with the Holy Spirit or the ego every instant. Those are our only two options and there are not any other. It seems like there is a "me" that can just make a decision without the Holy Spirit or the ego. But that is not the case. Jesus is very clear about that in the *Rules for Decision* section in Chapter 30. Your range is limited; you are choosing for one or the other. Every decision that you make brings you everything or nothing, even though it does not seem that way. It seems like there is a lot of gray area in between, like you are just floating along, saying: *Well, I will do this today or I will do that.* It seems like you can decide to have a brownie. But the whole point is that at the very bottom of the dungeon is the ego and Holy Spirit – way down in the mind. And, remember, a decision is a conclusion based on everything you believe. It is the Holy Spirit or the ego; they are your only two options.

What happens with all the layers of false beliefs? The decision is made way down here in the basement and then it comes out on the surface. *I believe I am subject to space and time. I believe in bodies. I believe I am a man. I believe I live in Cincinnati, Ohio. I believe I have a cat. I believe I am low on money. I believe it is Thursday. I believe it is 12:30 and....*

Friend: And I believe I have to have a brownie. [laughter]

David: I have to have a brownie! You see how it goes? No, no, no, you are making a decision from the ego or the Holy Spirit and that is the way it comes out on the surface. Now you have my attention, Jesus! "I will not value what is valueless." W-133 Everything you decide upon brings you everything or nothing. In that lesson (133) he gives you criteria you need to learn that will help you distinguish between what is valuable and what is valueless. This is getting pretty practical! He says that when you choose *anything*, unless it is *eternal*, it brings you nothing.

Friend: Oh, my goodness!

David: Yes.

> First, if you choose a thing that will not last forever, what you chose is valueless. A temporary value is without all value. Time can never take away a value that is real. What fades and dies was never there, and makes no offering to him who chooses it. W-133.6

And this is the first criteria! This is the first one! This is not number five or six! Then you read on and see there is something to this. All idols, all specialness, and all those layers and stacks in between that the mind invests in; that is where the guilt comes from. A clear mind has gone down through all the layers and levels. Jesus has transcended the ego and can see that the ego offers nothing. Not on floor 23 or 22, not in the closet! Nothing! There is nothing there that is valuable! Then you can see the choice for what it is. *This is no choice!* When you can get to the bottom then you can see that this is no choice at all. The Atonement is basically accepting a decision that has already been made. The Holy Spirit is really the only decision. There is no deprivation involved in that. But until you get to the bottom, oh boy, does it seem like sacrifice! Because I want what is on floor 23 and floor 9 down that hall, and in room 7, that one ... I call it the corral. *Here you go Jesus, you can have all those, but not these over here.*

Friend: But that is why it is a process?

David: It is a process until you start to generalize or transfer the training. We always talk about the main switch. The Course says in one instant you can choose ... perhaps today! There comes a point where you get so good at recognizing backward thoughts. You get so good at realizing that *the sun is not making me hot and that person did not make me angry.*

Friend: But you do not begin there.

David: No, you do not start there at all. In fact, when you are teaching a class with newcomers you do not even get into that, because you do not want to get into hypotheticals. That is why we are here now; we are here to go in as deeply as we can. Even with some of ideas we discussed you may think: *Maybe some of these are true but I still have my reservations.* It is like we are throwing out lots of seeds. It is not saying everyone has to take these seeds and everyone has to go home and plant them.

Friend: No one is guilty for not gathering up the seeds.

David: Just throwing out the seeds is the joy of it!

Beyond the "Image" is Abstract Light

Hi David,

Can you please explain the phrase: *We cannot even think of God without thinking of a body?* When I think of my brothers it seems their body separates and I find them with me and Jesus, sitting together looking at what is going on with us as bodies.

Beloved One,

Thanks for writing. When the mind seemed to fall asleep and forget the Abstract Light of Heaven, the ego projected a cosmos of specifics as a substitute for Divine Abstraction.

To the mind that believes it is in time-space, Abstraction has been completely forgotten or blocked from awareness. All that the deceived mind perceives is forms and specifics; this is why it cannot think of God without thinking of a body.

After the great amnesia, form became the "known" and the Abstract Light of Heaven became the "unknown." Forgiveness turns the mind back toward the Light and returns the experience of causation to the mind, which alone is causative.

The symbol of bodies together is a stepping stone, for truly bodies cannot join.

It is the Purpose of the Holy Spirit in the mind which is the joining; it is this Purpose that sustains peace of mind. With this Purpose comes the happy dream, for one dreams softly of a sinless world in a unified perception. The tapestry is one; all is well.

Questions and Answers on the Holy Spirit

Friend: Is there a specific technique you teach people on how to hear the Holy Spirit?

David: It is not so much a specific technique in the sense that the Holy Spirit's curriculum is highly individualized. There are so many different meditation techniques, tools, paths, etc. When I am asked: "Give me something specific that I can do to hear the Holy Spirit," or "How can I hear the Holy Spirit's voice," the short answer is to point to ACIM just because it is the path that I used and it was successful. I also studied many other paths and was well read and very open-minded about many teachers and techniques, but in the end it was ACIM that came to me. It was dropped in my lap. It was in English instead of Aramaic or Latin. It did not have to be re-translated. It was in a language that involved psychology, religion and Christianity.

Since I spent ten years studying in college and graduate school I was well versed in education. Terms like "curriculum" and "learning goal" were very familiar. It is perfectly delivered for me; it is a "how-to" book with a Text, Workbook, and Manual for Teachers. I have absolutely no excuses. So when people ask me specifically, I point them to the text of ACIM where Jesus says *study this text!* He told Helen and Bill, "I am giving it to you but you must study the notes." For me it was the same. Study the Text and then do the Workbook lessons. The Workbook is very explicit and has specific instructions. It has daily instructions on what to do, how to do it and how long to do it. It also has the Teacher's Manual for when you get to the point of really starting to hear the Holy Spirit's voice. There are helpful pointers there as you begin to fine-tune your learning and listening instrument.

That is my short answer as to how I hear the Holy Spirit's voice. I just point to the Course. The Course is not for everyone. But for those that feel the Course is their path, whatever language they are reading it in, I just say, "Hang in there with that Text, Workbook and Manual for Teachers."

Friend: *A Course in Miracles* says that only a few can hear the Holy Spirit or God's Voice. What is your take on that statement?

David: Within the realm of time and space where we seem to have a cosmos of billions of people, creatures and beings, countless other galaxies and solar systems—within that larger context, the relative context—I would say that there are very few that hear God's Voice. The distortions of the ego seem to be layers and layers of overlays that prevent a perfectly clear expression of the Holy Spirit through individuals.

I will use the example of Helen Schucman who took down *A Course in Miracles*. The dictation process took about seven years. It was not the dictation itself or the receiving that was difficult, but the ego resistance to hearing this message was enormous. So we have Helen who is a good symbol of very high scribal ability, yet it was still a seven-year process that could have possibly taken a year or a year and a half without enormous resistance. Frequently with this process the words were given and written down with short-hand dictation and even then there were distortions with what was received, in which case she was guided to make changes.

This shows that even for someone who had such a high scribal ability that she could hear the voice of Jesus Christ coming through – there were still ego distortions and ego interferences. They were really based on the fear of love which is what the whole ego realm is about. It took a very careful going back and going through it with Jesus to come up with what we call the Urtext, which was then edited and came to be the Hugh Lynn Cayce version. It was further edited to what is now the published version of *A Course in Miracles*.

You can see that this is a seeming process in terms of hearing the voice of the Holy Spirit, and that it is fairly accurate in the relative sense that very few can hear it. But the Holy Spirit uses many, many different symbols, and all kinds of sights and sounds. You can read words that are inspired from the Holy Spirit. They may show up in a novel, on a bumper sticker or on a billboard – just at that moment when you need to hear it most. You could have symbols, for example songs that just come; you feel the inspiration and you know just what to do after listening to a song on the radio that just happens to be playing when you get in the car. It could be little nudges from people ... your brothers and sisters talking to you just when you are in that struggling moment – giving you the answers through them voicing the very thing you need to hear. The Holy Spirit has countless ways to reach the mind. It should not be discouraging that very few can directly hear the voice for God, the voice of the Holy Spirit; you must remember that the Spirit can reach you in many ways if you truly desire it and are open and willing to hear and proceed.

Friend: When you started hearing this Voice, what within you helped in such a way that you started hearing that Voice in a clear way?

David: I would say that first of all it seems to contrast the human experience, which is full of so many upsetting, sorrowful and painful experiences. You might say that within me there was a feeling that there must be an answer to this, there must be an end, there must be a better way, there has to be a way out of this way of feeling; there has to be a way out of this way of thinking and perceiving. So the impetus was there. The motivation for a change of tune, a change of purpose, was very, very strong. The other thing was that before I was hearing the Holy Spirit clearly, I was intuiting the Holy Spirit. I was feeling intuitions and impulses and promptings that felt very wonderful. I would say that in the very beginning, before I was hearing the Holy Spirit's voice, I was feeling like someone had a feather in my heart chamber and was in there tickling my heart – the very core of my being. Initially, I thought: *Wow, this is not an intellectual experience. This is spectacular and I feel so good. The tickle is guiding me.* Initially, before it was: *Listen to the Holy Spirit* or *follow the Holy Spirit*, it was *follow the tickle* and I did. It got me into actually being able to hear the voice.

Friend: What do you tell people who ask you, "How do I quiet my mind? How do I get rid of this mind chatter? How can I get into that quiet place within?" How do you teach people to do that? What do you say to them?

David: There is an idea in the Course that really helped me. It was that when you find resistance high and dedication weak, do not fight yourself. T-30.I.1 This was a very helpful passage for me, particularly at the beginning of my work with the Course when I had extreme difficulty in quieting my mind for a sustained period. I would experience a lot of irritation and frustration, and then pray and open the book to a passage with a message like that, like, "do not fight yourself." I thought how wonderful a tool it is that is essentially saying *put the book down* rather than fighting yourself or trying to force your way through it. I think it is a very deep theme and topic.

I tried initially, in the parable of my life, to go off and live in the woods in a very simple way, with no running water and only bread and water to eat and drink. The ego resistance to the silence was enormous and it seemed initially like there was not a whole lot of success at reaching a consistent stillness. So I learned to relax and to just tune in with the Holy Spirit and ask, "OK what would you have me do here?" The guidance was not to just hang in with long hours of meditation. I was guided to go places and meet people. I started traveling and speaking with many different ACIM groups and instead of going at the ego through meditation and trying to do battle with it, I just decided to follow my joy. Then the sense of resistance started going down little by little as I did follow my bliss and got used to letting the voice for God speak through me. Years later I was guided to another hermitage experience where it was not a "trying" to be silent anymore; it was the silence of my natural Self just pervading my experience. It was like the silence found me instead of me trying to find the silence. That was so freeing. That would be my main advice for people. As you are trying to still your mind, be very gentle with yourself. Do not try to speed it up or force it. If you do—which is ego—there will be a sense of coercion, like you are being forced to do something that you really do not want to do. Come back and follow the Holy Spirit's intuition and prompts. That will gently guide you in.

Friend: I am curious as to what you think about the concept that in Truth there is no Father/Son/Holy Spirit; there is only One. I believe that the trinity gives us a framework and understanding so that we—in our present experience—can come to a more full experience that we are one with all that is. Does that make sense?

David: Yes, that is exactly it. People have talked for a long time about the trinity and have said that if there is only one and there is only perfect Oneness, then what is the need for a trinity? It is as you said. It is just a framework or structure to help the sleeping mind wake up. It is mainly in terms of functionality. God is the Creator and Christ or Son is Creation and Holy Spirit is the bridge to help the sleeping Son wake up to realize that *I am Christ, an Idea in the Mind of God. I am.* That is what this is all about.

Friend: What would you say is the biggest barrier to hearing God's voice and what is your advice for overcoming that barrier?

David: A lot of people report that they sometimes feel like there is static, or many voices. It is like trying to tune in to an FM station but you are between stations. You hear a lot of static and maybe even feel panic about that because you feel you need an answer. People feel or say: *Oh my God, I need an answer,* but this just makes the volume of the static go up. So I would say that the presence of fear is the biggest block to hearing the voice for the Holy Spirit because when the mind is in fear it is afraid of hearing the Holy Spirit's voice. As ACIM says, "No evidence will convince you of the truth of what you do not want." T-16.II.6 I have always kept in mind that I had to begin to really cultivate my wanting to hear and wanting to experience the Holy Spirit's use of symbols if I was really going to hear that voice consistently. So in short, fear is probably the biggest block to hearing the voice for God. And the answer to that is, of course, trust. Trust is the first of the ten characteristics of a Teacher of

God. He also says that when trust goes, all the rest goes. So you could imagine developing your characteristics and then getting into fear and losing your trust. In Christian terms they used to call this backsliding. With the Course, sometimes people do swing from being passionate about it—practicing it every day and working with it—to closing the book and locking it in the closet, swearing that they do not want to see it. They may flush it down the toilet, page by page, or throw it in the river.

Friend: How can people tell the difference between the Holy Spirit and the ego—or the Holy Spirit and their own voice? It seems to be a question that is repeatedly asked and I would love to hear your thoughts on that.

David: That is probably one of the most often-asked questions. I call it a question of discernment: discernment between the voice of the ego and the Voice of the Holy Spirit. It is a lesson in discernment. What was really helpful for me was when Jesus said that the one right use of judgment is to see how you feel. T-4.IV.8 That got my attention. When I read the first part of that statement my ears perked up. *The one right use of judgment* … wow. I am ready to let go of judgment and he is saying "the one right use." I would say the clearest, most straightforward, simple way is to really, really practice being in touch with how you feel. Of course there are many subtleties to this because if you have a lot of distractions going on and your mind seems to be very scattered and not really pointed in attentiveness, then you may seem to have an upset, an irritation, or an annoyance that goes unnoticed for quite some time and grows into anger and maybe even into rage before it gets your attention. But the more you get attentive to the mind and your thoughts, through mind training, the more you are able to pay attention and notice that upset, which is a clear indication that you are in alignment with the ego and wrong-minded perception and thinking.

In terms of distinguishing the voice of the Holy Spirit from your own voice: In the ultimate sense, since the Holy Spirit speaks for the Christ, which is your own self, the voice of the Holy Spirit is always your voice because it always knows your best interests in every perceived situation you seem to be in. It knows your best interests with anything you may be dealing with. The Holy Spirit is your own voice because you are created by God, and the Holy Spirit speaks for God.

In terms of sounding like a voice, it can sound many different ways. It can feel like a stream of consciousness, like a stream of thoughts, or it can have an audible quality to it. Many people who do not hear it consistently will say they have had moments when they were driving the car and they heard an audible voice saying "change lanes," and they paid attention and avoided what seemed to be an automobile accident. There are many ways that you can hear it. I would say that some people hear it as a sound that sounds like their own speaking voice. Others hear it as a masculine or feminine voice or as the voice of a young or elderly man or woman. But we must remember that these are all just forms and you are mainly paying attention to content, not to the form that it comes in. That is probably the most straightforward way I could say it.

Discernment is a very core topic; the way out of faulty perception is to tune into that voice and hear it clearly and consistently. That is the purpose behind everything I do. The purpose behind our lives is really to come to that discernment.

Friend: It seems like a lot of people worry that ego is going to somehow trick them into believing it is the Holy Spirit. Is that possible?

David: The definition of the ego is the belief in separation. The ego is self-deception and you might say that the ego's voice *is* trickery. All of the cosmos was made as a trick where figures seem to come and go. And all of what seems to be linear time – objects and figures moving in and out of awareness – are part of a trick, or sleight of hand, as Jesus calls it. It sounds almost like a poker game, but it is a trick.

As you go through discernment exercises it will seem like there are times when you follow the voice in your mind and it seems to lead you down a dead-end road or to a state of upset; but actually I think it is simpler to think of it as you just choosing your state of mind moment by moment. Every moment is a clean, fresh opportunity to choose again. That keeps it very simple and keeps it out of guilt. If you start looking at your life and your linear experiences and start analyzing them and saying: *I must have been tricked here and there,* you get into analyzing the past and trying to figure out the future. Those are always defenses against the present moment.

Friend: There are lots of questions asked about how to maintain the awareness of God and have some peace amidst what seems to be chaos. Can you speak to this?

David: Yes, a very often-asked question is: *How do I do this in the midst of work or chaotic situations?* At the beginning, I think you do the best you can. It is important to start the day very firmly open and connected by doing your Workbook lessons or by having quiet time and communing with the Holy

Spirit and asking for instructions. It may be walks in the woods or by the ocean. The more you start to fine-tune this, the more you may be guided to longer stretches of what seems to be silence, even in terms of the world's definition. As you move along this path, there may even be times when you are guided to go for a hermitage experience or for a longer retreat. It will look like finding quiet spaces and quiet times. Even this is just a phase because peace of mind is not circumstance-dependent, so you may find yourself sailing across the ocean-blue thinking: *This is it. I have finally left the world behind. I just have to live on the ocean.* That is not where this is leading, but those moments and periods of time can be very, very helpful and extremely nurturing as you go much deeper on the spiritual journey.

Friend: Now that you do not have the experience of having a split mind, do you ever find yourself talking to Holy Spirit anymore? Do you find yourself looking for guidance or is that not necessary? Do you just know in the present moment that all is well and will unfold as it should?

David: That is a very good question. Now when I seem to call on the Holy Spirit in prayer, it is more like asking a rhetorical question. It is not a real question but it is being used as a teaching device. For example, when I say a prayer and call upon the Holy Spirit's help in a group, it is really a symbol of being open to receive guidance. There is a sense of merging; I am identified with the Voice. It is actually not so much like the early days, where I was asking and receiving; it is more like a flow, almost like being carried in the river, where you are merged with the river. I am just enjoying the hum, or the flow, of all of life.

In terms of asking for specifics, that was again a very helpful phase for me. When you get into this state of seeing that all things work together for good, then that asking starts to fade away; it gets used in terms of rhetorical kinds of questions that are teaching devices. In ACIM, for example, Jesus seems to ask many questions even though the Christ mind is certain. Those questions are used as part of the teaching tool, as a model for a way of showing that it is helpful to ask questions and rely on the Spirit until a state of certainty is achieved or experienced. So it does feel like that. When questions are asked or guidance is sought as part of a group prayer, then that is just a symbol for me. There is not a two-ness there of asking a question and then waiting for this separate voice to give an answer.

Friend: So when the ego falls away there is a transition from seeking guidance to *being* it and watching the unfolding?

David: Exactly. I had a friend who visited many years ago. At first she had great difficulty in hearing the Holy Spirit and being in touch with her intuitions. Then, with a lot of practice with the Course – using movies and many meditation practices – she would hear the voice speak to her and direct her on specific things like what movies to watch and what job to take and so forth. Then she went through a phase after that where she was panicking because she would ask for help and would hear nothing. She was panicking because she thought she had almost blown it and disconnected from the Holy Spirit. At one point I laughed and said, "Silence is a wonderful gift." She looked at me in surprise. I can think of no greater gift than the stillness of God's presence. She was kind of assuming that the Holy Spirit should be chattering away all day to her if she were successful, and that when she was just having these quiet moments with no chattering going on, she was failing. A tranquil mind is no small gift. When you do have these moments you do not have to get into a panic state. You need not expect that the Holy Spirit should be speaking and giving lectures and sermons; just enjoy the stillness. That is where it all leads, to the silence and the experience where the voice for God is suddenly resting along with you, as you.

Friend: Can you clarify the difference between God and the Holy Spirit and why we cannot communicate directly with God?

David: God is abstract Love and Light. You might say that the term communion would apply to God in the sense that it is being in an experience of total oneness with God. Jesus expressed this through the words, "I and the Father are one;" a communion experience where there seems to be a creator and a creation. There seems to be a Father and a Son, a source and an effect of that source, but actually it is just one happy song of total Creation. That is a description – even though it is beyond description – of God and Heaven.

In terms of communicating with God, the Holy Spirit is the bridge. In other words, God reveals God to us through the Holy Spirit, and the Holy Spirit seems to take on the form of a voice for those that believe they have separated from God – the sleeping Son of God. He has to reach the sleeping Son of God in a way that can be understood. Since this is a cosmos of time and space and specifics, then that abstract light has to take the form of a voice. In Heaven, or abstraction, there are no voices. Everything is perfectly Known and you might say that there is a telepathic experience of perfect oneness and union. Abstraction seems to take the form of a voice for God and that is how the Holy Spirit is described in ACIM, not as the voice of God, which would imply that God has a voice. Abstraction does not even have a voice but the voice for God is the voice that speaks and represents God to a mind that has fallen asleep and needs help and instruction to return back to that awareness of perfect Oneness.

Friend: How would you describe the Holy Spirit's response to the ego?

David: I think the line "Forgiveness merely looks, and waits, and judges not," W-pII.1.4 is appropriate. There is a presence that is so peaceful and so tranquil and joyful. It is just certain in what is real and what is true. In one sense you can say that the Holy Spirit and the ego really have no meeting point. It is like light and darkness. You cannot have a room that has both in it. If the light is on, the darkness is gone. If it is pitch dark, then there is an absence of light. These are two thought systems that have no meeting point whatsoever. You might say that metaphorically speaking, the Holy Spirit overlooks error. That still implies that the error is there, but the Holy Spirit is good at overlooking it.

In *The Song of Prayer*, Jesus tells us to not see error. The first time I read that I was like: *Oh my God, do not see error?* What a state of mind is that where it is impossible to see error? You become so riveted in the truth that the error disappears entirely. "The truth is true," T-14.II.3 and "only the truth is true." W-66.10 That is what this is all aimed at. You get into such bliss and happiness and joy that there is not a sense of first discerning or experiencing the error and then releasing it and coming into the Light. You literally experience that the truth is all-encompassing. You need to put the purpose out front. It is only the ego that looks back and then tries to judge the situation. But when you hold the goal out front you will see everything that you perceive as witness to the purpose that you hold.

Put the peace out front. This was extremely helpful for me. In fact, when I was working with the Course in the early days I would say the prayer, "I am here only to be truly helpful." T-2.V.A.18 I would recite that whole prayer silently in my mind every time I would walk through a doorway, whether I was going to the grocery store or to *A Course in Miracles* meeting or to the laundromat, or wherever. It would really help me set the goal so that as I went into that grocery store I was in a state of humbleness, willing to be truly shown how to be truly helpful, to not prejudge the experience or have any agenda. For example, it was not to have preconceptions about how fast to get in and out, to look for the best prices, or to try and read through all the ingredients on the packages in order to get the most nutritious ones. It was to actually go in there with the goal—to have only holy encounters with everything and everyone— set in front. And when I actually started to practice that, I had so many miraculous and joyful experiences that I said, "Wow! This is very important and extremely practical." Just that shift of practicing brought me wonderful miracles that helped me gain confidence in practicing ACIM.

Friend: What would your experience be if you saw someone standing in front of you maybe yelling at the person next to them?

David: The words that come to mind are "unified perception," which is all things working together for good. When you have a single purpose, then all the images are unified and all the sights and sounds are unified. Smells and other perceptions that seem to be physical are all part of this unified experience. I experience the whole situation like a tapestry where I am simply flowing with Spirit and knowing that all things are working together for good. In one sense, that is what unified perception gives you. It takes away all the judgments and the preconceptions that would break the situation apart into separate behaviors and separate symbols. It just gives you a unified experience, even though here the Holy Spirit can speak about these things as if there were separate reactions and experiences. That is what the joy of enlightenment is. It is no problem. There is just happiness.

Friend: Do persons awaken? I do not think there are that many people in this moment that are actually awake. I think there are millions of people that are in the process, working it, practicing it, going through it, and yet I have not seen many people pop out the other side. Yet to have even a couple of people in my life where I can see that has occurred is really a blessing, so thank you. It is really incredible.

David: As we are going through the process we are grateful for all the signs and symbols – the Buddhas and Krishnas, Jesus and the mystics and the saints that seem to be sprinkled throughout history. We are so grateful for them. And the more you apply the teachings of the Course, the more you realize that it is just one mind waking up and recognizing itself. As Jesus says: *When I awoke you were with me.* He says it another way in the *Manual for Teachers*, "How many teachers of God are needed to save the world? The answer to this question is – one." M-12.1 One! That answer is amazing. There is one mind and there is only one of us and we are all the Christ. When people talk about awakened beings and say that Jesus was awakened, I remind them that Jesus the man was an illusion. That is quite a striking statement for many. I would say that persons do not really awake. It is just that the mind that was dreaming it was a person, realizes that it was mistaken. It is quantum physics. There is a big turn-around here.

Friend: In the world it looks like the hundredth-monkey syndrome, but it is really the one-monkey syndrome?

David: That is right; the one monkey sees that it is not a monkey.

Friend: You said earlier that the Holy Spirit is our own voice and the more we listen to it and spend time with that voice and experience it, the more we really do start to identify it as ourselves. That is the greatest news ever.

David: Yes, but do not step ahead of yourself. He says in the *Development of Trust* section of the *Manual for Teachers* that the Teacher of God has not yet come as far as he thinks. You hear *Not my will but Thine be done.* When you are starting out, that seems to be a great technique in the mind for surrendering to something that is greater than yourself. Then you read the Course and Jesus says that your will and God's will are the same. You are One. All of a sudden the old quote starts to seem funny. You think, *Oh yeah, God's will is my will and the voice for God is my true voice!* But at the early stages of mind training these seem like arrogant statements; they do not seem appropriate at all. Once you get into advanced mind training and you are feeling the peace of God, statements like, "I and the Father are one," and, "My will and God's will are one," seem very, very natural.

Reviewing the Idea of Karma

Hi David,

Can you talk about karma? People say different things. Someone said, "Even after awakening, there is still karma of the body." Does karma equal cause/effect? Then this whole hallucination, the belief in separation, is the karma. But even then, when there is a so-called "awakening," the body is still hanging out. It does not disappear. And sometimes it still hurts or sneezes or eats or sleeps. I really do not understand. Do you?

Beloved One,

Thanks for looking deeply at this universal law of mind. It has been written: "As you sow, so shall you reap," "Giving and receiving are the same," "What goes around comes around," "Cause and effect are one and there is no gap." This one universal law of mind has seemed to bring harm and destruction to the mind that seems to sleep and dream of a separate world of unreality. Yet this one universal law is the key to forgiveness. If you realize that you always choose your state of mind and that what you choose, you choose for the whole universe, the belief in victimization has been undone.

Misuse of a divine law seems to result in miscreation until the realization dawns that in Truth it is *impossible* to misuse or miscreate. What God creates is Spirit, and Spirit creates only Spirit. If you follow this divine logic, then there is the experience of Enlightenment: Truth is True. Love is Real. Nothing real can be threatened. Nothing unreal exists.

The body was a symbol of a separate self that could never be. The enlightened mind sees the tapestry of the forgiven world in which no object or specific exists "in and of itself." Illusions are one, thus the illusion of a "body" and the illusion of a "time-space cosmos" are the same illusion. In forgiveness there is nothing that is "still hanging out," for perception has integrated and is whole. There is nothing outside the mind and the cosmos reflects the Light of Heaven. Only a blessing remains and distortion has gone.

Since karma is a universal law, the only meaningful question is, "What is it for?" Will you use karma to demonstrate that healing is accomplished or to maintain the wish to be separate? The first use is inevitable and the second use is impossible. It is best to accept the inevitable and release the attempt to make the impossible possible. Such is simplicity, for Enlightenment is simple.

In Heaven, God and Christ, Cause and Effect are One. From the Holy Spirit's perspective, mind is unified and cannot be broken apart. The law of karma can therefore release or imprison the mind based upon the mind's use of this universal law of mind. Purpose is the only choice. Which purpose would you have it serve: love or fear? When you align with the Holy Spirit, your Answer is Love. And the experience which comes from aligning with God is so obvious that you will never doubt again.

Is it Possible to Reconcile Evil and Abuse with Innocence?

Hi David,

I have a couple of questions. I have studied ACIM and went through the Workbook once eight years ago, although I read the book on a regular basis.

I have found myself resisting some of the principles, so I am studying the Text and going through the Workbook again. Suddenly, ACIM teachings are affecting me differently. However, I understand that we must see the innocence in our brother and that evil is only of this world. Although I understand it, I find it hard to truly accept. How can you see the innocence in a man who has beaten and raped you? How can you give "tough love" to an individual who is hopelessly addicted to drugs and alcohol without being an enabler? You see, these are the areas where I feel blocked.

Could you help me understand why there is no opposite to God, to Love? In the Course, is the devil merely a synonym of perception of the ego? If God does not see evil, does that mean we have to accept rapists, pedophiles, and murderers without judgment? Please help me understand this.

Blessings Beloved One,

Thanks for sharing your inner ponderings. Your questions go to the heart of the matter called forgiveness. I have been told by the Holy Spirit that God is All-Loving, All-Knowing, and All-Powerful. God is a God of Pure Love. This description of God is an expression of the idea: God is Love and Love has no opposite. What God creates is like God. Spirit comes from Spirit. God is Spirit. Christ is Spirit. Creation is Spirit. Innocence is an attribute of Spirit, just as Perfection and Eternity are attributes of Spirit. If evil or error were possible, Divine Innocence would be impossible. Yet because Divine Innocence is Reality, evil or error cannot be at all. Forgiveness is for illusion, not for the Truth. Love does not need to be forgiven. In the Oneness of God there is nothing to forgive. Nothing God creates needs forgiveness, for Creation and Christ are like God in Spirit and extend God's Perfection. Forgiveness recognizes that what you think your brother has done has in Fact never happened.

In the Course, it is stated this way: "If God is real there is no pain. If pain is real there is no God." W-190.3 God is the Source of All; pain is therefore causeless and impossible. If there were an imposter "cause"—a claim made against the fact of the Allness of God's Love—that cause/error would need to be released *because* the error would be the denial of Divine Love. This is why you are drawn to *A Course in Miracles*; you have not been able to reconcile Love with fear, Truth with illusion, or Innocence with guilt. These seeming opposites can *never* be reconciled. To forgive is simply to accept the happy fact that Truth is true and nothing else is true.

To forgive is to happily release the belief in an opposite to Love. To forgive is to find the Innocence of Spirit. As the error of separation is forgiven, you humbly accept, "I am still as God created Me." W-rVI.in.3 You asked, "Is the devil merely a synonym of perception of the ego?" Yes.

The ego/error/devil was corrected by the Holy Spirit the instant the error seemed to arise. And now your only responsibility is to accept this Correction. What you believe you will perceive, as long as perception seems to last. Believe the error and you will seem to perceive abuse and addiction. Accept the Correction and you will seem to perceive a forgiven world shining in the Light of the Holy Spirit. Accept the Correction and you have given up the attempt to reconcile "opposites." Accept the Correction and lasting peace is the only possible result. Accept the Correction and see the impossibility of concepts such as "rapists, pedophiles, and murderers."

This is the Last Judgment: *Holy are You, Eternal, Free, and Whole, at Peace forever in the Heart of God.* Where is the world in this Loving Judgment? The world has ended in Laughter, for what seemed to be a world apart from God was attempting to take serious a silly, mad idea of separation. Once the past is released it is as if it never was, BECAUSE it never was.

You are not alone and Help is Given you. This message, the Awakening Mind website, the many Awakening-In-Christ messages, the travels and the gatherings are just some of the many witnesses to the Love you have Called forth in your awareness. The Joy I share heralds the end of illusion! The peace I experience is the peace that comes from acknowledging that Love is real and has no opposite.

The Bible said to have no graven images before God. This is because God knows no images, Being Pure Spirit. Forgive the images that never were, and experience indescribable Happiness! The dreamer of a dream first realizes the dreaming. Nothing can hurt the dreamer once the Holy Spirit has revealed the dream as unreal. Without judgment all dream figures are the same, for it was only the ego that made up the categories of victim and victimizer, abused and abuser, enabled and enabler to perpetuate itself. Once the ego is released perception has been healed, and nothing blocks the way to the experience of God's Divine Love. All Glory to the Living God!

How Practicable is this for the Fully Employed?

Friend: You have said that you experience a consistent, gentle peace and a feeling of accepting all things exactly as they are. I recall that Jesus teaches that we are holding grievances whenever we want something to be different than it is. Would I be correct in guessing that you are fully comfortable doing only what is in front of you without one thought of what needs doing beyond the "now?" How practicable is this for students who are fully employed and raising a family?

David: This peace is a natural state of mind flowing from the release of the belief in the future (and therefore any attempt to plan it) and the release of the attempt to control anything in the world. Without expectations are all things equally acceptable. In letting all things be exactly as they are, there is a realization that while one is always responsible for one's state of mind, this responsibility does not include the ability to control situations, events, circumstances, persons, places, and things.

In other words, the script of the world is written; it is the past. The remaining choice rests in selecting either the ego's personal perspective of the script or the Spirit's gentle Perspective of forgiveness, appreciating the simultaneous whole. In your e-mail you are asking how practicable and how practical it is to just do what is in front of you in peace without a lot of thought about the future, particularly for a student with a family. I shall address this question and context from the Perspective of unlearning error and undoing the ego.

In ACIM, the insight is revealed that there was only one problem and that problem has already been corrected via the Holy Spirit. It is also revealed that one cannot recognize the Answer or Correction to the problem until the problem has first been recognized as it is. We are told that "only the now is real." This is very literally true; it is only the ego that sponsors the impossible belief that the "now" is wedged in between two very real "realities" called "past" and "future." The ego's linear view of time sees the future as different from the past—that is, what has gone before is not the same as what is yet to come—and breaks time into separate persons, situations, events, increments, and segments that can be ordered or arranged in a linear fashion. From the ego's distorted perspective, the fear and guilt of the past is repeated over and over and over again and there is no escape from the cycle. Yet the present moment is the only reality because it remains constant and completely untouched by the error of separation.

The present moment is so simple that it seems beyond the grasp of possibility for a deceived mind spinning in complexity. The world was merely a representation of an identity-confusion, thus the world was but a symbol of the deep seated belief that love and fear can co-exist. This belief was the problem and only in imagination was the impossible made to be perceived. The self-concept made to take the place of Reality must therefore be unlearned or undone for Christ's Vision to return to awareness. Christ's Vision is the present moment; perception was only the apparent darkness of images arranged in a line. The Holy Spirit sees the line as a point. The ego saw the point as a line. The Holy Spirit's Perspective sets you free. The ego's perspective seemed to imprison.

How practicable and practical is the Holy Spirit's Perspective? That depends on whether you desire freedom or imprisonment. The miracle collapses the belief in linear time and brings the fruits of peace, happiness, freedom, and joy. The linear personal perspective attempts to reinforce an impossible identity as a "reality." Surrendering to the Holy Spirit's Perspective has no cost whatsoever. There is absolutely no "price" to pay for peace of mind. It increasingly becomes evident that experiences of "trials and tribulations" come only in the attempt to resist and defend against the Holy Spirit's Perspective. Yet the Holy Spirit's Perspective is the Atonement or Correction; one's only responsibility is to accept the Atonement for oneself. That is the utter simplicity of salvation.

What about the student who perceives a family to take care of? Can such a student hope to accept the Atonement and awaken to Reality, or must the student aim for a less lofty goal? The question is not so much one of context or situation as it is a question of desire. The mind that made up the cosmos and perceives itself as existing in a dualistic linear time-space continuum is insane by definition. This false self-concept is unreal, and there are no degrees of unreality or hierarchies of illusion. Though some situations may seem more complex than others to the ego, it must be remembered that "situational thinking" is the problem. Only the ego's "situational thinking" produces a world in which separate situations seem to exist. Yet what but a gap of time and space appears to separate one situation from another? And if there were no gap, then there could be nothing but the whole. In other words, the Holy Spirit is the reminder that it is impossible to order and arrange illusory images no matter how many different arrangements they may seem to take, because there was but one illusion. And that illusion has already been Corrected.

Peter the apostle perceived himself as married with children when he was approached by Jesus. Yet he was called out of the world to follow the Christ within and proclaim the good news of the Kingdom of Heaven. Siddhartha left his father's palace and wife and child to seek the truth beyond the illusion of the birth-death cycle. Peter would later proclaim Jesus as "the Son of the Living God" and go forth preaching the gospel. Siddhartha became known as the Buddha—the enlightened one. This is the question you must ask yourself:

Did these men abdicate their responsibilities or did they seek to accept their one responsibility? As you ask this question, you shall be answered in your heart.

Trust would settle every problem now. Trusting the Holy Spirit is not determined by the situation in which a mind believes itself. Whatever the apparent situation, Help is available and accessible. The "little willingness" asked for by Christ to open to the Guidance of the Holy Spirit is not limited by circumstances. If there appear to be earthly responsibilities and commitments which have been made, they will be handled with the compassion and love of the Holy Spirit's Plan of forgiveness. This cannot be understood from a personal perspective, but be assured that all things work together for good. There are no exceptions, for under the Holy Spirit's teaching everyone must gain. There can be no loss.

A general rule of Guidance can be stated this way: Pray, listen to and follow the Holy Spirit. Do just what you are given to do and be open to the "I need do nothing" solution of the stillness within. Question and raise to the Light all beliefs and thoughts which obscure the Light from awareness. Bring the illusion to the Truth. Be willing to change your mind and accept yourself as Changeless Mind. And be not concerned with the form in which the lesson of forgiveness appears to come.

Does the Holy Spirit Actually do things in the World?

Hi David,

Does the Holy Spirit actually do things in the world?

Beloved One,

The forgiven world is the Perspective of the Holy Spirit. Look carefully at the phrases "in the world" and "in the dream," and be open to the realization that there is no world apart from mind. Ideas leave not their source, and the world has not left the mind that made it. What could "in the world" really mean?

There is no "objective world" which exists apart from mind. Quantum physics is a witness to the realization that it is impossible to remove the "experiment" from the "mind of the experimenter" just as it is impossible to remove the "observed" from the "mind of the observer." Nothing exists "by itself" in the Perspective of the Holy Spirit.

There is no world apart from your ideas because ideas leave not their source, and you maintain the world within your mind in thought. W-32.10

Here is Christ's description in ACIM of distorted perception or the "darkened glass" spoken of in the Bible. The following perception is NOT the forgiven world Perspective of the Holy Spirit:

> You live by symbols. You have made up names for everything you see. Each one becomes a separate entity, identified by its own name. By this you carve it out of unity. By this you designate its special attributes, and set it off from other things by emphasizing space surrounding it. This space you lay between all things to which you give a different name; all happenings in terms of place and time; all bodies which are greeted by a name.
>
> This space you see as setting off all things from one another is the means by which the world's perception is achieved. You see something where nothing is, and see as well nothing where there is unity; a space between all things, between all things and you. Thus do you think that you have given life in separation. By this split you think you are established as a unity which functions with an independent will.
>
> What are these names by which the world becomes a series of discrete events, of things ununified, of bodies kept apart and holding bits of mind as separate awarenesses? You gave these names to them, establishing perception as you wished to have perception be. W-184.1-3

The undoing of the belief that *mind* and *manifestation of mind* are different, that inner and outer are different, is the entire focus of the Workbook of ACIM. Remember, complete forgiveness (Atonement) is the only goal there is, and acceptance of this Correction is the *only* responsibility there is. It is impossible to pull a thread out of the tapestry of the cosmos, give it a name and a meaning, and set it apart as something that has meaning in and of itself. Forgiveness is the realization that mind is singular and has no levels or aspects or hierarchies of illusion. Wholeness has no parts. Divine Mind is One, and the Holy Spirit's Perspective (cosmos as one) reflects the Oneness of Heaven. Some examples of the Holy Spirit's teaching include:

Yet what is by itself? And what does "in itself" mean? You see a lot of separate things about you, which really means you are not seeing at all. You either see or not. When you have seen one thing differently, you will see all things differently. W-28.2

If you can accept the concept that the world is one of ideas, the whole belief in the false association the ego makes between giving and losing is gone. T-5.I.1

The idea for today, like the preceding ones, applies to your inner and outer worlds, which are actually the same. W-32.2

I am alone in nothing. Everything I think or say or do teaches all the universe. A Son of God cannot think or speak or act in vain. He cannot be alone in anything. It is therefore in my power to change every mind along with mine, for mine is the power of God. W-54.4

A movie projector/theater analogy may be helpful here. In the projector room, inside the projector, is this glowing, brilliant, radiant light. That is a great metaphor for the Holy Spirit. That brilliant light *seems* to pass through the film, which is filled with a lot of dark images. We will call these dark images "attack thoughts" or "ego thoughts." As these thoughts are projected, what seems to be produced on the theater screen are shadows. To the sleeping mind watching the movie, these shadows appear to have meaning. However, the only meaning the movie seems to have is given to it by the sleeping mind, which has forgotten that what it sees is just a movie. It has identified with figures on the screen and thought of itself as a person among other persons. The only meaning the dream of the world seems to have is given to it by the ego, which has forgotten Christ and has made up a substitute "reality" and "identity" to take the place of Heaven. It has identified with dream figures in the dream and thought of itself as a person among other persons.

The world perceived through the body's eyes and heard through the body's ears is a screen of images. The world is just the shadowy reflection of the attack thoughts in the deceived mind. If one becomes aware of these attack thoughts and is willing to let them be released, one is willing to clean the film up, so to speak, and let go of the judgments that block the light from awareness. Miracles entail the willingness to let the light shine without obstruction. When this happens, the screen is going to *seem* to light up more and more. The world will reflect the light in one's mind, for there is no world apart from mind.

As the mind lets go of the ego belief system of separation/distorted perception, it opens up to the Holy Spirit's Perspective, which reflects healed perception. This is a Perspective which reflects Love and Oneness and offers a whole interpretation of the cosmos. As the mind is now in accord with the Holy Spirit's Perspective, the cosmos is a moment of unified witness to Abstract Love. Thus, to experience that there is no world apart from mind is to be open to the remembrance of Abstract, Eternal Oneness, which has no opposite. Truth simply Is.

A sleeping mind has to be willing to give up judgment, or more accurately, see the impossibility of judgment. The reason a sleeping mind seems to experience hot and cold, pain and pleasure, sickness and health, war and peace, death and life and all the variations, degrees, and extremes of the world, is simply because of judgment.

Judgment breaks apart and fragments. Let me use the thought of unity as a contrast. Just think of the word "unity." One. Oneness. Union. An unbroken continuity. The circle is a great symbol of unity; no beginning, no end, no duality, just one. The deceived mind looks about the world, the world perceived through the body's senses, and experiences fragmentation and duality. How does one reconcile duality with unity? They are not reconcilable.

The Holy Spirit's function is to replace duality and misperception with healed or true perception – the bridge to Oneness. This function is already accomplished and need only be accepted as complete to be experienced as such. The Holy Spirit *seems* to infuse through the ego belief system, so to speak, and reach the sleeping mind in "what" and "where" and "when" it believes it is. Let's say that it *seems* to be questioning its beliefs about everything. Well, what is on the screen of perception is just a motion picture of those beliefs. It seems like there is still a person who continues to do things in linear time – that is the dream or the story. That is the false interpretation or misperception of One Christ Self as a person in the world. This person may say, "I seem to be getting more peaceful" or "I seem to be getting more upset." Do you see that that is simply a false interpretation? Who is the "I" that seems to be getting more peaceful? Who is the "I" that seems to be getting more upset? The "I" in these examples is just a false interpretation or misperception. Yet the right mind is the Perspective of the Holy Spirit, the Point of Clarity that experiences all as mind. The "individual" or "personal" misperception has dissolved away entirely in the Light of Love.

Time and process are the same illusion. The Holy Spirit *seems* to be judgmental in the deceived mind, which *seems* to undergo the "process" of sorting out the two thought systems: love and fear. Here's an example of how that *seems* to play out: One tunes in to the Spirit and is quiet. One wants so much to join with the Spirit and has a strong willingness. Thoughts that still involve form come to mind, thoughts to call so and so, to meet with someone, to leave this job, to take that job, etc.

Obviously, those thoughts are still form thoughts. But the Holy Spirit understands that the deceived, split mind still *believes* it is a person in a world. The false belief system takes the form of projected shadows on the screen of the world, an out-picturing of dark beliefs. The Holy Spirit is working with the mind (for mind is all there is) to let go of the false belief that *seems* to project a cosmos of time-space. And so the mind feels disoriented as it starts to loosen and to question these highly protected and defended false beliefs. *I am not so sure anymore that I am a wife or a mother or a man or a construction worker or an American, etc. I am not so sure what I am.* Symbolically, things still *seem* to be happening on the screen, but these are just the interpretations and misperceptions of the deceived mind about itself. The Holy Spirit is not working "in the world," but is working with the mind (for mind is all there is) that thinks it is in the world so it can first realize that it made up the world (that is, I have invented the world I see). Once the mind has released the attempt to project the error of separation outward—as a cosmos apart from it—it accepts the Atonement and realizes that there is nothing outside of mind.

Healed perception and Atonement are identical. Do you see how this is completely different from saying: *Spirit, come into the world and change the circumstances—find me a parking space, help me win the lottery, heal my body, etc.?* In Atonement, illusion has been brought to truth; darkness has been brought to light. It *is* error to retain the belief that the Holy Spirit can change an "objective" world that is "outside." When attack thoughts have been released, the awareness of wholeness (the forgiven world as all-inclusive mind) is apparent.

> There is no point in lamenting the world. There is no point in trying to change the world. It is incapable of change because it is merely an effect. But there is indeed a point in changing your thoughts about the world. Here you are changing the cause. The effect will change automatically. W-23.2

> In gentle laughter does the Holy Spirit perceive the cause, and looks not to effects. How else could He correct your error,

who have overlooked the cause entirely? He bids you bring each terrible effect to Him that you may look together on its foolish cause and laugh with Him a while. *You* judge effects, but *He* has judged their cause. And by His judgment are effects removed. T-27.VIII.9

The world you see is a vengeful world; everything in it is a symbol of vengeance. Each of your perceptions of "external reality" is a pictorial representation of your own attack thoughts. One can well ask if this can be called seeing. Is not fantasy a better word for such a process, and hallucination a more appropriate term for the result?

You see the world that you have made, but you do not see yourself as the image maker. You cannot be saved from the world, but you can escape from its cause. This is what salvation means, for where is the world you see when its cause is gone? Vision already holds a replacement for everything you think you see now. Loveliness can light your images, and so transform them that you will love them, even though they were made of hate, for you will not be making them alone.

The idea for today introduces the thought that you are not trapped in the world you see, because its cause can be changed. This change requires, first, that the cause be identified and second, that it be let go, so that it can be replaced. The first two steps in this process require your cooperation. The final one does not. Your images have already been replaced. By taking the first two steps, you will see that this is so. W-23.3-5

In summary, with regard to the false belief that the Holy Spirit does things in the world, I offer this: The ego is the belief in the concrete and specific and can *only* misinterpret the dream of the cosmos. Yet the Holy Spirit does not "come into" the world/cosmos. Truth does not come into illusions. The Holy Spirit shines away false belief as it is brought to or raised to Light. There is actually no "activity" or "doing" in forgiveness. Forgiveness calmly, passively shines, seeing the false as false:

Forgiveness, on the other hand, is still, and quietly does nothing ... It merely looks, and waits, and judges not. W-pII.1.4

> A miracle is a correction. It does not create, nor really change at all. It merely looks on devastation, and reminds the mind that what it sees is false. It undoes error, but does not attempt to go beyond perception, nor exceed the function of forgiveness. Thus it stays within time's limits. Yet it paves the way for the return of timelessness and love's awakening, for fear must slip away under the gentle remedy it brings. W-pII.13.1

The Holy Spirit thus works with the mind to entirely let go of the false belief system of ego. The ego is the interpretation of One Self as a body in a world external to the body, and thus it is the ego which attributes situations and events to Spirit, such as *Spirit found me a parking space* or *Spirit helped me to lose 20 pounds*. These interpretations are personal interpretations, as if the Holy Spirit was actually working with separate bodies, objects, events, and situations instead of with the sleeping mind, which believes in these specifics. The Holy Spirit (or Spiritual Eye, as in "Let thine eye be single") does not perceive the world the way it is perceived with the body's eyes. The forgiven world Perspective of the Holy Spirit is not personal at all, for It is all-inclusive and whole.

Why Guilt is Never Justified

God creates our Spirit Perfect and nothing can change what God creates. The mind seemed to fall asleep and believed in dreams of separation, though in Awakening there is only a State of Being One Love. Reality is perfection and innocence, though dreams of judgment seemed to bring fear and guilt and hatred. As judgment was laid aside, happy dreams came to replace the dreams of guilt.

All dreams of guilt were centered on the body, for such was the target of guilt. It is as if the ego demanded some "body" to change or act different or be a certain way or play a certain role. The ego was synonymous with guilt and advised that the source of its guilt could be found in the world. It could not, for guilt had no real source, no real basis, and no "body" was ever to blame. The seeming source was a false belief which had been given faith or assumed to be true. And the world of perception rested on this error. Yet forgiveness sees the error has gone.

Guilt was never the result of behavior, for behavior was only an effect or outcome. It was the attack thoughts believed to be real that were in need of release and not protection. Attack thoughts were referred to in the previous post as private thoughts, and these meaningless thoughts were what seemed to produce a meaningless world. Distractions and outlets of the world were designed to minimize the guilt without releasing it. Yet forgiveness is a doorway to true peace for it is the release of the error, the release of all attack thoughts. Forgiveness always gently reminds you that you cannot be unfairly treated. Why? Spirit is invulnerable and our Reality is only Spirit. The body seemed to be unfairly treated and seemed to treat unfairly only through the ego's lens. Yet innocence is seeing that the ego's lens was nothing but distortion and held not a shred of truth.

If ever the temptation seems to arise to feel guilty, remember that you are forever Created by a Loving God Who knows forever the Innocence and Perfection of Your Being. And in aligning with the Mind of God, Innocence is all that can BE experienced. There is no guilt in God, and God knows not of the ego concepts of guilt and punishment. And in our Sanity of thinking with God, we experience no guilt or fear or hatred. God is Love, and this Divine Love never changes or fades or disappears. It shines forever. As dark clouds are released, the ever shining Light now comes directly into awareness. This is natural, for Light is our natural State of Being.

I rejoice that guilt was never justified. I rejoice that forgiveness is always justified. For the Gift of the Spirit is the opening to remember the Spirit of the "I Am" Presence. The Gift is ours for the asking. I am very grateful for God's unconditional Love.

Destiny, Choice, Channeling and "I Need Do Nothing"

Hi David,

In *A Course in Miracles* Jesus at one point addresses a concept that he calls "the script is written" where he says that there is nothing that can be done to "speed up" our Atonement. He says that it is written that at a certain time we will simply awaken – regardless of what we think, do, or do not do. Can this be so? I kind of get the impression that we could decide this instant on the Atonement and it would happen. But maybe it was written that I should decide this instant?

If nothing we think, say, or do makes any difference one way or the other, it seems like a waste of time and money to continue with this spiritual quest. Can we hear your take on this?

I am kind of confused about a perception I am having and hope you can shed some light on it. There are several people that say they channel Jesus. I have never heard you contradict the Course, but these other fellows do *seem* to contradict it. In my latest discovery, one has written that there is *absolutely* nothing that can be done to assist in our Awakening. He says that it is predetermined exactly when it will happen. The Course, on the other hand, tells us in several places that we are saving time through its help. Now I realize that these guys and the Course and everything are all illusion, but I thought the Holy Spirit used illusion to assist us in our quest.

Now either these guys are wrong or the Course is wrong, because they contradict. My question is: Is it possible that ego could be trying to undermine my faith in the teaching of the Holy Spirit by presenting me with conflicting teaching that is reportedly all coming from the same place? Am I being deliberately misled or have I simply misunderstood something? If there is nothing that can be done at all to hasten our awakening, what is the spiritual search all about? What is the Course for?

Beloved One,

Ahhhhh! You have come upon the DEEPEST teaching on Being Awake! You are the One Now, and nothing of linear time that seems to be thought, said, done, or imagined has anything to do with our Eternal Oneness. This teaching is the Experience to which the Course points. This is the holy instant!

There is truly nothing to be "done" to prepare for It. Simply desire It wholly and It is Experienced Instantly. Remember Christ has called this a journey without distance to a goal that has never changed. Remember the instruction in the *I Need Do Nothing* section:

> You *are* prepared. Now you need but to remember you need do nothing. It would be far more profitable now merely to concentrate on this than to consider what you should do. T-18.VII.5

There are passages in the Text, the Workbook, and the Manual for Teachers that point directly to the holy instant, for the mind that is willing. In the timeless moment, the holy instant, there are no contradictions. Cause and Effect are together, and thus there is no gap between them. What does this mean? It means that there is no "past" which "causes" a "future," for only a bright, clear, shining moment remains in "memory." It means everything exists simultaneously this very moment and that nothing can be "pulled apart" from the Whole.

The phrase "the script is written" has a pre-determined ring to it and a sense of destiny. Yes, this world was over long ago. Yes, what is past has gone. Yes, Christ is Real and ever-Present. And yes, Now is the only "time" to be Awake. Heaven seems to be a decision for the mind which believes in opposites, yet Atonement is accurately described as an acceptance of what is Now. You cannot "prepare" for It without "placing It in the future." That is why surrender is necessary. Surrender the thought that anything of this world can be figured out. Forgiven—yes! Figured out—no!

The concept of channeling was but a tool of time. Channeling is therefore past. As with all concepts of linear time, channeling was dualistic, with source and scribe seeming to be apart. Yet the Oneness of the moment has no parts. Christ, as an Effect of God, is One with God forever. The Oneness that is God and Christ in God is Everything. Heaven is Abstract Light and extends as Eternal Creation. To the extent that any transitory concept seemed to point beyond all concepts to the Real, the concept seemed to be temporarily helpful. Yet it must be understood that the holy instant is Now, the Point at which all concepts are laid by.

Now is the time of the Great Awakening. For the willing mind, the Kingdom of Heaven is at hand. The Kingdom is recognized in the Divine Silence. The Experience is beyond words. Love is a State of Mind which knows no "other." Very literally, the Self is Christ is One. You need do nothing to Be as You already are. What You have is Who You are. God gives Everything in Creation, and Everything is You. Nothing can be added to Our Perfection in God. The Grace of God is the Gift of Creation. "I Am" cannot, need not, will not, be earned or achieved. "I Am" simply Is. "I Am" is before time was. And this is "why" You need do nothing to Be as You already are. Such is the Simple Truth.

Love and Blessings as the One Christ forever in the Mind of God. You are the One. And as You recognize the One, You recognize the All of God.

Dealing with Illusions

Hi David,

Since finding ACIM, I have been thinking about the ego and illusions, and I have some questions on how to deal with them. It seems as though there are some illusions that I should avoid, such as ones involving anger, and ones I should promote, such as acts of kindness. This brings up the idea of levels of illusions.

And it seems we all have certain group illusions where the illusion seems identical to all of us. The body is an illusion but don't we promote this illusion by giving the body food to "sustain" it? Also, there are "natural laws." If a large truck is going down the road at 70 mph and you place your body in its path, it is highly likely that the body will die. We know that there is only one illusion with no levels, but we react as though there *are* levels. I do not know of anyone who does not give food to their body, for instance. At this time I do not think there is any way out of this unless we have help to do so. That is the Holy Spirit's part, as far as I can tell.

If I give up some illusions, such as the need to make money, I feel that I will be doing something to other people's illusions; the people that depend on me for their food, housing, etc. If I take away their source, am I not being selfish? The idea of illusions and levels go together but where does a person decide where to stop? Even this thought implies levels, so are we not reinforcing illusions even when we are in the act of doing something seemingly good?

All this makes me wonder how to go about my illusory trip and how to react to something that did not really happen.

Hello Beloved One,

Thanks for taking the time to describe what is going through your mind. The belief in many levels is the ego's basis, for the ego was a fragmenting belief which seemed to splinter itself into many degrees, levels, parts, and intervals.

ACIM simplifies the approach to Atonement (Correction) and the remembering of Oneness by using the metaphor of two levels: Right-mindedness, which is the Perspective of the Holy Spirit, and wrong-mindedness, which is the perspective of the ego.

Right-mindedness recognizes that only mind is causative and sees that the cosmos is an unreal effect of an unreal cause (belief in the ego). Right-mindedness recognizes that cause and effect are together and that ideas leave not their source. It sees that the world is a world of concepts that have not left the mind of the "thinker." Right-mindedness sees the tapestry as one illusion. Wrong-mindedness, to the contrary, perceives cause and effect as apart and perceives "causes" and "effects" in form and apart from mind. Raising body thoughts to the level of mind (causation) is an example of level confusion. In simple terms this error is an example of attributing a trait of mind (i.e. causation, energy, memory) to the body. The concepts of "instincts" and "cellular memory" and "kundalini energy" are three varied examples of the attempt to spiritualize matter by seeing causation in form. They are but different forms of level confusion, which is seeing causation in form.

Becoming free from level confusion is the outcome of following the Holy Spirit toward acceptance of the Atonement. Once the realization comes to awareness that only mind is causative this makes way for the Correction (Atonement) which shows that the error of separation never happened. This is the realization that only Love is real and the ego has no existence. The miracle shows that there is no hierarchy of illusions, for illusions are one. The miracle shows that there are no levels in perception.

In the Holy Spirit's Perspective there are not separate illusions – the Perspective simply sees the false as false. Therefore from this Perspective there is nothing to "avoid" and nothing to "promote." Also from this Perspective it is apparent that mind is one and the concepts of "individual minds" and "group illusions" have no existence. Mind is singular and cannot be broken into pieces or parts or groups, and thus the concept of a "collective" has no basis in Reality.

Jesus seemed to put food into his body, yet this seeming action took nothing away from the teachings about Eternal Reality: "Before Abraham was, I Am," "I and the Father are One," "I am Calling you out of the world," "I am as God created Me," "I am Spirit." Many of Jesus' teachings were done at the table during dinner time, yet the backdrop of eating was just that, a backdrop. The Content of the teachings remained: "The Kingdom of Heaven is within." T-4.III.1 ACIM Workbook lessons 50 and 76 dispel the notion of "natural laws" of the world/body and teach the Spiritual Reality: "I am under no laws but God's." Love is the only "Law" that operates in Creation because God is Its Source and that which proceeds from God is All Reality.

Illusion means unreal, and that which is unreal cannot be "born" or "die." The body therefore cannot die or be born or have life, for what is nothing simply is nothing. There is no mind in matter. "There is no life, truth, intelligence, nor substance in matter." (Mary Baker Eddy, Science and Health) From the Holy Spirit's Perspective, which is the only one that matters, there is no dead matter or living matter, no good matter or bad matter, no beautiful matter or ugly matter. What is unreal cannot BE divided into categories or parts. Right-mindedness recognizes this is so.

The way "out" of wrong-mindedness is indeed the Helper, the Comforter, the Holy Spirit. Doing the ACIM workbook lessons under the Holy Spirit's Guidance is a way of discerning between right-mindedness and wrong-mindedness (the only two meaningful levels during the "process" of Awakening) and thus approaching the final decision, Atonement, which leads past the concept of error entirely.

It is important to remember that the "giving up" of illusion has no cost or sacrifice. Correction is actually "the illusion of giving up," or the illusion of "gaining" everything and "losing" nothing. Is this not an acceptance worthy of our holy mind?

In the seeming release of error or illusion there is actually nothing that is taken away. There is only the acceptance of what is and has always been true. A "person" cannot accept the Correction, but the mind can and must. It is the realization that the Holy Child of God is Mind, wholly Mind, Purely Mind, Perfect and Eternal in the Mind of God. Divine Mind is Whole and Complete and can play no "part." It simply Is. Your sincere questioning began with the concept of levels and came to: "...all this makes me wonder how to go about my illusory trip and how to react to something that did not really happen."

Let the Holy Spirit Guide you in the moment to think and perceive from the Perspective of right-mindedness. As false belief is brought to the Light within, it disappears; in this dissolving you will experience that there is no causation whatsoever in matter.

Be "Selfish" in the constructive sense by accepting the Magnitude and Power and Glory of Thy Christ Self, and understand that there is no "cost" to this recognition. It is indeed humble to accept OneSelf as God created OneSelf, and arrogant to believe that a make-believe self-cosmos could ever take the place of the Eternal Christ.

As error is released there is no necessity to react to illusion at all. For Love is real and Love simply extends and looks upon Love. All reactions, including the perception of pain, were false emotions that have no basis in Reality. And in Atonement it is evident that nothing the ego seemed to believe or think or make or feel had any reality or meaning. There is no reaction at all to something that never happened, and Love remains forever true. I Love You forever and ever!!!

On "Following" Christ—Will the World Hate Me?

Hi David,

Is it true that the world will hate me if I follow Christ? I would rather the world feel my peace. Is the first statement just a thought that is true only if I believe it?

I think there is a passage in the Course that says something about me not having learned my final lesson until everyone who even thinks of me feels peace? I am struggling with feeling that I have been led by Christ only to find myself in disagreement with those around me. Please help me free my mind.

Beloved One,

It will seem as though persecution, accusation, and attack are real as long as the belief in private thoughts and private minds continues to be given faith. The belief that an Idea in the Mind of God could leave Its Source and enter a world of time and space and form, and that a wall of flesh could contain a private mind with thoughts of its own – all this springs from a belief which is erroneous.

The "role of the accuser" will appear in many places and many forms and it will seem to be accusing you, but have no fear it will go at last and leave you in peace. The recognition of our Self as Christ is the end of the concepts of "leader" and "follower," for Who is Christ but OneSelf. And with this recognition is attack seen as impossible. For Oneness cannot attack or be attacked, Being One.

Divine Mind is singular; attack of any degree or kind is impossible in truth. Peace cannot enter a mind which perceives itself in a world of duality. God's peace transcends the personal perspective; it can truly be said that God is no respecter of persons.

What you seem to see and encounter around you are doubt thoughts which have not yet been raised to the Light. Yet "seeing" through the five senses is not to See with Christ Vision. The images seem to hate "you" who follow Christ, yet they but witness to a belief in a tiny self. The images have all the meaning that the ego gave them, yet nothing of the ego has meaning. This is the turning point in which you allow the meaning of "Nothing I see means anything" to dawn in awareness. This is the point of going within to the experience of "There is no world," the idea presented in lesson 132. This is the Mysticism, the experience within Mind that cannot be explained or described. What is now at hand is the "giving up" of nothing for the experience of Everything. There is nothing outside of You, Holy One of God.

The finding Christ is seeing the impossibility of the search. The search was the sickness. The search was the confusion. Peace is its own reward, for Cause and Effect are together and never separate. One Mind transcends the concept of parts. When healing (Atonement) is accepted, gone is the concept of separate "individual minds." That concept WAS the confusion, for it was the belief that attack was real. It was the belief that Mind could be splintered into many, many separate pieces. Peace and Oneness are the Same, and cannot be found apart. Peace of Mind is forgetting the concept of "piece." The test of perfect peace to which you refer applies to our Holy Mind, Beloved One.

The interpretation I give you now is: The experience of the Peace of God includes everyone and everything, for there is nothing outside the Mind of God. What You recognize as your Self is true of All, for Christ is All. Let the images recede from your awareness and rest in our Father's Love. Peace can never be found in attempting to reconcile images with truth. Let them fade away in a prayer for the eternal. I am witnessing Now that You are It, the Whole of Creation, for We are One Self.

The invitation that Christ Be but Itself remains the same. Again, let us look at Workbook lesson 189:

> Simply do this: Be still, and lay aside all thoughts of what you are and what God is; all concepts you have learned about the world; all images you hold about yourself. Empty your mind of everything it thinks is either true or false, or good or bad, of every thought it judges worthy, and all the ideas of which it is ashamed. Hold onto nothing. Do not bring with you one thought the past has taught, nor one belief you ever learned before from anything. Forget this world, forget this course, and come with wholly empty hands unto your God. W-189-7

You are the Gift of God forever. The end of doubt about our Self is the end of confusion.

Chapter Six

How Can One Surrender to God?

Hi David,

Thank you for all you do. I am beginning a treatment program for chemical dependency. For years I have struggled with this problem, and when I first walked into an NA meeting, I had a very limited God concept. Now, years later, after having read and practiced ACIM, I almost feel like my God concept is now far too complicated an idea to trust, and everything I have ever believed, I feel like I must let go. How can one surrender to God? Is it a matter of practice, or is it a matter of simply letting go, which just does not seem to be simple? Thank you for any thoughts on the matter. Namaste.

Namaste Beloved,

Thanks for writing and thanks for your devotion to Awakening.

It rapidly becomes apparent that the "human condition" was one of ego dependency. Ego thoughts can but seem to veil the truth of One Self. Our Christ Self is untouched by illusion.

You wrote: "I almost feel like my God concept is now far too complicated an idea to trust, and everything I have ever believed, I feel like I must let go." You are right on, for holding in awareness any concept (including a "God concept"), with the exception of complete forgiveness (the final concept), is a block to true release.

How can one surrender to God? How is forgiveness accepted? These are the same question, and the Answer is the Holy Spirit. The Holy Spirit is a decision and all that is asked of you is willingness to decide for God. Each moment you do this is a miracle. And with total willingness the need for time and miracles is over. Application of ACIM, with willingness not to make exceptions to the Workbook lessons, is what you might call "practice." And each moment, if accepted for the Holy Spirit's Purpose, is a full opportunity for "simply letting go." I am joined with you in this Purpose and we cannot fail. For God's Will is done. Nothing can change eternal Love.

With each willing moment a momentum seems to grow, and a confidence and certainty about the Holy Spirit's Guidance seems to grow as well. This momentum is like a tidal wave of Love. And as the last sands of ego are washed away, it is obvious that Love is all there is. The belief in opposites has been undone! Be open to this happy and true thought with each step you are Guided to take on the road to Recovery or Recognition of Spirit. It has been said: "Let go and let God," and this is sound advice. Leave the "how" to the Holy Spirit, for means and ends are one to Him. Only be willing. More you cannot do. The rest will be given you. I Love You!

Coming to Consistency

Hi David,

How does one remember to hold the hand of the Holy Spirit or Jesus every minute of the day? I seem to be helpless and wandering to commit errors again and again, and find out only that I am not holding His hand. Please teach me. Thanks.

Beloved One,

Teaching and thinking are synonymous. The mind is constantly teaching itself what it is by the thoughts it has. The deceived mind is confused and conflicted for it attempts to hold in mind two irreconcilable thought systems: God's and the ego's. When the mind is untrained, vacillations in thought simply describe the deceived condition of the sleeping mind. The mind that seems to have forgotten its wholeness (and holiness) believes it has two parts. The Holy Spirit's function is the sorting out and release of the false (forgiveness) and the remembrance of the true (Awakening).

The first important thing to remember is that an error is a mistake in thinking, and just a mistake. The only thing to do when you recognize a mistake is to release it immediately. Hand the mistake over to the Holy Spirit or Jesus and trust that it has been released from your mind. Hop off the ego's train of thought. Do not repeat or compound the mistake by continuing with it, by staying on the train. Now is the moment of release and the present is free and clean and untarnished by the past. Practice being still in the present, for such is meditation.

The second important thing to remember is that you are worthy of healing and receiving and remembering God's Love. The belief in unworthiness is the ego, and You are not the ego. You are an Idea in the Mind of God, wholly loving and wholly lovable. You are not capable of changing Eternal Love or of becoming something apart from Love. Errors are corrected as they are brought into awareness and released. This is the same as saying mistakes are forgiven or released when they are raised to the Light of Truth. Awakening to Christ is inevitable, so relax and do not judge yourself, not because you "shouldn't" but because you are incapable of judgment. God gives creative ability to His Creation, not evaluative ability. Only the ego evaluates and analyzes, for only the ego divides and separates. The ego is not You. You are the Gift of God.

Consistency comes with practice and transfer of training. Remember the mantra: "This does not mean anything." Apply it to all the thoughts and sights and sounds of the world, and great will be your reward, for peace of mind comes to the willing mind which has been emptied of idols. And the feeling of gratitude will grow stronger and stronger in your heart. The strength of the Stillness, the Silence within, will carry you gently to the remembrance of Christ. And the Christ will dawn in awareness: I am still as God created Me.

What Is Real?

Hi David,

Are you real? Or are you just part of the dream, representing my desire to awaken.

Am I the only being in the world? There is no spiritual community center, is there? Unless of course I decided to go there, then it would all be exactly as I made it up to be. There never really was a man named Jesus. This is all contrived. I made you up, didn't I?

Beloved One,

I am real. There is only One. You are the One. I am the One. There is no person in Reality, yet the symbol of a person can be used by the Holy Spirit as a symbol or reflection of the desire to Awaken. The same applies to Jesus. There is only the Spirit God created Eternal. There is no spiritual community center in Reality, and yes if you seemed to decide to go "there" it would be exactly as the ego made it up to be. Perception is selective and subjective through the ego's lens, and there is no objective world apart from the perceiver. The ego made the cosmos, yet the Holy Spirit uses what the ego made to lead to the Kingdom of Heaven within. Love is All there Is. Eternity Shines!

Two Basic Questions Regarding Miracles and Stepping Stones

Hi David,

I have a few questions for you on my mind:

1) ACIM says as a Miracle Principle that "Miracles should not be used as spectacles to induce belief."

2) If this is true, then how would you define Jesus' miracles such as feeding the multitudes, raising the dead, etc.?

3) Wayne Dyer really speaks to my soul! I see him and ACIM in perfect alignment with their teachings. Do you see the same consistency in teachings between ACIM and Ernest Holmes? And ACIM and the Unity Church?

Thank you as always for your wonderful help in poking holes (miracles) in my clouds that are blocking the Sun. I also would like to share with you a verse I came up with: *Don't see the sun shining, be the sun shining!*

Beloved One,

Thanks for sharing your questions. Miracles are always only for the mind of the perceiver or dreamer. Mind is One, and what seems to occur in form is merely symbolic. Miracles are for the mind that has the ears to hear, so to speak, or the willingness and readiness to behold. Seeming changes in form reflect the shift in mind of the miracle-minded, and though some of these changes seem to transcend "known physical laws," in Reality there are no "known physical laws." The Law of Love (Spirit) is the only Reality.

Feeding the multitudes and raising the dead were symbols of the Divine Law of Love, which has no limit or lack. It is truly the beatitudes or state of mind that demonstrates the miracle has come. It is this state of mind in which consistency is possible and this is a characteristic of Awakening.

"Consistent form" is a contradiction in terms, although behavior can seem to become more "stable" for the miracle-minded. The easy way to remember that miracles are not intended to be used as spectacles to induce belief is to remember that miracles are the means of Awakening for a mind that already "believes," yet is also willing to go beyond belief and "be still and know that I Am."

The teachings you mention are all very helpful stepping stones in Awakening to Oneness. The Holy Spirit will Guide you to discern the true from the false in all regards, and the deeper you seem to go you will seem to transcend all linear concepts and come to an experience that will end all doubting.

The teachings you mention have Oneness as their main focus, yet there are subtleties of ego concepts that are transcended completely in Enlightenment. Your inner work with the Holy Spirit will instruct you on your inward movement and Help you lay aside every linear (past-future) concept (such as balance and process and growth and personality). You are moving steadily inward to the experience of Atonement, Christ, and God's Love.

Is the Devil Real?

Hi David,

Could you bring clarity to a question I just have not been able to get a consistent answer to. Is there an entity of evil such as Lucifer, Satan, Demiurge, etc., as mentioned in the Bible, *The Urantia Book*, Gnostic writings, etc. that is out to sabotage mankind's awakening? Or is that which appears as an evil force just another one of the ego's attempts to confound, frighten and confuse the sleeping mind?

Thank you for your help and patience on this topic. And if there is a real devil do we need to forgive him also? Wanting to wake up!!

Beloved One,

Thanks for writing. The devil/Lucifer/Satan is just a belief held in mind. When the belief is exposed and released it is apparent the belief was never real at all. The ego is synonymous with belief, and in Heaven there is no belief. Everything of God can only be Known.

The ego is dispelled by withdrawing faith from it, not by attempting to fight or resist it. What a mind seems to fight or resist seems to persist in awareness because the struggle comes from the belief in opposites. To believe that Divine Love can have an opposite, which is the ego, is clearly insane.

Forgiveness is the release of illusion; the ego is to be released. It only seems to be a battle while the belief in opposites is held as real. Illusion is not dispelled by words, but it is dispelled by aligning with Holy Spirit and by accepting the Correction for error. Error is never to be fought against. It is only to be exposed as nothing and thereby released from awareness.

The concept of entities is nothing more than a projection, and it is more direct to say that the ego and the Holy Spirit are decisions. Decide for God by accepting the Correction for error. The sole responsibility of the teacher of God/miracle worker is to accept the Atonement. This acceptance brings consistency and peace and stability to the mind. This opens the way for the remembrance of the Kingdom of Heaven/Divine Mind/Christ/God.

Clarification on Passion, Action, Free Will, and "The Script is Written"

Hi David,

My first set of questions is around the idea of passion: In a popular spirituality book it says something like: Passion is the love of turning being into action. Is that true, or is passion really just a drive based on the ego's symbols? After enlightenment is there still a love of turning being into action? Is there any passion, or just total and complete bliss?

My second set of questions is around the idea of free will: If the script of my life is already set and I cannot change it, then isn't it also pre-scripted as to when I choose forgiveness and when I do not? Or is only the "physical" stuff scripted; that is, those things which relate to the five senses? Are ALL my thoughts scripted?

Beloved One,

Thanks for writing. In Enlightenment there is only Being (complete and total Bliss). True passion is extending Love and therefore is without desire. There is no "doer" or "action" in Pure Being.

As for the phrase "the script is written" and the question about free will, I wrote the following:

God's Will is for Perfect Happiness. God's Will is unified and abstract, Being Oneness and Divine Love. Creation is God's Will, and creation has no meaning in this world. The cosmos was made to deny God and Spirit and creation; even the forgiven world or happy dream is but a temporary helpful illusion that offers a bridge back to the Divine Abstraction called the Kingdom of Heaven.

God's Will has no meaning in this world. Therefore do not attempt to "figure out" or "understand" in perceptual terms the meaning of "God's Will." The closest approximation of Eternity that this world offers is the Present Moment. You might say that the Present Moment is the gateway to Eternity. You cannot prepare for the holy instant without placing It in the future. Therefore I have simply Asked you to desire the holy instant and have told you of the "I Need Do Nothing" Solution. Since you believe in linear time you believe that the Holy Spirit's Plan involves linear time. All your questions arise from the assumption that time is linear instead of simultaneous. The attempt to order thoughts in a linear manner, to make a hierarchy of illusions, to make a series of unanswerable questions—all of these delusions are the ego's defenses against the Atonement, the Present Moment, which Is "before" time was or seemed to be.

"The script is written" statement from the ACIM workbook is still a linear concept since "the script" is made of linear time. The emphasis of the statement rests on the past tense of the word *written*. The world was over long ago. You who seem to sleep and dream a world of linear time with events sequenced one after the other are attempting to relive an ancient instant that is over and gone and in Truth never was. Let's keep everything very, very simple. You seem to be dreaming a dream that involves duality and multiplicity. Your questions assume that this duality and multiplicity are real. You assume that the "I" that is asking the questions is real. I have told you that illusions are one, not many. There is only one mind and there is only one dreamer of the dream. Once this is realized the dream is a happy, unified dream of non-judgment or forgiveness. This unified dream might be called healed perception or the real world, for it is a reflection or symbol and is the closest perceptual experience to Heaven, which simply Is and does not involve perception at all.

The miracle simply sees the false as false. The miracle is the Perspective of the Holy Spirit which is aware that time was (or seemed to be) simultaneous and is over (and never was). The ego offers the distorted perspective that time is linear and is still happening. The choice of purpose is the seeming choice between the

Holy Spirit's Perspective and the ego's perspective. One choice brings peace, love, freedom, joy, and happiness. The other choice brings pain, guilt, fear, anger, and depression. You can tell which choice you have made by how you feel.

You could say that the thoughts of linear time (past and future) are scripted because the thoughts you think you think and the world you think you see are the same. The Atonement, however, is an acceptance of the Correction to all mistaken thoughts and misperceptions and is independent of time – being for healing the belief in linear time. Now is the only time Atonement can be accepted. The Holy Spirit's Purpose is the only meaningful Choice.

Getting Back on Track – Feeling Like the Worst ACIM Student

Hi David,

I have decided that I am the worst student to ever study ACIM. I have been right through the book dutifully doing all the exercises to the best of my ability.

Forgiveness: Just when I think, *yes, I do forgive*, something else pops up and there I go again; ego rationalizing my decision as to why I should not. I know that the message of the Course is my truth but I just don't get it.

Fear: I had an experience lying in bed late at night. I told my Higher Self that I had no fear, so please, return me to love. Within a few minutes, I can only describe what appeared like dark clouds rolling towards me and the energy in the room changing. Terrified, I said *Stop!* And it did. I am obviously full of fear, and do not forgive – a pretty useless student if I must say so myself!

I opened the ACIM book at the page where it talks about, "You may think that I was mistaken at choosing you as a channel," and I did laugh.

Can you tell me where I go so obviously wrong?

Beloved One,

Thanks for writing. The sleeping/dreaming mind is very, very deep and unknowingly afraid of God's Love as long as it believes in the ego. The ego is the belief in separation from God and must be completely exposed and released before the mind is restored to its natural state of Peace.

You are not "the worst student to ever study ACIM" because comparison is only an ego device and Love makes no comparisons or evaluations or judgments. The ego knows nothing, being nothing. You need not attempt to share in the thoughts/beliefs/emotions/perceptions of insanity. The Course is to be studied and practiced diligently if you wish to experience the Peace that Jesus and the Holy Spirit and I promise you. You have been told that Peace is inevitable, and that you must go through the darkness to the Light. The decision to follow and practice ACIM demonstrates a willingness to move in the direction of healing the mind; the decision to heal with the miracle is a moment by moment decision.

"Be vigilant for God and His Kingdom" is a statement that Calls forth the willingness to watch your mind for ego thoughts and let them go. It takes practice and sustained willingness to be so very attentive to the mind and to withdraw attention from pseudo "problems" that the ego set up as distractions to Peace.

I am joined with you in our shared Purpose. Together there can be no failure. What God Wills is Perfect Happiness for everyOne in the Mind of Creation. To recognize Creation it is necessary to see the nothingness and unreality of images that seem to be "fabricated" to block the Light from awareness.

A mistake is not a reason to give up hope in your mind training, and neither is a seeming series of mistakes. Release all past mistakes to the Holy Spirit and come again with an open heart to the Present Moment of Innocence. I will meet you there. We have a date! It is wonderful, I assure you. You will not regret keeping this appointment.

What Distinguishes an Authentic Spiritual Path From a Cult?

Hi David,

What distinguishes an authentic spiritual path from that of a cult? What exactly is a cult?

Beloved One,

The best indicator of an authentic spiritual path is one that instructs that responsibility for your state of mind at any given moment rests with you. The truth is within and cannot be found in persons, places, or things outside. Truth is not something that can be found in a book or object. Truth is an experience of the living moment that will dawn of Itself. The Spirit uses the symbols and sights and sounds of the world, including people and music and words of inspiration (scriptures), to help the deceived mind to the point of Realization or Recognition. These are all stepping stones or metaphors; they all dissolve at the point of Recognition, which is an experience within!

True spirituality rests on open communication, the release of all attack thoughts (and the fear, guilt, and anger that they produce), non-judgment, true humility, defenselessness, gentleness, and divine mercy. Any authentic spiritual path will promote forgiveness and advocate laying aside grievances. All are included in the experience of love, for it is unconditional and impersonal. Everyone is equally loved and appreciated.

A cult is a symbol or representation of the belief that your state of mind is dependent on a person, place, event, or circumstance and is not a decision of your mind. Faith is placed in "external authorities and forms and rituals," and the underlying experience will always be based on fear, no matter how endearing or adoring the devotion seems to be. Ultimately you can never really love or adore or be devoted to anything specific or anything in form, for truth cannot be found in images and symbols.

When you attach to the form or scenario or script you believe will make you happy, a substitute or idol image has been made and accepted as real, and is being worshipped. Truth is denied in such an attempt. And the pseudo "love" will turn to hate and anger in the mind of the "leader" or "follower." What can turn to hate was never the Love of God, but was instead the desire to be special and "loved" in a personal sense. There appears a "holier than thou" mentality in cult-thinking, which attempts to raise some people up and put other people down and perpetuates a "we/they" division. Hence there is always a fear of an external "enemy."

In true spirituality everyone is always welcome, for it becomes apparent that we are always meeting our Self. No one is turned away or "judged against." Acceptance of the truth is an experience in which no one is "labeled and dismissed," for the experience of truth is vast and expansive and All-inclusive! The experience is freely given by God, and the Peace and Joy and Love of God is beyond the possibility of commercialization. There is no reciprocity (giving to get) and authentic spirituality cannot be bought or sold. Love is freely given, and by giving it, it is retained in awareness. What you share is strengthened in your awareness, so by giving love you become aware that you have love and are love. This is how the mind is awakened by the Holy Spirit from the dream of scarcity, guilt, fear, and death. First you learn to forgive; then you are awakened unto Eternal Life!

The opposite of a life of love and forgiveness and trust in God is a "condition" of fear, guilt, scarcity, and anger. This "condition" is the simplest way to define "cult-thinking." Because of intense fear and suspicion, "cult-thinking" involves threats, privacy, secrecy, hierarchies and "chains of command," attempts at control and manipulation through breaking off communication or using communication to "make guilty." It may seem to manifest as scarcity (hoarding of food, money, possessions, and supplies out of a fear that they may run out). It may also manifest under the guise of abundance (power, wealth, fame, psychic powers, energy experiences and phenomenon that are valued in and of themselves). These pursuits, under the guise of spirituality and religion, are distractions and detours to true peace and happiness. When the ego is highly threatened, it may even resort to confrontation, the use of firearms and weapons, violence, or suicide as an "escape."

"Cult-thinking" rests on judgment, for it raises some people up as special "good ones" and lowers others down as the "bad ones." The "good ones" are praised and loyally adored, while the "bad ones" are attacked, avoided, blamed, abandoned, excluded, or rejected. "Cult-thinking" involves forming cliques around worldly and historic beliefs and values of ethnicity or heredity or tradition or geography or nationality or race or gender or age or formal religious practices and rituals. "Cult-thinking" may involve anything specific in the world, as long as boundaries can be kept. "Cult-thinking is quick to anger and accuse and sometimes as quick to flee. It is particularly threatened by open, direct communication. Future loss is not the greatest fear of "cult-thinking," for present joining and union is what it dreads most. The ego sees complete joining as the abolishment of privacy and separation. This it cannot tolerate. To protect itself, the ego will attempt isolation and rely heavily on "fight or flight" strategies. Decisions are made hastily and always based in fear. Reason and patience and cooperation and clear-thinking are de-emphasized, and shared opinions, gossip, and grievances are rallying points against the perceived "external enemy," hence the "group-think" mentality. Moral and ethical systems of behavior (around sexuality, money, and possessions, etc.) and arbitrary standards are often cited and defended as good reasons for attacking, condemning, avoiding, blaming, excluding, or rejecting the persons, things, groups, institutions, or countries that have been labeled "bad or wrong." This "judging against" based on perceived differences is the rationale the ego uses for the dismissing, isolating, and separating tendency that is so highly valued by the ego.

All "cult-thinking" is based on fear, though it is not seen that the fear is not really based in the images of the world (persons, places, things, events, etc.). The underlying fear is the fear of God and the Holy Spirit, which strikes terror in the ego. Darkness is afraid of the approach of Light. The opposite of love is fear, but love is all-encompassing and has no opposite! "Cult-thinking" is therefore no real threat to a mind that is devoted to loving. A clear mind, free of judgment, is very capable of forgiving, or seeing the false as false. The still mind rests in God. And who can fear when there is love?

I am so grateful to teach and learn that Innocence is real and guilt and condemnation are false witnesses. I am so grateful to learn that nobody is ever to blame and that it is impossible to be unfairly treated. "Cult-thinking" is just another name for the ego or the world of darkness. Jesus tells us to be of good cheer and to be happy learners, for he has overcome the world! A misperception can always be corrected by a miracle. "Cult-thinking" and "cults" are errors, for they come not from our Heavenly Father. A child of God need not seek outside and fall for the ego's games of attack and defense. "Judge not, lest ye be judged" is an instruction not to attempt something you are incapable of. A mind that values stillness and quiet and peace is a mind that does not attempt judgment. Forgiveness and non-judgment are synonymous.

If we want peace, we must hold every thought up to the Light of Truth. If a thought does not come from God, the only thing to do is to release it and harbor it no longer. "Manipulation" is of the ego, for God did not create it. "Betrayal" is of the ego, for God did not create it. "Abandonment" is of the ego, for God did not create it. "Attack" is of the ego, for God did not create it. "Rejection, exclusion, avoidance, isolation, condemnation, scarcity, fear, anger, guilt, and even death" are all of the ego, for God did not create them. If these or any of the fearful beliefs, thoughts, and emotions the ego sponsors are believed in as the truth, the world will out picture or witness to this belief. That is why these beliefs must be questioned. When the mind clings to and protects these beliefs, thoughts, and emotions, upset is unavoidable. Forgiveness is the laying aside of all these transitory beliefs, thoughts, and emotions. Forgiveness of illusions brings peace, happiness, love, and freedom!

How magnificent is the Perspective that simply sees the false as false! How glorious is the Mind that recognizes Itself as One! The Mind that is shared

185

with God is Pure Oneness and knows not of judgment. For in Oneness there is nothing to judge between! This Mind is forever Innocent, for Life and Being are in the Mind of God.

Holy Child of God, You are Innocent forever! Hallowed be Thy Name and the Name of Our Creator God! Thy Kingdom has come! Thy Will is done! Amen.

What About Jesus Christ? – Religion and Theology

Hi David,

Lately when I have talked to some who are studying *A Course in Miracles*, they get upset with me when I talk about Jesus Christ. Yet is it not Jesus Christ who brought us the Course? What does Jesus Christ have to do with religion? Was it not Jesus Christ who overcame death by rising from it, by not believing in death's power to take life from him, because he believes in eternal or everlasting life? Am I wrong about the strong Love that I feel for Jesus Christ for all that he has done for us, in proving to us that we can overcome the greatest of obstacles, even death itself, if we just believe?

Beloved One,

Thanks for writing. Yes, your love and gratitude for Jesus is very natural since he is a Wayshower, and Guide, and the Living Christ.

Some people confuse religion with theology; this brings resistance to anything that is associated with a theology. True religion is inner peace, thus religion is *experience*. Theologies are stepping stones and pointers. With practice and willingness Christ comes alive in awareness as an experience of Divine, Unconditional, Universal Love.

The ego has made many bitter idols of Jesus, for the ego does not know Love. The ego belief is a denial of Love, so Jesus is either hated or idolized by the ego. Jesus teaches that Love is real and eternal. The ego teaches that time, space, guilt, fear and sin are real. Until the mind withdraws faith and belief from the ego, it experiences a resistance to Divine Love. This resistance seems to play out in many forms. One way is for Course students to dissociate from Jesus Christ. This is actually quite common, for the depth of resistance to Divine Love is the basis of all emotional upsets. Human beings are never upset for the reason they think, for it does not consciously seem like the mind is afraid of Love. Belief in the ego and projection make it seem like the people and circumstances of the world are the "cause" of upset, yet this is never the case.

Jesus Christ is a symbol for Love not of this world. To love Jesus Christ without reservation or exception is a pathway to remember the Love of God. Jesus will seem to be whatever a mind believes until the mind accepts Atonement (complete forgiveness); then Christ is recognized as Self. Self is Spirit. Remembrance of the Spirit is the Awakening to the Kingdom of Heaven within. All glory to God for this Great Awakening!!!

Is there Really Only One Mind?

I only remind you of and reflect what is already deep within. It is not surprising that Mind is whirring with the energy and the high vibrations of Reality, because Enlightenment is close at hand. The Living Moment is being unveiled by the Holy Spirit. There is only One Divine Mind, and the gateway to remembering Divine Mind is complete forgiveness. Complete forgiveness is identical to the realization that there is only one dreamer and this Perspective is the Atonement.

From the one dreamer Perspective "there really are no enlightened folks running around the world, because there is no world and no 'others' to be enlightened." This idea I shared many times. There is no such thing as an "enlightened person," for mind dissolves into Mind; "personhood" was nothing but a false concept, a false construct.

Enlightenment is a State of Mind and the "step" to experiencing the only True State of Mind is seeing the falsity of the belief in private thoughts and private minds (i.e. human beings or persons). This is the dreamer of the dream Perspective, and joined with Holy Spirit in this Perspective is the Correction or Atonement to the error called ego (the belief in private minds). From the Holy Spirit's Perspective of the single dreamer, the mind is no longer at the "mercy" of the images, for it sees them for what they are (unreal effects).

You said it very accurately: "Actually, the only thing that needs to happen is for the dreamer to awaken.... That would even mean that there was no Jesus, but only a dream of a fellow like that. Also, there was no Hitler, et al. There is no meaning in physical existence because it does not exist." This is what the first lesson in ACIM teaches and what every non-dualistic teaching aims at. The

Perspective of the Holy Spirit is the highest aim of learning, for it is the complete unlearning of the belief that mind can be separated into minds (plural). It must first be realized that there is only one mind, one dreamer, one consciousness before the mind Awakens from the dream entirely and experiences ItSelf as Divine Mind, Eternity, Infinity, Love (i.e. the Kingdom of Heaven).

You are (((((zooming))))) in rapidly, very rapidly, to the realization that the sole responsibility of the teacher of God is to accept the Atonement for himself! The Simplicity of Salvation is seeing the one error as it is (i.e. one dreamer). This is what the dreamer of the dream sections of ACIM point to very directly. You are ((((zooming)))) in on the Homing Beacon; the Light at the "end of the tunnel" is very close at hand.

You wondered if God is waiting for His Son to awaken. God is Completeness and Wholeness and Eternal Perfection. God knows not of time, and therefore the concept of "waiting" does not pertain to Eternal Oneness. Only the ego seems to "wait," and in "time terminology" its days are numbered, so to speak. The forgiveness of the belief in linear time is the end of the illusion. Jesus says: "Why wait for Heaven. Heaven is in You and You are Home." One Instant: The holy instant!!! I love You forever and ever Beloved One.

Opening to the Experience of One Mind and Unified Perception

Hi David,

A thought came to me a while ago which I tried to put aside because I perceived it to be total arrogance. It would not leave though, and eventually I asked the Holy Spirit to help me look at it. The thought was that I am really all there is. God created one Son and everything and everyone I perceive as outside of me is really me. I am the one dreaming the dream. All the characters in the dream are of my making. There really is no one out there who can make me angry or be angry with me. Nor can there be anything out there that I can fear, because everything out there is what I made up. I have made the bodies of my friends, my children and I use them to maintain my own illusion. I am the dreamer of the dream and all figures I encounter are dream figures of my own making only.

Now the arrogance of even entertaining a thought that "I" could have done all this, made me shirk away. And yet, if this is true, which I really sense it is, so many things fall into place. All anger that I perceive then has to be within me.

When I forgive anyone, I really only forgive myself, because "they" are made in my mind. I would not have to hold on to any belief system, because who would I need to prove something to, what can I judge against, what would I need to defend myself against. If it all starts within me, all of the judgment, beliefs, attack etc. would be pointless, because I would only be attacking what is within me. If all is within me and everything "out there" is my dream, experiencing oneness would become effortless.

Part of me wants to grab wholeheartedly onto this, because I can sense the total release that would come with its acceptance, yet another part of me says "You are finally losing your mind! If anyone has to know what you are thinking you will be locked up!" Please help me.

Beloved One,

Blessings of Love. You are finding our mind, the mind that shares the Holy Spirit's Purpose. The idea of everything being one mind is the introduction of the idea of the forgiven world, the happy dream of forgiveness. The ego made the cosmos. This is reflected in the early workbook lesson "I have invented the world I see." The idea that everything is one mind does eliminate the possibility of attack, of proving something, of defense, judgment, and separate opposing beliefs, for oneness has no parts to conflict.

The Holy Spirit Asks that you accept the idea of one mind wholeheartedly, for this is the Correction to the error called ego. The ego was the belief in private minds with private thoughts, but if mind is one the ego has no foundation on which to stand. Forgiveness reflects the Oneness that shines beyond perception. Forgiveness unifies and shows the world anew. You are not going insane, you are going inward to sanity of mind. And unified perception is the gateway to the remembrance of God and Christ.

The idea you have shared is the key to the puzzle of the ego. The door is open wide. Now you will begin to realize that there are no exceptions to the idea. This transfer of training is the end of the puff of nothingness that never really began. The end of illusions is the final illusion of forgiveness, for the ego was but one illusion—not many. The sameness of illusion seen in mind is the end of multiplicity and complexity. Only a blessing remains!

How blessed is the mind that sees there is nothing but itself. There is no subject/object split, no perceiver/perceived split, and no observer/observed split in one mind. Oneness is simple. Truth is simple. Happiness is simple. Love is simple. I rejoice in our Oneness! In Happiness and Peace.

A Question about "Private Minds"

Hi David,

I would like to know more about private minds because Jesus was one with the Father, but did he not have his own thoughts and feelings? Or are you saying that Jesus did not feel the thoughts of this world that he was walking in? If he did not have the thoughts of people in this world, how could he know what Peter was thinking when he said "Get thee behind me Satan"? (Mathew 16:23)

Beloved One,

The belief in private minds assigns the attributes of the body (separation) to the mind, and thus the mind seems fragmented, isolated, and alone in distorted perception. The belief in private minds with private thoughts assumes that the mind can pull itself apart from the Mind of God and be fragmented into separate pieces, each one different from the rest. The assumption is that "individual" minds have their own unique set of thoughts and also that each "mind" has the ability to make its own decisions.

The Christ Mind, however, reveals that Divine Mind is One, a unified Whole which cannot be divided. What is One with God cannot be divided or become unlike the Mind of God which created It Whole. The Reality of One Mind transcends the illusion of "parts," for what could separate What God created One forever. Only the Thought of God remains eternal. And this is why there can be no private thoughts.

Jesus and the Holy Spirit are synonymous as symbols of Awakened Mind, which sees the error but knows it is unreal. This is why Jesus Christ knew that the thoughts of man were but temptations to believe that the impossible had happened. Jesus was an example of the Purity and Innocence that transcends the belief in private minds. For seeing no one as separate from God, Christ recognizes the Self as Whole.

"Get thee behind me Satan" (Luke 4:8) is the declaration that what is created as One cannot become something else, giving no credibility to the "something else." It is a statement that Love and Truth can have no opposition, since Oneness knows nothing "other" than Self in God.

Jesus demonstrated the Christ Mind, which entered not a body and shines endlessly in Eternity. The Mind of Christ simply Is, and in Being can be but remembered or recognized. The Mind of Christ is beyond perception. Forgiveness (or overlooking error) is how perception gives way to the Light of God. Error is the belief in private minds and thoughts, yet forgiveness sees that mind is whole and that nothing exists "in and of itself" apart from the whole. Nothing is private in the Light of Divine Love. This means that "human" thoughts and emotions and beliefs have no meaning, for they were based on nothing at all. Identity in God is All Meaning, and the world dissolves away in God's Holy Presence.

Getting to the Bottom of Belief

Hi David,

I have a resurging question: If I believe that I am the only one, that there is no one out there, it is all a movie screen, then why do I believe in being helpful to the characters in the script? Who is there to be awakened? Why do some figures seem to have awakened while others seem not to have? How can some of the mind be asleep and some of the mind be awake. When I lay the body aside and the dream is ended... what about the other dream figures? I think you know what I am getting at. There is something here I have not resolved, something I cannot explain.

Beloved One,

Thanks for your devotion to Awakening. Being helpful is being tuned in to the Spirit, and this helpfulness is in a Purpose of mind that offers only benefit.

Your happy, joyful, peaceful, free-flowing state of mind is the gift, for it is our beatitude. This state of mind comes from being in Purpose and thus not taking anything personally. In the joy of the Living Moment there is no concern or worry for any of the characters of the script, for one has stepped back and is identified with mind – not body.

There is only one mind to be Awakened. One mind Awake sees all the characters as the same. No character is ahead or behind; no character is awake or asleep. All of the characters were constructs or symbols of the wish to have private thoughts and private minds. Awakening sees the impossibility of such an attempt, for one mind is unified and cannot be divided and alone and separate.

The happy dream brings an end to dreaming, because forgiveness is a dream of non-judgment. Then, as the Mind remembers It is Creation, Self, the illusion of dreaming is over and never was. When the body is laid aside in Atonement the cosmos is laid aside as well. Eternity remains as God creates. There is no time in what is Forever Spirit.

On Joining

Joining is usually seen as an action in this world. As with everything of this world, the true meaning of joining is approached as old definitions are laid aside. What could never leave need not return; what could never separate need not join. Mind is One and can never be broken into separate, private, isolated fragments, each with private thoughts and a different perspective on the world.

Likewise truth is not a collection of parts that unite to make a whole, for truth is One. The Whole is One and is far beyond the so-called "sum" of the parts. To join is to forgive, for to see illusions as one (tapestry) is simply to release the thought of parts. Nothing exists apart from the One, for connection is just another name for Union and Oneness. Forgiveness is the Point of the world, and no amount of "connecting the dots," "networking," or "trying to bring people together" is necessary to solve a problem that does not exist.

To join is to accept the Changelessness of Mind. How simple and easy is the truth! Seek not to change the world. For one can but accept that which Is, now, always, and forever. What is the same (forgiveness) cannot be different. What is One (Heaven) cannot have separate parts. Forgiveness seems to collapse time, while Oneness is beyond time entirely. I join you in the Purpose of forgiveness, for what else could joining mean? Forgiveness is Content and has nothing to do with specific forms.

On Psychic Abilities

Friend: Do you feel that since you are so connected to that unified mind that maybe you have opened up to other types of abilities, whether it is knowing other people's thoughts or seeing auras or having different types of psychic abilities? Have you had that experience or is your experience more just that feeling of knowing your oneness and being connected?

David: I will talk about the idea of reading thoughts, what seems to be other people's thoughts. When you remove the limits and the parameters of what communication is from your mind, it seems like you pick up thoughts. It is almost like you have a giant satellite dish like the ones that picks up very tiny little impressions, even from outer space. This is a phase you go through and it may be experienced as disturbing. I spent some time seemingly picking up thoughts during that phase and I went to Jesus and the Holy Spirit saying, "What is the purpose of this? I am picking up other people's thoughts and some of them are disturbing or unsettling." The Holy Spirit said: *This is just a phase of your mind training. It is not really that other people have the thoughts. These are thoughts in your mind that have to be released.* This is another opportunity for discernment, tuning into the Spirit and letting go of reactions and judgments and identification with these thoughts. They seem to be negative but they really are just unreal. When you completely unplug your mind from them then they seem to not even be in your awareness because you have not given any faith to them. That is a good example of a phase that I passed through.

Things like intuitions, precognitions, or premonitions can seem to have some value but as you go even much deeper, present peace of mind is the greatest gift. I will mention a little about precognitions that seem to involve the future. Future and past are the same. The ego has just made up a different form so that the future seems to be different from the past. The more you see that the future is already the past, the more you can understand how the psychics can read the future. They are really just reading the past. Once you get into these experiences, the fascination with psychic abilities and seeming powers just starts to fade away because it is still the ego being fascinated. God is the power. Spirit and the present moment is all power and glory. Those abilities can seem to come but you never need to be frightened by them. They are actually very, very natural. It helps to realize that you are going for awakening and that you are not going to be delayed by any ego judgments about what seems to be supernatural powers. They are very natural and when given to the Holy Spirit to use they are very productive and helpful. The ego will always try to jump on these so called psychic abilities and make an identity. It could try to make a lot of money out of a psychic ability.

On Private Minds

David: This coming together and really sharing of the heart is the dispelling of the ego. To the ego communication is abandonment. Think about close relationships or significant relationships where you thought: *I cannot tell him that. If I told him that he or she would leave me.*

The whole basis of the ego is that you have a private mind with private thoughts, and you have some hideous things in there—things that if your husband or your best friend or your lover ever knew about they would be gone in an instant, if you ever shared yourself completely. But the desire to communicate attracts communication. As we start to desire to let the Spirit be the guide of our lives, we begin to attract witnesses to the Holy Spirit. We can See the Spirit more and more.

You cannot see the Holy Spirit perceptually but you can see the witnesses to the Holy Spirit in your life. That is how you know that He is there; that is the effect of miracles. It is helpful to always keep that in mind because the temptation when coming together in groups, or family, is to only go so far with communication—to keep areas of privacy and to not let go of your mind completely. But when you do let go of your mind completely you spring into the oneness of One Mind.

Friend: A friend was talking earlier about the collective consciousness, the Christ Mind Consciousness. There are a lot of belief systems that are dealing with the human pool of consciousness, sometimes referred to as the "raised mind consciousness." I am thinking of large groups in which there are several specific types of thought manifestations all the way to mass hypnosis, etc. How does the Course deal with this specifically? I have only seen references to individual thought and not collective thought.

David: To look at this idea of the collective, let's turn to *The Ego and False Autonomy* section. Often I hear people talk about there being a difference between dealing with "their own" ego vs. the "collective ego." Or I hear comments like: *my friend's ego is really acting up. What am I to do since I am doing pretty well at handling mine right now but my friend is out of control?* The first two sentences of the second paragraph are very helpful:

> Everyone makes an ego or a self for himself, which is subject to enormous variation because of its instability. He also makes an ego for everyone else he perceives, which is equally variable. T-4.II.2

Oh! Now we are getting past the trick of the collective! You see, that is where the individual mind thing comes in. Jesus is saying that your mind is twisted; not only have you made an ego for yourself, which you might call your personality, but you have made an ego for every other person you meet! It is your dream; you are the dreamer of the dream; you have made this whole thing up. Now that is a huge leap. There is another place in the Course where he hints at this with the question: "How many teachers of God are needed to save the world?" M-12.1 When thought of in the "collective" sense, you might wonder how many thousands it will take to handle this mess. The answer that Jesus gives is: ONE.

It cannot be a collective thing since it only takes one teacher of God to handle this seeming mess of multiplicity. This is pretty deep. It goes back to the idea that there is only one mind. The whole idea of the collective, or of multiple minds, or even of egos, is a metaphorical construct that Jesus uses often in the Course, for example, when he talks about "your brother's mind," or about "minds" in plural. These are metaphorical constructs. We get a hint that he is using the plural in a metaphorical sense in the *Clarification of Terms* section where he talks about Mind and Spirit. At the bottom of the first paragraph he addresses what you mentioned earlier – the unified spirit.

He describes and uses the metaphor of the individual mind, as if we each have one. He knows that the mind is so convinced of the illusion that it would make no sense to come right out and describe things in terms of the one mind. The Course is written at the ego level – where it is needed. It would do no good to just have two words – God is – because the mind is not in touch with "God Is." It believes in fragmentation and needs a system to help undo that fragmentation.

Once again it is described *as if* it has two parts. The split mind is a metaphor because in reality the separation did not happen. Separation must be impossible because God did not create it. But he knows that when the mind is in the deluded state, you have to have something to work with. So, as a structural component or metaphor, it is described *as if* it is split in two parts – a right mind and a wrong mind. When we get into the belief that the collective is causative in some way, that it influences individuals, this is still part of the ego's backward thinking. It is a big thing to remember that:

> I am responsible for what I see. I choose the feelings I experience, and I decide upon the goal I would achieve. And everything that seems to happen to me I ask for, and receive as I have asked. T-21.II.2

This does not leave a lot of leeway for projection. If all my feelings and perceptions come from my decision – then I am responsible. That is the good news. That is where the empowerment is; I do not have to rely on anything or anyone outside myself to accept the Atonement. But I cannot project the responsibility for the ego anywhere else.

Christ-Mind Interview

Friend: What, for you, is Christ Mind?

David: It is a vast, vast experience of unconditional Agape love; nothing else in mind but that love and the expression of that love – not of this world. To me Christ Mind is even beyond a unified field. It is so vast that it transcends perception; it transcends what for centuries has been called matter. In quantum physics the unified field is completely overthrowing the laws of Newton – the behavior of objects, the physics, etc. I would say that the quantum physics term "observer" is the closest that we come to Christ Mind in this world, which is vast love – One with the Creator.

Friend: Tell us more about this witness or observer in the context of Christ Mind – what it actually is and how people can enter into that?

David: I would say that Jesus was a demonstration of this Witness Self or this observer. He said things like: *before you remove the speck out of your brother's eye, remove the log or the beam out of your own.* He was talking about perception; he was talking about distortion in perception.

Friend: Are you saying that the Witness is clear perception, without any distortion?

David: Yes, the Witness is clear seeing. It is total, all-inclusive seeing. And even that is not the Christ Vision; that is only the gateway. I was doing an open-eye meditation once with someone sitting across from me and I got so deep in my mind that the figure/ground, the 3-dimensionality collapsed. It started to look like a painting, then just a flimsy veil, and all of a sudden this amazing light started streaming through it and the veil started to disappear. Perception was just a veil drawn over this Vision. I got a glimpse into the Vision of Christ, which was this blazing light that was non-perceptual.

I could tell that the ego was terrified of that light, and more than anything, of losing control of the picture. I had a real taste of the Vision of Christ – the abstract light that is beyond the veil. Since I had experiences like that I knew that my whole life would be dedicated to that light.

Friend: So the Witness is the gateway to the Vision of Christ, which is a blazing light? How can people who are reading this start to access that gateway?

David: Yes. These people have to be authentic. We were just talking about holding onto the mask of spirituality, or holding onto differences, such as emphasizing one teaching over another, comparing, contrasting. All of that needs to come up into awareness. Emotionally you can feel it; it does not feel like joining. It does not feel like joy and happiness when there is a "my" way or a "your" way, because there are still preferences. I would say the most striking characteristic of the Witness Self is that it has no preferences; it is all inclusive. It is so aware of the unity in the unification that it does not prefer this or that; all is equally acceptable to the Witness Self.

Friend: It is very interesting because when I look at someone for a few minutes they just dissolve completely like there is nothing there, and it all becomes like a dream. So the Witness becomes the actual experience or tangible "seeing" of the dream. So what is the dream?

David: The dream is a group of images, just like when you go to sleep at night. They are all generated by the ego. There seems to be a lot of emotions associated with them, like being chased – there is a monster or a tsunami wave coming to get you. The dream is meant to take the place of abstract light. The dream is the veil. The key is not to judge the dream as good or bad; the key is to come as the observer, the dreamer, the Witness – to see it as a dream while not identifying with the dream figure. As soon as the mind identifies with the body, then it identifies with the figure in the dream. And then we have the split within the dream – the perception of the subject and the object, the perceiver and the perceived. Really the whole dream is the perceived and there is no perceiver. The Witness Self knows this; it knows that the dream is unified.

There are really no "believers" and "non-believers;" no one who "has it" and others who do not "have it;" no "enlightened ones" or "ignorant ones." In the Witness Self everything and everyone is lit up, because everything is unified. You will never hear a spiritual teacher who is truly enlightened saying: *I have it and you do not*, because immediately there is duality there. What you will hear from an enlightened teacher is: *Come you who are weary, Judge not; Be ye perfect as your Father in Heaven is perfect; I and the Father are one; Before Abraham was I Am.* This is the Witness Self; this is the Gateway.

That is why I speak often of forgiveness, not to forgive somebody for wronging you, not to make the grievance real. What is important is coming to a moment of humility when you realize that everything that occurred was perfect – no sense of victimization, no one was harmed! In the Witness Self attack is seen as impossible; it never was the case that anybody was mistreated; it never was true that anyone was harmed. In the Witness Self there is no attack.

In humanistic psychology everything is good at the core. Transpersonal psychology emphasizes our oneness and our connection. Then as you move to parapsychology, you reach lucid dreaming – the awareness of dreaming. Think how happy, how free, how defenseless you could be if you were *watching* this dream. There could be monsters and dragons, or a whole army coming with machine guns, and you are stepped back in mind, in the state of lucid dreaming – you know you are dreaming. What does it mean to know you are dreaming? It is to know that what you are watching is not real.

The Witness Self knows it cannot be harmed. No matter what the content of the dream is, the observer knows everything is connected. This requires a lot of mind training. It is why we are traveling the world to share this, and to demonstrate that this Witness Self is not only attainable – it is inevitable. It is natural. We keep coming back to the same note: how easy Oneness is and how difficult fragmentation is. That is why we have a happy tune. We are saying, give up your funeral dirges of the peoples of earth; come and rejoice in the Witness Self and open to the Christ Mind – to this Oneness that is forever true.

Opening to this requires an invitation. I have discovered that everything happens by invitation; love will not force anything. At this moment, we are sitting together due to an invitation. Love will not try to convince or push something; love just is. It Is what It Is. There is an invitation to come into that love. As we travel, as we speak through the media, we have fun with many forms of expression; we are sending out an invitation. An example is our friend's Skype slogan: "I am the One, won't you join me there?" He is sending out the invitation. And that is what we are all doing through all these means of expression. People see we are happy and joyful. They can see that we are non-judgmental, that we do not need to put anybody down to be in this awareness. In fact, it is inconceivable that love would put anybody down. Then people feel drawn to us; they show up. We are witnesses to our Mind, and the witnesses are growing. It is so spacious when there is no judgment.

Friend: What are three of the simplest ways for people to access the Christ Mind and get themselves out of the way?

David: Trust your intuition or your Higher Power. Pay attention to your emotions; they are barometers. Awakening takes a lot of mind training and part of it is paying attention to your emotions, and to be genuine. Use simple language and do not pretend to be somewhere you are not. If you are hurting, that is OK, if you feel guilt, shame, and pain coming up, that is OK. Let your tears flow, let your anger come out. Let whatever is down there come to the surface; give yourself permission to move through it. Then finally, give yourself an opportunity with stillness. Whether you call it meditating, fishing, sailing on the ocean, whatever the form is, give yourself that peaceful easy feeling, a time to decompress, to unwind and relax; that makes the intuition much, much clearer.

Friend: It is beyond the words; it is a way of being. No words can describe the true teaching, a teaching that is a way of being.

David: Like Gandhi, when someone asked him what he believed, he replied: *Follow me for a while and you will see.*

Touching on Teaching and Learning

Friend: Does it happen very often that someone sincerely goes into the Course, works through the whole book, and then says, *been there, done that,* and walks away? It seems like it would change your thinking so much. How could you walk away and say, *I do not need to work on it anymore?*

David: This revolves around what Jesus calls "transfer of training:"

The ego can learn the Course and then compartmentalize it in the mind so it can just talk the Course, which would be a defense against applying it. The ego says: *Do not apply it. Do not start looking at the various aspects of your life because that would literally bring about an experience of awakening.* The message of the Course is so simple and so direct that people will often attempt to fit the Course into their life instead of letting go of what they conceive of as their life – and just letting go to the Holy Spirit. What happens is people try to mix the Course with all sorts of different things. This can be another diffusing mechanism. *I do not want to really hear what it is saying. I do not want to really see what it is saying, so I interpret against it.*

But there can be a genuine experience with the Course if the mind is ready and willing to use it. At the end of the Workbook Jesus says, "Our use for words is almost over now." W-pII.14.2 If the mind is really open and ready, it can approach mysticism, where it sinks more and more into that quietness. It sinks more and more into the revelatory experience and then, for a period of time, it seems to come back into the world, until it does not come back. It just sinks into the light and that is it.

People can say, *I took that Course*, but the Course has such a depth and is so profound that it is rare that someone seems to come in and just go through it. We need to step back and see that even "taking" *A Course in Miracles* is not a choice that the mind really has. At the very introduction Jesus says that only the time you take this Course is up to you. Even the form is not up to you. In the ultimate sense, here is the world and here is the screen, and here is where *A Course in Miracles* is (on the screen). It is all about my mind's readiness and willingness to turn back to the light beyond the screen of the world. As I do that, purely in a mind sense, it will seem like there is a form going on out here; I seem to be a person with a book, with eyes moving over the pages. All of that is out there on the screen, and is just a symbol. Really, I am a mind and I am coming back to the light. There just seems to be form; it is symbolic.

That really gets away from defending the Course. You begin to see that it seemed to be a path a person was taking, but really it was just another symbol. That brings such joy. I do not have to get into defending the Course or worrying about *60 Minutes* ever doing an exposé on it. I do not have to get into that because all that is out there on the screen. What I do need to do is watch my mind. Jesus says that being a miracle worker does not have anything to do with how long you have been in it, but it has to do with your willingness and readiness. Ultimately he says to trust implicitly in *his* readiness; you cannot really trust in your own readiness.

Friend: That teacher within us, right? It is not a teacher *out there*.

David: Yes, it is to be seen as symbolic. In the *Manual for Teachers* there is a section about levels of teaching. Jesus begins the section by saying that there are no levels or progressions of teaching; God's plan for Atonement was accomplished in an instant. But Jesus knows that Idea is too big a quantum leap, so he goes on to offer three levels. He talks about the casual encounters, sustained relationships, and lifelong teaching/learning relationships. In the

Song of Prayer he also talks about rungs of a ladder as a metaphor for going deeper with the teachings. He begins the *Manual for Teachers* by saying that you are teaching and learning every instant. That takes it out of a realm of form, of teacher or student appearing. If you are teaching every instant, then it is all in your mind. There are two thought systems in there. I am teaching myself depending on which one I am lining up with every instant. I always go back to that. That is how I keep it simple, every instant. I do not have to think about who the teacher is for me, or who the student is. Actually, most of the *Manual for Teachers* is written at the relative or metaphorical level. He talks about healers and patients, but in the ultimate sense our minds are what need healing. He does give a sense that there will be some who seem to have trained their minds or will seem to be a little bit more miracle-minded. It is described as teacher/pupil or healer/patient relationships. He is clearly talking at the metaphorical level of how it *seems* to be.

We see this same thing in the sections on holy relationship. In the ultimate sense, holy relationship is nothing more than accepting the Holy Spirit's Purpose. It is not dependent on you and your spouse agreeing on a holy purpose because ultimately there is just one mind. But a lot of the text on special and holy relationships is written at the level of the seeming split mind. For example, in the Workbook: "Two minds with one intent become so strong that what they will becomes the Will of God." W-185.3 And there is a passage in the text where he says, "Whoever is saner at the time the threat is perceived should remember how deep is his indebtedness to the other and how much gratitude is due him, and be glad that he can pay his debt by bringing happiness to both." T-18.V.7 This is obviously written as if there is a relationship between two people. These are helpful metaphors while the mind seems to be split and believes in separate persons. At this stage the world is not yet experienced as nothing but a world of ideas. Until there is a significant shift in the mind, it is experienced as relationships of bodies.

Friend: Is there a difference between teaching, which we all do by our thoughts and actions, and a teacher who seems to be able to verbalize and express concepts a little better, like you do?

David: I would say when you read the *Manual for Teachers*, just be aware of these different metaphors. At the beginning he says that a teacher of God is anyone who wants to be one. Well, that is one way of talking about it; it is one that is often quoted. People will say: *we are all teachers*, but there is another "metaphor" in the *Manual for Teachers* as well: "He cannot claim that title until he has gone through the workbook, since we are learning within the framework of our course." M-16.3 To be a teacher of God you have to be teaching what comes through from the Holy Spirit. Otherwise, you are seemingly teaching with God part of the time and teaching with the ego the rest of the time. That is why it is helpful when he uses all these educational metaphors. In the Manual he says this about the teacher of God: "…somewhere he has made a deliberate choice in which he did not see his interests as apart from someone else's. Once he has done that, his road is established and his direction is sure." M-1.1

There are only two lessons in your mind. The Holy Spirit is a lesson and the ego is a lesson and if you continue to try to teach from both you will be a conflicted teacher and a conflicted learner. It is a very confusing curriculum to try to teach two opposing thought systems that do not meet at any point. It gets back to the willingness to unveil the wrong mind. I cannot choose the Holy Spirit consistently until I see that the wrong mind has nothing to offer. I cannot choose the Holy Spirit as long as I think there are some parts of the wrong mind that are attractive. For example, maybe I still believe that there is some "good guilt." For most people innocence is good, but there are certain heinous crimes that are unacceptable. As long as you believe there are certain injustices and certain grievances that are valid, then you still believe in "good" guilt. The Course's message is that guilt is never good. Guilt always comes from the ego.

Ultimately, it seems as if there is an ego, a Holy Spirit, and a decision maker. But as long as you believe there is an autonomous decision maker that can choose one or the other, or at times neither, you are falling into another trap. You are always, every instant, either in the wrong mind or the right mind.

In the *Rules for Decision* it says, "Today I will make no decisions by myself." T-30.I.2 He says you may perceive this as coercion, but, think about it: you have two advisers in your mind, and every decision you make comes from listening to one or the other. It is not a question of coercion here. He says you will make a decision based on one of these advisers. The purpose of the Course is to take a look at what I really want. I cannot make a choice for the Holy Spirit as long as I believe there is something attractive about the ego. As soon as the ego gets raised up from the unconscious into conscious awareness, I can see that none of these beliefs serve me. That is it!

On Teachers and Learning without Limits

Hi David,

It is very tempting to me to hold a teacher of high regard as an idol. The ego will use spiritual teachers and books and writings for its own goal if you allow it. "He is your only example of one who has successfully completed the work that you are putting so much time, effort and sacrifice into," the ego raves and rants. I find it best to "come back to the breath," as I learned from meditation, which really means to not follow the mind, but return to the Truth. Continuously returning to the Truth is showing me that I am becoming much more peaceful in situations that before really stirred me up while I protected myself and attacked in retaliation.

Faith in God is all I need to follow in the path back to Him. Faith in man will only lead me into illusions. Faith in your brother does not mean in what he says or does, but in the Truth about him—his innocence. This is the way home, in my belief.

Thank you all for showing me the specks of dust on the altar, and thank you, Spirit, for the duster I have in my hand, called Forgiveness! In other words, thank you all for all.

Beloved One,

Thanks for sharing the private thoughts and emotions that were bubbling to the surface of consciousness for healing. It is truly an inside job. I have always said, "Do not follow the flesh; follow the Spirit within." Jesus taught me the one right use of judgment—asking myself *how do I feel?*—as a tool for coming to an authentic transformation of consciousness and emotional honesty—a State of Joy! This I now express freely, and if that seems to inspire someone to forgive and be happy, that is a blessing beyond measure.

I no longer identify with the "roles" of teacher/student or leader/follower or guru/devotee, for I rest in the Present Moment and am content to simply Be.

I was always inspired by the passages about the characteristics of God's teachers in the fourth chapter of the *Manual for Teachers*. I invite you to look them up and take Comfort as well, particularly the sections on: Honesty, Tolerance, Gentleness, Joy, and Defenselessness, and:

Except for God's teachers there would be little hope of salvation, for the world of sin would seem forever real. The self-deceiving must deceive, for they must teach deception. And what else is hell? This is a manual for the teachers of God. They are not perfect, or they would not be here. Yet it is their mission to become perfect here, and so they teach perfection over and over, in many, many ways, until they have learned it. And then they are seen no more, although their thoughts remain a source of strength and truth forever. M-in.5

I am grateful for God's Eternal Love that simply *is*, ever available as the Source of Help within.

Mastery through Love

Hi David,

I have followed a teacher for years who has been called and declared himself an awakened "master teacher." He has taught that mind is singular, that this world was over long ago, that he speaks from out of time, and that he and all of his followers are going to flash out of time together. He makes many references to the Bible and *A Course in Miracles*, yet in the Bible Jesus teaches to turn the other cheek, resist not evil, and says if someone asks you for your coat to offer them your cloak as well. In ACIM Jesus even teaches: "In my defenselessness my safety lies." My teacher has in recent years, however, advocated and participated in an ongoing campaign and lawsuit against the copyright holders of ACIM, and justifies this action as taking a stand for Christ against those who would attempt to distort the teachings and block the spreading of the Word. This is confusing. I do not understand how it is possible to engage in a lawsuit, have legal representation, prepare a case against a brother, and defend a position—all in the Name of Jesus Christ. Jesus says, "If I defend myself I am attacked." Could you explain this?

My second question has to do with the teachings from my teacher about physical transformation. If the body is an illusion how is it possible to transform or change an illusion? My teacher refers to the transfiguration of Jesus, yet I cannot understand how a change in form or in the physical has anything to do with the transformation of mind called Enlightenment? Am I missing something?

My third question has to do with spiritual specialness. My teacher has referred to himself and has been referred to as an insertion of light into the time-space continuum, yet at the same time he speaks of being out of time. There is great importance placed on being *with* the master teacher and staying in the high energy and fast time of the master teacher and the association. Yet in ACIM I read that the holiest spot on earth is where an ancient hatred has become a present love. Would you speak about the trap of making somebody special and different from everybody else? I have heard this called the guru trap and it seems to be yet another ego ploy to set one brother above others and to maintain a sense of uniqueness, specialness, and separation in a subtle way. If we are One Mind then it seems that no person, place, event, or thing will have more importance and that there is nothing to compare in truth. Is this so?

Hello Beloved One,

Christ is Spirit, created by God, and needs no defense. Concepts were made by the ego and thus seem to need constant defense. Truth needs no defense for Truth has no opposite or opposition. Concepts of self are fragile and no matter how puffed up they may seem to get in this world, they have no foundation in truth and offer no peace of mind, safety, or security.

Mastery through Love sees the folly and the impossibility of defense. Mastery through Love sees that a lawsuit is a joke, for defense and authentic spiritual practice have no meeting point. Defense is an ego attempt to teach that vulnerability is real and that something exists which is in need of protection. Yet the central teaching of *A Course in Miracles* is: "Nothing real can be threatened. Nothing unreal exists. Herein lies the peace of God." Peace and understanding go together and cannot be found apart. Be glad that you CANNOT understand a lawsuit justified and engaged in under the Name of Jesus Christ. What you have described is a good example of the joke of the world, the foolishness of the ego's antics under the pretense of a "spiritual cause."

In answer to your second question, "physical transformation" is an oxymoron or contradiction in terms. This is the error of the world of contradictions. It is indeed impossible to transform or change the physical, for the change of illusion is simply the illusion of change. That is why I say: "Seek not to change the world. Rather change your mind about the world." The *Serenity Prayer* is the same reminder: The world cannot be changed but you can change your mind about the world. And the Holy Spirit is the Wisdom to know (discern) the difference.

The transfiguration of Jesus described in the Bible was a "phenomenon" or "window dressing." At best it is seen as a symbol or representation of going beyond the veil of images to the Light of Christ beyond. It is helpful to be reminded, however, that ALL perceptions are false. Abstract Light is Universal and not specific or particular. Spirit never "comes into" matter and Truth cannot be brought to illusions. Eternity never "comes into" time and Infinity never "comes into" the finite. This is also why the concept of an "insertion of Light" is impossible, for the Word does not literally become flesh. Reality cannot be translated or transformed into unreality. Instead, bring the darkness of false belief (including the physical) to the Light of Truth and Know Thy Self as Spirit. Time-space-matter-physical dissolves, and the Spirit remains. Accept Atonement and this realization is obvious.

In Answer to your third question, the ego IS the belief in specialness or uniqueness. The attempt to single out a person, place, thing, situation, or event from the whole tapestry of the cosmos IS the attempt to make and worship an idol or God-substitute. This ego temptation (the wish to make illusions real) of "guru worship" is but one example of the death wish of specialness. Whenever a comparison is made, duality has been accepted as real and Divine Love is seemingly blocked from awareness. Yet Love simply Is.

Spirit Love is the Energy of Life in God. This Energy is never "high" or "low," "bright" or "dim," "strong" or "weak." Spirit is Timeless and Changeless. Time is an illusion, thus there is no "fast time" or "slow time." It is impossible to be "close to" or "far away" from Spirit because Spirit transcends the false concepts of distance and increments of measurement. The ego attempts to use such concepts to maintain its "existence," and its "existence" rests on the belief in differences and uniqueness. Happily Oneness cannot be broken into different, unique pieces or parts. Wholeness means One!

Divine Mind is real. Personhood, a concept of body-mind-soul, is not. It is impossible for a concept to be real, for God did not create concepts. God creates Spirit and Spirit shares in God's Reality. ACIM is but one seeming "pathway" of releasing past associations, accepting the wholeness of the forgiven world, remembering Self and God. Where would "the association" begin? Where would "the association" end? You see, the false is false and cannot be broken into parts or pieces. There is no we/they split, no in/out split. The "association" or group is but another self-concept. Remember that only self-concepts require the illusion of defense; this will offer insight to the Answer to your first question about the lawsuit. Salvation is nothing more than the escape from self-concepts.

Forgiveness, the last illusion, the last self-concept is not made by you alone. The Holy Spirit offers Atonement as the Perspective of wholeness that transcends the ego's personal perspective of parts. To the Holy Spirit, GURU means: Gee You are You. The "I Am" Presence is Spirit, One Self forever in the Mind of God. Nothing else exists.

Truth is an experience. It cannot be organized.

Look not to the flesh for the experience within.

Look not to man or woman or "master teacher" in form.
Spirit neither leads nor follows. Spirit simply Is.

Enlightenment is but a recognition, not a change at all.

Atonement is the Point of recognition which transcends the ego traps of "leader" and "follower."

There is nothing "outside" of One Self. Such is Enlightenment!

Transcending the Teacher Concept

Wanting to be a "teacher of God," in the personal sense, is part of the ego's illusion. Heaven is pure desireless Oneness; the step toward Heaven is a unified "Goal" or "Purpose" which dissolves the belief in time. The many goals and desires of the ego are meaningless, since the ego has no existence. The ego's game becomes obvious: Seek and do not find. The end of seeking is Finding.

Teaching and learning are not separate, for the mind is teaching/learning all the "time" as long as it believes in time. Teaching/learning can be equated with thinking; Awakening is the conversion which occurs as past/future thoughts are released and the Mind realizes It Thinks only as God Thinks. It Creates exactly as God Creates.

As long as the mind believes in lack, it seems to want, and seeks to fill the empty feeling. When lack is seen as impossible, the Mind realizes only Wholeness and Fulfillment and Oneness. Peace and contentment are experiences of the Present Moment. "Teach only Love" means you think with God and are with God.

To let forgiveness be your "learning goal" is to be willing to unlearn everything you believe and empty the mind of all it thinks it thinks. You are coming inward to discern the valuable from the valueless, the meaningful from the meaningless, the true from the false. It will dawn in awareness that the "detour" was the illusion. You remain as God created You, Beloved Light Bearer. You are God's Gift as you shine so brightly! Happily God's Child is beyond change.

The Importance of an Invitation

Friend: How do you deal with people who have all these beliefs about the body? It may be that they are taking lots of supplements or have certain types of diets or exercise regimes? Do you ever say anything to them unsolicited?

David: No, it is really upon invitation. Someone who is sincere about the mind training may say something like, "Please help me out in any way that you can. Please point out anything that you see that could be helpful in releasing the ego." That is an open invitation. Even then, what would be shared is not so much an attempt to correct a brother but rather just answering the call. When I travel, people around me may talk about dietary things or they may seem to be addicted or trapped or enslaved by a number of things, I am there to join and to rejoice in the joy of the moment and not to point things out. We have stayed with people who seem to be struggling in many areas but are not actively asking for things to be pointed out. It has been a great experience for me. People will say, "Oh I so enjoyed your visit and I just loved your being here;" they appreciate the joy and the peace and the sense of non-judgment.

That feeling is more likely to inspire them to make the inner changes necessary for letting old patterns fall away—more so than being told to look at specific things. Correction like that can feel like judgment or criticism. The invitation is essential before I will point out specifics. But when we are joining in the awakening, as we go much deeper we will uncover many ego defense mechanisms, which is really where the problem is. It is in the mind; it is not in the behaviors. Behaviors rise automatically out of beliefs and the thoughts. I try to join with people in purpose—and to work with the beliefs and the thoughts. I really do not notice the behaviors. Just live as you would live and let's share the joy.

Opening to God's Voice

Hi David,

I am having difficulty listening to the voice for God. I am continually on and off between peace and conflict. I have been studying ACIM for three years and I no longer see things as I did before. But, although in meditation I feel a wonderful, peaceful and loving sensation, during the rest of the day I almost feel enraged and furious. I really feel I am going crazy, I feel I have a split mentality, I see myself as evil and awful and also as innocent and impeccable. It takes an effort to remember to breathe and recall Who I am. Intellectually ACIM has been a constant awe for me, I can see how teaching and learning work, how perception, illusion and ego work. I do not know how to express myself. I feel terrible at this moment and feel I need help.

The Course has become my almost obsession for the last years. I would only like to be around ACIM students, only talking about God and the Holy Spirit, only feeling peace and love. To realize that I am voluntarily trying to believe differently than I had always believed seems so crazy. If instead of just myself I had a "guru" or someone else telling me to brain-wash myself to believe this, I would indeed be very afraid. But I have felt the love and peace that this belief offers and I want it. I suppose I am desperate. Could you please send me some words of comfort? Am I the only one having these problems with the practice of ACIM?

Beloved One,

You are soooooo Loved. I am with You all the way in Awakening! The conflict of belief is surfacing in consciousness, as it must. Though it may feel to the ego as though you are going insane, the false is merely being exposed and brought to truth. The darkness is being brought to the light.

The emotions you experience are part of the illusion of undoing and are not unusual in the purification of thought—in the transformation of mind to Mind. ACIM is your path and you follow it with devotion. It is an accelerated path of going through fear to love. As you Call on God's Love, everything that blocks the awareness of Love is being brought to awareness so it can be released. As you approach the core of the ego thought system, the feelings can seem very intense, for the ego is highly threatened by the Light and identification with the ego produces the illusion of upset. Take heart, for the end of dreaming is close at hand.

The Holy Spirit will direct all unlearning. If you are having difficulty hearing His Voice I suggest asking the question: "What is this for?" about the situations and events you experience daily. This questioning, if done sincerely and persistently, leads deeper and deeper into the ego's belief system and is helpful in relinquishing faith in the ego. This will help in the task of releasing linear perception and allowing the miracle to rearrange perception to the simultaneous Perspective. To use the symbol of the cross, the horizontal collapses and dissolves; all that remains is the vertical (Communion with God).

At some point you may be Guided to participate more fully in a "spiritual community," and this form will be a symbol to you of open communication and the safety and stability to allow error to surface and be released. Everything is a reflection of thought. Happily it is learned that changing thoughts by releasing attack thoughts is our salvation. The world can only reflect belief, yet belief can change from judgment to forgiveness as the willingness to lay aside all judgment arises. This is the surrender into God's Grace.

"Spiritual community" is a reflection of willingness to Call for Help and to be used in extending Help. This will open up even greater willingness to hear God's Voice. The key is not hiding or protecting false thoughts and beliefs. Sharing with your brothers and sisters is symbolic of hiding nothing from the Loving Light of the Holy Spirit. This opportunity is readily available in all apparent forms of community, including physical contacts and the Internet. It is always helpful to remember, however, that laying aside the horizontal (belief in a linear world "out there") at the point of intersection (the miracle) leads to the vertical (Vision of Christ). "Spiritual community" is a helpful step toward recognizing the Communion with God within.

I join with you in your devotion, for Christ Calls and we Answer. What more Holy aim could there be? I love you and walk the Selfsame road to God.

Truth Has No Exceptions

What is true for you is true for me and is true for all if it be the Truth. Divine Principle has no exceptions; there is no misperception that forgiveness cannot heal. God has no favorites and since there is no order of difficulty in miracles, one seeming situation is as forgivable as the next. Yet by "forgivable" I mean that no illusion can stand in the Light of Divine Principle. Upsets give way to Joy in awareness as attack thoughts are released. Joy is natural to the Spirit.

The important point to see is that the world is distorted perception, a darkened lens. The ego distortion seemed to split the world in two and perceive subjects/objects, victims and victimizers, saints and sinners. Yet the split was in the mind and not the world; the Correction is in the mind, not in the world.

A change in perception is literally to look on the world anew, with the Spirit, and see a forgiven world. Once the error is healed or seen as unreal, gone are the effects as well that the error seemed to produce. The body in the ego's perception can seem to be born, to live, to grow sick and old, to be either victim or victimizer, and to die. Yet the Spirit is eternal and therefore incapable of any of these illusions.

Am I Spirit or body is the distinction or decision that is key, for One is Real and the other but a dream. Forgiveness sees illusions as illusions and dreams as dreams, and thus sees the past as past. Such is true empowerment, for to be aligned with a Higher Power is to truly be invulnerable.

To find, seek no further. Be willing to discover that you are a "seeker" no longer, but One Who Is. Just what would change in experience (besides everything) if the Real You experienced True Identity and flowed from knowing Union with God instead of clinging to doubt and walking on fearful eggshells seeking it? You know the Answer. You ARE the Answer.

It would mean having no excuses for holding onto the belief in victimhood.

It would be an end to the cry: "But what about me?"

It would mean being Free to Love without limits.

It would mean not coddling anyone who appears to be settling for less by saying, "Yeah, I know what you mean."

It would mean choosing prayer, meditation, etc., each morning instead of jumping onto the train of ego meanderings and busy nothings.

It would mean that responsibility for the Atonement, for Complete Inner Peace, has been accepted.

It would mean seeing the nothingness of the belief in "the crowd of mass sleepiness," and basking in the Light of Heaven within.

It would mean eye contact (from the window of the soul) with the grocery clerk and the person on the street and everyone that comes to mind ... Real ... Deep ... Contact from within the Core of Beingness.

It would mean feeling deeply without resistance.

It would mean a depth of Peace that is so All-encompassing that for an Instant the world disappears and the experience of True Vision dawns.

It would mean dancing in indescribable Joy and experiencing Awe about the Power and Glory and Everlasting Love of God!

It would mean living in a Universe that makes no mistakes, thus having not one thing to judge.

Peace Comes with Acceptance

David: There comes a time when all searching and seeking and desire for improvement comes to an end. There is a moment in which the mind is still and content. There is an instant that transcends time/space and all the things of time/space. In this instant is the world forgiven – seen from a point of reference that knows not of judgment. All things are seen as they really are, without distortion or distinctions. The sameness of all things is radiantly apparent! Such is Acceptance! Such is Peace!

Friend: Can you talk about what my purpose in life is?

David: The clearer you get and the more you go into it, there is a joy that is just impelling. It is a joy to start getting clear. Then when you connect and join with people, what you say is what you need to hear. The awareness of that comes in more and more.

Friend: How do you know when you follow that desire to share that the ego is not going to take over?

David: The Holy Spirit is purpose. The ego does not know what purpose is. It does not know what meaning is because it does not come from meaning. It never had a consistent role model, so to speak, and it is very inconsistent and erratic. It does not know what it wants. It just keeps grabbing and searching for things in the world: the perfect relationship, the perfect car, the perfect college degree. The ego is always playing this game, *I will be happy when* ____ (fill in the blank). Behind this game is the belief that if you get the right situation, your dream world of form will bring you happiness – so you go for the dream. Some people want the American dream and when they finally get the wife, the house, the dog and even the picket fence, then they do not know why they wanted all that. The ego is always saying there is some form that will bring you happiness.

The Course teaches that there is a Purpose in mind, not in form, that will bring us happiness. "When you decide upon the form that you want, you lose the understanding of its purpose." T-30.III.2

Opening to Divine Love

It always feels heart-warming to extend Divine Love. Releasing the temptation to look outside for the "source of love" and instead extending the Love within is the key to lasting happiness. For Love is like a never-ending well-spring bubbling up; the more we extend It the more we are aware that we have It and are It. Love makes no distinctions and does not discriminate, for Love bathes all in its kindly Light. This is what makes Love a gift to all.

The world was made as a substitute for Divine Love. The world's "love" involves bargains, reciprocity, control, specialness, and its core characteristic is possessiveness. While Divine Love radiates and shines without limitation, condition, or restriction, possessive "love" is full of rules, boundaries, demands, and expectations. Divine Love is free and freely given. Possessive "love" is always looking for what it will get in return. Possessive "love" has many strings attached to its "gift." Divine Love knows not of strings or attachments, for it flows as powerfully, silently, joyfully, and freely as a Grand River.

We cannot direct the Course of Love. We can surrender into the Current of Divine Love and it will carry us until we happily realize that the I Am Presence of Divine Love is our very Self in God. The Love of God is Everlasting, and thus everything else that seems to be will fade and disappear as we remember the Everlasting Light of Divine Love. Glory to God for creating Divine Love as One!

A Parable of Forgiveness – The End of Seeking

Forgiveness is the means to be in the miracle, where all questions are answered. This beautiful parable, told by Hugh and Gayle Prather in *A Book for Couples*, expresses it well.

There was a seeker who went before God and said, "You have told me that my training is almost complete. You have said that I am nearly ready to leave the world of form and enter into our Heavenly Kingdom. But You Who are Love have given me no instruction in the ways between a man and a woman."

"Yes, my child," said God, "there is a question that saddens you. But do you see it clearly?" And as he had been trained, the seeker went within the Silence and abode there awhile. Shortly he said, "I have many questions that sadden me. Am I to marry or be alone? And if I am alone, am I to be celibate? And if I am to marry, are we to be alone or with children? And if I have a spouse and children, do they join me in the work you have given me? And if they are to join me, what am I to do if they refuse?"

"Yes, my child," said God, "these and a thousand questions more could you ask. Yet do you not see a single question beneath all the others?"

Again the student touched the Silence, and this time he remained Still for a long while. Presently he said, "I believe the one question I have is 'Am I alone'?"

And God said, "You have seen well. You have seen the only question there is. The world you are about to Ascend from was merely this question."

Still the seeker did not laugh. And so God said, "Perhaps, my child, you think you do not know the Answer."

The seeker said, "Are there no thoughts you can give me to answer the many little questions that are born of this one?"

"There are indeed many while you believe that the One is many," said God, "but they are all answered in the one Answer."

And then God spoke to the seeker from deep within the depths of Love:

You are the miracle you must perform. And whenever you seem to fail in this function you will feel alone, and by this choice you will abstain from all life, all truth, all reality.

You will know when you have remembered your function by the Love that overwhelms judgment and desire. For the miracle is your function: To be the reflection of My Love, and then see our Divine Spirit as all there is—to give Love easily and thus receive it easily. Nothing you say or do in the world will have any meaning without Love.

To Love is to be in the shining Heart of Me and thus within the hearts of the "least" and the "greatest" of My children. For when you are in the Heart of Me you do not look through the faults of your brother. You do not look past them, or over them, or around them. You look within Me. For only in My Heart will you recognize the Pulse that courses through all Creation.

In this world you will be tempted to believe that to Love one you must first Love all. But I tell you now that you must forgive one brother before you can love all. For there is only One. It matters not if you seemed to take a spouse or have no spouse, seemed to have children or have them not. For this brother you forgive is every child, woman, and man you look upon. But until you treat at least one brother as you would be treated and come to recognize that his heart is your own, you will seem to wander alone through space and time and dream of death. You will seem to think of hurting your brother and dream of hurting Me. But when at last you Wake to Who your brother is, you will Waken as One in Me.

During that Instant you will return Home. And I will sing You the Eternal Song of Happiness. For You are my Child and there is no other. And I will rock you Awake to Life in Me: You who are My joy and My Meaning and My Completion."

I hold a place in Eternity for You where We dwell as One, I in You and You in Me forever. Know Love and You will know that You are never alone.

Glory to God for Everlasting Love. Forgiveness is always a gift to our Self, and thus forgiveness has no price or cost.

BOOK TWO
UNLEARNING THE WORLD

CONTENTS

Chapter Seven

Chapter One

Healing and Atonement are Identical

David: There is absolutely, positively nothing in time, matter, or space that is causative at all. Out of everything that seems to come out of the mouth, you need to just watch for *content*. For example, just now when you were talking about the dog you expressed the idea that if you lock the dog up she will feel deprived, and then when you let her out she will be excited – cause and effect. Just about anything you can think of is based on causation in the world.

To accept the Atonement and hold to the fact that my mind is causative and there is absolutely nothing on the screen in the entire cosmos that has any kind of causation whatsoever – is healing. That is what this lesson in the *Manual for Teachers* is about:

> Healing and Atonement are not related; they are identical. There is no order of difficulty in miracles because there are no degrees of Atonement. It is the one complete concept possible in this world because it is the source of a wholly unified perception. Partial Atonement is a meaningless idea, just as special areas of hell in Heaven are inconceivable. Accept Atonement and you are healed. Atonement is the Word of God. Accept his Word and what remains to make sickness possible? Accept his Word and every miracle has been accomplished. To forgive is to heal. The teacher of God has taken accepting the Atonement for himself as his only function. What is there then he cannot heal? What miracle can be withheld from him? M-22.1

The next paragraph touches on the self-concept and transfer of training. What will I hold back from the Atonement?

> The progress of the teacher of God may be slow or rapid depending on whether he recognizes the Atonement's inclusiveness or for a time excludes some problem areas from it. In some cases there is a sudden and complete awareness of the perfect applicability of the lesson of the Atonement to all situations but this is comparatively rare. The teacher of God may have accepted the function God has given him long before he has learned all that his acceptance holds out to him. M-22.2

Friend: If I knew what was in store for me....

David: [laughing] Mother Theresa said something like: *If I had known when I was young what was coming, I would never have stepped into this.* She was being slightly facetious.

> It is only the end that is certain. Anywhere along the way the necessary realization of inclusiveness may reach him. If the way seems long, let him be content. He has decided on the direction he wants to take. What more was asked of him? In having done what was required would God withhold the rest? M-22.2

I think of that line, "If the way seems long let him be content." You get a sense of how quickly you want to climb the seeming ladder. You cannot really go to the next rung until you get a really good push off from the prior one. Desire and willingness are the only things that determine whether it is going to be a long ladder or....

Friend: That feels reassuring to me; be content where you are. Do not worry about whether or not it seems to be taking a long time.

David: Do not get into judging based on increments in the world, or comparisons.

Friend: Just be content and stay on the path.

David: "That forgiveness is healing needs to be understood if the teacher of God is to make progress." M-22.3 Forgiveness is the reversal of the thoughts in the mind, all the backwards ones having been turned around. "The idea that a body can be sick is the central concept in the ego's thought system." M-22.3 That is an underlying assumption. Whenever things are brought up, like the issue with your toe or flu symptoms, the underlying assumption in the presenting problem is that you have a sick body. "I feel it," or "I have been through this." The idea that a body can be sick is the central concept in the ego's thought system. As we see in this paragraph, it is very important for the ego to hold onto the idea that a body can be sick. That is one of its strongest witnesses to separation—its ace in the hole!

Friend: And the more you think of it, the more power you give it.

David: Focusing on pain "...gives the body autonomy, separates it from the mind, and keeps the idea of attack inviolate." M-22.3

Friend: As if the body has power over my mind to keep me distracted from the truth.

David: Underneath that is the thought: *I cannot change my mind.* That is what I hear when people say….

Friend: "I am in pain."

David: Yes. I also hear: *I tried. I asked the Holy Spirit to see things differently. I want to not be in pain. I cannot do it. It has power over me.* There is a feeling of frustration and powerlessness. The mind has chosen it and then forgotten exactly what it chose in order for it to seem that the body has power. As we get into this deeper you begin to see the mind's desire to hold onto the concept of itself as it perceives itself. It wants to hold on dearly to the separation, to the small self. It is invested in holding on to that. It is so terrified of letting that go and just going into the light that it seems like sickness is a great device that has value. It clearly provides a witness.

Friend: It gets your attention.

David: It draws the attention off of the mind and back out there onto the body and the screen.

Friend: Instead of watching what I am thinking now, all I think about is the pain in my toe or elbow.

David: And as we go deeper into the metaphysics, the next thought is like our friend's comment: "I want to understand this thing. I made myself sick." Now the mind has taken responsibility for the attack thoughts and for what it perceives as sickness. That is where the guilt comes in. The guilt is coming in from lining up with the wrong mind, from raising body thoughts to the level of mind. In other words, saying I am responsible for behavior, for things that the body seems to do and has done and so on and so forth. If that is true then sins are only in bodies, but the mind has associated itself with the body and that is where the guilt comes in.

Friend: Is that level confusion?

David: Yes, it is about level confusion. Body thoughts are of the ego and not of the right mind. But saying that body thoughts are causative is really what "to raise body thoughts to the level of mind" means. It is simply to say that the body, or something in matter, is causative or creative. And you can see that is where the level confusion occurs—in the belief that bodies actually act. It seems in this world as if there are autonomous persons that act autonomously. It seems like, in the deceived state, that we each have different minds; one can decide to come or to stay, each of us can decide to do this or do that. It really seems that way. There is a pretty well-accepted belief that we are all persons. And part of being a person is to have a mind of your own. The deceived mind has assigned to the mind the properties of the body. The metaphor here is that we have these separate bodies sitting on the couch and that each of these minds is also separate.

Really there is just one mind and all the characters on the screen, all of them, are part of the playing out of a script that is already played out; it has all been played out. In other words, when I say that the mind wrote the script: it hired the characters, it gave out the parts, and everything that is said is its own invention. This one sleeping mind has invented and projected out all these other bodies and all these other minds and has given out all these parts; it has done the whole thing.

There is absolutely nothing to be upset about when somebody says or does something. When another dream figure or the dog seems to do something and you feel upset, that is part of the script. It is believed to be apart from my mind, though. If I am a person and that is a dog, it is not a child but just a dog, and I am upset at the dog's behavior or whatever, I have simply denied that that is just a thought or an image in my own mind. I mean, if it is just another image, what is the big deal? You see when the meaning gets written into it: *I am a person; this is my house; we have guests coming over; this is just a dog; the dog should not inhibit our social life; the dog should not be doing this.* You can see where all this stuff gets read into as meaning and then, by golly, before you know it you are upset at something that the dog has done. Or, you can look at it from the perspective that bodies are not autonomous, they do not act apart from your mind; they are thoughts in a concretized form, acting out.

Friend: So I am not responsible for the roles that I assign, for what is said or done by the characters, but I am responsible for how I perceive that?

David: Yes.

Friend: I am responsible for my reaction. That is all it is really. Everything is how you feel—everything. It is like when I walk along and think that I will see somebody to talk to; I know there will be somebody there, and sure enough there she is!

David: The only thing you want to do is always keep it in past tense because the miracle sees it as having already happened; I put someone there to talk to. "I will put," has a linear sense to it.

We are getting back to this causation thing. For example, it really seems that at times when I think I would like water, a pool shows up. There is a lot of talk about concepts like abundance, about using your mind to attract things to you, but the script is written! The only thing we really have a choice about is seeing it through the miracle – from above the battlefield – seeing that none of the images are true and none of it is me. That is where the peace comes from. It only seems as if symbols are being brought forth, as if people are using their minds to get cars and stuff. Then they make the association that the mind is powerful and creative but it is linked in with the form again. They do not have that clarity of the levels that the Course brings. The right mind sees it all as false. The right mind is not full of images; it is above the images and looks on all of them as equally false. The teaching is very clear on causation and that all of these are unreal effects. If they are unreal effects, then their cause is unreal. The Holy Spirit looks to the cause and knows that the "cause" of these effects is unreal. He has judged their cause and overlooked it. He does not look to the projections on the screen. He has judged their cause and knows that it is unreal and therefore knows that everything in the wrong mind is false. In that sense then, defenselessness makes perfect sense. There would never be a reason to have any kind of care, worry or concern.

> Can you imagine what it means to have no cares, no worries,
> no anxieties, but merely to be perfectly calm and quiet all
> the time? Yet that is what time is for; to learn just that and
> nothing more. T-15.I.1

That is it. That is the lesson. And it is not something you strive for either.

Friend: Yes, this quote really spoke to me: "You would not react at all to figures in a dream you knew that you were dreaming." T-27.VIII.10

David: Yes.

> Awareness of dreaming is the real function of God's teachers.
> They watch the dream figures come and go, shift and change,
> suffer and die, yet they are not deceived by what they see. They
> recognize that to behold a dream figure as sick and separate is

no more real than to regard it as healthy and beautiful. Unity alone is not a thing of dreams and it is this God's teachers acknowledge as behind the dream, beyond all seeming and yet surely theirs. M-12.6

I can hold onto that thought. Even though some may seem to be sick or dying, the mind sees that as impossible. It is impossible for the body to be sick; it is impossible to really die. Death gets redefined as being whenever you are upset in any way. That is death. That is helpful because it brings it back to the psychological, to the realm of mind, and gets away from the physical realm, as if something happens when a body quits breathing. You have heard the expression that someone "passed on," or "made their transition"? Transition into what?

Friend: Yesterday my son came in not just crying, but wailing. It was a great opportunity for me to not get stuck! I wanted to be loving but I did not know how to communicate without getting caught up in it. I just held the intention of being loving and not getting caught up, but I felt like I did not know how to communicate that. I didn't know how to express being loving or comforting. Does it mean holding him and hugging him? He told me that the log had fallen on his hand.

David: Yes, he wanted to show me too. I sat down with him and simply held my intention. In a matter of a few seconds he quit talking about the hand and started talking about other things. When it was not shared in the mind, the attention shifted from the hand to just sitting there. There we were on the bed just talking about other things for about 5 or 10 minutes. One of them was, "When will my mom be home?" and I said, "Oh she is running some errands." That is part of the conditioning too, of wanting to look for someone that is familiar and sympathetic. But once again, when it is not shared, the attention can shift. Like the example you always share about going to the Christian Science class when he had that scab on his face, like the elephant man. This was Christian Science, so neither the kids nor the teacher made a big deal about the scab. Nobody even mentioned it.

Friend: And it healed very quickly then. But for about a week, everywhere else we went people would say things like, "Oh my gosh, what happened to you? Are you okay!?" People really made a big thing of it. For me there was such contrast in going where it was never mentioned. Wow, what a difference that makes.

David: It really puts it into practice.

Friend: He did not feel the need to go in and tell them that this is not the way he usually looks. He did not explain it to anybody.

David: There was another story about an elderly woman in Christian Science who had experiences like that her whole life. Once she picked up her granddaughter at school after the girl was sent home by the school nurse. Her daughter was just going on and on in a panic about the nurse saying that it could be this or it could be that, but the grandmother was just not giving attention to it at all – not lending her mind to share that perception. She just let it diffuse naturally because the mind is literally calling out: *teach me that this is not so.*

Friend: One area where I feel at a loss is when the kids feel sick and want to stay home. I have said, "Okay, so stay home." But then the school requires that you write a note and explain why they stayed home. I feel like I cannot write that they were "sick." What do I say?

David: Sickness is, in a sense, a mind calling for help.

Friend: So, my daughter had a sick mind calling for help today. [group laughter]

David: In your mind you know it. You have to know the meaning and let the words be used. Jesus was so clever about saying the words and you can see his meaning from his perspective, but someone could read an entirely different meaning into it. The important thing is that I have to be in my right mind. Then the behavior will feel automatic; there will be hugging and holding *through* me, not by me.

You have to be anchored at that point where you know everything is okay and then whatever words come, let them come. They may be like an ice-breaker or a lead-in to something else. But the whole point of being anchored is that it is just impossible to perceive sickness; it is impossible that the Son of God would be sick. As you see your brother you see yourself. If your brother is a sick body then you cannot avoid seeing yourself in the same way – as a body. If you think of and see your brother as a body, you think of and see yourself as a body. There is no way you can un-mind, un-spirit your body. "As you see him you will see yourself ... As you think of him you will think of yourself. Never forget this, for in him you will find yourself or lose yourself." T-8.III.4

Friend: Even our friend limping—I still see that but to just say, "Well, I am not going to talk about it," is not the point either.

David: It is an interpretation. Bill Thetford was a psychologist and one time Jesus wanted him to go to a rehab conference. Part of Bill's resistance was that he just could not stand to see broken bodies because it reminded him of what he thought was his own frailty. And literally that is what is happening when we start interpreting behaviors, whether they are limps, coughs or the speckles you saw in some of the AIDS patients.

Whenever we start to make any interpretations we have made the error real. Then you ask: *What do I do now? How do I put the pieces together?* This is a perceptual problem. The more you get anchored into the Holy Spirit's thought system the more the unreality of sickness has to dawn on the mind. In your mind what you are doing when you come to your brothers is you are constantly reminding them of their wholeness. The mind of the healer petitions the mind of the patient, so to speak. There is another way; God's Son is whole and complete. And that is at a mind level. It is about being anchored in seeing your brother as whole, and then whatever is most helpful at a behavioral level will be given. Jesus is using the body to do the miracle. The doubt thoughts come in when we decide that we should have done this or we should have done that. Oh, you still think you can *do*? Then you do not realize that it is just a matter of aligning with the right mind or the wrong mind, with the behavior following automatically. You still think you could have *done this*, or that you should have *done that*? Then you are still playing God. You are still in the arrogance of trying to run the miracle yourself, and that means you still believe that the body is autonomous—that you can control your behavior, that there is a separate, individual person, the "*I*," and the "*I can*."

Friend: In the example you used with her son, is it like saying that instead of looking back and saying, *was I helpful to him* or *did I convey love to him*, it is just to look at how you felt and whether you were in your right mind? And if there is doubt then I guess you were not. I mean if there is any doubt about doing it right or if I should have done more, then I guess it cannot be the right mind.

David: In this moment. We bring it back to this moment. That is where the intention and passion to get clear comes in. The only way that we will be free of doubt forever is to be absolutely clear of cause and effect, absolutely clear of those thoughts, having watched our minds so closely; I will let that one go, I will let that one go…. When that is really done consistently, the mind becomes anchored and certain that love is really all there is. The stepping stone is to see everything as love or a call for love, but you realize that even that has to fall away.

Friend: So in the case of her son thinking that the falling log caused his pain, do I just need to see that the log was not the cause of his upset, that it was something in his mind or something in my mind? Can you explain?

David: Well, using the analogy of "his mind" and "my mind" means that the mind believes that it is guilty. My mind as a teacher of God is to be positive—absolutely certain—that the mind is guiltless.

Friend: So he was calling forth the witness that he was guilty. And if I reinforce that, then I am reinforcing that he is in fact guilty.

David: In your own mind, if you go to that level of the metaphor.

Friend: So if I see him in pain, then that is the witness to my mind that pain is possible and real?

David: Yes. You have to believe in pain before you can see it. Pain is a concept; you cannot see it in the world unless you believe it.

Friend: So there is a way to have this scenario going on, with the wailing and the cut in the skin, without perceiving any pain? And if you dreamed that happened, would there be anything to be upset about? Could her son be hurt?

David: That is where the "Oh" comes in. Like: *Oh, I feel pity; I have been through that too.* What "I"? Has Christ been through that? Has Christ been through pain; can Christ identify with pain? No. There is a belief; you think that you know that those things really happen and therefore you feel bad that someone else is going through it. That is giving it reality. It is saying that you know it is real. *Right now I happen to not be experiencing it, but you are, and I feel for you.* That thinking has to be given up. That is not healing.

Friend: That is the unhealed healer.

David: That is definitely the unhealed healer. You can be light. Not in a sense of cracking jokes or making fun of this or that, but there can be a sense of lightness and joy; that is what the whole day can be—a sense of lightness and joy. Regardless of whether the sun is shining and people are coming over expressing gratitude, or whether there seem to be wailing children, floods, hurricanes, or....

Friend: ...an annoying dog, or....

David: ...or your house burning down. That was a good example, just watching that big mansion burn down in a very detached way, knowing it was purposeful—seeing that there was a purpose there. For many that was an extreme example. The ego says: *Oh my gosh, what if that were my house?* But when you are the dreamer of the dream there cannot be loss and hurt. And it is not even a matter about going back and thinking: *Well, I blew it with my son.* That is the past too. That thought is a made up perception. You have to keep coming back to a present intention; what is my purpose now?

Friend: Then how do you use a situation like that?

David: It *is* being used. By talking about it in the way it is being talked about, it is given a new purpose. The whole purpose is to give it a new purpose. And when can that purpose be given? *Right now* is the only time it can ever be given. Words are just symbols.

Friend: I do find it helpful to use an example like that and run it through.

David: Yes, and you can see that you are absolved *now*. That is what you finally come to. Now is the only time you could be absolved, or feel guilt. It is a present-moment decision. It gets away from the linear sense of, *Well, ...*

Friend: *...I could have done it better.*

David: There is that linear person again. Whenever you go back and feel personally responsible for what you did or what you failed to do, you are raising body thoughts up to the level of mind. You are seeing yourself as a linear person—a person in linear time—and that is guilt inducing. It is the denial of your Self, your spiritual Self. The miracle on the other hand—regardless of what was said or done—literally lifts the mind. The mind is watching the dream and that includes all perceptions of everything that the body ever seems to do, or say, or think, even thinking of yourself as having judgment thoughts like: *I haven't got it yet, I will never get this.* Once you are above it, it is like *Ahhh*—instant release. And if we go on here we will see that is the whole point.

> The idea that a body can be sick is a central concept in the ego's thought system. This thought gives the body autonomy [there is the thought of personhood], separates it from the mind, and keeps the idea of attack inviolate. If the body could be sick Atonement would be impossible. A body that can order a mind to do as it sees fit could merely take the place of God and prove salvation is impossible. M-22.3

That is the reversal of cause and effect. If it was possible for a body to order a mind to do anything, then God is dead, as Nietzsche said; God is out of the picture. The belief then is that there is no God and I am helpless. I am the victim of this dream now. It tells me what to do. I have to follow its laws. I am a little dream figure that is stuck and helpless. I can only do certain things to hold off the inevitable. When this world closes in on me and the breath goes out of the body....

Friend: What is going to happen to me then? Am I going to hell or am I going to Heaven? How fearful.

Friend: Still, you can either be in your right mind or your wrong mind. [group laughter]

David: I think our friend is being facetious; that is how the ego looks at it. That scariness is the ego. You have every right to be fearful based on the way you perceive yourself.

Approaching the Idea of Forgiveness

The feeling of peace is how we can know when we are in a state of non-judgment. To get at the real depth of what forgiveness is takes study and understanding. There are many different approaches that Jesus takes in the Course to meet the mind at different levels. He even uses visualization exercises where he tells you to think of someone you are having difficulty with and to envision them in light, etc. I would say that these are more initial kinds of experiences. Beyond that, you get down to the deeper realms where there is nothing to forgive; you forgive your brother for what *he has not done.*

Let's look at this interesting idea that I forgive my brother for what he has not done. *But I just saw him growl at me; she did not pay the money back to me that she said she would;* or whatever the grievance is. I see the behavior right here, what am I supposed to do, deny what my eyes have seen? This is about perception. The most helpful way to look at perception is to first remember that what the Course calls our *real thoughts* are way down in our mind. They are the light. The mind ran away from the light. It made attack thoughts and the world of perception to cover over and hide from the light. In other words, the world is projected out there to keep the mind distracted from looking at these silly thoughts and seeing that the attack thoughts are not real. Forgiveness is being able, in a Zen sense, to step back into your mind and be able to turn within and look at these thoughts, without being horrified.

Now the mind believes that it *is* these thoughts. You know how identified you can be with cars, houses, bodies, body image ... and they are all really just a projection of thoughts. Imagine your own private world; you close your eyes and meditate and you hear all this chatter going on. You have all these judgment thoughts about the lady down the street or the boss, or whatever. The mind is horrified by these thoughts. It feels overwhelmed at times. *What can I do? My mind is just filled with these thoughts!* In a sense the ego is saying: *Right, you are guilty, you do not want to look at these thoughts. Go get involved in some kind of addiction out there in the world, get very busy so you can become so distracted that you won't ever have time to be quiet, because it is too scary to be quiet and look at those thoughts.*

The thoughts are not good or bad; they are unreal. They are nothing. But the mind is convinced that they are more than nothing. It is convinced that they are *me*; I am a judgmental person, I am a controlling person. All the attributes that we give ourselves have to do with the thoughts that are in there. Forgiveness is a stepping back from those thoughts.

A brilliant way to approach forgiveness is to remember that the mind is causative. The mind is the cause of everything. Once it bought into the crazy puff of an idea of separation and fell asleep, cause and effect were split off and turned around backwards. Now it believes it is a person in a world. It seems as if the cause of our state of mind is everything that is happening around us. In this world people think: *Yeah, but what do you do when a tornado is coming? There is danger if the news says there is a killer loose in the neighborhood. If the body seems to be ill or to be sick or to have cancer or something, what do you do?* All these things seem to be taking away your peace of mind; this is like a real problem; I have a sick body or something. But the body, as well as the entire world, is part of the screen that the ego counsels is where the problem is. Forgiveness, in the ultimate sense, is the reversal of that. It is being able to gradually transfer these ideas in more and more situations as you go through your daily life and to bring cause and effect back around—to see that the mind is the cause. Everything is a decision that I am making, and my state of mind is an effect. Literally, I can choose peace in a concentration camp or when my car has suddenly vanished from my sight. In any situation, peace is a choice.

A lot of questions come up when we get into these things. Knowing that your state of mind is a choice can be very empowering; you are not victimized by the projections outside of you. It is always a choice. But with sickness for instance, people can feel guilty about being sick, about "choosing" sickness. This is a very common trap. But ultimately, what is happening with sickness is that it is a decision that the mind is making. The Course teaches this in lesson 136 and in the *How is Healing Accomplished* section of the *Manual for Teachers*. The mind feels guilty, so it projects sickness out onto the body, which is like calling a witness up to the stand, and then saying: *See God, I am not whole and complete, eternal and changeless. I am this weak little frail body and I am right about it, you know, I am little and I am right.* In a sense sickness comes about out of the fear of healing, when the warm, gentle reminder of light comes into our mind, which the deceived mind is afraid of. It then chooses a defense mechanism to provide a witness that will say: *You are wrong God, and I am right.* This now leads us into the authority problem, which the Course tells us is the basic underlying problem in our mind behind everything.

The idea that there is an authority issue going on in the deceived mind, between itself and God, is just too big of a thing to think about. *Me? I have an issue with God?* It is too monstrous of an idea, so the mind literally projects it out into the world. Now I am a person in the world and I do not have an authority problem with God—I have an authority problem with my parents or a politician, or lawyer, with my husband or with my boss. It gets transferred and projected, when really the central authority issue or question is: *Was I created by God as Spirit, changeless and eternal, or can I make myself up? Can I make myself up as I go along; can I make something that is different than that?* Everyone who seems to come to this world and believes that they are a person in the world has this authority issue going on. Of course this is only within the deceived mind; in reality God knows his Son is eternal and changeless. But within the dream of the world there is an issue going on with God! This is not a conscious issue. If you look back at your journey you may have taken a few different routes before coming to the Course and to the idea that God is Love. There is something about that idea—that God is Love—that just resonates; *Yes! I have always known that had to be the truth.*

Then the Course comes along and tells you that every time you get angry at someone or make a special love or special hate relationship and every time you try to justify your thoughts—it is just an expression of that authority problem. The Course is helping us to really get down to changing our perceptions so that we literally can see the world differently. You may even come to a conscious thought that God is Love.

That is a synopsis of forgiveness. And it has to be an *experience*. We do not need another theology to talk about. We do not need another religion; we have had enough religions. Jesus says that there can never be a universal theology; there is never going to be a time on this planet when everybody has one religion. The ego is fragmented and everybody has different perceived self-concepts and beliefs. Within the perception of the world there will not be any universal theology—but there can and must be a universal experience.

The World Has No Real Cause

David: Lesson 182 of the Workbook refers to the metaphor that there is a child within you that needs your protection. This is not about protecting the ego. I would say that there is some confusion in the approach of therapies that talk about protecting the wounded child. You do not want to protect the ego because that is where all the defense mechanisms are. All defense mechanisms are attempts to protect the wounded split-off self. The defenses need to be laid down.

The Course's path differs from the inner child work of going into a safe place with the inner child or re-doing a scene. The Course is about looking at your interpretations, which includes your so-called present memories, your daytime dreams, where things are coming up. It is your interpretation of what is happening that you are reacting to. It is the interpretation that evokes emotion.

Friend: I remember one of the main messages in the twelve-step program was that we are powerless over alcohol, as if alcohol is the devil, which we have no power over. The message might as well be: I am a body!

David: This is about form and content. I see a parallel between AA's idea of being powerless over alcohol and "the script is written." You are powerless over the script. The script is written. You cannot change the form. The only remaining choice you have left is *how* you look upon it. It takes a real opening in the mind to really see that you do not have control over events but only over the way you perceive things; it means giving up the attempt to fix people or to change things on the screen.

Friend: Couldn't you say in a sense we are in control? We have a choice about who to identify with at all times. Isn't that what you are saying? That in a sense, who my guide is determines my perception? If I was driving home tomorrow night and got into a car wreck, I could look at it as if I have asked for this on some level. I am responsible so hence I am not a victim in any way, shape or form.

David: That is a good point. We can go into cause and effect a little deeper. In the next step people may feel like: *I have cancer; I am responsible for this* or, *I got in this car wreck and I lost my arm. I am responsible for this. Aack!* That is still big-time guilt! You ask: *What am I doing wrong*, or *why did I bring this upon myself?* The pure cause and effect relationship, the real one, is in Heaven. God is the Father and the Son is the effect. Thinking that you have any causative power on the screen, or with the script, is level confusion; all causation is in the mind. When we get into the idea of manifesting, the mind believes that there is some kind of creative ability that is connected with form. We have to start to realize that causation is always at the mind level.

Once we start to see that there is nothing on the screen that can take away our peace—that there is no effect out there that can take away our peace—we prove that there was actually no real cause for anything that happened. It is a backwards way of disproving the ego. Obviously, if this world has no effect then it can never take our peace away and we can generalize that to every situation. That is the way the Holy Spirit "proves" it; aha, then the world must not have a real cause and therefore the ego is disproved. That takes away all sense of guilt, because in reality we never did anything to ourselves. Like our friend is always saying, "We can say the script is written; but the script is unreal."

Friend: If there is nothing out there on the screen then we could not affect anything. Trying to teach the Course for example, or trying to teach that a change of mind is possible, we can't *really* do that, can we?

David: In the ultimate sense, that is true. Using expressions like "other brothers" and "helping" is using the metaphor of a seeming split mind. Think about the idea of affecting another person's mind; it is kind of like the old voodoo thing. Even if we use the metaphorical sense of everyone having a separate mind, Jesus says that minds are equal. He says that he cannot take away our fear because that would be tampering with the basic law of cause and effect. T-2.VII.1 He cannot come in between our thoughts and their effects. That is where another great relief comes in. *You mean I have never been able to hurt anyone ever? And no one has ever truly been able to hurt me?* That is a vast idea.

Friend: It says in *The Development of Trust* section of the *Manual for Teachers*:

> The next stage is indeed a period of unsettling. Now must a teacher of God understand that he did not really know what was valuable and what was valueless. All that he really learned so far was that he did not want the valueless and that he did want the valuable yet his own sorting out was meaningless in teaching him the difference. The idea of sacrifice so central to his own thought system had made it impossible for him to judge. M-4.I.A.7

We are not at peace yet. We still think that we have a way of determining what is valuable and what is valueless. Our belief in sacrifice makes this completely impossible because sacrifice is not real, but we think it is. So, we have no basis for judging anything?

David: The Course is about bringing causation back to the mind. In other words, before you can give another purpose to this dream, you have to first pull back from identifying as being "the dream figure" to seeing that you are the "dreamer of the dream." When you know that you are the dreamer of the dream you can accept another purpose and you can have a happy dream.

Friend: You are in such peace because you do not judge anything. It seems to me that you are not projecting any attack thoughts. When you are not putting out attack thoughts, then the love comes forth, the Love that we truly are. When that love comes forth you do not judge anything because love accepts everything as it is. When my state of mind is free from what is happening on the screen, I can see that there are no real effects, so there must not be any real cause.

David: We are getting pretty deep into this. Cause and effect relationships are the relationships of everyday life. In the world, if you water a plant and give it food, it will grow. That is seen as cause and effect. If the power goes out, the thought might be to check the fuse box, or to attribute it to the storm. Do you see how it is assumed that there are causes and consequences in the world?

Those are spurious cause and effect relationships. It is just a screen and there is not ever a cause. This is pretty drastic when you apply it to your own life. All of the "mature" judgments that we make about what is a good outcome and what is not—all the judgments of the world are based on learning these spurious cause/effect relationships. None of it is true. Starting to understand this can be kind of mind-blowing because the world as we know it is constructed on top of all these unreal cause/effect relationships.

Friend: Does the Holy Spirit use our cause/effect idea? Like if you practice the Course, the effect will be more peace of mind, which would have to be considered another spurious cause/effect relationship in the world? Does the Holy Spirit use these spurious effects to help us out of the illusion, towards right perception? It seems like it is helpful to think that what you are putting out is coming back. If you put out love then that is what you see.

David: The Holy Spirit looks not to effects. He is the presence of light in our minds. He works with the lower mind on its beliefs. The mind looks within and simultaneously calls forth external witnesses. The Holy Spirit is not doing anything with the slide show on the screen. He is just working with the mind to give up the dark beliefs that are producing the slide show. But it can seem as if, like our friend was just saying, "If I study the Course and I apply it daily there will be feelings of more consistent peace." This would be a spurious cause/effect thing because here is a person studying the book and going through life and it seems like the peace is coming more and more, but what really is taking place is that we quit judging and we quit interpreting things. It really does not have anything to do with reading a book. That was just the form in which this deceived mind could accept it. The symbol or the representation of the light of the remembrance of God is the seeming coming of this book into this world, to this person that seemed to read it. Do you see how our personhood and our individuality are all symbols too?

Friend: So you are saying that the script has been written and since all is an illusion you cannot affect it in any way?

David: If you can give it another purpose, it will seem to be happy.

Friend: So if you look at "the script is written" incorrectly, it is another way of saying the world is real. But the only reality is thought, the idea of God in the mind. So "the script is written," can be summed up as the tiny mad idea and the fact that we are all in pretty good shape. "The script is written" means that it is all over, that we are all back?

David: It is helpful to keep it in that context–that the script is in the past. As the Course keeps saying, the past is gone. If the past still seems to be present–if the "script is written" still seems to be experienced as a present thing there is a feeling of *Oh no!*

Friend: I see what you are saying. Thinking you can affect the script just makes it real. It is the ego that is trying to do something, trying to get into effect.

David: For me the joy has been in pulling back from participating in the script. You get so accustomed to "doing" and "striving" in the world. When you step back from striving you may hear messages all around you like, *You are nuts! You are crazy!* You almost need a metaphysical basis; you need something to put your foot on, so to speak, to start withdrawing from the constant striving and participation. That is where the Course helps. I can withdraw. I can approach more and more the *I Need Do Nothing* section where it says that to do anything requires a body. It says that you are mind and there is a place in your mind that is so quiet and so still. You can reach into that place and there is no *doing* there. At one point in that section it says, "At no single instance does the body exist at all. It is always remembered or anticipated." T-18.VII.3 That is a deep statement. You can see that only through thoughts about the past and the future does the body come in. And all the doings and all the strivings are just layered on top of that. That section is phenomenal! I know people who have studied the Course for years and when they get to those couple of sentences, they just flip out. Here you are working with the lessons and working hard to get through twelve-hundred pages, and then you come to the *I Need Do Nothing* section. You think: *Whoa, what is this about?* In that section he says, "It would be far more profitable now merely to concentrate on this [I need do nothing], than to consider what you should do." T-18.VII.5 *Oh my gosh! I am trying to follow this. I am reading and doing all these lessons and he is telling me that it would be more profitable to just concentrate on this.* Can you see how that section is really a plea to come into stillness and just let go of all the ideas and concepts?

> One instant spent together with your brother restores the universe to both of you. You are prepared. Now you need but remember you need do nothing. T-18.VII.5

Question Everything You Think You Think, then Enter into Stillness

Hi David,

I have been studying the Course for about 11 years. While I have made progress, I despair of ever really getting to the quiet, happy state so many students refer to. It took so long to calm the enraged feelings – years to stop being a victim, years to bring jealousy and judgment to a much lesser level. I am grateful for this. But although I appear quiet and loving, the tempest is so close, and my abdominal anxiety increases when I do the lessons and read the text. Do most students have this resistance, but whine less? I am not sure if I am asking for answers or for special support. I really do love us, mostly.

Beloved One,

Thanks for your e-mail and your devotion to Awakening. The abdominal anxiety you speak of is indeed resistance, and the fear of Love lies deep beneath the surface of consciousness. Many experience this fear as the fear of the Unknown. While Love has been denied from awareness, a self-concept image has been made, maintained, and accepted as the "known" and "familiar." In this world, the Reality of Love seems to have been replaced by a "reality" of dualistic perception, and the deceived mind is afraid to let go of that which it is accustomed to and familiar with. The undoing of the ego is what you are experiencing as you read the text and do the lessons, for the ego experiences its own undoing with great anxiety. When you identify with it you experience anxiety. This is a Call to faith, a Call to allow any upsetting emotion to surface and to move through it instead of attempting to stuff it or distract away from it. It does not matter if the upsetting emotion seems intense or merely irritating, for fear has no degree or direction and is always properly perceived as a Call to what it masks: Love.

The Call to Awaken and be glad is the Call to leave every scrap of belief in this world behind, and remember *What Is*, Our Natural State of Being. That is the meaning of "I am Calling you out of the world." Not one thought of the world is true. And yet Our Identity Given by God is Christ, and Christ is eternally true. To the ego, Awakening seems lonely and meaningless and filled with struggle, for there is no personal glory or gain in releasing the belief in separation. But Peace is its own reward, and the Peace of God is far beyond the personal perspective of the ego.

ACIM is a tool to open the mind to deep meditation. The lessons are designed to help train the mind to be still. Peace and stillness go together and cannot be found apart. As you deepen you will seem to question everything you believe, and as you are drawn into the Silence you will approach a surrender point. This is the point of not knowing or understanding anything about the world of appearances, a point of "I do not know what anything is for." And through this point of humility, the truth is made welcome in awareness. In happy laughter is the truth plainly apparent as All there is. Truth is One and "dualistic perception" is laughable, for there is nothing that can be an "opposite" to What Is forever One.

Mysticism is emptying the mind of everything it thinks it thinks and thinks it knows. Mysticism is seeing from the *dreamer of the dream* Perspective. Peace and forgiveness are the feeling and Perspective of non-judgment, for what is the same cannot be different and what is one cannot have separate parts. It is impossible to reconcile dualistic perception with God, yet happily remembrance of God's Oneness is inevitable. Let nothing come before you that you would not release, and open to the Call to Stillness. Divine Silence is our Heart's State of desirelessness.

Healing the Perception of "World Disasters"

Hi David,

I have been very bothered by the ongoing events that culminated in the Pakistan earthquake in which thousands died and thousands more will die without more help from the citizens and countries of the world. During the tsunami last year I saw an outpouring of world support and this is not happening this time. I have done what I can financially. I know that we are spirit, not bodies, but I am still distressed to see the lack of world understanding that all are our brothers and sisters.

My son, who is severely disabled and non-verbal with Angelman Syndrome (I see him as an angel and a blessing), came to me in a dream. He had gone missing and nobody cared to help search for him. This dream came shortly after the quake. When I woke I realized my nightmare was a blessing that was reminding me to go ahead and donate the money I had intended to but had not yet acted on. I see families searching for missing children and loved ones in rubble and families waiting for someone to carry out the injured, and bring supplies as winter approaches. Again, I know that who we are is spirit–that peace is inside each one of us. But I am here at home, warm, and fed, with a wood fire burning. Their bodies are cold and suffering.

What am I missing in my understanding? What I hope is the world will move to love all people as one.

Beloved One,

Thanks for writing and sharing what is on your heart. Your desire is to be helpful, and this desire is of the Holy Spirit. The ego has distorted what is helpful, for the ego is the belief in the reality of the body. Your perception of "world disasters" has triggered a need for healing in your mind. In this, the perceived disasters have served the Purpose of Awakening to Divine Mind. If any giving is extended out of pity, comparison or perceiving someone as lacking something that you already have, this "giving" is done out of guilt and only serves to reinforce the belief in separation.

If you would truly be Helpful then you must clear the mind of false beliefs and allow miracles to be performed through you. The ego and the Spirit do not give in the same way. Money offered to alleviate perceived suffering does little to heal the mind, while a simple, loving, non-judgmental attitude radiates a miracle that is so expansive it cannot be measured. To be truly supportive and helpful, be open to the metaphysics of healing the mind and recognizing the problem where it is (in mind) and the solution (inner peace). Recognize that there will be no partial healing. You must feel a deep, unshakable peace to recognize that healing has been accomplished. Direct your efforts inward and the benefits will be immense for the whole universe. Support that which is truly valuable by being very devotional in your mind watching and mind training. Anything which assists you in this endeavor is truly worth supporting and will move your awareness in the direction of True Giving as God Gives in Spirit.

Addressing Prophecy, the Script, and Private Minds

Friend: I was sent an invitation to a website set up by someone claiming to be the awakened prophet Daniel from the Old Testament, now awake as an angel.

The prophet said he would pass judgment on two American cities that were to be destroyed by nuclear weapons, unless he observed humanity moving closer to divine will.

Now I am wondering if I should draw this to the attention of the worldly authorities, given that this world is all an illusion. But if I could have prevented September 11th and didn't, I would be devastated. So now then, if it is not meant to happen, then it may be me who is supposed to speak up, and if it is supposed to happen, then it will happen regardless of whether I speak up. What are your thoughts on this?

David: The script is written. The most helpful thing one can do is accept Atonement and thus see that all form is the past. The ego would have you believe that the future is different from the past and also that the future will repeat the past. Yet the present is free of the past and Innocence can only be found in the present. The future is a construct that is an ego defense against the holy instant.

Thinking that you can or should or must "prevent" a future outcome reflects the belief that you have some control over the script. You have no control over the script of the world, but you do have control over your state of mind. You can choose peace – a miracle – which will show you that you "see only the past." W-7

The "future" past is the same as the "past" past. Prophecy is the foretelling of what is already written. As a miracle worker, time is under your direction, meaning you can choose in any moment to bring an end to the erroneous "linear" perception of time. I am joined with you in choosing just that, for there is literally no other Perspective of clarity than that of the Holy Spirit's forgiven world.

Friend: I cannot change the outcome of reality, however I think I can change the outcome of unreality (which is admittedly a paradox) while there are those of the Sonship who experience the unreality of events like September 11th as real.

David: There is one mind, and the mind asleep has only one option: To change its mind about itself and accept its changelessness. That is the only responsibility: To accept Atonement. As long as one perceives "other" or "multiple" minds, this is the error to be released. There are not differing perspectives in forgiveness.

Forgiveness sees the false as false, and as long as the sleeping mind sees cause and effect as apart and the future as different from the past, it is refusing to accept

Atonement for the error. It is truly a matter of letting go of the belief in private minds and private thoughts.

Friend: It is still necessary to have bodies to reach the deluded.

David: The body is purposeless other than as a communication device. Yet I have also said that mind reaches to itself. It does not go out. Within itself is everything – you within it and it within you. God has only one Son or Creation. Bodies are only shadow figures that are called forth from the past to witness to separation, and nothing of the five senses can witness for Oneness. The body is used by the ego to reinforce itself and to promote the belief in attack. Yet mind cannot attack, for there is only one mind and nothing outside the Oneness or wholeness of mind.

Friend: Yes, the body is purposeless other than a communication device, communicating its Oneness to the parts which think they are only separate parts rather than integral parts – everything which God created in its *totality*, the sum of everything which God created is His one Son. As an analogy, the brain is one brain because of its composition of billions of integral cells.

David: God creates no bodies. The body is a limit, a fence made to contain what is uncontainable. The infinite cannot create the finite, and the eternal cannot create the temporal. Forgiveness shows that images are unreal, and this includes the perception of the body as well.

Friend: Sure, but it still allows for the oneness of the one Son to be composed of integral parts; parts that are still parts but combined parts, not separate parts.

David: The whole transcends the concept of "parts." Forgiveness transcends the construct of "parts" and the mind which still perceives parts is in need of Atonement.

Friend: You are thinking in terms of reference of parts being separate. I am thinking in terms of parts which are integral, maybe even necessary to the oneness.

David: In climbing a ladder of consciousness, so to speak, one will never rise up unless one leaves one step for the next. I ask you to see that Awakening requires a willingness to release the concept of "parts" and accept the goal of Atonement, which is an experience beyond the words. The experience of complete forgiveness goes beyond the words – the parts – to constant peace. That is always the helpful barometer: inner peace. When inner peace is consistent, only then will one "know" what is real and what is illusion.

Exposing and Releasing Faulty Assumptions

Hi David,

I have been a student of ACIM for almost two years, but I have been curious about one thing: Do you watch the news or read newspapers or stay in touch with the world of illusion on a daily basis? The deeper I get, the further I get from even wanting to know other's opinions about this life. I have never enjoyed reading the paper, but I am finding that I feel distant from my family and friends and my partner because I cannot speak of what is "going on in the real world" anymore. It does not interest me. As a matter of fact, when Katrina hit New Orleans I was not emotionally attached to the drama at all. Although I have two young girls and do become concerned for their safety on a daily basis, this was not of concern to me. However, I did volunteer immediately for the shelters during the first few weeks the evacuees came to this area. Does that seem hypocritical, and should I be more aware of what is going on – for example, political interest and local drama – just to be aware of forgiveness lessons?

Beloved One,

Thanks for writing. What you are speaking about is very common for sincere ACIM students, and it is natural to seem to lose interest in news and newspapers as you progress with the goal of ACIM: forgiveness. The seeming emotional concerns and/or personal dramas with your daughters and those in your immediate proximity are offering you many opportunities to forgive.

It is helpful to be reminded that the degree and direction of error does not matter, so misperception cannot be placed on a scale or a continuum. There is no degree or comparison to fear, for all fear is appropriately and Helpfully Interpreted as a call for Love. Be grateful and glad that you are allowing the unconscious fear into awareness for healing. You are definitely on the right track, and even though you may feel distant at times from your family and friends and partner, this is just fear coming to the surface for release.

I am sometimes Guided to watch the TV briefly or glance at a newspaper when I am traveling, and at times these bits and pieces of "world events" are used by the Holy Spirit in the context of teaching examples during gatherings. I actually do not read much of anything anymore, with the exceptions of mail and e-mail.

If you find that you still have an aversion to words about political interest and local drama, or news and newspapers, it may be helpful to watch and read them occasionally as Guided or to rent some movies that deal with these topics and issues and use the movie watching as a mind watching experience. For years I have used movie watching (and many years ago, TV watching as well) as a mind training exercise. Allow the feelings to surface without censoring them, and then recognize that the feelings are coming from the desires and beliefs and thoughts held in consciousness.

This kind of mind exercise can help you to question what is believed and also help in exposing and releasing faulty assumptions. With willingness the mind becomes open to the Holy Spirit's reinterpretation of perception, which is the goal of all mind training.

The first of the fifty miracle principles at the beginning of the Text says that there is no order of difficulty in miracles, and this comes from a deeper understanding that there is no hierarchy of illusions. It is helpful to use the ACIM Workbook in daily practice and apply the lessons without exceptions. This mind training leads to a truly loving and detached Observation of perception that is the Holy Spirit's "real world" instead of the sleeping mind's version of "the real world."

A Question of Vigilance: Can the Ego Be Vigilant?

Friend: There is a sentence in the Text that says, "By deciding against your reality, you have made yourself vigilant *against* God and His Kingdom. And it is this vigilance that makes you afraid to remember Him." T-10.II.6 What kind of vigilance is this? Can the ego be vigilant?

David: That is a really good question. Let's look at this. In the Course Jesus says to be vigilant until you no longer need to be vigilant. But the vigilance in this sentence you are asking about is a different quality of vigilance. Vigilance is of the ego, as the perceptual realm is of the ego, but it can be used by the Holy Spirit for the purpose of attentiveness. Yet this is a different context being expressed here in the quote you gave. Let's take a look at it. "By deciding against reality you have made yourself vigilant against God and His Kingdom." What he means is that you will do anything to deny God's reality and uphold your own – being vigilant for your own perceived reality. *Deciding* is of the self-concept. Only the split mind believes in choice/decision.

For example the belief that there is a country called America, or Canada, is a concept. I am a Canadian, I am an American, I am an African American, I am British, I am Australian – all of these are concepts and we find ourselves defending them because we believe this is who we are. We believe we have a choice to be who we want to be. We are very vigilant in protecting what we have made. Do you see how complex this "I know" mind is? What am I not? I am not Canadian. I am not born in a body. I am not the perception. Jesus speaks of this in the Book of John. When the Jews asked him how he could not even be fifty years old yet and still claim to have seen Abraham, Jesus told them, "...before Abraham was, I Am." Jesus is telling us that before Abraham was "I Am." There is nothing that comes after "I Am." I am not the name "speaker." I am not the citizenship of the country the body was born in. The Christ is not a label nor is it a part of time and space. Every time you are upset and you think you know something, it means you want to be right. When you are defending your illusion over God's reality, you are being vigilant against God and His Kingdom. "And it is this vigilance that makes you afraid to remember Him." T-10.II.6

That is the key. Because we believe that we have really separated, now we are afraid that we have done something wrong by pretending that we know something other than God's knowledge which is changeless, eternal love. By pretending that the separation is real we become fearful of remembering God because we really believe in the impossible. This kind of vigilance is the ego's vigilance, the vigilance of defending illusions. One can only be vigilant in the perceptual realm. Be vigilant for the Kingdom because the mind is very resistant. The egoic mind is vigilant for idols. Be vigilant in the exposing of the idols.

> The calm being of God's Kingdom, which in your sane mind is perfectly conscious, is ruthlessly banished from the part of the mind the ego rules. The ego is desperate because it opposes literally invincible odds, whether you are asleep or awake. Consider how much vigilance you have been willing to exert to protect your ego, and how little to protect your right mind. Who but the insane would undertake to believe what is not true, and then protect this belief at the cost of truth? T-4.III.10

What you have made is false knowledge and the split mind is very vigilant in keeping it; this is what maintains the world seemingly in its chaotic state—thinking that we know something. In fact we cannot know anything in the perceptual realm. Right-mindedness is the correction of this wrong-minded attempt to order one's reality. Right-mindedness is not to be confused with the knowing mind, God's knowledge, because it is applicable only to right perception. This is why in the early Workbook, Jesus says, "… you do not know what anything is for." W-25.3 You think you know what a telephone is for but only at the "most superficial level." We have to be open to the thought that: *I do not know anything because I am attempting to decide reality for myself and this is why I am afraid, because every time I attempt to make reality for myself, I am misusing the law of the Kingdom, the law of love.* This attempt to decide reality is why guilt arises in awareness. There is a sense of knowingness that the mind is not being used for the purposes of creation, but to make illusions. This results in fear because we believe the illusions to be real and we will do anything to protect them. The ego is very vigilant against God and His Kingdom.

In order to be clear on the idea of vigilance, we must first look at the Holy Spirit's purpose for vigilance and the ego's idea of vigilance. There seem to be two alternatives, two choices. Out of all the choices in the world, all of the decisions that one could possibly make, this narrows it down to just two. There is a great simplification in this. Let's say these two choices are the potential solutions to any seeming problem. The first solution is to unmask the ego. The second solution is to continue in the state of achieving, becoming and seeking for surface-level changes. The former solution is to unmask and unravel the ego and its schemes to save itself. The latter entails a continuance of seeking for a better illusion, seeking for salvation where it cannot be found, a continuation of the "rat race." The first choice will take effort but it is like unraveling a ball of yarn which has an eventual end. The second choice also requires effort, but in this effort it perpetuates all sorts of suffering. Although both require effort and vigilance we can say that because of the outcome, only one of these choices is a real alternative. Only one leads to the Kingdom.

Friend: That must mean I really have no choice to be what I want to be? So there is really no choice at all?

David: If there is one choice then there must be no choice, because choice implies two or more. If there is only one real choice that leads to Reality then there is no choice. The choice for the right mind is really just a choice to have the Holy Spirit decide for you. One really never had a choice, but an illusion of choice.

But this is too simple for the ego. The ego needs something to be for or against, or it will cease to "exist." The ego uses concepts, ideas and beliefs; it attaches itself to these ideas and then thinks that this is who it is: "I am an American. I am Catholic. I am Buddhist. I am this and I am that and I am Christian. I know, I know, I know." It gets lost in the "I know" which is really just a defense against the memory of knowledge that is available in the holy instant. The holy instant is where knowledge is reflected and where love is remembered. It is where we meet the Holy Spirit, in the present moment – right now. The Course tells us:

> To teach the whole Sonship without exception demonstrates that you perceive its wholeness, and have learned that it is one. Now you must be vigilant to hold its oneness in your mind because, if you let doubt enter, you will lose awareness of its wholeness and will be unable to teach it. The wholeness of the Kingdom does not depend on your perception, but your awareness of its wholeness does. It is only your awareness that needs protection, since being cannot be assailed. Yet a real sense of being cannot be yours while you are doubtful of what you are. This is why vigilance is essential. Doubts about being must not enter your mind, or you cannot know what you are with certainty. Certainty is of God for you. Vigilance is not necessary for truth, but it is necessary against illusions. T-6.V.C.8

Specialness and Special Relationships

Hi David,

I feel the concept of marriage is exclusive, maintaining separation by forming its own personal, little bond that is more special than any other relationship. I feel the role of wife is very limiting. Yet, having a best friend here for me all the time is not only extremely enjoyable, it is comforting and "secure," too. We do almost everything together. It seems I am more than willing to accept a limiting role in order to get this friendship (specialness) I desire. I know this is a bargain, and therefore of the ego, but I am afraid to release it. I do not like being "alone."

There are other ego agreements my partner and I have made, too. Sex: sometimes I want it, and sometimes I just give it because my partner wants it and I want to give him the gift of whatever he wants. (Isn't the "love" behind the act real?) However, there are other ego agreements we used to have that we have given up.

We never support each other in attacking a brother anymore, and we do help each other ask Holy Spirit what everything is for. We try to remind each other to stay present, and we help each other practice forgiveness.

In one of my ACIM classes, we were reading about special functions, specialness, and special relationships. What was taught in this class is that although we make special relationships for separation, Holy Spirit uses even special relationships for healing and forgiveness.

> Such is the Holy Spirit's kind perception of specialness; His use of what you made to heal instead of harm. To each He gives a special function in salvation he alone can fill; a part for only him. Nor is the plan complete until he finds his special function, and fulfills the part assigned to him, to make himself complete within a world where incompleteness rules. T-25.VI.4

It was said that this text says that our special function is to forgive the specific symbols each of us has made in our seeming separateness. So I am to forgive the symbol of separation I have made by having a special relationship. So as I know my partner is no more special to me than any other brother because there is only One of us, my outer behavior will naturally change. My fear is that I must release this twenty-six-year marriage to my "best friend" in order to forgive the world and fulfill my special function. Is this true? Must we release all special relationships? I do not want to be lonely. I like being with people.

And also, if we must release the concept of marriage, then does it follow that we need release the activity of sex because it focuses on body thoughts? And then do we also have to release eating, breathing, and keeping warm? Do these things reinforce my thinking I am a body and keep me from Heaven?

My only goal is to heal. ACIM has released me from forty-seven years of pain, and I do not want to go back there ever again. I am willing to do *whatever* Holy Spirit guides me to do to further my healing and forgiveness. I *will* make whatever changes are necessary in this goal. However, right now, I see giving up special relationships as sacrifice. This means, of course, that I need a change of mind here, a miracle. Please help me understand what my special function is, and help me change my mind to see all of this rightly.

Thank you so much for your willingness to be God's Holy and perfect channel. I love you forever in eternity!

Beloved One,

Thanks for your devotion to Awakening and for your sincere questions about the subtleties of specialness, special relationships, and your special function. I feel the gratitude you express for the Holy Spirit's use of all the symbols in your perception. As you continue to ask the Holy Spirit what everything is for, the Purpose will become very clear: The sole responsibility is to accept the Atonement for oneself. The only Helpful Purpose a dream of separation could serve would be to offer a reflection of a Still, nonjudgmental mind. This is why forgiveness is the key to happiness and offers everything that you truly want: safety, security, intimacy, freedom, love, peace, joy, and happiness. In the realm of perception forgiveness is truly your "best friend." Salvation's task is the exchange of concepts, approaching the all-encompassing concept of forgiveness: the one concept that leads out of all the rest that the ego made.

The concept of marriage is a stepping stone along the path of Awakening. Its value rests in what the marriage is for. If the marriage concept is for getting needs met and focusing on an object of affection, or for companionship to alleviate loneliness or a sense of isolation, then the concept is being used by the ego to reinforce the belief in separation from God. If the marriage concept is being used as a means of mirroring the mind in a shared commitment to Awakening through exposing and releasing erroneous beliefs, thoughts, emotions, and perceptions, then the concept serves the Holy Spirit while the belief in time is undone.

Specialness and linear time are synonymous. The holy instant and Spiritual Union are synonymous. True Union is the Christ Mind at One with God and transcends all concepts, even forgiveness. As the mind is emptied of all concepts, the seeming needs and struggles and conflicts of interpersonal relationships are laid down, for they have ceased to have any meaning. Identity as Spirit is All Meaning. You are the goal the world was searching for, and in finding or recognizing the Self all goals have vanished.

Be gentle with your mind in the Awakening. Awakening is a change of mind that recognizes the Changelessness of Spirit. Awakening depends on willingness and readiness for a shift in perception and is never induced through attempts to change behaviors or circumstances to suit preconceived concepts of what is specifically more spiritual or less spiritual. As you immerse in the Purpose the Holy Spirit offers, you will be given a "special function." The meaning of the term "special function" simply refers to the Holy Spirit's use of the symbols that are in your awareness. The term in no way means "better" or "more holy than" in terms of behavior, but does represent the Purpose in mind that the Holy Spirit offers. As the mind opens to this Purpose the joy and glee of function fulfilled is obvious! The feelings of love and fulfillment and contentment replace all sense of lack and incompletion and unworthiness. In this experience there is no sense of sacrifice, for wholeness knows not of lack.

Love is a State of Mind which simply extends ItSelf. The approach to the remembrance of Divine Love is a path of miracles. The ego's lens of lack is replaced by miracle working. Miracles are experienced directly in awareness, and the former distorted miracle impulses (cravings for food, drink, sex, possessions, and form preferences) fade and grow dim in awareness as the Holy Spirit's Purpose is consistently experienced. The attachment was to the ego mechanism of judgment or preferences and never to specific objects or behaviors or persons. In healed perception nothing is seen as apart from mind and therefore there is no rejection. In healed perception there is no need to seek for sensory gratification, for the Holy Spirit's Purpose is wholly fulfilling and nothing is lacking. In Awakening the ego has simply been transcended. Be gentle. There is no need to fight against the ego or to attempt to tame it. Let it arise and simply see its nothingness. Be attentive to your mind by simply noticing ego thoughts and giving them over to the Holy Spirit, Who sees their nothingness.

Do not raise body thoughts to the level of mind. This simply means do not see causation in form or bodies. The body and all forms are unreal effects of an unreal "cause" – the ego. God is a real Cause and Christ is a real Effect. Body thoughts were only the attempt to believe that something real could exist outside and apart from the Mind of God. There is nothing outside the Mind of God. Christ remains a Pure Idea in the Mind of God. This is why Self-realization is Spiritual and not of matter or time-space.

In Awakening the Holy Spirit is the Comforter, and this is the true meaning of Friend. In Oneness there is no "best" or "worst," no "more" or "less." Bodies and world will fade from awareness because they are not Eternal. The Holy Spirit is the Friend that remains Eternal. The "Voice for God" will seem to cease when the illusion of time is not held in awareness and the journey to nowhere is forgotten. Turn to the Comforter and let the Holy Spirit give your weary mind its Everlasting Rest. Rest in God. Watch the Plan in Joy!

Yielding Special Relationship to Real Love

Hi David,

I have had a question in mind for some time, and I thought it would be a good idea to put it out there instead of working and re-working it in my head. It is a special-relationship question. The Course says there is no order of difficulty in miracles, but I have not been able to forgive my last special relationship partner (or myself in relation to him) for more than short periods at a time. I have done the exercises so many times, and I feel like I get closer to forgiveness, but it is not really forgiveness unless it is total, right? I know what is truly there between us is love, but my ego is riled up at the thought that he did not continue to think I was the most special person in the universe, and that he recently found a new person that he seems to fancy as "the new improved most special person in the universe!"

You would think that with my humor and my understanding of how ridiculous the ego is I would feel better about it. I have tried just acknowledging what I am feeling under the layers, and letting go of the anger and judgment. Loving does hurt less than hating, but I must be feeling the wrong kind of love, because it still hurts.

Should I be thankful for this experience? Maybe now that I have shared all these seemingly "private thoughts" with you it will all open up to more light.

I heard that William Thetford said something like: *The Course suggests that we forgot to laugh at the moment we first began to believe illusions were real.* I love that!

Beloved One,

Thank you for pouring your heart out and exposing private thoughts. Like you wrote, expressing it all and getting it off your chest takes the power out of the ego and dissolves it immediately. You wrote about partial forgiveness, about feeling like the thoughts come up again and again, and that it needs to be total forgiveness for it to be over and done with. This is much like watching the air bubbles coming up in a tank; you can watch the bubbles (thoughts), forgive them and release them but unless you get down to the bottom of the tank and dismantle the pump, those bubbles ain't gonna stop!

It is good to get really clear about the difference between "having something coming up" and simply "being in the wrong mind/listening to the ego."

When you find your mind re-hashing the past, repeating unhelpful meaningless chatter that goes nowhere, you can get staunch and give the ego a swift kick. The Holy Spirit gave me a great catch-phrase: "Stop, Drop, and Roll;" like the fire-fighters say to do if you catch on fire or you are surrounded by smoke and you cannot see straight! Perfect! Stop the ego in its tracks. Drop down from the swirling headspace that you are in, down into your heart space–into your right mind–and roll with the Holy Spirit. Feel the peace and ask for guidance. *Help me Holy Spirit, what would you have me say or do, if anything?*

This is different than the feeling of deep emotions that need to come up to be exposed. The ego will try to jump in and get you to act on your emotions, to act from a place of doubt, hurt or sadness and this simply takes you further away from the truth. Again, turn to the Holy Spirit, acknowledge your feelings, acknowledge that you do not know why you feel this way and that you are willing to be guided as to what to do, or what to say right now. When you have quiet time to yourself bring the feelings up again with the Holy Spirit and ask about them.

Reading the first sentence of every paragraph and a few paragraphs here and there in Chapter 24 offers a good overall reminder of what specialness is. It is twisted. It is not what we think it is. It is not love. If Love is a consistent state and your experience of love has involved inconsistency, pain, a bit of sadness here and there, then this is not real Love. This world is a cover, made to hide fear. The pseudo-love relationships that we engage in are not real Love. Even the love you feel for your family, for your ex-boyfriend, right now when you think of them, you are thinking of the past. They are thoughts in the mind. The moments of joy, of love, of happiness experienced together are experiences of the present moment, a direct reflection of God's Love. When you attach these moments to the figures in the dream you are wishing to have more of these moments with a particular person. When a relationship seems to come to an end or you are not close to them in proximity, there is a feeling of loss, of wishing it were different because you are making them special and attaching your memories of the present moment to them.

Special relationships, special love–they are a block to Love, to the awareness of God's Love. We think we are pursuing love by holding on to the past and trying to make it work out. We are holding on to illusions and we are blocking our awareness of the present moment–the only time and space in which we are free to experience love, happiness and joy.

Fear of aging, death, and loneliness are hidden beneath the cover of the special relationship. To believe we are separated from God—that we are a body, that we will grow old and die, that we can be alone—is the ego. Reaching out for love in this world to dispel these feelings is the purpose of special relationship. It can never result in freedom, peace and happiness. It is a cover over death. All thoughts of comparisons, all thoughts of superiority and inferiority are of the ego, based on its ideas of success and failure.

You are the Christ, the perfect, holy child of God; there is nothing and no one to compare you to. If you forget your true identity for a moment just Stop, Drop and Roll. Remind yourself that you desire only the Peace of God. Ask the Holy Spirit/Jesus to hold your hand and be with you right now, to help you with whatever you are experiencing.

Thank you so much for your willingness to let go of special relationships! This is saying yes to Love, to Real Love.

Releasing Specialness and Experiencing Enlightenment

Christ Calls everyone to Awaken to Agape, Eternal, Unconditional Love. The only block to this Awakening is the filter of specialness which projects a world where some images seem more important and valuable than other images. This is very apparent in what have been called special relationships, where some people are raised up and some people are put down. In any situation where specialness is cherished, Christ remains hidden from awareness. When Christ is recognized, the folly of specialness has been released forever. Specialness is another name for the ego. Specialness obscures equality and Oneness from awareness by its emphasis on form and disregard for content. Love is content. Forgiveness is the great equalizer, seeing all images as equally false. This Perspective opens the gate to the remembrance of God. Specialness is a belief that springs forth many concepts. Possession is one such offspring concept, and relationships based in possession serve their "master." Time and space and bodies are concepts of specialness, and the ego weaves its own picture of "reality" from the concepts of specialness.

I have been asked to share some ideas on the transition from specialness to holiness, the shift from death to life or from grievances to resurrection. This is the Awakening to Eternal Life through forgiveness of illusions. In simple terms it is being Present and Open to What Is. There are three seeming stages that precede Awakening to Divine Abstraction. I will share ideas about each stage.

The first stage is allowing the darkness of specialness held in mind to surface and to be exposed. The second stage is a stage of detachment in which specialness still persists in awareness and yet the practice of detached Observing is a very consistent perspective. The final stage is really nothing more or less than living in the Present Moment. It is a happy dream of nonjudgmental awareness in which the sameness of perception is recognized always and without exception. I call this experience Enlightenment.

For most people, in terms of experience, the first stage is the most challenging and difficult. The second stage can entail intense moments and periods of time, yet due to increasingly effective mind training and consistent transfer of training, these intense experiences seem mostly infrequent and passing. In the final stage these intense experiences have gone, replaced entirely by love, peace, happiness, joy, and freedom.

Allowing the Specialness to Surface

During this stage, being rooted in unconscious beliefs, people still seem to be people and things still seem to be things. The mind believes that it is a human being and that the world/cosmos is external to itself. It also seems as if the perceived surrounding environment of people and things is, at times, hostile to the perceiver. The mind which believes in the ego (separation from God) is unaware of the extent of self-hatred it is holding onto. It is also unaware of the ongoing attempts to project this belief in conflict onto an "external" world, a world/cosmos that is essentially nothing more than a neutral screen of images. Today, however, the many witnesses to the workings of consciousness are becoming more evident in awareness. For example, currently quantum physics demonstrates that consciousness involves potentials that are subjective and related to choice; there is no objective world "out there," apart from consciousness.

The deep, often unconscious feelings of unworthiness, lack, and guilt drive the mind to seek for love, meaning, and value in the images of the perceived world. Certain people, things, groups, organizations, animals, countries, etc., are valued in subjective preference patterns that have nothing to do with Truth or Eternity. The ego's need to belong and its inherent feelings of lack, drive it to search for affiliations and associations in form that offer only a fleeting, illusory sense of connectedness. True intimacy is of the mind and can only be experienced through shared Purpose. Unified Purpose in mind brings a unified perception of the world—the happy, non-judgmental dream that is the goal of all authentic spiritual practice.

Detached Observation

The Spirit offers detached Observation as an alternative to the personal perspective of the ego, though this replacement cannot be accepted as long as the mind still values the personal perspective. Love waits on welcome and not on time. With willingness to expose and release the ego belief system that hides the Light, the Observer seems to become more and more obvious. As form is seen to be an unreal effect of an unreal cause (ego) – false associations of cause and effect are exposed as unreal. Miracles show the power of mind, restoring awareness of the mind as the mechanism of decision making, thus releasing the false concept of the body as decision maker. This frees the mind, through forgiveness, which is simply seeing the false as false. As forgiveness is experienced consistently, the mind is aligned with the Holy Spirit's Perspective or the Observer perspective spoken about in quantum physics.

I often speak about the ideas of "no people-pleasing" and "no private thoughts." Essentially what this means is that there are literally no people to please when the mind recognizes that the world is a world of ideas and that nothing can be kept hidden or private in whole, unified perception. It is not that one should not have secrets or private thoughts; it is the realization that mind is whole and cannot be split or divided into the known and the unknown. As hurtful emotions surface in awareness there is another context for dealing with them, other than blaming the people of the world. The healing context of mind and the forgiven Perspective of the Holy Spirit bring relief from the guilt-inducing personal perspective of the ego. With the Holy Spirit's Guidance the mind realizes that it is not "the doer" and therefore has never "done" anything at all – right or wrong. In this realization, guilt, fear and anger are forever impossible and are therefore gone from awareness.

Enlightenment

You are not at the mercy of the world's concepts and images. Before you Awaken from the dream of the world, you will have a happy dream. You will see that you are the dreamer of the dream. You are vast and have dominion over images.

Chapter Two

The Reality of Life and the Unreality of Death

Truly there are no "obstacles to peace" we cannot transcend together in forgiveness. Forgiveness is letting go of valuing the ego, which could also be called death. The ego was an attempted denial of God. Yet such a belief cannot really change the truth of God's Love, for nothing can change Eternal Love. Yet while the ego seems to offer something of value, God's Answer cannot be completely heard or accepted. For the ego is the belief that there can be a substitute for God. And the Holy Spirit teaches that there is no Love but God's All-Encompassing Love.

The "attraction of death" is an attraction to a made-up identity image and to all the distractions and defenses that are part of the image. The image is the ego, or death, and it attempts to masquerade as a real entity with a life of its own with the power the sleeping mind gives to it. The ego cannot be an obstacle to peace if belief is withdrawn from it and faith is placed in the Holy Spirit.

The ego – death – seems attractive only because it seems to offer an alternative to God, who is feared by the sleeping mind as an angry and punitive god. God is nothing of the sort, but to a mind asleep that believes it has actually separated from God; this is its unconscious fear. It has projected its fear onto a made-up "angry" god and is afraid to turn to this god for help.

There seem to be pleasures associated with the made-up image and its world, fleeting as they may be. And to the sleeping mind, these pleasures are attractive and therefore sought after. Yet idols never give lasting joy and contentment, for they are temporal. They rise and they fall, for they could never substitute for eternal Love. While the ego and its idols are valued or attractive – by definition "death" still seems attractive to the sleeping mind, for again, the ego is synonymous with death.

There is no death. This is realized in the Light of God's Love. The ego has no foundation and illusions are but error. Once faith has been withdrawn from the error, the error is no more to be experienced as real. This is the meaning of Awakening, the overcoming of death. You allow the Spirit to raise the ego error to the Light of Truth (bring illusions to truth), and the darkness of death is no more.

Death is not the death of the body. Death is the belief that separation from God could actually occur. To transcend the ego then is to transcend a belief in the impossible. Once death is seen for the illusion it is, it is no longer attractive. For who would choose illusions when the Light of Truth is experienced as Love, and when Love is no longer feared?

I am joined with you in the Life and Love of God. You are as perfect and changeless as God created You. And I give thanks we are One Self. Amen.

Addressing the Subject of Death

Hi David,

If you have the time, could you expand one of your articles on the subject of death? When we are young, death seems so far away. When we are old, we just give into it as something inevitable. The situation changes somewhat when we face death or the threat of death due to illness such as cancer. It seems most important for people battling with this sickness to unlearn and learn what reality is. Can you help?

Beloved One,

Lessons 163 and 167 in the ACIM Workbook are excellent for exposing the belief in death, just as lesson 136 is a gem for exposing the belief in sickness. Death and sickness are different names for the same belief: the belief in separation from God. The perceived world was made by the ego as a cover to protect and maintain this belief. The Holy Spirit uses the symbols of the world to undo this belief.

Though sickness and death seem to involve symptoms and bodies, the symptoms and bodies are but effects of the false belief in separation. Yet what is not a real cause cannot have real effects, for only that which proceeds forth from God has Reality. Christ, Divine Love, is Reality, for the Christ Idea has not left Its Source (God). Love remains Eternal, and nothing can change Eternal Love.

The deceived mind appears to "battle" and "struggle" to maintain a tiny illusory identity apart from the Whole of Reality. It makes up a world of duality, of birth and death, of sickness and health, of pleasure and pain, to maintain a belief in private minds with private thoughts. Yet Divine Mind is One Unified

Mind and cannot be divided or separated into parts. The Whole transcends "the sum of the parts," for the Whole is a state of Mind which has no parts. The concept of parts dissolves in forgiveness, which sees that illusions are one. Forgiveness is the last concept, being the gateway to an Experience of Oneness that transcends all concepts.

As you proceed with the mind training ACIM offers – the unlearning of everything you think you think and believe you believe – you will begin to recognize that in every moment how you feel is life or death, health or sickness, love or fear. Every miracle is a moment of life and health and love, and every grievance or specific judgment is a moment of sickness and death and fear. The joy and freedom and happiness of the miracle will be the necessary incentive to allow the Holy Spirit to guide all your decisions. And as you learn to think with God consistently, you become consistently miracle-minded. You open to acceptance of the Atonement or Correction. You see that you are God dependent and always will be, for God is our only Source. The belief in separation is an impossibility, for God Wills that Christ be One forever. Thy Will is done.

Life is a State of Mind. And what is unlearning but the peeling away of the onion of false belief so that the Light of Love may be recognized as All there is to behold? There is no death. God's Child is Life Eternal.

Immortality

Friend: A question came to my mind before when you were saying that the body is not immortal but the ego would love to have me believe that it could be. And there *is* the belief that the body can be immortal. I can remember believing this, and I can remember being very excited about that whole idea. It seemed very logical to me when I learned that it is only the mind's belief that the body is not immortal that would make it die.

David: Well, if we really look at it we see that the ego is for something that is nothing. It has the illusion of being very ingenious and that is certainly the experience in the world. It seems to have made up a giant cosmos apart from Spirit and apart from abstract union and it seems to have great diversity and variety. There seem to be many different skills, many choices and menus to pick from. In the sense of projection, now as part of it we have televisions and camcorders and VCR's; this is like making movies within movies. The movie of the world is one movie and within that we have another projection.

The fragmentation continues into seemingly smaller pieces. But the one thing that the ego has tried to come up with for an answer for Heaven is the idea of immortality. It never has and never will be able to mimic or create immortality. Immortality is an attribute of God, of creation, and the ego is a defense against that. It is literally a puff of nothingness that did not come from God and that is not immortal. The ego seemed to have a beginning and it will seem to have an end. But this is all within the fabric or the framework of the dream. The ego has never been able to come up with or attain immortality, but that does not stop it from at least having the idea of immortality, the idea that the body can be made to live forever. Once again, the body is form. Form and Spirit have no reconciliation. They have no meeting point. One Spirit exists, and form and time and space do not exist.

Friend: The very nature of form is that it is finite, not eternal. It cannot, therefore, be immortal.

David: It has boundaries. Every form has boundaries and limits. God and creation do not.

Friend: At that time I heard about someone in India who seemed to be proof of the fact that the body is immortal. It seemed that he would be around for periods of time and then he would dematerialize and not be around for periods of time. And then he would re-materialize and stay for a while and dematerialize. That seemed to be proof that you do not have to die, that the body can be immortal if it is held in the mind that way.

David: Just to perceive a body or a vision, though, gets back to perception. This can be a symbol – for many, a very comforting symbol. It can be a teaching symbol, that the thoughts of those who have completely laid aside the body are always available to the deceived mind as part of help. And their vision may appear from time to time if that may be helpful, if this is something that the Holy Spirit can reach the mind with. These are nothing more than symbols. Seeing the Virgin Mary in Medjugorje is an example of a vision that can be helpful. But they are still perceptions.

Friend: So you are saying that it is still perceptual – that it is still unreal but it is helpful and it is reaching the mind where it is?

David: Yes. The error would be to make the connection that you were making – that it seems to have been around for a long time and so it seems to be immortal. Once again, knowledge of the Kingdom of Heaven is purely abstract. It is light–not light like the body's eyes see, but light in the sense of understanding and wisdom. Darkness is a metaphor for ignorance, for blockage or unawareness of that light. This knowledge and the Kingdom are abstract. Any kind of perception, however pure and however stabilized the perception becomes, is still not the abstract Kingdom. It is still perceptual and temporary and will not last.

What You Extend, You Are

Friend: I think relying on the belief that we are separate justifies our shortcomings. We identify with our shortcomings, thinking: *Oh well, it is just because I am human.* It is self-feeding. It may be the question of the chicken or the egg. Which came first, the mistake or the belief in being capable of making the mistake? And that is kind of a moot point–just a play of ideas. When things go wrong, when things are less than perfect, we have a rationale like: *Well, what do you expect?*

David: Those thoughts are held onto in the mind to justify the experience. After a while you start to get wise. There comes a point of feeling *enough of this.* Then there is a willingness to really look at your thoughts–to look closely at them with Jesus, and to give up trying to justify them. If you feel angry the ego tells you to blast it out–to blame it on something or someone out there in the world. *It will make you feel better. You will get rid of it by giving it away. Kick the dog, do this, do that, but just get it out!* But projection does not work. It is like a boomerang. Zap it out there and it comes around and gets you in the back, and you feel guilty.

After enough times of throwing the boomerang out and getting whacked in the back, the mind starts to see that there is a trick. *Something is not going right when I keep trying to project these things.* If you get the metaphysics of this, you know there is simply one law in Heaven. The law in Heaven is this: What you extend you are. God extends himself–love–so He is love. His Son is the same thing; when you extend love you are love. Jesus says that when you come into the dream world, it is just a misapplication, or distortion, of this one law in Heaven. Through the ego lens "what you extend you are" becomes "what you project you will believe." When I project a world out there, I am trying to get rid of this world, to get it out of my mind. I try to get rid of duality–the split in my mind–and I project it. As soon as I project it I believe it. And it sure seems believable, doesn't it? Doesn't this body seem real? The whole point is to question the beliefs and the thoughts. You have to start to see that they are attack thoughts and that they are unreal. As soon as you can see that they are unreal, you do not invest in them. They are false. You pull your mind away from them. But as long as you believe they are real it feels horrifying and you just want to project it out more. That way you continue to seem like a victim, like there is something happening to you.

Friend: There are so many backwards thoughts. It feels like: *Why start looking?* Say you are tired of being angry and hurt and you just kind of become a hermit. Then you are not seeing any projections around you. You think you are hiding from them. Then you get to the point where you feel lonely. What is that?

David: Backwards thoughts. In other words, you can remove your body from society....

Friend: You think you are removing yourself from the things that bother you. You think that is where the cause is. But where is the cause? The cause is inside. You do not remove yourself from the mind. Then you get back in there and what is pulling you back? Is that the ego?

David: People ask what the difference is between Mother Teresa seeming to reach out to everybody, versus, let's say, a monk or a mystic that goes off into the mountains? In a sense, as long as you are training your mind and trying to detach from these thoughts, then form is irrelevant. We all have very high functions. We are called to be teachers of God. He is literally training us.

Friend: All of us?

David: All of us. We all have a lofty function and the more we really give our minds to that function and really start to live it and practice it, there comes such joy that it makes you forget about the candy bars and all the whatever's. Before it was inconceivable to be without the hot fudge sundae; *I like my hot fudge sundae, Jesus!* But more and more, as you get into this function and purpose, there comes an intrinsic joy. It is like a well that bubbles up from within the mind from the Holy Spirit.

Friend: So you do not have that emptiness that you are trying to fill all the time with all these other things that do not really work?

David: Right, and instead of trying to wrestle with them, they become like little flakes of dandruff. You just have to blow them off. That is the way to let go of things – to blow them away like they are little specks of dust, instead of giant leeches.

Friend: I suppose the more you validate them or focus on them, the bigger they become?

David: Yes.

Concern for the Body

Friend: I watched my mind as I was running errands, feeling nauseous and disconnected from Source. I noticed that I had a lot of fear come up around my friend's safety, about her going hitchhiking. I noticed how much body stuff I have going on. I noticed how much fear I have about letting those things surface and just giving them to the Holy Spirit. I feel guilty; I feel unworthy. I noticed with my friend's trip that things kept surfacing over the weekend and I just kept seeing her having this holy encounter. But there is something deeper coming up and I am not even sure what it is. But I am willing to go into it and heal this.

David: So you felt concern for her safety in some way?

Friend: Basically that was what it was. I tried to look into my past and see what this touched in me. Obviously there are some thoughts about really being that open and that vulnerable with God, that I am feeling really unsafe and unsure about doing that.

David: There is a line coming to me from Workbook lesson 48, "There is nothing to fear." In truth – in reality – there is nothing to fear, but this is not true for those who believe in illusions. As long as you believe in illusions you do have need to fear because of the way that you have defined reality and defined yourself. It is interesting to trace in that whole concept of vulnerability and risk. The spiritual journey is often described as requiring vulnerability in order to see what is within. That is just the way it seems to the ego. The ego's interpretation of looking at the beliefs in my mind is that it is a very risky and vulnerable undertaking. Of course it would be perceived that way; it knows that if this process continues then it is out of business, so to speak. It would have to be perceived that way through its lens. Even if it is someone else in your life taking the steps, it can still require a leap of trust. If your friend is really opening up to the Holy Spirit's Guidance and seems to be throwing caution to the wind in terms of protection and safety measures—it will be perceived as threatening if seen through the ego's lens. *If someone else can do it that means I can do this! Oh my gosh! I do not know if I can do this.*

There is a basic belief in the ego's system that darkness can hide. One of the initial things that the teacher of God goes through is the idea that darkness cannot hide. This can be experienced as painful. It can even be delayed and drawn out when the mind is still going back and forth about whether it can hide. But once that is transcended, the mind comes to a place where it starts to see that even if it could, why would it want to hide anything from God? That is when the ease starts to come in; it starts to feel safer and safer. Our sessions this week demonstrated to me how strong your commitment is. You are looking at all kinds of thoughts that have come up. When you make such a concerted effort and have the willingness to *not know*, and to just share what you are thinking and to look at it—that is very threatening to the ego. A lot of times it can even seem like there is backlash.

Friend: I had to go into the dentist for a gum scaling and all this stuff came up about the body. It is not a place that I really want to be looking, because while I am focusing on that it is really hard to focus on Spirit and Oneness. So I am trying to just let that go and in the meantime I have to go for this gum surgery. I am not at all ready to cancel all the appointments—I am too fearful that there still is something going on with the body. I am still feeling that I am going to go through with it but I want to be as defenseless as possible with the nurses, because I am very fearful. I need to really look at the idea of sickness because there is a part of me that sees that if I can let go of the feeling of the body being real, then I can let go of all of this—and I am not ready to let that go yet.

David: So somehow healing is associated with loss of self.

Friend: It would be loss of the body.

David: Which would be part of the self as the ego has constructed it, so in that sense, healing is feared if that is the way we perceive it. It is not surprising that with you having a background in nursing, medicine, and health promotion, that the mind gets lessons in the area with the symbols it is familiar with. When we have a lesson to learn it will be learned in a form the mind can get. It is not accidental that you seem to have all these medical appointments lined up and that you seem to have been working in the medical field. It is all coming to a head because we have to really get at the contrast between mind and body and all this offers a very direct way of doing it. There is a concern for bodies that is in there. A lesson that is coming to mind is the beginning of lesson 135. It comes before lesson 136 which is "Sickness is a defense against the truth."

A good springboard is to start to get at what this thing is that you are so concerned about. What is it that you are defending? It would be good to start to trace it in – to take a look at what is going on at a deeper level, beyond all these surface concerns. Whether it is with medications, or locking doors, or whether it is taking safe rides when the bodies are being transported from one place to the other – those are all forms of magic.

When the mind is too fearful, a mix of magic and miracles may be helpful to reduce the fear. Jesus talks about that in the section called *How is Healing Accomplished?* He says that the mind of the patient can simply say "I have no use for this" M-5.II.2, and just rise up. Or it can be that "special agents seem to be ministering to him," which can be, for example, doctor appointments. Nurses and doctors can be seen as special agents, still seemingly outside the mind, that seem to be ministering to the patient, but that is just a form in which the mind can handle it, so to speak. It is an interpretation of the way the mind can see that healing could occur. It seems more drawn out; there is still a fear of instantaneous healing. Through the ego's lens instantaneous healing is fearful because of what it would have to give up. It asks: *What will be gone from me? What will I lose if I am healed?* And so it seems to play itself out more in linear time.

Let's use lesson 135:

> If I defend myself I am attacked. Who would defend himself
> unless he thought he were attacked, that the attack were real,
> and that his own defense could save himself? And herein lies
> the folly of defense; it gives illusions full reality and then
> attempts to handle them as real. W-135

Whenever we talk about things like getting a safe ride from one place to the next, it implies that they are believed to be real problems, real issues that I have to deal with and therefore that is why I am having all these appointments and everything. In a sense you have to pull back enough to take a look at how you are giving illusions full reality. Even when you use the thought: *Well this is where I am at now* – whether it is with nutrition or body symptoms or whatever – when you say that is the way a problem really is, you have defined it as being in the world. That is giving illusions full reality, and then what else is there to do? What would a mature person do but defend against and take steps to alleviate the problems? That is defining a problem in a way that makes it unsolvable. There is only one problem and one solution – and that is in the mind. The problem is defining the issue as out here in linear terms in the world of form. It is the same whether it is a problem with the gums or with having a big debt to pay off and wanting the integrity of paying it off. You can see how both of these things are defining the problem. Somebody does not have their money and I need to pay it back. That is defining it in specifics. And with the gums – I have been diagnosed by a dentist and the doctors have looked at it and I have these other complications that have come in. That is defining it out there in the world or in form. Or even the example of fear for a friend's safety, fear that something could happen to a body that is too open and trusting. Again, that is defining the problem as out there. That gives us three very different specifics. We begin to see that when we define a problem as being in the world, we make it real. I make the illusions real and then whatever I do as an attempt to deal with them is going to be in a defensive mode. We want to go deeper, to take a look at whether the problem is really what we think it is.

> It adds illusions to illusions, thus making correction doubly difficult. And it is this you do when you attempt to plan the future, activate the past, or organize the present as you wish. W-135.1

This week my friend and I got into some of the finer points of disorderliness in the home, things like finger prints on a mirror or coffee grounds on the counter. That would fit into that last category; organize the present as you wish. The mind can think that a good defense against the Spirit is to insist things be a certain way on the screen, as if that will bring order into a chaotic life and mind. You can see how that last sentence "it is this you do when you attempt to plan the future, activate the past or organize the present as you wish," really covers a lot.

> You operate from the belief you must protect yourself from what is happening because it must contain what threatens you. A sense of threat is an acknowledgement of inherent weakness; a belief that there is danger which has power to call on you to make appropriate defense. The world is based on this insane belief. And all its structures, all its thoughts and

> doubts, its penalties and heavy armaments, its legal definitions
> and its codes, its ethics and its leaders and its gods, all serve
> but to preserve its sense of threat. For no one walks the world
> in armature but must have terror striking at his heart. W-135.2

There is a lot in that paragraph. He just rattles it off about the way the world has been constructed, with all the legal definitions and codes. The whole medical profession that you have become familiar with through your training is part of the defense – the thought that there is a real threat and that all of these procedures are good at reducing the threat.

Friend: Even the idea of holistic or alternative medicine would be the same.

David: Yes. This is radical, but isn't it nice to start to really get to the bottom of things? It can seem threatening, like: *Oh my gosh, what have I got to question to get to the bottom of things?* But on the other hand – *Hallelujah! I have been on this wheel for long enough now. It is time to really get to the bottom of things.* I was looking at a book called *Ageless Body, Timeless Mind.* The mind is timeless but the whole thing of the body being ageless – no, no, no! We talked about expanding the life span, when the definition of life still would be seen to be within the body and longevity seems to be pushing it. Let's take a look at this. Whatever comes up is fair game to throw onto the table because we want to be really thorough in looking at this.

> Defense is frightening. It stems from fear, increasing fear as
> each defense is made. You think it offers safety. Yet it speaks of
> fear made real and terror justified. Is it not strange you do not
> pause to ask, as you elaborate your plans and make your armor
> thicker and your locks more tight, what you defend, and how,
> and against what? W-135.3

That is what it takes sometimes when the mind seems to go, go, go, into its defensive maneuvers; just pause for a reflective moment. It can seem frightening because it can seem like it is too big a ball of wax. Jesus is asking me to look at *every* belief that I hold in my mind. At times it seems easier to just go through some of the defenses and preparations like I have always done. You know, you have gotten through it before. That can be the ego saying: *You have done this before, go ahead!* But the point of release comes by pausing and doing what we are doing right now – taking a look at it. He asks us a question about pausing to ask what we defend, and how, and against what. Here we go:

Let us consider first what you defend. It must be something that is very weak and easily assaulted. It must be something made easy prey, unable to protect itself and needing your defense. What but the body has such frailty that constant care and watchful, deep concern are needful to protect its little life? What but the body falters and must fail to serve the Son of God as worthy host? W-135.4

Friend: OK, what is coming up for me is that I was reading about a serial killer who was being executed. I have a fifteen-year-old boy so as I am reading this there are lots of places where I need to pause. Where I become weak is the thought that my son could be hitchhiking and then a serial killer could pick him up and gruesomely murder him. So I have to go to the fact that *bodies are not real,* but just the thought of that.... What I am defending is that I think that this has such reality.

David: It is very frightening, just the thought of letting it into the consciousness.

Friend: It is, and to just let this go seems frightening. I have even thought that this body needs me to take care of it, and if I do not, it is just going to go to pieces. In the next breath, I think about all the times when my mind was not on my body and a symptom never occurred because my mind was not focused on a symptom; it was not focused on the body. This is big because this is happening right now with the body, the hitchhiking, and the whole thing. It is very hard for me to let go. I can see the freedom in letting go, but I do not have that right now.

Yet, the other night I said to my friend, "You cannot tell me I am not a body!" And she said, "I am not going to sit here and align with that thought with you." I asked her, "If I am not a body then what am I?" She said, "My friend, you are a mind." That really clicked in for me. I feel like that made a really big shift. The Holy Spirit was operating that night for sure. I have heard that so many times before and then all of a sudden it was just like: *Oh, yes!*

David: Yes, the thought that keeps coming is how helpful it is to come together and talk about our perceptions, beliefs and thoughts. Minds have beliefs, perceptions, and thoughts. When we continually keep tracing them back, there has to come a time when there is an experiential shift, a feeling of a loosening and a lightening from it. You can talk about a right mind and a wrong mind; from the wrong mind's perspective the body is the reality and bodies have private minds. Each body has a private mind associated with it and a "higher" wrong mind perspective is where you get into that stuff about souls and mind/body/spirit and a lot of the mixture of things which is still the wrong mind.

We want to really lift this above the battlefield, which is where the right mind is; it knows without a doubt that I am Mind and that all of these images and projections and false concepts and beliefs are not me. It has a good view from above, perched above it can see the wrong mind, the entire world and the cosmos. And each thing we do is an attempt to get clearer and clearer. If you come from a nursing background, you will need to see that the whole thing with the body, neurology and the brain and all those things that are seen as common wisdom are not wisdom at all. It takes coming from a higher perspective to start to see the fallacy of it. That is a great leap. Just keep at it.

Friend: Another body thing that came up this weekend was the idea of abortion. I have seen the baby inside on the monitor and I have thought: *That is a body in there; I can see how it is forming.* This body thing is really hitting me. It is a little bit disorienting; nothing is making sense. In fact, my body is falling apart, which is completely disorienting. My husband and I were talking about a career and I said, "Nobody would hire me right now." I could not complete a task. I cannot even think about working.

A whole other fear is my daughter's education. There was a great big thing in the newspaper the other day about education costs having gone up 9.4%. I have not let that go. I believe it is very important for her to get an education; my fear is that if I become *A Course in Miracles* teacher and if I am not making any money, I am letting everybody down. That is where I am at. All this is coming up. It is creating havoc right now.

David: The Course keeps coming back to perception; it is saying that your perception is twisted. What you conceive of as a good future and good education, a good way of growing up for your children, for other children.... That is all a construct. In the beginning just do whatever you can to bring it back to that one idea that it is a perceptual problem. It can seem like a long stretch to wonder how a solution to your perceptual problem can handle your daughter's college costs.

I remember your son asking you, "Mom, do I have to go to college or can I just study *A Course in Miracles*?" That is certainly a different twist. The theme is that there is something deeper that may not fit into the structure of how society and the world are constructed.

Friend: The idea of planning the future is very rattling for me right now, in terms of career. I just finished this degree, but what am I going to do with it and how is it even going to make any sense? Then I find myself falling back into the trap of the world; that I have come this far with school, that everybody thinks that this is necessary, and my kids have needs–but it is about trust; again I have to come back to that sense of Christ strength instead of ego weakness, because ego weakness can really make me feel very vulnerable.

David: There was a gentleman at a retreat who had been drinking before he studied the Course. He said, "Now the Course is my comforter instead of the alcohol." But it was also the same gentleman that said, "If Jesus lived today I do not know if he could get a date. I mean he walks around and he is talking about the Kingdom of Heaven and he is saying to leave everything behind and follow him. I do not know how many guys could get a date with that! He even told his apostles to leave their jobs and not work!"

We will keep going into the metaphysics, which are the underpinnings for all this, but until the mind can loosen up enough to let some of these things in, it needs symbols; that is why I would recommend reading *The Urantia Book, Part IV*. Jesus goes through a training period and continues to question things while still engaged with what seems to be his family. It describes how he is helping to take care of the children–his younger siblings–teaching them, not abdicating responsibilities. Further, as he goes along and even leaves the family, he seems to prepare them for his leaving. Then he calls on the apostles. Some of them are married; Thomas is married and has kids and Peter has three kids.

Once again it is very similar to the situation that our friend is in. She is studying *A Course in Miracles*. She is being called by Jesus just as directly as if he had come and knocked on her front door and said "Follow me." She seems to have a family, as did Peter and Thomas and others. But he is calling them into an intensive teaching/learning situation where they are focusing on these high ideas; make no bones about it–that is a very important calling. They go back for periods of time to visit their families. Didn't Thomas or Peter feel feelings of loss? I was just reading in *The Urantia Book, Part IV* that Thomas was such a moody fellow that when he got called to go off and follow the apostles, his wife thought: *Yay, go with my blessing!* That is a different twist.

That is what our friend is going through now in the sense that her husband is starting to talk about what is going on. There are all these interpretations from those who see themselves as mothers. They are angry at her; from their perspective as mothers, they find her choices very threatening. Another gentleman who her husband talked to said, "Well, she must have a man in another city. Why would anyone leave so urgently?" There are all these different interpretations, as there may be with you and your husband when you can lay it on the table and say, "Here is what is going on." Her husband is at the point where he understands that it is not a man that she is going to, or that she is leaving her children, or that she is a vicious mother who never has cared for or shown an interest in her children. He knows that there is something much deeper that she is called to. The conversations continue, but there is still the fear. There are physical symptoms and all kind of ways that it manifests. *The Urantia Book, Part IV* was a great help to me as far as putting it all into a larger perspective. I started to feel disoriented at times with the Course because I did not know where it was guiding me. *The Urantia Book, Part IV* gave me a bigger swath of how things are unfolding. A stepping stone towards letting go is to not put a lot of credence in the future, or to even plan at all.

Friend: This weekend, I was observing my parents. I was on the Workbook lesson "The power of decision is my own." W-152 I said, "Dad, it is an opportunity." He knows I am in this and it is like the opportunity to bait me almost. I felt like I just wanted to leave and he was saying, "We are all inspired. I believe that we are all inspired," and I said "That is true, Dad." and I tried to find common ground. I said, "According to the Course, which is something that has been really dear to me and helped me to understand these concepts, the Holy Spirit came in when we separated and it was given to us." He said, "Well now that has got to be the biggest joke I have ever heard!" This is a very powerful experience for me because my dad wrote a book called, *What Is Truth?* He has been lecturing and preaching to me all my life and now that I am in this I am seeing that he is really very fearful. "The power of decision is my own" kept coming in; I wanted this lesson to be for him. I kept explaining to him and it kept coming back, "The power of decision is my own." This is my own lesson; I am talking to myself! I kept thinking *if he would get this lesson I could come home and we could talk about this!* He loves to talk about things. *If he could get this lesson we could discuss this*; but then I realized that I was not getting this. When *I* get this, we might be able to discuss it.

I have been looking at control too. I was observing my mother calling everybody on the phone to go to church with her. Then I realized how much control I have had over my family, over my husband, and my house. When I saw the intensity of my desire for my father to look at the idea that: "The power of decision is my own," I began to see how many control issues I really have. I even left the book open when I went for my walk, so he could read it. I mean, do you hear that?

David: The Course is a new belief system and sometimes you feel like: *Here it is guys. Now, if you could just get this.* But even the theology of how the separation happened is just theology, because Jesus says it never really happened at all. So he is giving his own little story that the mind can kind of grab onto as something to believe in for a while. But in the end there is an experience that will come. Everything else has to fall away, even the Course stories. But, the whole thing of wanting to be right, to control, is something to go into very deeply.

Reading the introduction to the *Clarification of Terms* is helpful. It says that those who seek controversy will certainly find it and those who seek clarity will find that as well, as long as they are willing to overlook controversy. It is really only in the *experience*, rather than the theology, that consistency is found. The uncertainty only ends once there is an experience. The temptation in the beginning can be to try to put it into a theological framework but that is not ever going to bring peace. It is very direct. You could read that section before you go visit your dad.

Friend: "In my defenselessness my safety lies" W-153 is the lesson for today. There is a sentence that says, "Defenses are the costliest of all the prices which the ego would exact. In them lies madness in a form so grim that hope of sanity seems to be an idle dream beyond the possible." W-153.4 That sentence has been on my mind. I wonder if this is an idle dream that may really be impossible for me. Maybe it is possible for you. But then I have to come back to seeing that I can either play right into that, with that ego weakness, or I can keep the Christ strength. What helped me today was thinking to myself: *OK, you can sit there and be this little weak thing going to all these doctors, or you can be strong and see what you are supposed to learn from this experience!*

David: In the beginning, the mind is just starting to be aware of these ego defense mechanisms, like noticing your dad's seeming desire to be right, or your mom's seeming controlling tendencies, etc. For years, these defense mechanisms have been kept out of awareness. When you start working with the Course, everything starts getting raised up. All these devious schemes and maneuvers and games come right up into awareness, but the mind is still invested in the ego so it sees the defenses in others! When you feel angry or frustrated at a brother for using a particular defense—being controlling or whatever it is—you are failing to forgive yourself for the very same attempt; you still believe that the defense has a reality. You are seeing it *out there* but when you start to pull it back to your mind, you start to see the control in yourself. The guilt from transferring it from one seeming person/body to another seeming person/body is enormous. Instead of blaming your brother, the blame gets turned onto your own seeming body, but it is still the same error. We have to see that *I am mind*; this identity that I took off of my brother but still saw in myself is also just a construct in my mind. Otherwise, what good is the transfer? *I am not so much angry and blaming my father or my mother anymore, but I walk around angry, blaming who I believe to be me.* The error is transferred but is not released yet. It is only a step.

Friend: So, do not leave it with my body. What is the next step?

David: The next step is to get more in touch with the idea that *I am mind*. I am not a body on the screen, in the world. I am not a linear construct. You have to begin to let go of the ways you have always conceived of yourself—as a person with a past, with aspects you are not so happy about, with a closet full of grievances, with preferences for some people and situations, with the wish for things to be different than they are, etc. You also have to let go of the ways you have conceived of yourself being in the future, whether it is regarding a career or whether it is in the spiritual context of moving towards the Atonement. That puts salvation in the future; instead of a career in the world, now it is salvation. Even that you have to question; what good is future salvation? What good is future happiness? It seemed to be a helpful stepping stone to a point until you start reading *The Immediacy of Salvation*: "Be not content with future happiness." T-26.VIII.9 Do not project the Atonement into the future. You have to bring it back to the present. In order to bring it back to the present we have to let go of the way we have conceived of ourselves and of everyone else we meet.

If I conceive of persons as these linear constructs, with real pasts and real futures, and of myself as a linear construct, with a real past and a real future, then how can I avoid aiming the guilt I pull away from others towards this linear construct of myself? The shift is to see that mind is not in a linear construct. The right mind is in the present. The right mind does not have a past and it does not have a future. It is like a pinnacle on top of a mountain. If you can get to the top, the view is spectacular. You can look at all the little roads below and all the little lines that you seem to take and that others seem to be taking; from that point it can all just be seen as one false thing.

That is how it has gone for me. It always comes back to: *I am a point, not a line.* That is a simple way to remember that you are not guilty. Whenever you feel guilty about what is coming up, or worried about loose ends or a bad relationship, just come back to the thought that *I am a point and not a line.*

Friend: I am realizing that I have been trying to bring truth to the illusion instead of illusion to truth. Now I am just seeing my oneness with God and how everything pales beside that.

David:

> What but the body has such frailty that constant care and watchful, deep concern are needful to protect its little life? What but the body falters and must fail to serve the Son of God as worthy host? Yet, it is not the body that can fear, nor be a thing of fear. It has no needs but those which you assign to it. It needs no complicated health structures of defense, no health-inducing medicine, no care and no concern at all. W-135.4-5

Now that is obviously a hugely different view than the importance the world gives to the body. It is helpful to think of the body as a marionette or a puppet. Sometimes I like to think of it as a learning device, even like a pen or a pencil. I have to, in my mind, equate it with something that can be a symbol of how insignificant it is. I mean normally you would not consider putting all this care and concern and careful watching over a pencil. You use a pencil for what a pencil is for, writing, and then you lay it down. You keep sharpening it as long as you need it and then when it gets too short so that you cannot hold it anymore, it is gone. You lay it aside. In that sense, thinking of the body as being like a pencil is a helpful metaphor.

> Defend its life, or give it gifts to make it beautiful or walls to make it safe, and you but say your home is open to the thief of time, corruptible and crumbling, so unsafe it must be guarded with your very life. W-135.5

You could "defend its life" through security systems, carrying mace, or medical interventions. "Give it gifts to make it beautiful" can be adorning the body; giving it compliments is really making it out to be more than it really is.

Friend: Mom gave me this bracelet for my graduation and my response was not the response that she was looking for. She said, "Don't you like it?" And I said, "I really do! It is a wonderful symbol of you, thank you." She said, "What do you mean, a symbol!?" I tried to explain it to her. I said, "For me, I can look at it as a symbol, but I do not want to see it as something adorning because that kind of takes away from its purpose."

David: That was the best use of the bracelet because it was a starting point for you to just share. It opened up a conversation to go into something and in that sense it is neither good nor bad. The Holy Spirit can make use of everything, including bracelets on arms.

> Is not this picture fearful? Can you be at peace with such a concept of your home? Yet what endowed the body with the right to serve you thus except your own belief? It is your mind which gave the body all the functions that you see in it, and set its value far beyond a little pile of dust and water. Who would make defense of something that he recognized as this? W-135.6

All this fuss over a pile of dust and water! Who would defend this? But the key is to hear this: What endowed the body with the right to serve you thus is your own belief. It is your mind! We do not have to blame the body or the bodies of others if they seem to be acting out, if they seem to be using these defense mechanisms, or if they seem to be just heaping in the wealth and the possessions. None of that matters. It is my mind. What value have I assigned to the body and the world? The only place that you have power to change is within your own beliefs. Whenever you try to change the bodies, so to speak, or the situation—say with something like abortion—then you have already decided that there is a real threat. Once you make the illusions real, you have to come up with the right way of dealing with whatever is perceived out there.

"The body is in need of no defense. This cannot be too often emphasized." W-135.7 When Jesus says that he means it very literally.

> It will be strong and healthy if the mind does not abuse it by assigning it to roles it cannot fulfill, to purposes beyond its scope, and to exalted aims which it cannot accomplish. Such attempts, ridiculous yet deeply cherished, are the sources for the many mad attacks you make upon it. For it seems to fail your hopes, your needs, your values, and your dreams. W-135.7

If you believe it is your home, then of course it would make sense that you would have a lot of hopes for it, a lot of needs and values for it. You can see how the body would be thought of as more than a pile of dust if you see it as your home. Identity is the most powerful thing there is; whatever the mind identifies with, it will defend. If it is identified with Spirit then there is nothing to defend because Spirit is invulnerable. It is in a state of grace. If you identify another body as a close friend, then you might feel a need to defend their body. And that defensiveness will go beyond the body to other symbols of your identity, such as your car, or house, or job.

Friend: My kids....

David: Yes, your kids. Those are just extensions of this body self-concept.

> The "self" that needs protection is not real. The body, valueless and hardly worth the least defense, need merely be perceived as quite apart from you and it becomes a healthy, serviceable instrument through which the mind can operate until its usefulness is over. Who would want to keep it when its usefulness is done? W135.8

The experiential shift of coming to perceive the body "as quite apart from you," is something that comes gradually—more like a trickle into a stream, than a river! When I first started studying the Course I was just trying to grasp some of the ideas; light bulbs were going off, but I was not being used as a teacher of God yet. I was not in the river. But the trickle is a start and I am grateful for the trickle; it is what I had always wanted. Then when you really start holding onto this as your only purpose and you make the commitment to be used as a teacher of God, every single situation is used for that. Other roles start to recede because you have your commitment and purpose out in front. There is a shift from the trickle to a flow. For me, the experience was like: *Wow, it seems like it is all really orchestrated!* We have all had glimmers of that. As the commitment grows you are carried along on a stream, and it starts to seem like a pretty quick stream. Before you know it you find yourself in the river. By the time you are in the river, the body is perceived as "quite apart from you." That is when all the plans, cares, and concerns for it have so receded from the mind that the mind is just riveted on Purpose; there is so much joy and flow! That experiential shift of not thinking of myself as a body has happened for me. When you start to be really centered in the moment, all the things that seem to be happening, whether it is temperature extremes, or sharp things flying—it all just fades into the background. The body is not the focal point. It is more like a pencil that you are using.

The Topic of Diet and Health

Friend: I would like to ask you about diet. How important is a healthy diet while dealing with and practicing the teachings of Jesus? Is diet, as everything else, a matter of beliefs and perceptions about food? How do you deal with food and how big a role does food play in your life? One thing I noticed is that when I treat my body nicely and eat "healthy" food, it seems more pleasant to be in and I can more easily undertake spiritual practice and mind training. Can you speak about this?

David: The question about diet is another version of the prayer to step back and let the Holy Spirit lead the way. The curriculum is highly individualized, so I cannot speak in broad generalities about diet. It is most helpful with diet, as with all things, to be highly intuitive and thus very open to the Holy Spirit's Guidance. You may use the prayer: *Holy Spirit, guide my eating that I may be fed by You.* Truly it is not what you eat that is most important on the spiritual journey, but Who is guiding the mind is all important. It is not what you put in your mouth that defiles, but that which proceeds from an unhealed heart. Likewise, the miracle brings healing far beyond what the ego judges as "healthy food."

Healing always depends upon exposing and releasing the ego belief system, for thus is distorted perception healed. Problems are never in form, being always a belief in the deceived mind. The ego projected a body and food and weight issues and fitness issues, etc., to distract the mind from the Light within. In the reversal of thought that the Holy Spirit sponsors, the mind is empowered as the mechanism of Awakening. As you learn to think with the Holy Spirit, you will be truly healthy and vibrant and joyful and energetic. This health comes from sharing the Purpose of the Holy Spirit, which is forgiveness.

The body is a symbol, or representation, so when you feel well this is a sign that you are following the Holy Spirit. Let your feelings be a barometer to the voice that you are following, and learn to trust the Voice for God within the mind. Eat what you feel guided to eat and when you feel guided to eat, and let this be a practice of the ACIM Workbook lesson: "I will step back and let Him lead the way." W-155 The ego will attribute the feeling to form, as it always does. Yet as you deepen with the Holy Spirit, it becomes more obvious that health is a decision of Purpose; the form is always just a backdrop or stage. In Awakening, it becomes apparent that there is nothing causative in form. This includes the body, food, exercise and the environment. Every experience is a decision of the mind. With training, the mind is consistently miracle-minded, or right-minded, and this state of mind is healthy. The happy dream is healthy indeed, and peace of mind results from the Purpose and Perspective of the Holy Spirit. In quantum physics this is called the observer. In ACIM terms, this is the dreamer.

Digest the Holy Spirit's Purpose in your mind and you will never hunger again.

Healthy and Unhealthy Foods

Hi David,

I am writing regarding your post concerning exercise and food. I am in this exact struggle right now. I am a personal fitness trainer. I got involved with the Course about four months ago when I had just begun my new job. At first it was difficult for me to even feel good about working with people on fitness. Now I see it as an opportunity to have holy encounters rather than focusing on the fitness aspect so much. However, your post really hit a chord with me because I am struggling in the worst way with food. I find that when I eat what I consider healthy foods, I am happy and energetic. When I don't, I get extremely depressed. I have played with this idea since studying the Course. I have accepted that the body is neutral. In doing this I began eating whatever I wanted instead of relying on "healthy" food to keep my emotions grounded. Intellectually I could accept the idea that what I put into my mouth does not have an effect on my mind. But when I ate "unhealthy" foods, even while keeping this thought in mind, it seemed to backfire. I became extremely depressed and miserable regardless of my acceptance of the idea. I feel trapped with this.

Do you have any specific advice for me? I feel as if I am in a constant battle and I am not sure how to handle this in the most productive way. Can you give me some more information about how you were able to get beyond this particular struggle?

Beloved One,

Healing of the mind is a process (until it is realized as an instant), so although you can be open to the ideas and you can be open to the healing, you cannot direct the miracle yourself. Your willingness to heal your mind and to accept the truth is what you can offer the Holy Spirit, and then your role is to listen and follow your intuition as to what happens next.

Leading with the behavior and focusing on the form is not the way that that healing occurs. It is always at the level of mind that healing occurs, so continue to be open regarding the foods that you eat, being aware that there is nothing causative in form, but that your mind is very powerful and you will experience the effects of your beliefs.

Unconscious beliefs run very deep, so use the "healthy food" concept as a leaf that you can trace inward to the branches, looking at all of your thoughts and associations with this belief–its opposites, its contradictions, the fears and doubts and convictions around it, inward to the trunk, or the belief in separation–inward to the belief that you must be "a body" at the mercy of and affected by foods (the world).

Look upon these beliefs and thoughts from a place of innocence, from a place of enquiry. Know that all you need do is observe and trace in, being honest with yourself about what you do believe. Allow the emotions to come up and pass away, while handing it all over to the Holy Spirit. Visual imagery can be helpful for "handing over." At times I have visualized scooping up all of the associated thoughts, putting them in a basket with a big bow on top and giving them to Him like they were a gift-wrapped present! At other times, when the images had sadness associated with them, I placed them on a raft and watched them being taken gently across a river of light to dissolve into Love.

It is all about becoming highly intuitive and releasing fear from the mind. Through a gentle process of enquiry and release, you may be surprised to find that you are intuitively guided to eat foods that you once considered "healthy foods." God's Will for you is perfect happiness, so any feelings of sacrifice are coming from the ego.

Be gentle with your beautiful self, knowing that you are not the healthy thoughts, or the unhealthy thoughts, or even the thinker of these dualistic thoughts! You are pure Love, and the symbol of eating food can be used as a backdrop for joining; it can be used as a backdrop for joy while you continue with the holy purpose of healing your mind.

Does Diet Have Importance?

It is the diet of ego thoughts that seem to fatten or reinforce the self-concept and block awareness of the Christ. Nothing in form is causative. It is not what goes into a mouth which "defiles." All laws of nutrition are of the ego (read Workbook lesson 76). Food, like all the images of the world, is an unreal effect of an unreal "cause."

The ego wants the mind to see the split *in* the world, and dualistic "thought" seems to project a dualistic world. The ego sponsors divisions and categories (i.e. organic/non-organic, good nutrition/bad nutrition, high calorie/low calorie, high fiber/low fiber, high sodium/low sodium). Nutrition is like all magic in that, to the ego, it seems to work—it can seem to produce changes. Yet what is unreal is not capable of "change." What is the same cannot be different, and what is one cannot have separate parts. The unreal is one error, and only a change of mind brings healing. Nothing in form ever really changes, for all form is the past (see Workbook lesson 7).

Release the belief that the past and future are different, and the concept of diet and all "specifics" are released forever. Such is Atonement. Atonement sees that the "separation" never happened, for God and Christ, Cause and Effect are One and can never be divided. Glory to God for the Oneness of Being! Healing is the acceptance of the Correction to the split in the mind. The true workings of the mind are reflected in the following passage from the beginning of ACIM Chapter 21, *Reason and Perception*:

> Projection makes perception. The world you see is what you gave it, nothing more than that. But though it is no more than that, it is not less. Therefore, to you it is important. It is the witness to your state of mind, the outside picture of an inward condition. As a man thinketh, so does he perceive. Therefore, seek not to change the world, but choose to change your mind about the world. Perception is a result and not a cause. T-21.in.1

The concept of diet, like all false concepts, reflects a belief that something of the world is causative. Yet the Holy Spirit looks not to effects, having judged their "cause"—ego—as unreal. Bring all thoughts of false causation to the Holy Spirit, and instantly they are gone. For only that which comes from God is real. Happily, Christ comes from God, and the "I Am" Presence is real. Rejoice in the truth of our Being: "I am as God created me." W-94

Healing and Medicines—the Use of Symbols

Hi David,

I ordered and received the ACIM books and am just getting started. The Course teaches that believing in medicine is like believing in magic, and I can see that. I have, over the last several years, adjusted and increased vitamins, minerals, antioxidants, amino acids, herbs, etc. to try and improve several conditions that I had associated with age, inheritance, stress, etc. However, while doing this, I have been also implementing practices of recognizing belief systems and their origins, releasing the need for them, and also releasing others from blame as I discovered that some of the beliefs were based on unforgiveness.

I have relentlessly pursued releasing and forgiving life perspectives and people who might have contributed to such beliefs. Of course, I have had dramatic health changes, but have attributed my wellness to the change in my thoughts as well as to the nutrients. As I look at it though, most likely most of my healing has probably come about because of the release of those belief systems. However, some of those healings may have come about because of belief in certain nutrients.

Also, can you give me an understandable definition of "level confusion," as is mentioned often in ACIM?

Beloved One,

Thanks for writing. The saying goes: "Mind over matter." Illness and health are solely mental, and the belief in the physical or the manifest is the basis of all conflict, disease, stress, and upset. The mind is causative, yet the sleeping mind remembers not the making of the world. The sleeping mind believes that the world the ego made turned around and made the body self. This is the belief in physical "birth." Thus it appears that events and circumstances happen to the body apart from its asking or control. The first step in healing this cause-effect split and reversal is opening to the realization that everything which seems to happen is the result of belief. The mind perceives what the mind believes. Questioning what is believed is therefore a way of raising the ego belief system to the Light.

Level confusion is the belief that time-space-matter is causative instead of an unreal effect of an unreal "cause." There is nothing causative in the material universe, and the sleeping mind is imprisoned by its own beliefs. Once the ego belief system is exposed as having no foundation, the effects it seemed to produce are seen as causeless. Appearances and images are seen for what they are, illusion, and no longer are they endowed with "life" and "meaning."

Right-mindedness or miracle-mindedness is the end of level confusion, for the miracle simply sees the false as false. The miracle does not judge the contents of consciousness, for it sees their unreality. The Holy Spirit looks not to effects, having judged their "cause" as unreal. The ego is the unreal "cause." Trust the Holy Spirit in the transformation of the mind. The Holy Spirit will reinterpret everything perceived with a new Perspective.

If you do the Workbook lessons of ACIM and read the Text, with openness and willingness, you will see that the Holy Spirit orchestrates everything of time-space for your benefit. Time is actually under the direction of the miracle-worker, for the miracle-worker is aligned with the Holy Spirit's use of time.

The Holy Spirit will instruct you on what is most helpful in terms of using time and the symbols of time. The body, diet, medicine, exercise, and activity in general are best given over to the Holy Spirit. The specifics are used by the Holy Spirit in the Workbook practice until the Divine Principle is transferred and applied so consistently that the belief in specifics is completely undone. In accepting Atonement the mind is thus prepared for the remembrance of Light or Divine Abstraction in God.

Food, Exercise, and Physical Care

Friend: The first part of my question is: Have you noticed that you agree with certain foods more than others or are you totally free from body needs or complaints? The second is: Do you exercise? And part three of this same question is: Would you comment on how to deal with the fact that we have a body here in this plane that requires physical care?

David: The Holy Spirit's curriculum is highly individualized. The guidance that I heard was to "eat what is served." The Holy Spirit can prompt you not only in terms of dietary needs but also in terms of all that would be most helpful in your journey—wherever your mind seems to be in the spiritual awakening. My experience has been a reflection of the ACIM Workbook lesson "I will step back and let Him lead the way." W-155 I was guided to join fully with my brothers and not let food be an obstacle. There was to be no debate or sense of being separated off by what can be eaten and what cannot be eaten. The Spirit said that not only was I to just accept and eat whatever was offered, but the main focus was to join with my brother in love, without allowing anything such as food to come between us. Dietary requirements are part of the ego belief system.

I recall working with lesson 50: "I am sustained by the love of God." It highlights that beliefs in pills, money, and protective clothing are all defenses. I was glad that Jesus was so specific about these kinds of things because I really wanted to go deeper in my mind training. Then I came to lesson 76: "I am under no laws but God's." He mentions nutrition in there specifically. I realized that I had to question my beliefs in everything I believed about nutrition. I had learned a lot through seemingly growing in this world and from studying at the university for ten years. I had to let go all of the beliefs about healthy foods. I had to let go of beliefs about cholesterol and polyunsaturated fats, calories, etc. I really had to come to the realization that I do not know what anything is for; I had to come to a place of asking, "Please show me how to join with my brother and sister and let go of these thoughts and doubts and concerns about nutrition." That was how it progressed.

It is the same with exercise. Exercise is a belief that I certainly was involved with for quite a few years, all the way down to seemingly being a professional tennis instructor, belonging to health clubs, doing a lot of exercise routines, running a mini-marathon, etc. I was concerned about cardiovascular fitness and weight-training. Then it came to a point where everything began to be used as symbols. I began speaking to groups about the parables of letting it all go and learning to open up to God's love. Exercise and nutrition are just concepts. Health, if you come at it in a practical way, is inner peace; therefore health involves the thinking. Health is purely a mental state of mind that seems to be reflected in the physical. There is no inner or outer in enlightenment. Mind is unified. We cannot say that the inner world of thought influences the outer world of matter because everything is mental and nothing is physical. In that state, which is the state of enlightenment, you really do not have a care or thought for the body. It is really about putting full attention on your purpose, and that is very practical.

To round out this series of questions: as you really care for your mind, everything that seems to involve the care of the body is taken care of. Food is given; it is a backdrop for joining. You do not have to refuse things. I always use Jesus as my learning model because he still seemed to walk the planet when he was here and he still went through the same bodily processes as far as urinating and defecating and putting loaves of bread and fish in his mouth. He seemed to look like a lot of human beings even though he often responded to the apostles' concern about him not eating enough by saying things like *I have manna that comes from the Heavens.* But the symbol of Jesus was used in a way that people could still relate to him. If he never ate or drank he would have looked like an alien. It is easier to learn from someone that you can relate to rather than from someone you perceive as having dropped in from another planet! Though he transcended the physical laws, it was very helpful that he still seemed to do things that looked pretty human.

Use of the Body

David: Despite the fact that the body will break down and degenerate and will never be immortal—despite the fact that it is very temporal, like everything else in the projected cosmos—the mind has a big investment in trying to make it a good home. Therefore if you think that you can make it live longer and more comfortably by exercising and eating the right things, then you will do it. But the flipside of that is that there is a strong identification and belief in the body. The body in this perspective is not seen as *nothing*. It is seen as something; that is why the great search for health is in the wrong place. Health can accurately be described as inner peace, as a mind that has let go of judgment and the ordering of thoughts; a mind that reaches a true perception, a more stabilized perception, is a mind at peace. That is a mind that is healed and is truly healthy.

Friend: So even to consider the body as an instrument that the Holy Spirit uses, I have to regard that body as nothing? I think there is that trap of thinking that because it is going to be used by the Holy Spirit, that somehow it is *something*, so I have to take care of it in a certain way. I am responsible for the kind of food that I put in it and the exercises that I provide for it, etc. It is as if I am thinking: *This is a temple of the Holy Spirit, so I have to regard it with respect and that means this, that and the other.* But this, that and the other are just ways the mind validates that the body is something, when it is really nothing. It is only when it can be seen as nothing that it can be turned over and really used by the Holy Spirit?

David: Yes. There is also a subtle trap of denying the body. When we talk about the body as nothing, it is in a very deep, ultimate sense of what it truly is. We are not asked to deny the perception of the body. The most helpful way to come at this is with a sense of purpose, or with the question: *What is it for?* This brings it back to the level of mind. What is helpful here is to look at the ego's purpose for the body and the Holy Spirit's purpose for the body. As that gets sorted out in the mind, one is able to begin discerning the ego's purpose from the Holy Spirit's purpose. As the mind begins to voluntarily give up the ego's purposes, then the body becomes more and more peripheral in awareness. It approaches "nothing."

Friend: So there is never a necessity of focusing on the body; the thing to do is just focus on the purpose and the rest will fall into place accordingly? The way to get to a point of regarding the body as nothing is by focusing on the purpose?

David: Yes. The idea of the body as a temple is an important thing. It is regarded as the temple of the Holy Ghost in the Bible. This is a starting point, a stepping stone. It is a step away from making the body evil. It is one thing to call the body unreal or nothing, but the ego would take the step to say that the body is evil. Saying that it is a temple for the Holy Spirit is saying that it can be used for the Holy Spirit's purpose. In that sense and in that sense only is the body a temple. It has nothing to do with the body in and of itself. It has to do with that intention, that purpose in mind. We could say that the body that is used solely for communication is a body that is being used by the Holy Spirit.

Friend: And what exactly is communication? It is not necessarily what I have been educated to believe that it is. It does not have to include two bodies. It happens at a mind level and that is the only place communication happens, at a mind level? So why do I need a body to communicate if it only happens at the mind level?

David: Every mind that seems to believe in the world, believes in separation and in the body. It believes that communication has been limited so that communion has been blocked. Communion could be called mind communication or even telepathy. It is called by many different names. The mind believing in separation has pushed the experience of communion out of awareness. The body has literally been imposed as a limit on communication. It appears in this world that if two bodies are not together, communication is limited. They cannot talk to another unless they use a telephone or walkie-talkie, or some kind of aid. You need material aids to help with communication. But in the ultimate sense we are back to *belief*; when the body is believed in, when the world is believed in—there is a limit on communication. The world was made to defend against communication. The Holy Spirit is our communication link with the Father. The world was made to cover that over! The Holy Spirit has to work with these beliefs. As the mind lets go of its beliefs in the world, it appears, gradually, that the powers of the mind are returned to it; telepathy, clairvoyance and intuitions seem to become more prevalent. Actually the mind is just returning to its natural condition. These are not supernatural powers that only rare individuals can develop. They are very natural modes of communication.

Friend: So the communication is always there. It has always been there but we are unaware; it is covered over?

David: Yes, and it is a strong investment in the body that does this. The body is the chosen home of the deceived mind. It gets back again to purpose.

Communication is the sole function or purpose that the Holy Spirit gives the body, while the ego uses it for pride, pleasure and attack. The purpose of pride, pleasure and attack actually constrains communication.

Friend: If communication is solely at a mind level, why have a body to be used for communication? I think I hear you saying that as long as the mind believes in the body, then the Holy Spirit uses the body for communication. It is only the belief in the body that has the body enter into the communication at all?

David: Yes. There are no bodies in the holy instant. Revelation is beyond bodies; revelation is direct communication from God to God's creation. As the mind gives up its false ideas, beliefs and judgments, it gets drawn into the holy instant. In the holy instant communication is completely restored.

Bodies are like symbols. The Holy Spirit will reach the mind in whatever way He can. It can be through the voice of a friend, a song, a billboard, a record lyric, etc. There are many ways and forms. But in that sense the body is a symbol. The Holy Spirit is using symbols to reach the deceived mind because the deceived mind believes in symbols. Metaphorically, as we move forward and get clearer—more able to line up with the Holy Spirit's purpose—we are asked to reach our brothers who believe in the world of time and separation. We are asked to reach them using symbols they understand. Once again, Jesus was a great example of that. He spoke in parables when he spoke to the masses and he spoke of higher ideals and concepts with the apostles and disciples that had the ears to hear. In both cases it was the Holy Spirit speaking through him, using whatever symbols the mind could grasp. You also have examples of Jesus going off into silent communion with the Father where not a word was spoken. Here we have a range of communication with words, which is still very crude, but as the beliefs are let go of in the mind we get back to Communion, which is totally wordless.

Friend: Let's go back to the ego's uses for the body; can you address those?

David: We can take them one at a time. Pride gets at the subject/object split, or the belief in personhood. Pride really comes down to the desperate attempt to maintain a belief in personhood, of being an individual person and actually perceiving other individual persons. It keeps that split between self and other in the mind. It reinforces it by drawing attention to oneself, through pride in accomplishments, physique, country, sports teams, family, etc., things in the world that are considered very good.

Friend: Can you talk about spiritual pride?

David: Spiritual pride is taking pride in what one knows – turning the spiritual journey into a book-learning feat or a display of abilities. Underneath that is still the motive to draw attention to the small self, to the personhood. It is a very subtle trap. For example, as the belief in separation is let go of in the mind, seeming powers can arise, such as psychic abilities, telepathy, levitation or psycho-kinesis. The mind can latch on to those and say: *Look at me! Look at what I can do!* But the "I" is still the little "I," the personal "I." Someone could become a lecturer, a workshop leader, a healer – but when that gets personified, when the mind identifies with the person as being the focal point, it is still trying to draw attention to itself. Jesus pointed to Heaven saying always that it is the Father who speaks; it is the Father who is the Source of all healing. He always took the second place, pointing at all times to the Father in Heaven. This is a sense of true humility; this is a mind that knows what it is. It knows what its Source is and is not attracted to the role of being the center of the universe in the sense of placing the personal thought-form self at the center. It always points to the Father. Spiritual pride can take many forms. It can show up in a group, for example, where there is an identity of having found *the* way. This is yet another spiritual trap of identifying with the small "I," with the personal self.

Pleasure is also part of the world of duality. Pleasure and pain are equally unreal; both are defenses against the truth in that they are both techniques the ego uses to convince the mind to maintain the body identity, to uphold the belief that the body is real. The mind can perceive the flesh or recognize the Spirit; it is one or the other. They are mutually exclusive in awareness. If one is aware of the body and the world, then the recognition of the Spirit is kept from awareness. The pursuit of pleasure is a distractive device, a trick that anchors the mind in the belief that the body is real. It seems to be very attractive. This is what the Course refers to as the "attraction to guilt." The deceived mind does not equate guilt and pleasure. Pleasure is seen as something desirable, something to be sought after and enjoyed. A lot of times you will hear statements like: *God wants you to enjoy yourself. Enjoy the many pleasures of the world.* But from the metaphysical perspective, first of all, God is Spirit. God does not know about the physical, projected world. God only knows his Creations or his Creation which is the Son, and he knows him as perfect. This is a pure, abstract, infinite relationship that has nothing to do with form in any way. The mind is unaware that the pursuit of pleasure and the avoidance of pain are the same; by pursuing pleasure one is also pursuing pain. The pleasure is a guise.

Friend: And both of them act as substitutes for God.

David: Yes. The pursuit of wealth and the belief in poverty are another version of the same split, or guise. If someone is poor, it seems to be a world of scarcity. They yearn for better times, more possessions and an easier life. On the other hand, those that do actually accumulate wealth and possessions still feel the pain and anguish and the depression. We find the same thing; the mind is still seeking for happiness, peace and contentment, in the world. It is just seeking in the wrong place. Peace, contentment and happiness are in the mind and in the letting go of the false beliefs. So there is a quick look at pleasure.

Attack is also something that is very important as a defense against the truth. It is a witness that separation has occurred. To truly see that separation is impossible seems to be at odds with what the body's eyes show because as one looks around through the body's eyes and distorted perception, one sees attack in many different forms. There seem to be arguments everywhere—whether they seem to be verbal attacks or physical attacks with fists, knives, guns, tanks, or bombs. There seems to be a world where attack is a common experience. But the mind cannot attack. The mind is abstract; it is One. It can only make up body fantasies where attack seems to be real. The ego's use of the body for its fantasies of attack definitely makes guilt seem real. And if attack is perceived as real then guilt is justified. And if guilt is justified how can one be wholly innocent? How can one be the innocent child of God?

Friend: Are you calling it fantasy because it is all pretend and made up?

David: Yes, it is made up. It is just on the screen. The deceived mind wants to see the conflict in the world, not in the mind. Under the ego's counsel the mind will look for it in the world. Now, this is not to say that wars per se, or sports or verbal abuse is evil or bad. It is the interpretation that has to be looked at. A healed mind can calmly look upon any sight in the world. The body's eyes will still report to the mind changes in circumstances, changes in the way things look, such as symptoms, etc., but a healed mind just puts them all into one category: they are all unreal. You have to have a clear metaphysical idea of why this is so, of why sickness must be impossible, of why competition cannot be, of why there cannot be victims and victimizers in the world. You have to see clearly that it is all in the mind—that it all comes down to the subject/object split. Pride, pleasure and attack are all the same thing. Pride and pleasure are seeming forms of attack.

The mind that has identified with the ego is an attack on the Christ within that mind. It is an attack thought. Even though it has no basis in reality, it is given reality by the mind's acceptance. To the mind, it seems real. The ego's use of the body – for pride or recognition for the personal self or for pleasure and so on – is all just the attraction of guilt, a way of concealing the belief in separation and keeping the mind distracted out on the screen. They are all attack thoughts. Now, to pull it back to right-minded perception: the mind cannot attack. These thoughts are unreal thoughts; even the thoughts that are called "attack thoughts" in the Workbook are unreal thoughts. They are thoughts that have not come from the mind of God. They do not exist. Only the thoughts that come from God have existence.

Friend: To speak of attack thoughts is just a manner of speaking?

David: Yes. They are unreal. A mind that is invested in them is deceived and will experience the hallucination of pain, upset, despair, sorrow and depression. This is because it has invested in thoughts and a thought system that has not come from God. The right mind sees that attack is literally impossible. It sees the false as false. It is not invested in these thoughts; it sees them as false and knows them as false. This is no different than saying that the Holy Spirit sees the false ideas and the false beliefs but looks to the Atonement, the undefiled altar, and is certain of the Christ.

Chapter Three

Ordering of Thought

David: To see a world, to even perceive anything, means there is an authority problem going on. Ultimately, that is the basis of why the mind judges. The mind orders the illusions and makes hierarchies of illusions because it wants to be the author of itself. There is a very deep-rooted belief that reality can be selected from. That is what all judgments in this world seem to be. *I choose to go here or there. I prefer this and I choose to avoid that.* The assumption underneath all of that is that I can choose reality; reality is not something that I can accept but rather something that I can select from. There are parts of it that I want, and parts of it that I can actually reject. That denies the wholeness. Judging makes the split seem real. That is what maintains it. When we move away from the ordering of thoughts we can think of ourselves more as a mind. We start to see the fallacy of all of these things that we thought we were as a person. *I did this, I did not do that. I am hoping to do this in the future.* It takes it out of the personal context into the awareness that I am a mind and I have all these concepts and ideas that are just images. Thoughts are just images that I have made. The thoughts themselves are not the problem, it is the ordering and the arrangement of those images that keeps me from seeing that they are all equally illusory. It is not that a cup in and of itself is good or bad. The arranging of the images is where the problem is, such as believing that a car is more valuable than a cup, or that this body is more valuable than that body.

Friend: It is the decision.

David: The decision to judge presumes that reality is mine to choose from, to select from. If I continue to judge, I must therefore believe that reality is mine to choose.

Friend: What about valuing anything? I thought that the whole idea was to recognize that there was no value in anything that is not eternal.

David: Yes, but you cannot do that without allowing the Holy Spirit to reorder the mind, and to do that you must give up your own thoughts and images. As long as you talk about having no value in the world and you still hold onto judgment and ordering of images, then you are giving it value by that.

Friend: You are saying that what we want to do is value everything equally?

David: Yes. The only way that the ordering can be given up is to give one meaning to every image. You do not just try to say that, "Nothing I see means anything," because there has to be a purpose—the Holy Spirit's purpose—to unify the perception. The Holy Spirit gives equal meaning to a lamp, a body, a car, a trailer. Everything has one purpose. In the Holy Spirit's eyes, so to speak, the idea of these things having any meaning in and of themselves is meaningless. There is no such thing as a microphone defined as the deceived mind perceives it, because that always has to do with someone speaking into it, it involves voices and bodies. You see how there are a bunch of concepts. It is the same with a couch. A couch is where bodies sit down. Bodies are just images too. They are images just like the couch.

Friend: Sitting on another image.

David: Even the "sitting on" is another image because there is a relationship there. The Holy Spirit knows that there is no relationship between the images and the only meaning that any of the images have is the meaning that the Holy Spirit gives to the images. In that sense the miracle sees that they are all false. That is why true forgiveness is just seeing that the false is false—seeing that there is no cause in the images. They are just a bunch of images. This brings us up into the metaphysical realm of knowing that: *I am a mind, with all these disordered thoughts. I want to learn to perceive correctly. I want to learn to allow my mind to be reordered by the Holy Spirit.* This is to say that the same meaning will be given to everything.

> Only what God creates is irreversible and unchangeable. What you made can always be changed because, when you do not think like God, you are not really thinking at all. Delusional ideas are not real thoughts, although you can believe in them. But you are wrong. The function of thought comes from God and is in God. As part of His Thought, you *cannot* think apart from Him.
>
> Irrational thought is disordered thought. God Himself orders your thought because your thought was created by Him. Guilt feelings are always a sign that you do not know this. They also show that you believe you can think apart from God, and want to. Every disordered thought is attended by guilt at its inception, and maintained by guilt in its continuance. Guilt is inescapable by those who believe they order their own thoughts, and must therefore obey their dictates. T-5.V.6,7

The guilt comes in once thoughts are believed to be real, once the mind identifies with the body; *I did hit so-and-so. I did yell at them, and I feel guilty for doing that.* It has taken the body thoughts of person A and person B and it believes that a real attack took place. If all those thoughts were just seen to be illusory thoughts – not part of my right mind, the part that thinks with God – where would the guilt be? Literally there could be no guilt. It is the association of the mind with those thoughts that brings the guilt. As soon as we identify with those thoughts we also look back on a personal history that is filled with a closet full of things that we wish we had done and things we wish we had not done. The moment of release is simply seeing – as a mind – that those thoughts are not real. They never have been real and they never will be, nor are my fear thoughts about being provided for in the future. All the thoughts of the future are just as equally past tense. To believe in linear time is to take thoughts from the past and project them in another direction and call it the future. They are projected and given another name – future – when really they are both past. It is the future-past. The fear comes in when I am identified as one of those thoughts, which is a body, and I believe in all the conditions of the world such as economics and weather. The fear comes when I believe those thoughts are real, instead of just seeing the unreality of them. When you start to see some of these things, you are really coming to a release – coming to see that "My mind holds only what I think with God" W-r.IV.in.2, and "I am as God created me." W-110

Friend: It is only the mind's identification with the unreal thoughts that makes them seem real?

David: Right. And it believes it can order them. We are back to that ordering thing. Before believing in them, it is the ordering of them that makes them seem real. That is why we have to give up the judgment, or ordering.

Friend: ...to recognize that they are not real, that they are not me?

David: Yes. That is why it is important to notice even the tiny things, even the minor, little preferences. Until you get the metaphysics down, you cannot see how it makes any difference. What we are doing is getting down to the basic point that *all* ordering of thought maintains the split. The mind has to be identified with form and thoughts and believe they are real before it can feel guilty. There is a choice to identify with the wrong mind, and then it gets played out into various scenarios. But really it is all just symbolic; the world is nothing but symbols.

Friend: So level confusion then is trying to put wrong-minded things into the right mind?

David: We have to go really deep into this to get clear on level confusion. It is not bringing the wrong mind into the right mind, because the right mind is the miracle, the Atonement. When there is any causality given to the world of form and as long as there is any ordering of thoughts, the mind cannot be in the right mind. As long as there are hierarchies, even just a slight preference, you cannot be in the right mind. You cannot be in the right mind and have a slight preference for anything.

Friend: What is the relationship between having a preference and not being able to see that form is not causative?

David: Having a preference has to do with the hierarchy of illusions. It is impossible to think of that preference without a hierarchy. That is what it means to have a preference, to have some higher priorities and some lower priorities. Hierarchy is impossible without a split. The mind does not want to see that the split is in the mind so it projects images out onto the screen and is in chaos and panic, having projected the images. It then tries to order the images to bring some sort of security and control into a very wild and chaotic kind of situation.

The split in the mind is horrifying so the mind tries to project the split, to give itself some relief, or the illusion of relief. As we go on with this passage, it will get clear about how this ordering of thought has to be ended for the split to get healed.

> Guilt is inescapable by those who believe they order their own thoughts, and must therefore obey their dictates. This makes them feel responsible for their errors without recognizing that, by accepting this responsibility, they are reacting irresponsibly. If the sole responsibility of the miracle worker is to accept the Atonement for himself, and I assure you that it is, then the responsibility for what is atoned for cannot be yours. T-5.V.7

This is a major area of level confusion that is easy to fall into. People think that because they invented the world they see and receive as they have asked, then they must be responsible for their cancer, and for the starving children. He is saying right here that the responsibility for what is atoned for cannot be yours. The self-concept itself cannot be yours. The dilemma cannot be resolved except by accepting the solution of undoing. All we are responsible for at any time is for accepting the Atonement—for choosing the miracle. In the ultimate sense, that must be the way out. If I am responsible for the starving children, or this or that, then guilt has to remain. The starving children are just one example, since ideas leave not their source, and thoughts and images are one and the same. A more subtle example was when you flipped the thing up on the suitcase and said, "What have I done?" Just a twinge, even a minor twinge, indicates that we are responsible for doing it, that we are responsible for something in form.

> You would be responsible for the effects of all your wrong thinking if it could not be undone. The purpose of the Atonement is to save the past in purified form only. If you accept the remedy for disordered thought, a remedy whose efficacy is beyond doubt, how can its symptoms remain? T-5.V.7

"The purpose of the Atonement is to save the past in purified form only." What in the world does that mean? To save the past in purified form is simply to be the dreamer of the dream and see that all the images are false and that there is no ordering among those images. You are just watching a bunch of images on a screen. Of course you are defenseless if you are just dreaming it and you know that it is all false and it is all past and you are living in the present; you are watching the past from the present. Then you are saving the past in the purified form. We are still in the perceptual realm, but we are talking about saving the past in the purified form. It is simply being in the right mind – not caught in the story of the figures on the screen or in the ordering of thought – not caught in the illusion in any way.

Friend: Just to see it for what it is, that is the purified form?

David: Exactly. It is simple.

> Perhaps you have been aware of lack of competition among your thoughts, which even though they may conflict, can occur together and in great numbers. You may indeed be so used to this that it causes you little surprise. Yet you are also used to classifying some of your thoughts as more important, larger or better, wiser, or more productive and valuable than others. This is true of the thoughts that cross the mind of those who think they live apart. For some are reflections of Heaven, while others are motivated by the ego, which but seems to think. T-14.X.4

There is the ordering that we have been talking about; the mind projects images and then tries to bring order into chaos by ordering those images. It tries to judge and order to bring security, to bring a sense of wholeness into a chaotic situation. What is the chaotic situation? It is the belief in two thought systems that are completely irreconcilable.

Friend: "Lack of competition among your thoughts." What is that about?

David: That is when you think one thing, and then you think another thing. It happens so often that you are totally accustomed to the back and forth, *Do this. No, do that.* The chatter goes on all the time and the mind does not stop to say *wait a minute, it cannot be both!* The clear mind would see that there is something that needs to be discerned here; these are competing thoughts but they seem to be coexisting.

> The result is a weaving, changing pattern that never rests and is never still. It shifts unceasingly across the mirror of your mind, and the reflections of Heaven last but a moment and grow dim, as darkness blots them out. Where there was light, darkness removes it in an instant, and alternating patterns of light and darkness sweep constantly across your mind. The little sanity that still remains is held together by a sense of order that you establish. Yet the very fact that you can do this, and bring any order into chaos shows you that you are not an ego, and that more than an ego must be in you. For the ego *is* chaos, and if it were all of you, no order at all would be possible. Yet though the order you impose upon your mind limits the ego, it also limits you. To order is to judge, and to arrange by judgment. Therefore it is not your function, but the Holy Spirit's. T-14.X.5

That brings together some of the ideas that we have been talking about. The mind believes that it can order its own thoughts. It is still into the hierarchy. That is what is keeping reality and happiness—our true function—obscured from our mind.

> It will seem difficult for you to learn that you have no basis at all for ordering your thoughts. This lesson the Holy Spirit teaches by giving you the shining examples of miracles to show you that your way of ordering is wrong, but that a better way is offered you. The miracle offers exactly the same response to every call for help. It does not judge the call. It merely recognizes what it is, and answers accordingly. It does not consider which call is

louder or greater or more important. You may wonder how you who are still bound to judgment can be asked to do that which requires no judgment of your own. The answer is very simple. The power of God, and not of you, engenders miracles. The miracle itself is but the witness that you have the power of God in you. That is the reason why the miracle gives equal blessing to all who share in it, and that is also why everyone shares in it. The power of God is limitless. And being always maximal, it offers everything to every call from anyone. There is no order of difficulty here. A call for help is given help. T-14.X.6

That is the very first principle of the Course: "There is no order of difficulty in miracles." T-1.I.1 But as long as I have a hierarchy of illusions—as long as I am ordering my own thoughts—I cannot choose a miracle. I am literally choosing my judgment in place of a miracle. They cannot coexist. That is why in healing, whenever there is concern for the symptoms of the patient, there is ordering of thoughts. *I know what a healthy patient looks like, and I know what a sick patient looks like. I say this one looks sick.* But the sickness *is* the ordering of thought. This pulls it back from the realm of behavior. Even a good part of the *Manual for Teachers* is written at more of a metaphorical level, for the mind that still believes it is a body and believes that there are other bodies. Some are called healers, some are called patients, some are called teachers and some are students. But we are pulling it all back to the mind. You see how all of that dissolves when you come up to this level? It gets more and more simple; it is very empowering to realize that it is not complicated. There is nothing to figure out in the world of form!

Sexuality and Ordering Behaviors/Thoughts

Hi David,

The Course does not say anything about sex, as if it did not exist, but it very much exists for me. I am gay (though not presently in a relationship) and I have been interested in "Sacred Sexuality" for some time. Having no sexual partner, I arouse myself to orgasm on my own a few times a week and thanks to the books I have read, I consider it to be a sacred act.

As I move deeper into the heart of the Course, I am noticing that more and more often that I simply have lost interest in sex. It does not bother me—usually my thought is, "Oh, good, I will have more time for other things now."

My questions are:

1) Should sex just be ignored as it apparently is in ACIM?

2) Should students like me enjoy it until its attractiveness evaporates away?

3) Is there anything really "sacred" in the sex act, and should I use it as a springboard to transcendence?

4) And finally, if I decide to ignore my sex drives and live a life of abstinence and celibacy, will the repression of those sex drives cause any problems? I am inclined towards celibacy because my Catholic upbringing made sex a mortal sin punishable by eternity in hell, though that clearly is not the right motivation to take a vow of celibacy.

Beloved One,

Thanks for your direct questions about sexuality. What you do comes from what you think, and that is why Awakening is a purification of thought. Behavior modification is therefore never the goal, for behavior but follows the guide the mind chooses to listen to and follow. Sexual desire is not better or worse than any other desire in the world, yet Awakening is a state of contentment that is desireless. This is the peace that passeth the understanding of the world. All appetites are ego "getting" mechanisms, and fantasy is the attempt to make false associations and obtain pleasure from them.

As the miracle expands and becomes consistently experienced, these appetites fade, grow dim, and disappear. The ego was the belief in lack, and all apparent appetites reflected this belief. The ego attempted to put various behaviors into moral and ethical systems of judgment, yet in the healed Perspective only wholeness is experienced and the past is gone.

There is no hierarchy of illusions, no order of difficulty in miracles, and no preferences in the Atonement. The ego was one error and cannot be broken into "enjoyable" error and "punishable" error, or "moral" error and "immoral" error. Celibacy and monogamy and masturbation are all stepping-stone concepts along the path of emptying the mind of all concepts, forgiving the illusion, and Awakening to Pure Oneness.

Sacred sexuality is a contradiction in terms because Spirit transcends form entirely and it is impossible to mix Spirit and matter. Pleasure and pain are the same error. The miracle transcends the error by showing its falsity, its impossibility. It is impossible to seek for pleasure without finding pain, for both are the same error: the attempt to reinforce the "reality" of the body and world. Christ is Spirit, not a body, and to experience Divine Mind is to forget the body entirely. At no single instant does the body exist at all. It is always remembered (past) or anticipated (future) in dreaming. This is the error of linear time. As one experiences the holy instant the experience of bodies and time is no more.

Awakening involves mind training: Pay attention to the thoughts that come into awareness. Detach. Desire healing.

Preferences are judgments, and as the mind yields to the Nonjudgmental Perspective of the Holy Spirit, the Awakening is obvious. You will observe that as long as appetites seem to exist, these are the ego defenses of indulgence and repression. Neither is better or worse than the other, for they are the same illusion. The miracle offers a real alternative and when one is consistently miracle-minded, defenses are no longer needed.

Let the Holy Spirit Guide you in the moment to the experience of the holy instant. In the holy instant God is Known, Christ is Known, and "sexuality" is unknown and unknowable. The perceptual world disappears in the Thought of God. The Thought of God is Sacred. Christ is Spirit. God is Spirit. That which is born of the Spirit is Spirit. Such is the simple Truth.

Preferences as Ordering of Thought

Friend: Is it a judgment, a preference, that I like to play tennis rather than golf?

David: Yes it is. It is back on the surface, like choosing between a blue sweater and a green sweater. The likes and dislikes are at the surface. Anything that is an ordering of thought, even preferences, is a judgment and the only way you can tell this is by your feeling. Let me give you an example: Say you go to a familiar restaurant where you have a favorite dish you always get. You go in almost salivating while you wait for the waitress to come. Only this time when you tell the waitress, "I will take the usual," she apologizes and tells you they are out of that dish, and you have a little twinge of disappointment.

I use that example because it sure seems like a common experience; *I am just upset because they do not have my favorite dish*. Remember that if you run everything through the Course's teaching – the upset is not there because they do not have your favorite dish. The upset is coming up because in your mind you have chosen the ego, or you have let an expectation take the place of peace of mind. It seems pretty minor, but there are no small upsets. Either you are feeling a deep sense of peace or you are not. You are not feeling peace when there is minor irritation, or rage – to use an example from the other extreme. It is all upsetting. The way the Course is laid out you can tell that it takes a while for the mind to get this. Jesus teaches over and over that there are not any differences between upsets; they all relate back to judgment or expectation. There would have to be a judgment, or an expectation; *I really am expecting to have that blueberry pie*. The upset is coming from my interpretation of what is going on.

Friend: You are trading your peace in for that. I think any time there is a charge of any kind related to something that I want, it indicates that I have a preference, and that is the extent to which I will put that between me and my peace of mind. That is not to say that you are not to play tennis or you are not to play golf. If your intention is to stay at peace, if something comes up and intervenes....

David: You could still stay at peace. The Course has us ask the question "What is it for?" Jesus is having us train our minds to think of everything as holy encounters. I remember the old *win at all costs* competitiveness in tennis, but this is about giving a new purpose to the world. Going to that tennis or golf match, or going shopping, or to the laundry – give it all a different purpose; let the Holy Spirit's purpose be the purpose that is held in mind, out front. When I travel the country holding the intention for everything to be a holy encounter – it is such a joy. When you look at it that way everything lights up. You end up getting into conversations at supermarkets, rest stops, Course gatherings, everywhere! There is a different purpose that has been placed as a priority in the mind even though you are still doing things. I have used tennis examples often, so sometimes people come up to me in my travels and say, "I have a racket, let's go play," and away we go! And while we hit the tennis ball we are discussing things. It gets away from competition.

That is another thing I have noticed as I have gone deeper into this. The desire to win is just the ego – it is my own self-concept trying to put myself higher up in my mind. As you are able to see that, you gradually lose interest in those kinds of things. It is not like you make it bad, you just lose interest. They become the backdrop. Birthday parties, celebrations, fireworks, whatever – I just look at everything as a backdrop for seeing the Holy Spirit's purpose. That takes it away from being about the form. Often times people on the spiritual path will think they have to start giving things up, and it feels like a sacrifice–but that is basically level confusion. The mind is so conditioned to think in terms of form that when it starts to read this or that about worldly or materialistic ways, ideas of sacrifice come in, ideas of giving things up. Yes! You have to give up ego thinking! If you give up ego thinking you will give up ego perceptions and ego interpretations and the behavior will follow automatically! The focus does not belong on the behaviors. When the perceptions change the form follows. It is about looking at perception. It is good news.

Defining Sickness as Ordering of Thought

David: I want to talk about sickness and the whole idea of not focusing attention on symptoms. It is about really trying to maintain constant vigilance about what can be sick and watching the temptation of paying attention to the symptoms. It seems to be easy to slide back into focusing on symptoms. There has been a lot of talk about the temperature in this building. Up and down and so on and so forth. Can we really watch our minds and watch the blah, blah, blah and then withdraw our minds from the blah, blah, blah? Withdraw from all the chatter; just try to be very, very attentive to the mind all the time. Keep a close watch.

Friend: I am concluding that since I still have some passing symptoms, I must not be as clear as I could be about this. What else could it mean? I notice that when I cough, part of me feels like I shouldn't be coughing, that it is setting a bad example. It feels like I am failing to have a clear mind if I am coughing and blowing my nose.

David: That is good. You have said that you would like to be clear. That is important. I also think there is a tendency to get back into talking about the symptoms when they seem to manifest when you are with others. If you are at the point where you cannot have a miracle, if you cannot seem to have a mind shift to reduce the fear and alleviate the distress, do what you need to do with the magic so as to be as unobtrusive about it as possible. It is important not to give your mind to sharing ideas that cannot be shared; that is where false empathy comes in.

Friend: How do you be unobtrusive when you are hacking your head off?

David: If you are hacking and hacking and do not seem to be able to get still enough to reduce it with the miracle, or if you have taken magic and are feeling very guilty about what is being exhibited, the most helpful thing would probably be for you to just remove yourself. If you are feeling guilty and self-conscious, you are making an interpretation that is fearful. If you are feeling that you are not teaching what you should be teaching – or however you are interpreting it in your mind – that is a state where the fear is not getting reduced at all. There is no shift.

Someone who seems to mean well asks, "How are you doing today?" Then it snowballs into thoughts of fixing special foods, etc. It just goes on and on. It is counter to everything that we have been talking about. That it is lending support to something that cannot be shared. You do not want to give your mind to ideas that do not come from the Father and yet there is temptation to just go right along and do it anyway. It has to get very clear that this must be an either/or thing. It cannot be something that you talk about and give lip service to and then turn around and slide into. So it may be helpful in those situations to just remove yourself.

Friend: Isn't there a way to be in that situation – of coughing – and not be fearful? I mean isn't there a different way of having the same externals yet having a different mindset about it?

David: Yes. That is the miracle. There has to be a total shift in perception for there to be an ease and a comfort about that.

Friend: Is there no other choice when hacking than to leave?

David: A miracle.

Friend: OK, the miracle. But if I am not accepting the miracle, then there is no other choice than to remove myself?

David: You are saying you are interpreting yourself as being uncomfortable; you are feeling guilty or ashamed. Is that helpful? Do you find that interpretation helpful?

Friend: I do not think leaving is necessarily a solution if I still feel guilty. I could stay or leave but it is the guilt that is the issue. It is the interpretation that I am making that is the issue, not staying or leaving.

David: If the mind is too fearful of the miracle then a mixture of magic and miracle is recommended, which could be taking medication, or it could be getting up and leaving. The "magic" is anything external – doing something on the outside to try to bring about some sort of relief. Moving a body in or out of the room is a kind of magic as well.

As you said, the guilt comes from the interpretation of the symptoms, but what we are trying to get to is the idea that the body cannot be sick. A body being sick is the same as a pencil or a shoe being sick. The mind is the thing that can be sick. The wrong mind is sick. A learning device cannot be sick. The guilt is coming from the interpretation that is being given to what seems to be happening on the screen. And pain, for example, is great evidence for the separation being real. The ego interprets pain as punitive. It proves that you are small, frail, weak, and vulnerable. It proves the body has power over the mind because "obviously" the body is telling you how to feel.

That is why we have to get to the question of purpose. You want to get to the idea of seeing how it is that you look upon the body, and what you are using the body for. How do I use the body? How do I see the body? Do I just see it as insignificant and completely apart from me, just a learning device, or are there ways in which it still seems very important to me. It is really important to look into that. And you can take it to the broader realm of looking at your whole life through the lens of purpose.

We can use the vehicle of talking about sickness to go in as deeply as we can. Let's try to get clear on this. To see a chair as a chair is sick, to see a clock as a clock is sick. In the ultimate sense, to see anything as if it has a separate existence in and apart from everything else is sick. It is a sick interpretation. You see how different that is than the world's way of seeing a body as sick? Yes, a chair is a chair, a clock is a clock and a sick person is a sick person because they have symptoms that let us know that they are sick. It is the mind that is breaking the world up into little boxes and categories. That is where the sickness lies. That is what we have to see, rather than reading meaning into particular symptoms and thinking that some bodies are sicker than others or that cancer is much more serious than the flu or a hang nail. There are all these different categories, but it goes much, much deeper than that. We have to go back to the self-concept. The mind believes it is guilty and it is so determined to hang on to that concept that sickness seems like a very small price to pay. If sickness is a witness that the body can tell the mind how to feel – it is also witness that the smallness, the puniness, and the vulnerability must be true.

It can be as subtle as wishing something was different than it is. The ordering of thought and our preferences – that is what we are talking about. The mind that believes it can order its own thought is a mind that is sick, but it does not want to see how sick it is. It does not want to see that it is wrong. Making it seem as if things happen to the body, with no connection to the mind, gives proof of its vulnerability and justifies guilt. It is about bringing it back to the mind and seeing just what the cause of sickness is. Sickness is wrong-mindedness; it is a sick interpretation of reality. The wrong mind is an assertion that I am what I wish to be instead of what God created. Sickness has to be traced back to the question of where it came from. Did it come from God? That is the ultimate question it comes back to every time. It is just that simple.

Friend: I have used this and other ideas in the Course to feel guilty—because many times the healing is not automatic. I feel that I have a clue about what is going on, but then I think I must be kidding myself. I must not really understand it at all because I am not healed instantly.

David: If you see it in that context it can seem frustrating. It is kind of like our trip when we went to buy some audio equipment and you noticed the frustrations coming up about the attendant who seemed to be waiting on us. Once again, it is that whole backwards thinking of judging based on appearances. First, you see the attendant appear. He seems to have wandering eyes or something. You ask a straight-forward question and you see a sort of pause or hesitation—and the mind starts concluding immediately.

Friend: Concluding that he does not know anything about this stuff.

David: ...and the frustration there begins. But when you take little incidents like this you start to think: *By golly, I keep reading meaning into everything that I see!* You can see that the mind is just looking at the littlest things and reading meaning into them all the time. But what if you suspected that these are dream figures that you are just giving meaning to—and that the meaning you give has no meaning at all in reality? That throws the scenario of going shopping and expecting an attendant to know what he is doing into a larger context.

It had nothing at all to do with getting the audio equipment. Those are just the things that get done. It will get done but it cannot be the focal point or the intention because if it is, then forgiveness is not; then my one function is on a back burner or on a side burner at least because the mind is set—it is going to do something. It has an objective in mind. It does not matter if the objective is to buy something or to learn as much as one can about it from a knowledgeable, trained professional; it does not really matter what the expectations are. What matters is that it is an opportunity to hold your intention out front and to remove all kinds of judgment from the script, from the scenario, about how it should go. When I think I know how it should be going that is where the trouble starts. That is when the frustration comes up. There are thoughts like: *This is less than optimal. I have defined what optimal is and this is not meeting the mark.* You can see where impatience or frustration would come in with that.

Someone may say we are getting way off track; what does this have to do with sickness? It has everything to do with sickness. Sickness is exactly what it is. You could also say that we are being so picky. It perhaps seems awfully small, but in the end that is all we have to go for. We have to keep trying to train our minds to hold that intention and to let go of everything we think we know! There was another golden opportunity when the attendant was ringing everything up at the end. There was something about the price. It is funny to watch how the mind flips and jumps at things like that. The mind just thinks it knows how it has all got to work out. He is merely ringing it all up and coming up with his figures—but there was a lot going on in the mind. I know you just finally said, "I want to leave; is it OK if I just go out and sit in the car?" How were you feeling? Was it all a whirl or was there frustration involved at that time?

Friend: I was just feeling like it was useless for me to be there. I had some frustration and impatience and I did have some judgment about this man's lack of expertise. I had thoughts about how it would have been just as helpful if we had brought everything home and just played with it there, instead of spending all that time there with him, which did not seem particularly beneficial. A lot of it was spent just standing around looking at each other.

David: There was obviously a holy encounter there, right? Every encounter we have is a holy encounter and what is it that obscures the holy encounter?

Friend: Expectation, judgment, interpretation....

David: Interpretation. I mean this is the holiest of all encounters because every encounter we have is simply an opportunity to see our brother completely without the past. Take away the thought of "Radio Shack salesman," that is just a learned concept. Take away "Radio Shack." Take away "competent" or "incompetent." Take away "wasted time," and ideas of "just looking at one another." The mind always thinks there is something much more productive to be doing or that there is a better place to be. What about asking: "What is the purpose?" When you hold the purpose out in front the other things seem to get done anyway vs. wanting to jump in with the mind thinking: *If only I could just sit around talking about the Course, then I would be happy.*

If you put it in Course terms, only God's plan for salvation will work. What is God's plan for salvation? Change your mind about your mind! That is it. That is it! In this instant, change your mind about your mind. Then there is the ego's plan: If only something had happened differently, if someone acted differently, if I was in a different place, if this event had happened, if this circumstance was different than it is. Something on the screen has to change but the only thing that does not change in the ego's plan is changing my mind about my mind. *That I do not have to do! I can be right about who I think I am; it is something on the screen that has to change.*

That kind of lays it out. There is God's plan. There is the ego's plan. Jesus says in lesson 71 that this seems preposterous to you but in fact you will see that you do believe in the preposterous if you observe your life, if you observe your mind. Precisely what you are trying to do all the time is to change something external to bring about salvation. It will never work. Obviously, that is going to cost the whole world that you think you know and the whole world you think you see.

Friend: Can you talk about this idea of what is most useful? I guess I want some clarity on it.

David: You can put it in the context of the first few stages in the *Development of Trust* section of the Course. First you go through a stage where you begin to have a sense that everything is helpful. Wherever the body seems to be, whatever it seems to be doing – it is all helpful. The next step is about increasing the helpfulness. What will increase the helpfulness? It is still a phase; it is obviously an illusion because the mind still thinks it knows in some sense what will actually increase the helpfulness. It is a stepping stone. But the next stage is the realization that all the teacher of God wants is to let go of the false and to accept the true, but he has no sense of what the false and the true are. His mind is so tied into sacrifice and into the belief in the reality of form that he does not know. So that early stage of *what do I do to increase the helpfulness* is really a very early stepping stone because it still involves changing circumstances to suit.

There is a very subtle ego draw to want to make a haven to hide from the guilt. The Course talks about it in terms of the special love relationship but you could have a student on the spiritual path trying to find the easiest, most helpful path and still kind of sliding into that haven of thinking that it is most helpful to stay in a quiet environment forever, sitting around and talking comfortably – when actually it is really about just staying attentive. You can use any situation that seems to be on the screen to instantaneously bring your attention back – to look at your reaction and use that as a starting point, to catch it when you are making an interpretation that is hurting you. This gets away from wanting to find a certain place or a certain activity that will be most helpful. Remember, frustration always comes from our own interpretation. There is nothing happening "out there."

Lesson 136 and the Purpose of the Body

David: Are we on? [laughs] Right in the middle of a pretzel! Okay. We will start at the beginning of lesson 136.

Lesson 136: Sickness is a defense against the truth.

> No one can heal unless he understands what purpose sickness seems to serve. For then he understands as well its purpose has no meaning. Being causeless and without a meaningful intent of any kind, it cannot be at all. When this is seen, healing is automatic. It dispels this meaningless illusion by the same approach that carries all of them to truth, and merely leaves them there to disappear. W-136.1

By sickness here we mean bodily symptoms, upset, and even the whole realm of psychological issues. You can also go to the flip side – to believing that someone is really healthy. The illusion of the health of the body can be carried to the truth as well, "and left there to disappear." We want to get to the point of understanding that there is no order of difficulties.

> Sickness is not an accident. Like all defenses, it is an insane device for self-deception. And like all the rest, its purpose is to hide reality, attack it, change it, render it inept, distort it, twist it, or reduce it to a little pile of unassembled parts. W-136.2

That is what this whole world is. It is just a pile of unassembled parts, at every level – whether you are talking about the cosmos, the personality, community, family, or even microscopic things. When you look around a room and see coats, ovens, rugs, chairs, clocks, microwaves, and refrigerators–you are looking at unassembled parts. Each thing is seen as if it has existence in and of itself. The microwave is set off by space from the refrigerator, from the teapot, from the rug. This sickness runs very deep in mind; things that are assumed to be everyday reality are just piles of unassembled parts. "The aim of all defenses is to keep the truth from being whole. The parts are seen as if each one were whole within itself."

We are redefining what sickness is. It is not just symptoms in the body, or dysfunctional communication in a family. Even just looking out on a winter scene and seeing separate snowflakes, animals and trees is part of sickness. As long as the mind is seeing separation everywhere and believing that each tree, snowflake, car, road and river has existence in and of itself–that is sick perception. The mind wants to hang on to its sick, twisted perception. Sickness seems to be there to serve the purpose of seeing life as happening *to* you, without having anything to do with your intention–as if the mind then does not have a choice, as if it does not play any part in the matter.

Friend: So using that example, I only need to be aware of the purpose that I give everything? If I am using the ego's perception then I see a bunch of unassembled parts. If I am using the Holy Spirit's purpose, then what is it?

David: Unified. The entire scene, the entire scenario, becomes unified. It becomes a backdrop that in and of itself is unimportant because the shining purpose is being held out in front. Form becomes peripheral–unnoticed. Perception is selective and when you are zooming in and focusing on your intent, on your purpose–then specifics are unimportant, they are irrelevant at that point.

Friend: So when I focus on the heat, or on sickness or symptoms, I am picking out one of the pieces and holding it up as separate, trying to see how it fits into the whole, which I cannot do if I am holding it out as separate.

David: Right. And it takes two minds to agree that there is a sickness. If one mind absolutely will not buy the bait of doing what you are describing–that is what healing is. Healing is when I hold in mind how impossible that is. As soon as there is talk about symptoms, brothers seem to join in looking at the symptoms, treatments and solutions. That is just reinforcing and trying to share what cannot be shared. It keeps the seeming reality of the illusion going. Instead of dispelling illusions it is like an invitation to hold on to them and make them seem real.

Friend: So when I am coughing and someone asks me if I am coming down with something, then it is my job to get clear in my own mind about not joining with that?

David: Yes. When I first started going to Course groups I would be going along with my purpose in mind, and someone would give me a compliment – maybe about something I was wearing, or my haircut. It is important not to feel uncomfortable about not responding to comments like that. Just smile and go on in purpose, without missing a beat, instead of getting off track and directing attention to the story of where you bought it or who gave it to you for Christmas. That is just a way of directing the attention back down to the form, whether it is a cute shirt or a nice haircut. It is not to say that it always has to be that way in form. You may meet somebody and the exchange is just an opening to joining, but often those responses are very unnecessary.

Friend: That is my chance to be aware and grateful to the person who brought that to me to look at, and say I do not want to get hooked into that.

David: It is a good opportunity. And you would not necessarily do that with everyone. In a Course meeting that might be a very appropriate thing to bring up but if you are just chatting with your next door neighbor it might not make any sense at all to get into it. It is about being attentive. You do not want to draw undue attention to symptoms, clothing, hair, or anything in the world of form.

Friend: Because all of that just breaks apart the whole?

David: Yes, anything that is judged or valued as better or more attractive is getting into the ordering of thoughts. Judging is what makes the error real. As long as there are better haircuts and worse haircuts, good-looking clothing styles and poor clothing styles – that makes the error real; it is not "nothing" if it is valued positively or negatively. That is the metaphysical reason to not buy into those kinds of judgments. It just makes the error real. It makes the world real in the mind of the thinker.

> Defenses are not unintentional, nor are they made without awareness. They are secret, magic wands you wave when truth appears to threaten what you would believe. They seem to be unconscious but because of the rapidity with which you choose to use them. In that second, even less, in which the choice is made, you recognize exactly what you would attempt to do, and then proceed to think that it is done. W-136.3

This gets back to all the mind tricks and how quickly they are done. It is all part of wanting to forget that I made this whole thing up and that I perceive exactly what I want to perceive in the situation. The mind waves its magic wand, forgets that it did so, and then sees itself on the screen as events that are happening to it, quite unasked for. *He treated me unfairly; he should have paid more attention to me. She shouldn't have frowned. She shouldn't have yelled at me.* Once the mind forgets it is mind on the screen and it believes it is a person then it thinks that my foot is swollen because a rock dropped on it, or there is a feeling of being cold because the warm coat was forgotten at home. With something as simple as that there is still the belief that there is something outside of me on the screen that is bringing my discomfort about. When we talk about these kinds of things we are getting into more subtle realms – but the underlying thing is the belief that there is something external that is doing this to me, apart from my own wish.

> Who but yourself evaluates a threat, decides escape is necessary, and sets up a series of defenses to reduce the threat that has been judged as real? All this cannot be done unconsciously. But afterwards, your plan requires that you must forget you made it, so it seems to be external to your own intent; a happening beyond your state of mind, an outcome with a real effect on you, instead of one effected by yourself.
>
> It is this quick forgetting of the part you play in making your "reality" that makes defenses seem to be beyond your own control. But what you have forgot can be remembered, given willingness to reconsider the decision which is doubly shielded by oblivion. Your not remembering is but the sign that this decision still remains in force, as far as your desires are concerned. Mistake not this for fact. Defenses must make facts unrecognizable. They aim at doing this, and it is this they do. W-135.4,5

The next paragraph gets into the idea that the mind assembles the parts the way it wants to see them. In other words, the entire cosmos has been constructed by the deceived mind to be the way it perceives it. Even on the metaphorical level of fragments, no two fragments see the same cosmos, because it is that fragmented and made up. In the ultimate sense there are not even any two fragments. But using that metaphor, no two persons see the world alike because there is no objective world. The entire world is always completely subjective; it depends on the meaning that I give it or the way that I have constructed it—which can have enormous variation. I like this kind of temperature. *I like these kinds of foods. I like these kinds of climates, settings, and preferences.* The preferences all get laid on: "Every defense takes fragments of the whole, assembles them without regard to all their true relationships, and thus constructs illusions of a whole that is not there."

But once the Holy Spirit's purpose is held in mind there is divine order in everything that seems to exist. All realms of perception are seen to be the result of what the mind wants. The mind is causative and perception is always just an effect. That is what all true relationships are—divine order—which is quite profound if you think about it. Every single event that has ever seemed to occur in the perceptual world is all in perfect divine order, except to the deceived mind that breaks it apart and sees some things as favorable and some things as unfavorable. A flood to one may be favorable, to another unfavorable. Financial conditions to one may be favorable, to another unfavorable. But really it is all in divine order. There is nothing good or bad but thinking that makes it so. To me that is quite a comforting thought; all things work together for good and there has never been anything out of place. Everything is always exactly as it is. [laughter] It totally flies in the face of the thinking of the world, the thinking that you have to improve world conditions, crime, or hunger. It has all played out. It is all in perfect order.

Let's take another look at the statement that "Every defense takes fragments of the whole, assembles them without regard to all their true relationships and thus constructs illusions of a whole that is not there. It is this process that imposes threat and not whatever outcome may result." W-136.6 In other words, the outcome is the outcome; there can only be one outcome always, and that is whatever is on the screen. The script is written; whatever is playing in the movie is what the outcome is. The threat comes from the perception and interpretation of the outcome. The categories in the mind are what call forth witnesses.

> When parts are wrested from the whole and seen as separate and wholes within themselves, they become symbols standing for attack upon the whole; successful in effect and never to be seen as whole again. And yet you have forgotten they stand but for your own decision of what should be real, to take place of what is real. W-136.6

The body is a concretized form of fear, but so is a snowflake, a tree, a couch, and a rug. In other words, when they have been wrested from the whole there is an ordering that has taken place that is denying their unreality. Reality is purely abstract. Once the mind believes that separation is possible – once perception is believed to be real – then abstract reality is denied. Now whatever the mind perceives as separate, as a whole within itself, is literally an attack upon reality.

Friend: It still seems a little abstract. I am not sure I am bringing it down to a practical level.

David: Most people would not think of watching your mind and just holding on to this abstract intent and holding peace as your only goal as a very practical thing, but actually that is very practical.

Friend: For me, I have to go back to what the Course says about believing all of it or none of it. I choose to believe that I am in Heaven with God, and that I do not even have to wonder that I believe a snowflake is separate. That does not even come into mind. I prefer to believe that I am in Heaven with God and I am supposed to be here to be of help. That is what I go back to.

David: "I am in Heaven with God" and "I am a child of God" are high experiences. It is important not to try to skip steps. When we come together in groups we do not start with the fact that *I am a Son of God*. We really look at the specifics; we have to look at where there is upset or annoyance. These last couple of paragraphs give us the metaphysics of what it is that is going on – of how separate things are made up in the deceived mind. The value of this is that I want to be very vigilant and very clear that I do not still buy into the belief that I can attack God, even in subtle ways. If there are subtle things that are attacks on God that I do not know about – that I do not see as attacks on God – I need to know about them.

Friend: And when I say a practical level, what I mean is that the logic of this is lost on me when I am upset. It even says here, part of doing this is that we forget we have done it. And so for me to go back and trace this when I am feeling upset takes a real understanding of it because I have already deliberately forgotten what I did. It is a deliberate decision that is built into the ego system.

David: Yes, these are unconscious beliefs. Like with the roles we play – of mother, wife, father, husband – you can be in a situation and click into the autopilot of being in a role. All the roles are pulled out of the whole as well. If I have been used to cruising along on autopilot, defining myself as that role, then it takes a real vigilance and awareness to go back and make those connections.

It seems abstract in the beginning but we can train our minds to think this way. I remember watching fireworks a couple of summers ago, by the Ohio River. Afterwards people asked what I thought of the show. I said, "Well, I was doing my mind watching during the show." They said, "Even with the fireworks and all the spectacular explosions of colors and sounds and heights?" I remember just telling them that honestly that was what I was doing during all of it – just holding onto my purpose. It was not a strain. It was not like I was forcing myself to do this tedious thing during the fireworks display. It was a part of a natural flow of everything – of being there and holding onto that purpose, with everything I was seeing. It was not like a separate thing. Some say: *What is the point, where is the enjoyment in that?* The enjoyment or the entertainment does not come from the fireworks or the songs the band played that night, or the bungee jumper that was splashing in the river there. It has everything to do with holding onto my intention and just feeling very much in the flow. It has nothing to do with any of that other stuff. But it has taken an effort to align my thinking that way. That is certainly not the way I have experienced other Fourth of July celebrations.

With this next paragraph we get into what is going on in the mind. Why would the mind choose sickness?

> Sickness is a decision. It is not a thing that happens to you, quite unsought, which makes you weak and brings you suffering. It is a choice you make, a plan you lay, when for an instant truth arises in your own deluded mind, and all your world appears to totter and prepare to fall. Now are you sick, that truth may go away and threaten your establishments no more. W-136.7

Often, people will ask the Holy Spirit to help them see symptoms of sickness differently, and nothing happens. But sickness is of the mind. It is not about trying to deal with sickness per se, at the symptom level. Trying to address it at the symptom level is saying that it has reality. *I really do get these migraines every month.* It is going on a witch hunt to say that and then look for a specific mind change or a specific belief when what really has to be let go of is the whole world as it is constructed backwards, with outer things being seen as causative. It is the self-concept that is holding onto that. That is what is sick. The sickness is the mind that believes it is a self-concept of its own, constructing reality in a way that it wants it to be. It has nothing to do with migraine headaches, flu symptoms, cancer, rashes, or hives.

Friend: So what I hear you saying is not to wait until there are bodily symptoms. Pay attention to what is going on in the mind. There is no quick fix.

David: Yes, the whole message of the Course is: do not wait. In other words, salvation is offered to you this instant; be vigilant! Watch your mind. Be as attentive as you can this very instant. And the Course does not give specifics, like if this arises, do that. It is all based on sorting out the two thinking systems: the right mind and the wrong mind. That is where healing takes place. It draws attention away from symptoms level, whether it be financial problems, health issues, or whatever.

> How do you think that sickness can succeed in shielding you from truth? Because it proves the body is not separate from you, so you must be separate from the truth. You suffer pain because the body does, and in this pain are you made one with it. Thus is your "true" identity preserved, and the strange, haunting thought that you might be something beyond this little pile of dust silenced and stilled. For see, this dust can make you suffer, twist your limbs and stop your heart, commanding you to die and cease to be. W-136.8

There we have the ultimate of the reversal of cause and effect. The deceived mind wants to be sick; it wants to experience and interpret sickness as being of the body so it can prove that it is separate from God. It is vulnerable. It is guilty. It is a strong witness to have a throbbing headache or sharp back pain, etc. As long as pain is being experienced, it is seen as a strong witness. It is a decision. You think it is serving you in some way. As soon as you can see how it does not serve, it will be gone instantaneously.

Friend: And the only way it serves me is to help me keep my concept of the world in place? That could be the only purpose that it serves.

David: And the Course is teaching how insane, how ridiculous that is:

> Thus is the body stronger than the truth, which asks you live, but cannot overcome your choice to die. And so the body is more powerful than everlasting life, Heaven more frail than hell, and God's design for the salvation of His Son opposed by a decision stronger than His Will. His Son is dust, the Father incomplete, and chaos sits in triumph on His throne. W-136.9

That is quite graphically laid out. Once again, you need to trace it back and see it for what it is. Feeling a little bit cold or a little too hot, feeling an itch, or anxiety, or a nervous twitch—all of that is simply a decision, a defense that is being made against Heaven, even the more subtle things. Do not say, in a personal sense: *Oh my gosh, but I still have an itch,* or, *I still feel too hot or too cold,* but use it to bring to your attention how vigilant you have to be. Your mind watching has to be totally free of this backward thinking to let the light shine on all the false thoughts in your mind.

> Such is your planning for your own defense. And you believe that Heaven quails before such mad attacks as these, with God made blind by your illusions, truth turned into lies, and all the universe made slave to laws which your defenses would impose on it. Yet who believes illusions but the one who made them up? Who else can see them and react to them as if they were the truth?
>
> God knows not of your plans to change His Will. The universe remains unheeding of the laws by which you thought to govern it. And Heaven has not bowed to hell, nor life to death. You can but choose to think you die, or suffer sickness or distort the truth in any way. What is created is apart from all of this. Defenses are plans to defeat what cannot be attacked. What is unalterable cannot change. And what is wholly sinless cannot sin. W136.10,11

Let's look at the subtleties of this. Whenever there is concern for the body, concern about where I will get food to eat or where I will sleep or how I will get all the work done that I have to do, it is always related to the body—and the mind is defending the self-concept. What a relief to see that it is not necessary! It flies in the face of everything in this world to think that you can just hold onto your purpose and everything will click and flow in absolute perfect harmony, but that is what the lessons are teaching us. If this is absolutely practiced, then the mind will become so detached of judging anything that it literally just lets go of all preferences and all judgment thoughts. "Healing will flash across your open mind, as peace and truth arises to take the place of war in vain imaginings." W-136.16 The mind that believes in war and vain imaginings is a darkened mind; that is what is sick. Healing, or light, will flash across an open mind.

> There will be no dark corners sickness can conceal, and keep defended from the light of truth. There will be no dim figures from your dreams, nor their obscure and meaningless pursuits

with double purposes insanely sought, remaining in your mind. It will be healed of all the sickly wishes that it tried to authorize the body to obey. W-136.16

In the next paragraph he uses a metaphor: "Now is the body healed, because the source of sickness has been open to relief." That obviously has to be a metaphor because he told us many times that the body cannot be sick. There is an assumption here of a concept that a body can be sick. In a sense he is saying that when the mind is healed the body will reflect that health. There won't be any suffering involved in it. This gets back to the illusionary belief in separate parts that are seen as "wholes." This belief is very deep. Bodies and every separate thing in the world that has a made-up purpose is an illusion of a whole. This goes beyond the metaphor of even a body being healed.

And you will recognize and practice well by this: The body should not feel at all. If you have been successful, then there will be no sense of feeling ill or feeling well, of pain or pleasure. No response at all is in the mind to what the body does. W-136.17

On Duality and Forgiveness

David: You are not a body and you are not *in* a body. You are a mind. Initially that is an alien way of thinking but gradually you will start to think of yourself as mind, because that is what you are. This goes beyond the idea of reincarnation, of coming in and out of bodies. Again, you are not a body and you are not even in a body; that really flies in the face of experience in this world. It seems as if you are looking out from these eyes and hearing with these ears and smelling with this nose. Experientially, it seems very much that our experience is rooted in the body – but the Course tells us this is not a fact.

On the topic of mind the Course says, "Mind reaches to itself. It is not made up of different parts, which reach each other. It does not go out." T-18.VI.8 About the body it says, "The body is outside you, and but seems to surround you, shutting you off from others and keeping you apart from them, and them from you." T-18.VI.9 The world is like a movie screen. Sometimes when you watch a movie you feel identified with the characters. This is what so-called everyday daily life is like. You are so identified with the characters on the screen that you perceive them as yourself, as your family members, your boss, etc. This is a major perceptual problem. All our grief comes in when we identify with what is on the screen.

Another very fundamental idea is that mind cannot attack. Guilt arises from the belief that mind can attack. Mind can make up fantasies, like making up a movie; it can have characters act out and seem to attack one another verbally or physically, but it is just a fantasy. It is the split in the mind that throws the belief in attack out on the screen, where the figures seem to attack and be attacked. It is the mind's way of trying to escape the problem of thinking it has separated from God.

This is a very fundamental idea: the mind cannot attack. But this is not how we think in day-to-day life. There is the belief that one person, or mind, can manipulate another mind. This takes many forms, like the idea of someone being seductive, for example. Can you hear what that implies? There is an interaction, with one being made prey, as if manipulated to do something against one's own will. The Course says that is impossible. If it was possible, where would the equality be in that? If one mind could dominate another mind there would not be equality, and guilt would be justified. But you can see how deeply rooted these ideas are in the split mind. Minds cannot attack. They can just make up bodies to act out the fantasies. It is the perception of attack that brings on the defenses. As soon as the mind perceives attack in any form it cannot help but respond with defense. The problem is with the misperception of attack.

Early on in the Workbook Jesus tells us that we have not yet learned that attack and being attacked are the same. The same! That is not how it seems in this world. There seems to be a big difference between being attacked and being the attacker – but they are identical, they are just different forms of the same thing. If you have attack thoughts in your mind, it does not so much matter how you perceive it. It does not matter who you assign which role to; the attacker and the one attacked are the same.

You have to come to the realization that attack is impossible. Otherwise you are going to keep perceiving attack and keep responding and reacting in defensive ways. This can take the form of magical maneuvers, fancy health structures, medicines, and hospitals – all the different forms of armature. If you take it to the national level it will look like armies and bombs used to guard the country or the handgun issue, or crime. All of that is out there on the screen. There is not a problem with crime in the country. There is not a problem with guns. There is not a problem with defense spending and so on.

That is all out there. The problem brings it back to me and my mind – to the realization that I still believe in attack.

Friend: When you get into a situation of conflict, it is so easy to get sucked in. At work, at home, family stuff, in-laws – everybody is taking sides.

David: The key is transferring this to *all* these different circumstances. A situation is just a situation. Jesus knows that the mind in a deceived state does not believe that. It seems to be that some situations are more difficult. It is one thing for instance, to go to *A Course in Miracles* group where everyone is talking about all these ideas. But then I have to go deal with my in-laws or my boss at work. There is just a deep underlining belief that there is an order of difficulty in miracles. The first principle of the Course is that there is no order of difficulty in miracles.

Friend: When I have a conflict with someone sometimes I go home and start getting really angry. I feel like a little kid. I just want to kick my feet or hit somebody. When I think about it, I do not want to be responsible! I want to blame it on someone else! It is so hard for me to look at. I feel just like a little kid; I just want to lie down on the floor and kick my feet and scream and holler.

David: That anger is a good topic to look at. Here's a statement that sometimes just feels like too much: "Anger is never justified." T-30.VI.1 This comes pretty late in the text. It is not to say that you won't get angry. It is not even saying that you *shouldn't* get angry. It is saying that it is never justified. If you really trace it back, say to the idea that "I am responsible for what I see," T-21.II.2 then you could see the fallacy of it – but there is such tremendous projection of the cause of sacrifice and of guilt. The main ego dynamic is the belief that what you project out on the world is what you get rid of; that is how to get rid of it. Projection is the ego's way of minimizing or diminishing anger, threats and guilt. What the ego never tells the mind is that what you give away is what you keep! That is the fundamental law of Heaven. That is how the Son was created. God extended himself in his likeness and attributes. That is how the Son came into being; it is the fundamental law of Heaven. As soon as you start to see that, you begin to see that projection never gets you anything. Perceiving attack or responding with anger never brings you anything you want.

As you go deeper into the metaphysics you begin to generalize this principle more and more. It takes such a transfer of training. The Course says that as long as you perceive a physical world of duality, you are blind. It is not like when you have a healed perception that there is going to be a world there to see. "The world was made as an attack on God." W-pII.3.2   When the mind fell asleep, it took what was truly visible – light and love – and made it invisible. And it made what does not exist, visible. That is what this perceptual world is. Heaven disappeared as soon as perception was made. It is quite deep to see that the world is a perceptual hallucination. This is different from other paths that suggest you can come to a perfected world in some sense. There have been religions that have talked about paradise on earth, or even about making the body immortal, which is another extension of the same idea. The Course is saying that what you made visible, what you see now, does not have any existence and that when you can come to the vision of Christ it won't be there anymore to see. This paragraph really gives us a key to what true forgiveness is:

> Pardon is *always* justified. It has a sure foundation. You do not forgive the unforgivable, nor overlook a real attack that calls for punishment. Salvation does not lie in being asked to make unnatural responses which are inappropriate to what is real. Instead, it merely asks that you respond appropriately to what is not real by not perceiving what has not occurred. T-30.VI.2

That is deep. It merely asks that you respond appropriately to what is not real – which is the whole cosmos – by not perceiving what has not occurred.

That is reminiscent of some of those lines about forgiving your brother for what he has not done. The Course is getting us to start to really question what we are seeing with the body's eyes and hearing with the body's ears. We begin to question whether what our senses report is reliable. Many of us have had an experience of thinking that we knew all the facts about a situation only to find out we were really way off base. Our own motives and wishes had influenced our perception; we were reading into the scene something that really was not there at all. That is a good stepping stone.

"You are merely asked to see forgiveness as the natural reaction to distress that rests on error and thus calls for help. Forgiveness is the only sane response. It keeps your rights from being sacrificed." T-30.VI.2 Through the ego's lens forgiveness is shaky. The ego says we can *try* to forgive, or we can try to pull the old "forgive but do not forget" routine. Or there is the arrogant approach to forgiveness: *Because I have come along so far in my spiritual journey and I have really trained my mind, now I will stoop down to forgive you.* This is a move way beyond all of that. It is seeing that forgiveness is the only sane response. If you want to keep peace of mind in your awareness, then forgiveness needs to become a natural, habitual response to everything! That is pretty drastic.

> The real world is achieved when you perceive the basis for forgiveness is quite real and fully justified. While you regard it as a gift unwarranted, it must uphold the guilt you would "forgive." Unjustified forgiveness is attack. T-30.VI.3

When we use the word "attack," it conjures up images. The mind thinks that it knows what attack is, but there are many, many subtle forms of it that are not seen for what they are. The more you work with the Course the more you start to see that all judgment is attack, because it denies the wholeness and the unity of mind. It is attack whenever the mind engages in judging, or breaking apart. We are talking here about the ordering of thoughts and the hierarchy of illusions. It gets into very subtle realms. It is hard for the mind to grasp that preferring apple pie over cherry pie is a form of attack. You think: *Attack is what I see on the news every night! I know what attack is. Preferring cherry pie over apple pie has nothing to do with attack.* But the Course is saying that it is an attack.

There are all these hierarchies of preferences – preferences in the way people look or food preferences or sexual preferences, climate preferences, visual preferences, music preferences. These are ego configurations of what I call "my version of reality," which is not reality at all. It is just "my" version of reality, the small self's version. That is why there seems to be conflict; there seem to be all these tiny, disparate versions of reality and they all seem to collide. That is why we have debates and opinions and arguments! The "first chaotic law," or the ego's law, is that "the truth is different for everyone." T-23.II.2 "To each his own;" how many times have you heard that cliché? Or, "everybody is entitled to their own opinion."

I see forgiveness as the complete relinquishment of judgment in the worldly sense. This is not to say that as a stepping stone the Holy Spirit is not judgmental or evaluative. It clearly states in the Course that the Holy Spirit is evaluative as long as you believe that you are in a maze of duality. There are choices to make in duality: *Do I do this? Do I do that? Do I go here? Do I go there?* Then the Holy Spirit is evaluative. He gives the mind what it can receive and guides the mind out of the belief that it is in the world of duality. But how can I truly let go and listen to the Holy Spirit's judgment if I want to hang on to my own version of reality – my own preferences, my own likes and dislikes and opinions?

Friend: For a while I had the idea of "good" confused with truth and the idea of "bad," with false. I would immediately evaluate things to see if they were good or bad (true or false). It recently occurred to me that "bad" has nothing to do with false and that "good" has nothing to do with truth. I have a problem seeing what is false in this world except when I realize that everything I see is false and everything I do is false. Can you talk about good and bad, about this duality of good and evil?

David: We can talk about good/bad, beautiful/ugly—you could phrase it as desirable/undesirable and pleasurable/painful. There are a lot of different ways to come at it. You can tell there is duality in all those; there are two ends of the scale. In the deceived state you cannot tell the difference between pleasure and pain. The deceived mind "tries to teach itself its pains and joys are different and can be told apart." T-27.VIII.1 In lesson 12 Jesus tells you to look about yourself and list what you think you see "using whatever descriptive terms happen to occur to you." He says:

> If terms which seem positive rather than negative occur to you, include them. For example, you might think of "a good world," or "a satisfying world." If such terms occur to you, use them along with the rest. You may not yet understand why these "nice" adjectives belong in these exercises but remember that a "good world" implies a "bad" one, and a "satisfying world" implies an "unsatisfying" one. W-12.3

There seems to be a general consensus that there are a lot of wonderful, beautiful, good things in this world and also that there are certain things which are bad or negative. Perhaps the belief is that if I can just forgive the negativity then I will be left with what is good. Goodness, if we use it in the ultimate sense, is behind the veil of duality. It is when you cease to judge both ends of the spectrum of "good and bad"—and lay aside all judgments—that you are left with the truth. It is not by forgiving the negative or trying to give up all the negative judging; it is about giving up the belief that you even know what is good or bad.

Do you see where this is going? We are transcending morality and ethics—all the disciplines that are preoccupied with what is *good*. This points to a very high place because admittedly most all religions and philosophies have come up with a lot of rules about good and bad. You have to be very careful about how you define and construct that. You are back into making the error real as soon as you categorize. As soon as you have good and bad, you are denying that it is all an illusion. If I think some behaviors are good and some are bad, how can it all be equally unreal? Are there some illusions that are better and some worse? When I say "making it real," I mean giving reality to the projected world. Here we have the metaphysics of why we need to stop thinking we know what is good and bad—because we are giving reality to the projected world by doing that.

Friend: Some people believe that negativity should be dealt with—done away with. I know people who do not want to talk about the news or even look at it. They do not want to read anything negative. They think if they do not look at it, it will go away. No, it will just be further projected out. We must look at those things. If we don't, then we are denying that that is our mind that projected it out there. That is my thinking that did that; I am still holding onto these thoughts because I am seeing it out there. I am seeing it on the news. If I just hang on to this beautiful and lovely nature and sunlight and the glorious illusions, I won't ever wake up. I will stay in this dream.

David: It is about watching your thoughts, and watching your thoughts, and watching your thoughts! Just noticing the thoughts can be used in a helpful way. And you may get to the point of getting clearer and clearer in your mind. You may get to the point where you may not watch the news. It may not be the thing that you are guided to do; it may not be what is most helpful for the whole Sonship. But, it is *always* about watching our thoughts—whether it is during a movie, watching the news or being with the in-laws, or at work—whatever it is you are doing. It really is a full-time job to watch your mind all the time.

Friend: I did not realize it was my mind I was supposed to be watching!

David: That is the first step. You have to watch these thoughts to begin with, and then you have to stay aware.

Friend: It is my dream and when I get identified with it and start arguing with someone, or feel attacked—I have forgotten that I wrote the script and I am an actor in the play! I hope I can finally step back; *wait a minute! This has no reality at all! I am giving it all the reality that it has. I bought into it. I identified with it. I think it is real.* And it is real when I think it is real.

David: The key word is "identified." Jesus says in the *Manual for Teachers*, when he talks about the real meaning of sacrifice: "...self-condemnation is a decision about identity, and no one doubts what he believes he is. He can doubt all things, but never this." M-13.3 Whatever you are identified with, you are in it with your whole being. All of our defense mechanisms arise out of identification with the space/time world of form and bodies; all emotions come with identification with the illusion. As you begin to train your mind you learn to see that rage is no different than a little twinge of frustration. You start to see the subtleties. When we trace the emotions back we always find the identification with the personality.

Friend: The body concept.

David: That is where the defenses come in. The Course mentions the path of asceticism: "Many have chosen to renounce the world while still believing its reality." W.155.4 And in the next sentence something more familiar in our modern-day age of technology and convenience is mentioned: "Others have chosen nothing but the world, and they have suffered from a sense of loss still deeper." The world is like a playland of convenience and comfort, with an "I can do whatever I want" mentality. It can be very lulling. It can seem as though I have it pretty good; I have it better than earlier generations. Look at all the progress, conveniences and comforts. Convenience for what? Comfort for what? The body! The body is the centerpiece in all this "progress."

At some point you start to think: *Wait a minute, I want to have a free mind and if my mind is identified and attached to the body then how can I have a free mind and a free body?* "Do you want freedom of the body or freedom of the mind? For both you cannot have." T-22.VI.1 You want to get to the truth that is stable – that just *is* – beyond the good and bad. Everything that we perceive in this world can be used as symbols. Concepts can be used as stepping stones. The more you apply the Course the more you see the things of the world as merely symbolic. The more you withdraw your judgment, the more you can allow the mind to open up and expand. Forgiveness is a concept. It is the biggest, most all-inclusive concept/metaphor that there is, for it undoes all other concepts/metaphors.

Chapter Four

Delving into Form and Content

David: I am glad to be here with all of you. It is a precious thing to come together with the intention of looking at the false beliefs in the mind. As the Bible says, "Wherever two or more are gathered, there I am." When we come together with this purpose it accelerates the process of outgrowing or transcending the ego—so I feel really grateful.

It takes a leap of faith to come. There is always a bit of uneasiness when you do not know the people. The ego's way to deal with it is to have a lot of structure—to know what you are going to do ahead of time. Or repetition, the ego is big on ritual and method. To come together without a format is scary to the ego. I want you to feel free to say whatever comes to your mind so that we can go into it. If you have a reaction to something someone is saying, we can go into that. It is always a decision; everything we feel is based on our own decision. Let's get into the metaphysics and try to understand what is going on in our own minds so we can understand why we are choosing what we are choosing.

On a conscious level it can seem kind of crazy. *Why would I choose to be fearful, or sick?* It is strange to think of choosing to be sick. No one in their right mind would choose to be sick, but you are not in your right mind when you are choosing sickness. Why would someone choose to be fearful? You are not in your right mind. We need to go into the metaphysics to see what is going on with decision and choice. The passage that is coming to me to use as our springboard is in Chapter 24, *The Goal of Specialness.*

In the first couple of sentences he reminds us of the goal. It is nice to be reminded that the goal is peace of mind. It is so simple. Here is a book with 1200 or so pages, but it all comes down to:

> Forget not that the motivation for this Course is the attainment
> and the keeping of the state of peace. Given this state the mind
> is quiet and the condition in which God is remembered is
> attained. T-24.in.1

There are some heavy-duty things in this chapter but it starts off very simply, with a reminder that peace of mind is our goal. In the second paragraph he gets right down to the nitty-gritty: "To learn this Course requires willingness to question every value that you hold." That is very literal; when you really get into it you begin to see that the Course is very literal.

> Not one can be kept hidden and obscure but it will jeopardize your learning. No belief is neutral. Every one has the power to dictate each decision you make. For a decision is a conclusion based on everything that you believe. It is the outcome of belief, and follows it as surely as does suffering follow guilt and freedom sinlessness. T-24.in.1

Wow! What an enormous passage. Decision is an important theme in the Course. The final section of the entire Course is called *Choose Once Again*. In it he says: "My brother, choose again." And: "...you *will* choose again." He is telling us all through the day that we have decisions to make. He wants us to get to the point where we can choose peace, and to understand that peace is nothing more than a decision.

> The Holy Spirit, like the ego, is a decision. Together they constitute all the alternatives the mind can accept and obey. The Holy Spirit and the ego are the only choices open to you. T-5.V.6

Even the Holy Spirit is a decision! The Holy Spirit is a decision and the ego is a decision. It is interesting to see that the Holy Spirit is a decision. If we are a mind with decision-making ability, then that decision is available to us every instant. Of course the Holy Spirit is a decision that brings peace to our awareness. That is pretty straight forward; the Holy Spirit is a decision and in choosing the Holy Spirit I will be at peace – not in fear, upset, depression, anxiety, or any upsetting emotion. So what is it that prevents me from choosing that? That is a central question. What is it that seems to stand in the way of choosing peace? What about this other option for fear? He is really giving us a giant leap forward with this. He says that a decision is a conclusion based on everything you believe. Decision is the outcome of belief.

Friend: Whether I know what the belief is or not?

David: Whether or not I am aware of what the belief is. If a decision is a conclusion based on everything you believe then you can see why this Course "requires willingness to question every value that you hold. Not one can be kept hidden and obscure but it will jeopardize your learning." T-24.in.2 It is crucial to hear that. If you have hidden beliefs—decisions will spring from those beliefs. Two paragraphs later hidden beliefs are described as if they are warriors:

> Beliefs will never openly attack each other because conflicting outcomes are impossible. But an unrecognized belief is a decision to war in secret, where the results of conflict are kept unknown and never brought to reason, to be considered sensible or not. T-24.I.2

There is a war going on in the mind.

Friend: In the next paragraph after that he says, "All that is ever cherished as a hidden belief, to be defended though unrecognized, is faith in specialness." Does that mean we are giving our faith to specialness and making decisions based on a goal of specialness at all times? That seems so insane because I can see how specialness is complete upside-down thinking and how it is hurting us all.

David: Can we see that? That is a good question. Can we see how specialness hurts us?

Friend: There is so much going on in my mind about this goal of specialness. Can I recognize that it is an upside-down belief and just choose the goal of oneness? That does not seem to automatically block out this faith in, or goal of, specialness. There seems to be something else going on down there that needs to be brought up. It says here that all that is ever cherished is the belief in specialness. It is a barrier between me and everybody else. What I am trying to do is realize there are no barriers between me and everybody else.

David: The ego is the faith in specialness but it seems to take millions of different forms. It seems like we are healing things one at a time, healing this one and this one … It seems endless, like waves. You finally get through a whole wave and then you get the next wave and the next wave. I like to use the analogy of a skyscraper. We have to start at the top and go down, floor by floor, turning on the light. We also need to get to the idea that there is a master switch in the basement! In many parts of the Course he says it can take an instant; that would be like going down and flipping the master switch. *Help me get in touch with this master switch. I do not want this to take forever.*

This brings us to the distinction between form and content. Jesus lays it out so simply by saying that the Holy Spirit sees everything as love—everything is either love or a call for love. In the ultimate sense everything is just love.

The only judgment involved is the Holy Spirit's one division into two categories; one of love, and the other the call for love. You cannot safely make this division, for you are much too confused either to recognize love, or to believe that everything else is nothing but a call for love. T-14.X.7

The ego sees attack. It does not see everything as love or a call for love; it perceives everything as attack and judgment. In the next sentence we find out why: "You are too bound to form, and not to content. What you consider content is not content at all. It is merely form and nothing else." That is the reason. If you can really get at this form/content thing and loosen your mind from the grip of being bound to form, then you can clearly perceive with the Holy Spirit and see everything as being love or a call for love. Why is there such a huge, huge investment in form? It helps to go back to the overall metaphysics. If you can gather this theme into the overall picture of what Jesus is saying in the Course, it begins to make sense: *The world was made as a defense against love.*

We talk about the tiny, little mad idea, where the Son of God remembered not to laugh. He took seriously the silly idea that he could actually separate from his Creator, that he could be the king-pin, that there could be something more than Heaven. It is a ridiculous idea, but when taken seriously the little puff of nothingness tells the mind to run and hide in form. God is abstract, unconditional, infinite light; he is not going to chase you into form. "God knows not form." T-30.III.4 That means the Infinite does not look on the finite. The abstract does not look on the specific.

This is the trick the ego sets up, like hiding in the basement. *Let's go hide in form; we will make up a world that is a substitute for this infinite abstract light.* That is where the mind begins to get bound into form. It is not that the world is inherently evil; it is just being used as a hiding place. The cellar is not a bad place; it is just what it is being used for. It is kind of twisted to run away from a Father that loves you. The world was made by the ego for the purpose of hiding; it was made as an attack on God because it was made as a place to hide from God. The good news is that the Holy Spirit instantaneously gives the world a whole new purpose. The Holy Spirit's purpose for the world is to use it to bring peace to mind. You do not want this world you made. Your Father loves you. You have everything in Heaven and this is such a tiny little place.

"You do not ask too much of life, but far too little." W-133.2 You are entitled to everything. You are entitled to remember who you are. The mind runs to hide in form and then starts judging and ordering. To forgive the world is to see the false as false; this is what the Holy Spirit says. The ego says that you have done a horrible thing; *you have to order and judge.* That is where the hierarchy of illusions comes in. The whole point of the ego is to make hierarchies and order, to see differences in situations and scenarios and persons. The ego's focus is on seeing differences. These are the idols, the graven images!

This can be a springboard to make clearer the distinction between form and content. Content is the miracle, the Holy Spirit's lens of being able to see the false as false from above the battleground. Content is nothing more than remembering that it is my decision – my decision in mind. Form is forgetting that you are a mind. Form is forgetting that you can choose between the ego and the Holy Spirit. Form is thinking you are a tiny, little person in a sad, sad world of form; and all you have are choices between illusions, like where to go, what to see, what to buy, who to date, who to marry, and who to divorce. All these seeming choices are on the surface, or at the top of the skyscraper, to use our analogy. They are the outcome of all the false beliefs in the mind, leading you like a robot that has no choice but to seemingly follow the demands of the tyrant hiding in the basement.

Friend: Guarding the master switch. [laughing]

David: Guarding the master switch. *Do not come down here.* [laughing] That gives us a context. Now, what are the situations and issues that you cannot see as specialness, the things that seem to be real issues, real problems confronting you? To work it down through the floors of the skyscraper we have to start where we experience it – at the top: relationship problems, problems with the person at work, financial problems or a flood. You could say it is easy for me to say that it is just a perceptual problem but what if my house was under water? How would I feel then? I would start at the top with the experience, and work it back down all the way to the realization that it is just a perceptual problem.

Friend: I have this pattern that is getting really tiring. It is like I do not want to give up the ego. The way the Course has painted the picture for me, I can see very clearly the difference between choosing to focus on the light and choosing to run away. I keep running back to the ego's way of doing things as far as specialness and body identification are concerned, until I just cannot stand it anymore. Then I will turn to Spirit, but after a day or so it seems that I am ready for more punishment. It is silly. Even though I feel like I can see it for what it is, I just feel very stubborn, kicking and screaming, and crying. *Go to hell Holy*

Spirit; leave me alone. That is the way I have been feeling for a while. I have a recital coming up for example, and I do not want to know about peace and love. I just want to do well! It is a very uncomfortable place to be.

David: Observing behavior can be tormenting. You see the behavior as erratic; you seem to be doing one thing at one moment and then something completely contradicting the next moment. That is intolerable for the mind because the mind in its natural state is whole, integrated, and complete. The mind feels so fragmented when looking at this behavior and that behavior. It has to be pulled out of the realm of behavior completely.

It does seem to be a very big leap to let go of the belief that *I am a person and I have choice.* It seems like common sense to think that I can choose right now to raise my right hand. I can choose now to lower my right hand. These seem to be real choices that I as a person can make. I can choose to go out in the rain; I can choose to stay in from the rain. It seems that these are real decisions; it seems as if the behaviors are the outcome of these decisions. But the decisions are being made way, way back in the mind. We never respond to anything directly. We are always responding to an interpretation of what we are seeing.

If a giant bumble bee is flying right at your nose, it seems that you are responding to the bumble bee. If you are walking under an apple tree and you dodge a falling apple, it seems that you are responding to the apple. If your boss is screaming at you and you start to feel your defenses come up, it seems as if you are responding to your boss. But you are responding to your interpretation of the event. The only way out is to change your mind about the interpretation of the event. There will never be a way to find peace by trying to change the event. And isn't that what we all try to do all the time? We strive to have better relationships or to live in better places; we hope for better jobs. It just goes on and on and on. The ego says: *Yeah, change the form; you are a person in the world and if you can just get a better situation the problem will be solved.* Of course that is just shifting from one idol to another, which is more specialness. It is an endless game of continually trying to change the form. It takes a lot of energy to do that.

Friend: But we are not that familiar with content; that is what we need to learn. You cannot make a step until you know there is something there to step on. I think that is the biggest thing for all of us because it seems like the reaction is so automatic. I can see how specialness mixes me up. Without specialness where would I be?

David: Of course the ego's answer is *oblivion*! The ego says you would be nothing without this world because you have turned your back on God. You have already been kicked out of Heaven, the ego says, so you have no other choice but this world of judgment and specialness. But if there are Holy Spirit purposes for the body and the world, and there are ego purposes for the body and the world, and these are decisions that I can make, then the question is whether I choose to give my mind to the ego and specialness or the Holy Spirit. If all my misery comes from giving my mind to the ego's purposes, and all my joy and peace comes from giving my mind to the Holy Spirit's purposes, then I have to be able to tell the difference. If I can just begin to tell the difference, then I can begin to withdraw my investment; I can check in with the Spirit more often. The Holy Spirit's purpose for the body is simple: "The Holy Spirit sees the body only as a means of communication, and because communicating is sharing it becomes communion." T-6.V

Nice and simple; the Holy Spirit uses the body only for communication – not for striving and not for attaining some worldly end. It is *only* for communication. The ego uses the body for attack, for pleasure, and for pride. Now we have something to work with. If the ego uses the body for these three things, then all of my guilt continues to be reinforced. The world keeps showing me that I am guilty because I am holding onto the ego's purpose for the body; I am holding onto attack, pleasure and pride. All I have to do is clearly see the insanity of using the body and the world for these three purposes and let them go. If I look at that and think: *Oh, oh my specialness is in trouble here; I am going to be deprived*, I must not see the insanity of it. I clearly have to have it right in front of my nose. I have to really see the dynamics of what the ego is doing before I would voluntarily say: *No more of this. I do not want this anymore.*

We have to look at the nature of our attachment to all of this. Detachment on the other hand is the ability to be the observer. That is really what we want to do. We want to be the observer of the script rather than get caught up in it. We have to move beyond form. We have to see that the ego uses the body for pride, pleasure, and attack. And it does not work to just grit your teeth and try to control your behavior. For example, proclaiming to never yell and scream at anyone again won't get you anywhere. Attempting change at the level of form does not work.

Let's bring our discussion back to the level of content. Pride, for example, is very sneaky. Sometimes you arrive home expecting that smile or hug that does not come, or you look for recognition at work. You just want to be recognized, to stand out from the crowd. You buy a new car or new clothes to get a little attention. Pride is so sneaky. Look at the motivation in the mind; it is vanity. We spend so much time on bodies, hairstyles, makeup, clothing, cars, etc. Just look at vanity and how far the pride goes. It always comes down to the body identity. What difference would it make if I was famous or not? What difference would it make how my body looks if I was not first identified as a body?

Now let's look at pleasure. Pleasure seems to feel good, really good. [laughing] The body's pleasure seems to be a really big deal, whether it is favorite foods, certain kinds of sexual activities, or beautiful places like the mountains or the ocean. There are temperature preferences; some like it hot, some like it cool. The ego uses the body for pleasure. Metaphysically, why does that keep you so constrained and limited, and feeling so guilty? The five senses are part of the ego's way of gratifying itself by making the body seem real. Just try and get in touch with God when you have a throbbing headache. Pain powerfully reinforces frailty and guilt. It seems to be a very powerful witness – the opposite of "I am as God created me." It seems to be a witness to weakness, frailty, and powerlessness. Pain is a very powerful witness for the ego. It is the ego saying: *You have screwed up. You have left your creator and he is angry and this is a form of punishment.* You are feeling pain because you think that God is angry at you. You are feeling pain because you believe that God is punitive.

The flip side of pain is pleasure. In the moment of orgasm and ecstasy some people scream out *Oh God!* I do not think this is exactly what *A Course in Miracles* is talking about. [laughing] It is not exactly a feeling of detachment! Pleasure, being the flipside of pain, reinforces the belief that *I am a body. Not only am I a body, I am feeling pleasure in this particular spot in my body.* When you are having your favorite cup of coffee or looking at your favorite painting, it seems to be that there is a physical or psychological sensation. It is not uncomfortable and it is not painful; it seems to be different. The Course is saying: *My child you are hallucinating. Your mind is twisted and you think you can tell the difference between pain and pleasure.* Jesus is telling you that you are in such a distorted, twisted state of mind that you are seeing what does not even exist; you are hallucinating. These sensations you are feeling are not the real world; they are not the state of Heaven. Both ends of the spectrum reinforce the belief that the body is real.

> Yet to the One Who sends forth miracles to bless the world,
> a tiny stab of pain, a little worldly pleasure, and the throes
> of death itself are but a single sound; a call for healing, and

a plaintive cry for help within a world of misery. It is their sameness that the miracle attests. T-27.VI.6

How many times do we ask for forgiveness when we are experiencing pleasure? You are dreaming a dream and you believe that there are good dreams and bad dreams. I would say that most of us put the pleasurable dreams in the "good dreams" category. In fact we spend a lifetime pursuing them. Why would we chase after huge careers and climb corporate ladders unless it was for money? Money can be exchanged for a lot of the menus of the world. You get your Visa card and the world is your oyster. The flip-side is the belief that there are certain dreams that are better than others. Later in the Text he says that the miracle overlooks all dreams.

> Thus it is the miracle does not select some dreams to leave untouched by its beneficence. You cannot dream some dreams and wake from some, for you are either sleeping or awake. And dreaming goes with only one of these. The dreams you think you like would hold you back as much as those in which the fear is seen. For every dream is but a dream of fear, no matter what the form it seems to take. T-29.IV.I

Friend: I have a question that goes back to the use of the body. If we look at the three things that are the ego's purpose for the body (pleasure, pride and attack), and imagine a scenario for a moment where we wipe out all of those, what would we have left?

David: What you are asking is, if you begin to withdraw from the world and really start to give up these uses, what is it that you will be doing? The world is a hallucination. When you withdraw your investment from the hallucination, the hallucination fades and fades and fades until you wake up to your eternal reality. The phrase, *the dreamer of the dream*, refers to when you step back far enough to be detached. There will still seem to be things that are going on. Jesus is a good example as he certainly seemed to have a mission to be traveling places and doing things, but the mind reaches a point of detachment.

Friend: How do I practice seeing the hallucination throughout my daily life?

David: We know that repression and indulgence are two sides of the coin. Anyone who has been in any kind of addiction knows how hard it can be to control one's behavior. Obviously the ego is in on that; the ego is what is driving it. The other side of the coin would be repression, where you deny yourself that chocolate ice cream, that sex or whatever. With both, you are trying to change the form, the behavior, and hoping that the mind will follow suit. But the mind is what needs to be changed. The mind has to change first, then the behavior automatically follows suit. This is what a miracle is. It is painful to approach the Course from the backwards way of looking at all the things the ego is doing and say to yourself: *This is my specialness and I have to let it all go.* It is very difficult to let go of specialness when it is your focus.

Friend: It becomes sacrifice.

David: Jesus calls it fighting against sin. In the *I Need do Nothing* section he says that many have spent lifetimes battling against sin. "It is extremely difficult to reach Atonement by fighting against sin." The answer is to focus on the purpose—on the forgiveness, or healing, or whatever word is comfortable for you. Carry that with you into your everyday activities. Hold that purpose out in front. In the *Setting the Goal* section the steps are laid out for putting your goal out front. Do that and just watch how everything seems to bear witness to your goal, because your mind is very powerful. Hold your goal out in front. Do it right now as you are sitting here. Watch your reactions. Remember they are based on your interpretations of what seems to be happening. It is always your own lesson. The proper use of judgment is to use it to watch your feelings. How do I feel? Am I peaceful or am I upset? It does not seem to matter too much what the upset is; it is about noticing how you feel. This makes it a very practical Course. You get many opportunities to practice forgiveness when you hold your goal out front. Everything becomes a backdrop; you can apply the lessons in every circumstance.

You will begin more and more to see that the specifics are not important. The deceived mind believes in specifics. Everything in this world is specific. There is nothing outside of the mind. In the beginning the mind cannot quite conceive of that, it is too big of a belief. I can tell you from my own life, when I first began going to Course groups I was looking at the girls, at their legs and other body parts, and then I would bring my mind back. You notice your eyes and your mind. Your eyes get drawn to this and that but there comes a change when you hold your purpose out front. When you start connecting with the higher self you begin to really want to connect with people. Instead of telling your eyes not to look here or there, you just start to really want those heart-to-heart connections. There is an automatic shift that takes place. When you are totally focused on your purpose, you just stop paying attention to the body. You stop paying attention to how many people show up, or how many women there are. You do not notice weight, looks, or race. Racism is not in this world. Racism is in the mind. The ego makes a big deal about all the specifics, like color, age, attractiveness and gender. That is where sexism, ageism and racism come in. It is a phenomenal idea to think there is no racism in the world. The only place that racism could be is in my mind.

Raising the Self/World Concept to Awareness

Truth is peace, happiness, joy and freedom; Truth is an experience of the Heart. Truth cannot be described or explained. By the time it is experienced, the how's and why's have been dissolved. Truth is approached through negation, through becoming aware of all that is false—and from withdrawing belief from all illusion. All that is false is to be released.

Illusions are transcended by raising them into awareness. When all illusions are uncovered and revealed as one (i.e. the ego tree trunk and its many branches are all one tree), Truth is made welcome. Seeing the barrier completely and bringing it fully into awareness automatically shines it away. Seeing the barrier only partially, (i.e., some of the branches) is not to see at all.

Consciousness is the domain of the ego. It is made up of concepts and images. The subject and object, observer and observed, me and other, the individual and the collective, the dream figure and the dream—are not different at all. They are but concepts/images. They are the ego. Divine Mind is the Reality of Identity in God. Experiencing this is freedom!

Free Will is God's and Christ's. Ego "will" is the belief that reality is fragmented and can be chosen or selected from and that choice between images in the field is possible. Ego "will" is an effort to bring about a change, an improvement, by juggling and rearranging the concepts and images in the field, in the hope of future happiness. This illusion of change is not transformative because it is still within the field.

True change is a radical transformation of the mind. This occurs only when the mind sees the entire field—consciousness itself—from a completely different purpose or frame of reference.

The false self or ego is the image-maker *and* the images it makes. It is the persona (mask) which covers over or hides Abstract Reality from awareness.

It is a self-concept comprised of concepts. It is fragmented into the person (a fragment), other people (fragments), and the "surrounding" world/cosmos (still more fragments) *and* it is that which made or thought them all up. In other words, ego is both the "thinker" and the "thoughts," the image-maker and the images.

Freedom is the realization that Reality is whole and can only be accepted in this instant; it is not made up of and selected from images. The concept of choice vanishes with this acceptance, for in Reality there is nothing to choose between. It sees that future happiness was just a concept. It sees that past guilt was just a concept. It sees that striving and effort were just concepts. Present Reality is changeless and tranquil, devoid of all concepts.

Let us take an even closer look at letting go of the self-concept. As long as the mind identifies with the dream figure/s and the world, it cannot help but believe that there are real problems to solve and lots to be done in order to solve them. Action or doing implies a body to act or do. Yet whenever a decision in mind is made based on fear, the mind will retain fear. Judgment invites fear. Thoughts of consequences/outcomes, be they judged "favorable or unfavorable," "desirable or undesirable," are all merely self-concept thoughts about the dream and have nothing to do with one's Real Self.

The only choice available for a mind perceiving this world is which inner guide it will view the play of the world with—the Spirit or the ego. If anything in the script seems unsettling at all, it is just another chance to notice the mind's identification with the ego self-concept and to release the thought. When one remembers one's function of forgiveness (releasing illusions) and holds this Purpose clearly in mind, it does not matter at all what film seems to be playing or how the plot seems to be unfolding. Content is Purpose in the mind. The state of mind (that is, peace or upset) is not dependent on outcome/appearances, but only on which guide (Spirit or ego) is called upon to watch with. The ego's lens is always dark and the Spirit always views a clear and light and beautiful world. Spirit is without judgment and is therefore without condemnation.

It must surely become clear that one cannot retain a single shred of the self-concept and understand true forgiveness. One must choose between them and ultimately accept the Reality which Is, the Truth which has no opposite. True meditation is simply emptying consciousness of all its contents (i.e., time/space thoughts, concepts, ideas, and beliefs). All these concepts, images, beliefs, and thoughts are rooted in linear time. The only reason for the ego's complexity and busyness is its denial that Now is the only time there is.

The self-concept, which is a time/space/matter identity association, is what is atoned for, or Corrected. The acceptance of the Atonement, or the decision to hold the one Purpose of the Spirit, is what one is responsible for (that is, not for the error, but for accepting the Correction). Anytime one wishes for the script to go a certain way, one has made a judgment of form, and holds an expectation. Any expectation is a choice to forget the one Purpose of Spirit, and reflects the belief that there is something of value outside One Self.

All ego goals spring from the self-concept and have nothing to do with one's own best interests and everything to do with maintaining the self-concept. By first becoming aware of illusions, and then ceasing to invest in them by giving faith to a unified Purpose for the world, the illusions fade away and One remembers One Self as Spirit.

"Ye shall have no idols before God" translates into "you shall retain no self-concept if you shall know God." For One Self is created eternal and is far beyond any concept or image. Prayer is the desire of the heart. When prayer is purified, the remembrance of Truth springs to Mind as Divine Mind. *Let thine eye be single* is a way of saying, let thy prayer be for the Living One, for Love is What You are. Love is All there Is!!! Such is the Glory of God!!!

The Self-Construct

Friend: There was a time when I was feeling such desperation that there came a willingness to open up to something else. It seems that is often the case with people. As long as things seem to be going along smoothly, then the desire to question and to look at what is going on is not there; there is no motivation for it. But when things have obviously gone amuck, there is greater readiness and willingness to take a look and see what is possible.

David: When things have gone amuck in my perception, I have a perceptual problem. It really is not sane to project the problems, chaos and conflict of the world onto God, as if God knows about it, but chooses not to do anything. Any attempt to make a connection between God and the fragmented run-amuck world is an attempt to evade the responsibility I have for my own state of mind. Peace is a choice that I can make. When I choose to perceive myself as a victim or as part of a world run amuck, there is a distortion in my perception that needs correction.

Friend: The world never has run amuck. My mind has run amuck! Let's talk about the concept of victimization – all the different forms that that takes and how the concept really is not possible except in a deceived or sleeping mind.

David: To even have a sense of victim or victimizer, you have to have two. You have to have a subject and an object to have a victim and a victimizer. Conveniently for the mind that has two thought systems, the split can be projected out onto the world when the experience of it feels intolerable, reinforcing the idea that the split is in the world. It appears on the smoke screen so to speak, and not in the mind where the construct could be seen as a construct, illumining that there really is no problem. Early experiences of helplessness or victimization by parents are just part of a construct, set up so that the self-concept can perceive itself as victimized by other bigger people.

Friend: I guess dependency is another form of victimization. I set it up, for instance, so that physically I was dependent on my parents to provide food and clothing and shelter as well as emotional needs.

David: The scarcity and the lack of faith are projected out onto the world so that the world seems to be a place of scarcity. Now I am a subject, a person, in an objective world outside of me. This is a world of *kill or be killed*, where you have to fight to keep your head above water. The meaning that can be read into it is: *I am a dependent little child that will die unless I get food and shelter from mom and dad.*

Friend: I am helpless, of myself. I have to count on the adults in my world to take care of me.

David: That is a construct; we are back to it being a construct. You might have other children as part of that construct, an older sister or a younger brother. There is competition and I seem to be victimized. Sometimes I seem to be victimized and at other times I seem to be playing the victimizer role, the teaser and the tormenter. Then you go to school and there are teachers. The teachers have rules. Now I have to sit in a particular seat and do things when I am told. This can be perceived as a battle for control. The construct of victim and victimizer can take many different forms. The person may seem to be an adult or a child, which are both constructs.

Friend: The mind always wants to see inequality. So whenever there is inequality, somebody is always going to be the dependent one, the victim.

David: The deceived mind always needs the split in the world to be a distraction from the split in the mind. It does not want to see that it is just a decision. You have military and IRS and police departments and officers. We could bring it all back to the authority problem. There are authority issues all the way through all of these; basically there is an authority issue with God in the sense that the true self, the true Spirit is One, whole and complete. It is abstract. To believe that I am a person in a world is to deny my reality and instead make up something that is not real. The belief that I could have separated from God is so painful that these concepts are made up to cover over that pain – to be a substitute.

Friend: The idea of victimization really depends on the belief in separation and the whole authority problem; worked in through all that is the desire to be in control.

David: The belief that one can be unfairly treated by another person, by the world, or by society is part of the setup of the world to see the split outside the mind and emphasize the difference between the subject and the object. It is literally just a choice in the mind.

Friend: So let's bring this into what feels like a practical realm. Please address the issue of being abused as a child by a parent.

David: Okay. We see that this can be perceived as a problem. There can be a lot of pain or upset associated with it. The pain is coming from the sense of being victimized.

Friend: So that particular interpretation of being victimized is where the pain stems from?

David: Yes. That is a construct. Before you can have a belief that you were victimized by a parent comes the subject/object split. You have to believe that you are a person, a body in the world. You have to believe the circumstance took place and there was no decision or choice involved in it. It happened *to* you, as a person.

Friend: And that something outside my mind could bring me hurt or distress or upset of any kind.

David: If I believe I am a body and set up certain psychological and physical boundaries, I can say that I have certain inalienable rights as a person and there are other persons out there who can violate those rights. I have set up the whole construct; I believe there are things that are violations of my personhood, things that are against my will.

Friend: You are saying that if I think I have any personal rights related to this body and how it is used in relationship to other bodies – that is nothing more than a construct.

David: Exactly. It is made up, fictitious. One can have the illusion of being violated. It could be anything from traumatic physical or sexual abuse to someone frowning at you or failing to give you praise. These appear to be different degrees of rejection or victimization but it is all within the construct. The mind has to believe it is that construct before that can happen. There is an ordering of thoughts. There is a belief that there is something outside of me that can take away my peace. That has to be questioned. The construct has to be questioned; it has to be stepped back from and seen as a construct.

Friend: The very idea that I have rights about my body feels to me like it rests on my desire to be in control, and the desire to be in control rests on the fear that I am not in control.

David: You think you are given a little band of time between birth and death to be as you would like to be. It is like getting a blank canvas and a paint set; you may be painting and having a good time and then someone seems to come and disrupt your painting in some way. It seems to be a violation. This is a metaphor of course for what so called life in this world seems to be for a mind that believes that it is a construct or a concept. It says, "Hey! I have my uniqueness, my individuality. I will share some things with you and we may be able to agree on some things, but I will always be a separate person." In a sense, this is where the control comes in because it is perceived as if there are forces, external situations, and people that are taking away or eroding the "me" that I believe in. And until it is all seen as a made up mental construct there can be no peace.

Friend: The horror of being out of control is really the horror of no longer having this construct or self-concept to cling to.

David: Yes. What is the alternative? If I let go of this construct, then what? The ego counsels that you would be obliterated. Annihilated! You won't be you; there will be nothing left. You will be destroyed. The Spirit in the mind is reminding you that you will be you. You are you. But as you hold yourself as a concept, you do not know the magnitude of your own identity and your own reality. The Spirit is advising, reminding, and counseling the mind to let go.

Friend: So while the ego is saying: *It is going to be the worst thing that ever could happen, the Holy Spirit is saying: Ahh! If you only knew how wonderful the experience will be!*

David: And what are the implications of this? There is no racism in the world. Oh! What a statement. There is no sexism in the world. Huh! There is no ageism. There is no bigotry.

Friend: Where have you been? [laughing]

David: Yes, what place are you talking about? All of those perceived inequalities and problems are projected so that the mind will not have to look at the subject/object split in the mind. These two irreconcilable thought systems in the mind is where the problem is. I can crusade against racism and go out and try to convince other persons, other bodies, to shape up and think better, to pass better laws. It is the same with all the different controversies and social issues. It seems ludicrous in the world to say that there are no problems. Are we talking pie in the sky when we bring it back to it all being a construct? All of it is a construct – all the complexities and layers and levels of problems – from the interpsychic levels to global or international problems. Every single layer was made to obscure the simplicity that the split is in the mind and not in the world, that the problem is in the mind and not in the world, and that the problem has been solved. There is no problem. Once the mind can step back and see the world as nothing more than ideas, as nothing more than its own construct, then it sees that it is the dreamer of the dream. It is not in the dream; it is not a figure in the dream battling against other figures and forces of a wild and crazy dream. Once that is realized, the dream can be let go. It is a very happy dream for the dreamer when he sees he is the dreamer of it, that he is the cause of it.

Friend: Because then he sees there is nothing that goes on within the dream that matters.

David: Yes. He sees he is the dreamer, or the cause of the dream. That could be more accurately stated as: the dreamer can see that he *was* the dreamer....

Friend: That it is over and done. It is past.

David: It is over and done. It only seemed to have an existence in the past; it has no existence now. That is where we really get into the time aspect of the unholy instant and the holy instant.

Friend: Because the only thing that can have existence now is what is real. When you recognize that the dream is not real, then it cannot be something that is held in the present moment. It has to be something that was of the past.

David: All those lines in the Course about the past being gone start to click. The construct is past. When the construct is seen as a construct there is the awareness that the construct is also the past.

What it Means to Let Go and Live in Love

Trust is the key to letting go of fear, guilt, and pain through forgiveness and surrendering the worldly "identity" to the Spirit; the Spirit's Light is opposite to protecting and defending the body "identity." Letting go of attachment to externals and placing faith in the Spirit is the key to Enlightenment.

Anger and guilt will shift from scene to scene, place to place, until its source is unveiled and forgiven inside of us. Until there is forgiveness, the blame game, finger-pointing, and distractions to forget the pain are but follies that a deceived mind plays with in order to stay in denial. Once anger and guilt are seen as unjustified they can be released forever.

The lures of the world glimmer and tempt toward a "better life" of more status, more money, more power, more recognition, and more sex appeal. But once these "gifts" are seen to be fool's gold, the underlying illusion of the world (ego) is unveiled. As long as one gives faith to the ego, one will seem to be a pawn in the ego's game and world. When you see the ego exposed, it no longer is attractive. When faith is withdrawn from an illusion, the illusion disappears, much like darkness vanishes with the dawning of Light.

What faith it takes to move beyond inner fears and doubts and the seeming "opinions of the world" to find True Innocence within. What strength it takes to look past appearances and actions to the Love that resides inside, without taking sides or condemning any brother or sister. Yet faith is rewarded openly when we learn to truly forgive and let go of the illusions that were mistakenly held about our Self and the world. We experience a Joy not of this world!

All "relationship" conflict arises from the personal perspective of the ego. In self-deception the self-concept/body identity is held as a substitute for True Intimacy or the Union of Mind. The belief to be questioned is the belief in separation and all subsequent thoughts of rejection, betrayal, anger, and abandonment. It takes great faith to unveil what is believed to be true and to instead accept the Truth of our Self: that as a Spiritual Being we are incapable of being rejected, betrayed, or abandoned.

In a world of darkness controlled by time, images and roles shift and change by night as if part of a mad experiment. Everyone seems under the spell of sleep and forgetfulness, just vaguely remembering a distant memory of Light, of Home, though struggling to remember how to get back Home. When the plan of darkness is finally uncovered and exposed, the upside-down world is turned right-side-up and bathed in the light of Innocence in the Present Moment. There is no memory of a past in God. The games of fear and guilt are ended in the Light of True Love.

Holy Child of God, You are a Beautiful Creation of a Loving God. Let not the dreams of the world persuade You that you are unworthy of Love. You are Divine Love itself, and nothing can ever change the Real You: the One Perfect, Infinite, Magnificent, Eternal Love that You shall forever Be!

Beyond the Belief in Victimization

If there is such a thing as a "victim," there is no God. Yet since God is Real and All Loving, All Knowing, and All Powerful, victimization is impossible. What could victimization be but an illusion, a misperception? Questions about the "evil" or the "horrors" of the world are pseudo questions, for they but ask and answer from the assumption that error is real. The first question that ever seemed to be asked was asked by the ego: "Who am I?" And every question throughout history is but an illusory doubt about the Certainty of the "I Am" Presence. God is without question. Christ is without question. Follow the trail of the question to the so-called "questioner." Seeing the impossibility of the "questioner" is True Freedom, for Identity in God is beyond question.

Search and question you will while illusions seem to persist. Question what you believe, what you assume to be true. Question your perceptions and your desire for things of the world. Question the faith which has been placed in the ego. Then ask yourself if there is anything worth hanging on to that perpetuates guilt and fear and hatred. The ego made this world. Instead of questioning the seeming effects of error – the persons, events, and circumstances of the world – it is good to question the underlying error that separation is possible at all. Why question effects when their "cause" is unreal and has no foundation. God did not create the ego, so it has no Source. God created His Child as Spirit, and so Identity is Spirit. No dream of fear can veil the Truth of our Eternal Being.

I love You for such is Self Love! It cannot be difficult to accept the Truth. Illusions are difficult to maintain, for they have nothing to stand on. Let us watch them disappear like sand castles in the vast Tide of the Ocean!

Witnesses to my Fatherhood

Friend: This is a question about something I do not understand in the ACIM Text:

> With everyone whom you release from guilt great is the joy in
> Heaven, where the witnesses to your fatherhood rejoice. T-13.IX.6.9

My question is: who are these witnesses to my fatherhood? Whoever they are, they are already in Heaven. Who are these beings? Did I "father" them? And if I did "father" them, how come I am not aware of it; have I forgotten about my own spiritual children? Have my children awakened to Heaven before I have awakened? The above passage would have stimulated plenty of enlightenment if it said no more than, "With everyone whom you release from guilt great is the joy in Heaven," But the rest of the passage is completely meaningless to me, so I decided to let you know about this hole in my understanding so you can clarify what the rest of that passage means. Thanks.

David: Christ has creations that are Pure Spirit, just as God's Creation of Christ is Pure Spirit. When Christ seemed to fall asleep and forget Heaven, the creations that Christ had created or "fathered" (fathered is a synonym for created) were forgotten as well. These creations are Abstract Spirit, and there is nothing in the time-space cosmos that they even remotely resemble *because* they are Pure Spirit. These creations cannot be described or explained because their Meaning is Eternal and One with God, as is Christ. It must suffice to say that they will be Known as Thy Self and Creator are Known. In Light the darkness is forgotten, and when darkness seems to appear, the Light has simply been obscured from awareness.

Identifying and Removing Obstacles to Inner Peace

I am always happy to write about removing the blocks to the experience/ awareness of inner peace. Many sincere students and seekers cling to affirmations and metaphors and symbols only because there are unconscious fearful beliefs which remain unquestioned and hidden. Yet the consistent experience of inner peace comes only when nothing remains assumed to be real and true. If the awareness of falsity was applied equally to everything in the cosmos, without exception, there could be nothing but peace of mind. Only exceptions bring the illusion of conflict, and it becomes obvious that Truth has no exceptions.

Our Mind is holy and sacred, because Divine Mind is a creation of God. Nothing is special and no *thing* is sacred, for nothing exists apart from God's Allness and Wholeness. Love is a State of Mind that transcends the belief in differences of any kind. Love is Sameness and recognizes ItSelf. Love is whole and complete and all-encompassing. Love never deviates. Love never changes.

Errors are mental assumptions about the nature of reality. They are beliefs in the impossible and attempts to call forth witnesses to impossibility. Metaphysical errors attempt to make something in form causative, yet no form is causative and no form has "individual" existence. The parts do not make up the whole, for wholeness is real and reality cannot be broken into parts. Once the Divine Principle is grasped, it must be applied without exception to Be ItSelf. Transfer-of-training errors are only attempts to make exceptions to Absolute Truth, yet happily Truth has no exceptions.

Salvation is no compromise of any kind and non-judgment makes no compromises. Salvation might be described as leaving behind the attempt to live by two thought systems which can never coexist.

There is no such thing as partial trust, for trust is never partial. Trust must be as total and complete as the One the trust is being placed in, and faith in the Holy Spirit is always rewarded by peace of mind. Whenever you are tempted to think you know anything about this world, remember that the world was made to hide the Love of God. Then let go of the specific thought with a smile on your face, and happily relax into peace. Peace is natural to a mind that trusts.

Releasing the Ego Impulse to Blame or Change the Past

Hi David,

My motive for writing to you is for further clarification. As I am watching myself type this I am aware of feeling unsure and unsafe, with little confidence. Therefore I am also searching for reassurance that all is working together for good and that trust is deepening. Here goes: Babies are born to be dependent on humans and have something to blame for their unhappiness. This is so in an attempt to avoid responsibility for our own state of mind, which is our sole responsibility? I bring this up because I realize that I have set everything up in such a way to distract myself from relaxing into the living moment and Being in Joy!

I have chosen my family and they have chosen me. I have set it all up ... the world, family, friends, situations, circumstances, ideals, thoughts. The good news is that I am not any of these things. I am not the world. I am as God created me; Whole, Perfect, Changeless, Eternal!

Why do I seem to be so sad? I seem to be sad about having set everything up in order to prove to myself that the false self-image I made is true. Well, it is not true. I set my whole life up until now by using others and situations to prove that this lie that I made up about myself is true. This is the ego's game and I am no longer willing to play it because all it is doing is keeping me distracted from fully living in the Now.

I realize that the only way to stop playing the game is to stop running from the present moment. As I observe myself, I still have this hidden wish that the past did not happen the way I think it did. I wish that I had not set anything up with family. I wish I had not set anything up with that guy in Africa – of whom I still think about. I realize that I have a dependency on sex; a childhood rape seems to occur over and over in the mind (the seeming separation).

You have mentioned at some point last year that the form is not the problem, that it is a perceptual problem. Once again, I put everything in the Holy Spirit's hands, asked for the truth to be revealed, and trusted. I have come to the sole realization that I do not know what anything is for. Since the past did not occur the way I think it did, because in the same instant that the error seemingly occurred, the correction was made. The Holy Spirit was the correction, and I want to accept Him in my heart and let Him lead the way.

I find that I am still hard on myself. I watch and am aware of wanting everything right now. This is possible because *everything is right now* or *right now is everything*. However, I realize that I am still afraid because of all these seeming ego devices I made. But I am learning to be kind and gentle with myself. Thank you! Thank you Holy Spirit! Thank you God! Thank you to myself–for your willingness to let go and let God as you forgive yourself for what you think you did because you did not do it! Avec Amour!

Beloved One,

Thanks for pouring your heart out to me. Yes, just allow the memories and thoughts to arise in awareness, and gently be reminded that these are past thoughts floating through consciousness. The greatest ego temptation is to believe that things would have been better if they were different–and this is the desire to change the past or figure it out instead of releasing or forgiving it.

Last night I watched the movie *The Butterfly Effect*. It is a "mind watcher" that offers the forgiving lesson that it is impossible to fix characters or past memories. The main character keeps reliving scenarios and memories that were blacked out because of intense trauma and horror. Using the power of mind to remake the scenes and scenarios sends the script off in alternate directions, yet none of the life scripts offer any lasting satisfaction. Those who are destined to meet in form will meet, though the lesson in mind is always to see the past as past and the false as false. The past is over, though the ego wants the error to repeat over and over. The *dreamer of the dream* state of mind is tranquil and peaceful, and this is accepting the Atonement or Correction for the entire dream. I think you will find *The Butterfly Effect* a helpful resource in your healing.

Tonight I will, once again, be watching *Eternal Sunshine of The Spotless Mind*, a spectacular tool and symbol of memory deletion, surrender and forgiveness. Love transcends all of the perceptual memories, though the ego believes the memories *are* the love. The Light that shines beyond all perceptual memories is blazing with Eternal Love in a Spotless, Divine Mind. Beyond the temptation to judge and blame is a Love so deep and pure that the sleeping mind will rush to Love and abandon all images and trinkets the instant Love is remembered in Waking.

Pockets of Guilt

Hi David,

You say "Pockets of guilt must be exposed and voluntarily given to the Holy Spirit; as this occurs it becomes apparent that the guilt was never real."

I have tried to do this but I have doubt that I am doing it effectively. My thinking is very literal. The past that I hold in mind was very bad, violent, painful, etc. I have tried to let it go and think of it as just a really bad dream where nothing in it was real. I was/am the dreamer making everything in the dream happen. I constantly ask the Holy Spirit/Jesus to help me with everything I do.

This is on my mind almost every waking hour. It is like an obsession to "find my way home." I realize that there is nothing here in this world that is worth anything at all. I asked Holy Spirit about all the problems I seem to have. This is a simplified version of what I believe I got: I have only one problem, and that problem is that I believe that I can be separate from God. All other problems stem from this one belief and are only distractions to keep me from looking at the original problem. For if I look at the original problem, reason will tell me that it is impossible for me to be separate from God. I think this is true but I am not sure.

This leads me back to the letting-go-of-guilt idea. I have guilt for something that did not happen. It did not happen because it has no cause. But I can believe it happened, which does not make it real but generates guilt. Is this not insanity? How do I bring guilt for something that never happened to light and give it to the Holy Spirit? How do I know that I have been successful at this? I do not want anything to keep my mind from being healed, from awakening from the dream.

Hello Beloved One,

Thanks for writing. Your desire to find your way Home is a powerful force; it is pushing all the attack thoughts into awareness. You can relax, there is no need to feel like it is an obsession, since you are giving your mind permission to let the beliefs and thoughts surface. What you are hearing from the Holy Spirit is true:

"I have only one problem, and that problem is that I believe that I can be separate from God. All other problems stem from this one belief and are only distractions to keep me from looking at the original problem. For if I look at the original problem reason will tell me that it is impossible for me to be separate from God."

All of the "surface issues," which are form problems, were made to distract the mind from looking within at the beliefs. Think of the mind like concentric circles with desire in the center. The next ring is belief, followed by thought, followed by emotion, followed by perception. The inner areas determine the outer. You are using your desire (center) to Wake Up as the incentive to question everything you believe, and as false belief is dissolved the thoughts that sprang from the ego are released as well. This in turn releases fearful emotions and perceptions. This is why ACIM talks so frequently about the little willingness – it is this splinter of desire to Awaken (joined with the Holy Spirit) that ignites the undoing of the ego.

The Holy Spirit is the "how," and miracles, or shifts in perception, are the means. Cause and effect are getting turned back around and this means you are becoming aware that mind is causative. Quickly give over these thoughts to the Holy Spirit and He will show you that the thoughts had no real effects.

Pockets of guilt are fixed beliefs that have not been questioned and are still assumed to be true. The base of these beliefs is the belief that time is linear instead of simultaneous. As the pockets of guilt are released, peace returns to awareness. You will know of your mind training "success" by the peace you feel.

Forgiveness is Natural; Judgment is Impossible

Forgiveness is the most natural thought that relates to this world. To release what never was cannot be difficult. To give up what one never had is funny to behold. The joke of the world is very funny when one sees it as nothing.

How could a Child of God judge, since Creation knows not of judgment? And what is Creation but God's Beloved Child? Judgment is impossible in One Being, for there is nothing to "judge between" in Oneness. Such is Love. Love precludes the possibility of judgment. That is why forgiveness is so very easy. As a reflection of Love, forgiveness is the realization of the impossibility of judgment, condemnation or attack. How could there ever be an opposite to Love? The Law of Love is the Only Law, the Only Being!

God does not forgive, for God has never condemned. Forgiveness is the only need of this world, for forgiveness sees its impossibility. It cannot be difficult to overlook what is not there. And since Love is real, where could a world of separation really be? Nowhere indeed!

Rejoice and be exceedingly glad, for the time of illusions has passed. Forgiveness only seemed radical to the ego, the thought that never was. Forgiveness is the most easy, natural concept that can ever be learned, for once learned it disappears as well. Forgiveness is forgotten once it is learned, for Reality is all that "remains." All is One Being–Love! And Thank You God for creating Love as One forever! Amen.

Irritability

As you progress with your study and application of ACIM, you will be increasingly aware that a twinge of irritability or frustration is the same as intense anger or rage since there are only two emotions with regard to this world. The wide ranges of emotions that seem to be experienced in this world are variations of Love's reflection (alignment with God) or variations of fear (alignment with ego).

Wrong-mindedness is the experience of illusion as if it was real and regardless of the degree or direction of the error, the mistake is the same. This is why there is no order of difficulty in miracles and no hierarchy of illusions. Right-mindedness is the solution to wrong-mindedness, regardless of the form the mistake may seem to take.

If irritability or frustration arise at times, it is best to treat them the same as any upsetting emotion, situation or thought. Use your daily Workbook lesson as instructed by Jesus and apply it to whatever you are feeling.

The lessons aim at transfer of the Divine Principle to every situation and thought and emotion you seem to experience, to make way for the Vision of Christ. When the mind training exercises in undoing (learning complete forgiveness) are completely transferred to everything and everyone without exception, a complete conversion or transformation of awareness will result. This is the learning goal of ACIM, and it requires nothing less than unlearning everything you believe about yourself and the world.

Happily we are joined in the same Purpose and can ultimately experience only the Love that We are right Now. The mind watching is continuous and the vigilance Asked for by Holy Spirit remains essential until the realization dawns that Love has no opposite. Let us hide no thought or belief or emotion from the healing Light of Love and trust the Holy Spirit to lead the way.

Look Upon the Full Extent of Hatred, Then Let it Go

Hi David,

I am tired of ACIM. I have been studying it for over eight years. I have been going to Course groups. I have been practicing both forgiveness and seeing the face of Christ in my brothers and sisters. I have more than "a little willingness" to be guided by the Holy Spirit to see my oneness with God. I feel that I have been at the point of the "last step" for a long time. I have been waiting for Jesus, or somebody, to take me across that little bridge into the garden of joy and inner peace promised by the Course. I know that I cannot make it happen, and that it has to be done for me.

I have met over one hundred Course students, including you. But you are the only one whom I regard as enlightened. Now it seems to me that the Course is a lottery game. Only one out of 100, or 1000, or more ever wins the prize of Christ's final guidance into that garden. What kind of God is it that plays with us like this?

Beloved One,

Thanks for offering what is on your heart. We will lift it up together to the Holy Spirit.

Frustration and anger are the ego's reactions to the "god" it made, a "god" that plays with humans and grants "enlightenment" to only a select few in history. If this were God, then God would be cruel instead of loving—and you and I would be human. Our reality is Spirit and lives forever and ever and ever! The real God Wills only Perfect Love and Happiness and has nothing to do with dreams of games and numbers and groups. God is abstract, and to know God in Spirit is to remember the abstract. But first the forgiveness of illusions (seeing the false as false) is necessary.

It takes "great willingness" to see that all events, encounters, and circumstances are helpful – to see that all things work together for good. There is no amount of evidence that will convince a mind of what it does not want. Yet, since there is only One Mind, the experience of Love must be extended to be Itself. Love Is. One can seem to be aware of Love or not aware of Love. The latter is the illusion and must be forgiven or released. I am joined with you in this and we cannot fail to recognize God's Plan for salvation, for only this is possible. This is what is meant by sayings like: With God all things are possible; If God is with us who can be against us?

I have devoted everything to sharing and extending the experience of Enlightenment, and this is a natural expression of the Love I feel within. What I am I proclaim for everyone, for we are the same – not different. We have the same Source. We are the same Spirit. We are the same Self. Enlightenment is a State of Mind that looks upon the world from the inner experience of peace and sees no world apart from mind. I see our Innocence and I rejoice that Love is real! We are the same One!

The anger and frustration that seem to be surfacing in awareness for you need not be repressed. You must look upon the full extent of hatred before letting it go. In this sense, anger cannot be denied but must instead be exposed before it can be released to the Holy Spirit. The Holy Spirit cannot take away what is protected from awareness and must wait until the anger is willingly offered up. This is the meaning of: *Would you rather be right or happy?* Identity confusion is the root of all anger, and no self-image or concept will stand in the Light of Truth.

I am joined with you in emptying the mind of all false idols, images, and concepts, for God Wills that Light and Love extend forever and ever in limitless and infinite Being. This is truly Natural. Holy are You, Eternal, Free, and Whole, at peace forever in the Heart of God.

At one point, Helen asked Jesus to take her fear away. Jesus told her, in essence, that he could not do that because that would be tampering with the most basic law of cause and effect. He could, however, help her with removing the limits placed on the mind that were producing the fear. That is what I have to say to you. Your mind is as powerful as mine for we share the same mind. You cannot wake yourself, *and* there is nobody outside your mind who can Awaken you. We can, however, look together at the beliefs that produce the anger and frustration, that they may be exposed and released. And finally it all comes down to desire. Truth will be restored to awareness by your desire, as it was lost by your desire for something else. Desire calls forth witnesses. Here are some messages from the Course that witness to the help and clarity I am pointing to with the words I have shared:

> You may complain that this course is not sufficiently specific for you to understand and use. Yet perhaps you have not done what it specifically advocates. This is not a course in the play of ideas, but in their practical application. Nothing could be more specific than to be told that if you ask you will receive. The Holy Spirit will answer every specific problem as long as you believe that problems are specific. His answer is both many and one, as long as you believe that the one is many. You may be afraid of His specificity, for fear of what you think it will demand of you. Yet only by asking will you learn that nothing of God demands anything of you. God gives; He does not take. When you refuse to ask, it is because you believe that asking is taking rather than sharing. T-11.VIII.5

> Think not that happiness is ever found by following a road away from it. This makes no sense, and cannot be the way. To you who seem to find this course to be too difficult to learn, let me repeat that to achieve a goal you must proceed in its direction, not away from it. And every road that leads the other way will not advance the purpose to be found. If this be difficult to understand, then is this course impossible to learn. But only then. For otherwise, it is a simple teaching in the obvious. T-31.IV.7

> When you fail to comply with the requirements of this course, you have merely made a mistake. This calls for correction, and for nothing else. To allow a mistake to continue is to make additional mistakes, based on the first and reinforcing it. It is this process that must be laid aside, for it is but another way in which you would defend illusions against the truth. W-95.9

> Salvation is no compromise of any kind. To compromise is to accept but part of what you want; to take a little and give up the rest. Salvation gives up nothing. It is complete for everyone. Let the idea of compromise but enter, and the awareness of salvation's purpose is lost because it is not recognized. It is

denied where compromise has been accepted, for compromise is the belief salvation is impossible. It would maintain you can attack a little, love a little, and know the difference. Thus it would teach a little of the same can still be different, and yet the same remain intact, as one. Does this make sense? Can it be understood? This course is easy just because it makes no compromise. Yet it seems difficult to those who still believe that compromise is possible. T-23.III.3-4

This course will be believed entirely or not at all. For it is wholly true or wholly false, and cannot be but partially believed. And you will either escape from misery entirely or not at all. Reason will tell you that there is no middle ground where you can pause uncertainly, waiting to choose between the joy of Heaven and the misery of hell. Until you choose Heaven, you are in hell and misery. T-22.II.7

I am Guided to encourage you to revisit the epilogue of the *Clarification of Terms* section of the Course, as well as the closing five paragraphs of the *Song of Prayer*. Like a gentle caress, these beautiful passages call upon the mind to leave behind its "dreams of malice" and receive "the sweet embrace of everlasting Love and perfect peace."

Chapter Five

Releasing the Pain of the Past

Hi David,

Thank you for your kind words. I had wanted to ask a question when we saw you, but felt it was not appropriate and would be too difficult to ask. I will try and phrase the question to you without a long, drawn-out story.

As a child, I was raised in a family that was involved in a ritualistic organization. People would call it a satanic cult. Talk about the ugliness of the ego – it was personified in these people. All the horrors of abuse, torture, etc. were my life growing up on a daily basis. I won't get into the details. My mother and most of the extended family are practicing to this day. My brother is now also involved with them. My father killed himself when I was 10; I believe it was because he could not handle the guilt. I stopped all contact with them six years ago once I remembered they were involved with this. I have gone through extensive therapy, which has been ongoing for the past 18 years. I stopped having memories of the events and abuse that took place about three years ago. My journey has been incredible, and despite the obvious excruciating pain of surviving this as a child and reliving it through therapy to heal, I would not change my life. It has made me a strong person and I know I chose my life. I could not have survived this experience, and did pass over twice and was brought back at the ages of 7 and 17 at the hands of my mother. I know all this has a purpose. I know I chose this life and that God is with me every step of the way.

Yet, the fear of my mother and the things that were done to me seem so deep and affect so many areas of my life I do not know how to heal what feels like a humongous all-consuming fear and guilt within me. I have even had a holy instant of knowing my mother is my teacher and that she did nothing to me. But I am still afraid of her on what seems to be almost a cellular level. Throughout the 18 years, I have prayed and worked on forgiveness, asking for the grace to forgive her. But I know that as long as I am afraid of her I have not forgiven her. Consequently, this fear affects every area of my life. I cannot seem to get past it. Ultimately it is a fear of God and the guilt of the separation. Is there anything you might be able to tell me to help me heal this? I do not want this to rule my life anymore and I do not want to give my power away to this anymore. My mother is in a horribly dark place and cannot experience God's love; she is so shut down. It is painful to be cut off from all of that part of the family, but I have an incredible family with my husband and children and I feel very blessed. Studying the Course has been my greatest blessing and healing.

I do not know if this makes any sense to you. It is always on my mind and I feel like my life is defined by it even though I know that is not true. On this level, as a human being, it is a huge forgiveness lesson and one I want to get. Anything you can tell me would be greatly appreciated. Thank you again for all of the blessings you give with your work for God.

Beloved One,

Though your experiences and memories were very intense, you have a more accurate sense of the madness and depth of insanity of the ego. This has helped give you an impetus and calling to forgive the illusion and recognize the truth. The intensity is always a motivator to find another way of perceiving, and this disillusionment is always a helpful first step toward transcending the ego. Now the inner healing work must be nurtured, and it is very helpful to focus on all you have to be grateful for. The biological family was just a starting point or launching pad for the glorious experience of Communion with God to come. Be grateful that through the acting out of the ego, the mind did reach a turning point and has begun the inner journey to healing and wholeness.

Trust that as you accept the Correction for the error, everyone will be freed with you; when perception is healed, all is forgiven.

Dear David,

Thank you. Your response brought tears to my eyes and peace to my heart. I know my forgiveness will also release all those I hold on to as "hurting" me. I wish peace for them and peace for me. Thank you for reminding me of that. I know my experience will help someone else. I have had the opportunity to share and help someone heal that had the same experience. That was the most peaceful feeling—to know there is a reason I chose my life, even if it was just giving one person the hope that we can do anything and survive anything with the love and guidance of God.

Releasing Betrayal and Hurts

Hi David,

I have a question in which I would like your insight. I am having difficulty coming to Peace with my husband's leaving me and my nine-year-old son and going off with another woman who he is married to now, after our divorce.

In the beginning my mantra was "I choose Peace instead of this" and I was handling it for a while, but then I just fell apart. I feel more stable now though there is a lot yet to be released. Can you give me a way to let go of my ego's holding onto his betrayal, deception, breaking of vows, and hurtful threats? I realize the deeper the attachment, the deeper the letting go. Please help!

Beloved One,

Thanks for opening up and sharing what is on your mind. Aligning with the ego, in any regard, always invites the illusion of hurt to make itself at home in an illusion of self. Hurt always comes from the belief that something of the world can bring lasting peace and happiness or take it away.

Divorce and marriage are terms that refer to separation and union, respectively. True Union is the Christ Mind in Union with the Mind of God and is literally All That Is, far beyond the illusion of time-space. Think of forgiveness as representing Union on earth, and special relationships as representing hell on earth.

Christ devotes nine chapters of ACIM (from the end of Chapter 15 to the beginning of Chapter 24) to learning to distinguish between the ego's purpose for relationship and the Holy Spirit's Purpose. The ego sponsors special relationships to maintain itself, and the Holy Spirit offers the holy relationship as a safe substitute for what the ego made. "Betrayal, deception, breaking of vows and hurtful threats" are experiences of the special love relationship and the desire for some body outside of mind to fulfill and make oneself whole. Trust that when one door seems to close another opportunity to forgive is presented.

What you have written reflects the way the Awakening seems to go: "I realize the deeper the attachment, the deeper the letting go." The Holy Spirit would have you realize that peace and happiness and love and joy and freedom are not circumstance dependent. Ego attachment will never satisfy, and with each letting go, the awareness of the Truth within comes closer. Be happy for the release of attachment, for you shall know the Truth and in Truth You are free as the Christ. Teach this in every seeming situation, in countless opportunities, and the realization will dawn – I am still as God created Me. Love does not possess. Love has no object. These are the simple lessons salvation teaches, for Divine Love knows Eternity and has no limits or conditions on Its Giving and Receiving.

Be grateful for every emotion and belief that is flushed up, for nothing real veils the Love of God. As the ego is exposed it becomes apparent that the special relationship offers nothing and the holy relationship always offers a reflection of the Kingdom of Heaven.

Aspire only to holy relationship and pray to release all grievances that block the Light from awareness. Offer this blessing to everyone, including your former husband, and you will feel the blessing in your heart. Forgiveness is always a gift to our Self for it releases the illusions of an ego self that could never be. You are deeply Loved Beloved One.

Upsets, Values, and Beliefs

David: Does anybody have anything they are wrestling with other than communication? We can go into that.

Friend: For me it is about communication and control. It seems I have control issues lately.

David: How have they been expressing themselves? How are you perceiving them?

Friend: There are a bunch of things that seem to disturb my peace. First, I was irritated by things that happened at the restaurant where I work. We were so busy, and the cooks, waiters, and other staff were yelling at each other and yelling for managers. There was no teamwork. It broke down to an *every man for himself* kind of thing. I was trying to encourage people by giving them pats on their backs and telling them they were doing great, yet I was feeling I did not want to stay in that environment for very long. I was thinking it was not worth it to me for a few dollars. Physically I felt tired from standing in one place for that long, and it was hot in there. But I think all of those things could have been overlooked so much more if people had just encouraged each other and communicated. Also, they were throwing parsley on the plate just for the sake of having parsley on the plate, and it all seemed so phony. I had a hard time with that.

Then I had another issue with my partner. She wanted me to wax the van. I think she got it in her head that it should be something I should do to contribute. I said, "I will wax the van with you but I feel we are getting into expectations here and that van is a large vehicle and it would go a lot quicker if two people were doing it." She came and did it. Towards the end, I brought up the issue that the van is big, it is going to take more time and money to maintain, and it gets poor gas mileage. Then I questioned: "Why do we really need it?" She said, "I do not have to answer that. I like the van and that is good enough." I became frustrated that she would not even talk about it. She said, "Look, why should I talk about it? We are not going to sell the van." I was saying, "It is not about selling the van. I just want to talk about why you think you need it." After I had thought about it I came back and said, "I am sure it is not about the van but I am feeling upset about something, and it seems to be the van that is the focal point right now. The bottom line is that I think we need to be communicating." We came together with the group in a session and things got a little bit better and we felt good, but if we just stop there and say we are on separate paths and we are just going to live in this house and not communicate, I think things are going to break down again. She seemed to agree with that but said she was not going to run to the group every time I thought there was a problem. She basically said that she does not get anything out of the sessions.

David: We keep coming back to choice and we keep coming back to beliefs. I have talked about how you have to retrace the steps up the spiral to go up, so maybe we can talk more about the spiral, about what that spiral is. The beginning of Chapter 24 is a good starting point. Let's look at control. Perhaps in your case there is a perceived control issue about waxing the van, or maybe there are control issues about money or about things at work. Everyone seems to experience control issues all the time. They seem to take on so many different forms. Chapter 24 talks about decisions, and it talks about beliefs:

> To learn this course requires willingness to question every value that you hold. Not one can be kept hidden and obscure but it will jeopardize your learning. No belief is neutral. Everyone has the power to dictate each decision you make. For a decision is a conclusion based on everything that you believe. It is the outcome of belief, and follows it as surely as does suffering follow guilt and freedom sinlessness. T-24.in.2

All these decision points—whether or not to go for a job interview, or whether to send another resume here or there, or to wax the van or not—these are all just pseudo decisions. It is humbling to begin to realize that all seeming decisions in this world are just pseudo decisions. Like a computer program, the beliefs are part of what has already been programmed in. The running of the program depends on what has been loaded into the memory. You may often feel like a chicken with your head cut off because the program already seems to be loaded in; it seems to be executed and running, like a robot, even though there seem to be struggles about specific things that are taking place. A decision is a conclusion based on everything that you believe. Everything that you believe in a given instant determines the decision you make. A decision can be as small as whether to put parsley on a plate or not.

Friend: It seems arbitrary but it is not. Who cares if there is parsley on a plate?

David: In one sense it is total determinism. People say that the environment determines what we do, but we are going much deeper. It is the belief system that determines what you do every instant. A control issue which seems to be between persons is really the first belief that was taken seriously—the belief in separation from God. Tons of substitutions have been layered onto that, to try to compensate, to try to alleviate the guilt of that first belief. There are stacks and stacks and stacks of beliefs in the mind.

As I went deeper I started to sense that I wanted to be totally free of it all. I thought: *How can I be free of it as long as I am in relationships, the way I perceive them?* I perceived that control seemed to be involved in every kind of relationship, whether it was parent-child relationships, husband-wife relationships, boyfriend-girlfriend relationships, employer-employee relationships or even friendships.

For me it has been helpful to see that I have constructed this world in which I believe I am this person or this body. I believe that I am in all these kinds of relationships and situations, yet it is all made up based on the beliefs that I hold onto. It became apparent that there cannot be total integrity as long as there seems to be a dependency or reliance on persons, places or things that are on the screen. How can I have a total sense of integrity if I have to answer to anything or anyone on the screen, no matter who it appears to be, whether it is the United States government, a husband or a wife, a boyfriend or a girlfriend, or a parent? I think you can see, as I saw initially, that this is really going to take a thorough examination of everything in order to unplug. How can I participate in the world as if I am a part of the world, *and* be free of the world? I cannot! There is no reconciling mind with playing a game or a role there.

Everything we talk about is going to be about questioning the beliefs one has about the world and oneself. The beliefs you hold about the world and the beliefs you hold about yourself are identical. It is not like you are just dealing with a little personality. The whole cosmos is your self-concept. It is not that you have to somehow be free of and transcend the little personality. It is not like there is a little mask, and if you could just figure out how to lay aside the mask, you could be a true, genuine, authentic person. The whole world and the whole cosmos as it is constructed – the belief in economics, the belief in politics, the belief in medicine and sickness – the whole thing is the self-concept! None of it is true. None of it has any reality. If you believe in part of it, you really believe in all of it, since it is one. There is no way to give up any shred of it without having to really give up everything. When we read, "To learn this Course requires willingness to question every value that you hold," T-24.in.2 we are talking about every value – every single value!

Friend: And under every value is a belief, because I have to believe that it has some value. There has to be an ordering. If there is a value on anything, I have to have ordered it, and I have to have fit it somewhere into my hierarchy of high or low?

David: Literally, it is all or nothing. If the belief in separation is where this control issue is really rooted, and the belief in separation is what seems to maintain this whole world of illusion, then the whole world has to be questioned to come to an end of this authority problem or this control issue. As long as I believe I can make myself – as long as I believe that this menagerie of images is mine to choose from, then I am denying that my only real choice is to accept my reality as Spirit. That is where the control issues are going to seem to spring up over and over again. The problem will seem to keep coming. It is not about any specific issue of control, whether it be finances or relationships, or the government. It is not about the system; it is not about anything that it seems to have been about. It is about me believing that I can make myself, instead of accepting my reality as I was created.

Friend: And it is also not about avoiding the system or just saying: *I am not going to deal with any of those things out there.* When I was talking with my friend today at lunch, one of the things that came up was that you are always seeing what you believe. So if you look with the body's eyes and listen with the body's ears, you are just seeing and hearing what you believe. It is not like there'll be a time lag, like you will change your mind and then a few days later or a few minutes later you will see a corresponding change in form. You are always looking upon a world which represents what the mind believes, and it is nuts! Jesus was saying that whenever you are upset it can seem like, as in lessons 5, 6 and 7: "I am never upset for the reason I think." I think I am upset because it is so fast-paced here. I think I am upset because waiters are shouting at cooks and vice versa. I think I am upset because they are throwing things on plates, but I am never upset for the reason I think. I am upset because I see something that is not there. That puts it into a whole new context. I am seeing a world that does not exist. That is upsetting.

David: Hallucinating is upsetting.

Friend: And believing the hallucinations is upsetting.

David: That is the upsetting part. It is not anything specific. The flip side would be: *Oh, I am so peaceful. I am sitting here watching the waves come in, and I am listening to the waves lap on the shore.* You could even construct that as: *This is a much more peaceful environment than the wild Saturday night scene at the restaurant,* but you are still seeing a world that is not there; that is what is upsetting. The lessons continue on: "A meaningless world engenders fear." W-53.3 Why does it engender fear? It engenders fear because it is unreliable. The world being experienced through the five senses is totally unreliable. It seems to always be changing; there is no stability to it. It seems chaotic. That is what makes it seem fearful; that is what makes it seem…. You can fill in the blank with any derivative of fear.

Putting the Ideas into Practice

David: If the Course is not practical, if you cannot apply it to your life, then what good does it do? If there are any questions or issues in your life that you feel comfortable talking about as you perceive them, we can trace them back into the mind. That is how we can get at some of the beliefs and misperceptions.

It is like a spiritual psychotherapy. Basically, you do not go to a therapist and say: *Oh, I do not know what to believe about God and the nature of the universe.* There is probably a pretty specific group of problems you start with. What the therapist calls the "presenting problems," are the things the patient has to start off with. Since everyone who believes in this world believes they have specific problems, these can be used as a springboard to work them back into the mind. It can be a very helpful tool.

Friend: I have this tendency to start brightly in the morning, feeling good, reading the Course and feeling connected to God. With the way my work and circumstances are set up these days, I might not say "boo" to anybody until five o'clock. I practice a lot and I prepare for my lessons and recitals. I do not go to an office for work. I have time to read and really get into the things that I am reading. But there seems to be a pattern that around five o'clock it all starts to fall apart. I put it all away, forget it and run out and have an ego party; I start to feel down, or I go out and get ice cream or something like that. By nightfall everything is different. It is kind of like an alcoholic who wants to stop drinking but keeps *choosing* to drink. In my case, I would not have it this way but yet I would. How can I move through that? I realize in moments of clarity that when I am ready to let it go, I will let it go. It will be gone. But I often choose to retain painful patterns of behavior; sometimes I really prefer to stay in a state of pain. I want to move through that.

David: You are describing your day as having two parts. The initial part of the day is about working, studying, reading, going deeply into things, sometimes not seeing anybody until five o'clock. Then you seem to feel satiated, like you have just got to break out. Again it is the same dichotomy whereby the ego breaks the day into two parts; for you, the first part is before 5pm, and the second part is after 5pm. In the Monday to Friday workday world it is common to have a sense of "my time" and "their time;" when five o'clock comes around it is "my time." *I cannot wait until the weekend. Thank God it is Friday.* These are common expressions. There are categories that the ego uses to break things up as if there was a "my time" and a "their time," and a "study time" and a "party time." The more we lay aside judgment and take on the Holy Spirit's function the more it is God's time all the time.

I remember last time you said, "My God, the thoughts that go through my mind when I am practicing!" You were aware of all these judgment thoughts. What it comes down to is a 24-hour-a-day, 7-day-a-week job, so to speak, in that the mind is very active and very powerful. These judgment thoughts are like trains. You hop on the train for a while and when you try meditating you are able to hop off, but before you know it you are back on another train like, *I told so-and-so that I was going to do that today. I had better get going because if I do not do it …* or, *Why did she have to do that?* You hop on these trains and ride them. In your case you practice and study until you cannot read another line and then you go out and whoop it up. It is all about the form/content distinction. It is a matter of getting in touch with and watching those thoughts. While all this seems to be happening on the screen, you are learning to notice the backward, constricting thoughts that are fear-based, thoughts like: *I should do this or else the consequences will be this or that.* The majority of thoughts in the untrained mind have the fear of consequences behind them.

Friend: Who administers the consequences? We do ourselves. Nobody is there to bash you; you are bashing yourself.

David: It can seem as if there are other people. For instance, if you talk with your mother on the phone every day and you decide that today you have something else you want to do, it may seem that mom has a reaction. *Why didn't you call me?* It seems as if people are doing things to us and that events completely beyond our control are taking place. The mind in a deceived state says: *I am innocent. I did not deserve to be treated like that person treated me,* when in actuality the deceived mind believes it has separated from God; it has guilt. It actually believes it pulled off the impossible. It believes it was able to usurp the ability of God and to pull away from the Kingdom of Heaven, to leave the Garden of Eden. It really is convinced of this. It is a horrifying thought, a really guilty thought. The Course says that it is not true. The Holy Spirit is gently reminding the mind that it is OK; *Your Father loves you. You could never pull off such a silly thing as usurping your Father's ability or taking over God's role as the Creator.*

It is silly but the mind is convinced that the separation has occurred. It projects that thought out onto the screen, which is the world, and calls forth witnesses to reinforce the belief that it is guilty. It believes it is guilty and calls forth witnesses. Then by its interpretation of what seems to be happening on the screen it is convinced of its guilt. There seem to be mean people and evil forces, when really it is just the mind calling forth witnesses to its belief that it is guilty. The good news is that when you start to get past the insanity of the false beliefs and let go of the guilt, the mind is healed. The healed mind calls forth witnesses that show guilt is not real. You start to see everything as a holy encounter. That is the good news. Remember it gets back to the *interpretation*—that is the only thing that changes.

Friend: I have an example of that. During the first year I was teaching there was a little boy in my class who was extremely irritating to me. My supervisor directed me to move him to the front-row and to pat him on the back or stroke his hair or take his hand or make some kind of contact every time I went by him, to let him know that I was learning to care about him. I did so, and he began to change. But do you suppose it was *he* who really began to change? He was still the same kid of course, and behaved, I am sure, in exactly the same way. But I changed the way I thought about him. At the end of the year he was the only child I cried over when we said goodbye. The Course says that changing your behavior does not help because it is in your mind. And yet sometimes introducing a behavior seems to have an effect on your mind. Or does it?

David: It is never that way; that would be part of the backwards thinking. What the Course *is* saying is that when you change your mind and are willing to see something differently—your interpretation of the situation is different. Behaviors change automatically because of the change of interpretation. This does not mean we have the power to change other people's behavior.

Metaphorically you and all your brothers have equal minds; you are equally powerful. No brother has a more powerful or less powerful mind than another. In that sense you cannot influence your brother's mind positively or negatively.

> I have already indicated that you cannot ask me to release you from fear. I know it does not exist, but you do not. If I intervened between your thoughts and their results, I would be tampering with a basic law of cause and effect; the most fundamental law there is. I would hardly help you if I depreciated the power of your own thinking. T-2.VII.1

Your thoughts are causative and the thoughts you choose determine your state of mind. He is saying here that your mind is as powerful as his, and that he cannot tinker with that basic law of cause and effect. He cannot take your fear away but he can help guide you and show you your misperceptions and help you erase them from your mind; this will reduce the fear. With the Holy Spirit he helps you discern between the true and the false, so that you will be able to recognize the false as false and let it go.

That sure is a different interpretation than seeing Jesus as a deity on a higher level. He is an elder brother that is equal to us always, except in time. He seems to be higher on the vertical axis of rising up to God and laying aside the ego, but the vertical axis is in time and time is an illusion. Time is part of the ego's system, so in fact we are complete equals.

Friend: In our friend's case, when her boss basically ordered her to make a change in her behavior, she was really ordering her to make a change in her mind? And when she affected a change in behavior, perhaps the part of her mind that recognizes love recognized the change in behavior as representing what was already in her mind?

David: "Changes are required in the minds of God's teachers." M-9.1 When one has willingness for a shift of mind it may seem like externals are the impetus or the push. Take for example someone who feels too afraid to leave their job even though they really want to. It goes on and on and on like that until they eventually get fired. It could seem that getting fired from that job was the impetus to move on but that is just an interpretation. It always comes back to the mind; it all has to do with the willingness to open up to the Holy Spirit. Everything that occurs is coming from a decision in the mind but the mind quickly forgets the decision and whatever is out-pictured can seem to be what triggered the change. But it always comes back to our own responsibility.

Friend: Do you find that people who want to take full responsibility, and yet still believe in the illusion, start feeling even guiltier because they know they are responsible?

David: Yes, that is level confusion. I think the most common issue I find as I travel around is with sickness. Here you are, using a tool that says everything is a decision in your mind. You start to see that there is no external God punishing you or zapping you with AIDS or cancer, etc. You see more and more that the medical model does not really do anything. The Course is saying there is nothing outside in the world that is bringing any of this about. That is a big turnaround.

If everything is a decision and I have the ability to make those decisions, then when sickness comes up the ego is very happy to see the mind go through a guilt trip: *I am sick, oh my gosh! I am making myself sick.* But that really is level confusion because it is still a misidentification with the "I." *I am making myself sick* – self meaning the body, the tiny idea of myself. The mind still believes it is a little person; that is where the mistake is. We are infinite; we are magnitude; we are Spirit; we are abstract light. People who have had near-death experiences talk about a brilliant white light of unconditional love; in a sense, the Course is saying that is what your true identity is. The Christ is Spirit Created in the image of the Father. The Father is Spirit, the Son is Spirit.

The Father is infinite, the Son is infinite. But with sickness the tendency is to think: *I am responsible!* If you put the principle of self-responsibility together with, *look what I am doing*–there is guilt. It is still a misperception of who I think I am; it is misidentification.

The medical model tells us there are operations and pills, etc., that are necessary for good health but the Course calls all of that "magic." It is really about watching our thoughts and letting go of the ego thought system. Of course in the ego's system there are lots of external things that are "magic," but the Course is not anti-magic. It is not like pills and surgery and all these things are bad. Basically, if you are too frightened to open up to the Holy Spirit and have a mind-shift or a miracle, perhaps you need a mix of magic and miracles. Sometimes the mind can be in such a fearful state that it is too closed down to the Holy Spirit. You can have a mix of magic and miracle. You will go along and keep getting better. Your mind will get more highly trained, and there will come a time when you will be open to the mind-shift and the symptoms or pain will disappear. That is where the mind training comes in.

I have had miracles where there has been an instantaneous shift in my mind and symptoms left my body that same instant. Those are very powerful personal witnesses for me that the Course is not fooling. For example, there are thoughts that it will take 24 or 48 hours to get over the flu. But you can have such a powerful shift that all the symptoms–the nausea, the diarrhea, everything–disappear in an instant. That shows you the power of the mind.

Going Beyond the Obvious, Part 1
Wanting the Experience

David: As you become a better "forgetter," you become better at remembering. Forgetting helps you remember. As you forget the world–the ego belief system–you simultaneously remember Heaven; you remember right-mindedness.

Friend: Even when we get to this depth, I still have this sense that I want to know more, I want to go further. That is when I become really aware of the fear of letting go of the world, of the familiar; like this room here with these bodies, all that seems comfortable. It feels like I need some reassurance that what is real is going to be familiar. I can read the words but I have not had the experience yet. I keep hoping for an intermediate experience to assure me it is okay to let go of the world.

David: If you want it, how can you not have it? Desire is at the center, desire is your altar. All beliefs, thoughts, emotions, and perceptions spring forth from desire. When your altar is defiled, you have beliefs that are not of God; you have thoughts that do not come from God; you have emotions that do not have anything to do with God. You have perceptions on the outer ring that may seem comfortable and familiar, but they are distorted, twisted, and very unstable. How can you not have what you truly desire? The only thing you really need to have is that desire, that willingness.

The reasoning of the world says that you are the cause of what I do. While you attack I must be innocent – as if there was a cause or attack outside one's own mind. The Course says that this "… seems sensible, because it looks as if the world were hurting you. And so it seems as if there is no need to go beyond the obvious in terms of cause." T-27.VII.3 In the next line he says: "There is indeed a need." When you feel tired, the mind figures that the reason is because you only had so many hours of sleep, or you did not have the proper food or exercise. All those things are part of the thinking of the world. When you feel a lack of energy, or a sense of preferring to have a nice, breezy, relaxing day rather than looking at your mind so closely – that is because the mind believes there is no need to go beyond the obvious in terms of cause.

People may say they need to surround themselves with Course students, as if somehow having other bodies around that are using Course words would magically intensify one's desire to study the Course. You may think that, but what happens when people come together in community to try to live the Course? The very thing they thought would intensify their desire makes them run for the corners saying, *Get me out of here!* They do not really want to look so closely at their own thoughts and beliefs. It may seem as if there is no need to go beyond the obvious in terms of cause, but there is indeed a need to go beyond the obvious!

Friend: To go beyond the backward thinking.

David: Yes. You say you would like some intermediate experiences, not just the words. You can think of words as tools and symbols for the mind. They are just symbolic. Everything you are hearing has just the meaning you give to it. If your desire becomes single, focused, intense, and clear, then everything you perceive will be a witness to that. You will be able to hear the Holy Spirit in everything. All things are echoes of the Voice for God. All things are lessons that God would have me learn. That turns it around from thinking the words in these sessions are separate from the experience. For me experience is not apart from the words. When I have my intention to be truly helpful, the words just flow – they are just symbolic of the experience. What I am feeling is the experience and the words are like offshoots of that experience.

Let's look at the idea, "The truth is true, and nothing else is true." W-152.3 It is a nice idea and yet as long as there is still backward thinking involving exercise, food, sexuality, etc., as long as you believe there is something causative in the world, then what meaning does that idea have? It may sound good but if your experience is divorced from it then we need to investigate everything that seems to stand in the way of that being your experience.

Friend: This morning I was feeling tired and depressed, feeling like I do not have any future. I have gotten rid of this projected future and yet I am not sure what I have replaced it with. Then I knew that if I followed that out, the depression cannot be all there is. It does not all culminate in a sad ending. There *has* to be a way out of this. I started to think about how I really have to stick with being on purpose, and I do feel much better now.

David: This morning in our logistics meeting a mission statement came through as a short, concise, little thing: "God Is." If you feel depressed, like you have no future, well there you go – that can be your anchor! God Is.

Going Beyond the Obvious, Part 2
Seeing the Problem As It Is

David: "Now you are being shown you *can* escape. All that is needed is you look upon the problem as it is, and not the way that you have set it up." We are back to seeing that the problem is in the mind. Wrong-mindedness is the problem; right-mindedness is the solution. Right-mindedness is seeing the problem as it is. Wrong-mindedness is the way you have set it up: seeing problems as specific, in the world, and involving personhood in some way.

> How could there be another way to solve a problem that is very simple, but has been obscured by heavy clouds of complication, which were made to keep the problem unresolved? Without the clouds the problem will emerge in all its primitive simplicity. The choice will not be difficult, because the problem is absurd when clearly seen. No one has difficulty making up his mind

to let a simple problem be resolved if it is seen as hurting him,
and also very easily removed. T-27.VII.2

Friend: That is raising the darkness to the light. Just bringing it into the light
and exposing it results in its removal.

David: Yes. An idea came through today when writing the mission statement for the
Foundation for the Awakening Mind. One idea was to remove: "Messengers see that
they must look at the darkness and they must examine all beliefs and raise them to the
light." That is a pretty common statement; we talk about raising beliefs to the light,
but it needed to be deeper. The way the statement came out was: "They understand
that to receive miracles requires that they raise the darkened belief system—ego in
their minds—to the light of truth." It clumps the plural into a singular.

Friend: There is one false belief no matter how many forms it takes?

David: There is just one, though it seems to take many different forms. The
clarity and joy of enlightenment is in seeing that there are not many. It is just
one belief system; one belief that has to be seen where it is—in the mind. The
key is seeing *the* error. Raising *the* error to the light, and then all of the specific
forms (time, space, bodies, etc.) are seen correctly. It is like an overhead projector
with stacks and stacks of overlays—you could just look at *the* stack of overlays.
It has to be raised up. It can be helpful to talk about it in terms of concepts
because there does seem to be a process of looking at all the concepts, and the
deceived mind can relate to that process. That is why we have the stages of the
development of trust; that is why the Workbook has 365 lessons, and why Jesus
uses the term "process" at times—because that is what the deceived mind can
relate to. That is the only thing it can relate to because it believes in incremental,
sequential time. What else is a process but sequential timing?

> The "reasoning" by which the world is made, on which it rests,
> by which it is maintained, is simply this: "*You* are the cause of
> what I do. Your presence justifies my wrath, and you exist and
> think apart from me. While you attack I must be innocent.
> And what I suffer from is your attack." T-27.VII.3

The key line is, "While you attack I must be innocent." You see the subject/object
split? And can you also see how underneath that statement is the belief that attack
and innocence can coexist? But the Course teaches that if attack is real, innocence
is not. Since attack is unreal, innocence is real; they cannot coexist.

> No one who looks upon this "reasoning" exactly as it is could fail to see it does not follow and it makes no sense. Yet it seems sensible, because it looks as if the world were hurting you. And so it seems as if there is no need to go beyond the obvious in terms of cause. T-27.VII.3

Whether you are watching the news, reading the newspaper, or just looking around, it seems like the cause of all hurt and suffering is in the world. Not enough food, not enough clean air to breath, pesticides, diseases, burglars, and wars – there are so many things in the world that seem to be the cause of all the misery and upset. Because of all these seeming causes it *seems* as if there is "no need to go beyond the obvious in terms of cause." But none of those things are the cause. This is why we look so carefully at every single belief in the mind. There is a need to look for cause within the mind and not to keep relying on the belief that the cause of my upset is in the world.

> The world's escape from condemnation is a need which those within the world are joined in sharing. Yet they do not recognize their common need. For each one thinks that if he does his part, the condemnation of the world will rest on him. And it is this that he perceives to *be* his part in its deliverance. T-27.VII.4

I remember having thoughts about martyrdom. I thought: *this is so radical – so different from the world.* I would just get flashes of myself being a martyr. A typical interpretation of Christianity has been that anyone who would completely follow Christ must in some way be ready to "bear the cross" as he did. I remember one fellow who was writing about Christianity said, "It has been tried and found to be too difficult." [laughter] When you begin to look at the teachings and really follow them in, it can seem to be too difficult or impractical. In a sense, that is what we are reading about in this paragraph: "For each one thinks that if he does his part, the condemnation of the world will rest on him. And it is this that he perceives to *be* his part in its deliverance." As if somewhere along the line I am going to have to pay a price for following this Course; as if there is a bitter pill to swallow as a part of salvation.

It cannot be that there is a price to pay for what you are!

I remember hearing a discussion about someone who described his moment of awakening from the dream as excruciatingly painful. That is certainly not my experience of it. The Course mentions often that you will at first awaken to happy dreams. Why would there be passages about happy dreams? Happy dreams are dreams that are purified of all the intentions and purposes of the ego; you are right-minded, in the position of the *dreamer of the dream*. Wouldn't it be happiness to know you are free and there is nothing on the screen that can influence you, affect you, or take away your happiness?

My experience has been that of a gentle presence and easy-goingness about life. There is no more rush involved, and nothing to defend. There is nothing to prove to anyone anymore and nothing to be right about. There is a lot of peace and joy. Intuitively, that feels like it is the way it would be, and that has been my experience. The happy dream is addressing the mind that believes it is part of the world and that to give up the world is going to involve some sort of cost, retribution, or vengeance.

Friend: That scenario makes sense to the ego. The other scenario makes sense to Spirit.

David:

> Vengeance must have a focus. Otherwise is the avenger's knife in his own hand, and pointed to himself. And he must see it in another's hand, if he would be a victim of attack he did not choose. And thus he suffers from the wounds a knife he does not hold has made upon himself. T-27.VII.4

The projection of the guilt is out onto something in the world.

Friend: It is important to put the knife in someone else's hand. [laughter]

David: This is the symbol for all the things in the world that *seem* to be cause of upset. *You fired me! That hurt! I got this disease because I was near the canal. A flood washed away my home.* Putting the knife in another's hand is saying that I am victimized by a person or something in the world that is not myself. Or, to share an example which is a little more subtle, I could be beating myself up, inflicting wounds upon myself, but that is still something taking place out on the screen. The mind is still not aware that it is Mind. If it can believe it can attack itself, it certainly does not perceive itself as Mind, as Mind that cannot attack. There is no attack. Mind cannot attack.

> This is the purpose of the world he sees. And looked at thus, the world provides the means by which this purpose seems

to be fulfilled. The means attest the purpose, but are not themselves a cause. Nor will the cause be changed by seeing it apart from its effects. T-27.VII.5

That is interesting, "And looked at thus, the world provides the means by which this purpose seems to be fulfilled." Everything in the projected world is used to justify the mind's belief in separation; it is used as a means for reinforcing and holding onto the belief in separation. Every time you think about a scenario in which you did not get your way, or you were seemingly treated unfairly, those are like memories of images. And whenever those memories of images are called upon as justification for the feeling of upset or attack, they are being used as a means to hold onto the belief in a separate identity. There is nothing in any of those scenarios that is the cause of your upset. The stepping stone is to say: *I want a different way of looking at the world, where the body and the world and all the seeming objects in the world, are given over to the Holy Spirit and used for another purpose.* The miracle is the means. What is a miracle? Towards the end of the Workbook there is a section called *What Is a Miracle?* It says: "A miracle is a correction. It does not create, nor really change at all. It merely looks on devastation [the cosmos] and reminds the mind that what it sees is false." The miracle shows you that the false is false; images are images; illusions are the same. You can see that the top rung of the ladder would be just to see the false as false.

Chapter Six

Purpose is What We are Going For

David: Purpose is what we are going for. Forgiveness is the purpose. You could also call it salvation or Atonement; you can call it by many different names. There is a different purpose for this world which is very obscure and buried. When the mind falls asleep, it thinks of purpose in terms of specifics. What is the purpose of a house? What is the purpose of a pencil? What is the purpose of shoes? Everything seems to have a purpose. When you really start to look at it, the purpose almost always comes back to how it relates to the body in some way. Everything comes back to the body. You could say that cities grew up near waterways and interstates, and they seem to have an economic function. That purpose is based on economics. The economic system is based on supporting human life, which is directly linked to identification with the body. The purpose we are trying to come to is not natural to the deceived mind, just as forgiveness is not natural to it. When the mind fell asleep it learned of a false world. You have to carefully unlearn the world. You have to learn a new purpose. In the Kingdom of Heaven there is no purpose. There is just being. Purpose is like a goal and in the Kingdom of Heaven there are no goals.

Friend: So the purpose of forgiveness only came into play with the seeming separation? In truth there is no forgiveness? In truth there is no purpose?

David: Right. There is no need for Atonement and correction in Heaven. If we are talking about a single purpose, we are talking about the realm of Heaven. I am using the term "Heaven" as natural. Heaven is natural. When the mind fell asleep, that was very unnatural, and now it has to learn this very unnatural correction. It is like the needle in the haystack. The mind fell asleep and found itself in the haystack and now it has to find the needle. To do that it has to question every piece of straw in the haystack. It requires a very thorough going through. You cannot by chance just stick your hand in there and hope to pull the needle out. That is why it is so important that we keep coming together to look at all the obstacles and blocks to our awareness of that purpose. It has to be very carefully learned.

The New Interpretation section in Chapter 30 talks about purpose. It says that, "Only a constant purpose can endow events with stable meaning." Once the mind falls asleep, it perceives all these images; everything is distorted. Instead of having a single, unified purpose, there are seeming millions of purposes. Everything perceived seems to have a different purpose. This book seems to have a different purpose than that microphone. These shoes seem to have a different purpose than this couch. The table seems to have a somewhat different purpose than the chair. Everything seems to have meaning in and of itself. Jesus addresses this in the Workbook:

> At the most superficial levels, you do recognize purpose. Yet purpose cannot be understood at these levels. For example, you do understand that a telephone is for the purpose of talking to someone who is not physically in your immediate vicinity. What you do not understand is what you want to reach him for. And it is this that makes your contact with him meaningful or not. W-25.4

It is one thing to call somebody on the phone but what is my purpose for reaching him? What is this for? When you answer that question you are getting down to the mind level. That is a decision of mind. What is my purpose in reaching my brother, as opposed to the superficial purpose?

"Teach only love for that is what you are." T-6.I Again whether it is making a phone call, going to visit someone, or doing anything, tune into the *Holy Spirit and ask: Holy Spirit, what would you have me say, what would you have me do?* It may take the form of a phone call, but really it is about *intention*. That is another word for purpose. What is my intention? Am I trying to pull out the hooks to make somebody guilty? Am I calling to manipulate somebody to get them to do something that I want them to do?

Friend: You mean like if I try to reach my children because I am worried and I want to know how they are doing, that is one thing, but if I want to call somebody just to gossip about somebody, then that is my purpose?

David: You need to look at the idea of concern as well. If the Holy Spirit has a purpose, and if I line up with it and feel peace, then I want to learn what that purpose is because it does not feel good to feel scared or concerned. It is uncomfortable.

Friend: When they are not answering the phone I could think: *Oh, they are probably out at the lake. They are fine. They are having fun.* But then my next thought might be an effort to reassure myself that nothing happened, *hoping* that everything is OK. I get scared because I think maybe they have lost the phone number and are trying to call me and cannot reach me. Then I try to reassure myself again that they are fine.

David: Lesson 37 says: "My holiness blesses the world." And lesson 38 deals very practically with concern for how people are doing. The lesson is: "There is nothing my holiness cannot do." The first paragraph says:

> Your holiness reverses all the laws of the world. It is beyond every restriction of time, space, distance and limits of any kind. Your holiness is totally unlimited in its power because it establishes you as a Son of God, at one with the Mind of his Creator. W-38.1

And the specific applications, in italics, are the ones which are really useful. The way it reads is, "In the situation involving _____ in which I see myself, there is nothing that my holiness cannot do." Put your own name in the blank as you think of yourself calling home and feeling fearful about not getting an answer.

Purpose – Not about Action or Inaction

Hi David,

I am writing you with much hesitation and skepticism because I deeply believe that no one can ever help me find the truth. The decision to write this mail is primarily a spontaneous act!

One question that has always troubled me is about action. I have seen that awareness leads to so much sensitivity that it becomes tough to act at all, and I find it very hard to distinguish between this state of inaction, and apathy. Besides the practical implication of this inaction (that one needs money for living), there are some deeper implications too, like that of self-expression. With inaction there is no action at all: interesting, boring, no matter what kind. Is that what man is born for?

How is one supposed to find out what one loves most? Is there really such a thing as self-expression at all? Why is it that so-called "realized souls" always lecture around, trying to teach the world? Why is it that the Christ and the Buddha are always preachers? Why not, say, an engineer or a doctor? Is there an action that is not a product of thought? And is spontaneity lack of thought (both conscious and unconscious)?

I think the ready-made explanation of all our problems with terms like thought/ no-thought, consciousness/no consciousness have become so commonplace that they have very little meaning. I think that we fundamentally tend to find solace in paradoxes. Thought/no-thought theory provides us with excellent paradox to feel satisfied with – to stop questioning further, to wait perpetually to come out of it one day! How in your view can one find the true meaning of action?

Hello Beloved One,

Thanks for writing. The question is not one of action versus inaction, but always one of purpose. Discernment of purpose is very important, because one's state of mind is a result of the purpose one has chosen to align with (ego or Spirit). Peace of mind, happiness, freedom, and contentment are not dependent on whether the body seems to be active or inactive; the Spirit's Perspective reveals that all apparent behavior is a dream, an unreal effect of an unreal "cause."

Interpretation of behavior is always the ego's perception, for the ego recognizes only form and knows nothing of Content or True Meaning. True Meaning (Identity) is Abstract Light, and the world was made to cover over the Light and keep It out of awareness. An ego device for distracting away from questioning underlying false beliefs and concepts is to focus on behavior and ask endless questions about behavior. Behavior, as all of form, is the past and no meaningful questions can ever be asked about that which is over and gone.

What one "does" or "does not do" flows from the purpose the mind has chosen to identify with. The ego uses the body for pride, pleasure, and attack. The ego's purpose is to reinforce separation and protect the false belief in private minds and private thoughts. The Spirit uses the body solely as a communication device. The Spirit always communicates that mind is unified and that everything is connected, being one tapestry of wholeness. Apparent actions or inactivity inspired by the Spirit's Purpose are always helpful; apparent actions or inactivity motivated by the ego's purpose are never helpful. Discernment is, therefore, being clear about what Purpose is helpful and what purpose is not helpful.

Apathy is ego motivated. Joy is Spirit inspired. "Working" for a "living" is always ego motivated. Trusting Divine Providence is always Spirit inspired. The perception of "needs" is always ego motivated, the miraculous synchronicity of "all things working together for good" is always Spirit inspired. Real Self Expression is joyful, while ego "self" expression is but an attempt to reinforce an illusion that could never be. Be aware that as long as the mind believes in duality, the choice of which purpose to align with (Spirit or ego) is a choice of which Self/self to believe is real. This moment, "to Be or not to Be" is the choice, and in the ultimate decision to accept Atonement is "choice" undone forever.

"How is one supposed to find out what one loves most?" Forgive the illusion and recognize that Love is One and "most" is meaningless. Love makes no "comparison" for there is nothing to compare in Oneness.

"Why is it that so-called "realized souls" always lecture around, trying to teach the world? Why is it that the Christ's, and the Buddha's are always preachers? Why not, say, an engineer or a doctor?" The form may seem like a "preacher" or a "teacher," yet the Content is One Spirit. A mind emptied of all false self-concepts is freed to recognize the Self, the Spirit. Forgiveness is the release of all "tiny" ego self-concepts, and even forgiveness must give way to the Truth beyond all dreaming. Forgiveness shows the meaninglessness of fragmented perception and offers a happy dream for but a moment. You might say that this forgiven world is learned as the ego is unlearned, for the reflection of light and darkness have no meeting point.

"Is there an action that is not a product of thought? And is spontaneity lack of thought (both conscious and unconscious)?" All thought-forms (opposites), including apparent "action" and "inaction," are within the domain of the ego. A miracle is a spontaneous choice of the Spirit's Purpose in which form is one or whole and the cosmos is perceived from the Spirit's Perspective which sees the false as false – for there is no sense of "otherness." The miracle collapses time and seems to shorten the need for learning forgiveness or unlearning the ego. The holy instant is a Still Thought in God which time cannot touch and in which "action" and "inaction" have no meaning.

"I believe deeply that no one can ever help you find the truth." This is true, for truth is the recognition that there is no "other" than One Self. The opening to this recognition is discernment, and only the Spirit within can make the discernment of which I speak. Do not look to any "body" to make it for you, for there is nothing "outside" and the Voice for God alone can be understood. Meaning cannot be found in images, so seek not to "figure out" or "understand" what has no meaning. The recognition of Self as God created Self is everlasting Meaning, and nothing else has ANY meaning. This seeming leap of faith is but a simple recognition, and this natural and obvious "Ahhhh haaaaa" is Enlightenment.

You Cannot Mess it Up

Hi David,

I am pondering over how much is script and how much is not. I love it because if I could live it to its last consequences, it would leave no place for guilt and blame on myself or others. But I can see also the danger; I could use it to excuse myself for doing all kind of nasty things.

What about the decisions for which I let purpose be my guide? Are those decisions also part of the script? Or do "we" decide them? And, if so, how do we do this? Why is one a seeker of truth and another not?

Is even the decision to be guided by the Holy Spirit scripted? Is whether I will listen to His answer or not scripted? But if all is the script, where does willingness come in?

I have heard you mention the concept that the "script is written," and then I watch a movie like *What the Bleep Do We Know*, where the main message seems to be that I can change the dream/reality/illusion as I wish! Can I only change if the script allows it? Are the wanting-to-change-it and the actual changing it also just the script? I fear to screw it up somehow. Maybe I should just ask you: can I do whatever I most like to do, without endangering my awakening? Would enlightenment still happen in its scripted moment?

Beloved One,

I am happy to hear from you!

The entire time-space cosmos is scripted and is the past. It is impossible to change the past, though it is inevitable that the cosmos be forgiven. The only choice to make is the purpose you give to the script and the way you look upon it. The script is one and cannot be broken into the doer and the one who is done to. It is a script that is over and done and impossible to analyze. If you allow the mind permission to relax and enjoy the watching, peace of mind is inevitable. Purpose is a decision of mind and as such is not "in the script." You might think of purpose as a higher-order decision, a meaningful decision, whereas decisions between illusory forms have no relevance in reality. All of life is an opportunity to practice discernment and choose to align with the Holy Spirit's Purpose.

It is therefore not so important what you do as it is important to be clear of your intention or motive, and this comes back to purpose. The choice for the Holy Spirit is truly unavoidable, so be vigilant in watching your mind and harboring no scrap of judgment. Then you will experience how simple and easy salvation is. For Love asks for nothing except to be itself, and to extend.

Relax and enjoy the show, and allow your mind to restfully watch. That is always good enough, for the Might of the Holy Spirit is joined with our mind. You cannot mess it up, for the Holy Spirit is in charge. There is no burden in trusting the Holy Spirit. All the mind is left with is a feeling of lightness and Divine Ease.

Ambition and Specialization

David: In the movie *Gandhi* there was a reporter walking with him in South Africa. Gandhi was building ashrams and the reporter from America said, "Mr. Gandhi, you are quite an ambitious fellow." Gandhi smiled with his sweet, gentle eyes and said "I hope not."

In the world the response to: "You are quite an ambitious fellow," has been, "Thank you very much." Something resonated when I heard Gandhi say "I hope not." There was something inside me that leapt with joy; *Whoo, that is a different response.*

Whenever we are ambitious in the worldly sense, we also have a sense of ruthlessness because whenever I am striving to gain something of the world, then I will perceive my brothers at times as an obstruction getting in the way of my ambitions, of what I want. So Gandhi's little statement, "I hope not" took on new meaning. I grew up in America, the land of free enterprise and ambition and I really had very positive connotations associated with the idea of ambition. But when you go deeper into the Course you hear Jesus saying:

> You must have noticed an outstanding characteristic of every
> end that the ego has accepted as its own. When you have
> achieved it, *it has not satisfied you.* T-8.VIII.2

This is why the ego is forced to constantly shift from one goal to the next, hoping it will find something that will satisfy you. When I read that, I recognized that was what I had been doing my whole life. I did it in college with degrees—*this degree is not enough, I need this degree.* I have done it with relationships—*this relationship is good but I can do better.* I have done it with possessions—*this car is nice, it has all these extras, self-steering wheel, rear window defogger, but I am not really satisfied.* It seems never-ending. So in one sense we are just trying to expose the ego's thought system. A lot of times when reading the Course, there can be a sense of relinquishment. After learning so many things and getting accustomed to a certain lifestyle, the Course comes along and says that our perception is all messed up. Occasionally Jesus will say "Give up the world!" T-30.V He puts an exclamation point behind it; you know he must be pretty serious about this idea. But through the ego's lens the feeling is: *I do not want to give up anything.*

Friend: Right. That is how I feel.

David: Exactly. *I am accustomed to this. Thank you very much Jesus, but I enjoy this.* He is so eager to help us see that pursuing and seeking outside ourselves, instead of within where the Kingdom is, is a really painful pursuit. At times the attitude is like: *Jesus, I want you to take all the pain and grief and misery out of my life, and I want to keep things just the way they are.* You can see that it is like asking to reconcile truth and illusion in the sense of seeking outside myself. *I want to seek outside myself and I want to be peaceful.* The more I have gone into these things, the more I recognize that the need is to embrace the inner, to embrace that light within my mind, and to start to let go of the goals and pursuits. When I have goals and pursuits in the world then I have expectations of how I think the script needs to go to fulfill my goals. In other words, if I have real ambitions, such as being the best tennis player in the world, or the wealthiest man, or the best at anything—it does not really matter what the form of the ambition is—if I have ambitions, then I will have expectations about how I want the script to go. If I am seeking to become a renowned Course teacher then I may start having expectations about how many people are in the audience, or how many books I sell. Can you see how it is a set-up for pain to have expectations of how you want the script to go, to have outcomes in mind?

Friend: And the only way you can have good outcomes is to have those goals set in place from the beginning. It is an insidious thing that says if I accomplish this goal then I am better, not only better than other people but I am better than I was, and that is a lie. But in and of themselves, they really are not bad.

David: We have to get clear on what "in and of themselves" means, or if it has any meaning. Lesson 184 gives us the sense that everything we come here to learn is about separation and fragmentation. Every child learns how to label and categorize all of the separate objects. It is taught that this is very important; if you do not do this you won't be able to make it in the world. This is "mature" education.

> You live by symbols. You have made up names for everything you see. Each one becomes a separate entity, identified by its own name. By this you carve it out of unity. By this you designate its special attributes, and set it off from other things by emphasizing space surrounding it. This space you lay between all things to which you give a different name; all happenings in terms of place and time; all bodies which are greeted by a name. W-pI.184.1

You can see that this first phase of learning in the world must be released to really come to peace of mind. We must then enter another phase in which we start to let go of the meaning and purpose we have given to everything; we have to release the attachment to what we think they mean. We are convinced we know what they mean "in and of themselves," but Jesus is teaching us that we have read a lot of false meaning into everything. We need to have a complete transformation where we open our minds up to the idea that maybe we do not know how things should go. Maybe I am just going to take your hand and walk into this in trust! We need to start somewhere with the unlearning process.

The process of categorization is judgment, and like it says in the Bible, "Judge not." The Course makes it clear that all our pain comes from our own judging and categorizing, splitting and breaking apart. The good news is that the Holy Spirit has a different judgment that is also in our mind. We can totally tap into the Holy Spirit's judgment if we let go of our own judgments and get out of the way. That is good news!

Friend: I was thinking, any kind of specialization or expertise in anything is kind of like taking this to the nth degree, where I know everything there is to know about whatever. I know all the names for.... The mind just wants to break it apart, break it apart, break it apart and then feel like it has a handle on one of these little parts; it can be an expert.

David: Like in the old days, general practitioners had to learn about all the parts of the body and how everything functioned together, and perhaps also some psychological principles to help their patients get along in life. But the trend of medicine has been towards specialization of everything; gone are the days of the general practitioner. Once again the ego would teach you that you have to specialize in order to survive. That was the conflict I felt in my mind when I was in college. A little voice in my mind kept saying: *Step back, think further, and see the big picture.* And the other voice in my mind, sometimes coming from my parents or professors, would say: *You are not going to make it unless you settle down and pick an area of specialty, focus your attention, and become specialized.* For a long time there was a push-pull in my mind. The deeper I went, the more I questioned every field I was in; I questioned the assumptions. I could not stop questioning the meaning of life and decide to just be a good psychologist, or a good educator, or urban planner. I kept going deeper and deeper and finally I found the Course, which says that in order to learn this course you have to question every value that you hold. I thought: *Yes, that is what the little voice has been telling me all along! Am I nuts or not?* The Course keeps saying that you have sanity within you—if you keep listening to the little voice and not to the other voices.

One "Boss," One Function

Hi David,

Lesson 25 says that all goals are of the ego and asks me to relinquish them. Does this mean that I should not have any goals in my life? Should I then not even plan my day? How am I to survive in the business world where everything is goals and quotas?

Hello Beloved One,

ACIM gives the goal of forgiveness to replace the ego's goals of form outcomes that maintain the belief in separation from God. The Holy Spirit works with the mind, whatever and wherever it believes itself to be, and Helps loosen the self-concept the ego made to take the place of Christ.

I held a gathering many years ago in which the following Q & A dialogue took place:

Question: I have to go back to work today and do some computer work and some other things before tomorrow morning. I would rather stay right here. You talk about intuition and Spirit leading you. Now how do I do that?

David: The Holy Spirit starts from where and what the mind believes it is. Suppose you believe you are a woman who has a particular job, and tonight that looks like having to do work at a computer. Let's suppose that this scenario is all just a motion picture of a belief system you have, and this is simply the way you perceive yourself at this moment. The Holy Spirit does not try to yank this web of beliefs apart. The Holy Spirit will use those things that you believe in to help you realize that you are much more than the self-concepts you believe define you. This discussion, for example, is bringing witness to your mind's desire to wake up and remember your reality as the Son of God. All one has to have is the willingness, and the Holy Spirit will undo the false self-concepts and replace them with forgiveness. Start with this prayer:

Abide with me, Holy Spirit. Guide me in what to say and do and where to go. If you welcome and trust Him, you will experience immediate results.

Question: I am having some trouble with the description of duality and with the idea that it is our perception that is the problem. I work in a business where I have to see things exactly as they are happening, not as I might like them to happen. How do I get to the place that you are talking about?

David: When one has identified one's self say, as an employee in a business, there certainly seem to be "external" constraints and restrictions to abide by. For example, let's say one is identified as a manager. As a manager, one seemingly has to hold other people accountable for doing certain things. A manager monitors and evaluates employees, directs them, conducts performance reviews, and so forth. Also, every manager has a "boss" whose job it is to make sure the manager is accountable. What one must do is look closely, going deeply into the belief system that is producing the faulty perception which is producing the scenario I have just described. One must be willing to examine what the priorities are, what is most important in life. Is peace of mind one's only priority?

I have had to take a good look at everything I believed, turn inward for strength and support, and realize with certainty that the Holy Spirit is my only "Boss" and forgiveness my only function. One may ask, "How practical is that? What do you do when you have two bosses, if you have the Holy Spirit and your employer telling you two different things?" Again, the Holy Spirit meets the mind where it believes it is. He works with the mind, helping it to exchange accepted self-concepts for the more expansive self-concepts that approach true forgiveness.

As you lay aside judgment and change your mind about the world, what happens on the screen of the world will be a symbolic representation of that mind shift, and of your perception of relationships. So really we are back to just saying: *Okay, Holy Spirit, work with me right now where I believe I am and help me loosen my mind from these false beliefs. Help me let go of the ego and my perception will be healed.* Trust in the Holy Spirit for everything and He will take care of you in ways you cannot even envision.

Let the Holy Spirit Guide you in all things and everything will work out for the best. The inner journey goes very deep, but the Holy Spirit Guides surely and there are many free resources available for the asking. I am joined with you in the Awakening. You are dearly loved.

What is Life without Goals and Ambitions?

Hi David,

What is life without goals and ambitions? I have heard so many times people quoting, "Man without a dream or a vision shall perish." An aim or a goal in life drives us to do work or action and that keeps us busy and occupied. Now even if we try to do action just for the sake of action and not for any rewards or fulfillment of desires, still how do we pick any action without a purpose?

I mean I brush my teeth to keep them clean and it is a hygienic thing to do. If you say you reply to people's e-mails and do talks, I am sure there is a goal, aim, or purpose behind it. But choosing you as an example would not be the right thing to do as you are an exception! So many people with good intentions are still action-driven by an aim or goal, basing decisions on future goals, like: *What should I do today that takes care of my family now and also in the future?*

Goal, ambition, and aim are things of the future. So my question is what is living in the present if the essence of the "present" is the past and the future? Present does not exist without a past or future, right?

Beloved One,

Thanks for your sincere question. It seems that life is moving forward in this world and that time and progress move forward towards the future. Future goals seem to aim at something better than the past or present. Yet the past is gone and the future is but imagined. Both are defenses against the Present Moment and the realization that everything is Perfect right Now.

In Awakening, time seems to collapse; it seems to shorten, and it seems to move backward toward the original error and then disappear entirely in the Innocence that precedes the error. In Awakening, time is like a carpet that rolls back until it rolls up completely, so that nothing is left at all. The Present is before time was. This is another way of saying what Jesus taught: "Before Abraham was, I Am." Awakening is remembering Original Innocence, and this Enlightenment experience has everything to do with Now and nothing to do with time. The essence of the Present Moment is Eternity, and Now has nothing to do with linear time or past or future.

Life is a State of Mind. With regard to this world, the closest approximation of Eternity is Now. Now is the rebirth of Spirit in awareness. Now is free of past regrets and grievances and future worries and anxious plans. There is a meaning to the quote you share, "Man without a dream or a vision shall perish." Without the happy dream of non-judgment, without the Vision of Christ, everything of this world does seem to perish, for nothing of this world is everlasting.

Goals and ambitions seem practical in the world, yet they are aimed at the future. Future outcomes, I assure you, are ego motivations. Present Peace is a "goal" worth desiring, for it is more than possible, it is inevitable. The experience of Present Peace results from listening only to the Spirit within, and to the Spirit, there is no tomorrow. The Holy Spirit uses time to teach that there is no time. This is the Purpose that inspires and blesses and even seems to motivate action until the awareness dawns that nothing is really happening. The happy dream is like a lucid dream in which the dreamer is aware of dreaming. Dreams are not taken to be Reality, and sleep is not taken to be Wakefulness. If you feel like you are driven to "do things," ask yourself if there is a fear of consequences. If you believe that to not "do things" will result in fearful consequences, then it is wise to examine what is believed. As long as fearful beliefs are held as true, thoughts and actions will be fear-driven.

Forgiveness is a miracle and it releases the mind from the fear of consequences. Let the Holy Spirit be the Purpose that gently Guides and you will never feel "driven" again! Value not one belief the ego sponsors and enjoy the experience of Divine Ease. Not one seeming difficulty but will melt away before you reach it.

Accept Present Bliss as our Purpose, and watch how bright the world seems in awareness. Seek not to change the world, seek rather to change your mind about the world. Enlightenment is as simple as accepting the Changeless as True. For there is nothing else but Love! All Glory to God!

Goals, Doing, and Purpose

Hi David,

I feel compelled to say that if there were no goals, then I would never have listened to the voice for God, which spoke to me and told me that opening my store was my path. I feel I was specifically "directed" to do this. And now that I am here, I have to do certain things which are more "of the world" in order to pay the rent, support my family, and continue on with what I have started.

My question is: you talk about goals like they are "counter" to the Holy Spirit. And yet, in order to get the messages out there into our brother's hands, we, including you, have to "do things," and those of us with children and payments have to "do things." One step has to go before the other in order for things to fall into place. It has been my experience over the past year, that as long as my Goal is Truth, then as I move forward, I do not need to see the next step, I just have to take it. I could lie in bed all day and not do anything and still survive for a while, but how is that helping my brother?

In the Course it talks about "setting the goal," and if I understand it correctly, if your goal is Truth, then all you need is faith, and all will be given you. So my sister, when she talks about writing children's books, as long as her goal is Truth, shouldn't it work the same way? Clarity on this would be appreciated.

Beloved One,

Thanks for your loving witness of the answer to prayer and for the deeply sincere question. If you read *The Real Alternative* section of ACIM it becomes apparent that all of the roadways of the world were made to lead away from Truth, and thus Christ teaches that all the roadways of the world lead to death. Happily, Christ also teaches that there is no death and that the Real Alternative leads to heights of happiness.

So every seeming "step" the Holy Spirit offers as Guidance to Help the mind Awaken is valuable, for every "step" in Purpose has the value of forgiveness.

Yet the context of Awakening is that the Holy Spirit uses the symbols of time to teach that there is no time. Miracles are temporary devices to collapse time, and the Atonement is the complete collapse of time in which the mind loses track of time entirely.

The "doer" dissolves in Watching. This is referred to in the *Manual for Teachers* of ACIM when Christ says that judgment "through you" rather than "by you" occurs. The "through you" refers to the Holy Spirit. Goals which are specific are used by the Holy Spirit along with specific Guidance while the mind still believes in "process." The sleeping mind made up and believes in time and specifics.

The mind is never hurled into Reality, and though there is some uneasiness with every seeming self-concept shift, there is no destruction of perception or of the status quo. The Holy Spirit's Plan is a retranslation of the past to a Perspective that might be called a purified past. The purified past is whole, thus not divided into the parts the ego offers in its perspective of the past.

The reply to the previous post also dealt with the same topic, as the writer perceived herself as a writer Awakening to the Christ Self. These symbols called words (which are twice removed from Reality) can be used in Purpose to recognize a State of Mind that is beyond the words entirely. The Beatitudes – the tranquil state of consistent peace, love, freedom, and happiness – are the goal of the Course. These attitudes come from accepting the Atonement. The Atonement is complete forgiveness.

In the third chapter of the supplemental pamphlet *Psychotherapy – Purpose, Process, and Practice* there is a section you may find helpful, called *The Question of Payment*. In the *Song of Prayer* Jesus tells us that the truly humble have no goal other than God because the need for idols and defenses is past.

And from Workbook lesson 131: "No one can fail who seeks to reach the truth."

> Failure is all about you while you seek for goals that cannot be achieved. You look for permanence in the impermanent; for love where there is none; for safety in the midst of danger; immortality within the darkness of the dream of death. Who could succeed where contradiction is the setting of his searching, and the place to which he comes to find stability?

Goals which are meaningless are not attained. There is no way to reach them, for the means by which you strive for them are meaningless as they are. Who can use such senseless means and hope through them to gain in anything? Where can they lead? And what could they achieve that offers any hope of being real? Pursuit of the imagined leads to death because it is the search for nothingness, and while you seek for life you ask for death. You look for safety and security while in your heart you pray for danger and protection for the little dream you made.

Yet searching is inevitable here. For this you came, and you will surely do the thing you came for. But the world cannot dictate the goal for which you search unless you give it power to do so. Otherwise, you still are free to choose a goal that lies beyond the world and every worldly thought, and one which comes to you from an idea relinquished yet remembered, old yet new; an echo of a heritage forgot, yet holding everything you really want.

Be glad that search you must. Be glad as well to learn you search for Heaven, and must find the goal you really want. No one can fail to want this goal, and reach it in the end. God's Son cannot seek vainly, though he try to force delay, deceive himself, and think that it is hell he seeks. When he is wrong he finds correction, when he wanders off he is led back to his appointed task. W-131.1-4

Dreams – Are they Idols?

Hi David,

Your e-mail a few days ago caught my attention. I have read it and re-read it a few times and will probably re-read it a few more times before I can take it all in.

I am afraid that I am just getting to a point in my life when I would very much like to wholeheartedly bring forth some beautiful seeds, or at least one of the seeds. This is one of my dreams. Now it would seem quite useless to bring forth a dream such as an alphabet book.

Are dreams also idols? Lots of aspects, in fact almost all of the supporting or un-supporting members of my life, are fast falling away. All the props are being taken away. I am stressing out and from time to time buy into anxiety about how my personal future will work itself out. If my house sells, then I can go on with a pilgrimage dream, and jump out of this dream of living in a house and working on a children's book and some art work and from time to time participating in *A Course in Miracles* activities or other spiritual avenues which call me Home.

Beloved One,

Thank you so much for your heartfelt and sincere e-mail. You are on the cusp of understanding that the specific dreams of the ego mean nothing and the forgiving, unified dream Perspective offered by the Holy Spirit is Everything in terms of perception of the world. Yes, the spiritual experience that brings Awakening requires a release or letting go, or including in, of all specific dreams and specific goals.

Abstraction Calls, and those who have the ears to hear and the eyes to see gladly Answer the Call. The world of ego familiarity begins to dissolve and fall away in awareness as you enter the realms that the mystics and saints and sages have spoken about for centuries. Your trust in the Holy Spirit grows strong as you withdraw faith from the ego, and the body, and the five senses the ego made to reinforce its error of separation.

I love you dearly. You are not alone Beloved One, though the dissolving ego would have you believe and think and feel and perceive that you are. I am with you always, closer than the breath which seems to animate the dream figure. Our Comforter is ever Present, reminding all that the dreams of seeming fear and guilt and isolation are almost over now, and will change to happy dreams of non-judgment through forgiveness of illusions and nonattachment to form. The only "outcome" worthy of our Holy Mind is peace, and this is independent of form. Heed not the ego's witnesses, for false images appearing real cannot keep you from Awakening unless this be your desire. Nothing happens by accident.

In relative terms, very, very few seem ready to release illusion entirely and accept the Atonement. This has been written as a symbol to not be discouraged when you look upon the images of the world. The Plan of Salvation is always Now and always is simply the Moment of Grace that you experienced waiting for your snow tires to be mounted. The ego wants to join the spiritual journey with its goals of economic success, material prosperity, and special ones to call family, whether it be a "biological" or "ethnic" or "spiritual" family. The ego judges against the One and the ones who do not support its form goals and outcomes. Yet there are no form goals or outcomes that will not instantly dissolve into the Light of Peace when they are no longer valued.

Ascend in Love by giving complete forgiveness priority over everything the ego's world can seem to offer. No one who would realize the Truth can be associated or affiliated with any of the specific dreams or symbols of the world. Truth, Being Present, cannot be organized in form. Love, Being Abstract, cannot be objectified and focused on persons, places, events, things, groups, or organizations. Let all projects of form give way to Purpose, to accepting the Atonement. Everything is already accomplished, and so Watch the dream in Happiness with the Holy Spirit and let all things be exactly as they are.

Live in Integrity. If you feel out of accord with the Harmony of the Present, let go of the thoughts of the future. Feel the Peace of our Holy Mind right Now, the Mind that is shared with God. Grace is experienced when the mind lets go of trying to control anything of the world of form. Remember: In Peace I Live. In Grace I am released. You are ever in my heart Beloved of God.

Abilities, Work, and Purpose

David: We live in a false world; everything in it is false. What can we do with that? We can get up in the morning and tell ourselves it is all false, but that does not make the feelings of constriction about consequences go away. What we really need is to turn it all over to the Holy Spirit. The section called *Healing as the Recognition of Truth* starts to articulate what that will be like. "The Holy Spirit teaches you to use what the ego has made, to teach the opposite of what the ego has 'learned.'" T-7.IV.3 This world is learned; anything that can be learned can be unlearned. The ego is learned. In the *Self Concept versus Self* section, it says: "The building of a concept of the self is what the learning of the world is for. This is its purpose; that you come without a self, and make one as you go along." T-31.V.1

From the moment we can speak we learn to label things; this is a ball; that is a table; you are a boy, or a girl, etc. There we go. The mind wants a false self-concept and now it seems to be learning separation—learning that everything has a different purpose. The learning of the world just reinforces what the mind believes. But, again, the Holy Spirit can use what the ego made.

> The kind of learning is as irrelevant as is the particular ability that was applied to the learning. All you need do is make the effort to learn, for the Holy Spirit has a unified goal for the effort. If different abilities are applied long enough to one goal, the abilities themselves become unified. This is because they are channelized in one direction, or in one way. Ultimately, then, they all contribute to one result, and by so doing, their similarity rather than their differences is emphasized. T-7.IV.3

It seems as if everyone has different aptitudes, but all abilities, if put towards the same purpose, will be channelized; the differences between them will fade from awareness. Playing the violin, for example, is a very highly developed ability but the question underneath all this is: "What is it for?"

Friend: So after a while it does not really matter whether I am spreading butter on bread or playing the violin because all of my abilities are channelized in one direction and become unified?

David: The good news is that I do not have to pretend not to have skills. I can still use them but the purpose is changed. As we move our attention towards forgiveness as our one purpose, some things will start to fall away. We may no longer find ourselves involved in things that seemed to serve before, but nothing is wasted in the sense that all abilities can be used as long as they are being channelized.

> All abilities should therefore be given over to the Holy Spirit, Who understands how to use them properly. He uses them only for healing, because He knows you only as whole. By healing you learn of wholeness, and by learning of wholeness you learn to remember God ... Healing is the way to undo the belief in differences, being the only way of perceiving the Sonship as one. T-7.IV.4,5

Healing could be equated with having one, unified purpose for everything. When you *so* desire to look through the Holy Spirit's lens at everything, however it seems to be used in the world of form, changes in behavior will come automatically, as a by-product of that desire. Miracles should not be consciously chosen. All you have to do is be ready, the Holy Spirit will do the miracles through you. You have to let go of the component of behavior; it has to be a by-product of your thoughts. When there is still a sense of trying to control, the miracles will not be pure. What a strain it is to try to figure out what to do and what to say. There is an enormous amount of strain when you want to do it all *just right*; you are caught in the level of form, which is guilt inducing.

Friend: And if someone is not accepting the miracle as you are offering it to them you feel like you have done something wrong.

David: There we go again: guilt! "The body is nothing more than a framework for developing abilities, which is quite apart from what they are used for. *That* is a decision." T-7.V.1 Here is the form/content theme again. A decision in mind is content. A decision of purpose can be made by asking about every single thing: *What is it for?* Training the mind to ask that question in every situation is so opposite and backwards from the way in which the deceived mind thinks. The deceived mind goes plunging into things already thinking it knows what they are for. The deceived mind is convinced that it already knows what everything is for. It always has something to do with form and outcome—whether it is shopping, laundry, going to work, playing tennis, etc. We must accept the Holy Spirit's purpose of healing or forgiveness as our only function, but this is only part of it. The other part is letting go of the ego's goals. The self-concept is in on anything we have expectations about or an investment in. The ego has all kinds of goals and outcomes that it wants.

Remember, the deceived mind thinks the self-concept is its existence, so it perceives the Holy Spirit's purpose as requiring sacrifice. We want to bring this into the context of what we are moving *towards*, knowing that things are going to fade away automatically rather than thinking we have to fight the ego every step of the way and give things up that we value. Workbook lesson 154 articulates what we are moving towards: "I am among the ministers of God." How many of us have thought of ourselves as ministers of God? A key thing to keep in mind as we go into this is that it is all about a loosening, beginning to get the "me" and the "my" out of there. You do not write down all of your abilities and then try to figure out how you are going to unify it so that it all works out. You are not the one that is going to figure it out. That is good news! You do not have to feel the weight of trying to put these things together. Turn your skills and abilities over to the Holy Spirit. He is the one that has to make those decisions. He can see how best to use them.

> Let us today be neither arrogant nor falsely humble. We have
> gone beyond such foolishness. We cannot judge ourselves, nor
> need we do so. These are but attempts to hold decision off,

and to delay commitment to our function. It is not our part to judge our worth, nor can we know what role is best for us; what we can do within a larger plan we cannot see in its entirety. Our part is cast in Heaven, not in hell. And what we think is weakness can be strength; what we believe to be our strength is often arrogance.

Whatever your appointed role may be, it was selected by the Voice for God, Whose function is to speak for you as well. Seeing your strengths exactly as they are, and equally aware of where they can be best applied, for what, to whom and when, He chooses and accepts your part for you. He does not work without your own consent. But He is not deceived in what you are, and listens only to His Voice in you.

It is through His ability to hear one Voice which is His Own that you become aware at last there is one Voice in you. And that one Voice appoints your function, and relays it to you, giving you the strength to understand it, do what it entails, and to succeed in everything you do that is related to it. God has joined His Son in this, and thus His Son becomes His messenger of unity with Him. W-154.1-3

There is a sentence in there with three parts to it: "And that one Voice appoints your function, and relays it to you, giving you the strength to understand it, do what it entails, and to succeed in everything you do that is related to it." You can see how much this relies on listening. It is like the prayer, "I am here only to be truly helpful. I am here to represent Him Who sent me. I do not have to worry about what to say or what to do, because He Who sent me will direct me." T-2.V.A.18

The only way our abilities can be unified is to literally take instructions moment by moment, on faith. That is the flipside of the way it seems in this world. The world says that in order to be secure and confident you must plan and have everything well scoped out. But this is a totally intuitive approach to listening. The analytical abilities that you have relied on are all out the window. It can seem a little scary, like walking off the ledge and trusting there is something there to catch you. There is a little section in lesson 135 that can help us tease this theme out further:

A healed mind does not plan. It carries out the plans that it receives through listening to Wisdom that is not its own. It waits until it has been taught what should be done, and then proceeds to do it. It does not depend upon itself for anything except its adequacy to fulfill the plans assigned to it. It is secure in certainty that obstacles cannot impede its progress to accomplishment of any goal that serves the greater plan established for the good of everyone. W-135.11

You can see that we are talking about completely letting go.

Friend: That is such a contradiction to what the world is like.

David: It is such a contradiction. When I was taking classes in urban planning, I had a class in problem-solving. You define the resources, analyze the factors, and generate all the different approaches. Then you decide which one you want; that is what you get good at. Everyone does it to some degree whether it is at the supermarket or with a career or getting our car fixed. Which place has the best price? It is the same kind of thing. Now we are coming to the letting go of all that, letting go of doing it based on our past experience, letting go of saying that you know from experience that you can get a product cheaper at store A, or that you know from experience if you take a certain class it will take you further ahead than another one. Here is one of the most amazing paragraphs in this whole book:

A healed mind is relieved of the belief that it must plan, although it cannot know the outcome which is best, the means by which it is achieved, nor how to recognize the problem that the plan is made to solve. W-135.12

You cannot know what the problem is ahead of time, whether it seems to be your problem or someone else's. He is saying that you cannot recognize ahead of time the problem that the plan is made to solve. We have all been taught that the best outcome is achieved by defining the problem and knowing what goals are best. That is what all of the judgment of the world is based on; you know the good outcomes and the bad outcomes so that you can strive to achieve the good outcomes and avoid the bad ones. He is saying that you cannot know that, nor can you know the means by which it is achieved. You have to trust Him.

"The mind engaged in planning for itself is occupied in setting up control of future happenings." W-135.15 That has been your whole life! Look at all of our lives. What kind of life is this if you are not trying to plan for or control future happenings?

Friend: That is exactly what I was going through last week. I knew this was a lesson for me. It is something that I deal with all the time in my business and it is time for me to learn that lesson. I do not know how much of it I learned, but I do know to quit reacting to things that happen – to recognize that I had an outcome and expectation planned.

David: And when you trace it back a bit, there is the fear of falling behind and being in debt, and when you trace that in, it gets back to "my security;" security of what? In the beginning of this lesson it tells us that it is the body's security we seek to protect – to save it from death. You can see that when you trace it back. The more we do this, the more we see the insanity of constantly defending and protecting the body and working for its betterment. There is a heavy investment in that. The more we see that it is foolish, that it is tightening the grip on our mind, the more we begin to let go of it.

It was a great example to take something concrete like that and work it back. I appreciate you bringing it up because we need to start like that. If we get too much into a theoretical conversation it is not truly meaningful. We want to keep it practical. And that was a good example. When we do that we all get clearer.

Friend: I can see that in business this just would not work at all. If I told my boss that I did not have a plan or any goals, they could not deal with it. I was doing some of this when I was in twelve steps, but I still had to play the game at work. Do people integrate that or do they leave these jobs?

David: We feel guided by the Spirit. The shift takes place in the mind and then what takes place on the screen is the witness or the out-picturing. Otherwise it seems like we are trying to put round pegs into square holes. If we tell Jesus that we cannot apply this Course at our jobs, his answer is: *Come back here into the mind and we will question the beliefs.* You start to loosen the identification of being a worker or being in the mode of planning outcomes. When you begin to step back you will call forth witnesses; you begin to have a more expansive concept of yourself. In other words, Jesus is not taking us from this little tiny self-concept straight into abstract reality. It does not work that way. Salvation's task is changing concepts.

Maybe someone sees himself or herself as just a factory worker and then they begin to think there is more than just being a factory worker. It seems like we develop abilities and our concepts start to expand, we seem more fluid and flexible. Really what we are doing is that we are changing concepts in our mind. We are starting to approach the one concept that leads out–which is forgiveness. Forgiveness is an all-inclusive concept. It is still a concept; there is no forgiveness in Heaven as there is not anything to be forgiven for. God does not forgive because He has never condemned. It is illusions that need forgiveness. So we take these little steps more and more and more. We are being led towards a concept of a "teacher of God" or a "minister of God," which is a lot different than "production manager." Ultimately we are being led towards a concept of total forgiveness.

We had a friend in Cincinnati who was working in a sales job where his manager kept telling him to set sales goals. He kept feeling more and more that there was a conflict and the whole point was to see that the conflict is in the mind. Eventually it became a very competitive situation where the boss insisted he stick to the goals and accomplish this and that. All the while he was feeling more and more drawn to meditating and studying the Course. In the end there was a shift of mind, and he ended up leaving the position. But leaving does not relieve the conflict. The ego wants you to believe that if you leave one situation and go to a better one, then you will be in good shape. But the whole point is to see that the competition is not in the sales job. The competition is in my mind; the belief in competition is what the problem is. As we continue to move towards what the Course is talking about, things get taken care of. You may start to move away from the work ethic and the five or ten year plan; you may open to the Holy Spirit and trust that it will work out. But you will not get it in writing from Him. [group laughter] *This is what you will be doing next year as part of phase one of the plan.* It is not like that. It is about taking the step for today, for right now.

In the beginning I needed experiences that let me know I was going to be provided for. There were many synchronistic moments. I was guided to a garage sale and got a car for $100. I was guided there, and my other car broke down in front of the garage sale and had to be towed away. It was so synchronistic; I could not have planned that in a million years. It was obviously hand-off time. I needed that. That was the Holy Spirit going before me saying: *You are going to be okay. This seems scary, but you are okay.*

There can be a temptation to get stuck in this thing of manifesting. You hear in some circles, "I manifested myself a job, I manifested myself a new mate, just the way I wanted." [laughter] The Course is saying that you have a powerful mind so why not use it for peace of mind–to wake up and be totally free? Do not rest in bringing about certain outcomes; do not pray for the *effect*. Ask to be shown a different way of looking at the world. There is a natural progression towards that. As we traveled we had so many synchronistic experiences where things would seem to show up just as we needed them; you could write a whole book on that. It makes for good reading because it is exciting and fun, even magical in a way, but after a while you just become completely focused on your purpose and convinced that you will be provided for. The fear level goes down, and then the whole focus is just on seeing the world differently, on seeing the ego belief system and getting to the bottom of it.

Finding Your Special Function–Help With Guidance

Hi David,

On January 1st I started the Course over from scratch. I rapidly and dedicatedly read the Text and started out strong on the Workbook, but have fallen off now from the lessons. I am still doing it, but not as willingly as before. I do feel like I have learned a lot and feel very differently about things, but the best way I can describe my inner feeling is like I am a fish out of water, floundering all over. I have so many pieces of information in my head but they are not coming together, like puzzle pieces on a table that are not put in place. Do you have any suggestions? I keep having these feelings that I cannot do this. Although I understand the words intellectually and feel like I know what is being said, I cannot relate at all to the feelings. I am hoping you have some advice for me.

Beloved One,

Thanks for sharing what is on your heart. The feelings you are experiencing are very common for those who use the Course and attempt the Workbook lessons. Remember that it is up to the Holy Spirit to use your little willingness to eventually convince your mind of true forgiveness through the experience of many, many miracles. Miracles light the way, and you can already feel yourself looking upon the world a little differently than before. Each miracle convinces the mind and is a step in becoming completely right-minded.

The Holy Spirit wants to use your interests and skills and abilities in the process of Awakening. In my case He has used my university studies and communication abilities, my interest in music and movies, and my willingness to travel and express His Purpose. The use of these things is highly individualized for each person. The Holy Spirit uses what you like and are drawn to so artfully that the ego resistance to the Light within fades and fades and falls away as miracles come and light the way.

Allow your mind the permission to open to the thought that Awakening can actually be fun and enjoyable, and that resistance to the Course is only the ego's judgment of progress and growth. Of course the ego resists the Course. Be not dismayed by the ego, for You are not it and it will never be You. You are the Christ, and every step in Awakening to Know Thy Self is for rejoicing! You can remind yourself often of our Worthiness of Love and our Holiness, and remember that Jesus and Holy Spirit are worthy of trust and gratitude.

Make a list of everything you love and appreciate about yourself. Then offer the list to the Holy Spirit to use in a highly individualized way in the Plan of Awakening. Pay attention to the way you feel, and be aware of ways your passion can be used by the Spirit and focused toward the Purpose that benefits everyOne. I am with you all the way!

Chapter Seven

Beyond the Body

The home of vengeance is not yours; the place you set aside to house your hate is not a prison, but an illusion of yourself. The body is a limit imposed on the universal communication that is an eternal property of Mind. But the communication is internal. Mind reaches to itself. It is *not* made up of different parts, which reach each other. It does not go out. Within itself it has no limits, and there is nothing outside it. It encompasses everything. It encompasses you entirely; you within it and it within you. There is nothing else, anywhere or ever. T-18.VI.8

That paints a picture of Mind. In the very next sentence he contrasts it with the body:

The body is outside you and but seems to surround you, shutting you off from others and keeping you apart from them, and them from you. It is not there. T-18.VI.9

The body is kind of like on the surface of the Mind, where all the projections and attack thoughts are, way on the outside. It is outside you but through the experiences of the deceived mind it seems to be wrapped around your mind. It seems like consciousness is somewhere in the head looking out through these eyes.

Friend: That is because we cannot seem to deny the brain. Tell me again, what is the real story about the brain and the Mind?

David: The Mind is not in the brain; it is not in the body. I think the best analogy that the Course uses over and over is that of the *dreamer of the dream*. A friend recently said to me, "I was reading the Course the other day and I just got something that I never got before. I used to think of the script in terms of all these other people out there but I did not include my own body in it, but it is *out there* too." To me that is the best analogy of the Mind, in the sense that the *dreamer of the dream* is watching all the characters on the screen, including its own character. But the Mind has no reference point in this world. It does not go out. The Mind is so expansive that there is no limit. When you ask where the Mind is, you have to understand that *place* is a concept in the split mind. Only a deceived mind could even have such a crazy idea as *place*.

Friend: It says in Chapter 16: "His Kingdom has no limits and no end and there is nothing in Him that is not perfect and eternal. All this is *you* and nothing outside of this is you." T-16.III.7 and somewhere else it says, "There is nothing outside you." T-18.VI.1 Here it says that the body is outside of you; obviously that means that the body is nothing because there is nothing outside of us. Even the body is not outside of us, because we are Mind. We are having this nightmare and are sitting there drawing these little stick figures. This one burns up in a car wreck and this one does this to that one, but it is *us* feeling guilty because we think that we could get away from God and we think we are playing with this until we just take our hands away from the controls and recognize that we did not do any of it.

David: All the roles were assigned and everybody is just playing their part. Every time you hate somebody, it is because you believe they are not fulfilling the role the way you want it to be fulfilled.

Friend: I assigned you a certain role and you are not doing it.

David: The Course tells us that a metaphor for the assigned role is that they are always our savior, whether it is the wife, husband, child or boss that you think is supposed to act a certain way or give you a certain thing. The ego produced all these forms because the deceived mind is trying to use relationships to take vengeance out for the past. It really believes that it was deprived in the past and is therefore attracted to certain people and situations; it wants these people to fulfill roles and needs that it thought it was deprived of. It never works. The whole idea of deprivation is a scam; it comes from the attraction to guilt. As long as we set people up to be God substitutes from which we have all these expectations, of course there is going to be fury and anger when they do not seem to get fulfilled.

Friend: It is just another of the countless ways of making sure that we stay in ego. The ego is one nasty decision, just one, but there are so many ways that we are attracted to staying in that thought – because of our belief that we are the ego and our fear that love will swallow us up. The only thing the ego does is weaken us either by separation or by trying to convince us that we are weak or no good – because without that thought we would remember who we are. We are scared to be happy and attracted to misery. It is like I believe that as soon as I get happy, somebody is going to come along and burst my bubble, and I will be the fool. To me, that demonstrates my attraction to pain.

David: To pry away from the ego you have to have a sense of how the ego thinks. That is why we have all these sections on *The Laws of Chaos* where Jesus lays out the ridiculous things we believe. There are myriad forms that seem to obscure the content, like you were saying—thoughts that separate or weaken. The ego makes all these forms as a mirage of complexity to keep obscure its basic way of thinking. As soon as we can get in touch with the backwards ways of thinking, which is what the ego is, then we can tease it out and start to feel into something that is apart from these thoughts. But while they are swirling in our minds, we feel the feelings and we think the thoughts. There is such a strong belief that the thoughts are real, that they really are "my thoughts." But they are outside you; they are not who you are.

I am reminded of the section in the Course called *The Immediacy of Salvation*. A line that gets me every time I read it is, "Be not content with future happiness." T-26.VIII.9 It is so common for people to see themselves on a spiritual journey, thinking, *I am certainly not there now but in another year or ten years, or maybe in another lifetime I will get there.* Do not project this out into the future. Do not project salvation into the future.

Friend: It is just another excuse for not being happy right now.

David: Right. You were not deprived in the past. If you are feeling upset, it is a present decision. It has nothing at all to do with anything that seemed to happen in the past. It has everything to do with your interpretation right now. Do not project your anxiety off into events that you are afraid are going to happen in the future. Bring it back; it is a present decision right now. Jesus says that you really believe there is a gap between the time that you forgive and the time that you will receive the gifts of forgiveness. That is the fear in the mind, the fear that if you follow Him, the rage of the world will rest on your shoulders! There is such a fear of chaos and here Jesus is telling you to be totally defenseless. The key is to just totally let go.

Wanting the Experience of Forgiveness

Hi David,

Does forgiving illusions mean forgiving what a body does? If a body cheats or lies, hurts another body, or takes something away by deception, it is still not deception? It is our attachment to illusions and things like the body that can make us judge others or feel hurt or angry or say it was unjust. If we recognize that Spirit is all powerful, and cannot be hurt, and that only Spirit exists, then nothing that happens here matters. And we see everyone and everything from the point of wholeness. Even the deceitful thing that happened is probably to teach us a lesson not to value anything of this world, including the body. Thus we see sinlessness in all persons, things, and events.

If something happens that feels disturbing (fearful), do we just have to think that it will not have any effect on our living? This is really hard. We are afraid of losing our friends, family, our living conditions etc. I just have an understanding of these principles but have no firm conviction. Then we also have to develop present trust that the Holy Spirit will provide for all our needs as long as they are necessary. But first we have to experience miracles and that we are Spirit for conviction and inner knowing to come. Otherwise, it will be just based on theory. How do we get these miracles and Spirit experiences? In spite of doing ACIM, I have not had any such experience to speak of. At least this is my understanding of Christ's vision. Would you provide us with some insight into this? As always your valuable vision is tremendously appreciated.

Beloved One,

Thanks for sharing what is on your heart and for your sincere opening to the Spirit within. You have written what you are just beginning to grasp: "It is our attachment or belief in illusions of things or body that can make us judge others or feel hurt or angry or say it was unjust. If we recognize that Spirit is all powerful, and cannot be hurt, and that only Spirit exists, then nothing that happens here matters. And we see everyone and everything from the point of wholeness. Even the 'deceitful' thing that happened is probably to teach us a lesson not to value anything of this world, including the body."

Miracles bring conviction for they demonstrate what you have just written – the valuelessness of the body and world and the value of the Spirit, which is unchanging.

Miracles are experiences that dissolve belief and collapse time. If you are willing to question what you seem to believe and apply the words you have spoken to everything in your awareness, the experience of inner peace will be evident. If you seem to be afraid of losing friends, family, living conditions, etc., then there is an identity attachment to these things which is blocking the experience of the miracle. The miracle costs nothing and offers a glimpse of Everything. There is no sacrifice in Knowing God's Will and our Will is One with God's Will. Nothing real is lost or given up in serving God because the temporary never had any value whatsoever.

Releasing Roles; God Asks No Sacrifice

Hi David,

I am having a really hard time with the idea of letting go of the "mother story." I have children at home and elderly parents that I help. I am afraid that if I give my life into the hands of the Holy Spirit, I will happily dance away with Him and leave them to struggle on by themselves. That thought breaks my heart. Interestingly enough, I have recently begun to doubt my success in my chosen role—my son is angry, bitter, and filled with rage despite a near idyllic childhood. When you said that with the Holy Spirit obligations will be met as long as the belief in obligations exists, does that apply to emotional obligations? Any thoughts you can share will be accepted with an open heart.

Beloved One,

Emotional obligations that are interpersonal are dissolved away by the miracle. There are only two emotions that spring from opposing thought systems, and of the two, only love is real. One is always responsible for one's state of mind and this is actually one's only responsibility as a teacher of God.

The beatitudes of happiness, peace, joy, and freedom are reflections of the one true emotion, Love. This is God's Will, and nothing else exists.

The ego is the belief that Love has an opposite and that fear can be fragmented into many different forms of emotion: anger, guilt, pain, shame, envy, greed, etc. Whenever you feel as if following the Holy Spirit would leave a "loved one" abandoned to struggle and suffer, allow your mind to be reminded that God asks no sacrifice.

The temporal will not last and therefore is without value. The Eternal lasts forever and therefore is all value. This is the great emotional reversal, for the mind asleep believes it has thrown away Eternity and must search for, keep, and maintain the temporal for its survival and sustenance. The miracle re-translates the symbols of the world and demonstrates that nothing is ever lost.

Only the anticipation of Awakening is frightening. Awakening is always Loving. The ego interprets Awakening as death, for in Awakening there is no ego. When the fear of loss arises in awareness, step back and Call on the Holy Spirit for the Comfort of God. As you align with the miracle, the experience will show you that there is nothing to fear. Your Family is the Family of God in Spirit and Divine Mind and therefore has no beginning or end.

Going Deep with the Early Lessons

Lessons 51-54 are a review of the first 20 lessons of the Workbook. Let's use them to take a close look at the early lessons. Lesson 1 starts out with perception, with what the deceived mind seems to see: "Nothing I see means anything." The first three lessons deal with distorted perception and then *BINGO!* In lesson 4 he introduces thinking for the first time. Then he introduces the past in lesson 7:

> When I have forgiven myself and remembered Who I am, I
> will bless everyone and everything I see. There will be no past,
> and therefore no enemies. And I will look with love on all that
> I failed to see before. W-52.2. (7)

Lesson 8 combines time with thinking: "My mind is preoccupied with past thoughts." In this lesson he is talking both about the past and about thought: "My mind is preoccupied with past thoughts." The three main elements that are being worked with are time, perception, and thought; three different aspects that keep being interwoven.

> My mind is preoccupied with past thoughts. I see only my own
> thoughts, and my mind is preoccupied with the past. W-52.3. (8)

If we replace "my own thoughts," with "ego thoughts," we have, "I see only ego thoughts and my mind is preoccupied with the past." This means that ego thoughts are the past. What then can I see as it is?

> Let me remember that I look on the past to prevent the
> present from dawning on my mind. Let me understand that
> I am trying to use time against God. Let me learn to give
> the past away, realizing that in so doing I am giving up
> nothing. W-52.3. (8)

Let's look at the line, "Let me understand that I am trying to use time against God." That is the basic problem. The mind is trying to use time against God; everything we go into will be about getting clear on what that is. Time in and of itself is not harmful but time used for the ego's purposes is harmful in the sense that it takes away peace of mind. You lose the awareness of peace of mind. The ego's construct of time is linear; the ego tells the deceived mind that you are guilty in the past. The ego says: *Look at you, as a person. Look at your past. Look at all the mistakes you have made. Look at all the things you have done wrong. Look at all the things that you have messed up. You are convicted. You are guilty in the past.* There is no doubt about that, and then it wants to skip over the present and say to the mind: *And your future is going to be as bad as it was before.* It is a closed system. You can see why there would be fear of retribution or fear of pain to come in the future if the mind listens to the ego's belief that pain and guilt were real in the past. It wants to skip over the present and see that there is going to be more of the same. That is the ego's use of time. You can see that if you listen to the ego about time, guilt will be reinforced. There will be fear of future consequences.

The Holy Spirit does not skip over the present; the Holy Spirit emphasizes the present as the only aspect of time that is valuable – the only aspect of time there really is.

> I see nothing as it is now. If I see nothing as it is now, it can truly be said that I see nothing. I can see only what is now. The choice is not whether to see the past or the present; the choice is merely whether to see or not. What I have chosen to see has cost me vision. Now I would choose again, that I may see. W-52.4. (9)

Here He introduces the idea of vision. Vision has nothing to do with the physical eyes. This is one of those things to keep your mind open about. You do not want to fall into a sense of complacency, of thinking about how far you have come or how spiritually advanced you are. Remember, "The choice is not whether to see the past or the present. The choice is merely whether to see or not." If you perceive a world where there are separate images and you still feel a charge about anything, that is the indicator that you want to ask for Help. *Lord, help me today. I am determined to see. Help me to see.* That is where the openness and the humility come in. If you feel a charge about something, you not only are not seeing clearly, you are not seeing at all. This gets away from the thinking of seeing better or more clearly than ever before. That can sometimes feel like a little pep talk, but you can fall into complacency and be content with "seeing better." Ultimately we have to come to understand that even seeing the door handle is an attack thought. It does not seem to be an attack thought but you actually make all things your enemy because everything that the deceived mind sees is something that exists in and of itself, as a separate thing. That is a picture of attack thoughts. It thinks it sees all these separate things that exist apart from my mind, but it cannot be so.

There are so many expressions of the mind thinking of itself as a person, as a separate person, like all your feelings of longing or restlessness, for example. Restlessness is the thought that there is something different you could be doing or someplace else you would rather be. That is a pretty common thought that rolls through consciousness; if only I had the resources I could…. That is an expression of the mind thinking of itself as a person that is imagining other situations and events that it likes more than its current circumstances. This is impossible. Where else can you go? You have always surrounded yourself with projections and illusions. What is the difference if the constellation seems to move a little bit from this scene to that one? Attack thoughts are still attack thoughts, no matter if the body seems to be here or there. You can imagine the body with the ideal soul mate in the ideal setting, Hawaii–Waikiki beach. There you go. You could fantasize about scenes with this ideal soul mate, what you would do, where you would go, what you would eat. But the whole basis behind this is a belief that reality is yours to choose from and that you can imagine things a lot better than they are now–if only something was different.

If cause and effect are apart, you ain't seen nothing yet; *I have seen glimmers of more pearls on distant shores that I have not yet partaken of.* What we are trying to see is that there are no pearls on any distant shores. There *seem* to be so many options. It would not be difficult at all to use the word infinite to describe the choices of the world, and what about in the cosmos? *The Urantia Book* says earth is one tiny speck out of the whole projected time/space cosmos. Just in the realm called earth there seem to be an enormous number of choices. Some might use the word infinite, but infinite ultimately means having no end and everything in form has an end. There are a finite number of choices.

The key is the Atonement. Atonement was built into the whole time/space continuum, or the whole thought of separation. The Atonement put an end, a limit on the mind's ability to miscreate. It can seem as if that is an infringement on free will, but it is kind to have that built in. Jesus says it would not be kind to let you go on and on and have to choose from every option. Talk about taking a long, long time. It is precious when you can start to generalize the transfer of training from a trip to Hawaii or switching around relationships, or all the different things that are attempted. When seekers come together and start sharing their stories, even though the forms vary they are all really the same in terms of the underlying content. Ah, we have all been seeking in the wrong place! Even though the forms of our seeking have varied, we see very clearly that this is not the way; there is no rest in being a seeker. The only rest comes from being a finder. That is the experience we are pointing to. It is not good enough to work your way to the edge of the cliff. The only reason you got to the edge was to jump! There is no rest in being at the edge of the cliff because even though it seems like there is been quite a progression in getting there, there is no release aside from jumping.

In a sense you could say that to try to pierce the veil and just go directly into the light – without having questioned the darkness – is kind of like a bungee jump. You go into the light and then you seem to get hurled back; it is very disorienting. It is not satisfying because you have a burning yearning to return and yet there is still a fear of it. There are many things that are still unquestioned. That is why the mind has to stay with what is, to let go into the water, or to let go into the light.

OK, we are up to lesson number 10; now let us recap a bit. The Workbook starts off with: "Nothing I see means anything ... I have given what I see all the meaning it has for me ... I do not understand anything I see." Three different lessons to start off on the topic of perception; not only does it not mean anything, it is not even understandable. The reason is that everything in the world is entirely subjective, or, you could say, seen entirely from the ego's perspective. The subject in that sense is subjective; it is the ego, which really has no meaning at all. Therefore nothing I see means anything, and I do not understand anything I see. Lesson 4 does not yet make the overt connection that thoughts produce the perceptions, it just introduces the idea that your thoughts do not mean anything. Lesson 5 continues with "I am never upset for the reason I think." Once thinking has been introduced, upset comes into the picture. Lesson 6: "I am upset because I see what is not there." The upset is being related to hallucination, or seeing a world that does not exist. Then in lesson number 7 we have our first lesson in time: "I see only the past." We jump from "I am upset because I see what is not there," to "I see only the past." What is not there is the past! There is a connection between those two. My mind is preoccupied with past thoughts. The idea of "time" or "past" is associated with the thoughts that are first brought up in lesson 4. I see nothing as it is now.

It is foreshadowing the idea that the holy instant and the world do not have anything to do with each other. The holy instant is non-perceptual. The holy instant is revelatory and therefore I see nothing as it is now. "My thoughts do not mean anything;" that is lesson number 10:

> My thoughts do not mean anything. I have no private thoughts. Yet it is only private thoughts of which I am aware. What can these thoughts mean? They do not exist, and so they mean nothing. Yet my mind is part of creation and part of its Creator. Would I not rather join the thinking of the universe than to obscure all that is really mine with my pitiful and meaningless "private" thoughts? W-52.5. (10)

It could be said in general that people often feel that their lives seem meaningless, that they run around doing a lot of stuff, feeling out of control, and feeling helpless, feeling like they are part of a larger system from which they cannot escape. And that is just the *doing*—the feeling that the actions of life seem meaningless. Why am I going to work? Why am I doing this same task over and over? Why am I cutting my lawn for the 979th time? Why am I polishing the silverware? Why am I doing this oil change? Why am I stacking this wood? Why do I keep repeating these same things? What is the purpose of all these repetitive actions that seem like toil at times? And those are just the actions! This lesson is saying my *thoughts* do not mean anything, meaning all the trains of thoughts that just seem to roll through the mind over and over. It is not only that all the physical actions do not mean anything but the thoughts that rumble through the mind do not mean anything either. The thoughts are perceived by the deceived mind as what it is; it is identified with those thoughts.

The basic ego belief is that the truth is different for everyone; *to each his own*. That is ludicrous! It cannot be so. It cannot be the reality; *to each his own*. You could use *to each his own* as the metaphor or stepping stone, to say each has his own experience and experience is non-transferable. But in the end there is an experience that is universal and there is no individual in that experience. It is truly an impersonal experience. *To each his own*, or *the truth is different for everyone* are basic ideas that have to be questioned. They represent the belief in private thoughts and private minds. Notice as we go along where the resistance comes up. Watch how tenaciously the deceived mind tries to protect the idea of private thoughts, because if that goes, everything goes. Once the dam that is holding onto the idea of private thoughts breaks, then there is nothing that will hold the river back.

We have learned about thoughts, and we have learned about a world that does not mean anything and is not understandable. Now the connection is made in lesson 11 that the thoughts are producing the world. The meaningless thoughts are producing the meaningless world.

> My meaningless thoughts are showing me a meaningless world. Since the thoughts of which I am aware do not mean anything, the world that pictures them can have no meaning. What is producing this world is insane, and so is what it produces. Reality is not insane, and I have real thoughts as well as insane ones. I can therefore see a real world, if I look to my real thoughts as my guide for seeing. W-53.1. (11)

This sets the stage for ideas like "Therefore, seek not to change the world, but choose to change your mind about the world." T-21.in.1 "Seek not to change the world" makes sense if my mind is producing the world. Of course, I will have to change my mind if I want a significant change to take place. It is important to really open oneself to this idea. It cannot be just an intellectual idea where I continue to play the part of being a person. It is to see that those roles, and that person, and everything that seems to be happening is just a projection of meaningless thoughts. It cannot be both ways. This is why I call a lot of what seems to be going on, a transitory phase, because what is approaching, as quickly as you want it to approach, is a real devotional life – an inward life; a life that is perhaps best symbolized by monasteries and convents where you focus the mind on God, only on the thought of God, forgetting everything else. The image or metaphor that is coming is a priest without a parish, a monk without a monastery, a philosopher without a profession.

The other day our friend asked why not get a job and work the spiritual activities in around the work schedule, as if you can do that. The very essence of this is you do not work anything into a schedule. You put God first in your mind. How does that look on the outside? Well, it does not have any particular form, but I guarantee you, symbolically as you start devoting your mind solely to thinking of God every minute and every second of every day, you end up approaching what I call mysticism. That is why the mystics in India would go off into the woods and just sit there and do nothing, or do some teaching, but generally live very simple lives in silence. They were focusing their minds on God and nothing but God. The children of the village would go out and bring a bowl of rice once in a while or a piece of bread. It would be their joy to drop off a piece of bread to this kind, gentle, funny man or woman that was sitting out there in the woods saving the world by accepting enlightenment in their own mind – by withdrawing their mind from the world. That is why it just seems on the outside to get simpler and simpler, because what is the point of devoting your mind to trying to keep the game going once you see that the game of the world is in one's own mind? And the only way that you can let go of the game of the world is not through doing but through meditation.

Lesson 11 is a key element: "My meaningless thoughts are showing me a meaningless world." Until you start to make that metaphysical connection you are going to believe there is an external world outside your mind that is real. You are going to continue to try to adjust to it and still try to make your way in it, even if it is by being *A Course in Miracles* teacher, or trying to leave behind a legacy as a renowned Course teacher. Someone could say Jesus left behind an enormous legacy, all of Christianity, but in the ultimate sense he did not. It is a hallucination. There is nothing real about history or Christianity or anything like that. It is not like Jesus came, lived a real life in the flesh and then left the flesh to go to another real place, the Kingdom of Heaven, or to be on the right hand of the Father, as if that is coexisting now with the world. How does this world coexist with Heaven? How does duality coexist with Oneness? Do not get into the trap of trying to think of *A Course in Miracles* as a system and go around talking about it as a system. Do not even get into the trap of focusing on it as a tool. The key thing is to go for the experience. The Course is just symbolic of your Mind's desire to go for the experience and nothing more. It certainly is not causative.

Lesson 12 follows. "I am upset because I see a meaningless world." That can also relate back to lesson 6, "I am upset because I see what is not there." You could combine them and say: *I am upset because I see a meaningless world that is not there.*

> Insane thoughts are upsetting. They produce a world in which there is no order anywhere. Only chaos rules a world that represents chaotic thinking, and chaos has no laws. I cannot live in peace in such a world. W-53.2. (12)

"I cannot live in peace in such a world." Isn't that nice to know right off the bat that I do not have to try to live in peace in such a world? I do not have to try to be a peaceful person living in the world. I do not care how many people come to me quoting the passage from the Bible, about being in the world but not of it. I cannot settle for being in the world anymore. It could be a stepping stone but that line, "I cannot live in peace in such a world," is pointing to something other than the Kingdom of Heaven on Earth or Paradise in this world. It fits with every other lesson that we are reading. My insane thoughts are producing an insane world. My chaotic thinking is producing a chaotic world and there is no way that I can live in peace in such a world because it is made out of chaotic thinking.

> I am grateful that this world is not real and that I need not see
> it at all unless I choose to value it. And I do not choose to value
> what is totally insane and has no meaning. W-53.2. (12)

That is what it takes. I remember when I used to go out into the woods and deliberately eat bland foods. I would take bread and water and simple foods with no spices. I would spend a while just noticing the contrast. Then when I would go back into the city I would just notice the feelings about the soft couch to lie down on, or the movie playing, or the talk show; I would just notice the thrill of seeing a talk show again.

Friend: So you are talking about just noticing there was still attraction there?

David: Noticing the attraction, noticing an attraction to the stimulation, noticing an attraction to the busyness.

Friend: And the body comfort.

David: Yes, and the false associations, like with a long, hot bath in contrast to the sponge bath every several days in the woods. That is all that it comes down to, associations. There is still an attraction to this kind of insane thinking. There is still an attraction to being a personal, private, little self. That is what is underneath it; it is not the long hot bath in and of itself, or the Hershey bars, or the long couch to stretch out on. Those are just the associations. Behind all the associations is both the desire to hold onto a private self, as well as the fear of letting go into the light.

Friend: The wish to be separate.

David: The wish to be separate, still unquestioned, and a sense of restlessness and discontent. Here we are. We are back to, "I cannot live in peace in such a world. I am grateful that this world is not real and that I need not see it at all unless I choose to value it." Sometimes there can be a feeling of being caught between a rock and a hard place. On the one hand there is the fear to go within and question, and on the other hand there is a specific irritation or grievance, let's say for example, feeling used. It feels upsetting to feel used, and the only alternative is to question everything you perceive. EVERYTHING! Or would you rather feel hurt and used than to question everything deeply? That is just one example but for each of you, every time you are upset, it comes down to that very same thing. Will you continue to question personhood and question private minds, or will you continue to feel_____(fill in the blank), whatever that is: depressed, upset, restless, tired, fatigued, etc. Just fill in the blank with the form of the upset. Lesson 13:

> A meaningless world engenders fear. The totally insane engenders fear because it is completely undependable and offers no grounds for trust. W-53.3. (13)

The thinking is undependable and the world that out-pictures the thinking is also undependable. The world is undependable. Even computers are undependable.

Friend: I can vouch for that.

David: Computers are inconsistent because the thinking that produced the computers is inconsistent. No wonder the world is unstable. No wonder it seems to behave in ways that the mind thinks it shouldn't. It is not perfectly consistent because there is nothing perfect in this world.

> Nothing in madness is dependable. It holds out no safety and no hope. But such a world is not real. I have given it the illusion of reality, and have suffered from my belief in it. Now I choose to withdraw this belief, and place my trust in reality. In choosing this, I will escape all the effects of the world of fear, because I am acknowledging that it does not exist. W-53.3. (13)

Instead of taking a stand for good or a stand against evil in the world, take a stand of saying that the world you see is not real, and the thoughts which you are thinking that are producing it are not real. Take a stand not to believe in it any more. The dream figures around you may say: *You fool, what do you think you are doing? You are losing your mind.* They may seem to accuse, and rather sharply at times.

> I choose to withdraw this belief and place my trust in reality. Choosing this I will escape all the effects of the world of fear because I am acknowledging that it does not exist. W-53.3. (13)

We are up to lesson 13. So far we have heard a little about cause and effect. In lesson 11 we get some reflection about the cause and effect relationship: "My meaningless thoughts are showing me a meaningless world." But, we still haven't heard much about the Cause. Lesson 5 did say: "Yet my mind is part of creation and part of its Creator," with a capital C, so there is a glimmer that there is something beyond it. The Creator or the Source is mentioned for the first time.

Now we go to lesson 14. Yay for the Big Guy! Glory Hallelujah! "God did not create a meaningless world." That is the hallelujah lesson. You go through all this other stuff about projecting out a meaningless world and my thoughts showing me a meaningless world, but here we are being introduced to the Kingpin and He has nothing to do with the chaotic world at all.

> How can a meaningless world exist if God did not create it? He is the Source of all meaning, and everything that is real is in His Mind. It is in my mind too, because He created it with me. Why should I continue to suffer from the effects of my own insane thoughts, when the perfection of creation is my home? Let me remember the power of my decision, and recognize where I really abide. W-53.4. (14)

This is a foreshadowing of the leap that must come; it is not like you have to whoop it up and throw your arms around everyone, but that is the kind of feeling inside your mind and inside your heart and that is the feeling that should be *the* feeling of the day. Jesus says there is one thought you can hold throughout the day and that is the thought of pure joy.

Friend: If I am in the Mind of God what else would it be?

David: Develop gratitude; let go into the joy! If you do not know what to be thankful for just thank God. This lesson shows us what to be thankful for. God did *not* create a meaningless world. That is stated in the negative; but I can be grateful for what he did create—for who I am. That is what you want to be grateful for, not specifics. Specifics are all just little reflections of that. Underneath a sense of gratitude for anything specific is the enormous gratitude that none of this is so! Thank God! The joy is not circumstance-dependent; it is not personal or specific. It is unfettered and unbound. It is just this feeling. Of course you can share words of thanks. They are like beams coming off the brilliant sun, little reflections of it. The joy can be expressed in various ways, but the expression points to the intrinsic joy. There is no need for a lot of praise; that is just the old way of pep talks and flattery. This is very much an intrinsic joy and the mind is really afraid of that light. All specifics are just backdrops. If you really go into it deeper you find there is nothing to be grateful for in specifics. For me, gratitude is no longer aimed at persons, places, or things.

> My thoughts are images that I have made. Whatever I see reflects my thoughts. It is my thoughts that tell me where I am and what I am. The fact that I see a world in which there is suffering and loss and death shows me that I am seeing only the representation of my insane thoughts, and am not allowing my real thoughts to cast their beneficent light on what I see. Yet God's way is sure. The images I have made cannot prevail against Him because it is not my will that they do so. My will is His, and I will place no other gods before Him. W-53.5. (15)

My thoughts tell me where I am and what I am. The deceived mind is wound into a web of dark thoughts, into a perception of feeling caught. Our thoughts are like a golf ball. When you tear the little white cover off you find one gigantic rubber band that you can unravel. It is wound very tightly but you can just keep pulling and pulling; it is a rubber band that has been wound all these times around a core. All my thoughts, wound tightly around the core, are telling me where I am and what I am. Until I question all that is wound around the core, I will really believe I am a person in the world, and I will really believe that I am all these roles. I will deny my reality in God in the process of doing that. Workbook lesson 16:

> I have no neutral thoughts. Neutral thoughts are impossible because all thoughts have power. They will either make a false world or lead me to the real one. But thoughts cannot be without effects. As the world I see arises from my thinking errors, so will the real world rise before my eyes as I let my errors be corrected. My thoughts cannot be neither true nor false. They must be one or the other. What I see shows me which they are. W-54.1. (16)

This puts thoughts into the black/white, all or nothing category. It is not that certain thoughts are more powerful than others. Sometimes people are impressed with specific thoughts, as if they are powerful, and see other thoughts as weak. But this lesson teaches that there are not any powerful thoughts or weak thoughts. There are not any big thoughts or little thoughts. There are only true thoughts and false thoughts. These are the only categories that are helpful. And they are just meant in a metaphorical sense. This lesson is very early on. Later the teaching is that ultimately there are not any false thoughts; they do not exist. But this is a helpful stepping stone.

Friend: So wouldn't the true or real thoughts be the powerful thoughts?

David: No. False thoughts are as powerful as real thoughts.

Friend: I guess they are very powerful; they created this world.

David: Ego thoughts are not weak. In fact, they are endowed with the power that the mind gives them and believe me, the mind is very powerful. That is why Jesus says "Thought and belief combine into a power surge that can literally move mountains." T-2.VI.9 It moves planets around the sun; it can certainly move mountains, little tiny bumps. But in this world, where the mind perceives itself as a person, mountains seem enormous and impenetrable by comparison to persons. But mountains are the result of the combination of thought and belief.

The deceived mind believes that attack thoughts are real and it feels guilty, so it tries to forget about them. It tries to keep them out of awareness. It seems to alleviate the guilt to believe that private thoughts do not exert any real influence on anything anyway. To down-play the power of one's thinking seems to alleviate the guilt, but the cost of that defensive maneuver is that the mind is seen as impotent. How does that fit with the power, glory, and magnitude of having been created by God? How can I be magnitude and also have a tiny mind with tiny little thoughts?

It is a stepping stone to see that God did not create a meaningless world and my mind holds only what I think with God. The first thing is seeing that there are judgmental thoughts that seem to be in my mind. And there seems to be something producing them—thinking them up. But I am not that thinker, nor the thoughts. I am not the judgmental thoughts, nor the thinker that produced them. That would have to be the wrong mind. Was Christ producing judgmental thoughts?

Friend: Right, did Christ produce the ego?

David: No.

Friend: If Christ and God are one, then nobody produced the ego and yet the ego seems to exist. But does it?

416

David: That is the question. It seems to, but you have to look at it closely so as to see that it cannot.

Friend: How can something seem to exist and not exist?

David: The key thing is going for the experience that negates all perception. To perceive oneself as a person in a world or in a room denies the fact of reality.

Friend: I have a hard time with that. I understand the goal is to undo this, but it certainly seems ludicrous to say the ego never happened while it seems to be happening. That seems insane to me.

David: Let's look at it this way: the Atonement is the awareness that the ego never happened. The statement you are making is that the Atonement seems ludicrous to you. That is the ego's point of view—that the Atonement is ludicrous. The Atonement is simply the awareness that nothing happened.

Friend: When you talk about it in that context I can see how I am either on one side or the other. There is no transition period or anything.

David: It is not a future goal. It just comes down to right now, it is this or it is that.

Friend: Which makes it clear why I have to leap. I cannot slowly become enlightened.

David: Very good deduction.

Friend: I have to let go of one to grasp the other. And if I try to do both simultaneously, it feels like I am doing the splits. I can see the need for being detached in my mind about what people think. As long as I am worried about what my mom's going to say, I cannot leap.

David: I would not even say I *cannot* leap. You could say that if you are concerned about what your mom is going to think, then you haven't leapt. We can leave the "can't" word out of it. It is not a matter of can or can't. It is a matter of have or haven't. The capability is not in question. The pain of not leaping will become intolerable.

Friend: It is just the weirdest thing to be in this situation because I want to know what it is going to be like before I do it. I want to know that it will be okay. And then I think I do not really feel that I have a choice anyway. I feel like it is not up to me. The only thing I can resolve myself to do is keep hitting the books and coming to these sessions. I feel like I am making these adjustments in my lifestyle to a life that has a purpose. I am kind of seeing where it leads, but often I do not feel that I can just choose it.

David: It has to be an internal decision. You have to put your mind to it. Looking around for externals will not help. You cannot even use "challenge" as a motivator, like to enjoy the challenge of it, because the experience you are coming to is that there is nothing challenging about anything. Even that fades away, as it says in the Teacher's Manual, "There is no challenge to a teacher of God." M-4.II.2

Friend: I have always wanted to get to know God, but I have always wanted that to be something separate from me, some greater power that is not me. This idea that the Father and the Son are One seems frightening. I have ego ideas caught up with that. There is an idea of loneliness, of just being in the middle of time and space all alone; like I am going to wake up and realize that I am really just this one person and I made everything else up. That kind of oneness is very isolating and scary. The Oneness that we are going for is not that of course. It is very expansive and very inclusive, complete and full.

David: You do not have to forgive the truth. Everyone who walks this world and believes that they are a private mind and a person in this world believes that they have to forgive the truth. They come to sessions with all these specific things, with grievances, irritations, annoyances and rage, etc. They believe that what seemed to happen really did happen; they believe they have to forgive the truth, as if I really did lose my job, I really did get yelled at, I really did get walked on, I really did get mistreated, and so on. And now I have to forgive that. But that which they describe is an illusion.

Forgiveness means to overlook. Forgiveness is for illusions. Overlook illusions. See illusions as illusions and look past them to what is real, to what is Spirit. If you believe that you are a real person in a real world in a real room—that simply denies truth. That is why the person and the world and the room have to be overlooked and seen as false. See that it is all just a projection of thought. Meaningless thoughts produce a meaningless world. Where can there be a grievance if I see that it is a meaningless world that I made up? Who mistreated me? Who can I think of that ever mistreated me? Did I ever mistreat me? This "I" is just a projected image. This body is just a projected image too.

What is forgiveness? It is seeing the false as false. It is nothing more than that. It is not seeing that there is something true and then overlooking it. It is just seeing it is false. Forgiveness is seeing that there is nothing causative in the world. Nothing ever got me to this point in the world. It is a common metaphor to think that everything I have ever done has gotten me to this point. Impossible! It is utterly ridiculous to think the past has brought me to the present. Mind is causative and to believe that anything in the world causes anything is a denial of the fact that Mind is causative. Forgiveness is the awareness that Mind is causative.

Freedom is of the Mind, Not the Body

David: Let's read from the section called *The Light of the Holy Relationship*.

> Do you want freedom of the body or of the mind? For both you cannot have. Which do you value? Which is your goal? For one you see as means; the other, end. And one must serve the other and lead to its predominance, increasing its importance by diminishing its own. Means serve the end, and as the end is reached the value of the means decreases, eclipsed entirely when they are recognized as functionless. No one but yearns for freedom and tries to find it. Yet he will seek for it where he believes it is and can be found. He will believe it possible of mind or body, and he will make the other serve his choice as means to find it. T-22.VI.1

Now that is pretty clear and simple. It fits right into the metaphysics; the world was made up for the mind to run away from pure abstract light, abstract Oneness, and hide in specifics – identified with form. The purpose was to forget, dissociate from the light, and even forget about the mind. As I was growing up, I remember a lot of talk about brains and bodies, about the concrete and about form – but there was not a lot of discussion of mind. Mind and thoughts were hazy, vague kinds of things to talk about.

This paragraph helps put that into perspective: Which do you value, and where do you want your freedom? Do you want freedom of the body or freedom of the mind? They are mutually exclusive in that whichever one you decide on is going to be your value; it is going to be your freedom. Whichever one you decide brings freedom you will automatically pursue as your end, and you will use the other one as a means to reach that end.

You could say I was sleeping all those years spent in college. All the education, all of the skills and abilities we learn with our mind, if they are seen as the means, then the end is the body. The end is to buy bigger, better things for the body, to shelter it in better ways, to provide more conveniences and comforts for it, using the mind as the means. Which do you want? Do you want to be in a free and open mind? To do so, you have to let the body be the means. Here's a companion paragraph, from the *I Need Do Nothing* section:

> You still have too much faith in the body as a source of strength. What plans do you make that do not involve its comfort or protection or enjoyment in some way? This makes the body an end and not a means in your interpretation, and this always means you still find sin attractive. No one accepts Atonement for himself who still accepts sin as his goal. T-18.VII.1

It always gets back to interpretation: How do I perceive the body? As long as I perceive the body as the end, I am misperceiving it and sin is still attractive. That might seem to be a big stretch. Why is it that if I see my body as an end then I find sin attractive? How does that connect? A paragraph in the *Manual for Teachers* will help bring that connection into focus. He points to how the body is the focal point of all of the things of this world.

> It takes great learning both to realize and to accept the fact that the world has nothing to give. What can the sacrifice of nothing mean? It cannot mean that you have less because of it ... There is no sacrifice in the world's terms that does not involve the body. Think a while about what the world calls sacrifice. Power, fame, money, physical pleasure; who is the "hero" to whom all these things belong? Could they mean anything except to a body? Yet a body cannot evaluate. M-13.2

In a worldly sense, power, fame, money, and physical pleasure are all rooted in the body. That is what all the striving is about – trying to get ahead, trying to move up in the world, trying to get more than the next person. You could throw the term "intelligence" in here too, in the sense that although it is a mental thing, it is tied into self-image.

Politicians talk about the need to sacrifice for future generations. Just notice all the ways that sacrifice comes in; there is a belief that there is a benefit to sacrifice. But if you listen to the speeches, it always has to do with better money, better jobs, and better living quarters—for the body! Here is the key point: "Could they mean anything except to a body? Yet a body cannot evaluate." He rules out the body because it is simply a learning device. The body just responds to the intentions of the mind. Bodies do not judge; bodies do not evaluate; bodies do not learn. They do not even react, they are simply *told* to react, like a robot or a puppet responding to the intentions of the mind. Now we shift to the mind:

> By seeking after such things the mind associates itself with the body, obscuring its Identity and losing sight of what it really is. M-13.2

There is our key sentence. That is why making the body an end makes sin attractive. Once again, the natural condition of the mind and the true identity is pure Spirit; it is purely abstract. There is no form connected with it at all. But once the mind starts associating with the body, and with form, with the finite, it starts to seek outside of itself. It believes it has thrown away its eternal home—its eternal identity—and it is going to cling and attach onto that which is finite. The next sentence is the kicker:

> Once this confusion has occurred, it becomes impossible for the mind to understand that all the "pleasures" of the world are nothing. But what a sacrifice,—and it is sacrifice indeed!—all this entails. Now has the mind condemned itself to seek without finding; to be forever dissatisfied and discontented; to know not what it really wants to find. M-13.3

In this profound confusion the mind is completely turned around and twisted because it is identifying with something it is not. In doing so it completely discards all remembrance of its natural state.

> Where freedom of the body has been chosen, the mind is used as means whose value lies in its ability to contrive ways to achieve the body's freedom. Yet freedom of the body has no meaning, and so the mind is dedicated to serve illusions. This is a situation so contradictory and so impossible that anyone who chooses this has no idea of what is valuable. Yet even in this confusion, so profound it cannot be described, the Holy Spirit waits in gentle patience, as certain of the outcome as He is sure of His Creator's Love. He knows this mad decision was made by one as dear to His Creator as love is to itself. T-22.VI.2

Who has not experienced this? This has been our whole lives! Now he is telling us it is all backwards, but he is also telling us that the Holy Spirit is in the mind and He has great patience.

> Be not disturbed at all to think how He can change the role of means and end so easily in what God loves, and would have free forever. But be you rather grateful that you can be the means to serve His end. This is the only service that leads to freedom. To serve this end the body must be perceived as sinless, because the goal is Sinlessness. The lack of contradiction makes the soft transition from means to end as easy as is the shift from hate to gratitude before forgiving eyes. You will be sanctified by your brother, using your body only to serve the sinless. And it will be impossible for you to hate what serves whom you would heal. T-22.VI.3

There are many forms of attack that are not seen as such. The mind in its deceived state does not even know what they are. In the *Special Love Relationship* and various other sections, the Course says that you do not know all the forms of attack but if you can get clear about that, you can withdraw your mind from them; you can stop attacking yourself.

> In the holy instant, where the Great Rays replace the body in awareness, the recognition of relationships without limits is given you. T-15.IX.3

Relationships without limits!

> But in order to see this, it is necessary to give up every use the ego has for the body, and to accept the fact that the ego has no purpose you would share with it. For the ego would limit everyone to a body for its own purposes, and while you think it has a purpose, you will choose to utilize the means by which it tries to turn its purpose into accomplishment. This will never be accomplished. Yet you have surely recognized that the ego, whose goals are altogether unattainable, will strive for them with all its might, and will do so with the strength that you have given it. T-15.IX.3

We gradually get more accustomed to a sense of *mind*, of abstractness. In a section called *Beyond the Body*, the Course says:

Everyone has experienced what he would call a sense of being transported beyond himself. This feeling of liberation far exceeds the dream of freedom sometimes hoped for in special relationships. It is a sense of actual escape from limitations. If you will consider what this "transportation" really entails, you will realize that it is a sudden unawareness of the body, and a joining of yourself and something else in which your mind enlarges to encompass it. It becomes part of you, as you unite with it. And both become whole, as neither is perceived as separate. What really happens is that you have given up the illusion of a limited awareness, and lost your fear of union. The love that instantly replaces it extends to what has freed you, and unites with it. And while this lasts you are not uncertain of your Identity, and would not limit It. You have escaped from fear to peace, asking no questions of reality, but merely accepting it. You have accepted this instead of the body, and have let yourself be one with something beyond it, simply by not letting your mind be limited by it. T-18.VI.11

And when people speak about near-death experiences, this passage always comes to mind:

This can occur regardless of the physical distance that seems to be between you and what you join; of your respective positions in space; and of your differences in size and seeming quality. Time is not relevant; it can occur with something past, present or anticipated. The "something" can be anything and anywhere; a sound, a sight, a thought, a memory, and even a general idea without specific reference. Yet in every case, you join it without reservation because you love it, and would be with it. And so you rush to meet it, letting your limits melt away, suspending all the "laws" your body obeys and gently setting them aside. T-18.VI.12

In the next paragraph it says: "You are not really 'lifted out' of it; it cannot contain you." That is a great sentence; it gets away even from the idea of being lifted out of the body.

Friend: There is no out-of-body experience. There is no in-the-body experience.

David: Jesus asks this question of us all: "Do you want freedom of the body or of the mind? For both you cannot have." T-22.VI.1 Whichever one you pick as the answer to this question, you will use the other one as means. That is what we have done in our so-called lives in this world. We have picked the body as the end and used our minds as the means to serve the body. Now the Holy Spirit is suggesting a turnaround: *You wanted to have a free mind didn't you? Let Me use your body to express miracles.*

The beginning of the section we just read is one of the clearest statements in the Course about mind and body. "Minds are joined; bodies are not." T-18.VI.3 And here is an idea repeated over and over in the Text and the Workbook as well, "Mind cannot attack." T-18.VI.3 If minds could really attack, then guilt would be real and justified. The deceived mind is so convinced that minds can attack; it is so convinced that it is guilty. The section goes on about how the deceived mind tries to displace or get rid of the guilt which it believes is absolutely real. It is positively sure that it is guilty. It is convinced, locked in, split, and fighting itself. This is one of the best sections of the Course for getting into these two levels – into the idea that minds are joined and bodies are not.

The second paragraph in the section *Beyond the Body* really gets to the heart of it! First we see how the deceived mind tries to hold onto the guilt:

> What could God give but knowledge of Himself? What else is there to give? The belief that you could give and get something else, something outside yourself, has cost you the awareness of Heaven and of your Identity." T-18.VI.2

Now he gets into the main thing that is going on with deception:

> And you have done a stranger thing than you yet realize. You have displaced your guilt to your body from your mind. T-18.VI.2

The mind is so convinced that it is guilty; it is not going to try to mince words with God on this. Being convinced that it is guilty, it displaces its guilt onto the body.

> Yet a body cannot be guilty, for it can do nothing of itself. You who think you hate your body deceive yourself. You hate your mind. T-18.VI.2

There it is! There are so many ways that people express hatred for their bodies, like *Oh, I am too fat,* or *I am too thin; my body is breaking down; I turned 40; I turned 50; I turned 70; I am getting old; I am getting wrinkly.* That is all just trying to dump the hate off on the body. You hate your mind! But as soon as we start to see how deep this hatred is we can start to change our mind, now that we know where the problem is. The body has nothing to do with it.

He continues, in that same section:

> You hate your mind, for guilt has entered into it, and it would remain separate from your brother's which it cannot do. T-18.VI.2

> Minds are joined; bodies are not. Only by assigning to the mind the properties of the body does separation seem to be possible. T-18.VI.3

This is where that whole idea of separate minds comes in, as if every person in this room has their own private mind. That is what the ego claims, but the Course says, *No way!*

> And it is mind that seems to be fragmented and private and alone. Its guilt, which keeps it separate, is projected to the body, which suffers and dies because it is attacked to hold the separation in the mind, and let it not know its Identity. T-18.VI.3

BOOK THREE
TRANSFER OF TRAINING

CONTENTS

Chapter One

Transfer of Training

The experience of joy comes to a willing mind that has given up all attempts to make exceptions to the miracle. Only exceptions block the awareness of ever-Present miracle mindedness. Let's look at some ideas that will help clarify what "transfer of training" is, as described in *A Course in Miracles*. This clarification will have tremendous benefits for anyone desiring to experience the State of Mind called Enlightenment.

Many have heard the teaching, *Love does not possess.* This world of time-space, made by the ego, is a construct of possession. Everything and everyone that makes up distorted perception is the result or outcome of the desire to possess. To be free of limits of any kind it is imperative to expose and release the concept of possession from the mind entirely. There is no such thing as partial forgiveness or partial healing, and no such thing as partial possession. Either the mind believes in possession and experiences the illusion of imprisonment, or the mind has forgiven or released the concept of possession and is naturally free and whole. There can be no compromise, middle-ground or "balance" with the release of possession. If you believe you can actually possess anything, you have allowed your mind to be possessed by error/illusion. Freedom is nothing more than the escape from concepts, and all ego concepts rest on the assumption of possession. Once this error is abandoned, all errors vanish immediately.

Think awhile on what seems to attract so much attention in the world: the body. What plans do you make that do not involve the comforts, conveniences and care of the body? You treat it like it is your home, a valued treasure in a world of transient images. Yet the body is nothing more than a temporary learning device that you can use awhile to expand your perception beyond its current limits. That is all. A free mind is one that no longer sees itself as in a body, firmly tied to it and sheltered by its presence. Without the concept of possession you would not believe that you can even possess a body. Yet your beliefs extend far beyond just seeing the body as a possession; you have identified yourself with the body and therefore see yourself as temporary and transitory. How can there be consistency and stability at all if your identity is in constant flux and change? And this self-concept, this "identity," seems to change and be as unstable as the things with which it has surrounded itself. No stability is possible in an impossible situation, and this world of time-space is just that—an impossible situation. Every day the deceived and untrained mind concerns itself with survival of the body, and the state of this mind often seems stressed and at times angry, fearful, and guilty. Though these conditions of mind are illusions, they seem very real to a mind that believes in the error of possession. Possession is a synonym for the ego, for the ego desires to *get* and has no awareness of True Giving, which is the natural attribute of Spirit. Only the mind can be freed and it can only be freed through the peace of forgiveness (the release of illusion). How simple is salvation.

Trust in the Holy Spirit is a basic requirement for experiencing freedom of mind. Without trust in the Holy Spirit the spiritual journey will seem like an intellectual endeavor, an impossible undertaking or a sorrowful, intense series of trials and temptations. What is temptation but the wish to make illusions real? And who will Awaken to God's eternal Love who still values the illusions of the ego? As you answer the Call to Awaken and be glad, the Purpose of forgiveness is strengthened in awareness and the need for the concerns and the dramas surrounding the body fade away. Thus it can accurately be said that without trust in the Holy Spirit and devotion to this Purpose, the Awakening will seem to be delayed until there is a willingness to trust. As you develop trust in the Holy Spirit all perceived problems will disappear from awareness, and with acceptance of the Atonement, it is certain that "problems" will never return again.

Since the topic is transfer of training, our brief discussion will eliminate aspects of this world that seem most problematic, for they are all the same. All of the aspects I discuss are based on the concept of possession, and therefore the Answer or Solution will always be as simple as the release of this erroneous concept. Trust in the Holy Spirit undoes the concept of possession, and as possession dissolves away only the Light of Spirit remains in awareness. The Light of the Spirit simply Is; when the obstacles have been removed, the Light shines unobstructed in awareness. The Light of Love is perfect Oneness. There is nothing lacking or incomplete in perfect Oneness. This is the Unity and Purity of Heart that Christ radiates forever, being God's Love.

In the time-space cosmos this Love has been temporarily forgotten—pushed out of awareness. The sleeping mind has therefore experienced a kind of amnesia about the Kingdom of Heaven. It seems preoccupied with bodies, environment, food, clothing, shelter, entertainment, competition, betterment, pleasure, attack, economic advancement, education, and striving for progress or destruction in a variety of ways. These pursuits leave the mind mired in an unnaturally stressful state that is highly busy and exceptionally unproductive. Productivity and Creativity are synonymous, yet the makings and the strivings of the ego have nothing to do with true Creativity. The imaginations and goals of the ego serve only to perpetuate the illusion of linear time-space.

The linear time-space cosmos of distortion is a game. The only way the game becomes consistently happy is when you allow the Holy Spirit to interpret the game from the lofty Perspective of non-judgment. Possession is a belief (the ego) which seemed to set the game of time-space in motion. The game cannot be won or lost. The game can only be forgiven or Observed in a beneficent way. The game is in the mind. Though the ego projects a world which seems to be the game, it is not.

The game cannot be forgiven or observed correctly until you realize that the game is in the mind. Economics are therefore in the mind. Sexuality is in the mind. War is in the mind. Competition, attack, defense, education, entertainment, pleasure, suffering, bodies, striving, etc. are all games that the sleeping mind is toying with. The game of time-space is only a game in the mind and has no reality whatsoever. It is a game of belief and has no real Substance or Spirit. The only thing necessary to be free of the linear time-space game is to stop playing the game and trust in the Holy Spirit for absolutely everything–absolutely everything. If you open to experiencing the Holy Spirit as the Provider you can open to experiencing your Self as Christ, as God, as the Creator. The Way is very simple, and it is only the ego that obscures the Way, the Truth, and the Life.

Dedicate your "life" to experiencing the peace that passeth the understanding of the world. Drama is replaced by Certainty; striving is replaced by rest; depression and boredom are replaced by joy and freedom; loneliness is replaced by intimacy of shared Purpose; and you are happily in Love with God and everything and everyone. So peacefully Present Am I, there is no longer an expectation that people, places, events, or things be any different than they Are. By Grace one lives in the Heart of God, serenely unaffected by the journey that never was. "How" did this awareness seem to happen? By trusting the Holy Spirit absolutely. The Holy Spirit is the "How," the Means and the End together as One. There is nothing left to search for, nothing left to attain. There is no problem to solve and nowhere to go. There is nothing left to do. Enlightenment is a Present experience.

The Experience beyond Theology

Friend: I am touched by your concern for me and the intensity of your passion for the Course. Its message of salvation was clearly demonstrated in your most recent post. You stress repeatedly that we tend to perceive only what we want to perceive, and that my perception represents what I want to see and not what is really there. I trust you will accept that this propensity to misperceive based on prejudice is not unique to me, and that you might also share it?

David: I love You as my very Self. The Joy of Christ is the intensity of the passion I express. I am aligned with the Holy Spirit's Perspective and do not share the "propensity to misperceive." I now see that illusion cannot be shared. Only the Holy Spirit's Perspective can be shared, for the "personal perspective" of the ego based on the premise of "private minds/private thoughts" was the only error. Only love can be shared, and the attempt to "share" an illusion is literally impossible. I know of your desire for true freedom, and therefore point out that your questioning must be aimed at what you believe freedom to be; it is what you believe it to be that is covering the Experience over in awareness. "It is of them who learned of freedom that you should ask what freedom is." T-20.IV.4.5

Friend: With "a little willingness" the Holy Spirit corrects our perception and then what we project is the Love of God, not the confusion of the ego?

David: Actually the Holy Spirit extends and the ego projects. Love extends and error projects. Projection is always of the ego.

> The difference between the ego's projection and the Holy Spirit's extension is very simple. The ego projects to exclude, and therefore to deceive. The Holy Spirit extends by recognizing Himself in every mind, and thus perceives them as one. Nothing conflicts in this perception, because what the Holy Spirit perceives is all the same. Wherever He looks He sees Himself, and because He is united He offers the whole Kingdom always. T-6.II.12

Friend: I will tell you also that almost everything I thought was true about the world and God forty years ago, I do not agree with today. My mind was changed about many things, and it was changed mostly by people with whom I initially disagreed totally. I was "a little willing" to listen when I came across a persuasive case, whether I "wanted" to believe it or not. So it is not true that there is no amount of evidence that can change my mind.

David: You are beginning to discover that everything that "you think you think" is completely meaningless. This is a reflection of the "undoing lessons" of the Workbook, particularly lesson 4 and lesson 10.

Friend: I will tell you one more thing; I spent three years in Biblical studies at a church college. Some of my teachers were spiritual giants and they taught me a great deal more than they knew they taught me. One thing they taught me was how to do theological and scriptural exegesis, carefully and professionally. I love doing both, with those who are capable of doing either, and that is not everyone, which is fine.

David: The concept of theology has only temporary value as a "stepping stone" to the Awakening Experience. The text of the Course is intended to make the Workbook lessons more meaningful, yet it is application of the lessons (without making exceptions) that is the key to the transformation of consciousness or the happy dream. The goal is true forgiveness, and theology must be laid aside for this Experience to occur in awareness.

Theology rests on belief. Because belief is not universal, argument and debate play a central role in theology. That is why Jesus tells us in the *Clarification of Terms* that though a universal theology isn't possible, a universal experience is! It is the *experience* that brings an end to all doubt.

Friend: We do not talk theology, we just DO IT. Whether talking about it or doing it with others, I usually learn something, which is where the joy comes in. God knows I am not always right; one cannot learn if one thinks one is. It does say after all: "Blessed are the peacemakers," There is nothing that says: Blessed are the theologians of peace.

David: Talking about theology can be summed up in the following passages:

> The study of the ego is not the study of the mind. In fact, the ego enjoys studying itself, and thoroughly approves the undertakings of students who would "analyze" it, thus approving its importance. Yet they but study form with meaningless Content. T-14.X.8.6

> All unhealed healers follow the ego's plan for forgiveness in one form or another. If they are theologians they are likely to condemn themselves, teach condemnation and advocate a fearful solution. T-9.V.3.3

Do not let the attachment to theology delay the application of the daily lessons, for all learning inspired by the Holy Spirit is aimed at the Experience of

Awakening. The ego is the seeming block to the awareness of this Experience and therefore it is the ego that must be unlearned or undone to wake up to Reality.

Friend: While studying the New Testament I also had time for a few psychology courses, including one in perceptual psychology. The bias of perception, so often stressed in the Course, was presumably well known to the psychology professors, Helen Schucman and Bill Thetford. They would also have known about a similar phenomenon called "extension transference," whereby a pattern of thinking can be transferred from one arena to another, unconsciously, whether or not it is appropriate. An example that is related to the bias of perception is when we take a principle such as: *It is a good idea to stop at stop signs* and apply it as an absolute, suggesting for example that in all cases all laws should be strictly obeyed, including for instance the law that required one to "rat" on Jews in 1943 Germany.

David: What you are calling a principle is a make-believe thought that is part of a false self-concept that God did not create. Spirit transcends the belief in the physical. If you read the Principles of Miracles at the beginning of the Course, you will see examples of what I call the miracle principle. The miracle principle does apply "in all cases," and if you apply the Workbook lessons without exception you will Experience this as true. There is no order of difficulty in miracles precisely because the principle is equally applicable in all cases. This is the transfer of training at which the ACIM Workbook aims and on which the Experience of true forgiveness depends.

Our Spiritual Being, represented by the Holy Spirit, is shared as one Purpose or Perspective. The Holy Spirit knows what is truly most helpful "in all cases." The Holy Spirit is always present within to Guide our thoughts, emotions and perceptions, and to inspire the seeming "actions" of the body. Whether or not one listens to the Holy Spirit appears to be a choice. But remember – the Holy Spirit is always within, ever present, and always waiting to be heard.

In any situation, if you quiet the thoughts, quiet the emotions, quiet the urges of your mind and listen within to the Holy Spirit, you intuitively know the right thing to say or do. It follows that if you are a willing listener you do not need a legislature or a philosopher or a psychologist or a church authority of any kind to tell you what is right-minded and what to say or do. If you are honest with yourself you know the answer is inside of you. The Holy Spirit is the Guide that always leads to the Peace of God.

When the mind seemed to fall asleep and forget Divine Principle as Being One with God, the Holy Spirit was Given as the Guiding Light whose Purpose is forgiveness and Awakening to Oneness. But a sleeping mind does not always want to listen to the Holy Spirit. Sometimes a sleeping mind listens to the ego. This is a mistake, for the ego is not real and knows not Reality. Thoughts, emotions, perceptions, and actions of the body which proceed from the ego produce the illusion of enslavement of the mind. Does the Holy Spirit know that the sleeping mind is not going to always listen to the Guidance offered? Of course! The Holy Spirit knows about the sleeping mind's fear of Awakening.

The Ten Commandments were given mostly as behavioral "guidelines" intended to remind the mind about Divine Principle. I say "mostly" because there were a few Commandments that are not behavioral in that they apply directly to the altar of mind: to Love the Lord Thy God, to covet not, and to have no graven images or idols before God. But the other ones address behavior. The Holy Spirit was basically saying: *Since you often forget to listen to Me within, I will let you know in advance that I, your Memory of Spirit, am never going to Guide you to kill, commit adultery, steal, or bear false witness against your neighbor, etc.* You may call these laws, yet they are simply crude guidelines which help lead you Home to Heaven. Christ is the Divine Principle to which these "laws" point. The Christ is the Spirit of God's Love, and the only real "Law" is Divine Love. This "Law" cannot be broken for it has no opposite. Yet this "Law" can seem to be unremembered. This seeming amnesia is the time-space cosmos of a sleeping mind.

The commandments, or "laws," were inspired by the Holy Spirit as stepping-stones towards turning within and following the Guidance of the Holy Spirit "in all cases." When the Eternal Principle of Spirit, of God, of Christ was forgotten, ego "laws" were "made" or "projected" out of fear. Listen deep within. Do not listen to the ego's reasoning. Listen to the Holy Spirit. The "laws" made up by the ego are nothing and lead nowhere. Yet the Holy Spirit leads the sleeping mind to a gentle Awakening.

Examples from the Holy Spirit are Given and used to show that there are no exceptions to the miracle. They teach "resist not evil" by proving there is nothing real to resist. The context or content of all the examples I share IS the miracle principle. What you perceive as "extension transference" is but the attempt to deny that the miracle applies in all cases.

Every conflict you perceive is a Call for Love. Peace comes to the mind which sees that conflict is impossible because attack is impossible. Only the ego believes that attack is real, yet without the concept of attack there is only peace. The ego is not real and there is only peace. Forgiveness is impersonal in a very literal way, for it transcends the belief in private minds, private thoughts, and separate persons. The detached Perspective of the Holy Spirit reflects the Biblical phrase "God is no respecter of persons." (Acts 10:34) "Intrapersonal" is another word for the self-concept, yet the miracle shows that no self-concept can stand in the Light of Truth. The Truth is: I am as God created Me. The Truth and the belief in attack do not coexist, for perfect Love casts out fear.

There is no order of difficulty in miracles and no hierarchy of illusions. The miracle simply sees the false as false.

Relationships: Lack, Completion, and Ownership

David: Does anyone have anything they want to bring to session as a springboard for discussion?

Friend: I had an intense dream last night that was all about the desire for a mate, an ideal mate. It was not even so much about wanting a physical mate. It was about the desire to be with someone who wants me as much as I want them, and the feeling of completion that comes from that. I can see the fallacy of how human relationships do not achieve that, but there is still an intense yearning that I was getting in touch with. I was thinking it was probably a distorted miracle impulse.

David: Yes, it is nice you can make that observation. Even when you think of it along the lines of just companionship rather than sexual attraction, it is still coming from the ego. Companionship still has that element of wanting another body just to be there. It is a sense of *being with* someone else in body and it still involves the idea of relationships; it involves bodies instead of the pure mind relationship. The feeling of "intense yearning" really gets to the core of the ego. The ego is continually telling the mind that you must seek outside yourself to complete yourself. The thrust of that yearning comes from a deep, deep feeling of incompletion and the desire to be complete. In the *Beyond all Idols* section it says that you have every right to ask for this; completion is your inheritance. It is just that you are looking in the wrong place.

You believe completion lies outside yourself, on the screen. Even the sense of companionship or just someone to be there with you is still a form of that. The "special love" relationship is the ego's most boasted gift. It is the ace card of the ego – the yearning that seems to be the strongest. There are many yearnings for specific things but this one seems to be the one the mind believes is kind of the end all. *If I could just have that!* Then life would be bearable. Everything else would matter not if I had that.

That is just another trick. People who have tried to play that out find that even what they think is the ideal companion of course is not. There is not that sense of completion. It is not like they come to the end of the rainbow with that. The mind is still looking. *This is great. Now, what is next, what else can I add?* The feeling you can add something else should be a clue the ego is at work.

As we join in community, this topic will come up. One person will seem to stand out more than the rest and be attractive in some way. You will notice it come up and it will obscure the complete equality of the Sonship; it will always obscure the true identity. Until it is completely transcended the draw will always seem very attractive, at times intensely attractive. What you are describing is kind of like the jewel in the ego's crown.

The Aquarian Gospel of Jesus Christ is a book about Jesus going through all these temptations. In Egypt he gets to number six I believe, and it is described as the "angel idol." A woman of entrancing beauty comes to Jesus as he is sitting in contemplation. She does not even say a word; she just sits down and starts to sing songs of Israel. She sings these beautiful songs, some of them of his upbringing, of his life, and then she gets up and leaves; not even a word is spoken. The way it is described is that the passions were stirred in the heart of Jesus. She would periodically come back and it was a period of unrest for Jesus and very much a temptation. After all these other temptations, deceit and different things, it is like here is this. It was a forty-day temptation again. The forty days seems to be a number that comes up; for forty days was he tempted. Then he arose and said: *Am I to be the demonstration of unconditional love, this Divine Love that comes not from this world?* He talked to her. He told her that their paths would cross but that he had to go on and do what he had to do.

Reading those kinds of stories while working with the Course helped bring it all together for me. You cannot have impersonal love *and* personal love. They cannot go together. That is a great little parable about temptation. Eventually, when you really follow it in and come to your right mind so to speak, you see that they cannot come together; they cannot be mixed.

Thinking about that yearning in terms of a distorted miracle impulse gives you a sense of the power of love or the power of the miracle–just by the strength of it! Because it seems to be coming through the ego's lens it is perceived as a lack. Can you imagine the strength of it without that lens? When it comes through the ego as a distorted miracle impulse, it is felt as an intense yearning. But when you are able to lay aside the ego, it comes straight into consciousness without going through the ego's lens. It is quite powerful. Our friend was feeling this enormous urge to extend, feeling like she is going to explode. It is hard to stifle it. Once you really go with it for a while, it becomes just a tremendous urge to extend and be of help.

It is kind of like in the movie *Groundhog Day*. Phil goes through all these things over and over and over, trying to manipulate people and get Rita in bed, etc., until finally he gets this uncontrollable urge to be helpful. He starts going around fixing tires on cars; he catches a child falling out of a tree; he saves a guy's life with the Heimlich maneuver! Everywhere he goes he looks for some way to be helpful. It is like an uncontrollable urge. And that is what got him out of the loop.

Linear time is a loop where the past just seems to repeat, over and over and over. That is what makes the movie Groundhog Day such a powerful metaphor. Not only can you see the loop, which is symbolic of the loop that everyone has experienced, but you also see a metaphor for the way out of the loop, which is just to be totally helpful–to completely lose yourself in the urge to be truly helpful. It is intense. You will experience that; there is no doubt about it.

Friend: Can we talk about expectations? In meditation I was feeling that to have expectations of anyone based on what they said in the past will always be hurtful. I cannot trust what anyone says; I can only trust who they are. I can only trust the Holy Spirit, or the Holy Spirit in them, and I cannot trust anything in form nor have expectations in that area.

David: The deceived mind has a very deep-rooted belief in scarcity, lack, unworthiness, and guilt. That is what the special relationships of the world are all about. Perceiving oneself as a person and perceiving your brothers as persons and bodies is all set up to solve the problem of guilt. In other words, the world was made as an attempt to solve the problem of guilt. The world was made as an attempt to solve the problem of lack; the world was made as an attempt to solve the problem of scarcity. The belief that one can adjust to the world and find fulfillment and completion in that adjustment is erroneous.

440

When you trace expectations back you will find that they are always about a belief in incompletion or a belief in lack that is still there in the mind. Why would it be important what someone else said? Why would it be important what somebody else did? Why would anything in the world be important for that matter, if one had an inner sense of completion? The lack and the incompletion are what have to be questioned. "Those who see themselves as whole make no demands." W-37 That is a great line. Can you see how it does not leave any room for expectations? Those who see themselves as whole are not at the mercy of anyone or anything.

Friend: Consequently they would have no expectations because there would be nothing perceived as needed.

David: And of course in that scenario they could not be upset. They could not be unfairly treated based on a seeming change in what someone said or did. They could not perceive themselves as unfairly treated. They could not perceive someone as breaking their word or doing something against them when they see themselves as *the dreamer of the dream* and no longer perceive attack.

Lack, incompletion or scarcity is what has to be addressed. The fundamental thing that we will keep going over many, many, many times is that the deceived mind does not know what giving is and therefore it does not know how to extend. It does not see that giving and receiving are equal – the same. How many times have we heard clichés in this world about the importance of giving? Or even the clichés about it being better to give than to receive? Even that is off.

Friend: Because you cannot give without receiving?

David: The mind gets exactly what it wants. And it is always giving and receiving. It is impossible that it be better to give than to receive, because they are the same. You cannot place one higher than the other. The key thing is that the deceived mind does not have a clue what giving is. It believes in the ego; it believes in form and specifics. Believing in specifics, it does not know what giving is. Giving does not, in the end, have anything to do with specifics. Neither does extending.

As long as the mind feels incomplete and has expectations of other people or even expectations of the person that it identifies as its self – that *has* to be the ego talking. Christ does not put pressure on himself; it is the ego that does the pressuring. It is the ego that sets up personal expectations, like living up to somebody else's standards or living up to standards one sets for oneself. It is not the capital Self doing that; it is the ego. In the end the only realization you are ever asked to come to is that *having* and *being* are the same. Having and being or giving and receiving are the same.

The mind that is asleep thinks it is in a world; it associates itself with a person, with a body, and it associates everything in the world with specifics – therefore it believes in personal possessions. It believes it possesses a body. The body is probably the deceived mind's most prized possession of all the things in this world of possessions. That is why in cases of rape and incest there seems to be such a deep wound; the mind feels like it has been personally violated. Because the mind identifies with the body, when something is done to the body there is a strong sense of violation and victimization.

The deceived mind thinks it possesses a body and it thinks it possesses other things, like green paper strips, houses, cars, clothing, jewelry, and computers; just fill in the blank of all the things of the world: dogs, cats, biological family members, etc. It may even think it possesses a religion. The list just goes on and on and on and on. All of it reflects the confusion about "having." It thinks it has these things but in truth that is not what having means. You cannot have a hundred dollars. You cannot have a husband, you cannot have a body, and you cannot have talent, say for playing the piano or playing baseball. You cannot have mathematical ability, you cannot have high IQ, or verbal ability; you cannot have any of that because none of it is real. How can you have something that is not real?

The Course teaches that *what you have is what you are.* That is it. That is what having means. Having and *being* are identical. Do you see how the recognition of that would bring an end to all seeking outside oneself on the screen? It brings an end to expectations, to expecting others to do what they said they would do, or however you have it constructed. This is all it takes. It is free. This realization is free. It does not cost anything. There is no cost associated with recognizing that what you have is what you are. It is given. It was given to you when you were created by God and nothing can take that away from you. You can cover it over in your consciousness, you can bury it, you can deny it, you can keep it out of awareness, but you cannot destroy it and you cannot change it. You can just accept it.

Friend: And it is the associations that cover it over? All those things you said you cannot have, it is like you can associate with them but you cannot have them. And it is one or the other; actually it is only one but it seems in awareness to be one or the other.

David: I will read a helpful passage from the *Attainment of the Real World* section:

> Ownership is a dangerous concept if it is left to you. The ego wants to have things for salvation, for possession is its law. Possession for its own sake is the ego's fundamental creed, a basic cornerstone in the churches it builds to itself. And at its altar it demands you lay all of the things it bids you get, leaving you no joy in them. Everything the ego tells you that you need will hurt you. For although the ego urges you again and again to get, it leaves you nothing, for what you get it will demand of you. And even from the very hands that grasped it, it will be wrenched and hurled into the dust. For where the ego sees salvation it sees separation, and so you lose whatever you have gotten in its name. Therefore ask not of yourself what you need, for you do not know, and your advice to yourself will hurt you. For what you think you need will merely serve to tighten up your world against the light, and render you unwilling to question the value that this world can really hold for you. T-13.VII.10

Along the way the Holy Spirit can use the concept of ownership while the mind still believes in it. The Holy Spirit works with the mind where it perceives itself. The concept of ownership can be part of the backdrop, however once you pull the concept of ownership out of the backdrop so to speak, and you really believe you can own things, then it is "dangerous." Notice that your peace of mind is out the window when you really believe that you possess something. Whether it is a body, money, a car, a jewel; it does not matter what, it could be anything. You will notice immediately that your peace of mind is gone because you will be defending that thing, whatever it is. There have been those that have misinterpreted this issue, thinking that renting something is not owning it. It does not bring you peace to think that you can just shift the form of owning something to that of leasing it. It should be so easy that you just lease everything! A little shift in form does nothing. You have to question every value in your mind if you want to let go of ownership and release the ego.

Sex and Spirituality: Do they go together?

I have been asked to share my thoughts on this topic and have taken the request to prayer. The spiritual journey is voluntary if it is authentic. Everything that is real is experienced through acceptance, and everything that temporarily appears to be real is experienced through desire and belief, until Awakening. The Spirit is Eternal, a State of desireless Being. The linear time-space cosmos spins with desire. The aim of spirituality is to experience the Changeless Being of Spirit. This aim involves dissolving the belief in sacrifice. It cannot be a real sacrifice to accept Reality, but the process of Awakening seems to reflect the belief in sacrifice until Awakening.

Sexuality is one among many experiences on the linear continuum of illusion. It is no better or worse than any other experience on the continuum, though it can seem to be lifted up and glorified or put down and regarded as shameful by the ego. The desire for receiving and giving sexual love to a partner is a sign that ego beliefs and desires are still active. Yet it is possible and helpful to allow a committed relationship to be used by the Spirit to raise these beliefs and desires to the Light within; with willingness these beliefs and desires will vanish and leave the mind at peace.

Trials and struggles in relationships expose falsity in the mind and this will help in making the ultimate decision which opens the heart to the remembrance of God's Love. The mind will naturally outgrow body thoughts, yet as long as the body seems to be part of the self, its renunciation would be an inappropriate use of denial. When struggles arise, expose and release the beliefs and thoughts by not protecting them. Give them to the Holy Spirit. Multiple desires will fall away, yet this cannot be forced. The mind must be ready.

Express love and affection as Guided and allow the mind to receive it. Be willing to hand over to the Holy Spirit anything in the mind that does not feel loving. Every relationship is about recognizing the One Mind. This is discovered as it becomes apparent that there are no thoughts that can be kept private. Keep no secrets and it becomes apparent that only love can be shared. This Divine Love is beyond the body entirely, but one must start with how one currently perceives oneself. All are worthy of God's Love; through the lesson of forgiveness all will experience what they seek deep within.

The fear of attachment is really a fear of Intimacy. This fear is not about sexual intimacy, but it is the fear of revealing the Innermost Self, believing that rejection or attachment may result. Love and affection are held back because of the belief in expectations attached to them. Love must be freely given to be Love, and it is the same with affection. If there are strings attached to love and affection, there are also unfulfilled expectations. One always has the opportunity to open up and feel how good extending love feels. As one practices extending love and cultivates expressing affection as the Holy Spirit Guides, it will seem more and more natural. There will be Guided opportunities for this, and as the mind allows the Holy Spirit to shine through it, the feeling will seem more and more natural. Old inhibitions are washed away in our shared Purpose. The limits that were once placed on the mind begin to loosen and dissolve. The motive shifts from getting to giving without expectations. And a feeling of Ease Guides one unfailingly.

As one does the Inner work of forgiveness one feels more vibrationally attuned to the Spirit and calls forth witnesses to that state of mind. Everyone reflects the state of mind which is maintained. The miracle demonstrates the warmth and affection that flows from our shared Purpose. As the Purpose becomes the focus it may seem as if one is wearing a smile almost always, noticing smiles and laughter everywhere. Love and affection are apparent when our Purpose is apparent.

Is sexual expression good or bad, helpful or harmful? What one does, comes from what one thinks; that is why Awakening is a purification of thought. Behavior modification is therefore never the goal, for behavior but follows the guide the mind chooses to listen to and follow. Sexual desire is not better or worse than any desire for the world, yet Awakening is a state of contentment that is desireless. This is the peace that passeth the understanding of the world.

All appetites are ego *getting* mechanisms. Fantasy is the attempt to make false associations and obtain pleasure from them. As the miracle expands and becomes consistent in experience, these appetites fade, grow dim, and disappear. The ego was the belief in lack, and all apparent appetites reflected this belief. The ego attempted to put various behaviors into moral and ethical systems of judgment, yet in the healed Perspective only wholeness is experienced and the past is gone. There are no hierarchies of illusion, no order of difficulty in miracles, and no preferences in the Atonement. The ego was one error and cannot be broken into "enjoyable" error and "punishable" error, "moral" error and "immoral" error, "ethical" error and "unethical" error. Masturbation, monogamy and celibacy are all only stepping-stone concepts along the path of emptying the mind of all concepts, forgiving the illusion, and Awakening to Pure Oneness. Sacred sexuality is a contradiction in terms because Spirit transcends form entirely and it is impossible to mix Spirit and matter.

Pleasure and pain are the same error. The miracle transcends the error by showing its falsity, its impossibility. It is impossible to seek for pleasure without finding pain, for both are the same error: the attempt to reinforce the "reality" of the body and world. Christ is Spirit, not a body, and to experience Divine Mind is to forget the body entirely. Awakening involves mind training. Step back and pay attention to the thoughts that come into awareness. Feel your desire for healing. Preferences are judgments, and as the mind yields to the nonjudgmental Perspective of the Holy Spirit, the Awakening is obvious. Observe that as long as appetites seem to exist there are the ego defenses of indulgence and repression. Neither is better or worse than the other, for they are the same illusion. The miracle offers a real alternative and when one is consistently miracle-minded, defenses are no longer needed.

Sex in a loving relationship dedicated to the Holy Spirit and Guided by the Holy Spirit is (in this sense) an act of affection and can continue to be so until the mind has become so unified in Purpose that there are no cravings or desires for form of any kind. When this desirelessness happens there is truly the miracle of Atonement, and Christ is fulfilled in the Divine Love of Knowing God in Spirit. The miracle of Atonement transcends or dissolves the attraction to guilt in the sleeping mind. Sex for the purpose of pleasure and sensual gratification is an ego motivation, attempting to reinforce the "reality" of the body, and this always involves the illusion of guilt. As one deepens in Awakening the desires for anything of this world evaporate and Joy radiates from within! All seeming needs are gone in Divine Love.

The ego uses relationships for gratification – and the ego, being impulsive and unstable, has no conception of commitment. Commitment to a monogamous interpersonal relationship is a step that the Holy Spirit can use, as with any commitment or discipline, to open the mind to the sole or ultimate commitment that one can make: accepting the Atonement – Awakening to God's Love.

I have referred to the ego's purpose for relationships as "Dixie-cup relationships." The ego seems to throw its relationships away once it seems to get what it thinks it wants and moves on to the next relationship for another drink. Simultaneous sexual relationships or "open" relationships, as they have been called, simply appear to add to the complexity. A monogamous interpersonal relationship can offer a full plate of opportunities to expose and forgive the ego. The undoing of the ego (forgiveness) is the only Purpose for all relationships. The ultimate realization (Self-realization) is the recognition that Creator and Creation share the same Spirit of Love. At best all perceptual relationships reflect the Love of God and this Agape Love inspires forgiveness and miracles.

Attraction to the body is the attraction to guilt. Enlightenment is recognition of the Spirit beyond the body and the experience of Divine Innocence. The seeming Awakening "process" is an unlearning or undoing of the ego in which the mind is emptied of all specific concepts to make way for forgiveness – seeing the false as false.

446

Miracle impulses are the Call to return Home to God, yet they become distorted in consciousness as appetites, fantasies, and "getting mechanisms" when they pass through the ego's filter of lack and need. Agape Love knows no need or lack. Romantic sexual "love" springs from the attempt to find "love" in form. True joining opens communication and dissolves the filter, allowing miracle impulses to reach consciousness directly. Relationship is truly only a means for working miracles and extending Love. This Purpose shows the body as meaningless and reveals the Spirit as All.

Learning to give in the fullest sense will draw one out of the sense of having a separate will apart from God's Will. As long as one holds on to a self-concept one must want to get something outside of One Self, and must believe it is possible to do so. One's assignment with a sexual partner, and indeed with everyone one meets, is to learn how to give totally, completely, without distinctions or conditions of any kind. Everyone is calling on the Sacred. Listen carefully to the Spirit, for what one is asking for is what everyone is asking for. Giving and receiving are the same. This is a path of devotion. In devoting oneself to one goal—forgiveness—one loses all sense of separate interests and separate selves. No request is too large or small in this Perspective. One can only join in this Perspective, the Perspective of the dreamer—never in the dream. Love does not oppose. There is nothing to fight, defend against, or be right about. And devotion requires trust, for trust in the Spirit dissolves all doubt.

Until the mind is Awakened—through retraining and re-translation via the Holy Spirit—it will seem as if there are causes in the world. Hunger, thirst, sexual desire, and the desire for stimulation seem to be based in the body and brain, yet they arise from distorted miracle impulses that pass through the lens of lack. All fears and cravings and needs are wrong-minded perceptions, yet answering the Call to be a miracle worker will yield many miracles and dissolve the lens of lack. Until the lens of lack is dissolved completely the sleeping mind will experience cravings. Cravings are either acted upon and temporarily satisfied, or pushed down and denied from awareness. Neither approach will satisfy in a lasting way, yet miracles open the door to lasting peace, joy, freedom, and happiness. In miracles are all seeming human needs met without effort. The final miracle of Atonement brings an end to the belief in need, lack, and fear forever.

Perception is selective. One can choose to aim the mind to the Purpose of the Holy Spirit, which brings Joy. There is no sacrifice. The pleasures of this world are fleeting, transitory. If one looks at this honestly, one will see that this is so. The pleasure of delicious food, a pleasant scene, the pleasure of sexual orgasm – all have time limits. They start and they stop. They do not offer lasting joy. They are not really gifts, because they are offerings of the ego. They perpetuate the amnesia about the Christ Self. The judgments of the world make some images attractive. The mind believes that they are valuable and does not want to let them go. It is still convinced that they are real, and therefore values outcomes that will bring about the things it still wants. They are like "fool's gold." They look very beautiful, but when you touch or embrace them, they dissolve away; they do not last.

Let the Spirit within Guide in all things, moment by moment. The ego is flushed up and exposed in relationships. Aligning with the ego brings illusory experiences of pleasure and pain. Distorted miracle impulses reach awareness as cravings, and in this regard sexual cravings are the same as cravings for food, drink, temperature, stimulation, etc. Cravings always involve lack and preferences, and the miracle leads past this distorted perception of the world. As the ego belief system is questioned, exposed and released, the "lens of lack" is cleared of all obstacles to peace. When this happens, miracle impulses are experienced directly in awareness as Love and Calls for Love. Wholeness and completion are the natural characteristics of the mind; the miracle returns these characteristics to awareness.

What about Marriage?

Hi David,

I was wondering about something I read in ACIM about special relationships and how the ego uses them as proof for guilt, separation, and the death of God. I am married. Is the Course basically saying no one should get married?

Your insights would be greatly appreciated. I have more questions I would like to ask but I almost feel like they are pointless. To some degree, I think the above question is pointless as well because it is like trying to understand that which is insane – the ego.

Beloved One,

The ego is synonymous with special relationship and is a belief held in mind. ACIM is about exposing the error of belief in the context of what seems to be interpersonal relationships. Even though the ego made the distorted world of separation, the Holy Spirit uses what the ego made and reinterprets it. Thus forgiveness is a reinterpretation of error.

The real meaning of marriage is Union, and this Union is the marriage in Spirit – Creation in and of God. What seems to be marriage in the worldly sense, between two people, is actually a backdrop for healing the mind. Relationships mirror all that is unconscious, all that has been denied from awareness, so that the ego can be exposed and released. This release is the awareness that the ego is not real and the experience that there is only Love.

As you continue your inner healing work with ACIM, the distinction between form and content will become clearer and clearer. Love is content. It is not form of any kind. And though all form is a projection of the ego, the Holy Spirit uses the symbols and images the ego made to Guide the sleeping mind to Awaken and be glad. The Holy Spirit uses time to teach that there is no time, and interpersonal relationships to lead to an experience of the only real relationship: Christ in God. Mystical experience transcends the personal just as the Whole transcends the sum of the parts.

Hidden error is synonymous with unconscious belief. Healing does indeed dissolve the questions, and in Divine Silence is everything Known. Yet until the experience of healing dawns, it is helpful to question the ego's belief system. Questioning error and exposing error brings it to Light, thus dissolving it forever.

Holy Spirit Vows of Union

We come together today to join our minds in a shared Purpose and to demonstrate the true meaning of Union. Our joining is a symbol to be used for the expression of Divine Love and Oneness. To join together in and of itself is not a cause for celebration – for in itself it has no meaning. But cause for celebration and joy is in the Purpose which this joining serves. Our Vow is God's Will, to follow the Voice of the Holy Spirit. In this purpose we will find the source of our joy and peace.

In loving you as I love myself I see that there is nothing of you to be possessed – for what you are, I am also. I acknowledge that Love is allowing you to be Who you are, to shine your Light and to follow the voice of the Inner Guide.

We remember that faithful Allegiance is to the Father and His Voice alone.

We come together to support one another, to be witnesses of love and non-judgment. We come together for forgiveness.

In releasing one another we are freed.

In forgiving one another we are forgiven, and in loving one another we are loved.

May our joining be a symbol of the commitment we are making to this highest Calling.

We have come together only to serve Him who sent us.

We are here only to be truly helpful and to fulfill the commitment we are making to our Father in Heaven, that we may remember our True Identity as a Child of God.

In God we are Joined, and what God has brought together can never be separated.

In Love All Is One. Amen.

Releasing Guilt and People-Pleasing

Hi David,

You have said that guilt comes from accepting ego roles. The Course seems to say that guilt comes from believing you can attack your brother and therefore yourself. Can you clarify this for me? Can the Holy Spirit help with willingness, or is it solely our own responsibility?

I read your letter titled "Experiment in Forgiveness," about a child returning home as a house guest. My 25-year-old son has been in my home for about a year now. I have felt led by the Spirit to treat him as a house guest; however, I believe I have been doing things I have not been asked to do. We had agreed that he could live in a trailer that is behind my home, that he would refurbish it and I would supply what he needed to do so. He was separated from his wife when he first came here, but now she has moved in and his two children are here. I seem to find myself taking care of them a lot. I do their laundry, cook, and clean up messes. He sort of stopped doing the things he agreed to, and talking about it has yielded no results. I felt the Holy Spirit was prompting me to really begin listening to, and following my inner guidance, and just let him follow his own path. I suppose the thing that hangs me up is not wanting my house to become upside down, dishes piled up, and the regular stuff that accrues when one does not clean up after oneself. It seems the more I clean up, the more it is sort of left there for me to clean up. I have a flower shop that I would love to work in, which I have not been able to work in for a couple of years because I had my mother to tend, who could not go with me to the shop. She is now completely bedridden, and I still tend to her but the schedule of her care gives me the opportunity to work in my shop a couple hours at a time.

How do I untangle from being the caregiver of the children, from being the one who cleans up after that family, cooking for them and doing their laundry, etc. Our initial agreement was that he would take out the garbage, pick up groceries (because I was housebound with my mother), clean up after himself, and work on his place. He seems to be unwilling to do any of that now. In exchange, on the days of their visitation, I would take care of his children when he was working, do most of the cooking and do his laundry. He is not working now but draws unemployment. The whole family is living here. He seems to need me to watch the children when he goes fishing, plays golf, or goes out to get some alone time with his wife. This has all sort of slipped up on me. It seems that trying to discuss it gets him riled up, but I want my life. This sounds like a soap opera, which I created, and out of which I cannot find the exit. I know you are not "Dear Abby," but if you would help me, I would appreciate it so much. What I would love to do, and what I feel led to do, is to go out in my shop, turn on the CD player, and play the ACIM tapes while I get creative. I want to let that be my hermitage for a while, in between the times I have to go in to turn my mom, clean her and feed her.

Beloved One of God,

Thanks for your sincere questions. The belief that a Divine Mind in Union with God can be broken apart into bits and pieces and fragments is the belief that attack is possible. To see a brother as a separate individual with a private mind and private thoughts is a reflection of the belief in separation from God.

Mind is One and forever Eternal, yet the "mortal mind" that is the ego invention is an illusory belief in fragmentation. The ego assigns each fragment a "life" of its own and calls the fragment by a name, and this false memory package is assigned a series of roles. This is how the ego attempts to make something from nothing. It tries to see "life" in graven images made to take the place of Christ. None of the make-believe roles are true.

Indeed all the world is a stage, though Divine Mind can play no part. Oneness can never shrink into a little role that seems to play out on a time-line. All that is asked is that you be willing to call upon the miracle and see the world anew with the Holy Spirit. The willingness is our responsibility, and this joins with the Might of the Holy Spirit. The reason willingness is required is because the Will of God can only be experienced voluntarily. If it is your single desire, you will recognize that what is whole has no need of healing, and this is the Atonement or Correction to the error that never was.

This world is based on false roles. Guilt is kept buried and hidden in awareness as the mind attempts to identify and act out these roles, for the ego belief that made them is kept out of awareness as they are blindly pursued. The ego uses guilt to keep the mind in the illusion of bondage because it is impossible to live up to ego ideals that never had any life or substance in Reality.

The "person" never lives up to the "ideal" and this is where the guilt SEEMS to arise. Yet neither the person-construct nor the ideal or role-construct is real. You have been measuring your "self" against an illusion, yet you are not two selves. You are One Self united with our Creator and far beyond any measurement or comparison. Not being a good enough mother, father, sister, brother, son, daughter, neighbor, student, citizen, Course teacher, etc., is never the source of the guilt that imprisons. It is the ego belief beneath all the roles that is the "source" of guilt as long as it is believed to be real.

Your work with the Course and with music is calling you into your true function, and that function IS your happiness, freedom and peace! You are not your brother's keeper and the mother role was but a temporary role to be laid aside in the undoing of the ego. You are Spirit, yet you will not remember this until you release the little roles the ego made to keep you unaware. The Holy Spirit will offer more expansive roles (i.e., teacher of God) in exchange for the limiting roles of the past, as you begin to Awaken. Yet even the seemingly more expansive roles will be transcended as you learn to forgive illusion entirely. The stepping stones to Enlightenment are just backdrops of scenes and scenarios that allow you to practice releasing all limiting belief and accept the only belief that will set you free, Atonement.

You will see your "son" as what you believe you are. Are you flesh? Then is your "son" flesh and confined to the flesh. Are you Spirit? Then your "Son" is the Christ, our very Self, and the past has been forgiven of all the images and memories that seemed to hide the Face of Christ. When you play the "caretaker" role you lay the limit upon your own mind in awareness, for you witness to the belief that the ego is still in charge and still responsible. Give this "care-taking role" to the Holy Spirit, Who careth for our Holy mind. As you follow the Holy Spirit's Guidance you will see that you are not sacrificing anything to fulfill the function Given you. Forgiveness suits your need, and you have no other.

Be straightforward and honest in this matter and let the Holy Spirit put the words in your mouth when you speak to your son. You will feel a calm assurance when you speak from your heart and say what is truly most helpful. And as you do, the past patterns, habits of people-pleasing, and thoughts of guilt will dissolve away, for they were never truly a part of the Real You. Once they are given to the Holy Spirit they are already gone, and if you cease to protect and cling to these people-pleasing thoughts they will seem to vanish quickly.

Your true function is waiting in your mind for you to immerse into it. Take the lid off the pot of past thoughts, for it is a waste of energy to try to keep the lid on and pretend to be what you are not. When you pray, remember this: You do not ask for too much, but for far too little. Do not limit your asking, for Joy is what you deserve in awareness, and Joy is what You are in Reality. Your true function will show you this. In your true function I will come as a witness to your willingness to Awaken. And we shall "gather" and give all the Glory to God, for the Light has come!

Awakening to Relationship

Hi David,

I have been amazed at your succinct interpretations of the Course. I print out some of your discussions for use in a Circle Meeting which I lead at a Unity church.

My problem is this: My wife and I believe so differently on the surface of things, that there is conflict or friction every time we are together. I moved out some 10 months ago so that at least the time spent together in this friction would be lessened. But we have a son together, and so are often in each other's company. I keep telling myself to step back from the emotions that arise, and that any form of "attack" is false, but the same stuff keeps coming up. I know I must change my thinking– "forgive" – and know that in the silence of no-thinking only love will shine and be reflected to me, but it seems the closer I get to it, the harder it is. I do not know how to explain to my son why his mom and dad do not get along, or to explain the falseness of the world and illusions of attack, when I cannot model the same for him. Do you have any advice?

Beloved One,

Thanks for writing and sharing your experiences and ponderings. Changing your mind and demonstrating this wondrous change in attitude, with honesty and integrity, will yield great peace. This demonstration goes far beyond the words that are spoken and the concepts that are described. There are two passages from ACIM that come immediately to mind:

> I am alone in nothing. Everything I think or say or do teaches all the universe. W-54.4

> No thought of God's Son can be separate or isolated in its effects. Every decision is made for the whole Sonship, directed in and out, and influencing a constellation larger than anything you ever dreamed of. T-14.III.9

Everyone who seems to walk this world is concerned about the effect that their decisions will have on other people, including partners, children, parents, friends, co-workers, bosses, neighbors, etc. The context of decisions is always seen in terms of a small circle of people that seem most important in a person's life. Yet each and every thought that passes through the mind, and every decision made, is actually made for the entire universe, for the whole Sonship. A decision is a conclusion based on everything you believe. Until unconscious beliefs are raised to the Light and released then most decisions in daily life are dictated by the ego. The ego is like a computer program which runs your perception of everything until it is exposed and deleted.

Be grateful that your interactions with your wife have been a means of exposing the friction of holding onto ego beliefs. Offer her full appreciation in your heart for the beliefs which have been flushed into awareness that they may be offered up to the Holy Spirit. Relationships and Silence will expose ego beliefs and thoughts in an accelerated manner; this is so because deep down you are Calling for healing. As you progress in the mind training discipline, as trust in the Holy Spirit grows, and as judgment is relinquished you will experience waves of gratitude for the blessing everyone offered by mirroring, and thus exposing, hidden beliefs. You will also draw forth many witnesses to your peace of mind, and your mind will be flooded with these glorious witnesses to the Truth of You.

Relationships will seem more and more vibrational as you move inward, and this means they will obviously reflect the Purpose you hold dear in your heart. These mighty companions will reflect the love and intimacy that has remained forever in your Heart, for which God created Divine Love.

Your happiness and joy will be the best demonstration to your wife and son. Every time you meet someone there is an opportunity for a holy encounter. Every child you encounter or think of is yours. Those who see God's Will as their Own see beyond ego distinctions and roles to the Living Christ. Who is just a father, mother, sister, brother, son, or daughter—when everyone you meet or even think of shares the same Self in Spirit? Every decision you make teaches the whole universe what you believe you are. Every thought proclaims the identity of the Sonship. Let the thoughts be of gratitude for a Creator that creates Perfect Oneness and Divine Innocence. Embrace everyone and everything as a reflection of our holy mind, for our holiness lights up the perception of the cosmos. Everyone brings a blessing as soon as the desire is to offer only blessings. Giving and receiving are the same. Be a happy witness, and if your son sees this joy and comes to you with questions, the Answers will flow effortlessly through you from the Holy Spirit.

Friction is always an indication of a control issue. Friction seems to be between persons, but the "authority problem" Christ speaks of in the Course is never interpersonal. Whenever there seems to be friction in an interpersonal relationship the real question is this: Am I as God Authored Me in Spirit or do I still believe that I can make myself?

Christ is invulnerable because Christ is Spirit. The self-concept seems threatened by many things of this world because concepts were made up by the ego and the ego is a shaky substitute for the Truth of Spirit. As all ego self-concepts are laid by, the altar is made clean for the Truth to return to awareness. Our "Identity" is far beyond the concepts of the time-space cosmos. "I am as God created Me," is a humble statement of the Truth.

Be blessed in all ways, Beloved Child of the Living God. You are magnificent just as You are!

Love Knows No Opposite; Relationship and Perspective

Conflict in "personal relationship" is inevitable as long as perspectives are divided and variable. No two people see the same world, or the truth inside until separate interests are laid by. When the ego enters a "relationship," competition, pride, possessiveness, and control come with it. Yet True Love prevails as Light shines away darkness. Divided and variable perspectives give way to one perspective—forgiveness—in which the sameness and union become apparent. What God created One, remains One. Love is a unified whole and knows no differences. Love knows no opposite. Thank You God for creating Love as All in All—Whole, Complete, Perfect, and without an opposite.

Relationship is Divine

Relationships without a Divine Aim always "break up," for they are based on nothing. Divine Purpose could be described as forgiveness—the undoing and releasing of the ego. Belief in the ego prevents awareness of True Union and Intimacy. The underlying fear of Intimacy and Union is the ego's fear of loss of itself, the "personal self" and the "personal world." There are pseudo experiences of attraction and repulsion, bonding and hatred, that seem to be part of what the world calls "relationship," but underneath there is always the unconscious wish to separate and "go separate ways," or the wish to maintain the private, independent sense of self (i.e., individuality). This is the futility and confusion of all worldly relationships and attempts at the "union of bodies." True Love is of the Spirit (beyond the body) and lasts forever! The Real is What Lasts. The illusion of "relationship" fades and disappears from awareness as the Light of Truth dawns, for duality is without a foundation. What has no foundation will be washed away, for it has nothing to stand on.

Fear not when the mind seems disoriented and the world seems to teeter on its shaky underpinnings. The Truth of Light Divine is within; our Home is not of this world. Keep the faith as you sink inward into meditation. Watch the insights into True Reality light up your mind and lead you to an entirely new Perspective on the world: the forgiven world. Contemplate Love Divine, for you will never be content with anything else. Human companionship will never substitute for knowing and loving your Self as God created You. Self-realization is the only Aim of this world worth giving attention to, for all other goals are attempts to stay distracted from healing within and Awakening to your One and Only Identity.

There is Beauty Untold within. Let nothing distract You from remembering the Beauty which shines forever and ever. You are the Meaning of Life. For what is Life except eternal Spirit? My Peace I give to you. Nothing can separate Whom God created as One Spirit.

Releasing the "Family Concept" to Experience the Family of God

On the theme of releasing the self-concept and accepting One Self as Christ, it is important to emphasize that wholeness is a Perspective that includes all and excludes none. It is inclusion based on Purpose or Content in the mind and really has nothing to do with specific forms. It is okay to release the thoughts which no longer serve our peace of mind.

The Holy Spirit leads the mind inward, beyond past concepts and roles, to the recognition of Spirit in the Present. That which is born of the flesh is flesh; that which is born of the Spirit is Spirit. One can never distance One Self from our brothers and sisters in attitude, for everything and everyone is simply a reflection in mind. You are Awakening to the Family of One Mind, the Family of God, so to speak. This Oneness is the Family of God and Christ. You seem to go through what could be called *a release of past associations* so that the mind may be born again in the Spirit, first through healed or whole perception. One that knows the Will of God sees everyone and everything as Family, for there is nothing apart in the wholeness of the forgiven world.

> Ultimately, every member of the family of God must return.
> The miracle calls him to return. T-1.V.4

Here is a song that the angels once sent that is helpful in the retranslation of the idea of family. Gratitude comes from including all in mind and seeing that rejection and abandonment were always impossible:

Family

They're the ones I depend on when I need some help, helping me do what I can't do myself.
They set no limits on what I am worth.
They make it joyful to live on this earth.
They support me and bless me and call me their own,
and help me remember the Brightness of Home.
Refrain: Family, family, holy and whole is my family.
Kindness and love are the sweet ties that bind the family that lives in the Mind.
No one's excluded, and everyone's kin in the arms of forgiveness, the Spirit within.
Mothers and fathers and daughters and sons,
brothers and sisters: we're all of us one,
not bodies, not separate with no one to care,
but joined as the Child of one Parent we share.

Refrain: Family, family, holy and whole is my family.
Kindness and love are the sweet ties that bind the family that lives in the Mind.
My brother, come home now, there's no joy out there.
Throw off the mask of the stranger you wear.
Join with me, sing with me, praises of God.
Share with me, love with me,
laugh at the thought that the One could be broken,
the Whole could be part, that anything can be outside of God's heart.
Refrain: Family, family, holy and whole is my family.
Kindness and love are the sweet ties that bind the family that lives in the Mind.

Blessings on Family of the One! You live forever in My Heart, though the forms may seem to come and go, change and part. Never forget the Love I feel for You Beloved One! I am never more than a Thought away from awareness.

Help Releasing Fantasies

Hi David,

Thank you for forwarding the messages on to me and the kind help you and your friends are offering. What seems to underlie much of my distress is a crushing sense of loneliness, incompleteness, and inadequacy; my life is a picture of never-ending poverty, loneliness, isolation, failure, guilt, and fear.

It is very difficult to have a quiet mind in the midst of this as I have this desperate need to feel "at one," "connected," "loved," and I am very much aware how my mind gets its feeling of oneness (and creativity) from its relationship to its thoughts – a kind of substitute for the real thing because the real thing is unavailable, and because the emotions are so horrible to live with.

I have been totally unable to form stable relationships with women or hold down a job due to all this stuff and have therefore sought solace in spiritual ideals. However, the utter failure of my spiritual seeking has made me wonder whether it was all just a cover up for my emotional mess.

Up until a couple of years ago I had told myself all this spiritual stuff about being a Holy Son of God, etc., and had managed to "live" on the energy of my spiritual idealism (though not on the real energy of connectedness), and hoped that enlightenment might be just around the corner or even "now."

That was until I became painfully aware of my emotional desperation (through an experience of unrequited love). Since then I have sunk into increasing disillusionment with all things spiritual.

I am left craving and fantasizing about living with a beautiful woman in a beautiful cottage in the highlands of Scotland, not spiritual enlightenment. It just seems that I have been deceiving myself about wanting it. Yet I know all too well just how hopelessly unfulfillable my fantasies are since they are based on the very lack that prevents them from ever having the possibility of being fulfilled. Of course if the lack were resolved and I did feel connected and at one and loved, then I would not need these worldly substitutes, but that just seems impossible, at least not without some unimaginable trauma to push one over the other side—which is all so cruel and which is one reason why I hate the spiritual process so much. Something in me hangs on to the idea that there must be a better way, but I am utterly at a loss....

Beloved One,

The ego judges your experiences as failure, yet still the Inner Wisdom comes shining through as evident in the following words: "I know all too well just how hopelessly unfulfillable my fantasies are as they are based on the very lack which prevents them from ever having the possibility of being fulfilled. Of course if the lack was resolved and I did feel connected and at one and loved then I would not need these worldly substitutes..."

You hang on to the idea that there must be a better way, and there is. What the ego judges as "loss" is truly gain, for the world is backwards and upside down. What the ego judges as "failure" is truly success. The ego seems to offer substitutes for Reality and seems to thrive "from its relationship to its thoughts," but illusions have no Reality and the ego is not real. It is not wise to identify with an illusion and you need not do so. As it dawns that the ego has nothing to offer there is no need to follow its advice or seek after its "substitutes."

The ego's self-concept seems to be crumbling, and now the Spirit offers forgiveness as its replacement. Is this not an exchange you would gladly make if you realized it offers only happiness and fulfillment?

Spiritual seeking ends in Finding Stillness, for in Stillness there is nothing to seek for. To the ego Stillness is death, yet knock on the door of Stillness and It will open. You are Spirit and the Beauty and Glory God created as One forever.

Vision is a replacement for every misperception. The body's eyes and ears see not and hear not. Do not accept false witnesses that would deny the Glory of the Eternal Spirit. You are not a failure, Beloved One. Trials are but lessons repeated, so mistakes about time may be released forever. The ego judges Awakening as cruel, for it feels threatened by Reality. Reality has no opposite. The only question which seems to remain is one of identity. The Self God created as One remains invulnerable. The attraction of Love leaves Awakening inevitable and entirely unavoidable. This is the Good News!

Wait on No Body

The Kingdom of Heaven is Now. There is one "step" of Surrender to be experienced to know the Kingdom of Heaven as One Self: *Wait on no body.*

Cause and Effect are simultaneous, not separate. Salvation from illusions is immediate. There is no "gap" between God and Christ. This is the end of the illusion of linear time. Our only "task," therefore, is to accept and receive Atonement Now, in this moment, as an opening to the experience of God and Divine Grace. One cannot step from fear to Love unless they see the results of such a choice. When there seems to be a "wait," this is an apparent denial of our Reality, yet must this be impossible, for Reality remains Real and is unchanged by the illusion of denial.

Rest assured, if there is any "body" for whom "you" are waiting to "get it," "you" have limited what "you" are willing to give, willing to receive, and willing to demonstrate to the world. It is in Giving that One Receives. Present Giving is natural to the Christ, for Christ is Given Life by God's Eternal Giving and extends the Gift forever. You are the One Holy Child of God! Such is the simple truth. Rejoice and be glad!

Chapter Two

Living in Community – Demands and Requests

Friend: My desire to see you as uncooperative must be my desire to see the Holy Spirit as uncooperative. It feels helpful to delve into that; why do I not want to trust the Holy Spirit? Why do I want to see him as giving me a rough time?

David: Anytime you feel an upset towards any person or you feel that anybody is being uncooperative, that is an expression of the authority problem. The whole idea of respect and cooperation has to come from within. Anytime there seems to be friction or something that is not going the way I want it to go, that is just an expression of the authority problem, of: I can still make myself and *I can still have things work out to my liking, to my satisfaction.* Start with the specifics; notice that there are specific things you have an investment in.

Friend: In this case the specific I have an investment in is having you be cooperative, and I think I know what that is, or how that is supposed to look, or that I would recognize it if I saw it.

David: So you have a picture of what cooperation looks like and in the attempt to compare it with others, it is still the mechanism that is being used. It is very simple when you realize that the deceived mind will tenaciously try to find things that it can pick apart or that it can find wrong on the screen in order to hold on to and justify its position that it is right about its own unique identity and its own separate will.

Friend: I feel it; I feel that tenacity of trying to hold on.

David: And how does it feel? You are in the middle of *The Rules for Decision* section of the Course. You have to come to the point where you can say, "At least I can decide I do not like how I feel."

Friend: Well, I don't like how I feel. That is why I am here. Otherwise I would still be upstairs lying on the couch.

David: Well, whether it is something specific or something more general – like why won't this friend be more cooperative with me – it is the same in either case. As *The Rules for Decision* point out: If you decide to have a happy day and you are going along having a happy day and then all of a sudden you find yourself upset about anything at all, then the basic statement is that you forgot what to decide, or you have asked a question by yourself and have set an answer in your own terms. That is what the deceived mind does all the time. It thinks it knows what it needs to have a happy day. In this case you can go back to the original perception of what you reacted to and see that it has asked a question by itself and it has set an answer in its terms. Notice how tenaciously it hangs on to its own question, to wanting the answer to come in its terms. It does not want to step back and go: *Oops, I forgot what to decide. I tried to ask a question by myself.* Go back to the basic thing of: *Father, What is your Will for me. I do not know what clarity or Vision is, but I am willing to be shown.* It is going to keep coming up in a whole variety of forms where that tenacity just really wants to hang onto an individual will. It wants to be right about a separate self. And it will use anything in the world to justify itself.

Friend: Right. It feels like I *want* you to be uncooperative when I get down under it a little bit. You know, it probably does not matter what you say or what you do. If it was not the request about this, it would be something else. I want to get underneath that to see what value it seems to hold.

David: It is the thinking of the world. It is summarized in this passage:

> The reasoning by which the world is made, on which it rests, by which it is maintained, is simply this, you are the cause of what I do. Your presence justifies my wrath and you exist and think apart from me. While you attack, I must be innocent. And what I suffer from is your attack. T-27.VII.3

That is a pretty direct statement of the ego's purpose for the world; the cause of my upset and suffering is outside of me! You must begin to understand that all special relationships are entered into with anger. The ego's purpose for all relationships is anger. It does not state that on a conscious level; it does not allow that to be brought into awareness, but all special relationships were forged in anger. This anger is just looking to come out—to be projected onto somebody or something. Everyone who believes they are here in this world, everyone identified with the world, has this anger. Another way you can say it is that you asked for special favor from God and God said no. He could not grant that special favor. God would cease to be God. Love would cease to be love if it would have said yes to the special request that the deceived mind made. It asked for special favor.

That is where the anger is coming from; it is just that it is under the surface. If you think someone is not fulfilling your expectations or not living up to the role you assigned to them, there will be anger. The perception is: *you are not living up to my idea of cooperation,* or whatever the expectation is. If you are angry it is because your mind is constructing it so. That is the reason you are unhappy–because someone is not living up to the role you assigned them. Turn it around and see that you assigned the roles; you are the one who gave them out. Everything happening is by your own election. There is nothing out of place. There is nothing out there that has the power to make you weak or to take away your peace of mind, or to make you happy or peaceful. "Suffering is an emphasis upon all that the world has done to injure you." T-27.VII.1 That is when you forget you are dreaming a dream; you think that you are on the screen and you think that things are not working out well. You think you are being mistreated and abused. The specialness of even trying to compare is still the belief that you are not getting a fair shake in this. You have to question the thinking that is saying you are not getting a fair shake, instead of trying to arrange things on the screen in order to get a fair shake. There will never be a way to arrange the effects to get a fair shake when, as they say in Alcoholics Anonymous, it is the *stinkin' thinkin'* that has to be looked at. It is the belief that you can be unfairly treated. It is the belief that you can be treated as "less than." And there is a belief there. If you believe you are unworthy then you will just look for witnesses for that. You find what you are looking for.

Friend: This all seems absurd in the sense that being the *dreamer of the dream* makes it so simple. There is only one thing to think about. There are not millions of things to think about; there is one. Well that is pretty nice, that I can live with! And all the other benefits that come with being the *dreamer of the dream* ... There is no upset in it; there is no: *Who did what to me?* On the other hand, being in the dream is just a mess. What is it that wants to hang on to that? There is nothing beneficial about it. It does not feel good; it is not fun. It is exhausting. I am sitting here thinking: *Why would I ever want to do that?* It makes no sense whatsoever. So, why would I want to see you as uncooperative? Why do I not want to trust the Holy Spirit?

David: The Atonement is seeing that you are the *dreamer of the dream*. You have to see yourself as the dreamer before you can accept another purpose for the dream, which would be the Atonement. And the Atonement, as described earlier in the text, is a total commitment. The deceived mind is not so big on commitment to begin with, but total commitment? It seems to all come down to the need to overhaul the mind, to question every value and belief. You cannot shift and change circumstances. You cannot cover over things and compromise a little here and there. You have to find the total commitment to no compromise whatsoever. You must take a stand; it is time to take a stand.

That stand can seem awfully steep. It seems easier to pick away at things in the world that you want to be different than to change your thinking. It seems easier to compromise here and there than to have a transformation of mind. When faced with a choice between compromising and having a total mind overhaul, it seems easier to choose compromise; it seems easier to not take a stand than to take a stand. If you stopped someone on the street and asked them if they have ever considered what the purpose is to everything they are doing, you would probably hear answers like: *Yes, I have had those thoughts from time to time but I do not let them occupy my mind very often. What is the point? They are unanswerable anyway. Nobody has ever found an answer for them, so why entertain them?*

That was my experience when I was in college and seemed to be searching and questioning. I had this sense that there had to be something much deeper, yet it seemed fruitless and pointless at times. It seemed easier to compromise. *Just go ahead David, work on your urban planning project, go through the motions, do what everyone else is doing, survive, get the job done, keep the wheels rolling, go forward.* But these questions would not go away – because I did not want them to go away. I really believed there had to be something that was a permanent or a lasting solution. That is where we are coming to now. You ask why you would want to choose to perceive me as not cooperating, why you would choose to perceive misery or even just irritation. It is because the mind would rather choose a compromise approach. It would rather use something on the screen to justify its feeling of unworthiness, lack, and guilt.

Friend: Even though it knows that is going to be painful?

David: Yes.

Friend: Because it believes that the alternative is more painful than the compromise?

David: Yes. The alternative is obliteration to the deceived mind.

Friend: So I hold on to the delusion that if I get what I want, the pain will go away; if I get my friend to be cooperative or get people to do things my way, then I will not be in pain.

David: We think: *I am certainly not choosing this consciously.* That is something often said in relation to sickness. There is this extensive discussion about what is conscious and what is unconscious, as if somehow what is unconscious is such a powerful ego thing that it just dictates everything. Here is what Jesus says about that:

> Defenses are not unintentional nor are they made without awareness. They are secret magic wands you wave when truth appears to threaten what you would believe. They seem to be unconscious but because of the rapidity with which you choose to use them. In that second, even less, in which the choice is made, you recognize exactly what you would attempt to do and then proceed to think that it is done.
>
> Who but yourself evaluates a threat, decides escape is necessary, and sets up a series of defenses to reduce the threat that has been judged as real? All this cannot be done unconsciously. But afterwards your plan requires that you must forget you made it, so it seems to be external to your own intent; a happening beyond your state of mind, an outcome with a real effect on you instead of one effected by yourself.
>
> It is this quick forgetting of the part you play in making your "reality" that makes defenses seem to be beyond your own control. But what you have forgot can be remembered, given willingness to reconsider the decision which is doubly shielded by oblivion. Your not remembering is but the sign that this decision still remains in force as far as your desires are concerned. W-136.3-5

You have a belief in separation. A belief is just a decision that has become unconscious, pushed out of mind. That is how beliefs are made; they are just decisions – decisions to separate from God. That decision is covered over and all the other seeming decisions and maneuvers are "doubly shielded by oblivion." The mind does not want to remember God. It is terrified of God. All its beliefs and decisions are part of a delay maneuver or a defense against going back to question that original decision. That is what the mind wants to forget. It really believes it has separated from God and it wants to forget that. It really believes it is at war with God but it does not want to remember that. It says: "forget the battle;" M-17.6 forget the size and strength of the "enemy." It really believes God is a vengeful enemy that is going to come and get the mind for what it has really done wrong. So whether it is about someone being cooperative or respectful or doing things "right," all the things that are on the surface are just part of the smoke screen to try to forget.

Friend: Not wanting to trust the Holy Spirit is the same as not wanting to be mistaken about how I think I separated from God.

David: Either you are mistaken about the whole world as you constructed it or you are right about it. If you are right about it, then you are also right about the little, tiny you. That is really what it comes down to. The mind wants to be right, the deceived mind wants to be right about what it thinks it is, which includes the whole cosmos as it has been set up. "All that is needed is that you look upon the problem as it is and not the way you have set it up." T-27.VII.2 The way it is set up is that there is a world that is external to you; ideas have left their source—there is a world of duality, conflict, and competition. You seem to be teeny, unworthy, and lacking; the problem is not seen as what it is—just a false belief in the mind. All the solutions that the mind now seeks are solutions of the world, including things like your comment, "I am making just a small request, all I am asking is that...."

Friend: Pause. It seems a lot easier to pause than to change my mind about my mind.

David: You can tell by the charge you feel that it is not really a request. It is a demand. It is inconceivable to think of Jesus, fully awakened, making a request of one of his apostles and having a charge about it if they say no to his request. Can you see him saying: *You are my apostle, do you know what I have just told you to do?* [laughter] *Do you know who I am?* You know it would be ridiculous to think of Jesus doing that because that would be a demand instead of a suggestion or a request. If you make a suggestion and you feel a charge when that suggestion does not seem to be carried out, or you feel like someone is violating something, or bringing irreparable harm because they are not paying attention to the suggestion—then you need to turn it around and look at your own mind. Is this truly a request or is it a demand?

Friend: I have to question if there is always the wish that my requests be honored. I think there is always the wish that it be honored. What is the point of asking for something unless it is something you think you do want? It does not make any sense.

David: You know when the requests are being made *through* you instead of *by* you, so to speak. When the requests are not coming from a personal standpoint they are very helpful. You do not feel a charge about requests or suggestions that are being made through you.

Living in Community – Looking at Wants and Preferences

Friend: The preference or the "I want" that I associate with "request" is the thing that has to go?

David: You have pictured that "I want" comes with an expectation attached to it. You have asked a question by yourself and set an answer in your own terms – as described in *The Rules for Decision* section of the Course. That is the picture. The other day when you were talking to your friend and she seemed to be upset, I remember you saying, "Well it seems like maybe you had a picture in your mind of how it was supposed to go." You were helping guide her to the point of seeing that if she has a picture set in her mind, if she has an investment in the outcome, then she still must believe there is a specific form that would be best.

The whole purpose of everything we do is coming to hold the torch out in front so to speak, to stay right-minded, where you can see that you are the dreamer of the dream. When you are just watching the dream you can see that things are orchestrated; there is no sense of personal requests. You see that when you are lined up with the Holy Spirit and just trying to be truly helpful, suggestions or requests that serve the whole will just come *through* you. There is no charge attached to how it works out in form. The gift is in the giving. The suggestion is part of the gift; there is no expectation of when, or if, or how the gift will be opened. That is the distinction we are trying to get at with everything we go into.

Believing in the ego is to have a hierarchy of illusions, including preferences, and the key thing we have attempted to talk about over and over has been to watch and examine those preferences. As you start to see that judgment and ordering of thoughts offers nothing of value, you will begin to question it; you will get set on your one function, your single purpose – to see that you are the dreamer of the dream. That is the simplicity of it. And you see that you cannot be the dreamer, you cannot step back from it all while you continue to judge, and order, and have hierarchies. They do not go together. All the peace and joy and love comes from being in the dreamer position, from seeing the world differently and giving it another purpose. Pain and misery come from ordering, judging, fragmenting, and perceiving yourself as caught in the dream.

As long as the mind believes in specifics (in the ego) it has ordering of thoughts. That is what it means to be wrong-minded. That would include requesting special items be added to the grocery list. You can see how the logistics of it could spin out if we decide to just get everybody whatever they want. I heard one of you say just the other day, "Oh my gosh, I never realized how strong my food preferences were and how many I had." It was not just about eating out or specific things; it was even as specific as the kind of coke! Those kinds of things can seem very miniscule and yet when you are in that mode, they seem to be important. They have to be questioned.

Friend: I may just go for a week without buying groceries until the food supply goes down a bit. If all the chips get eaten up, all the peanut butter and jam gets eaten up [laughs], all the bread gets eaten up, then people will have to cook pasta or rice or something, I guess. I felt myself stepping back from it and just thinking that I do not really know what any of this means, but that I am just to watch what happens.

David: Yes. Eat what is there. That is the same as the Guidance I received, to just eat whatever is served. The followers of Saint Francis sometimes went for days without having anything but bread. Can you imagine them sitting around complaining about running out of things?!

The Secret Dream

David: "...you must see the causes of the things you choose between exactly as they are." T-27.VII.10 I am as God created me; I am either a real effect of a real cause, or I have separated from God and this is a world of reality. Thinking in the ego's terms, I am a person at the mercy of all the forces of the world, including other people. It seems to be real. This brings it down to right mind, wrong mind, and present decision.

It is a choice of purpose. It is not a choice of specifics between objects, things, persons, and behaviors. For example, the thought that I can choose to raise or lower my hand is an illusion; it is a trick. It is an example of magic since it is not a real choice, even though in this world it appears to be a real choice. It seems as if I can choose between two behaviors but that is all automatic based on the choice of purpose. It is pointless to try to control one's behavior. You can control the direction of your thinking; that is the only thing you can control. You cannot control the script; you cannot control the screen. All of the seeming upsets that come up around specifics are just the mind denying that – insisting that it does have a say in controlling what is on the screen!

This is about moving towards mysticism. Perceiving yourself as in the world, working in particular roles, with particular obligations, etc., all flies in the face of what we are talking about. Keep questioning. Keep tracing it in. It cannot be this way *and* that way; it has to be one or the other. The strain always comes when you try to make a compromise between Spirit and ego, between right mind and wrong mind. The strain comes from trying to mix a little of this with a little of that. Ease and effortlessness comes from following the thinking inward and saying, *Hallelujah! It cannot be both ways!* I am not going to tell you that you have to stop judging. Come with me, let us look at all this so deeply that you begin to see that judgment is impossible – it is absolutely impossible!

An early step is to see that judgment is a device to maintain separation. That is still speaking about it as if it is something real you have to deal with. It is just a stepping stone. We want to go into this deeply enough to see that judgment is impossible, to see that you do not have to do anything. That is where the peace and effortlessness come in. If you are in the mode of thinking that you have just *got* to stop judging because it is killing you, making you depressed, angry or furious – who is the "I" that has to stop judging? A friend was recently talking about having to give up a belief. She was aware that it was not about her actions but about a belief. She said, "I have to give up this belief and I still feel wrong about having to give up beliefs." Even the idea that you really have to give up a belief has to be questioned; the Christ does not have to give up beliefs.

Friend: Once you see the belief for what it is, there is nothing to hang onto or give up? It just dissolves?

David: Yes. The ease comes in when you see the impossibility of judgment. There is no feeling wrong when you see something is impossible. If you still think you are a real "I" that has to give up the belief in separation, just keep questioning. Who is the "I" that likes a certain climate, or the "I" that likes certain foods? Who is the "I"? Keep looking at who the "I" is. Can that "I" be real?

Friend: As I identify less with that "I" then that stuff has no meaning?

David: Even the metaphor of identifying less or more does not work. It is about coming to the clarity that it is one or the other, it cannot be both. One has to be impossible, and that is good news! That is where the non-compromise comes in. It is not about trying to make a bargain. It is not about holding onto a construct, or even talking about it. When you begin to see the impossibility of it all, even the need to have sessions like this begins to fade.

I always think of Ramana Maharshi as a great model. It was his very presence that people would come to be in. He did not do a lot of teaching in a verbal sense. I remember the first time I saw a photograph of his face. *Wow!* When I looked into his eyes I just saw his very, kind, sweet eyes and gentle smile – it was such a symbol for me. I had read some of his writings and they were a great symbol as well. We want to get to that clarity.

Friend: I know I still talk in terms of more and less, and I even hear it when I say it because I realize that it cannot be, but it still seems to be that way for me.

David: You cannot help but talk that way. The words are just a reflection of where the mind is.

> What choices can be made between two states, but one of which is clearly recognized? Who could be free to choose between effects, when only one is seen as up to him? An honest choice could never be perceived as one in which the choice is split between a tiny you and an enormous world, with different dreams about the truth in you. T-27.VII.11

It seems to be that there is this struggle going on "…in which the choice is split between a tiny you, a person, and an enormous world," whether you call it society, the world, or whatever – it has nothing to do with anything. There is no conflict between the individual and society. There is no conflict between the individual and the system; they are both made up. The individual is a fictitious construct. This system is a fictitious construct. The battle between the individual and the system is a fictitious battle.

It is a great joy to begin to see that it has to be that way. This is all just made up; it is all make believe. Once I see it for what it is, I am never going to be in conflict with the US government or with the IRS again, nor with a religious institution or my family of origin. You know how people seem to have difficulties with their families? They do not go back to see their families, or they see their families too much and feel all enmeshed. The basic thing underneath all of it is the belief in personhood, the belief that there is a difference between this person, or this subject, and these other people. It is an illusory difference. There is no difference; they are all just images.

> The gap between reality and dreams lies not between the dreaming of the world and what you dream in secret. They are one. T-27.VII.11

The "dreaming of the world" is the projected cosmos—all the images that are perceived through the body's eyes. "What you dream in secret" is the unconscious belief in separation, the belief that you have separated from God. The dream you dream in secret is the tree trunk; the dreaming of the world would be all the seeming fragments—the branches and the leaves. Everything in the projected universe is the dreaming of the world and what you dream in secret is the belief in separation. They are one.

> The dreaming of the world is but a part of your own dream you gave away, and saw as if it were its start and ending, both. T-27.VII.11

It seems as if the dreaming of the world started back in historical times. The Big Bang seems to be its start. Scientists are now speculating about its ending. They call it implosion theory. Einstein and a number of scientists have said the universe is expanding and will reach a point of equilibrium when it will start coming together and eventually implode; the beginning and the end. In the dreaming of the world it all seems grand and large.

Let's bring it down to a simpler scale. It seems like the mind is dreaming that it is a person and so "...the world is a part of your own dream you gave away and saw as if it were its start and ending both." If you believe your existence is as a person, what is the start of personhood? It is birth. And what is the ending? The ending is death. That is the same as the grander scale of the Big Bang and eventual implosion. The same thing on a smaller scale is the birth and death of the body. The ego has all the complexities explained, how bodies are born, sexual intercourse, the sperm and the egg, gestation, etc. And it likes to classify all the ways that bodies can die, such as AIDS, cancer, on and on.

Friend: Let's debate when birth really starts.

471

David: Yes, we can debate when birth really starts and when life ends. Is someone a vegetable? Are they hooked up to life support? Are they brain-dead? Are they dead when electrical brain activity stops? The ego is working so hard. The whole thing is made up and it is trying to cover both ends of it. And near-death experiences, oh then....

Friend: You go and come back?

David: [laughing] You go and come back!

> The dreaming of the world is but a part of your own dream you gave away, and saw as if it were its start and ending, both. Yet was it started by your secret dream, which you do not perceive although it caused the part you see and do not doubt is real. How could you doubt it while you lie asleep, and dream in secret that its cause is real? T-27.VII.11

Ah! The belief in separation is where the dreaming of the world came about. Has anybody seen the belief in separation from God? And did they perceive that?

Friend: Not lately.

David:

> ...which you do not perceive although it caused the part you see and do not doubt is real. How could you doubt it while you lie asleep, and dream in secret that its cause is real?" T-27. VII.11

If you believe the ego is real, how could you doubt the dream? We have just read in the previous pages, "Look, then, beyond effects. It is not here the cause of suffering and sin must lie." T-27.VII.5 And later on in the next paragraph, "Seek not another cause, nor look among the mighty legions of its witnesses for its undoing." Hah! All those epidemiology studies that try to find the causes of things, as if science was somehow better than myths and old wives' tales. Epidemiologists study things that are happening normally and governments do it on purpose. But *you* put it out there anyway; it is all in your dream! Do not get angry at the government; there is no government outside your mind! [laughter] You just constructed it that way. You had the government be the evildoers, or the bad guys, and you had the people in the subway be the good guys. You start to see that it cannot be so. It is all made up. That is good news.

> A brother separated from yourself, an ancient enemy, a murderer who stalks you in the night and plots your death, yet plans that it be lingering and slow; of this you dream. Yet underneath this dream is yet another, in which you become the murderer, the secret enemy, the scavenger and the destroyer of your brother and the world alike. Here is the cause of suffering, the space between your little dreams and your reality. The little gap you do not even see, the birthplace of illusions and of fear, the time of terror and of ancient hate, the instant of disaster, all are here. Here is the cause of unreality. And it is here that it will be undone. T-27.VII.12

You could think of this as "the little gap;" every time we come together we are going inward toward the little gap, toward this itty bitty gap, this little blip, this "tiny mad idea" that the Son of God remembered not to laugh about. It is buried, covered over and protected. That is what has to be exposed. That is the tree trunk from which all the branches and all the seeming beliefs seem to come.

But the gap is impossible; there is no gap. A stepping stone might be to say that the gap is past. Here I am Lord, *now*; the gap is past! If the gap is past, then everything that seemed to have sprung from the gap is past as well. Hence we get statements in the Course like "This world was over long ago," T-28.I.1 and lesson number 7, "I see only the past." I see only the past in the sense that what is producing the world is past and what it seems to produce (the world) is also past.

If I do not experience that the past is gone, then the past and the ego seem to have a reality; guilt and fear seem real. You cannot bring the unholy instant and the holy instant together. The meaning of the holy instant is that it is all there is. To keep trying to bring the unholy instant into the holy instant is just another way of saying that you are not aware of the holy instant. There are a number of ways we can come at it, but it is really just about getting very clear about the past and the present.

Friend: You said the gap is analogous to a tree trunk?

David: In a sense, the whole tree rests on the trunk; if you look at the branches, they are all funneled into one place. The trunk is the base from which they all come. This tiny gap is the base from which everything springs. Another way to describe the gap would be that the gap is the wrong mind. Or you could use the idea of the thinker and the thoughts; sometimes you hear people talking about feeling terrible because they are having judgmental thoughts. They feel guilty about it, but those thoughts and the thinker that seems to be thinking them are both illusions. They are both the wrong mind. The image maker and the images are both the same thing. That is why the right mind just sees the gap as the gap; the right mind sees the gap as false. That is a very simple definition for the right mind. The right mind is not part of the gap, tucked in there somewhere. It just sees the gap as false. That is where the simplicity comes in.

> You are the dreamer of the world of dreams. No other cause it has, nor ever will. Nothing more fearful than an idle dream has terrified God's Son, and made him think that he has lost his innocence, denied his Father, and made war upon himself. So fearful is the dream, so seeming real, he could not waken to reality without the sweat of terror and a scream of mortal fear, unless a gentler dream preceded his awaking, and allowed his calmer mind to welcome, not to fear, the Voice that calls with love to waken him. God willed he waken gently and with joy, and gave him means to waken without fear. T-27.VII.13

There is such a stark contrast between "...the sweat of terror ... a scream of mortal fear," and "...unless a gentler dream preceded his awaking, and allowed his calmer mind to welcome, not to fear, the Voice that calls with love to waken him." The awakening process perceived through the lens of the wrong mind, the lens of the ego, will seem like "the sweat of terror and a scream of mortal fear." Is there anybody in this room who has not experienced that?

Beyond the Subject/Object Split

David: Today we will go through *The Dreamer of the Dream* section.

> Suffering is an emphasis upon all that the world has done to injure you. Here is the world's demented version of salvation clearly shown. Like to a dream of punishment, in which the dreamer is unconscious of what brought on the attack against himself, he sees himself attacked unjustly and by something not himself. T-27.VII.1

That last sentence highlights two central ideas: "attacked unjustly," and "by something not himself." Attacked unjustly; you know: *It's not fair!* And the idea of "something not himself" brings in the subject/object split. That "something not himself" could be another person other than himself that he identifies as a person or it could be a dog; someone could perceive being attacked by a hurricane or a tornado, but it is something that is "not himself." Beneath all of those things, which seem to be quite varied in form, there is still the subject/object split; there is something that is doing the attacking and there is something that is being attacked.

If we go a little deeper we see that it is the body identification, or the personhood, which is the subject. A body or a person can also seem to do things to himself, like the statement: *I keep beating myself up over this.* Of course this is not the real self; it is just an image. Even with self-inflicted wounds, it is still broken up as if the self is an image in linear time. It would seem that somebody who cuts their own arm with a knife is causing a self-inflicted wound, but that still is not Self, it is the image. It is just the past. It is another image just like an image of an intruder coming into a house, so to speak, and inflicting a wound which seems to be different from a self-inflicted wound. In both cases bodies can seem to harm other bodies, and bodies can even seem to harm themselves. But all of them are projections. All of them are just images that seem as if they are inflicting harm, on oneself or another seeming self.

The basic premise of the Course is that Mind cannot attack. That is why mind is innocent, because mind cannot attack. The wrong mind is part of this construction in which it believes that it has left its abstract reality and has taken on form. Bodies can seem to attack. The illusion of attack seems to occur in form.

Friend: And there is a sense of that in expressions like: *I am warring with myself,* or other commonly-held notions we have which allude to having two parts of me. Even the expression "part of me feels…" alludes to parts that do not agree.

David: Whether it is a self-inflicted physical wound or whether I am having a war in my mind right now, they are both just statements of the wrong mind. What mind is at war with itself? You even have to be careful when you talk about warring and different parts; again, the right mind and the wrong mind are not at war because the right mind does not respond. The wrong mind you could say attacks, or, even better, the wrong mind is just a belief system of attack. It is not like it is an entity; it is the illusion of attack. The images that seem to be at war are always different segments or aspects of an illusion. For example, a runner might say: *I am not really competing with someone else, I am competing with myself.* There are still two images. The mind is holding onto an ideal time for running the mile, maybe a record that was set in the past. Now it believes it is a separate image from that, and it is going to try to beat that time. Whenever we are talking about competition with or attack upon the self, there are still images that are involved.

Friend: Where are the images when someone inflicts a wound on oneself?

David: The hand holding the knife, you could say, and the arm that is getting cut.

Friend: What I hear you saying is that it is just a demonstration of the duality which is the wrong mind. It does not take two of anything, not two bodies, not an attacker and a person being attacked, or a victim and a victimizer. It is the duality in the mind, not even the physical duality of a subject and object.

David: It is projected out that way. Even if you say self-inflicted wound, there is a hand holding a knife and a wounded arm. You can still see the duality perceived in the world even in that example. You could say there is just one person, one body, but there is one holding the knife and one receiving the blow, so to speak. The deceived mind does not want to see that it is holding onto a false belief system, so it projects the split out into the world and it sees duality—a cleaving of what is One into all these parts. That is where all the extremes come in: hot/cold, fast/slow, male/female, high/low, on and on; right arm/left arm, right arm with knife/left arm without knife; you could break it up any way you want. The key is to begin to see that there is not any duality in the world. The world is just a screen.

The key is to learn to discern what is all the same and what is different. What is the same? All the images, everything on the screen is the same. What is different? The right mind and the wrong mind are different; they are two different purposes in mind. They are not alike at all. One is the reflection of reality and the other one is non-existent. That is different! They are different in every way. So what we keep coming back to is a clear understanding and recognition of what is the same and what is different. All seeming upsets involve an ambiguity about that distinction. You have to believe that specifics are different from one another for them to seem important, whether it is a full cookie jar or an empty one, whether the rug is clean or not. You could go on and on and on. All the seeming difficulties that come up have the underlining assumption that there are aspects of this world that are different from other aspects, and that some can be better than others.

The whole point of all of this is to come to the awareness that images are images are images. Illusions are one. There is not any causation in the world. Talk about rest! What would you need to do? What conflict could you feel if you realized that there is no duality in the world, that there is no hierarchy of images? Miracles would be universal. There would be no order of difficulty in miracles. You would have on your hands the last miracle and the first – the Atonement!

To understand how miracles are used, you can think of the idea of Atonement as a string of beads. The first bead and the last bead are the same – the Atonement. Miracles are all the beads in between, helping to collapse the string (in the mind that still believes in linear time), until the first and last beads come together to be seen as one and the same. The reason the Course is a course in *miracles*, training the mind towards *miracle mindedness*, is because the mind believes in linear time. Miracles are like a metaphor representing all those beads in-between the first and last miracle. It is the same with holy encounters:

> Whenever you meet anybody, remember it is a holy encounter. As you see him you will see yourself. As you treat him you will treat yourself. As you think of him you will think of yourself. T-8.III.4

There is only one miracle; that is the Atonement. There is only one holy encounter. There is only one holy instant. It is about transcending the metaphors and coming to the state of mind that sees all the stepping stones for what they are, just stepping stones. There is only one holy relationship! It is not always described that way in *A Course in Miracles* because there are rungs along the way. There are many statements such as, "Two minds with one intent become so strong that what they will becomes the Will of God," W-185.3 but when we shift into the context of one mind, one solution, we are in the one instant that can be received NOW – the Atonement. Everything has to collapse into that instant. That is what immediate salvation is about. "Cause and effect are one;" "Ideas leave not their source;" "Time is simultaneous." There are many different ways of saying the same thing.

I would like to go back to that sentence:

> Like to a dream of punishment, in which the dreamer is unconscious of what brought on the attack against himself, he sees himself attacked unjustly and by something not himself. He is the victim of this "something else," a thing outside himself, for which he has no reason to be held responsible. He must be

innocent because he knows not what he does, but what is done to him. Yet is his own attack upon himself apparent still, for it is he who bears the suffering. And he cannot escape because its source is seen outside himself. T-27.VII.1

One major version of this is the feeling of powerlessness or blame, the belief that the world is the cause of one's suffering. Another version is the belief that the ego's thought system is so powerful that it is dictating one's decisions and actions. But the ego is not an entity that is outside the mind. The Course says you made this thing up and seem to be ruled by it; it seems to be the dictator of what you think and say and do. That needs to be questioned as well. Where is the escape in thinking that the "devil made you do it"? Where is the peace in that? The Course says: "Do not project this fear to time, for time is not the enemy that you perceive." T-26.VIII.3

Do not project the ego onto anything or anybody else and do not project it to time. Do not even think that you are in chains from which you will be released at some point in the future. That could be thought of as a helpful stepping stone, to think that at least there will be some future release, but even that has to be questioned. That is still projecting responsibility for the ego onto time, onto the future, like the thought that *time heals all wounds* or, *in time I will reach enlightenment.*

Friend: You are saying that is actually a denial of the decision for the Atonement?

David: Yes. Everything is always a present decision. The ego is a present decision. If you project to the future, that is like trying to hide it away in linear time. Linear time is a construction of the ego that is being held onto *now*, and it has to be let go of *now*. It is a metaphor to say that the decision for the ego is now, in the sense that the deceived mind does not know what *now* is.

Friend: The decision for the ego is past, not now.

David: It is the belief that it is still present. It is the belief that the past is still present, which is another way of saying the mind does not know what the present is. That is where *not knowing* comes in; *I do not know but I am open to be shown—to be shown the present. I am willing to desire the holy instant above all else.* That is the focus and the intention of what we do. You can see there are a lot of metaphors in there. When we say that peace and upset are both present decisions, we are still operating from the same metaphor that there is a right mind and a wrong mind, and that the mind can vacillate and choose one or the other every instant. You have to come to the point where you see that it is just a metaphor. You cannot hang out there. You have to come to understand that even the idea of right mind and wrong mind is a metaphor or construct. We have to keep going over it from all different angles to really raise all the level confusion and backwards thinking up into awareness. What good does it do to say, "The truth is all there is," if there are still aspects of level confusion that have not been exposed? What do you have then?

Friend: Denial.

David: That is what you have. That is why it is imperative to be very thorough and to look at everything. You certainly do not have the *experience* that truth is all there is when there is still level confusion in the mind. If you are hanging onto aspects of personhood or obligations you still have to fulfill in this world, you are still seeing causation on the screen. That is level confusion. The mind is causative. The screen is not. There are no aspects to the screen, and there is no causation on the screen.

"Truth is true, and only the Truth is true" is a common catch-word phrase we have heard as we have traveled around. It sounds great, but then we go into discussion about what seems to be daily living and find that there are inconsistencies being taught about all kinds of things, whether it is how often you should bathe, or the foods you are to eat or not eat to become enlightened, or the amount of exercise, or the positions or the times of meditation – backwards, backwards, backwards! All of it is backwards! People talk about ideal community environments, energy spots, vortexes, etc. Wait a minute! Which is it? That denies that Truth is true and only the Truth is true.

Opening to the Dreamer of the Dream Perspective

Friend: What is the Holy Spirit's use for the past?

David: It is symbolic. Words are the past. These teaching sessions are the Holy Spirit's use of the past. For example, as I bring up the events our friend described about his time in college in order to point to something beyond it – that is the Holy Spirit's use of the past.

Friend: I see. We are talking about the past right now and we think this is the present. I do not get that, but that is because I am deceived?

David: It is the reference point. Picture it as a symbol. Here is the cosmos, the time-space cosmos. You perceive yourself as within the time-space cosmos, we will say in a galaxy in a solar system on a planet, call it Earth, on a continent, call it North America, in a state, within the city limits, in the upper room of a home, in a bedroom, sitting on a couch, in a body that is six feet tall. You are observing the time-space cosmos from that reference point which seems to be from behind two eyes and between two ears. It can seem as if the sense of self is perceived to be in the head. You perceive the cosmos from that specific reference point within the cosmos.

But it seems to be possible to perceive the cosmos from a point that is not within the cosmos. You could say the *dreamer of the dream* is the mind that is watching all the images in the cosmos, including all the images that seemed to take place in history, Abraham Lincoln and Gandhi, and Julius Caesar, and Jesus Christ, and Confucius, and including all of the images that seem to be coming in the future.

Friend: The dreamer is watching all that simultaneously.

David: It does not matter what specific part of the cosmos is being seen; there is an awareness that they are all the same. If you have a giant structure that has all these different facets to it, as you turn it around it does not matter what particular facet seems to be in front at any given moment, so to speak. They are all seen as the same.

Friend: How do you get to that awareness from feeling like you are inside? How are you getting outside of it?

David: Realize first of all that you do not value judgment and you do not value ordering of thoughts. Everything we go into is about beginning to see that judgments, preferences, and the ordering of thoughts are not valuable. Judgment is a device for maintaining the experience of being within the cosmos. The relinquishment of judgment is coming to the point of seeing that not only do I not have to give it up, but I never had it. I just have to realize that I cannot judge, that I am incapable of judging. Isn't that wonderful? That is the release point. It is not that you are giving up something that is real. You are not giving up something you had and are now losing. You never had it! You are incapable of judging. That is the point of perceiving it not from within the cosmos but from the *dreamer of the dream* perspective.

Friend: And is there a way to see that? I seem to enjoy chocolate ice cream with hot fudge on it. Is that a judgment? How do I look at that? I am having a hard time because I do not want it to just be an idea. I do not want to play mind games.

I want to understand how that is achieved, if it can be achieved. How do you adjust your mindset?

David: You question the perception. The "I" that perceives that it enjoys ice cream with fudge on it is a construct.

Friend: So if I just start being more aware of all the judgments I make, it will undo itself?

David: That is symbolic of unwinding yourself, of coming to clarity or discernment between what is real and what is unreal. This came up recently; our friend was saying, "But I like nature," just like you are saying about ice cream with fudge. "I like nature! And I feel wrong because I like nature!" Follow the metaphysics of this in and question the "I" that seems to like nature; just question that "I" that seems to like the ice cream. Follow it in.

I began questioning my roles, what I was doing and why I was doing it. I thought, *Well, I am doing this because it is my job. Well, why do I have this job? I took the job because I need money. Why do I need money? I need money so I can have these things. Why do I need these things?* Well if you trace it back down, if you keep tracing it down, you come to the belief in body identity.

Friend: Right. I feel like I have done all that with the job and the roles and the relationships with other bodies; I started to question all that because if there is no purpose then I do not want to have anything to do with it. But if I do not have an experience of not being a body, I do not see how I can get beyond that, unless the experience will come by questioning. I guess that is what my question is: Do the questions bring on the experience?

David: The questions are still coming from the ego but the questioning of your beliefs and your thinking is meaningful in the seeming process of awakening. You desire an experience that will take the place of you as a body, and *by* your desire that experience will be brought to you. It will seem to come first through miracles. The holy instant is the experience of being the Holy Son of God, not this body and not confined to this world in any way.

Miracles will seem to precede that experience. You had one the other day, so to speak, when you came in and said, "I was resting and for an instant I had this beautiful feeling of detachment, of total release, not worried about anything, not concerned. A miracle! That is a miracle! It felt great!" It came to you by your desire for it. It is not like you have to go around collecting miracles; your desire brings them to you. Your desire for the holy instant will bring it nearer to your awareness.

That is why we say there is nothing you can do. Moving your eyes over the lines in a book is not going to bring you the holy instant. The desire and the intention of opening your mind to go beyond the words to the meaning of the ideas will bring the experience. The reflection of a person reading a book out on the screen is just a symbol but the desire is in the core of your being.

Friend: And that is what the questions are too? They are a symbol of that desire until I get past everything else? I guess asking the question is not causative. What is causative is the desire to ask the question?

David: Let's look at time for a moment. If you believe with the ego that the past happened, you believe you are guilty in that past. And the present seems very minuscule; it seems to get covered over so easily. In that scenario you believe that there is no power, no real opportunity for change in the present. The past is like solid granite, the present is like a teeny blip that is so easily covered over and the future is just a repetition of the past. Guilt–past, guilt–future. Fear–past, fear–future. If you really believe that, why would you question at all? The belief in linear time inhibits questioning. If you do not believe there is hope of ever getting out of the pattern, you feel locked in. It feels like everything is set and determined; you are condemned to a life of sin, guilt, misery and upset. If you believe that, why would you even raise a question? The mind is closed and has concluded that life is hell.

Friend: And there is no way out.

David: Like the bumper sticker, "Life's a bitch and then you die." If that is your conclusion, then why question? The questioning comes in when there is a sense that there is more than what meets the eye. There is something more than all of this. The questioning comes in when the mind is not so convinced that it knows everything there is to know. Then the questioning begins inwardly; you begin to question more and more and more. You question the mind and the beliefs and the thoughts–everything. One has to come to a point though where you reach the edge and leap off the cliff into certainty. There is no questioning in certainty. Christ is not a questioner. Questions are not inherently valuable. Christ asks no questions.

Friend: I assume that I will know when I am at that cliff because I do not feel like I am there right now. I do not feel that I could just jump from this point that I am at.

David: You do not feel it and you do not believe it. We are back to Atonement, or what seems not to be Atonement.

Friend: Because I do not see how. I feel like I need to know how to do it. I do not see a doorway. I do not see the cliff.

David: Stay attentive. It is right there under your nose. In the parable of David, so to speak, I remember metaphorically being so drawn to these ideas. I was still having my doubts but I sensed that there was something there. You sense that there is something, that there is a hope for emancipation, for happiness, peace, and freedom. But it is not really anchored; it is more of a hope than an assuredness.

Friend: From experiences I had on mushrooms, I can say I know that it is there. Even though it seems to have been years ago in linear time, the intensity with which I experienced that lets me know it is real. And the little experiences like the one I had the other day, are letting me know it is real. But I feel like I am in a maze. I need direction how to get to the cliff so I can jump, or how to get rid of the fear so I can jump. I want to not be afraid. I have always had an idea that God is gentle and he knows I am afraid. I always envisioned a process where the fear is slowly minimized to the point where the jumping is natural.

David: That has been a helpful metaphor but now the veils are starting to fall away on that one as well.

Friend: I still had this sense, even then, that I had a choice. And now it is no different. I have to make a choice about whether I want to go for it. I did not feel strong enough at that time to let it be my reality.

David: You believe that choices and decisions are in linear time. You are describing it as if you had a choice back then. Who was the "I" that had that choice? The body! The body! The body seems to have choice. Or beyond that, what are you, a person? So you must believe that persons have choices. Not only does the body have choice but it seems like other bodies can also make choices. Do you think these other bodies had choices to make in their past, like the one you are talking about? You believe that too! [laughter] There we go. Now we are getting down to some of the fundamental building blocks of what you believe. You believe that persons have choices. You believe there were real choices in the past. Do you believe there are some real choices coming up in the future? [nods from group] There we go! So it is obvious you believe that choice is within the realm of linear time and that persons are the instruments or the agents of choice, the entities that have choice. We have to follow that in to see if there is a choice or a decision that will end all choice. When would that have to be?

Friend: Now. Because now is the only time there is. But I still think of now as a moving now.

David: Oh, a moving now; so there is a past *now* and a future *now*?

Friend: The past is always following now and the future is always being pushed off by the new now. That is the way I think of it, as this marching *now*.

David: Yeah! That is good! Now we are getting into your beliefs about time; we have past now and future now. [laughter]

Friend: I was reading something once where a teacher was saying that if you have an appointment next week on Thursday at noon, you write that down and when that becomes *now*, you go to that appointment. It certainly seems like there are weeks to come and I have made commitments, like to be at work at 3:15 today. Even though I understand the clock is just going around and really nothing is changing, when the clock shows three o'clock I will make every attempt to get up and go, until I can see something else that allows me to say: *No, I am not going to do that anymore.*

David: You believe it and therefore you have experiences that witness to it, including reading what that teacher was saying. The mind gets exactly what it wants; the mind sees what it believes. If the mind believes in linear time, it sees a world in which time seems to be linear. It sees other figures in the dream as well, that also seem to be moving around on the clock. So we question, question, question, question, question. If there is a choice that will end all these seeming choices, then it has to be *now* and it has to be a choice that is very different than the choices of the world, different than choosing to buy a car, to work somewhere, to marry someone, or to leave the house today.

The choice that we are talking about is a choice of content, not of form. You have to question all the personal choices of the world, to have children or not to have children, to go to work or not to go to work – all the choices you believe are real in the past and all the ones you believe are real in the future. You have to question them and ask if there really is a choice. Are you open to a choice of purpose, to a choice of content that you can only make right now?

Friend: But isn't it always right now? Could I have made that choice yesterday?

David: Who? Who is it? You still believe there is an "I."

Friend: OK, let me take it away from that. When I begin to realize that I am not a body, I will realize I have always been in eternity and that will be right now because it is always now in eternity?

David: It is important not to get too hung up but I think it is great that you are seeing how it all boils down to time. You are, just by sitting here and talking about it. You are saying that yes, you do believe in past choices and yes, you do believe in future choices, and yes, you believe in that person that had past choices and will have future choices. All of that is the wrong mind. As you continue to be willing to take a closer look at it all and to be open to the idea that perhaps you have been mistaken about everything, you are opening up to an experience that is different than the way it has seemed to be. It will come. It has come. You will accept it. You will be aware of it.

Friend: I still have this feeling there was a time when I did not accept it. I have a feeling that what life seems to be about is this acceptance.

David: "The sole responsibility of the miracle worker is to accept the Atonement for himself." T-2.V.5 Sole responsibility! Not your responsibilities at work, or as a parent or as a husband. It is not about your responsibilities as a law-abiding citizen. It can be as simple as that; your sole responsibility is to accept the Atonement.

Friend: I guess we need to talk more about what that involves because I do not know. Those are just words to me right now.

David: Have we talked about anything other than that in these sessions? That is what a teaching session is; we look at what is in the way of that acceptance right now. What a joy to begin to see some of the assumptions you believe in, even though it may not feel comfortable! To believe in illusions but not have a clue that you believe in illusions, is that what you want? You think you are living in a real world and you do not even have a clue there is anything beyond this: *Mind? What is a mind? I cannot see it. I cannot taste it. I cannot touch it. I do not even know that there is such a thing as mind.* You are twice removed from reality when you believe in the reality of what the senses show you without realizing there is anything beyond that.

Once removed from reality is when you begin to see that this is a world of your own making. You read in the Course that you have made this world up and that it comes from your beliefs. Well, that can still be uncomfortable; where is the rest in the belief that you have bought into false beliefs? But now you are just one step from reality! You are going back into the mind and seeing that this is not you. The ego is history.

Before you can come to accept the Atonement you have to first raise the ego into awareness and see it for what it is. Do not be fooled by all the changing forms; you have to raise ego thinking to awareness. This has to come. The awareness that the ego is history has to be perceived. The ego is false. The ego is past. The ego is nothing. You have to question time. You have to question linear time; you have to question cause and effect. You have to look into those things before you can meaningfully and experientially say that the ego is nothing. Otherwise it would be denial: *Oh great, nothing happened. But how do I feel? It sure feels like something happened.* That is where the questioning comes in.

There is no amount of words that will ever deny the ego. There is only an experience. The miracle is a denial of the ego, but the miracle is not just a bunch of words. It is not like you can memorize the book until you reach a certain point where you say: *I have got it! I have generated enough words to dispel the ego!* That will not do it.

That is why we are not into studying the ego for the sake of studying the ego. The purpose is to come to the awareness of the miracle. The miracle dispels the ego. Traditional psychotherapy is a symbol of studying the ego. Where does studying the ego's defense mechanisms get you if it does not give you peace, joy, and happiness? What good does it do to know about defense mechanisms? What is the good of scrutinizing the ego or even studying the Course if you are not happy? Why read the words if you are not applying them, if you do not go within your mind to find a clear inner sense of discernment? It is just another ego maneuver. The ego will use the Course to protect itself by hiding behind fancy-sounding words.

In the *Clarification of Terms* section called "The Ego – The Miracle," Jesus tells us that we cannot really define the ego but the miracle is its opposite; the miracle shows us what the ego *was*. That is the key. You have to see that the ego is past, not present. There is no ego now. Can you grasp the clarity of that? There is no David now; there are no friends now. There is no past, present, or future now! There are no private minds now! There is a singular mind *now*!

Personhood and everything we talk about *was*! Singleness of Mind *Is*! That is the key distinction.

Let's use our metaphor of the cosmos. It is distortion or wrong-minded when you are viewing the cosmos from a perspective that seems to be within the cosmos. The miracle is seeing the cosmos for what it is, from a perspective that is not in the cosmos — seeing the false as false, seeing that the past is past.

Questioning is helpful initially because you are open to receiving another answer; you are open to receiving the Holy Spirit. But an experience will come that will put an end to the questions. The questions will seem meaningless. You are getting a glimpse of that now. A lot of the questions that seemed to be asked before do not seem as meaningful as they once did; they do not seem as serious.

The deceived mind makes up questions to still God's Voice. It asks what I call "wonder questions," seeming questions that are really statements. Every time you hear thoughts like: *I wonder why so and so did that to so and so*, just imagine a little sign going up behind you that says: I am an ego! *I wonder why?* I am an ego. And, what might a meaningful question be? *Am I willing to help the Holy Spirit save the world?* Hmmm, that is a different question than: *Should I buy the burrito or the soft chicken taco?*

Lucid Dream Realization: One Mind Dreaming

Friend: The scenario starts with the ever-present question here: One Mind dreaming or six billion scheming? I put this in a hypothetical context and ask that you take a moment to imagine that only one mind exists, and that is all that exists in all of existence. Place yourself in bed, right before you fall asleep. As you leave the world and your body and all that is your mind, you have a clean slate upon which you can draw whatever it is that you desire. Now you fall asleep, and you have this dream of the zany antics of these six friends: Monica, Ross, Joey, Phoebe, Rachel, and Chandler.

Now, there are two ways to have this dream: one is just as an observer, where you are watching these people, like on a TV show. With this type of dream, waking up is like turning the TV off. In another type of dream, you actually identify yourself as one of the characters in this scenario, it really does not matter which character you identify with.

So, in tonight's dream, the six friends go to visit the Swami of Pastrami to learn meditation and find their True Self (which we know is really you who is dreaming this particular dream). Suddenly Ross becomes enlightened through a perfect remembering of his Source. He realizes that he is not Ross, but the mind dreaming of Ross (you). Now, do we say that Ross has awakened? No, of course not! Ross was not sleeping, and even enlightened Ross is a dream figure. And even though Ross is enlightened, the dream continues. It continues with enlightened Ross replacing dilrod Ross.

Nobody has awakened, for the only anybody in this scenario is you, and you are still dreaming about an enlightened Ross and friends. So you see, even enlightened masters are part of the dream.

David: Bingo! There is one dreamer, observer, witness. This is the Perspective of forgiveness that happily sees a forgiven world, for causation has been returned to mind, and images are seen as unreal effects of an unreal "cause." The ego was not a real cause and had no real effects. This happy dream is a waking dream, for though it is an illusion as well, it leads out of illusions to Mind Awake. The ego was the belief in private minds with private thoughts, the belief in individuality, in being a person.

In the lucid dream – the Perspective of the Holy Spirit in which the dreamer has awareness of dreaming – the dream is seen as a whole. There are no differences, levels, or distinctions in a whole dream, and conflict is therefore impossible. The whole dream is peaceful for it reflects the waking state of Reality. Mind awakens, dream figures do not.

Atonement sees no differences, for there are none. Atonement is the recognition that the separation never happened. Ideas leave not their source. Just as Christ never left the Mind of God – the dreamer of the dream never left the right-mindedness of the Holy Spirit. It is therefore impossible to be a dream figure in "someone else's dream," for there is only one mind asleep and this dreamer is happily sharing the Holy Spirit's Perspective. Eureka!

> Forgiving dreams have little need to last. They are not made
> to separate the mind from what it thinks. They do not seek to
> prove the dream is being dreamed by someone else. T-29.IX.8

Holy Relationship is a Shift of Mind, a Shift Away From the Personal

A friend recently asked me to share more personal miracle-shifts from my journey so she could relate to the ideas I share. The Spirit uses the parables. People smile and nod in recognition of the Divine Principle that glimmers beyond the stories. Abstraction is the natural condition of the Mind. Parables are very specific examples that serve to point to a State of Mind that experiences nothing as special and perceives everything in the cosmos as a happy dream and a reflection of God's Love.

I experience God's Love as universal, expansive and unlimited. God's Love is literally beyond definition of any kind. The Holy Spirit uses many examples and metaphors to point to the Present Moment, which is the Presence of God's Love. The examples are witnesses that God's Love is not dependent on form or specifics at all. The Holy Spirit can use any symbol to help the sleeping mind recognize this Pristine and Tranquil Moment.

Holy relationship is not "between" people. It is very simply the Purpose of acceptance and non-judgment held firmly and surely in mind. It looks and waits and watches and judges not. It does not seek to change the world, for holy relationship is the symbol of a forgiven world. The Purpose is equally applicable to every person, place, thing, situation, and event. The Purpose is the understanding that there are no real differences possible in unified awareness. Love is all-inclusive because Love is One. Love is friendly because everyone is a friend in the experience of extending Love. The cosmos of time and space was made to hide Love and push It out of awareness, so examples of "Love in action," so to speak, are extremely helpful in Awakening to Love's Presence, which is ever-Present.

Here are some specific examples that point to holy relationship or what I refer to as Holy Union. Name 1 and Name 2 are symbols. They are symbols which represent two people. Holy relationship is not between Name 1 and Name 2. The symbols of people, like all symbols, are used by the Holy Spirit to point toward Divine Love. The symbols are never the actual experience of Love, for representations and reflections of Love always reflect the belief that Love and symbols are the same. Love is God's Will and thus has no object, and symbols can but point to the experience of Love. Never mistake a symbol for anything Real, for symbols are temporary and Reality is Eternal.

The holy relationship can be described as loving, trusting, open, honest, kind, free, spontaneous, present, affectionate, nonjudgmental, inclusive, happy, joyful, peaceful, extending, communicating, healing, and, very simply, as wonderful!

The holy relationship is not romantic, sexual, possessive, exclusive, time-based, judgmental, controlling, fearful, angry, guilty, jealous, or comparative, and the holy relationship is definitely not insane or sick in any way. The holy relationship is therefore unlike any and all interpersonal relationships that seem to be so very common and "natural" in this world, relationships based on separation, autonomy and individuality.

Holy relationship is shared Purpose. Only the Holy Spirit's Purpose can truly be extended or shared. The attempt to share ego concepts and beliefs is therefore the attempt to share nothing, but "nothing" cannot be shared; only Love is capable of being extended or shared. Love simply extends and shares, Being What It Is.

What form does holy relationship take? It takes whatever form is helpful to demonstrate the lesson that form is meaningless and Love is All Meaning, that Love is Content and not form of any kind. Love is a State of Mind and cannot be reduced to objects in a field of ego consciousness within linear time. In Holy Union there is no past and there is no future. In this world, saying "our relationship has no future" means that a relationship has come to an end, but under the Holy Spirit's Guidance these same words take on a very different Meaning—a Present Meaning. Live for the Moment, for Now is truly Everything. This is the key to Happiness not of this world, to the Happiness that comes from God.

In *A Course in Miracles*, Jesus teaches that "minds are joined, and cannot separate. Yet in the dreaming has this been reversed, and separate minds are seen as bodies, which are separated and which cannot join." T-28.III.3 He also teaches that "The Holy Spirit's purpose lies safe in your relationship, and not your body." T-20.VI.7 The relationship is thus the loving attitude you share and cannot be defined in terms of bodies. Bodies seem to come and go, and thus relationships that are defined by bodies are temporary. The attitude of Love is ever lasting, and this can only be experienced when all body thoughts have been released to the Holy Spirit. How is this done? Let the Holy Spirit tell you where and when to bestow miracles, and let Jesus perform them through your mind. Feel the Joy of Purpose as you step back and let the Holy Spirit lead the way. Do not attempt to tell the Holy Spirit who needs miracles and where and when, for only by receiving the miracles first can you be directed and instructed by the Holy Spirit.

The desires of the ego fade, grow dim, and disappear in holy relationship. The desires for bodily comforts and conveniences, preferences, appetites, and the countless distractions of the ego become more and more peripheral in awareness. Then in the holy instant they are gone, and the mind rests in Peace at last.

In form it seems that I meet countless brothers and sisters as I travel. There seems to be a gigantic spiritual family joined in shared Purpose. It is a vast holy relationship in which the faces and places seem to change, and the names and languages seem to change, yet the Purpose is constant. Holy relationship is so vast that it feels very Abstract, for all scraps of the personal are washed away in the River of Love. The River sees no special bodies and no couples. The River sees no groups or congregations for the River empties into an Eternal Ocean that is completely Abstract. The memories of time-space fade and grow dim and disappear in Oneness, and the River of Revelation shows glimpses of this boundless Ocean.

People always seem to be very interested in the script. The feeling of Love inside one's heart has nothing to do with the script. Form is eclipsed by Content, and this experience renders the form irrelevant. Such is the Mysticism of Love. For the mind that comes to a Single desire, creation is Revealed as What Is. Let our Beloved holy relationship lead the way. Let all symbols merge in a forgiven world, and welcome the disappearance of the cosmic universe. The Universe of Spirit is All, and nothing unreal exists. Herein lies the Peace of God!

Questioning the Reality of Debt and Reciprocity

David: The decision to get out of debt in a worldly sense is a decision within the unholy instant. You have to really take a look at the concept of debt and to begin to come into the mystical state of seeing how the whole idea of debt is really just as funny as the idea of "worldly justice." First you believe that there is fairness and justice in the world but when you get deeper into the Course, you start to question the concept of fairness and justice. You start out that way with debt as well and then as you go deeper you begin to see it as kind of funny. You have to believe in the laws of economics before you can believe in debt. You have to believe in exchange and reciprocity before you can believe in debt. It would make no sense to talk about debt without a belief in the laws of economics and the laws of reciprocity and exchange.

Seeming to pay off your debts in form is just the beginning, a stepping stone. You have to question the laws of economics, and the laws of reciprocity and exchange. Getting the debts paid off is on the surface but then you have to do the real work—you have to question the reality of debts. [laughter] As you question the reality of debts and reciprocity, I guarantee that you will come back to looking at personhood. You know that you are going to come back around to that again because there certainly are not any debts or reciprocity in Heaven. There are not even any debts and reciprocity in the real world and you have to go through the real world to get to Heaven.

It seems simple; it seems like we keep talking about the same things, just coming at them from all these different angles. That is the way the process seems to go until you can make the leap. The paying off of debts and the parting of ways that seems to take place in relationships of this world are just symbolic representations on the screen of the mind going back and retracing its steps. All the false beliefs that the mind has made are out-pictured in the seeming experience of being a person in the world, with debts and obligations, responsibilities and duties. That is how it looks out there on the screen. As you start to retrace these decisions, it may seem like the screen changes; things may seem to be getting more simple in your life—but really those are all still interpretations that are being made on the screen.

One could say: *I am completely free. I have nobody counting on me anymore in relationships. I have no more bills to pay. I have cleaned up my act.* And where are you? Have you reached an enlightened state if you have not come to understand that cause and effect are simultaneous, that there is no sequential time, and that there is not any sequencing of events? If you still have judgments and you think you have given up all these things, then where are you? You are still nowhere. You are still having the illusion of being in the world. When we say to take care of business and clear up your debts on the screen, it is just symbolic of loosening....

Friend: Of pulling back.

David: Pulling back in your mind. You want to retrace the steps that you seem to have taken, the steps that seem to have you thinking you are a body in the world. And if the retracing seems painful at times, do not be fooled by that voice. Jesus talks about the uneasiness that may seem to be part of the process in the *Self-Concept versus Self* section:

> A concept of the self is meaningless, for no one here can see
> what it is for, and therefore cannot picture what it is. Yet is

all learning that the world directs begun and ended with the single aim of teaching you this concept of yourself, that you will choose to follow this world's laws, and never seek to go beyond its roads nor realize the way you see yourself. T-31.V.8

We need the Holy Spirit!

Now must the Holy Spirit find a way to help you see this concept of the self must be undone, if any peace of mind is to be given you. Nor can it be unlearned except by lessons aimed to teach that you are something else. For otherwise, you would be asked to make exchange of what you now believe for total loss of self, and greater terror would arise in you. Thus are the Holy Spirit's lesson plans arranged in easy steps, that though there be some lack of ease at times and some distress, there is no shattering of what was learned, but just a re-translation of what seems to be the evidence on its behalf. T-31.V.8-9

As long as the mind believes in separation, it will see evidence of separation. The world you see is what needs to be retranslated: "…but just a re-translation of what seems to be the evidence on its behalf."

The only way out of this seemingly terrifying situation is to re-perceive the world, or to have the perception of the world retranslated so that mind no longer looks for witnesses of pain, suffering and hurt but rather looks for other witnesses, because it holds onto another purpose. Though it may not be comfortable, "there is no shattering of what was learned, but just a re-translation…" Resistance is just the ego's idea of progress. When you seem to have difficulty with some of these ideas it is just the ego's interpretation. Progress and growth so to speak are happening. The movement is taking place, the movement of the Kingdom, the movement of Christ. Do not be alarmed; you are right on schedule, you are right where you need to be. Do not get hung up on the ego's interpretations of events.

Friend: I am right where I need to be.

Chapter Three

Time, Space, and Personhood

David: This morning our friend was saying, "I want it now!!" This would be a good time to go into the section, *The Immediacy of Salvation* and examine the whole idea of whether you can really want it now and not have it.

> The one remaining problem that you have is that you see an interval between the time when you forgive, and will receive the benefits of trusting in your brother. This but reflects the little you would keep between you and your brother, that you and he might be a little separate. For time and space are one illusion, which takes different forms. If it has been projected beyond your mind you think of it as time. The nearer it is brought to where it is, the more you think of it in terms of space. T-26.VIII.1

There are a lot of metaphysics to look at right there in that first paragraph. It kind of eases into it but the last three sentences are the basis of everything we look at. They are zeroing in on the one remaining problem that you have. Everything is a thought in the mind, so every memory is just a thought. If it has been projected beyond your mind, you think of it as time. Memories are just thoughts about something that seems to have happened in the past. All those images that have been projected beyond one's own mind are thought of as time, as if I am a person in time and I have a private mind – instead of seeing that all the circumstances and events that have ever happened in a personal past or in any past are in the mind. Julius Caesar, Cleopatra, Abraham Lincoln, Gandhi, they are all images of the wrong mind.

When something seems to be beyond one's own personal private mind, it seems to be projected onto time, as if it has happened in the past or it will happen in the future. There is nothing that happens apart from me. When I say, "I am the universe," that is in the deepest sense of the word, the universe of creation, God and His Creation. There is no aspect of the cosmos that is apart from me in the sense of the right mind. It is a Perspective that sees that the entire projection was made up; there is no ordering of any of the concepts and images – they are all equally made up. Without that ordering there is no sense of being in the cosmos or of being a teeny little speck, a tiny part. There is more of a sense of the vastness of the idea that *I dreamed this up!* This is the *dreamer of the dream* analogy. In the *dreamer of the dream* experience there is no sound, image, light or variation of light, there is nothing within the cosmos that is apart from one's self, so to speak; one is the dreamer of it all!

Now for the second part: "The nearer it is brought to where it is, the more you think of it in terms of space." You perceive yourself as a body or as a person in the world, and you think of it as if the deceived mind has surrounded itself with the cosmos. The first thing it seems to have surrounded itself with in terms of space is a body. Then seemingly outside of that body there are other bodies, walls and furniture, trees and grass, sky above and earth below, moon and sun, planets and stars. It seems to have wrapped the whole cosmos around it, beginning with the body; "The nearer it is brought to where it is, the more you think of it in terms of space." If you think of a projector, the closer you bring something to the projector, the more it is thought in terms of space. That is how it is described. Stars are described in terms of light years because they seem to be so far away from the projector that they start to be described in terms of time, just like all those events that seemed to happen before or all those events that will happen in the future.

Friend: At any rate, whether it is time or space, it is a means for distancing. And it is the same thing; it only sounds like something different.

David: Time and space are one illusion that takes different forms. We can use the tree analogy again; all the branches come back to the trunk. You can look at time and space as the seeming branches of the trunk but the ego is the ego and everything that is of the ego is the ego!

Friend: No matter what you call it or how you conceive of it.

David: Or how many times it seems to have been multiplied. Talk about the ego belief system—it seems like it has oodles and oodles and oodles of beliefs.

Friend: A billion times zero.

David: Yes. But if the ego is zero, the ego is zero.

> There is a distance you would keep apart from your brother,
> and this space you perceive as time because you still believe
> you are external to him. T-26.VIII.2

Do you see the idea of personhood in there? You would have to have a belief in personhood to see yourself as external to your brother; if your brother is a body or your brother is a person and you are a person then you seem to be external to your brother. If you are a private mind and your brother seems to have a private mind, then your private mind seems to be external to your brother's private mind. This is what we keep looking at, from all these different angles; personhood and the idea of private minds are both made up and cannot be so.

"This makes trust impossible." T-26.VIII.2 You could say the subject-object split makes trust impossible. When the mind seemed to fall asleep, it began to believe in the ego. Now it had two opposite thought systems – two thought systems that have no meeting point. That is where the intolerable sense of strain came in; the mind tried to dissociate from and forget about the light. It tried to spiral out away from the light so that it could keep the two thought systems apart, because if they were ever brought together it would be seen that they cannot coexist. One denies the other. The mind tries to hang onto the split and the separation; it tries to keep the darkness, as if it can have an existence by itself, apart from the light.

Due to the intolerable strain of trying to hold onto both, the split and the cosmos were projected out rather than recognizing that two irreconcilable thought systems were in the mind. The split is seen as on the screen, rather than in the mind. The mind identifies itself as a person and sees everything else as outside itself; this is the subject-object split. Now there is fear because the mind has done all this and in a sense it has tried to forget what it has done. It has tried to forget the way it set things up but the Holy Spirit is a reminder that this cannot be forgotten; God cannot be forgotten.

The mind still has the guilt and the strain but seems to have relieved itself with this projected cosmos. It seems to have loosened up the strain a bit but it is really afraid of God. It has projected the fear out so it seems that it is afraid of all these things in the world. It is a setup; it is a scam; the subject-object split has not resolved the conflict! The mind tried to forget the wholeness that it truly is and made up a concept of a whole person to replace it. Now it thinks it is a whole person separate from the cosmos; *there* is the subject-object split. The fear is maintained. Until the fear is found to be just an unfounded hoax, the mind is in a fearful state, full of doubt. It is in a state of deception and lack of trust. It cannot trust anything because it does not know itself. This is why the split has to be seen as not on the screen; it is not a split between a person and another person/subject in an objective world. The split has to be seen in the mind for trust to be possible. Listening to the Holy Spirit would be the basis of trust and if one truly listened to the Holy Spirit, one would see that one is the *dreamer of the dream*, one is not a person or a little figure in the dream.

The one thing that can truly be trusted is invisible in terms of the body, and that is the one thing the deceived mind is afraid of. As Jesus says in a number of places in the Text, "… you are afraid of what your spiritual sight will show you." T-2.V.7 You believe that spiritual sight, i.e. the Holy Spirit, would rob you of something or that you would lose something if you had spiritual sight. You are fearful that you would lose the world you see, which you would! [laughter]

Friend: And as long as that seems like something, then it feels like loss.

David:

> This makes trust impossible. And you cannot believe that trust would settle every problem now. Thus do you think it safer to remain a little careful and a little watchful of interests perceived as separate. From this perception you cannot conceive of gaining what forgiveness offers now. The interval you think lies in between the giving and receiving of the gift seems to be one in which you sacrifice and suffer loss. You see eventual salvation, not immediate results. T.26.VIII.2

The mind is afraid of giving and receiving true forgiveness. That is where the loss seems to be. To give and receive the gift of forgiveness seems to entail loss.

Friend: Why?

David: What seems to be lost in forgiveness is personhood – the little gap that makes one a separate, unique, individual person, with personal interests, a personal past, a personal future, and a personal will. The mind is terrified of losing its sense of a separate self. That is that little space, the little distance it would like to retain. Forgiveness just sees the false as false.

Earlier when there was all that anguish coming up, you said, "It goes much deeper than just this talk about bodies moving around. It feels like I have to give up my whole world." From the ego's perspective that is exactly how it looks. The ego is a sense of a separate self, with all its preferences and memories and all of its ambitions that seem to be private, that seem to be unique and separate from everyone else; all that is part of its concept.

Friend: It feels like the ego is just kicking in with everything it has; it is seeing more and more clearly what is going on here and is pulling out all the stops. It feels so strong and powerful when that happens.

David: We have certainly used the metaphor that the ego is pulling out all the stops, as if the ego is an entity with life of its own—as if it exists. But ultimately it comes down to the idea that the ego is a decision and the Holy Spirit is a decision; either you are an ego or you are not an ego. Can you see how that goes beyond the idea that the ego is "kicking in." Describing it as if it really could "kick in" just seems to give it reality.

Friend: So instead of describing it that way it would probably be more helpful if I just say, "I am deciding for the ego."

David: Everything is a statement. Everything the mind thinks and says and does is teaching what it believes it is. You cannot leave it at that. That has to be a stepping stone or a metaphor. Where are you if you say, "I am presently deciding for the ego"? That is a definition of hell.

Friend: Again who is that "I," right? Is that what you are getting at?

David: Yes. It is a helpful stepping stone to say: "I am not upset because of what happened yesterday or what happened ten years ago or what I think will happen tomorrow. I am upset because it is a present decision." That is a definition of wrong-mindedness. A present decision for the ego is wrong-mindedness and wrong-mindedness is the problem. All sickness is wrong-mindedness, even though it does not seem that way. To the deceived mind it seems like there are many problems and many forms of sickness that do not have anything to do with wrong-mindedness but Jesus says that the decision for the ego, for wrong-mindedness, is sickness. Right-mindedness is the correction for wrong-mindedness. We are back to discernment between the right mind and the wrong mind. That discernment is the key.

The key is really in coming to see that right-mindedness is the only possibility. You felt such glee earlier, when you said, "I am the right mind!" We traced it and traced it back until you came to see that was the only possibility. I am the right mind. I am right-minded. That is the only possibility. Not, *I am right-minded some of the time*, but I am right-minded, period! In that clarity the wrong mind is dissolved.

Another way of saying it is that the right mind must be a constant state because in reality there is no vacillation back and forth between right mind and wrong mind. That is just a metaphor. When the right mind is seen as a constant state, the wrong mind is no more. As we said earlier, these two thought systems are mutually exclusive.

The *Immediacy of Salvation* section is about really coming to see that there is no gap between me and my brother because there is just one mind. There is no gap between private minds.

Friend: *I am deciding for the ego* could be reworded as: *I am the right mind, but right now I am denying it. I am going to deny it in this instant.*

David: Which you can see is meaningless when you really look at it. A body can say the words: *I am the right mind*; there is no doubt about that. A body can say the words: *I am as God created me.* The reason why we go so deeply into preferences, judgment and ordering of thoughts is because the right mind is a state where there is not any of that—no ordering of thoughts, no preferences, and no judgments. Images are just seen as images. They are not arranged; they are not constructed and put together in a certain way. They are seen as impossible, as laughable. If ordering of thoughts seems to automatically bring about pain, guilt, and fear—what is the point? Jesus says that those in Heaven or of the real world, so to speak, have seen temptation but have seen the falsity of it. They see no value in judgment.

Friend: And until I see that, I cannot stop judging.

David: You could say it that way or you could say: *I do not know who I am.* You just said, "Until I see that..." Here we are again with *The Immediacy of Salvation...* [group laughter] Let's question that "until."

> Salvation *is* immediate. Unless you so perceive it, you will be
> afraid of it, believing that the risk of loss is great between the
> time its purpose is made yours and its effects will come to you.
> In this form is the error still obscured that is the source of fear.
> Salvation *would* wipe out the space you see between you still,
> and let you instantly become as one. And it is here you fear

the loss would lie. Do not project this fear to time, for time is not the enemy that you perceive. Time is as neutral as the body is, except in terms of what you see it for. If you would keep a little space between you and your brother still, you then would want a little time in which forgiveness is withheld a little while. And this but makes the interval between the time in which forgiveness is withheld from you and given seem dangerous, with terror justified. T.26.VIII.3

If a mind believes in the reality of the ego, it believes in a false cause, or we could say cause with a little c. It must be that the mind is holding onto the belief in that false cause *now*. "Do not project this fear to time, for time is not the enemy that you perceive." Do not project the error! The old cliché about time healing all wounds is not true. Time does not heal wounds. Metaphorically you could say the Holy Spirit's use of time heals all wounds, but even that you have to see as just a metaphor because the awareness that brings the release is that there is no linear time. There is only now; there is only the holy instant.

Friend: Time is not in the healing. Time is in the sickness, as it were.

David: The belief in linear time is the sickness. Does everyone have an understanding of what the word hypothetical means?

Friend: Ah, no. [group laughter]

David: Every thought you hold in your mind right now is hypothetical.

Friend: Even the thought that we are gathered here this morning for a teaching/learning session is hypothetical?

David: Yes. You shared a thought about needing to leave this session at noon; that is hypothetical. You said that you are off on Wednesday next week; that is hypothetical. We have talked about looking for a job; that is hypothetical. Anything that you think you have done, experiences that seem to have happened in the past, those are all hypothetical as well.

Friend: Is it the relationship to time that makes it hypothetical?

David: The hypothetical is the whole projected world as well as the belief in linear time.

Friend: Anything I could talk about or have talked about or think I can talk about is hypothetical? Because what is there to talk about if there is no time, no space, no images, no form; how do you talk about that?

David: Go for the experience! Often as we go deeper into the ideas, we hear: *But! But David! What if you were at such and such a city at night and what if a man came up to you with a knife and said such and such?* Hypotheticals! The mind wants to come up with a lot of hypotheticals. It believes in an objective world.

Friend: But that is no more hypothetical than an experience that you seemed to have actually had?

David: Right.

Friend: I cannot get that. I do not understand.

David: What we are coming to is that "now" is all there is.

Friend: And "now" is free of images and form completely?

David: When we say now, the present moment, do not think you know what that is. We have heard these phrases for a long time: *Live in the moment. Be totally present.* The deceived mind does not have a clue.

Friend: *Now* does not mean just now—the five of us sitting here.

David: Right. *Now* is unknown to the deceived mind, but in the ultimate sense, now is all that can be known because....

Friend: ...that is all there is.

David: The Course says that there are no bodies in the holy instant. "At no single instant does the body exist at all." T-18.7 That is a direct line from the *I Need Do Nothing* section. [laughs] Very interesting: "At no single instant does the body exist at all."

That is what makes this seeming perception hypothetical. Hypothetical is the belief that cause and effect are apart, or that there is a gap between cause and effect. Everything in this world is part of a fixed delusional system made up of distorted cause and effect relationships. At the beginning of

Psychotherapy—Purpose, Process, and Practice, there is reference to the idea that a stepping stone for coming to the holy instant is to see that all perceptions that seem to be occurring in linear time are actually simultaneous.

Another way of saying that everything within the cosmos is simultaneous is, "Ideas leave not their source." T-26.VII.13 There is no gap; there is no space in between events. There is no span of minutes or seconds or days or months or years that separate events, because "Ideas leave not their source." All events are of the wrong mind. There is no gap. Like what we just read:

> …time and space are one illusion, which takes different forms.
> If it has been projected beyond your mind you think of it as
> time. The nearer it is brought to where it is, the more you
> think of it in terms of space. T-26.VIII.1

Time and space are just this little gap in between cause and effect. But the Course is telling you and I am telling you: there is no gap between cause and effect. And if there is no gap between time and space, there is no personhood.

Friend: Because that is where personhood is, in that gap?

David: The gap that isn't.

Friend: That isn't. Well it seems to be. [laughter]

David: That is the subject-object split.

Friend: I feel like I am running to catch up here. Can you say that in another way?

David: It can be said in many ways. The subject-object split that we talked about can only be equated with that gap. No matter how you come at it you just have to see the impossibility of that gap. The whole teaching of the Course is that there is no gap between cause and effect; there is no such thing as linear time.

Friend: But by hanging onto linear time and personhood I hold on to the gap. It is like I am struggling to hold cause and effect apart.

David: The whole point of mysticism is to come to see that cause and effect are not apart and there are no logistics to handle. Everything that seems to be done in the world is perceived within the basic assumption that cause and effect are separate – that you have to do certain things to have other things happen. If I apply for non-profit status, fill out all the forms and continue to be persistent then non-profit status will be granted – cause/effect. If I plant some seeds in fertile soil in the sun and water them, the seeds will grow.

The teachings of the Course are saying that is ludicrous. The world of images is a projection of unreal effects that are coming from an unreal cause. Think about the motion picture projector analogy for a moment; there is a projector and there is film going through it. The film would be the false cause and the images that are seen on the screen of the movie theatre would be the effects. If the film is an unreal cause then the images are an unreal effect. But when you watch a movie, from a deceived point of view it seems as if it is real. The mind identifies with the images; it feels startled or happy or sad because it believes in these false cause/effect relationships. It really believes that people do things to other people, like in science: for every action there is a reaction. The mind really believes in the reality of that idea. That is why it can seem disorienting when going deeply like this. The world as one has known it, does not seem to be as it was. Things are not as they appear to be in the world.

Friend: There is nothing in the world. There is no cause in the world that is producing an effect in the world; it is all generated from my mind. That is where cause and effect are simultaneous. It is all in my mind. The effect goes along with the thought of a cause, because "Ideas leave not their source." If the idea is in my mind, that is what is generating it, that is where it is coming from, then the effect is there as well. There is nothing in the world. It is not as if the thought produces something in the world, the cause and then the effect.

Friend: How is knowing this helpful? Is it even a valid question to ask you if you experience differently? Because if I do, then I am assuming that you are a person.

David: You do not have to assume that I am a person. Just think of it as a symbol speaking to you.

Friend: Whoever I am speaking to now, do you experience it differently? I want to know….

David: You want the experience. You asked how this is helpful. If the goal is peace of mind then this is the most practical thing. The recognition that cause and effect are not apart is imminently practical in the sense that it is the state of peace and restfulness, and that is the state of joy. The whole purpose of time is to see that there is no linear time. It can seem like a mind bender. *Whoa!* But look at the statement we just read, "Do not project this fear to time, for time is not the enemy that you perceive. Time is as neutral as the body is, except in terms of what you see it for." T-26.VIII.3 What is the purpose that I have for time? What am I using it for?

Nothing is a waste of time, no perceptual image, no event or circumstance is a waste of time, if you use it to get in touch with what you believe and how you perceive the world. Anything can be used for your healing and for seeing that cause and effect are not apart. You can use any experience for getting back, back, back in the mind and moving into the experience of not knowing what anything is for, of not thinking you know how things happen in the world, of not thinking that if you do A, then B will happen. It takes a lot of effort and strain to hold onto that kind of a conception of the world.

So, how is this practical? The state of mind that comes from the recognition that cause and effect are not apart is one of joy, peace, happiness, and rest. That is the experience you want. We go into these metaphysics as a way to bring the mind to an experience. It is not to get into philosophical metaphysics so you can pontificate and prove how deep you can go, or how fancy the words can sound. No. This is imminently practical because it is about coming to the awareness of peace of mind.

Another way of looking at it is: if you really come to the awareness that the script is written and there is no cause and effect in the world, then that awareness takes the entire struggle out of life. What would you be striving for? What would you be striving to attain in the future? When you really come to see that cause and effect are not separate, what a joy!

Friend: That is what all striving is for, future results.

David: Future results, future outcomes. I have been saying over and over that I have this feeling and this experience that everything is complete *now*, non-profit status or no non-profit status, teaching-learning sessions or no teaching-learning sessions, coming together with people or no coming together with people, it is all the same from this perspective, from this state of mind. Nothing that has to evolve or unfold. Those metaphors will still be helpful at times but I want you to look at going beyond the metaphors. I want you to leap into the experience. That is what you really want; you want the experience. You do not want the words. You want to go beyond the words.

And, what is my purpose for time?

> Do not project this fear to time, for time is not the enemy that you perceive. Time is as neutral as the body is, except in terms of what you see it for ... If you would keep a little space between you and your brother still, you then would want a little time in which forgiveness is withheld a little while. And this but makes the interval between the time in which forgiveness is withheld from you and given seem dangerous, with terror justified. Yet space between you and your brother is apparent only in the present, *now*, and cannot be perceived in future time. No more can it be overlooked except within the present. Future loss is not your fear. But present joining is your dread. T-26.VIII.3-4

Friend: "Future loss is not your fear;" it sure doesn't *seem* that way.

David: To the mind believing in linear time, future loss seems significant, but really it is "present joining" that the ego dreads. It is afraid of this "present joining" business. You know all the chatter people do at the beginning of gatherings, the discomfort and anxiety about joining, avoiding eye contact. That is another great symbol of the mind's dread of present joining, like on the streets of New York City where there seem to be so many people, but no eye contact.

A contrast can be found in a book about the Aborigines, called *Mutant Message Down Under* by Marlo Morgan. They were asked how it is that they can communicate telepathically, mind to mind, without words. Their answer was that they hold no secrets! That is a symbol of becoming totally transparent, of not dreading the joining at all. You are transparent if you have no sense of a private self, mask, or pretense that you have to hold up; you just totally reveal your right-mindedness, you have no belief in private minds with private thoughts. You do not have anything to hide from anybody. In that state telepathy, or the connection of minds, seems to come in and one mindedness can be experienced. "The willingness to communicate attracts communication to it...." T-15.VII.14 At a deep level of the mind a choice has been made to be in communication with the Father. These holy encounters, these teaching-learning sessions, are symbolic expressions of the willingness to communicate – of the willingness which attracts communication. It is still at the metaphorical level of persons, but it is a helpful symbol. You think: *Hmm, I seem to be in contact with other people who are really committed to waking-up.* Of course, willingness to communicate attracts communication! This is a symbol of your own mind coming to that awareness.

Personhood is very deeply rooted. It is easy to say the words "I am mind. I am not body," but as we go into this you will see that you do not perceive yourself as purely mind. Every concept held has to be looked at and questioned because that is what is keeping you from the awareness or experience of yourself as mind.

Friend: It is my beliefs that hold up what I think I am. That is why it is not just a matter of sitting around reading and talking; it is really about looking at and questioning those beliefs because they are what seems to be holding up this "person."

David: The most beneficial form of practice is completely unstructured. It is not dependent on a time, a place, or a body posture; it is not dependent on repeating something so many times a day. The most beneficial form of practice in salvation is to sink into your mind – to sink down and let go of everything you think you know. That is what you come to as you progress towards the end of the Workbook. But the majority of the Workbook, especially in the beginning, is highly structured. That is for a reason. The repetition of ideas and thinking of them frequently is important. The mind that is not highly trained cannot remember its purpose. It spins off into all kinds of specifics; it cannot remember its purpose because it is tied into thinking in terms of goals, into thinking that there are so many things that need to get done.

As we continue along in the mind training, the specifics and the tracing back will become less a part of the teaching-learning sessions. There will be more and more times of just sinking into the silence and not bringing up all these scenarios, because the mind will be open and ready for the stillness; it will be attracted to the stillness.

> But present joining is your dread. Who can feel desolation except now? A future cause as yet has no effects. And therefore must it be that if you fear, there is a present cause. And it is *this* that needs correction, not a future state. T-26.VIII.4

The present cause is the belief in separation. That is the one thing the mind has tried to conceal. It made up a world with linear time and all these separate parts as a hiding place or a smoke screen to conceal this "present cause" that must be examined.

Right now there is a present cause. That is all it really comes down to, but the ego pulls out all its magic tricks to avoid being looked at. Of course that is a metaphor, as if the ego is this identity. Ultimately it has to just be looked at as thoughts; you come to a point of knowing that "My mind holds only what I think with God." W-142 That puts the ego out of business, without any life of its own.

> The plans you make for safety all are laid within the future, where you cannot plan. No purpose has been given it as yet, and what will happen has as yet no cause. Who can predict effects without a cause? And who could fear effects unless he thought they had been caused, and judged disastrous *now*? T-26.VIII.5

The deceived mind believes that the hypothetical is real and that it is disastrous! [laughs] It has judged disaster in the past and it believes that disaster will inevitably be repeated in the future. It believes that there is cause for fear because of the disastrous effects it thinks really happened in the past. Real pain! Real misery! Real scarcity! It thinks it has proof that scarcity will come about in the future. More pain, scarcity, lack, and loss; that is what the whole ego system is based on.

> Belief in sin arouses fear, and like its cause, is looking forward, looking back, but overlooking what is here and now. Yet only here and now its cause must be, if its effects already have been judged as fearful. T-26.VIII.5

> In gentle laughter does the Holy Spirit perceive the cause, and looks not to effects." T-27.VIII.9

The Holy Spirit does not look to, or judge the projections of the world. He is not working in the world. He is not finding people jobs, parking spaces, and sunny days for picnics. He is not helping people to lose weight or...

Friend: ...find a soul mate.

David: And so on and so forth. The Holy Spirit looks not to effects but has judged the cause. The ego is the belief that produced all the effects. All the images on the screen come from the ego and the Holy Spirit knows that the ego is not true. He is simply judging; he looks at the ego and sees that it is untrue. He does not judge the images that have been projected from the ego. He "looks not to effects."

Friend: If I was very sad a few days ago, I had to believe there was a cause for that pain. I experienced pain and now I look back on it and say, "That was disastrous." To turn that around is to see that it was a total misperception; there was not anything that happened that caused me to feel what I felt. It was all a projection from my own mind. I was looking at the script, making a judgment about it and misperceiving what was happening.

David: Even the "I" that seemed to feel the pain was a misperception. From this moment it is just seeing how that must be so.

Friend: Yes. I was misidentified.

David: Take it even a step further back from "I was misidentified." Who is that "I?" Who is the "I" that is misidentified? The deception is thinking that there was this real being, this real person back then that experienced this pain or that was misidentified. Can you see how that reels it back to the present? Do I believe that there is a present cause (small c) that is disastrous?

Friend: And as long as I do then I have to believe that disaster is imminent in the future.

David: If it was real in the past....

Friend: Hang onto your seats because it is coming again.

David: Even if it is constructed that salvation and Atonement are *coming*–if it was real in the past, then I am going to have to wait. I have to go through a period of more pain. The wrong mind wants to see the pain as real; it has been real and it will be real. That is what has to be questioned.

> Yet only here and now its cause must be, if its effects already have been judged as fearful. And in overlooking this, is it protected and kept separate from healing. For a miracle is *now*. It stands already here, in present grace, within the only interval of time that sin and fear have overlooked, but which is all there is to time. The working out of all correction takes no time at all. Yet the acceptance of the working out can seem to take forever. The change of purpose the Holy Spirit brought to your relationship has in it all effects that you will see. They can be looked at *now*. Why wait till they unfold in time and fear they may not come,

although already there? You have been told that everything brings good that comes from God. And yet it seems as if this is not so. Good in disaster's form is difficult to credit in advance. Nor is there really sense in this idea. T-26.VIII.5-6

Friend: Yeah great. Thank you for adding that. [group laughter]

David: That relates to what you were saying earlier. You want the experience! It can say all kinds of things in here but until you have the experience … and Jesus is saying, right! "Good in disaster's form is difficult to credit in advance."

Friend: I do not understand what you are saying by that.

David: If you are experiencing confusion, frustration, and lack of peace in any form, then words like "you have been told that everything brings good that comes from God," might sound nice but it is not your experience; it does not make any sense. If God gave answer to the separation, where would he have placed it? Would he have placed it in the future or would he have placed it in the present? Wouldn't it be cruel to place it in the future instead of the present? That would mean there would be a gap between you and the acceptance of it. What if He has laid it right under your nose, so to speak? What if it is right here? And what is blocking your awareness of it if it is right under your nose?

Friend: Do not leave me hanging there. "Why should the good appear in evil's form?"

David: God has given you the present answer. The Holy Spirit is right here, right now!

Friend: How can who I am, be yet to come?

David: "Why should the good appear in evil's form? And is it not deception if it does? Its cause is here, if it appears at all." T-26.VIII.7 "Its cause is here" is referring to the good; the cause of the good is here if it appears at all.

> Why are not its effects apparent, then? Why in the future? And you seek to be content with sighing, and with "reasoning" you do not understand it now, but will some day. And then its meaning will be clear. This is not reason, for it is unjust, and clearly hints at punishment until the time of liberation is

at hand. Given a change of purpose for the good, there is no reason for an interval in which disaster strikes, to be perceived as "good" some day but now in form of pain. This is a sacrifice of *now*, which could not be the cost the Holy Spirit asks for what He gave without a cost at all. T-26.VIII.7

Look at that reasoning, "Why should the good appear in evil's form? And is it not deception if it does?" I mean there is cause for joy right now! If I am not experiencing the joy and the peace and the rest, it cannot be that God is withholding anything. It is not like the sun is not shining if I am covering my eyes with my hands, wishing it was not so dark. [laughter] That is what the deceived mind is doing. It says: *Father! Father, help me!*—as it holds up its shield against the light. *Take my fear away!* [laughter]

Friend: But even if the Son of God is doing that, wouldn't the Father still....

David: Shine! Shine, shine, shine; the shining does not stop. All the Father can do is shine. But will the mind be aware of it?

Friend: Won't the Father pull your hands away?

David: No way! No way! It cannot happen; that would prove the Son is helpless and needs to be rescued. It would prove that perfection needs some help to be perfection. God would not be Himself if He reached down into air and said, *That is awful! That is real! [laughs] Your shield is real. I will help you out.* The Father knows his Son is perfect. That is why it has to be voluntary and totally from within. You come to the point of looking at the shield and knowing that it is not you and that you do not need it.

The thought that salvation is in the future has to be questioned, as does linear time, cause and effect, ordering of thought, and judgment. It is not complicated. It is not like working through college requirements, studying each category and then regurgitating it back: *I will get this thing down on judgment and ordering of thought, and then I will work on special relationships.* It is about an experience. Even seeming to read this book is symbolic.

Friend: Will it help us get clear on how to take this shield down?

David: The Holy Spirit will. And if the blue book is a symbol of the Holy Spirit's thinking in a form that you can understand, it can be helpful. It is like you are turning to the light in your mind and this is what seems to be happening on the screen. It seems to be that this person is reading this book and coming to these sessions; these are just images out on the screen. That is the way it *seems* to be happening.

Really it is just your intention, your burning desire to turn to the light. It is not caused by this book. The Course dropping into your lap was not a magical thing; it is an effect! Just like this is an effect [pointing around the room to specifics], and this is an effect; everything in the world is an effect. There is nothing special about the Course, or about these conversations, as if there is one form or technique that is better than another.

Let's look at these last two paragraphs:

> Yet this illusion has a cause which, though untrue, must be already in your mind. And this illusion is but one effect that it engenders, and one form in which its outcome is perceived. This interval in time, when retribution is perceived to be the form in which the "good" appears, is but one aspect of the little space that lies between you, unforgiven still. Be not content with future happiness. It has no meaning, and is not your just reward. For you have cause for freedom *now*. What profits freedom in a prisoner's form? Why should deliverance be disguised as death? Delay is senseless, and the "reasoning" that would maintain effects of present cause must be delayed until a future time, is merely a denial of the fact that consequence and cause must come as one. T-26.VIII.8-9

There it is again, the statement that cause and effect are together. Any kind of reasoning that says Salvation is coming in the future is a denial of the fact that consequence and cause must come as one. Enlightenment must be simultaneous; it must be instantaneous. That is what it means to recognize something that is already here.

It is not like enlightenment is something new and that somehow if you read the Course enough or do enough good deeds, you will come to a point when you have finally filled the cup. The cup is full. The cup is overflowing this very instant; the only choice is whether you will recognize and accept it. If there still seems to be some vagueness – if you are thinking that it sounds simple but does not really seem to be simple – then there is something to question.

You still must believe in personhood and preferences; you still must believe in linear time—in a past where real things happened and in a future where more real things are going to happen. If you believe any of that you are just denying the awareness that is available right now. You are denying enlightenment. Salvation is immediate. When objections come up in your mind like concerns about debt, or your wife, or your kids: *but, but, but, but, but* ... remember that "trust would settle every problem now." T-26.VIII.2

Line up with the Holy Spirit. Just allow it all to be turned upside down and fly in the face of everything you ever believed. Be content and listen to the Holy Spirit. He will direct you. It is not like you have to deal with all these problems first so you can then be open to the Holy Spirit. The Holy Spirit is available right now and he will dictate. He will give you what to say and do, so to speak. That is comforting.

> What could you not accept, if you but knew that everything that happens, all events, past, present and to come, are gently planned by One Whose only purpose is your good? W-135.18

> Once you accept His plan as the one function that you would fulfill, there will be nothing else the Holy Spirit will not arrange for you without your effort. He will go before you making straight your path, and leaving in your way no stones to trip on, and no obstacles to bar your way. Nothing you need will be denied you. Not one seeming difficulty but will melt away before you reach it. You need take thought for nothing, careless of everything except the only purpose that you would fulfill. T-20.IV.8

You cannot have it spelled out any clearer than that. That is cause for rejoicing. Right now, not in the future. "Be not content with future happiness." T-26.VIII.9

Friend: It seems that a helpful question to ask myself is: *What it is that I want?* If what I want is what I get, then I want to be very clear and focused about what I want. I can trust that the mind gets exactly what it wants.

David: As we go deeper, you will observe your thoughts. As the words come out of your mouth, you notice where the thinking is coming from. There is a sense of monitoring. Like when you say, "Oh never mind," as soon as you hear the first few words in a sentence. You develop a quick sense of monitoring, of not condoning the mind-wandering. You are watching the thoughts rather than sleep walking. Catching your words like that means you are watching your thoughts – unplugging the ego! Right there in the thought "never mind" is the awareness that there is no point in finishing the sentence because it is pointless.

The awareness that you must not be ready or that you have investment in the false belief system if you do not have the experience of peace now – that is good! That gives you impetus to question. If you have a sense that salvation is available right now and yet there is something that is holding you back from experiencing it right now, then wow!

> Look not to time, but to the little space between you still, to be delivered from. And do not let it be disguised as time, and so preserved because its form is changed and what it is cannot be recognized. The Holy Spirit's purpose now is yours. Should not His happiness be yours as well? T-26.VIII.9

"And do not let it be disguised as time...." It seems as if all problems within this world have to do with time, whether it is paying off debts or resolving an issue with your wife, or moving towards becoming a mystic; it seems like there is always some time involved. There is so much strain and upset in thinking about how things will work out in the future or how they have not worked out in the past. When you are upset, "look not to time." Do not let time disguise it or be the preserver of it; be open to the present correction that is always available. There seems to be a tracing back only because there is a belief in linear time but the whole idea of tracing back falls away when you can just see the falsity of the ego. That is where the constant joy and peace come in – you do not bite the bait first and then have to trace it back. You no longer bite the bait in the first place!

To Desire Wholly is to Be

Friend: I just read about some guy having his awakening. Certainly I am glad that anyone can have such an experience, but I have a question. I keep hearing that there is nothing to do but remember. There is no doubt the experience of "just remembering" seems to be very elusive. I also keep hearing that it all comes together when we finally give up seeking for the light. Once we have had a taste of that light, giving up seeking it is unthinkable. I know that the desire for it is of key importance, but how can one desire something so much and not try for it?

David: To desire wholly is to experience the desirelessness of creation, of *Being*. To "try" is to make an effort to achieve something that is believed to be missing. Seeking and searching are thus activities of lack, whereas in accepting Atonement or Correction, the search has vanished. The search itself was the sickness. The experience of the present moment is the peaceful contentment of forgiveness. The seeking was the stress; the tranquil surrender or release offers only relaxation and divine ease. The "taste" of the light is always a present experience. Only the attempt to place the "taste" in the past or future is erroneous. Remembering the present and forgetting the past go hand in hand. It cannot be difficult to *be* as one is, now, but the belief in linear time introduces the illusion of the "necessity" of change. What could it mean to change our mind about our Mind but to accept our changeless oneness? Desire is not a matter of degree. Nor is our One Self in God. Simply forgive the "trying" to be any "thing." Being is beyond the concept of change. Even vigilance vanishes in the holy instant, for there is nothing to be vigilant against in the full experience of *now*.

I rejoice in the Living Moment! Now is wholeness true, and happily wholeness has no "opposite."

Spiritual Practice is Nothing without Integrity

Integrity is a symbol of an integrated or whole mind, a mind in which there is no conflict and nothing is out of accord. Integrity follows from honesty, as honesty follows from trust. By honesty I mean consistency and by trust I mean trust in the Holy Spirit.

It is impossible to believe in the ego and have trust, honesty, or integrity. Those who claim to teach or follow the simple teachings of forgiveness in the Bible and *A Course in Miracles* are called to expose and release the ego/judgment. This exposure and release of ego/judgment is a path to Enlightenment/salvation that succeeds only through complete forgiveness. There is no partial forgiveness as there is no partial healing. The mind which seeks to compromise between the teachings of forgiveness and the self-image concepts of the ego is asking for the impossible. Truth is beyond options; there can be no compromise in the gateway of forgiveness that leads to Divine Love.

The belief system of greed, possession and control must be released entirely for trust, honesty, and integrity to be realized. Jesus said you cannot serve two masters and you cannot see two worlds. The mind which attempts to possess has denied its Spiritual Reality and the Truth of our Being.

Many come to Christ and say, "Lord, Lord," but their hearts are filled with desires for control and possession. Christ says, "Depart from Me, I know you not." Christ lives in God, and in God there are no illusions. Keep not one concept apart from the Light Within or you have raised an idol image in belief and have blocked the Light of Love from awareness. Give away the belief in possession and control, and be happy! Recognize the Integrity of Whole Mind, Pristine, Innocent, Pure, and Bright with Love.

You shall know them by their fruits. Love is neither boastful nor proud, for Love accepts ItSelf as One with Its Creator. To be humble in the Lord is to know One's True Identity in God: Pure Magnitude! Without consistent purity of thought there is nothing to spirituality except a "show" of grandiosity; this "show" is but deception. Be humble in God's Love by releasing every scrap of possessiveness and pride and by accepting the glory of: "I am as God created Me."

The fruits of forgiveness and mind watching are Pure Joy! Accept the Gifts of the Spirit Now! Be not tempted by specialness and the littleness of form when the Content of Spirit is available for the Asking. Behold the Good News of the Kingdom Now.

Integrity: Living in Divine Purpose

There can be no more important trait in authentic Awakening than Integrity, for without Integrity, peace of mind remains an affirmation instead of an actual experience. Integrity depends on consistency and purity of thought. Without alignment with the Holy Spirit, Integrity will seem out of reach and guilt will seem real in awareness.

It is possible to desire, believe, think, feel, perceive, and act with consistency by following the Holy Spirit and ONLY by following the Holy Spirit. Another name for the ego is deception; when deception is believed in, the illusion of guilt seems very real indeed. Affirmations, mantras and well-wishing can never become substitutes for looking within and exposing the belief system of the ego. Pockets of guilt must be exposed and voluntarily given to the Holy Spirit; as this occurs it becomes apparent that the guilt was never real.

Confusion results from the attempt to serve two masters and see two worlds. Yet it is impossible to see two worlds that have no meeting point. There is no going back to the past; there is no way to really repeat the past. The past can only be forgiven or released.

Innocence and guilt arise from two different thought systems. One is real, one is not. God is a God of Pure Love and Innocence and therefore Union with God can only be experienced in a State of Innocence. Guilt is always a sure sign that the mind is listening to the ego and afraid of the Holy Spirit's Voice. Guilt is a way of closing down and shutting off, an attempt to be separate, alone, and isolated. The Holy Spirit offers healing and waits patiently for guilt to be exposed willingly, voluntarily. That is why I often emphasize that it is important to share what is on your mind and keep nothing hidden. For in Truth there is nothing to hide. Yet this is only experienced by not attempting to deny or protect the guilt as it rises into awareness. Unprotected guilt dissolves in the Light of Love so effortlessly. It takes enormous effort to hide guilt and keep it concealed behind multitudes of appearances and idols.

Have you ever asked yourself: "Why am I attempting to hide the guilt I feel?" "Why do I hold on to guilt so tightly?" "What am I afraid will happen if I let go of this guilt?" "What is it that I value in this world that I really believe the Holy Spirit will take away?" Resistance is futile for it has no Purpose. Salvation is no compromise of any kind. Yet salvation has no cost. Could the giving up of nothing for the remembrance of Everything ever be considered a cost?

The perceived world may have seemed comfortable and familiar at times, yet it always carried a sense of guilt, insecurity or uneasiness. The insane "reason" that the mind fears letting go of the familiar and opening to God is the terror of the "Unknown." Yes, that is right—the distorted world has become the "known" to a mind asleep and dreaming and God has thus become the Big "Unknown." As long as it seems valuable to cling to the "known" (ego), guilt will seem real in awareness. The Moment the mind decides to accept the Big "Unknown" (God), guilt is gone forever and Christ and God are Known. It really IS this simple.

Say what you mean and mean what you say. Listen to the Holy Spirit and this is not difficult. Listen to the ego and this will seem impossible. Do not hide from Me, Beloved One, for I Love You forever and ever. Hiding presumes the arrogant belief that there is something that must be hidden. In God there are no secrets, no mysteries. In God Everything is openly revealed. God is only Light. Pull up the shades and open the blinds. Only the anticipation will seem to frighten a mind so accustomed to the dark. Bathed in God's Light it is obvious that there is only Light.

God's Plan is to be happy, joyful and at peace. If you do not feel these emotions springing up and bubbling over, you are trying to follow an alien voice and a plan for keeping guilt concealed. Be not afraid to change course immediately, to change your tune at once, for you are entitled to miracles and the joy of working miracles. There is no way to experience Joy fully if people-pleasing still holds an attraction for you. For people-pleasing is the attraction to and maintaining of guilt. Should this temptation arise in your holy mind, pause a Moment and remember the gratitude you have experienced deep within. Let the Strength of gratitude carry your awareness beyond the fear and the guilt. Remember All that our holy Purpose offers; step forward in the Strength of our Divine Innocence.

You have taken many steps inward. You have experienced many miracles. The openings and shifts have seemed swift indeed. There are many more that will seem to follow. Make fast your unlearning, for our Purpose can have no exceptions or compromises to be Itself. The perception of the multitudes fades into one healed tapestry of forgiveness. Now is the time.

Be not afraid to Call on Me, My Beloved. Be not tempted to turn away. I see our Perfect Innocence. There is nothing to seek in the world. There is no body's approval that is required to accept our retreat into Eternal Innocence. The seeming advance into the world was always an illusion. Let go of the "business" of the world for it has served and it is forever behind Us Now. Heaven is approached as the world is seen as meaningless. You are the Meaning that the world was made to hide. You are God's Glory as the Christ! You are not letting anybody down in accepting Atonement. There is no cost to Salvation. Everyone is with Us in Atonement. How could it be otherwise? All shines brightly in the Innocence of Love Divine.

> In you is all of Heaven. Every leaf that falls is given life in you. Each bird that ever sang will sing again in you. And every flower that ever bloomed has saved its perfume and its loveliness for you. What aim can supersede the Will of God and of His Son, that Heaven be restored to him for whom it was created as his only home? Nothing before and nothing after it. No other place; no other state nor time. Nothing beyond nor nearer. Nothing else. In any form. T-25.IV.5.1-10

I am with You always, Beloved of God, for there is only One Self.

The Truth is True and Only the Truth is True

The truth is true and only the truth is true. This profoundly simple statement, applied directly to every seeming problem of this world, has the power to bring the mind out of confusion and fear. It has the power to bring the mind back into the simplicity and safety of the present moment in an instant.

What is the truth? When Jesus said, "I am the way, the truth, and the life," the Holy Spirit was speaking. The truth is an experience that God Is; it is a state of mind far beyond form. Words can be reflective of it and can point towards it, but the truth can only be known as an actual experience.

In this world the ego made up its own version of the truth. It involves six billion separate minds, each with its own version of truth. This distorted idea of the truth is nothing more than a judgment based on the past, subject to change, and therefore unreliable and unreal. Nothing about this world is true, for you are not of this world. This is a world of shifting, changing images and the Christ–being like God in every way–is eternal and changeless. The mind seemed to lock itself into time and space, exchanging Reality as God created it for a pseudo reality based on images. Forgiveness is the escape from illusions and the return to the truth.

Seeing the false as false requires humility and a great willingness to be wrong–to come to an admission that "I have been mistaken in my thinking, I do not know what the truth is and I am willing to be shown." As the mind continues deeper and deeper inward toward the truth, one realizes that nothing the world believes is true and it (the world) offers nothing of real value. All beliefs around survival, nutrition, exercise, love, relationships, life and death, sickness and health, causation of any kind, and the purpose of every separate thing of this world are to be raised and questioned, seen as false, and handed over to the Holy Spirit so that another way can be chosen.

Workbook lessons 9, 14 and 15 are helpful in supporting the initial step of seeing the false as false. Lesson 9: "I see nothing as it is now." And from the second paragraph of lesson 9: "It is difficult for the untrained mind to believe that what it seems to picture is not there." Lesson 14: "God did not create a meaningless world." This idea is "another step in learning to let go the thoughts that you have written on the world, and see the word of God in their place. The early steps in this exchange are what can truly be called salvation…" And lesson 15: "My thoughts are images I have made … It is because the thoughts you think you think appear as images that you do not recognize them as nothing." Not only are the images seen as real but the deceived mind then orders the thoughts/images into hierarchies.

As an example, let's apply lesson 14 to the thought of a plane crash: *God did not create that airplane crash and so it is not real.* When the event seems to be past and related to "other people" and to have occurred "elsewhere," it seems to be more acceptable. There is a seeming gap of time and space, a split between the perceiver and the event/object perceived. But when applied to persons, events and places in one's immediate environment, one's immediate life experience, the ordering of thought seems to cause great resistance to accepting and applying the teachings. Greater importance or "reality" is given to chosen "special" ones and "special" things. If only the truth is true and nothing else is true then every thought held in mind right now, relative to every person, object, and event in time and space—such as my best friend, my mother, my spouse, my pet, my house and my wedding day—are all equally unreal.

This transfer of training without exceptions is fundamental to the healing of the mind. To hold one exception out from the rest is to refuse the acceptance of the correction, the acceptance that all illusions are equally unreal. When Jesus said: "Be as little children," he was speaking of an open state of mind, a willing and humble attitude that happily releases any belief that it knows what the world is for, and how it should be.

In lesson 184 Jesus says: "You live by symbols. You have made up names for everything you see. Each becomes a separate entity identified by its own name. By this you carve it out of unity..." This carving up, this establishment of perception is wish-fulfillment. What is named is given meaning, seen as meaningful, and seen as causative. This establishment is set against the given truth. The name of God is the replacement for all the separate names, purposes, and meanings of the world. The Holy Spirit uses all of the symbols of the world, including words, to point towards the truth, remembering Creation has one Name, one Meaning, and a single Source which unifies all things within Itself.

Remember this world is a substitute for Heaven. It is not your home. All memories, thoughts, relationships, places, events, and people can be used by Me (Holy Spirit) for the glorious purpose of awakening. Tread lightly amongst the images. With gratitude, allow them to be released from your mind. Only through true forgiveness can the mind be freed from illusions and be free to accept the Name of God as the replacement for all of the little names, free to accept Reality as It was Created by God the Father.

When I speak of true forgiveness, true perception, and true love, I am speaking of a perception that is unified, that no longer perceives separation and fragmentation. I am speaking of the Love of God that is not of this world. The ego's version of forgiveness, perception, and love are inconsistent and subject to change. You can tell by the way you feel whether you are in alignment with the truth or not. Do not waste another precious moment searching for meaning in images. It is the past. It is over and done with now.

Come, abide with Me, trust in Me, release the past and give your Self to Me in this holy instant. There is no alternative but to accept Gods plan for salvation. To pretend there could be another way is nothing but a distraction, meaningless in eternity, but tragic in time—tragic because of the unnecessary conflicted state of mind that is being chosen. You have cause for freedom now. You have cause for happiness now! Acceptance is all that is required. Come rejoice with Me in the simplicity of the truth.

Rest In Me–A Message from Christ

Beloved Ones, be comforted. You are not asked to do anything. There is a time when stepping back is all that is asked of you. It is a time of rest, not strain; a time of peace, not conflict. That time is almost here. It seems fearful because it is not under your control but think honestly about what your control has done for you. What has it brought you?

You have been caught in a trap from which you never could escape. Conflict, guilt, and fear have come with you and never left your side. Each one of you has done this differently, yet each has come to the same place, the same impasse. And now it seems to each of you that there is no escape, for it is true that you cannot escape alone. Your stories seem to differ, for they do take different forms. Yet their one content makes you brothers. Dwell not upon the differences or you are lost. It is in recognizing the common content, the common need, that you are saved!

The mess that is your lives is an illusion. What can the form of dreams resolve? There is no answer to a question not yet asked, for it would not be recognized. Ask only this: Will I fulfill the function given me? What else is there to ask? Why must I know the form in which the answer comes to me? God answers, "Yes," and it is done. No more than this is meaningful to you.

It is not He Who would withhold the future and leave you fearful. You could not accept His "yes" in forms you would not understand. Things still in time unfold as is appointed them, and many things remain undone as yet. Plans based upon intangibles cannot be fully shown to you. And what has not as yet occurred must be intangible. This phase of learning has a single lesson for all the forms your problems seem to take.

To God all things are possible, but you must ask His answer only of Himself. Perhaps you think you do, but be you sure that if you had you would be quiet now and wholly undismayed by anything. Do not attempt to guess His Will for you. Do not assume that you are right because an answer seems to come from Him. Be sure you ask, and then be still and let Him speak. There is no problem He cannot resolve, for it is never He Who keeps apart some questions to be solved by someone else. You cannot share the world with Him and make half of it His while half belongs to you. Truth makes no compromise. To keep apart a little is to keep all separate. Your life, complete and whole, belongs to God or none of it is His. There is no thought in all the world that seems more terrible.

Yet it is only when this thought appears in perfect clarity that there is hope in peace and safety for the mind so long kept dark and twisted to avoid the light. This is the light. Step back and do not dwell upon the forms that seem to keep you bound. You will fulfill your function and will have whatever you will need. God does not fail. But lay no limits on what you would give to Him to be resolved, for He cannot offer a thousand answers when but one is all there is. Accept this one of Him and not one question will remain to ask.

Do not forget if you attempt to solve a problem, you have judged it for yourself and so you have betrayed your proper role. Grandeur, which comes from God, establishes that judgment is impossible for you, but grandiosity insists you judge, and bring to this all problems that you have. What is the result? Look carefully upon your life and let it speak for you.

Is this frail breath and deep uncertainty your choice for you? Or would you rather rest in surety, certain you would not fail in your request to have all problems happily resolved? Do not mistake the fine disguises you can use to cover judgment. It appears as charity, as mercy and as love, as pity, understanding and as care. And yet you know it is not what it seems because the problem still remains unsolved; it comes to haunt your mind in evil dreams. What have you kept from God that you would hide behind your judgment? What have you concealed beneath the cloak of kindness and concern? Use no one for your needs, for that is "sin" and you will pay the penalty in guilt.

Remember you need nothing, but you have an endless store of loving gifts to give. But teach this lesson only to yourself. Your brother will not learn it from your words or from the judgments you have laid on him. You need not even speak a word to him. You cannot ask, "What shall I say to him?" and hear God's answer. Rather ask instead, "Help me to see this brother through the eyes of truth and not of judgment," and the help of God and all His angels will respond.

For only here we rest. We cast away our little judgments and our petty words; our tiny problems and our false concerns. We have attempted to be master of our destiny and thought that peace lay there. Freedom and judgment is impossible. But by your side is One Who knows the way. Step back for Him and let Him lead you to the rest and silence of the Word of God.

You need do nothing now. There is no use in trying to work out specific plans, however important they may seem to be. They will all fall into place.

The Passive Nature of the Correction

David: There are a couple of passages we can use as a springboard for coming to see the passive nature of correction. These passages are about stillness, about going beyond the words. Many have heard the quote before, "Love does not oppose." In the *Song of Prayer* Jesus talks about humility in the same way. He says that the truly humble can allow their holy mind to rest without concern for the world, without thought of "enemies" and without need to judge or defend, because humility does not oppose.

What also comes to mind are the first few pages of Part II of the Workbook. This is where the Workbook seems to move into its final phase. After 220 lessons have been completed, the emphasis of the lessons shifts towards silence. There are probably two forms of practice that commonly come out of working through the latter part of the Workbook. One of them is to attempt to use a central thought to guide the mind into the meditative state. Another is more free form – not trying to think of anything, not trying to even hold onto a central thought.

That is the one that leads into the revelatory state, the one that becomes your common means of practice. The other forms were all preliminary to this, whether they were visualizations or moving your eyes around the room or even holding onto the central idea. This is probably the form of meditation the advanced teacher of God should embrace and try to practice.

I thought we might read through the introduction to the second part of the Workbook together, but first I will read from the *I Need Do Nothing* section in Chapter 18:

> Save time for me by only this one preparation, and practice doing nothing else. "I need do nothing" is a statement of allegiance, a truly undivided loyalty. Believe it for just one instant, and you will accomplish more than is given to a century of contemplation, or of struggle against temptation.
>
> To do anything involves the body. And if you recognize you need do nothing, you have withdrawn the body's value from your mind. Here is the quick and open door through which you slip past centuries of effort, and escape from time. This is the way in which sin loses all attraction *right now*. For here is time denied, and past and future gone. Who needs do nothing has no need for time. To do nothing is to rest, and make a place within you where the activity of the body ceases to demand attention. Into this place the Holy Spirit comes, and there abides. T-18.VII.6-7

And now from the *What is Forgiveness* section that follows the introduction to Part II of the Workbook:

> Forgiveness ... is still, and quietly does nothing. It offends no aspect of reality, nor seeks to twist it to appearances it likes. It merely looks, and waits, and judges not ... Do nothing, then, and let forgiveness show you what to do, through Him Who is your Guide, your Savior and Protector, strong in hope, and certain of your ultimate success. W-pII.1.4,5

All these passages point to a sense of correction being passive, not active in any sense. Truth is not about battling against illusions. It is about being able to see that only illusions can battle. In that awareness and in that recognition you do not attempt to take a side. You do not even attempt to perceive that injustice or unfairness is taking place because you realize that if you perceive injustice or if you perceive someone being unfairly treated, that it is just another way of saying that you are denying the Father. There could be no injustices *and* God, Being Who He Is. It just has to mean that injustices and conflicts are all misperception.

Now we will read from the Introduction to Part II of the Workbook:

> Words will mean little now. We use them but as guides on which we do not now depend. For now we seek direct experience of truth alone. The lessons that remain are merely introductions to the times in which we leave the world of pain, and go to enter peace. Now we begin to reach the goal this course has set, and find the end toward which our practicing was always geared.
>
> Now we attempt to let the exercise be merely a beginning. For we wait in quiet expectation for our God and Father. He has promised He will take the final step Himself. And we are sure His promises are kept. We have come far along the road, and now we wait for Him. We will continue spending time with Him each morning and at night, as long as makes us happy. We will not consider time a matter of duration now. We use as much as we will need for the result that we desire. Nor will we forget our hourly remembrance in between, calling to God when we have need of Him as we are tempted to forget our goal. W-pII.in.1-2

A beautiful sentence: "We will not consider time a matter of duration now."

And the bottom of the fourth paragraph continues:

> We say the words of invitation that His Voice suggests, and then we wait for Him to come to us.
>
> Now is the time of prophecy fulfilled. Now are all ancient promises upheld and fully kept. No step remains for time to separate from its accomplishment. For now we cannot fail. Sit silently and wait upon your Father. He has willed to come to you when you have recognized it is your will He do so. And you could have never come this far unless you saw, however dimly, that it is your will.
>
> I am so close to you we cannot fail. Father, we give these holy times to You, in gratitude to Him Who taught us how to leave the world of sorrow in exchange for its replacement, given us

by You. We look not backward now. We look ahead, and fix our eyes upon the journey's end. Accept these little gifts of thanks from us, as through Christ's vision we behold a world beyond the one we made, and take that world to be the full replacement of our own.

And now we wait in silence, unafraid and certain of Your coming. We have sought to find our way by following the Guide You sent to us. We did not know the way, but You did not forget us. And we know that You will not forget us now. We ask but that Your ancient promises be kept which are Your Will to keep. We will with You in asking this. The Father and the Son, Whose holy Will created all that is, can fail in nothing. In this certainty, we undertake these last few steps to You, and rest in confidence upon Your Love, which will not fail the Son who calls to You.

And so we start upon the final part of this one holy year, which we have spent together in the search for truth and God, Who is its one Creator. We have found the way He chose for us, and made the choice to follow it as He would have us go. His Hand has held us up. His Thoughts have lit the darkness of our minds. His Love has called to us unceasingly since time began. W-pII.in.4-8

And one paragraph down:

Now is the need for practice almost done. For in this final section, we will come to understand that we need only call to God, and all temptations disappear. Instead of words, we need but feel His Love. Instead of prayers, we need but call His Name. Instead of judging, we need but be still and let all things be healed. We will accept the way God's plan will end, as we received the way it started. Now it is complete. This year has brought us to eternity.

One further use for words we still retain. From time to time, instructions on a theme of special relevance will intersperse our daily lessons and the periods of wordless, deep experience which should come afterwards. These special thoughts should be reviewed each day, each one of them to be continued till the next is given you. They should be slowly read and thought about a little while, preceding one of the holy and blessed instants in the day. W-pII.in.10-11

Singularity and Silence

The body is a limit imposed on the universal communication that is an eternal property of mind. But the communication is internal. Mind reaches to itself. It is *not* made up of different parts, which reach each other. It does not go out. Within itself it has no limits, and there is nothing outside it. It encompasses everything. It encompasses you entirely; you within it and it within you. There is nothing else, anywhere or ever. T-18.VI.8.3

The belief in separation from God and the misidentification with the body is the block to vertical communication in the Mind of God. The body, brain, and senses seem to communicate information, yet nothing on the horizontal or linear plane has any meaning whatsoever. As the Holy Spirit uses words and symbols to help move beyond the need for them, a re-translation of perception occurs. Thus the Holy Spirit uses words to go beyond the words, uses the body to teach that, literally, there is no body, and uses time to teach that there is no time.

Healed perception is the realization that the cosmos is a singular cosmos of ideas, and that there is nothing outside of mind. The singular mind is a forgiven cosmos, for the subject/object split of misperception has been unveiled as impossible. There are no private minds with private thoughts, walled off from each other by flesh and separated by time and space. Universal communication, which reflects the Mind of God, has been restored.

Complete abstraction is the natural condition of the mind. But part of it is now unnatural. It does not look on everything as one. It sees instead but fragments of the whole, for only thus could it invent the partial world you see. The purpose of all seeing is to show you what you wish to see. All hearing but brings to your mind the sounds it wants to hear.

Thus were specifics made. And now it is specifics we must use in practicing. We give them to the Holy Spirit, that He may employ them for a purpose which is different from the one we gave to them. Yet He can use but what we made, to teach us from a different point of view, so we can see a different use in everything.

One brother is all brothers. Every mind contains all minds, for every mind is one. Such is the truth. Yet do these thoughts make clear the meaning of creation? Do these words bring perfect clarity with them to you? What can they seem to be but empty sounds; pretty, perhaps, correct in sentiment, yet fundamentally not understood nor understandable. The mind that taught itself to think specifically can no longer grasp abstraction in the sense that it is all-encompassing. We need to see a little, that we learn a lot. W-161.2-4

This is the importance of meditation, the sinking beneath every thought of past and future to the Silence within. The time-space cosmos is a tapestry, whole and complete. No thread, no star, no planet, no person, no thing, no atom can be pulled from the tapestry and set off as a "thing apart." No thing can be named as if it has a separate existence in and of itself. Wholeness has no parts.

A whole mind is a happy, joyful, free mind, for it no longer attempts to define and label Reality. In order to forget the Reality of Heaven, the cosmos was made as a substitute "reality." Time and space seemed to crack and divide into trillions of parts, with none occupying the same point in the matrix of illusion. Levels and hierarchies seemed to arise, but be of good cheer! The Holy Spirit sees the illusion as one tapestry, and what but this is Atonement?

What is the same cannot have separate parts. This is the simple Correction to the error of fragmented perception. This is the reference Point of non-judgment, for what is one is beyond comparison. The Point of release looks on the past as one illusion; this is the change of mind which brings with it the reflection of the Light within. The present is actually before time was. "Before Abraham was, I Am" is the form in which this idea is expressed in the Bible. Singularity is the gateway to the remembrance of Abstract Light. Christ is the Light, and You are That.

Happiness can never be found in duality or multiplicity. Rejoice!

Why look for happiness where it can never be found? God and Christ, Creator and Creation, Cause and effect are One Being. Deep within is everything perfect. Be still and know that I am God – One forever.

You are the Kingdom of Heaven Now.

> Simply do this: Be still, and lay aside all thoughts of what you
> are and what God is; all concepts you have learned about the
> world; all images you hold about yourself. Empty your mind
> of everything it thinks is either true or false, or good or bad,
> of every thought it judges worthy, and all the ideas of which
> it is ashamed. Hold onto nothing. Do not bring with you one
> thought the past has taught, nor one belief you ever learned
> before from anything. Forget this world, forget this course,
> and come with wholly empty hands unto your God.
>
> Is it not He Who knows the way to you? You need not know
> the way to Him. Your part is simply to allow all obstacles that
> you have interposed between the Son and God the Father to
> be quietly removed forever. God will do His part in joyful
> and immediate response. Ask and receive. But do not make
> demands, nor point the road to God by which He should
> appear to you. The way to reach Him is merely to let Him
> be. For in that way is your reality proclaimed as well. W-189.7-8

You are the One Christ Holy Child of God.

I am that I am. It is humble to accept My Self as God created Christ—as One
Spirit. It is arrogant to cling to specifics and humanness. Let Everything Be
exactly as It IS.